External/Sales Proposals (continued)
Site-preparation section, 484
Training-requirements section, 485
Statement-of-responsibilities section, 486
Description of vendor and sales pitch sections, 487
Conclusion, 488

Grant Proposals
Cover letter, 471
Title page, 472
Introduction, 472
References section, 472
Statement of need, 473
Program description, 473
Goals and objectives, 474
Budget narrative, 474
Time line, 475

Instructions

Illustrations for instructions, 437, 438, 439, 440
Informal instructions, 425
Internal instructions, 426
Introduction for instructions, 430
Product-maintenance instructions, 427
Visual instructions for international customers, 429
Warning icons, 435

Résumés

Format: ASCII résumés, 591

Parts of Résumés
Headings, 581
Education section, 583
Experience sections, 579, 580, 583, 584

Sample Résumés
Résumé for an entry-level position, 593
Résumé, highlighting professional credentials, 594
Résumé, highlighting management experience, 595
Advanced résumés, 596, 597
Résumés tailored to specific job listings, 600, 601

Presentations

Pattern of presentation slides, 503
Sample presentation, 505
Computer-presentation setup, 508
PowerPoint notes page, 521
PowerPoint slide-sorter view, 522

Brochures and Newsletters

Format: Text columns, 218
Format: Layout and design choices, 211
Format: Thumbnail sketches for newsletter, 217
Sales brochure (draft), 88
Sales brochure, 119

Research

APA sample page, 191
APA sample list of references, 192
MLA sample page, 201
MLA sample list of works cited, 202
Questionnaire, 155

Visuals

Images
Clip art, 244
Drawings, 242, 243, 244
Flowcharts and organizational charts, 245, 246, 247
Graphics, 253, 254
Illustrations for instructions, 437, 438, 439, 440
Maps, 248, 249
Photograph, 250
Symbols, 255
Visual instructions for international customers, 429
Warning icons, 435, 436

Data
Bar graphs, 229, 233, 234, 235, 236
Column graphs, 239, 240
Line graphs, 231, 232, 241
Picture graph, 238
Pie graph, 237
Tables, 226, 227, 229

Web Documents

Acknowledgments page, 558
Chunked content, 544
Linked table of contents, 546
Links, bad and good examples, 547
Lists and bullets, 544, 556
Online press release, 542
Privacy statement (excerpt), 556
Corporate blog, 560
Blog post showing keyword tags, 562

For Bedford/St. Martin's

Developmental Editors: Rachel Goldberg, Amy Hurd Gershman
Editorial Assistant: Erin McGhee
Assistant Production Manager: Joe Ford
Marketing Manager: Molly Parke
Text Design: Books By Design, Inc.
Project Management: Books By Design, Inc.
Cover Design: Sara Gates
Cover Photo: Closeup of a Personal Data Assistant and a Stylus. Glow Design/Getty.
Composition: Laserwords Maine
Printing and Binding: RR Donnelley & Sons, Inc.

President: Joan E. Feinberg
Editorial Director: Denise B. Wydra
Editor in Chief: Karen S. Henry
Director of Marketing: Karen R. Soeltz
Assistant Director of Editing, Design, and Production: Elise S. Kaiser
Director of Editing, Design, and Production: Marcia Cohen
Manager, Publishing Services: Emily Berleth

Library of Congress Control Number: 2009921705

Manufactured in the United States of America.

4   3   2   0   1
f   e   d   c   b   a

For information, write: Bedford/St. Martin's, 75 Arlington Street, Boston, MA 02116   (617-399-4000)

ISBN-10: 0-312-54182-1
ISBN-13: 978-0-312-54182-8

Acknowledgments

Figure 2–21: "Common Hearing Aids and Their Placement." From The American Academy of Audiology, <www.audiology.org/consumer/guides/hafaq.php>. Copyright © 2006 by American Academy of Audiology. Reproduced with permission of American Academy of Audiology in the format Textbook via Copyright Clearance Center.

Figure 3–7: Steve Coffel and Karyn Feiden. "Drinking Water Treatment Process." Excerpt from *Indoor Pollution* by Steve Coffel and Karyn Feiden. Copyright © 1990 by Steve Coffel and Karyn Feiden. Used by permission of Ballantine Books, a division of Random House, Inc., and Barbara Lowenstein Associates.

Acknowledgments and copyrights are continued at the back of the book on pages 676–678, which constitute an extension of the copyright page.

Preface

Writing That Works has been successful through nine editions because it effectively prepares students to apply the writing process to the documents and situations they will encounter in the workplace—regardless of their academic background or occupational interest. Informed by the decades of professional and academic experience we have between us, the book integrates practical coverage of the writing process with clear guidelines for specific types of workplace writing—correspondence, reports, proposals, instructions, presentations, blogs, podcasts, FAQs, wikis, and more—supported by a wealth of sample documents, hundreds of exercises and projects, and the most current advice for using technology in today's workplace.

The tenth edition continues to offer the structure and features that instructors have told us are effective. Workplace communications, however, is not a static field. Tools, sources of information, and practices continue to evolve, in both the classroom and the workplace. In preparing this edition, we looked critically at every facet of the book and added and updated material to keep it current. As we have added new material, model documents, and visuals throughout, our focus continues to be on helping students prepare for today's electronic workflow, an increasingly global and technical environment, and the critical ethical concerns of workplace writing. (For a detailed description of what's new to this edition, see pages ix–x.)

About This Book

Rhetorically Focused Guidance on the Writing Process at Work

The advice, assignments, and features in *Writing That Works* all draw on our workplace and classroom experiences and have been honed by the suggestions and contributions of hundreds of teachers and writers over the years. They take as their premise the belief that strong workplace writing comes from an understanding of the rhetorical framework of audience and purpose.

Divided into four parts, the book is structured so that it begins with an overview of the writing process and then applies that process to the specific tasks and types of workplace writing, all of them illustrated by an impressive number of samples that are annotated to clarify what they demonstrate.

- **Part One: The Writing Process**   Chapters 1 through 4 guide students through the steps of planning, organizing, drafting, and revising, with a focus on the contexts and practices distinctive to workplace writing.

- **Part Two: Essential Skills**   Chapters 5 through 7 help students develop additional communication skills essential to workplace writing. The collaborative writing chapter includes advice on how to peer-review and edit shared documents; the research chapter covers primary, print, and online research, with updated guidelines for documenting sources; and the design chapter offers concrete advice and examples for creating effective visuals and integrating them into documents and presentations.

- **Part Three: Writing at Work**   Chapters 8 through 16 help students apply the skills learned in Parts One and Two, guiding them through the many types of writing and communications they will face in any workplace. They provide detailed advice on routine correspondence—e-mail and instant messages, letters, and memos—informal and formal reports; instructions; and internal, sales, and grant proposals. These chapters also cover creating and delivering presentations, conducting meetings, writing for the Web, and finding a job.

- **Part Four: Revision Guide**   This self-contained handbook provides help with sentence errors, punctuation, and mechanics, and it features a section tailored to students who speak English as a second language (ESL).

Easy to Use, with an Emphasis on Practical Skills

Long appreciated for its clarity and comprehensiveness, *Writing That Works* is flexible enough to accommodate different courses and teaching styles. It is also thorough enough for students to use on their own.

Boxed features integrated throughout the text summarize important information and include helpful checklists for considering audience and purpose, drafting and revising, designing effective documents, and using the latest communications and word-processing technologies, as well as tips for ESL students. Marginal notes show students where to look for more support in the text and on the companion Web site. Recognizing that today's students are more visually oriented, *Writing That Works* uses design and color effectively throughout, with screened edges, shading, and color to highlight the most-referenced material (documentation models, the Writing @ Work portfolio, and the Meeting the Deadline features).

More than 300 assignments in the book and on the companion Web site give students unparalleled opportunities to practice their skills, either on their own or in class. Most of them class-tested, the assignments at the end of each chapter include exercises, collaborative writing projects, and Web-based research projects that are equally well-suited to face-to-face, online, or hybrid courses.

Focused on Workplace Success

To connect the book's advice with the real world, each chapter features salient observations from experienced professionals, conveying their firsthand experience and advice for writing, communicating, facing challenges, and succeeding on the job.

Recognizing the often demanding schedules of professional life, *Writing That Works* offers advice for writing successfully, even under the pressure of a tight deadline. The book's popular Meeting the Deadline sections offer practical help for approaching time-sensitive memos, proposals, and presentations.

■ New to This Edition

As with each edition of *Writing That Works*, this revision has been guided by the thoughtful reviews and suggestions of business- and technical-writing instructors across the country. In response to their feedback and to better address the demands of the contemporary workplace, we have made several improvements.

Greater Focus on Web and Multimedia Documents

Because workplace writing continues to evolve with the ongoing development of business-networking media, Chapter 15 now includes expanded coverage of common Web genres, such as blogs, wikis, podcasts, and FAQs. Discussions of tone, style, and design address the rhetorical choices writers face in drafting and posting these documents on the Web.

Fresh Sample Documents and Visuals

More than 50 new or revised figures—including letters, memos, informal reports, résumés, charts, graphs, drawings, tables, photographs, illustrated descriptions, and visual instructions—reflect the increasingly global workplace and the prominence of electronic communication.

New Writing @ Work Portfolio

Recognizing the diversity of fields and industries that attract business-writing students, this new visual feature provides a window into what workplace writing looks like across many different professions and expands the already extensive range of samples throughout the text and Web site. The portfolio builds on the design principles discussed in Chapter 7 and showcases real workplace writing across a range of disciplines, including arts and media, sciences, and social sciences.

Updated Guidance on Research and Documentation Styles

Chapter 6 includes the latest information on finding, evaluating, and documenting primary and secondary source material, including current, reliable links to a variety of Web sources across the disciplines conforming to the latest guidelines of both the Modern Language Association (MLA) and the American Psychological Association (APA). Extensive citation models offer examples for dozens of source types and adhere to the seventh edition of the *MLA Handbook for Writers of Research Papers* (2009) and the *APA Style Guide to Electronic References* (2007).

Expanded Coverage of Grant Proposals and a New Section on Requests for Proposals

With grant proposals playing an increasingly large role in institutional and academic fields, Chapter 13 includes a comprehensive research-proposal sample and new material on "repurposing" in-house information when drafting proposals. A new section on requests for proposals (RFPs) explains how organizations set requirements as they solicit proposals for a service or product from outside vendors.

Updated Advice on Finding a Job

Chapter 16 addresses how Internet technologies can aid in the job search, covering social-networking sites, Internet discussion groups, and blogs. A brief new section also discusses how internships can help students learn about a new field or make connections in an industry.

A Variety of New and Expanded Digital Tips

These new digital tips give advice on using collaborative writing software (Chapter 5), working with electronic search engines and storing search results (Chapter 6), creating tables (Chapter 7), and conducting meetings remotely (Chapter 14). All the tips throughout the book are up to date, and several are now enhanced by illustrated step-by-step instructions at the companion Web site.

Ancillaries

Free Book Companion Web Site: *bedfordstmartins.com/writingthatworks*

Updated and revised, the companion Web site for *Writing That Works* (illustrated on the back cover of this book) augments the material in the book with a wide range of resources:

- A gallery of model documents
- More than 100 additional exercises and writing projects

- Expanded Digital Tips with step-by-step guides
- Additional advice and resources for finding a job or an internship
- Step-by-step tutorials on designing documents, designing for the Web, evaluating sources, and preparing presentation slides
- Links to helpful and reliable Web sites related to every topic in the book. (See the On the Web marginal notes throughout the book, which point to specific resources and activities available online.)
- Re:Writing (<bedfordstmartins.com/rewriting>), a robust collection of re-sources on writing, including plagiarism tutorials, style and grammar exercises, diagnostics, technology help, and research guides — all written by our most widely adopted authors.

Online Instructor's Manual: *bedfordstmartins.com/writingthatworks*

The comprehensive online Instructor's Manual provides everything instructors need to create a successful business-writing course:

- Chapter overviews and teaching tips
- Chapter quizzes
- Suggested responses to the exercises and writing projects in the book and online
- PowerPoint slides and transparency masters for chapter content
- Classroom handouts for individual, group, and online work
- Course-planning help
- Sample syllabi for in-person, online, and hybrid courses

Content for Course-Management Systems

A variety of student and instructor resources developed for this textbook is ready for use in course-management systems such as WebCT and Blackboard.

Additional Resources for Business and Technical Writing

Team Writing

A print supplement with online videos, *Team Writing* provides guidelines and examples of collaborating to manage written projects by documenting tasks, deadlines, and team goals. Short two- to five-minute videos correspond with each chapter to give students the opportunity to analyze team interactions and learn about communication styles. Practical troubleshooting tips show students how best to handle specific conflicts within peer groups.

ix visual exercises for techcomm

This CD-ROM, which can be packaged free with *Writing That Works*, introduces the fundamentals of visual composition in an interactive medium, using brochures, instructions, reports, and other examples of technical communication. To see a sample tutorial, visit <bedfordstmartins.com/ixtechcomm>.

For ordering information, contact your local sales representative or e-mail us at <sales_support@bfwpub.com>.

Acknowledgments

We are grateful to Barbara Fister, academic librarian and associate professor at Gustavus Adolphus College, for her good advice and contributions to the research chapter, and Stuart Selber of Pennsylvania State University, Altoona, for his help in reviewing the Writing for the Web chapter. We also acknowledge Lisa-Anne Culp of the University of South Florida for her thoughtful work on the previous edition's writing assignments and projects, the companion Web site, and the Instructor's Manual, and Sandy Petrulionis of Pennsylvania State University and her student Mike Rishel for the short unsolicited sales proposal included in this book. Thanks also to Johan De Beer of Mitsubishi Engines North America for permission to include an adaptation of one of his trip reports, to Chris Helms of the *Cambridge Chronicle* for providing a model of a functional résumé, and to Peggy Edwards for letting us include the student résumé that helped her land her current job as an inspector for the Salem County Department of Health in New Jersey.

We wish to thank the following instructors who have substantially strengthened the tenth edition by generously sharing their helpful comments and recommendations: Shanti Bruce, Nova Southeastern University; Naomi Couch, Columbia College Chicago; Deborah Coulter-Harris, University of Toledo; Rick Duet, Nicholls State University; Sonia N. Feder-Lewis, Saint Mary's University of Minnesota; Kendra H. Gaines, Pima Community College; Jennifer Price Mahoney, Indiana University–Purdue University Indianapolis; Rita C. McMahan, Eastern Oregon University; Leslie L. Miller, Indiana University–Purdue University Indianapolis; Mary J. Monette, University of North Dakota; Alice Myatt, Georgia State University; Rita R. Owens, Boston College; Amber Quarles, California State University Monterey Bay; Renee Rallo, Florida Gulf Coast University; Yvonne N. Richter, Georgia State University; Angela M. Rogers, Clemson University; Linda Saulsby, University of Arizona; Jason Thompson, University of Arizona; and Jennifer R. Veltsos, Minnesota State University–Mankato. We also gratefully acknowledge the ongoing contributions and help of the students and faculty at the University of Wisconsin–Milwaukee, as well as our colleagues in the United States and abroad.

We are also greatly indebted to the leadership of Bedford/St. Martin's, beginning with Joan Feinberg, president; Charles Christensen, retired president; Denise Wydra, editorial director; Karen Henry, editor in chief; and Leasa Burton, senior executive editor, for helping us to re-imagine our approach to this edition and for their unstinting support throughout the revision process. Many thanks as well to

Erin McGhee for her work on the companion Web site and instructor resources. We thank Emily Berleth, who, with the help of Herb Nolan at Books By Design, oversaw the difficult task of producing this book. We are grateful to Janis Owens at Books By Design for the creative design, and to Kathleen Benn McQueen for her careful copyediting.

This edition benefited significantly from the invaluable collaboration with Rachel Goldberg, our developmental editor at Bedford/St. Martin's. Her contributions in matters large and small helped us rethink and upgrade key features throughout the text. Astute in pinpointing issues for resolution and creative in collaborating on their solutions, she has been especially helpful in designing the Writing @ Work feature and in locating effective samples for it. This edition is stronger throughout because of Rachel's professionalism and superb editing skills. Finally, we're pleased to acknowledge Amy Gershman, associate editor at Bedford/St. Martins, for her careful attention to the myriad of tasks associated with the final stages of this edition.

Walter E. Oliu
Charles T. Brusaw
Gerald J. Alred

About the Authors

Walter E. Oliu served as chief of the Publishing Services Branch at the U.S. Nuclear Regulatory Commission, where he managed the agency's printing, graphics, editing, and publishing programs. He also developed the public-access standards for and managed daily operations of the agency's public Web site. He has taught at Miami University of Ohio, Slippery Rock State University, and, as an adjunct faculty member, at Montgomery College and George Mason University.

Charles T. Brusaw served as a faculty member at NCR Corporation's Management College, where he developed and taught courses in professional writing, editing, and presentation skills for the corporation worldwide. Previously, he worked in advertising, technical writing, public relations, and curriculum development. He has been a communications consultant, an invited speaker at academic conferences, and a teacher of business writing at Sinclair Community College.

Gerald J. Alred is Professor Emeritus of English at the University of Wisconsin–Milwaukee, where he teaches courses in the Professional Writing Program. He is the author of numerous scholarly articles and several standard bibliographies on business and technical communication, and he serves as the associate editor of the *Journal of Business Communication*. He is a recipient of the prestigious Jay R. Gould Award for "profound scholarly and textbook contributions to the teaching of business and technical writing."

Brief Contents

PART ONE   **The Writing Process**   1

Chapter 1   Assessing Audience and Purpose: A Case Study   3
Chapter 2   Organizing Your Information   25
Chapter 3   Writing the Draft   64
Chapter 4   Revising the Draft   94

PART TWO   **Essential Skills: Collaboration, Research, and Design**   127

Chapter 5   Collaborative Writing   129
Chapter 6   Researching Your Subject   148
Chapter 7   Designing Effective Documents and Visuals   209

PART THREE   **Writing at Work: From Principle to Practice**   273

Chapter 8   Understanding the Principles of Business Communication   275
Chapter 9   Writing Business Correspondence   320
Chapter 10   Writing Informal Reports   358
Chapter 11   Writing Formal Reports   385
Chapter 12   Writing Instructions   422
Chapter 13   Writing Proposals   448
Chapter 14   Giving Presentations and Conducting Meetings   498
Chapter 15   Writing for the Web: Rhetorical Principles   539
Chapter 16   Finding the Right Job   570

PART FOUR   **Revision Guide: Sentences, Punctuation, and Mechanics**   623

Sentences   625
Punctuation   643
Mechanics   662
English as a Second Language (ESL)   670

Contents

List of Sample Documents   *(inside front cover)*

Preface   *v*

About the Authors   *xiii*

Brief Contents   *xv*

PART ONE   **The Writing Process**   **1**

Chapter 1   **Assessing Audience and Purpose: A Case Study**   3

Writing Systematically   4
Determining Your Purpose   5
Assessing Your Audience's Needs   6
Considering the Context   8
Generating, Gathering, and Recording Ideas and Facts   8
  Brainstorming 9 • *Using Other Sources of Information 11*
Establishing Your Scope   11
Organizing Your Ideas   12

Writing for Results   14
Chapter Summary 21 • Exercises 21 • Collaborative Classroom Projects 23 • Research Projects 24

Chapter 2   **Organizing Your Information**   **25**

Outlining   26
Traditional Roman Numeral Outline   26
Decimal Numbering System Outline   28

How Audience and Purpose Shape Organization: A Case Study   31

Essential Organizing Patterns   34
Sequential   34
Chronological   36
Spatial   36
Division and Classification   40
Decreasing Order of Importance   44

Increasing Order of Importance   45

General to Specific   47

Specific to General   50

Comparison   51

Chapter Summary 58 • Exercises 58 • Collaborative Classroom Projects 61 • Research Projects 62

Chapter 3   Writing the Draft   64

Time-Management Tactics   65

Allocating Your Time   65

Preparing Your Work Environment   66

Remaining Flexible   66

Keeping Your Audience in Mind   67

Writing from the Audience's Point of View   68

Accommodating Multiple Audiences   68

Writing for an International Audience   70

Persuading Your Audience   70

Establishing Your Role and Voice as the Writer   71

Development Strategies   75

Explaining a Process   76

Describing Information   77

Defining Terms and Concepts   79

Explaining Cause and Effect   82

Writing an Opening   84

Writing a Closing   86

Case Study: Drafting the Lifemaker Brochure   87

Chapter Summary 89 • Exercises 90 • Collaborative Classroom Projects 91 • Research Projects 92

Chapter 4   Revising the Draft   94

Content and Organization   96

Coherence   97

Paragraph Unity   97

Transitions   98

Transitions Between Sentences 99 • Transitions Between Paragraphs 100

Emphasis   101

    Active and Passive Voice   101

    Subordination   102

    Parallel Structure   104

    Lists   104

    Other Ways to Achieve Emphasis   105

Point of View   106

Language   107

    Context and Word Choice   108

    Conciseness   109

        Redundancy 109 • Padded Phrases 109 • Bias 110 • Sexist Language 110 • Other Types of Biased Language 111

    Plain Language   112

        Affectation 112 • Technical Terminology 113 • Jargon 114

Proofreading   115

Physical Appearance   116

Case Study: Revising the Lifemaker Brochure   116

Chapter Summary 120 • Exercises 121 • Collaborative Classroom Projects 123 • Research Projects 124

PART TWO   Essential Skills: Collaboration, Research, and Design   127

Chapter 5   Collaborative Writing   129

Advantages and Disadvantages of Collaborative Writing   130

Functions of a Collaborative Writing Team   131

    Planning   131

    Research and Writing   133

    Review and Revision   134

The Role of Conflict in Collaborative Writing   137

Leading a Collaborative Writing Team   139

    Schedule   139

    Review Transmittal Sheet   141

Collaborating with Other Departments   141

Chapter Summary 142 • Exercises 143 • Collaborative Classroom
Projects 144 • Research Projects 145

Chapter 6   Researching Your Subject   148

**Conducting Primary Research: Experience, Interviews,
Observations, and Questionnaires   149**

Beginning with Experience   150

Interviewing for Information   150

*Determining Whom to Interview 150 • Preparing for the Interview 151 •
Conducting the Interview 151 • Expanding Your Notes After the
Interview 152*

Observing Firsthand   152

Using a Questionnaire   152

*Selecting Questionnaire Recipients 153 • Preparing and Designing
Your Questionnaire 153*

**Conducting Secondary Research: The Library
and the Internet   157**

Developing a Search Strategy   157

Library Research   158

*Using Library Catalogs to Locate Books 159 • Using Databases to Locate
Articles 161 • Using Reference Works to Locate Facts and Topic Overviews 162
• Other Library Resources 165*

Internet Research   166

*Using Search Engines and Web Subject Directories 166 • Locating Business
and Government Sites 170*

**Evaluating, Recording, and Acknowledging Research
Sources   171**

Evaluating Sources   171

Authority 172 • Accuracy 173 • Bias 173 • Currency 173

Taking Notes   174

Quoting from Your Sources   176

*Direct Quotations 176 • Indirect Quotations 176 • Deletions or
Omissions 177 • Inserting Material into Quotations 177 • Incorporating
Quotations into Text 177*

Paraphrasing   178

Summarizing   179

Avoiding Plagiarism and Copyright Violations   180

*Acknowledging Your Sources 180 • Common Knowledge 180 •
Copyright 181 • Public-Domain Materials 181 • In-House Materials 181*

Documenting Sources   181

APA Style   182

APA In-Text Citations 182   •   APA Citation Format for a References List 184   •
APA Documentation Models 186   •   APA Sample Pages 191

MLA Style   193

MLA In-Text Citations 193   •   MLA Citation Format for a List of Works
Cited 194   •   MLA Documentation Models 197   •   MLA Sample Pages 201

Other Style Manuals   203

Chapter Summary 204   •   Exercises 205   •   Collaborative Classroom
Projects 207   •   Research Projects 207

Chapter 7   **Designing Effective Documents**
and Visuals   209

Designing Documents   210

Typography   212

Typeface 212   •   Type Size 212

Highlighting Devices   213

Typographical Devices 213   •   Headings and Captions 213   •   Headers
and Footers 215   •   Rules, Icons, and Color 215   •   Page Design   216   •
Thumbnail Sketches 216   •   Columns 216   •   White Space 216   •
Left- or Full-Justified Margins 219   •   Lists 219   •   Illustrations 219

Creating Visuals   220

Designing and Integrating Visuals with Text   220

Tables   224

Graphs   228

Line Graphs 228   •   Bar Graphs 233   •   Pie Graphs 235   •   Picture
Graphs 238   •   Dimensional-Column Graphs 238

Drawings   241

Flowcharts   244

Organizational Charts   247

Maps   247

Photographs   248

Highlighting Photographic Objects 249   •   Using Color 249

Using Visuals to Communicate Internationally   250

Colors 252   •   People, Parts of the Body, and Gestures 252   •   Cultural
Symbols 254   •   Reading Practices 255   •   Directional Signs 255

Chapter Summary 256   •   Exercises 257   •   Collaborative Classroom
Projects 259   •   Research Projects 260

Writing@Work: A Portfolio   261

Nursing 262 • Radio Disc Jockey 265 • Elementary Education 266 •
Public Relations 267 • Microbiology 268 • Casting Agencies 269 •
Structural Engineering 270 • Research Consulting 266 •

PART THREE   Writing at Work: From Principle
to Practice   273

Chapter 8   Understanding the Principles
of Business Communication   275

Selecting the Appropriate Medium   277
E-mail   277
Instant Messages   277
Memos   278
Letters   278
Faxes   278
Telephone and Conference Calls   278
Voice-Mail Messages   279
Face-to-Face Meetings   279
Videoconferences   279
Web Communication   280

Developing Style and Tone   280
Audience and Writing Style   281
Goodwill and the "You" Viewpoint   282

Structuring Effective Correspondence   283
Direct and Indirect Patterns   283
Direct Pattern 283
Openings   288
Closings   289
Clarity and Emphasis   290
Lists 290 • Headings 290
Subject Lines   291
Observing Protocol   291
Organizational Rank 291 • Copy Protocol 292

Meeting the Deadline: The Time-Sensitive Message   293
Understand the Assignment   293
Gather Information   293

Organize Your Thoughts   294
Write the Draft   294
Polish the Draft   294
Take a Well-Deserved Break   295

Writing E-mail and Instant Messages   295
Review and Confidentiality Implications   295
Observing Netiquette   296
Design Considerations   297
Salutations, Closings, and Signature Blocks   298
Writing and Managing Instant Messages   301

Designing Memos   303
Memo Format and Parts   303
Additional Pages   305

Designing Letters   306
Heading   306
Inside Address   309
Salutation   309
Body   310
Complimentary Closing   311
Writer's Signature Block   311
Continuing Pages   311
End Notations   312

Chapter Summary 313 • Exercises 315 • Collaborative Classroom
Projects 317 • Research Projects 319

Chapter 9   Writing Business Correspondence   320

Routine and Positive Messages   321
Covers (or Transmittals)   321
Acknowledgments   321
Inquiries   321
Responses to Inquiries   325
Sales and Promotions   325

Sensitive and Negative Messages   330
Refusals   330
Complaints   331
Adjustments   336
Collections   339

Writing International Correspondence   343

Culture and Business-Writing Style   343

Language and Usage   346

Dates, Time, and Measurement   347

Cross-Cultural Examples   347

Chapter Summary 352 • Exercises 352 • Collaborative Classroom
Projects 355 • Research Projects 356

Chapter 10   Writing Informal Reports   358

Planning and Writing Informal Reports   358

Considering Audience   359

Collecting Information   359

Parts of the Informal Report   360

    Introduction 360 • Body 360 • Conclusions and Recommendations 360

Types of Informal Reports   361

Progress and Periodic Reports   361

    Progress Reports 362 • Periodic Reports 364

Investigative Reports   365

Trouble Reports   370

Trip Reports   373

Test Reports   374

Chapter Summary 379 • Exercises 379 • Collaborative Classroom
Projects 382 • Research Projects 383

Chapter 11   Writing Formal Reports   385

Transmittal Letter or Memo   388

Front Matter   389

Title Page   389

Abstract   390

Table of Contents   394

List of Figures   394

List of Tables   394

Foreword   395

Preface   396

List of Abbreviations and Symbols   396

Body   396

Executive Summary   398

Introduction   400

Introducing the Subject 400 • Stating the Purpose 400 • Stating the Scope 400 • Previewing How the Topic Will Be Developed 400

Text (Body)   403

Headings 403 • Explanatory Notes 408 • Graphic and Tabular Matter 410

Conclusions   410

Recommendations   410

Works Cited (or References)   411

Back Matter   414

Bibliography   414

Appendixes   415

Glossary   415

Index   415

Chapter Summary 417 • Exercises 418 • Collaborative Classroom Projects 419 • Research Projects 419

Chapter 12   Writing Instructions   422

Planning Instructions   423

Learn to Perform the Operation Yourself   423

Assess Your Audience and Purpose   423

Coworkers 424 • Consumers 425 • International Readers 427

Organize the Instructions   428

Writing Instructions   432

Write Directly to Your Reader   432

Include Warnings and Cautions   433

Language of Warnings 434 • Visual Symbols and Signal Words 434

Using Illustrations and Design Principles   436

Illustrate for Clarity   436

Design for Ease of Use   438

Testing for Usability   442

Chapter Summary 443 • Exercises 444 • Collaborative Classroom Projects 445 • Research Projects 445

Chapter 13   Writing Proposals   448

Planning and Writing Proposals   449

Audience and Purpose   449

Project Management   451

Repurposing Content (Boilerplate)   451
Organization   452
Persuasive Writing   452

Internal Proposals   454
Routine Internal Proposals   454
Formal Internal Proposals   454

External Proposals   463
Solicited Proposals   463
Unsolicited Proposals   463
Grant and Research Proposals   468
  Cover Letter 470 • Title Page 470 • Introduction/Summary/Abstract 470 •
  Literature Review 470 • Project Narrative 470 • Project Description 470 •
  Project Outcomes 473 • Budget 473 • Schedule 475 • Conclusion 475
Sales Proposals   475

Meeting the Deadline: The Time-Sensitive Proposal   488

Requests for Proposals   490
RFP Structure   490
Information about Your Company   490
Project Description   491
Delivery Schedule   491
Proposal Description   491
Vendor Qualifications   492
Proposal-Evaluation Criteria   492
Appendixes   492

Chapter Summary 493 • Exercises 494 • Collaborative Classroom
Projects 496 • Research Projects 497

**Chapter 14   Giving Presentations
and Conducting Meetings**   498

Preparing and Delivering Presentations   499
Determining Your Purpose   499
Analyzing Your Audience   500
Gathering Information   500
Structuring Your Presentation   500
  Introduction 501 • Body 502 • Closing 502 • Transitions 503
Using Visual Aids   504
  Using Presentation Software 507 • Using Flip Charts, Whiteboards,
  and Chalkboards 509 • Using Overhead Transparencies and Slides 510 •
  Using Handouts 511

Delivering Your Presentation   511

Practicing Your Presentation 511 • Using Delivery Techniques That Work 512 • Dealing with Presentation Anxiety 514

Reaching Global Audiences   515

Listening   516

Fallacies About Listening   516

Steps to More Effective Listening   517

Make a Conscious Decision 517 • Define Your Purpose 517 • Take Specific Actions 517 • Adapt to the Situation 519

Meeting the Deadline: The Time-Sensitive Presentation   519

Conducting Productive Meetings   523

Planning a Meeting   523

What Is the Purpose of the Meeting? 523 • Who Should Attend? 524 • When Should the Meeting Be Held? 524 • Where Should the Meeting Be Held? 524 • What's on the Agenda? 525

Running a Meeting   527

Dealing with Conflict 529 • Making a Record of Decisions and Assignments 530 • Closing the Meeting 532

Chapter Summary 533 • Exercises 535 • Collaborative Classroom Projects 536 • Research Projects 537

Chapter 15   Writing for the Web: Rhetorical Principles   539

Writing for Rapid Consumption   540

Crafting Content for the Web   540

Using the Inverted Pyramid   540

Using a Simple Style and an Appropriate Tone   541

Writing Concisely   543

Chunking Content   543

Linking to Internal Content   545

Linking to External Content   547

Highlighting Information   549

Using Headings and Subheadings   549

Using Bulleted and Numbered Lists   549

Giving Directional Cues   550

Providing Keywords for Content Retrieval   550

Using Graphics and Typography   550

Graphics 551 • Font Size and Style 551 • Line Length 551 • Special Font Characters 552

Enhancing Access to Content   552

Ensuring Access for People with Disabilities   553

Considering International Users   553

Repurposing Existing Content   554

Protecting the Privacy of Your Users   555

Documenting Sources of Information   557

Contributing to Collaborative and Multimedia Content   558

Blogs   559

Organizational Blogs 559 • Writing for Organizational Blogs 560 • Tagging Blog Postings 561

Wikis   563

Podcasts   563

FAQs (Frequently Asked Questions)   564

Questions to Include 564 • Placement 564

Chapter Summary 565 • Exercises 567 • Collaborative Classroom Projects 568 • Research Projects 568

Chapter 16   Finding the Right Job   570

Determining the Best Job for You   571

Networking   572

Campus Career Services   572

Web Resources   572

Advertisements   574

Trade and Professional Journal Listings   575

Private and Temporary Employment Agencies   575

Internships   576

Government Employment Services   577

Letters of Inquiry and Informational Interviews   577

Job-Search Record Keeping   577

Preparing an Effective Résumé   578

Analyzing Your Background   578

Organizing Your Résumé   580

The Heading 581 • Job Objective 581 • Qualifications Summary 582 • Education 582 • Employment Experience 582 • Related Skills and Abilities 586 • Honors and Activities 586 • References 587 • Portfolios 587 • Salary 587

Electronic Résumés   587

Scannable and Plain-Text Résumés 587 • E-mail–Attached Résumés 590 • Web Résumés 590

Sample Résumés   592

Writing an Effective Letter of Application   602

Opening Paragraph   603

Body Paragraphs   603

Closing Paragraph   604

Sample Letters   605

Doing Well in the Interview   609

Before the Interview   609

During the Interview   611

Behavior 611 • Responses 611 • Salary Negotiations 612 • Conclusion 612

Sending Follow-up Correspondence   613

Sending a Resignation Letter or Memo   615

Chapter Summary 617 • Exercises 618 • Collaborative Classroom Projects 619 • Research Projects 620

PART FOUR   Revision Guide: Sentences, Punctuation, and Mechanics   623

Proofreaders' Marks   624

Sentences   625

Sentence Faults   625

Run-on Sentences and Comma Splices   625

Sentence Fragments   626

Dangling and Misplaced Modifiers   627

Pronouns   627

Pronoun Case   627

Determining Case 628 • Using Who *or* Whom *629*

Pronoun Reference   629

Pronoun-Antecedent Agreement   630

Person 630 • Gender 630 • Number 631

Adjectives and Adverbs   632

Comparatives and Superlatives   632

Placement   633

Verbs   635

Subject-Verb Agreement   635

Intervening Words 636 • Inverted Word Order 636 • Collective Subjects 636 • Compound Subjects 637 • Indefinite Pronouns 637 • Relative Pronouns 637 • Singular Nouns Ending in -s 638 • Book Titles 638 • Subject Complements 638

Voice   638

Mood   639

Tense   640

Punctuation   643

Commas   643

Linking Independent Clauses   643

Introducing Elements   644

Clauses and Phrases 644 • Words 644 • Quotations 645

Enclosing Elements   645

Separating Elements   645

Items in a Series 645 • Adjectives 646 • Dates 646 • Numbers 647 • Addresses 647 • Names 647

Using Commas with Other Punctuation   647

Avoiding Unnecessary Commas   648

Semicolons   648

Colons   649

Apostrophes   650

Showing Possession   650

Singular Nouns 650 • Plural Nouns 651 • Compound Nouns 651 • Coordinate Nouns 651 • Possessive Pronouns 651

Indicating Omission   652

Forming Plurals   652

Quotation Marks   653

Identifying Quotations   653

Setting Off Words, Phrases, and Titles   653

Words and Phrases 653 • Titles of Works 654

Using Quotation Marks with Other Punctuation   654

Periods   654

Question Marks   655

Exclamation Marks   656

Parentheses and Brackets   656

Hyphens   657
  Linking Modifiers   657
  Separating Prefixes and Suffixes   658
  Other Uses   659

Dashes   659

Ellipses   660

Slashes   661

Mechanics   662

Capitalization   662
  Proper Nouns   662
  Common Nouns   662
  First Words   662
  Specific Groups   663
  Specific Places   663
  Specific Institutions, Events, Concepts   663
  Titles of Works   664
  Professional and Personal Titles   664
  Abbreviations, Letters, and Units   664

Numbers   664
  Words or Numerals   665
  Money   665
  Plurals   665
  Measurements   666
  Time and Dates   666
  Addresses   667
  Documents   667

Abbreviations   667
  Names of Organizations   667
  Measurements   667
  Personal Names and Titles   668

Italics   668
  Foreign Words and Phrases   668
  Titles   669
  Proper Names   669

Words, Letters, and Numerals   669
Subheads   669

English as a Second Language (ESL)   670

Count and Mass Nouns   670

Articles   671

Prepositions   672

Gerunds and Infinitives   673

Adjective Clauses   673

Verb Tenses   673
Present Perfect   673
Present Progressive   674

Helping Verbs   674

Conditional Sentences   675

Index   679

Menu of Tips and Checklists   (inside back cover)

PART 1

The Writing Process

Chapter 1
**Assessing Audience and Purpose:
A Case Study, 3**

Chapter 2
Organizing Your Information, 25

Chapter 3
Writing the Draft, 64

Chapter 4
Revising the Draft, 94

In Part One, you will learn techniques for developing, drafting, and revising letters, memos, e-mails, and a wide array of other on-the-job writing tasks. These techniques will help you produce clearly written, well-organized documents because effective on-the-job writing always reflects the writer's attention to the work that goes on before the finished document emerges from the printer.

◆ **Determining Audience and Purpose.** Chapters 1 through 3 provide discussion and exercises to help you clearly define your reader's needs for the message you intend for your document.

◆ **Brainstorming and Gathering Information.** Chapter 1 includes a detailed case study to illustrate methods you can use to generate ideas, to select only those that are relevant, and to begin organizing them clearly for your audience.

◆ **Outlining.** Chapter 2 describes in detail how you can organize your information into an outline that is appropriate to your purpose and audience. It also offers examples in a wide range of outline styles.

◆ **Writing the Draft.** Chapter 3 discusses and offers examples of the process by which writers turn an outline into a workable rough draft.

◆ **Revising.** Chapter 4 describes the kinds of problems you need to evaluate when you revise your draft. You will learn to review your draft to see how well it communicates to its intended audience, to be sure it is complete and coherent, to look for ways to emphasize key ideas, to check information for accuracy, to consider the ethical implications of your writing, and to proof

1 Assessing Audience and Purpose: A Case Study

AT A GLANCE: The Writing Process

This chapter describes how one employee successfully completed an important on-the-job writing task from first thought to final product. The process occurs in a series of steps applicable to all workplace writing:

- Following a systematic approach / 4
  - Determining why you are writing / 5
  - Thinking about your audience / 6
  - Considering the context for your writing / 8
  - Gathering information with your audience, purpose, and context in mind / 8
  - Choosing the scope of information most pertinent to your purpose / 11
  - Organizing your information / 12
- Writing for results / 14
  - Writing a rough draft / 15
  - Revising and editing / 17

Christine Thomas was aware of a potential opportunity at HVS Accounting Services, where she worked as the company's systems administrator. The company was prospering. In just the past year, Harriet Sullivan, the president and founder of the small company, hired five new employees to handle the increasing workload of tax preparation, financial planning, and investment services. HVS now had 12 full-time employees, about half of whom commuted over an hour each way. Christine was also aware that the company recently had lost several promising job applicants because they did not wish to spend two or more hours a day driving to and from work.

With this information in mind, Christine had carefully reviewed several management magazines and Web sites about the benefits of telecommuting for companies and their employees. Companies that offered this option to their employees had a more satisfied workforce, less absenteeism, and greater productivity per employee.

> **To:**   Harriet V. Sullivan, President
> **From:**   Christine Thomas, Systems Administrator
> **Date:**   May 5, 2010
> **Subject:** Telecommuting and HVS Accounting Services
>
> I believe that HVS Accounting would benefit greatly if we permitted our employees to telecommute one or more days a week. A growing number of companies, large and small, permit employees to perform company work at home on a schedule they jointly agree to. The companies can communicate with these employees during the workday in a variety of ways — by phone, e-mail, and fax.
>
> Such a policy has many advantages that would help HVS and our employees. Employees would save the time and expense necessary to commute every day. They would also suffer less stress and be in a better frame of mind to tackle their work. This would result in greater worker productivity. Please consider my suggestion that we offer our employees the opportunity to perform their HVS work at home one or more days a week.
>
> Christine

Figure 1–1   First Proposal (E-mail)

So, with all the information in hand and confident of the value of her suggestion, Christine wrote an e-mail message to Harriet Sullivan (Figure 1–1). Two days later, Christine received the following terse return e-mail from Harriet: "Not right for HVS." Christine was not only disappointed but also puzzled. She knew that her suggestion was timely and reasonable because she had checked all the facts before writing the e-mail. Yet she had failed to convince Harriet Sullivan.

Writing Systematically

In writing her e-mail message, Christine Thomas committed the most common mistake made by people who write on the job: She lost sight of the purpose of her message and overlooked the needs of her audience. Christine was so convinced of the value of her suggestion that she did not consider that Harriet may not be familiar with the information her research had produced and could not see the situation from her perspective. Had she kept her primary purpose and her reader clearly in mind, Christine would have been able to generate ideas, establish her scope, and organize her thoughts in a way that ultimately might have achieved her objective. The last three steps are important: Even with her reader and her purpose clearly in mind, Christine would not have been ready to write her e-mail to Harriet. She would simply have established a framework in which to develop her message. Once they have identified their purpose and their audience, some writers don't know what to do next and stare at a blank page or computer screen waiting for inspiration.

A systematic approach helps writers over this hurdle. Before beginning to write, careful writers not only identify their purpose and audience but also think seriously about the context of their writing and strive to organize and present information for ease of understanding. This process involves first listing all the ideas and facts the writer might wish to include, refining that list by examining each item from the perspectives of audience and purpose, and organizing what's left in a way that satisfies both the writer's purpose and the audience's needs.

WRITER'S CHECKLIST
Planning Your Document

✔ Determine your purpose.

✔ Assess your audience's needs.

✔ Consider the context of your writing.

✔ Generate, gather, and record ideas and facts.

✔ Establish the scope of coverage for your topic.

✔ Organize your ideas.

Determining Your Purpose

Everything you write has a purpose. You want your readers to know, to believe, or to be able to do something when they have finished reading what you have written. Determining your purpose is the first step in preparing to write; unless you know what you hope to accomplish, you cannot know what information you should present.

Purpose gives direction to your writing. The more precisely you can state your primary purpose at the outset, the more successful your writing is likely to be. (You may also have a secondary purpose, such as to motivate or to reassure.) Christine Thomas might have said that her purpose was "to allow HVS employees to telecommute"—but permitting employees to telecommute was the *result* she wanted; it was not the precise purpose of her memo. Further thought would have led Christine to recognize the specific goals of the e-mail itself. To make sure that your purpose is precise, put it in writing. In most cases, you can use the following pattern to guide you:

▷ My primary purpose is to   so that my audience   .

By filling in the blanks, Christine Thomas might have developed the following statement of purpose:

▷ My primary purpose is to explain the advantages of telecommuting to Harriet Sullivan so that she agrees to permit it at HVS Accounting for a trial period.

With this statement of purpose, Christine would have recognized that her purpose was more complicated than it had at first appeared and that she would have to present persuasive evidence to be effective.

Assessing Your Audience's Needs

Your job as a writer is to express your ideas so clearly that your audience cannot misinterpret them. An important element of the purpose statement is the phrase "so that my audience . . .". Simply identifying the response you would like is very different from actually achieving it. Although a purpose statement addresses a problem from the writer's point of view, the audience's needs must also be taken into account if you are to be persuasive. Yet many writers often forget that they have an audience, and they focus solely on their own purposes.

After you have stated your purpose, ask yourself, "Who is my audience?" Often you will know the answer. For example, if you are writing a memo attempting to persuade your manager to fund a project, you know who your reader is. In another situation, however, you might be writing a letter to someone you do not know in another company. In this case, you would try to imagine your reader, taking into consideration what you know about that company, your reader's position in the company or department, and his or her responsibilities regarding the topic you are writing about. You could not know what your reader's needs are until you know at least that much about him or her.

VOICES IN THE WORKPLACE

Thinking About Audience and Purpose

In her role as president and chief executive officer of the Children's Museum of Phoenix, Deborah Gilpin knows the importance of audience and purpose to her organization's communications: "Thank-you notes for contributions express gratitude and strengthen the personal connection the donor has to the museum's purpose. Proposals, on the other hand, serve as an invitation to contributions, participation, and collaborative work."

When you know enough about your reader that you can actually picture him or her responding to what you have written, you have an advantage. However, even if you know your audience very well, a little reflection is necessary. Without careful thought, Christine Thomas might have answered the question "Who is my reader?" from only one point of view:

▶   My reader is Harriet Sullivan, and she's been my manager for ten years. We've worked together since she founded the company, so she'll no doubt understand that I have her best interests in mind.

Had Christine carefully analyzed Harriet as the reader of her e-mail, she would have considered Harriet's role in the company, her lack of familiarity with the

▶ CONSIDERING AUDIENCE AND PURPOSE

Writing for Your Reader

Try to answer each of the following questions in as much detail as possible to help focus on your reader's needs in relation to your subject. This process is helpful for all types of writing, but it will be especially important for longer, more complex tasks.

- ■ Who is your audience?
- ■ Do you have more than one audience?
- ■ What do you want your audience to know, to believe, or to be able to do after reading your writing?
- ■ Have you narrowed your topic to best focus on what you want your audience to know?
- ■ What are your audience's needs in relation to the subject?
- ■ What does your audience know about the subject?
- ■ If you have multiple audiences, do they have different levels of knowledge about your subject?
- ■ What are your audience's feelings about your subject—sympathetic? hostile? neutral?
- ■ Does your writing acknowledge other or contrary points of view about the subject?
- ■ Have you selected the right medium—e-mail, memo, letter, advertising flyer, and so on—for your subject and audience?
- ■ Is your tone respectful?
- ■ Does your format enhance audience understanding?

topic, and her anxiety about taking such a step. Bearing these concerns in mind, Christine might have answered the question differently.

▷ My reader is Harriet Sullivan, president of HVS Accounting Services. Harriet founded HVS ten years ago with modest savings and a substantial loan. Cautious, industrious, and a stickler for detail, Harriet has built HVS into a sound business and is now beginning to see some return on her investment. Harriet is also a hands-on executive. She puts in long hours at the office and is in frequent contact with the staff by e-mail, telephone, and face-to-face conversations. In addition to a regularly scheduled staff meeting every Wednesday, she holds informal meetings several times a week. She may strongly resist the loss of hands-on access to her staff when they work at home. She values computer technology and purchased laptop computers for the accountants and financial analysts to help them as they visit clients throughout the metropolitan area. However, although she uses e-mail regularly, she does so reluctantly and prefers memos.

Based on this analysis, Christine would have been better prepared to provide the information that Harriet needed to understand, to agree with, and to act on Christine's proposal.

ON THE WEB

For online resources for determining audience and purpose, go to Chapter 1, bedfordstmartins.com/ writingthatworks

Considering the Context

In the workplace, everything is written in a context. The environment, or situation, in which you write a document (such as a proposal, letter, or report) will affect how your audience interprets its meaning. Even a good idea will fail to get support if the writer does not take into account the circumstances—both inside and outside the organization—that could influence its acceptance.

Christine Thomas, for example, had to consider her manager's style and the company's infrastructure. Aware of Harriet's hands-on approach to management, Christine needed to address Harriet's potential anxiety about the staff being away from the office one or more days a week. Christine also had to consider the larger context of how telecommuting might affect the company as a whole. For example, she needed to think about each staff member's personal situation and commuting habits, equipment requirements, communications technologies, customer confidentiality and convenience, jobs most and least suitable for telecommuting, and any expenses her suggestions might incur. Without addressing these issues, she could not adequately develop a proposal that would merit Harriet's serious consideration.

WRITER'S CHECKLIST
Assessing Context

Use the following questions as a starting point as you assess the context for your topic:

- ✔ What is your professional relationship with your readers, and how might that affect the tone, style, and scope of your writing?
- ✔ What is "the story" behind the immediate reason you are writing; that is, what series of events or previous documents led to your need to write?
- ✔ What medium do your readers prefer—memo, letter, report, or e-mail?
- ✔ What specific factors or values, such as competition, finance, and regulation, are important to your readers' organization or department?
- ✔ What is the corporate culture in which your readers work?
- ✔ What are the professional relationships among your readers?
- ✔ What recent or current events within or outside an organization or a department may influence how readers interpret your writing?
- ✔ What national cultural differences might affect your readers' expectations for or interpretations of a document?

Generating, Gathering, and Recording Ideas and Facts

When you have determined your purpose, assessed your reader's needs, and considered the context for your writing, you must decide what information will satisfy these demands. Several techniques are available for gathering and recording information.

Brainstorming

A good way to start generating ideas is to tap into your own knowledge and experience. You may find that you already have enough information to get started. The technique of interviewing yourself, commonly known as *brainstorming*, may also suggest ways to obtain additional information. To begin, list as many ideas as you can think of about the general subject of your document as they occur to you. (This type of research also works well with a group of writers or project team members.) Jot down what you already know and, if possible, where you learned of it, using a computer, a dry-erase board, a pad of paper, or note cards.

Journalists and other writers have long used the following questions as a guide to ensure that they have answered the questions their audience is likely to have about a particular story: *What* happened? *Why* did it happen? *When* did it happen? *How* did it happen? *Where* did it happen? *Who* was involved? Rarely will you be able to apply all these questions to any single on-the-job writing situation, but the range of information they cover can help to start your thinking.

Once you have assembled a list of ideas, examine each item and decide whether it contributes to your purpose or satisfies your audience's needs. Then mark the item with a *P* for purpose or an *A* for audience. Some items will satisfy both your purpose and your audience, others will appear to satisfy only one, and still others will appear to have nothing to do with either. When you have finished marking your list, cross out any item not marked with a *P* or an *A*. Be sure to reconsider an unmarked item from the perspectives of both your purpose and your audience, making certain that the item fits neither before eliminating it. Ideally, you will have a comprehensive list of items beside which you have placed both a *P* and an *A*. The more common ground your purpose and your audience's needs share, the more effective your writing will be.

As you review your list, you will find that items relating clearly to both your purpose and the needs of your audience are easiest to work with. Items that your audience might need but that would get in the way of your purpose are trickier. Harriet Sullivan, for example, needs to know that after the program begins, she will have less direct access to employees working from home. Because she's a hands-on manager, this break with her customary practice will be difficult for Harriet to accept. Christine, however, might be reluctant to mention this fact because it appears to undermine her purpose, which is to persuade Harriet to support telecommuting. To reconcile Harriet's interests and her own, Christine would have to point out this aspect of the program. To have credibility, you need to acknowledge opposing points of view when they are relevant; doing so allows you to respond to your audience's objections rather than leaving them unanswered.

ETHICS NOTE

Be honest in acknowledging any real or potential conflicting opinions. Doing so not only is ethical but also allows you to anticipate and overcome possible objections. It helps build your credibility by showing readers that your coverage is balanced.

Turning a writer's list of ideas into a reader's list of information should be neither difficult nor mysterious; thoroughness is the key. Christine Thomas, for example, might have generated the well-balanced list shown in Figure 1–2, using one or more of the methods described here. Such a list will give you an idea of the content of the project. The list will probably be sketchy or have missing information, but that's actually helpful in showing where additional research is needed. It will also give you a framework for where to integrate the details of the additional research.

ITEMS FOR TELECOMMUTING PROPOSAL

A	Harriet needs to see benefits of new practice
P	Current commutes too long
AP	Employee morale down because of long commutes
A	Good feature for recruiting and keeping skilled staff
A	Productivity gains
P	Saves employees time and money
A	Done elsewhere?
P	~~Eliminate the need for current office space?~~
P	Need for additional equipment — computers? phones? faxes?
A	Cost of additional technology
A	Do on trial basis
A	Is home work space OK?
A	Need to establish home working hours
P	~~Advantages to community~~
P	Benefits to employees of avoiding long commutes
A	Advantages to customers?
PA	Benefits to employees with special needs
P	~~Employee isolation~~
P	Is this a program for everyone?
A	Management can't look in on workers — not physically in office
P	Not all jobs lend themselves to telecommuting
A	What about staff meetings?
A	What about meetings with clients?
A	What about taking confidential information home?
A	How can Harriet assess employee productivity?
A	Danger of losing employee loyalty?
A	What are the benefits for HVS?
A	Will employees be distracted at home?
AP	Does program apply to all HVS employees?
A	~~Will those not in program resent those who are?~~
A	How will work be coordinated among employees?

Figure 1–2   Brainstorming List for a Proposal

Using Other Sources of Information

Brainstorming may not produce all the information you need. Christine, for example, read about telecommuting by reviewing trade journals and Web sites in the field. To get enough information to meet the needs of your audience, you may have to conduct formal, systematic research. In such cases, you should have some idea of how thoroughly you will cover your subject. To consult the appropriate sources, you will have to know how much detail is required. If you know what you are looking for and where to find it, research presents few problems.

The library contains books, articles, and reference works. In addition, reference librarians also provide expert assistance, including access to search tools and online databases not available on the Internet. The Internet, used carefully, provides access to information from commercial, educational, governmental, and other sources. A personal interview with an expert can provide you with up-to-date information not readily available in printed material. A questionnaire permits you to obtain the views of a group of people and requires less time and money than numerous personal interviews.

These different sources of information are discussed in detail in Chapter 6, Researching Your Subject.

Establishing Your Scope

Having refined your list of ideas and facts, you must review it once again to establish the scope of coverage for your topic. Your *scope* is the degree of detail you decide is necessary to cover each item in your list, and you must determine it based on your purpose and the needs of your audience. As you contemplate each item, ask yourself, "How much information should I include to support my purpose and satisfy my audience's needs?" Often you will find that you have omitted important points or that you need to research your subject further to obtain necessary facts or figures. At other times, you will find that your list is cluttered with unnecessary detail.

Had Christine Thomas drawn up the list shown in Figure 1–2 and then reviewed it to establish her scope, she would have discovered that some of the items on her list needed detailed information to satisfy Harriet Sullivan's concerns. Entries such as "Cost of additional technology" would tell her that she had to either provide detailed figures for the cost of this equipment or explain why no additional expense is necessary. However, other items requiring more detail might be more difficult to identify: "How can Harriet assess employee productivity?" indicates Christine's sense that evaluating productivity would present a cost-conscious person like Harriet with a challenge. She would want to know how this could be done effectively.

Figure 1–3 shows the list in Figure 1–2 after the scope has been established. Christine eliminated the ideas outside the scope of her purpose, such as concerns about employee morale and office space. She crossed out the first item, too. It's unnecessary because Harriet's need to see the benefits of the new practice is the overall topic of her proposal, not a separate topic within it.

POINTS TO COVER

- *Good feature for recruiting and keeping skilled staff*
- *Productivity gains — note industry data*
- *Saves employees time and money*
- *Our competitors permit telecommuting*
- *Costs of additional technology and types needed — although HVS is set up well right now*
- *Do on trial basis — recommend three months, two days/week*
- *Need to establish home working hours*
- *Advantages to customers — maybe?*
- *Benefits to employees with special needs — two HVS employees can use now!*
- *Employee morale down because of long commutes*
- *Management can't look in on workers — not physically in office*
- *Not all jobs lend themselves to telecommuting — such as receptionist*
- *Scheduling staff and client meetings*
- *Need to protect confidential information when home*
- *Show how Harriet can assess employee productivity*
- *Possible danger of losing employee loyalty*
- *Address possibility that employees will be distracted at home*

Figure 1–3   Notes for Proposal

Be careful when establishing your scope. Writers who know a lot about a subject tend to unload information on audiences who have no time or need to wade through a catalog of topics or details to get to the point. Understand, too, that establishing your scope in the classroom may be different from doing so on the job. Classroom assignments must often be limited because of accessibility of information, the goals of the course, or other learning objectives. Consider these limitations as part of the purpose of an assignment. Whether in class or the workplace, however, be guided by your purpose and your audience's needs in establishing your scope of coverage.

Organizing Your Ideas

Once you have established your scope, you should have a list of the ideas and facts to be included in your writing. Examine this list and look for relationships among the items in it. Group the related ideas and arrange them under headings, using short phrases that identify the kind of items in each group. As you group the related ideas, consider the following questions: Is the time sequence _a Case Study_

.ow risk

.and retention

.ERNS

.dditional equipment

.o establish home working space and hours

.t for all jobs or employees

- Can't observe workers firsthand
- Staff meetings
- Client meetings
- Confidential information
- Assessing productivity
- Employee loyalty
- Distractions at home
- Coordinating work

3.   EMPLOYEE BENEFITS

- Help special-needs employees
- Improve morale — less time on the road
- Save time and expense

Figure 1–4   Revised Notes for Proposal

among items important? If so, organize them chronologically. Do you need to compare the features of one item with those of one or more other items? Organize accordingly. Should you present the most important information first or, instead, build a case that ends with the most important information? In other words, should you organize items by decreasing order of importance or by increasing order of importance? As you assemble and arrange the groups of ideas, add, delete, and move ideas around until you feel that you have the best possible organization. For example, Christine turned her brainstorming list of thoughts, shown in Figure 1–2, into the Points to Cover list in Figure 1–3 after narrowing the topic. She then organized these points into the three major subtopics covered in Figure 1–4.

◆ _For a detailed discussion of organizing techniques, see Chapter 2, Organizing Your Information._

◆ _For large or complex subjects, a more formal outline is often helpful. See Chapter 2, Organizing Your Information._

@

DIGITAL TIPS: **Using Word Processors**

■ Avoid the temptation of writing first drafts without any planning. After brainstorming a list of ideas, use the outline feature to organize them. As you create the draft, you can use the cut-and-paste feature to try alternative organizations.

■ Set your word processor to automatically save your draft at regular intervals. Routinely create backup copies of all of your files.

■ Use the Find-and-Replace command to locate and delete wordy phrases (such as "that is," "there are," "the fact that," and "to be"); to find technical terms that may need further explanation or inclusion in a glossary; or to find words you have a tendency to overuse.

■ Use a spell-check or grammar-check feature to identify and correct typographical errors, misspellings, and grammar problems. Remember, however, that a spell checker cannot determine that you meant "here" if you incorrectly typed "hear." Also, consider grammar-check recommendations as suggestions only because the software cannot interpret the context of your writing.

■ Practice effective document design by defining styles for headings and other repeated text elements, by using the Copy and Paste commands to create and duplicate parallel headings throughout your text, and by allowing extra white space to set off examples and illustrations (refer to pages 210–220 in Chapter 7, Designing Effective Documents and Visuals, for more information). Style sheets from your instructor or employer will help you create uniform document designs.

■ Writing for Results

Soon after she received the disappointing response to her e-mail, Christine found the courage to step into Harriet's office. Christine explained, "I've really investigated the situation, and I'm sure my suggestion would be in our best interest. Perhaps if I gave you more information, you'd reconsider my suggestion." Harriet thought for a moment and then said, "All right. Give me the major benefits and any associated disadvantages and costs by next Monday. If they are convincing, I'll meet with you and Fred Sadowski as soon as I get the chance. And, by the way, give me the information in a memo. An e-mail is too informal for what you're suggesting." Christine Thomas left Harriet Sullivan's office both relieved and determined that this time she would convince Harriet.

Christine realized that she would have to summon all of her thinking about the proposal and shape it into a persuasive memo. To do so, Christine wrote a statement of purpose; determined the general needs of her reader; generated, gathered, and recorded the key ideas and facts; and established her scope of coverage. As she prepared to organize her information, Christine thought again about Harriet as her reader. Knowing that Harriet is a practical businessperson concerned about money and wary of change, Christine realized that she must organize her ideas to first convince Harriet of the advantages of telecommuting before going on to address what Harriet would see as the potential disadvantages. After organizing her notes (see Figure 1–4), Christine was ready to write a rough draft. Note that a first draft is less concerned with creating a coherent, correct, and persuasive memo than it is with getting all the needed information down in a reasonably organized manner.

Christine wrote a draft and put it aside, planning to reread her work the next morning to discover any problems with clarity, coherence, and correctness. She also e-mailed the draft to a trusted colleague and asked for suggestions. The coworker said that Christine had obviously researched her subject with care and that she presented the appropriate information about starting the new program, but she needed to do a better job of anticipating some of Harriet's questions. The coworker suggested also that Christine might rephrase and reorganize the memo with a sharper eye for Harriet's needs. She noted, for example, that the memo would benefit from headings to introduce subtopics and commented that Harriet would appreciate being told that the new program would benefit both the company and its employees. Finally, she told Christine that the writing was too choppy and needed to be smoothed out. She handed Christine a copy of the draft that included her handwritten suggestions (Figure 1–5).

◆ *For a discussion of specific revision techniques and strategies, see Chapter 4, Revising the Draft.*

◆ *For detailed guidance on memo format, see pages 303–305 in Chapter 8, Understanding the Principles of Business Communication.*

◆ *For help in locating and correcting sentence-level errors, see Part Four, Revision Guide.*

****D R A F T****

Memo

Date: May 9, 2010
To: Harriet V. Sullivan, President
From: Christine Thomas
Subject: Telecommuting and HVS Accounting Services

I believe that HVS Accounting Services and its employees would benefit if we permit our professional staff to telecommute two days a week. Telecommuting is becoming increasingly common throughout the United States. I suggest that we try the program for three months. That would give us a trial basis. I suggest that we begin on September 1. That would be before our busy end-of-year and winter tax-preparation period.

Such a program offers a lot of advantages to HVS. The biggest advantage is that employee productivity could increase. I looked at a dozen trade-journal articles and they show average gains of from 15–30%. I spoke with other financial-services companies at monthly Accounting Society meetings. They mention gains in the 20–30% range. We need to pull even with the competition.

Make subject line more descriptive

Sentences too choppy — smooth out

Add topic headings for readability

Include list of articles and publications they appear in?

Reasons?

Figure 1–5   Draft Proposal (with Notes from Coworker) (continued) page 2

This would also benefit our employees. They save time and money on the days they work at home. They also wind up being less frazzled. Employees say that the time savings and better frame of mind are two reasons why they can better focus on their jobs. Also, the competition is doing it. They say they have an easier time recruiting and keeping employees. This is an important option that we can offer to our employees. The current job market is very competitive.

Name one or two specific competitors doing this?

The program would also be good for Bill Mayhue and Mabel Chong. Bill is having a hip replacement next month. He will be away from work for up to 6 weeks. Part of this time away could be used productively if he's allowed to work at home. Mabel's baby is due in September. She plans to spend 3 months at home after the birth and wants to keep up with her projects. Instead of losing their services, we would all mutually benefit. This would be a great boost for employee morale, too.

Note that staff has well-defined tasks

Will the program work in practice? One key issue is keeping track of employees working away from the office. HVS currently has details on staff productivity by billable hours. This system would apply to work-at-home employees. I will work with Fred Sadowski to set up and maintain measurable goals for those in the program. We would then review these goals in the middle and at the end of the 3-month trial period with you.

I wouldn't approach Fred w/o Harriet's permission

OK for all jobs at HVS?

I believe that Mondays and Fridays would be ideal work-at-home days. That would leave Tuesday through Thursday as core business days. Keeping in touch with employees at home will not be difficult. Everybody has a telephone. Our staff also has home desktop computers with Internet access. They also have fax machines and printers. Several also have small copiers. HVS has secure electronic information exchange. That's how we send and receive confidential client information electronically. Those in the program can be given password access to this information with their current remote-access software. In other words, they can log into and work on their office computer from their home computer. Finally, we can put home e-mail addresses and phone and fax numbers on our internal Web site. We can give that information to clients, also.

Long-distance calls?

Who pays for paper? for other supplies?

Any costs to HVS?

Will employees mind sharing their info?

Everyone I have spoken with already maintains a home office, so they have access to private work space at home already. They also believe that they would not lose touch with everyone else at HVS if they're only gone for a day or two a week. Our staff has a proven record of getting the job done. This makes them well-suited to a work-at-home program.

Any evidence?

Maybe auditors?

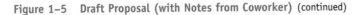

Figure 1–5　Draft Proposal (with Notes from Coworker) (continued)

Christine considered her coworker's suggestions and reviewed the brainstorming lists she'd written earlier. She added them to her introduction and conclusion and reworked the body of the memo. The extra attention she gave to Harriet's needs provided a helpful point of focus she could use to restructure and polish her writing. She also heeded the format advice to add topic headings to guide Harriet through the proposal. When she finished her revisions, Christine proofread her work for grammatical and mechanical errors and sent the final version of the memo to Harriet Sullivan (Figure 1–6). Note that the content and style of the finished memo reflect the suggestions made by Christine's coworker. Christine's story had a happy ending: Harriet was persuaded by Christine's final memo and started the work-at-home program on a trial basis that September.

◆ *Handwritten initials on printed memos are based on organizational practice. See page 304 in Chapter 8, Understanding the Principles of Business Communication, for more information.*

HVS Memo

DATE: May 12, 2010
TO: Harriet V. Sullivan, President
FROM: Christine Thomas, Systems Administrator   CT
SUBJECT: The Advantages of Telecommuting

I believe that HVS Accounting Services and its employees would benefit if we permit our professional staff to telecommute one or more days a week. Telecommuting is becoming increasingly common throughout the United States for several important reasons. I have researched the topic and talked with colleagues here and among our competitors. This memorandum presents the results of my findings and proposes that HVS set up a work-at-home program on a three-month trial basis beginning September 1. The trial period would occur well before our busy end-of-year and winter tax-preparation period.

What Are the Advantages?

The program would offer HVS several important advantages:

- Improved employee productivity
- Enhanced ability to recruit and retain good employees
- Mutually beneficial arrangements for employees with special needs

Preprinted memo stationery

Memo heading

Author's handwritten initials on paper copy

Introduction to proposal

Heading signals a new topic

List of key points focuses attention on advantages to company

Figure 1–6   Final Proposal (continued)

Harriet V. Sullivan   2   May 12, 2010

Development of key points

The foremost advantage to HVS is that employee productivity for those in a work-at-home program would very likely increase. I have reviewed a dozen trade-journal articles in our field and several Web sites that show average productivity gains of from 15 to 30 percent. In conversations with other financial-services companies at monthly Accounting Society meetings, they mention gains in the 20 to 30 percent range. This is an area where I believe we need to pull even with the competition.

Advantages to employees

Telecommuting would provide important advantages to the staff that would help us to recruit and retain qualified employees. Several of our employees commute over an hour each way daily. Telecommuting would permit them to save time and money on the days they work at home. They would also be less frazzled on those days. Employees who telecommute report that the time savings and better frame of mind are two reasons they can better focus on their jobs. As you are aware, we have lost qualified job candidates because of their objections to long commutes. Our competitors note that they have an easier time recruiting and retaining valuable employees when they offer telecommuting as an option. This is an important benefit that we can offer to our employees, especially in the current competitive job market.

The program would also be strongly beneficial to HVS and two employees in particular: Bill Mayhue and Mabel Chong. Bill is scheduled for a hip replacement in late summer and will be away from work for up to six weeks. Part of this time away could be used productively if he's allowed to work at home. Mabel's baby is due in September. She plans to spend three months at home after the birth and would also be a good candidate for this program. Instead of losing their services for extended periods—and their ongoing contacts with their clients—we would all benefit. This would be a great boost for employee morale, too.

Figure 1–6   Final Proposal (continued)

Harriet V. Sullivan   3   May 12, 2010

How Would Telecommuting Work at HVS?

Any new program of this kind raises questions about how well it will work in practice. I believe that the key questions are the following:

- How can we track the work of those in the program?
- Should everyone participate?
- Which days of the week would work best?
- Are there startup or ongoing costs to HVS?

List focuses attention on company concerns

HVS Accounting Services is in an ideal position to be able to keep track of employees working away from the office. Each member of the professional staff has well-defined tasks in financial and estate planning for families, in tax preparation and auditing for financial and estate planning for families, and in tax preparation and auditing for both families and small businesses. As you know from our monthly reports, HVS currently maintains detailed information that quantifies staff productivity by billable hours. This system would apply equally well to work-at-home employees. Also, with your approval, I will work with Fred Sadowski to set up and maintain measurable goals for those in the program. We would then review these goals in the middle and at the end of the three-month trial period with you. Not all jobs at HVS would be suitable for the program. The receptionist, mail staff, several of our temporary employees, and I need to be at the office during business hours, so we would not participate.

Development of key points

I believe that Mondays and Fridays would be ideal work-at-home days. That would leave Tuesday through Thursday as core business days for staff meetings, client conferences, and other activities better done at the office. Even on Mondays and Fridays, keeping in touch with employees at home will not be difficult in this electronic era. In addition to telephones, everyone eligible for the program already has home desktop computers with Internet access, fax machines, and printers. Several also have small copiers. Essentially, no startup expenses for HVS are associated with the program. The staff can keep a log of long-distance business calls and bring in their telephone bill monthly for reimbursement.

Figure 1–6   Final Proposal (continued)

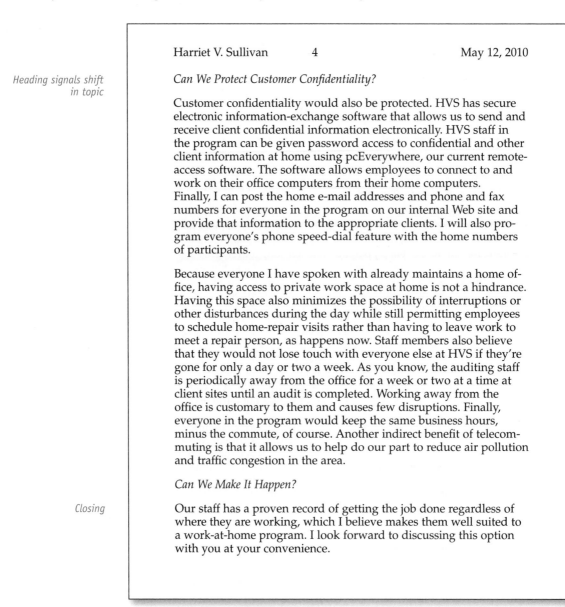

Harriet V. Sullivan   4   May 12, 2010

Heading signals shift in topic

Can We Protect Customer Confidentiality?

Customer confidentiality would also be protected. HVS has secure electronic information-exchange software that allows us to send and receive client confidential information electronically. HVS staff in the program can be given password access to confidential and other client information at home using pcEverywhere, our current remote-access software. The software allows employees to connect to and work on their office computers from their home computers. Finally, I can post the home e-mail addresses and phone and fax numbers for everyone in the program on our internal Web site and provide that information to the appropriate clients. I will also program everyone's phone speed-dial feature with the home numbers of participants.

Because everyone I have spoken with already maintains a home office, having access to private work space at home is not a hindrance. Having this space also minimizes the possibility of interruptions or other disturbances during the day while still permitting employees to schedule home-repair visits rather than having to leave work to meet a repair person, as happens now. Staff members also believe that they would not lose touch with everyone else at HVS if they're gone for only a day or two a week. As you know, the auditing staff is periodically away from the office for a week or two at a time at client sites until an audit is completed. Working away from the office is customary to them and causes few disruptions. Finally, everyone in the program would keep the same business hours, minus the commute, of course. Another indirect benefit of telecommuting is that it allows us to help do our part to reduce air pollution and traffic congestion in the area.

Can We Make It Happen?

Closing

Our staff has a proven record of getting the job done regardless of where they are working, which I believe makes them well suited to a work-at-home program. I look forward to discussing this option with you at your convenience.

Figure 1–6   Final Proposal (continued)

WRITER'S CHECKLIST
Drafting with Ethical Considerations in Mind

On the job, ethical dilemmas do not always present themselves as clear-cut choices. To help avoid ethical problems in your writing, ask the following questions as you plan and review your draft:

✔ Is the communication honest and truthful?

✔ Am I ethically consistent in my communications?

✔ Am I acting in the best interest of my employer? the public? myself?

✔ What would happen if everybody acted or communicated in this way?

✔ Does the action or communication violate anyone's rights?

✔ Am I willing to take responsibility for the communication, publicly and privately?

CHAPTER 1 SUMMARY: ASSESSING AUDIENCE AND PURPOSE

Successful writing on the job is the result of careful preparation. Review the following check-list to ensure that your writing assignments—in the classroom and on the job—are adequately planned.

▓ Have I determined the purpose of my writing?

▓ Have I considered my audience's needs and perspectives?

▓ Have I considered the context in which my audience will evaluate the document?

▓ Have I gathered and recorded all the ideas and facts necessary to fulfill my purpose and to address my audience's needs?

▓ Have I established the appropriate scope of coverage?

▓ Have I organized my ideas into related groups and determined the best sequence to link these groups for my audience?

▓ Have I revised the draft to emphasize the points most important to my audience?

▓ Have I reviewed my draft for problems with clarity, coherence, and correctness?

▓ Have I formatted the final draft to highlight key ideas?

ON THE WEB

For an online quiz on audience and purpose, go to Chapter 1, bedfordstmartins.com/ writingthatworks

▓ Exercises

1. Select a problem at your place of employment (past or present) or on your campus. Using the pattern in this chapter, create a statement of purpose for a memo you could write about a suggested solution for this problem. Your reader should be able to make a decision regarding your suggestion. Give the reader's name and position in your statement of purpose. As your instructor directs, prepare the following:

   a. Brainstorm a list of items for the subject selected. Try to list 15 to 20 items; even if they seem inappropriate, just keep listing. Mark the items with a *P* for purpose or an *A* for audience.

   b. Eliminate the items in your list from 1a that clearly do not meet the audience's needs or contribute to your purpose. Then establish your scope and rewrite the list, grouping the items into three or more categories. Next, arrange the items in each category in sequence.

c. Using the groups of items created in 1b, write a memo suggesting a solution to the problem. (See Chapter 8, Understanding the Principles of Business Communication, for memo-format examples.)

2. For three of the following topics, or topics of your own choosing, list the topic, the audience, one possible purpose for a document, and the information needed to achieve that purpose. (List kinds of information, not sources of information.) Because the following topics are broad, you will need to select some particular aspect of each topic that you choose.

Banking	Marketing	Printing
Computer programming	Music	Real estate
E-commerce	Occupations	Small businesses
Electronics	Office procedures	Sports
Health care	Personal computers	Television
Highway construction	Photography	Welding
The Internet		

The following is a sample list:

Topic	Internet faxing
Audience	The average computer user
Purpose	To instruct the average computer user on how to set up and send a fax message to a friend, a fellow student, a coworker, or an instructor.
Kinds of information	Required hardware, Internet access, e-mail address, fax number, location (Web address) of one or more Internet faxing services, detailed instructions on how to send and receive faxes over the Internet

3. Using the techniques described in this chapter, write a memo explaining how to perform your job (or a job you've had) for an employee who will be replacing you while you are on vacation. Write two versions of this memo: Write one to a temporary employee hired through a temporary job agency and write a second to an employee who works in your department but not in the same job. (See Chapter 8, Understanding the Principles of Business Communication, for memo-format examples.)

4. Write a memo to your manager asking for tuition reimbursement to attend this or another course. Assume that you work for a large organization that does not have a regular procedure for such a request and thus requires approval beyond your department. Therefore, you will need adequate background information and detail for someone who may not be familiar with your job duties or this request. Use the course, text descriptions, and the syllabus to prepare your memo. This memo will be most successful if you help your audience see the value of this course. You may wish to attach supporting material (such as the course syllabus). (See Chapter 8, Understanding the Principles of Business Communication, for memo-format examples.)

5. Your company is experiencing financial difficulties, which has resulted in a hiring freeze. Because of limited support-staff positions and internships, upper-management personnel will now have to do more of their own office tasks, such

as photocopying and faxing. First, consider the possible reactions and feelings regarding the change in responsibilities. Then write a memo from the human resources department to upper management, describing the situation and explaining the new policy.

6. Your company's human-resources manager has asked you to create an employee manual that details how to use the following office machines: the fax, the photocopier, and the phone system. Brainstorm about the amount of detail (the scope) that you would have to provide in this manual for the following groups of employees: interns with no office work experience; administrative assistants with one to two years of office experience; and senior-management personnel who have over ten years of office experience but who have relied on staff to complete faxing, copying, and telephone tasks. Write a brief e-mail to the human-resources manager, suggesting the number of manuals needed and for whom. Support your claims.

7. Using the list of topics in Exercise 2, select a product or service and write a complaint letter about a problem you, the consumer, have had with this product. Before writing, consider the purpose of your letter, the exact nature of your complaint, the audience you are addressing, and what you want the company to do about the problem or what you think the resolution to the problem should be. Bring your letter to class. (For advice on writing complaint letters, see pages 331–333 and 336 in Chapter 9, Writing Business Correspondence.)

Collaborative Classroom Projects

ON THE WEB

For more exercises and collaborative classroom projects, go to Chapter 1, bedfordstmartins .com/writingthatworks

1. Divide into groups as directed by your instructor. Discuss similarities and differences between writing for the audience in Exercise 3 and writing for the audience in Exercise 4. Make a list that you can share with the class.

2. The manager of your company's publications department believes that sharing a printer among four employees is slowing down their productivity on company manuals, brochures, and other communications pieces. In the long run, this slowdown might cause his department to miss publication deadlines. The manager of the information technology (IT) department, however, doesn't want to purchase a new printer because it is near the end of the fiscal year and an equipment purchase could push her department over budget, making IT look bad to upper management. Part c may be completed outside of class.

   a. Divide the class into two groups, one that represents the publications department and the other the IT department. Instruct each group to brainstorm separately a list of reasons that support your manager's concerns and needs.

   b. Debate your position with the other group. Acknowledge each other's concerns and address them. At the end of the debate, discuss what you have learned and research possibilities that would benefit both sides (for example, would a used or refurbished printer be a possible solution?).

   c. The publications department group should now draft a memo to send to the IT department manager. The IT department group should draft a memo to send to the publications department manager. For either memo, state your group's needs, acknowledge the other side's concerns, and suggest possible compromises or solutions that could resolve this issue amicably.

3. Divide into groups of four to six students. For 20 to 25 minutes, brainstorm and develop a list of problems that make studying on campus difficult. Then take 15 minutes to revise the list into two versions: (1) a list for the dean's office committee whose assignment it is to make studying on campus easier and (2) a list for the residence-hall planning committee in charge of designing a new dormitory on campus. Discuss how the different purposes and audiences affected your lists.

ON THE WEB

For more research projects, go to Chapter 1, bedfordstmartins.com/ writingthatworks

■ Research Projects

1. Find an article on a subject of interest to you in two different types of publications — for example, a newspaper or a general-interest magazine (such as *Discover*) and a technical journal (such as the *Journal of the American Medical Association*). After you have read the two articles, do the following:

   a. Identify the target audience of each publication. Compare the approaches taken in each article toward the intended audience. Look specifically for indicators of the audience's knowledge of the subject, such as the presence or absence of technical terms and the kind and number of illustrations used.

   b. Create statements of purpose for each article, as if you had been the writer.

   c. Discuss or report on how well the writers met the needs of their audiences. (Respond only after you have completed a and b.)

2. Interview at least three current or former instructors about how they prepare their class lectures for their different groups of students. For example, you might ask them how their style of teaching first-year students differs from teaching juniors or seniors (or graduate students). Or, you might ask how the style of their exams or essay questions varies, depending on the class for which they are written. Write your findings and present them to the class. (*Note*: Before you begin, read page 150 about interviewing for information in Chapter 6, Researching Your Subject.)

3. Suppose that the company you work for provides a week's paid vacation package as a reward to the Employee of the Year and his or her immediate family. Your manager has asked you to select this year's vacation package at a location that has educational value. You have a budget of $6,000. Using the Web, compare and contrast different vacation packages and then outline your reasons for your recommendation. Keep the checklists Planning Your Document on page 5 and Writing for Your Reader on page 7 in mind as you write a concise memo to your manager.

4. Imagine that you volunteer several hours a week at an adult community learning center where you teach basic computer skills to people over the age of 65. They usually are interested in learning how to use e-mail or research information on wills or planning trips. However, their lack of experience with the Internet leaves them vulnerable to scams, particularly ones that require them to send e-mails to receive free things or that ask them to verify bank-account or credit-card information. Go to sites that debunk online scams and sites that offer advice on how to spot scams. Write a memo to your students warning them about these scams and how to avoid them. Be sure to give examples.

2 Organizing Your Information

AT A GLANCE: Organization

How do business and technical writers arrange facts and ideas to serve their purposes and meet the needs of different audiences? This chapter reviews proven organizing techniques and describes a wide range of organizing strategies that you can apply to your own writing.

- Using an outline / 26
- Considering audience and purpose / 31
- Choosing an organizing pattern / 34
  - Sequential / 34
  - Chronological / 36
  - Spatial / 36
  - Division and classification / 40
  - Decreasing order of importance / 44
  - Increasing order of importance / 45
  - General to specific / 47
  - Specific to general / 50
  - Comparison / 51

When a motion picture is being filmed, the scenes are usually shot out of sequence. Different locations, actors' schedules, weather conditions, and many other circumstances make working out of sequence necessary. If it were not for a skilled film editor, the completed film would be a jumble of random scenes. The editor, following the script, carefully splices the film together so that the story moves smoothly and logically from one event to the next, as the screenwriter and the director planned. Without a plan, no such order would be possible because the editor would have no guide for organizing the thousands of feet of film.

Organizing a movie and organizing a written document are obviously different tasks, but they have one element in common—both must be planned ahead of time. For a film, planning means creating a script. For a written document, it means organizing information into a sequence appropriate to the subject, the purpose, and the audience.

■ Outlining

Organizing your information before you write has two important advantages. First, it forces you to reexamine the information you plan to include to be sure that you have sufficient facts and details to satisfy your audience's needs and achieve the purpose of your writing. Second, it forces you to order the information in a sequence that your audience will understand as clearly as you do.

The importance of these advantages has been confirmed by research studies of workplace writing. According to one study in a corporate setting, more than three times the number of good writers as compared with poor writers use a written outline. In fact, 36 percent of the poor writers said they never use an outline or plan, either written or mental.[1]

Not all writing benefits from a full-scale outline, of course. For relatively short documents, such as memos, letters, and important e-mails, you may need only to jot down a few notes to make sure that you haven't left out any important information and that you have arranged the information in a logical order. These notes then guide you as you write the draft.

Longer documents, such as formal reports or larger proposals, require more elaborate planning that benefits from a formal outline. In addition to guiding your first draft, an outline can be circulated for review by your colleagues and superiors. They can easily see in the outline the scope of information you plan to include and the sequence in which it is organized. Their reviews can help you find and fix major problems before you've committed a great deal of time to writing your draft. Any outline is tentative and represents your best thinking at that point. It need not be labored over so that it becomes virtually an end in itself. This chapter introduces conventions for creating simple and complex outlines and provides techniques for verifying that your outline is sound.

◆ For an example of informal organizational notes, see Figure 1–4.

ON THE WEB

For online resources for outlining, go to Chapter 2, bedfordstmartins.com/ writingthatworks

VOICES IN THE WORKPLACE

Thinking About Organization

In noting the importance of organization for workplace writing, Steve Bramlage, president of Vectren Energy Delivery of Ohio, points out, "If you don't organize your thoughts before you hit the keyboard, you're sure to end up writing several drafts instead of getting it right the first time."

Traditional Roman Numeral Outline

The most common type of outline emphasizes topics and subtopics by means of Roman numerals, letters, and Arabic numbers in the following sequence of subdivisions:

---

[1]Christine Barabas, *Technical Writing in a Corporate Culture: A Study of the Nature of Information* (Norwood, N.J.: Ablex Publishing Corp., 1991), p. 188. "Good" and "poor" writers were so classified by their readers within the corporation.

I. Major section
   A. First-level subsection
      1. Second-level subsection
         a. Third-level subsection
            1) Fourth-level subsection

Your subject will seldom require four subdivisions, but dividing it this way allows for a highly detailed outline if one is necessary. Stop at the level at which you can no longer subdivide into at least two items. Where possible, for every Roman numeral *I* you should have at least a Roman numeral *II*, and for every *A* you should have at least a *B*, and so on.

Begin your outline by writing down its major sections. For example, if you are writing an article about the development of the Internet for a company magazine, you might start with the following major sections:

  ▷ I. History of the Internet
     II. Growth of Internet technology and future societal issues for the Internet

After a moment's reflection, you decide that the first-level heading is actually the overall topic of the article. After reviewing your research notes, you realize that the topic of the first section should be the background and developments that led to Internet technology, so you revise the outline accordingly:

  ▷ I. Background of Internet technology
     II. Growth of Internet technology and future societal issues for the Internet

You quickly decide, however, that you have put too many topics in your second major section, so you make another effort:

  ▷ I. Background of Internet technology
     II. Growth of Internet technology
    III. Future societal issues for the Internet

Once you establish your major sections, look for minor divisions within each section. For example, you might first arrive at the following minor divisions within your major sections:

  ▷ I. Background of Internet technology
      A. Pioneers
      B. Later developments
     II. Growth of Internet technology
      A. Network technology
      B. Improvements in network technology
    III. Future societal issues for the Internet
      A. E-commerce and intellectual stakeholders
      B. Domain space

  C. "Digital divide"
  D. Privacy issues

This outline is a start, but the second-level divisions (A and B) are too vague to be useful. After considering Growth of Internet Technology, for example, you might produce the following revision:

▷ II. Growth of Internet technology
   A. Competing network techniques and protocols throughout the mid-1970s and early 1980s
   B. Improvements and standardization of techniques and protocols with increased users in the mid-1980s
   C. Transition from a community of scholars, scientists, and defense contractors to widespread infrastructure in the late 1980s and early 1990s
   D. Expansion of Internet in business, academic, and government institutions from the late 1990s and beyond

   After evaluating the whole outline, you are ready to insert the information you compiled during your research under the appropriate major and minor divisions, as shown in Figure 2–1. When you have finished, you have a complete outline. However, although the outline looks final at this point, you still may need to revise it. Make sure that corresponding divisions present material of equal importance (that is, that major and subordinate divisions are equal to one another in importance). Likewise, ensure that every heading is divided into at least two parts if it is to be divided at all. Subtopics are typically divided into at least two parts (for every 1 there should be a 2), although doing so may not always be possible.

NOT   A. Pioneering communications technology
      1. Morse and telegraph, calculating machines, silicon chip, and remote-access computers

BUT   A. Pioneering communications technology
      1. Morse and telegraph
      2. Calculating machines
      3. Silicon chip
      4. Remote-access computers

   Finally, review your outline for completeness, determining whether you need additional information. If you find that your research is not really complete, return to your sources and locate the missing material.

Decimal Numbering System Outline

The sample outlines shown to this point use a combination of numbers and letters to differentiate the various levels of information. Many science and technology authors use a decimal numbering system instead, such as the following, to develop their outlines.

HISTORY OF THE INTERNET

I. Background of Internet technology
   A. Pioneering communications technology
      1. Morse and telegraph
      2. Calculating machines
      3. Silicon chip
      4. Remote-access computers
   B. Development and evolution of network technology
      1. Galactic Network envisioned by John Licklider of the Department of Defense's DARPA (Defense Advanced Research Projects Agency) in 1962
      2. Packet-switching theories published by Leonard Kleinrock of MIT in 1961
      3. First wide-area computer network developed by Lawrence Roberts and Thomas Merrill of MIT in 1965
      4. Computer networks, packet-switching networks, and packet-networks research presented at 1967 conference by three groups whose research took place without knowledge of one another
         a. MIT
         b. RAND Corporation
         c. National Physical Laboratory (UK)
      5. Interface Message Processor (IMP) developed by Bolt, Beranek & Newman
      6. ARPANET created with the connecting of four host computers at UCLA, Stanford Research Institute, UC Santa Barbara, and the University of Utah (1969)
         a. Person-to-person communication (e-mail) introduced in 1972
         b. Host-to-host protocols developed in early 1970s
         c. Transmission control protocol/Internet protocol (TCP/IP) developed in 1974
II. Growth of Internet technology
   A. Competing network techniques and protocols throughout the mid-1970s and early 1980s
   B. Improvements and standardization of techniques and protocols with increased users in the mid-1980s and the early 1990s
      1. TCP/IP adopted as standard protocol in 1984
      2. Domain Name System (DNS) introduced in 1984
      3. U.S. Congress funds national research and infrastructure improvement through High Performance Computing Act
      4. World Wide Web browser/editor program released to public in 1991, simplifying global information sharing
      5. Mosaic browser created in 1993, making Internet easier to use and graphically richer
   C. Transition from a community of scholars, scientists, and defense contractors to widespread infrastructure in the late 1980s and early 1990s
      1. Governments encourage use of Internet throughout higher education system
         a. JANET serves British universities (1984)
         b. NSFNET serves U.S. universities (1985), eventually becoming the backbone of the Internet
      2. Internet workshops target private sector in the mid-1980s

*Labels (right margin):*
— Major topic
— First-level subsection
— Second-level subsection
— First-level subsection
— Second-level subsection
— Third-level subsection
— Second-level subsection
— Third-level subsection
— Major topic
— First-level subsection
— Second-level subsection

Figure 2–1 Sample Outline (continued)

Major topic ——

> 3. Commercialization of networking products influences vendors of technology to be competitive as well as interoperative
> 4. E-commerce era begins in 1990s, transforming Internet to a "commodity" service
>
> III. Future societal issues for the Internet
>   A. E-commerce and intellectual stakeholders to drive evolution and innovation
>   B. Contending stakeholders to vie for control of domain space
>   C. Protection of privacy to continue to be a challenge
>   D. "Digital divide" between developed and developing countries to narrow
>   E. Internet 2.0: effects of evolving social-networking sites

Figure 2–1   Sample Outline (continued)

1. FIRST MAJOR IDEA
    1.1 Supporting idea for 1
    1.2 Supporting idea for 1
        1.2.1 Example or illustration of 1.2
        1.2.2 Example or illustration of 1.2
            1.2.2.1 Detail for 1.2.2
            1.2.2.2 Detail for 1.2.2
    1.3 Supporting idea for 1
2. SECOND MAJOR IDEA

This system should not go beyond the fourth level because the numbers get too cumbersome past that point. In many technical articles and reports, the decimal numbering system is carried over from the outline to the final version of the document for ease of cross-referencing sections. Typical uses for the decimal outline include procedural manuals, technical reports and specifications, mathematical texts, and scientific and technical material of many kinds.

An outline is preliminary by its nature—a means to an end, not an end in itself. Don't view it as a final product. If you suddenly see a better way to organize your material while you are writing the draft, depart from your outline and follow the better approach. The main purpose of the outline is to bring order and shape to your information before you begin to write.

◆ *For a discussion of decimal numbering in formal reports, see page 408 in Chapter 11, Writing Formal Reports.*

◆ *For detailed information on researching information, see Chapter 6, Researching Your Subject.*

WRITER'S CHECKLIST
Creating an Outline

✔ Complete your research and know your topic well enough to be able to write about it. Break a large topic into its major divisions and write them down. Does the sequence fit the organizing pattern you have decided to use? (See pages 34–58 for organizing patterns.) If not, re-sequence and label the topics with Roman numerals (I, II, III, and so on).

✔ Repeat the process for each major topic. Break each into its logical subtopics and list them under each major topic. Then sequence the subtopics to fit your pattern of development and label them with capital letters (A, B, C, and so on).

- ✔ If necessary, repeat the process for each subtopic. Divide each into its logical sub-subtopics, list them under each subtopic in the appropriate sequence, and label them with Arabic numbers (1, 2, 3, and so on).

- ✔ Now go to your notes and key each one to the appropriate place in your outline (for example, placing II-C beside any note that fits the portion of your outline labeled II-C).

- ✔ Merge your notes and your outline, placing every note under the appropriate head, subhead, or sub-subhead in your outline. Then organize the notes under each head in the most logical sequence.

- ✔ To convert your detailed outline into your first draft, put the first head on your computer screen and expand the notes listed under it into sentences and paragraphs.

How Audience and Purpose Shape Organization: A Case Study

The kinds of information and organization that shape your outline will vary according to your purposes for writing and your audience's specific needs. Let us say, for example, that a writer needs to prepare two documents about the Lifemaker System, a home gym that combines the features of ten separate resistance machines into a compact weight-and-cable exercise system. The first document will be a sales brochure directed at potential purchasers of the Lifemaker; the second document will be a maintenance manual written for customers who have already purchased the system.

◆ *For an explanation of written statements of purpose, see pages 5–6 in Chapter 1, Assessing Audience and Purpose.*

ETHICS NOTE

Readers are persuaded in part if they believe the source is credible. Therefore, be careful not to overstate the claims you make. Although comparing your product or service with that of a competitor is an effective persuasive strategy, speaking negatively or disparagingly about a competitor is not.

Both documents share several aspects of audience and purpose. The sales brochure and the maintenance manual both need to describe the design and structure of the Lifemaker System, although they will do so in different ways and for different reasons. The audience for each document is composed of nonspecialists, so each document should contain minimal technical language and avoid terms that would be familiar only to technicians, engineers, and sales representatives. Whether they are potential or current customers of Lifemaker, readers will likely be familiar with exercise systems, so descriptions of the exercise equipment for either document need not be too detailed. Much of the information gathered and used for brainstorming and outlining will be useful for both the sales brochure and the maintenance manual.

However, these documents reflect different purposes in two important ways. Consider how a written statement of purpose might look for each.

SALES
BROCHURE   My primary purpose for writing is to describe the benefits and features of the Lifemaker System so that my readers will want to purchase it.

MAINTENANCE   My primary purpose for writing is to explain the assembly and
MANUAL   maintenance requirements of the Lifemaker System so that the cus-
              tomer knows exactly how to put it together and take care of it.

The writer of a sales brochure will need to select and organize the information so that it persuades the reader to purchase the system. The brochure's outline, then, should highlight the benefits of buying the system and offer more general comments about the design and structural features of the system.

The maintenance manual will be directed at readers who have already purchased the system, so the writer will not be concerned with organizing information to form a persuasive argument. Instead, the writer will want to create an outline that will lead to clearly written, step-by-step instructions on how to assemble and maintain the Lifemaker. References to structural features will be very specific and more technical than they would be for the sales brochure. (The audience is still made up of nonspecialists, so the writer needs to keep the use of technical terms to a minimum and might leave places in the outline for diagrams that will eventually appear in the manual to clarify the instructions.)

The outline for the sales brochure (Figure 2–2) notes specific design details (cast-iron plates, adjustable cables, 4-ft. by 7-ft. size), but the information is organized to support the brochure's persuasive purpose. The purpose of the maintenance manual is to instruct rather than to persuade the audience, so the manual's organization would differ from that used for the sales brochure. Figure 2–3 is an excerpt from the outline for the maintenance manual. This outline follows a *sequential* (*step-by-step*) organization of information (see pages 34–35), which is an ideal pattern to use when instruction, rather than persuasion, is the major purpose for writing. In contrast, the outline for the sales brochure uses a *general-to-specific* sequencing of information (see pages 47–50), which is more appropriate when the purpose for writing is to persuade the audience with a general argument supported with specific details. Within the major topic divisions, the sales brochure also uses two other types of organization: *comparison* (see pages 51–57) to emphasize its features against those of its competitors and *division* (see pages 40–44) to illustrate how its features (weights and cables) function in the system. These differences are summarized as follows:

	Lifemaker Sales Brochure	**Lifemaker Maintenance Manual**
Purpose	Describe benefits and features to attract purchasers	Explain maintenance requirements for system customers
Audience	Nonspecialists who are potential Lifemaker customers	Nonspecialists who have purchased the Lifemaker system
Organizing patterns	General to specific; comparison; division	Sequential (step by step)

◆ *For drafts and revisions of this sales brochure, see Chapter 3, Writing the Draft, and Chapter 4, Revising the Draft.*

Thus, although both documents are drawn from the same source and speak to nontechnical audiences, their different purposes call for different patterns of organization.

LIFEMAKER: The Compact, Affordable Home Gym

I. General benefits of owning Lifemaker
  A. More compact than other systems
  B. Provides better training programs than other systems
  C. Lower-priced and easier to assemble and maintain than other systems

II. Design benefits/features
  A. Multiple stations, so two people can work out at the same time
  B. Takes up minimal space (measures only 4′ by 7′)
  C. Designed to work all muscle groups (40 different combinations of exercises)

III. Structural benefits/features: Weights
  A. Dual weight stacks that total 200 pounds of cast-iron plates
  B. Adjustable weight stacks with resistance range of 10 to 150 pounds
  C. Varied individual weights with resistance adjustable in 5-, 10-, and 15-pound increments

IV. Structural benefits/features: Cables
  A. Adjustable cables that increase tension at stations working strongest muscle groups
  B. Reconfigurable weight stacks (cables permit reconfiguring of weights without dismantling entire system)
  C. Reversible tension (cables can increase/decrease tension in mid-set)

V. Financial and maintenance benefits
  A. More reasonably priced than leading system: $999.99
  B. Two-year guarantee for all parts
  C. Easy maintenance (no oiling or solvents necessary)

Organized to compare benefits with other systems

Organized by division of features, according to function in system

Organized to compare benefits with other systems

Figure 2–2   Outline for a Sales Brochure

MAINTAINING YOUR LIFEMAKER

I. Maintenance and troubleshooting
  A. Inspect and safeguard all parts each time you do the following:
    1. Inspect parts for wear.
       a. Check cables for fraying.
       b. Check weights for cracks.
       c. Replace worn parts immediately.
    2. Tighten tension on cable #1.
       a. Find end of 125″ cable (#43 on diagram).
       b. Turn end of cable clockwise.
       c. Thread cable farther into weight tube (#35 on diagram).
    3. Tighten tension on cable #2.
       a. Find end of 265″ cable (#46 on diagram).
       b. Turn end of cable clockwise.
       c. Thread cable farther into weight tube (#35 on diagram).
    4. Clean parts.
       a. Clean with damp cloth.
       b. Use nonabrasive detergent.
       c. Use no solvents or oils.

Maintenance steps organized sequentially

Figure 2–3   Outline for Instructions for a Maintenance Manual (Excerpt)

@

DIGITAL TIPS: **Formatting Your Outline**

Using the outline feature of your word-processing software enables you to do the following:

- Format your outline automatically.
- Fill in, rearrange, and update your outline.
- Experiment with the organization and scope of information while retaining the outline format.
- Rearrange sections and subsections easily.
- Create Roman numeral or decimal numbering outline styles.

Experiment with the default settings of the outline feature to make the best use of this software. For step-by-step instructions, go to <bedfordstmartins.com/writingthatworks> and select Digital Tips, "Creating an Outline."

■ Essential Organizing Patterns

The choice of a pattern for organizing information comes naturally for some types of writing. Instructions for how to process an invoice or operate a piece of equipment are arranged step by step. A trip report usually follows a chronological sequence. When a subject does not lend itself to one particular pattern, you can choose the best sequence or combination of sequences by considering your purpose and your audience's needs. Suppose, for example, that you report on a trip to several offset-printing companies to gather information on the most efficient way to arrange equipment to improve workflow through the printing shop where you work. You would probably organize information about visits chronologically, but your description of the various shop layouts, emphasizing the physical locations of the equipment, would be organized spatially. If you went on to make recommendations about the most workable arrangement for your shop, you might organize them according to decreasing order of importance by presenting the most efficient arrangement first, the second most efficient arrangement next, and so on. Table 2–1 lists and describes the most common ways to organize, or sequence, information in on-the-job writing.

Sequential

In the sequential pattern, you divide your subject into steps and then present the steps in the order in which they occur. This arrangement is the most effective way to describe the operation of a mechanism, such as a digital photocopier, or to explain a process, such as cardiopulmonary resuscitation (CPR). Sequencing is the logical pattern for writing instructions. For example, the instructions for installing printer software on a desktop computer follow a step-by-step sequence.

TABLE 2–1   Patterns of Organization

Pattern	Description
Sequential	Consecutive order of steps, not connected to a specific time
Chronological	Sequence of steps or events related to time
Spatial	Description from top to bottom, front to back, and so on
Division and classification	Division into parts and grouping of parts by class
Decreasing order of importance	Order beginning with the most important item and leading to the least important item
Increasing order of importance	Order beginning with the least important item and leading to the most important item
General to specific	Order leading from an overview to a detailed explanation
Specific to general	Order leading from the details of a topic to a broad overview or conclusion
Comparison	Assessment of traits or characteristics of two or more items to describe their similarities and differences

▷ To install printer software:
  1. Make sure that your printer is plugged in and connected to your computer.
  2. Turn your computer on.
  3. When you see the "New Hardware Found" screen, insert the Printing Software CD-ROM into the CD-ROM drive.
  4. The printer's installation software loads automatically, so follow the instructions on the screen.

The greatest advantage of presenting your information in sequential order is that it is easy for a reader to understand and follow the process because the sequence of steps in your writing corresponds to the order of the process being described. If you were to write instructions for the proper way to download images from a digital camera for e-mailing, for example, you would present the information in a step-by-step sequence (Figures 2–4 and 2–5). When you present your information in steps, you must carefully consider the needs of your audience. Do not assume that your readers are as familiar with your subject as you are; if they were, they wouldn't need your instructions. Even for a simple process, be sure that you list all steps and explain in adequate detail how each step is performed. Sometimes you must also indicate the purpose or function of each step. Note the description in step 3, modifying photos, of Figure 2–5 on page 37, for example. It explains both the purpose and function of this feature before an image is given a unique name and saved.

OUTLINE: How to E-mail a Picture from a Digital Camera

1. Transferring photos from camera to computer
   a. Connect camera to computer by plugging the camera cable into the computer port.
   b. Click on Camera icon on desktop to view images stored in the camera.
   c. Decide which photos you want to transfer.
2. Saving photos on computer
   a. Create and name a folder on your hard drive or on your desktop.
   b. Open and view images (as described in step 1).
   c. Select images you wish to save; drag them to the designated folder or save them by using imaging software.
   d. Delete images from camera.
   e. Back up images on an external medium.
3. Modifying photos
   a. Crop, change resolution, or add effects, using imaging software.
   b. Save the edited image by using the Save As or Export command, renaming the image to reflect changes.
4. Attaching photos to an e-mail
   a. Open e-mail box and click on Attachment icon.
   b. Locate designated folder and click on file to be sent.
   c. Before sending, check with recipient about file size restrictions.

Figure 2–4   Outline for Sequential Instructions

Chronological

Sequential and chronological patterns overlap because each describes steps in a process. In a chronological sequence, however, you focus on the order in which the steps or events occur in time, beginning with the first event, going on to the next event, and so on, until you have reached the last event. Trip reports, work schedules, minutes of meetings, laboratory test procedures, and certain accident reports are among the types of writing in which information may be organized chronologically. These documents use clock times or dates to denote the time frames for each step. In the outline and memo shown in Figures 2–6 on page 38 and 2–7 on page 39, a plant superintendent reports the course of an accidental fire at a chemical plant.

ON THE WEB

For another example of chronological order, go to Model Documents Gallery, bedfordstmartins.com/ writingthatworks

Spatial

In a spatial sequence, you describe an object according to the physical arrangement of its features. Depending on the subject, you may describe the features from top to bottom, from side to side, from east to west (or west to east), from inside to outside, and so on. Descriptions of this kind rely mainly on dimension (*height, width, length*), direction (*up, down, north, south*), shape (*rectangular,*

HOW TO E-MAIL A PICTURE FROM A DIGITAL CAMERA

The following step-by-step instructions describe how to transfer images from your camera to your computer, save them, and then e-mail the images to your friends, relatives, or business colleagues.

1. Transferring Your Photos from Camera to Computer

Connect the cable from the camera to your computer at the USB, or serial, port to enable the camera to serve as its own disk drive. If your digital camera includes a docking station, place the camera in the docking-station cradle to automatically connect it to the computer. In most cases, an icon of your camera or a folder for it will appear on your screen after you hook it to your computer. Double-click on the icon to open and view the image files stored on your camera.

2. Saving Photos on the Computer

To save images to your computer, create and name a folder on your hard drive. If you're working on an ongoing project that will have many images, include the dates of the images or other useful identifying information. After you create the folder, open and view the images stored on your camera as described in step 1, select the files you wish to save, highlight them, and drag them into the folder you've created on your hard drive. You can also save the images in software, such as Adobe's Photoshop, using the software's File/Open command to select a file directly from your digital camera.

Most digital cameras will default to save images in either GIF or JPEG format. However, if yours does not, then the imaging software that came with the camera should provide a way to save the image in either of these formats.

3. Modifying Photos

Use imaging software, such as Adobe's Photoshop, to crop your image, to change the resolution, and to add other effects. Once you're done making changes to your image, use the File/Save As command or, in some imaging programs, the File/Export command, to make a copy of the image. At this point, you can give the image a more useful name than your camera will have given the file because digital cameras typically assign images a number.

4. Attaching Photos to E-mail Messages

To attach the file to an e-mail message, open your outgoing e-mail box and click on the Attachment icon or box. When your file directory opens, select the folder where your photo images are stored, highlight the file you wish to send, and click Open. Your photo file is now attached to your e-mail box.

5. Checking on File Size Restrictions

Before e-mailing an image, check with your recipients to ensure that their e-mail program can accept a file of the size you're sending. Some recipients have mailbox quotas that may not accommodate your image. E-mail attachments are sometimes used to transmit computer viruses, so letting recipients know in advance that you intend to send an image makes them feel more comfortable opening the attachment.

Introduction

Instructions organized by sequence in which steps must occur

Figure 2–5   Sequential Instructions

OUTLINE

I. Conditions Before Fire
   A. Building A
      1. Three piles of scrap paper 100 ft. outside building
      2. Six pallets of Class I flammable liquids along west wall
   B. Building B approximately 150 ft. from scrap paper outside Building A

II. Chronology of Fire
   A. 6:00 a.m.
      1. Spark initiated fire in electric shop of Building A
      2. Night watchman called Ardville Volunteer Fire Department and the plant superintendent
      3. Fire spread to drums of flammable liquid, engulfing Building A
      4. Fire spread to scrap paper
   B. 6:15 a.m.
      1. Watchman hosed down scrap paper
      2. Watchman set up lawn sprinklers between Buildings A and B
      3. Watchman noticed smoke coming from Building B
   C. 6:57 a.m. (approx.)
      1. Volunteer fire department arrived
      2. Firefighters began pumping water

III. Results of Fire
   A. Building A destroyed
   B. Building B suffered $250K damage to roof

Figure 2–6   Outline for a Chronological Description (Excerpt)

square, semicircular), and proportion (*one-half, two-thirds*). Features are described in relation to one another:

▷   One end is raised six to eight inches higher than the other end to permit the rain to run off.

Features are also described in relation to their surroundings:

▷   The lot is located on the east bank of the Kingman River.

The spatial pattern of organization is also commonly used in descriptions of building layouts; emergency evacuation plans; proposals for landscape work; fashion design; construction-site progress reports; and, in combination with a step-by-step sequence, many types of instructions. These descriptions commonly include drawings or photographs to further clarify the features being described, as in Figure 2–8 on page 40, a concise dress description by the designer.

Contrast the description in Figure 2–8 with the installation requirements (in English and SI units) for facility construction compliance with the Americans with

Memorandum

To: Charles Artmier, Chairman, Safety Committee
From: Willard Ricke, Plant Superintendent, Sequoia Chemical Plant   *WR*
Date: November 17, 2010
Subject: Fire at the Sequoia Chemical Plant in Ardville on November 12, 2010

The following description provides an account of the conditions and development of the fire at our Sequoia Chemical Plant in Ardville on November 12, 2010. Because this description will be incorporated into the report that the Safety Committee will prepare, please let me know if I should add or clarify any details.

Conditions before Fire

Three piles of scrap paper were located about 100 feet south of Building A and 150 feet west of Building B at our Sequoia Chemical Plant in Ardville. Building A, which consisted of one story and a partial attic, was used in part as an electric shop and in part for equipment storage. Six pallets of Class I flammable liquids in 55-gallon drums were temporarily stored just outside Building A, along its west wall.

Cause of and Response to Fire

A spark created in the electric shop in Building A started a fire. The night watchman first noticed the fire in the electric shop about 6:00 a.m. and immediately called the Ardville Volunteer Fire Department and the plant superintendent. Before the fire department arrived, the fire spread to the drums of flammable liquid just outside the west wall and quickly engulfed Building A in flames. The fire then spread to the scrap paper outside, with a 40 mph wind blowing it in the direction of Building B.

During this time, the watchman began to hose down the piles of scrap paper between the buildings to try to keep the fire from reaching Building B. He also set up lawn sprinklers between the fire and Building B to protect Building B from the fire. However, he saw smoke coming from Building B at 6:15 a.m., in spite of his best efforts to protect the building.

The volunteer fire department, which was 20 miles away, reached the scene at 6:57 a.m., nearly an hour after the fire was discovered. It is estimated that the fire department's pumps were started after the fire had been burning in Building B for at least 20 minutes.

Results of the Fire

Building A was destroyed, along with its contents, and the fire burned into the hollow-joisted roof of Building B, which sustained a $250,000 loss.

Clear headings allow readers to see major steps at a glance

All steps are timed to inform the audience of the sequence of events

Figure 2–7   A Chronological Description (Excerpt)

A handkerchief-style dress with elbow-length sleeves; V-neck in front and back; bodice (*top*) backed in matching fabric; 3-inch back at center; long belt at side ties around waist; polyester/cotton blend fabric in deep mustard yellow.

Figure 2–8   Spatial Description with Photograph.   *Source:* fashionmefabulous.blogspot .com/2008/02/project-design-flowing-cotton-dresses.html. Accessed June 26, 2008.

Disabilities Act (ADA) in Figure 2–9. The fashion designer uses general descriptions like "elbow-length sleeves" and "long belt"; the writer of the installation requirements uses precise measurements and a scaled illustration.

Spatial descriptions are also important to site descriptions in environmental studies. Figure 2–10 presents an outline and Figure 2–11 on page 42, a design basis description of access and summit road requirements for a proposed 18-turbine wind farm on a mountaintop in Maine.

Division and Classification

An effective way to organize information about a complex subject is to divide it into manageable parts and then discuss each part separately. You might use this approach, called *division*, to describe a physical object, such as the parts of a home backup generator; to examine an organization, such as a company; or to explain a system, such as the channels of communication that make up the Internet. The emphasis in division is on breaking down a complex whole into a number of like units—because it is easier for an audience to consider smaller units and to examine their relationship of each to the other.

Figure 2–9   Spatial Description with Precise Measurements.   *Source:* access-board.gov/ adaag/html/figures/fig27a.html. Accessed June 26, 2008.

OUTLINE

    I. Primary Access Roadway Width
       A. Roadway = 12 ft.
       B. Shoulders
          1. Uphill = 2 ft.
          2. Downhill = 4 ft. (or less for flatter slope)
       C. Wideouts for Passing
          1. Width = 20 ft.
          2. Length = 200 ft.
          3. Distance = every ¼ mile
          4. Locations
             a. Along incoming access roads
             b. To avoid wetland areas
   II. Summit and Mountain Roadways
       A. Width = 32 ft.
       B. Shoulder = Same as for access roads

Figure 2–10   Outline for a Spatial Description

3.3 Roadway Width

The access roadway width for road segments leading to the mountaintops in tangent sections is approximately 12 feet. Shoulders should be 2 feet on the uphill side to aid in some snow storage. A 4-foot shoulder is used for the downhill side except where the fill height is less than 4 feet and a 3:1 or flatter slope can be constructed. In these areas, the shoulder can be reduced to 2 feet. Wideouts approximately 20 feet wide and 200 feet long for passing will be constructed along existing and proposed incoming access roads every ¼ mile for vehicle passing. Locations of wideouts along existing roads will be selected to avoid wetland areas. The roadway width increases in curve sections, especially the switchback areas. The summit and mountaintop spur roadways width is 32 feet. Shoulder requirements will be the same as those for other access roadways noted.

Figure 2–11   A Spatial Description.   *Source:* "Black Nubble Wind Farm Project: Basis for Design for Primary Access Roads and Summit Roads" from revised application for Black Nubble Wind Farm Project, submitted by Maine Mountain Power, http://www.maine.gov/doc/lurc/projects/redingtonrevised/Documents/Section13_Maintenance/Section_13_Access_Road%20Maintenance.pdf. Accessed October 21, 2008.

If you were a financial planner describing the types of mutual funds available to your investors, you could divide the options into three broad categories: money-market funds, bond funds, and stock funds. Although this division is accurate, it is only a first-level grouping of a complex whole. These three can, in turn, be subdivided into additional groups based on investment strategy. The second-level grouping could lead to the following categories:

Money-Market Funds
- Taxable money-market funds
- Tax-exempt money-market funds

Bond Funds
- Taxable bond funds
- Tax-exempt bond funds
- Balanced funds — mix of stocks and bonds

Stock Funds
- Balanced funds — mix of stocks and bonds
- Equity-income funds
- Growth and income funds
- Aggressive growth funds
- International growth funds

- Domestic growth funds
- Small capitalization funds
- Specialized funds

Specialized funds can be further subdivided as follows:

Specialized Funds
- Communications
- Real estate
- Energy
- Financial services
- Technology
- Environmental services
- Metals and materials
- International
- Health services
- Utilities

After you have divided the variety of mutual funds into accurate categories, or parts, you could classify them by their degree of relative risk to investors. To do so, you would reorganize your original categories based on the criterion of risk. Depending on how risk is defined, this classification might look as follows:

Low-Risk Funds
- Taxable money-market funds
- Tax-exempt money-market funds

Low- to Moderate-Risk Funds
- Taxable bond funds
- Tax-exempt bond funds
- Balanced funds
- Equity-income funds
- Growth and income funds

High-Risk Funds
- Domestic growth stock funds
- International funds
- Aggressive growth funds
- Small capitalization funds

High- to Very High-Risk Funds

- Specialized stock funds

The process by which a subject is classified is similar to the process by which a subject is divided. *Division* is the separation of a whole into its parts (such as a piece of equipment, a company's organization, the U.S. budget); *classification* is the grouping of a number of units into related categories (such as herbicides for weed control, allergens affecting people in Hawaii, or types of virus-checking software for desktop computers).

When dividing or classifying a subject, you must observe some basic rules of logic. First, divide the subject into its largest number of equal units. The *basis* for division depends, of course, on your subject and your purpose. If you are describing the *structure* of a four-cycle combustion engine, for example, you might begin by dividing the subject into its major parts—the pistons, the crankshaft, and the housing that contains them. If a more detailed explanation were needed, each of these parts, in turn, might be subdivided into its components. A discussion of the *function* of the same engine, however, would require a different logical basis for the division; such a breakdown would focus on the way combustion engines operate: (1) intake, (2) compression, (3) combustion and expansion, and (4) exhaust.

Once you have established the basis for the division, you must apply and express it consistently. Put each item into only one category so that items do not overlap categories. An examination of the structure of the combustion engine that listed the battery as a major part would be illogical. Although it is part of a vehicle's ignition system (which starts the engine), the battery is not a part of the engine itself. A discussion of the parts of the ignition system in which the battery is not mentioned would be just as illogical.

An outline provides a clear expression of classification and is especially useful in preparing a breakdown of any subject at several levels. In the following example, two Canadian park rangers classify typical park users according to four categories; the rangers then discuss how to deal with potential rule-breaking by members of each group. The rangers could have classified the visitors in a variety of other ways, of course: as city and country residents, backpackers and drivers of recreational vehicles, U.S. and Canadian citizens, and so on. However, for law-enforcement agents in public parklands, the size of a group and the relationships among its members (the bases of the comparison) were the most significant factors (Figures 2–12 and 2–13 on page 46).

Decreasing Order of Importance

◆ *For an example of this way of organizing information, see pages 540–541 in Chapter 15, Writing for the Web.*

When you organize your information in decreasing order of importance, you begin with the most important fact or point, then go on to the next most important, and so on, ending with the least important. Newspaper audiences are familiar with this sequence of information. The most significant information usually appears first in a news story, with related but secondary information completing

OUTLINE

    I. Types of campers
        A. Family groups
        B. Small groups
        C. Large groups
        D. Hostile groups
   II. Dealing with groups of campers
        A. Groups A and B
           1. One on one
           2. Courses of action
        B. Groups C and D
           1. Large groups
              a. Make the leader responsible
              b. Course of action
           2. Hostile groups
              a. Make the leader responsible (once determined)
              b. Course of action

Figure 2–12   Outline for a Memo Organized by Division and Classification

the narrative. Minor details go last, where they may be cut to accommodate a last-minute need for column space.

Decreasing order of importance is an especially appropriate pattern of organization for a report addressed to a busy decision maker, who may be able to reach a decision after considering only the most important points — and who may not have time to read the entire report. This sequence of information is useful, too, for a report written for a variety of audiences, some of whom may be interested in only the major points and others in all the points. The outline and memo shown in Figures 2–14 on page 47 and 2–15 on page 48, respectively, present an example of such an approach.

Increasing Order of Importance

When you want the most important of several ideas to be freshest in your readers' minds, organize your information by increasing order of importance. This sequence is useful in argumentative or persuasive writing when you wish to save your strongest points until the end. The sequence begins with the least important point or fact, then moves to the next least important, and builds to the most important point at the end.

Writing organized by increasing order of importance has the disadvantage of beginning weakly, with the least important information. Your readers may become impatient or distracted before reaching your main point. However, for writing in which the ideas lead, point by point, to an important conclusion, increasing order of importance is an effective pattern of organization. Reports on

Memo

To: All Employees
From: Canadian National Park Service, Office of Rangers
Date: June 15, 2010
Subject: Dealing with Campers in Violation of National Park Rules

To respond to campers breaking National Park Rules and Codes for Safety and Conduct, first recognize the various types of campers. They can be categorized as follows:

A. Family groups
B. Small groups (up to six well-acquainted members)
C. Large groups or conventions (organized, but not always well-acquainted)
D. Hostile groups (may not have an evident leader)

Groups divided into major categories

Groups A and B

Persons in groups A and B can often be dealt with on a one-on-one basis. For example, suppose a member of the group is picking wildflowers, which is an offense in most of our park areas. Two courses of action are open. You could either issue a warning or charge the person with the offense. In this situation, a warning is preferable to a charge. First, advise the person that this action is an offense, but, more important, explain why. Point out that the flowers are for all to enjoy and that most wildflowers are delicate and die quickly when picked.

Group C

For large groups, other approaches may be necessary. Every group has a leader. For a large group or convention, find out who the event organizer is (this is likely to be the person who reserved the campsite). Hold the group's leader responsible for the group's behavior and take action — issue a warning or charge the leader with the offense — according to the guidelines of the National Park Rules and Codes for Safety and Conduct.

Group D

For hostile groups without an obvious leader, observe the group's behavior to learn which person(s) assumes control of the group's actions, and try to deal with that person. Ultimately, it is best to regain control over a group through one or two individuals within the group. In a potentially hostile environment, always request backup of at least one other ranger on duty. Issue a warning or charge the leader of the group with the offense, according to the guidelines of the National Park Rules and Codes for Safety and Conduct. If necessary, eject the group from the premises, as outlined in the Codes.

Each group is then classified according to specific criteria

Figure 2–13   Memo Organized by Division and Classification

OUTLINE

  I. Most qualified candidate: April Jackson, Acting Chief
     A. Positive factors
        1. Twelve years of experience in claims processing
        2. Thoroughly familiar with section's operations
        3. Strong production record
        4. Continually ranked "outstanding" on job appraisals
     B. Negative factors
        1. Supervisory experience limited to present tenure as Acting Chief
        2. Lacks college degree required by job description
  II. Second most qualified candidate: Michael Bastick, Claims Coordinator
     A. Positive factors
        1. Able administrator
        2. Seven years of experience in section's operations
        3. Currently enrolled in management-training course
     B. Negative factors
        1. Lacks supervisory experience
        2. Most recent work indirectly related to claims processing
 III. Third most qualified candidate: Jane Fine, Administrative Assistant
     A. Positive factors
        1. Skilled administrator
        2. Three years of experience in claims processing
     B. Negative factors
        1. Lacks broad knowledge of claims procedures
        2. Lacks supervisory experience

Figure 2–14   Outline for a Memo Organized by Decreasing Order of Importance

production or personnel goals are often arranged by this pattern, as are oral presentations. Figures 2–16 and 2–17 on page 49 present an outline and a memo, respectively, that show the use of increasing order of importance as a pattern of organization.

General to Specific

In a general-to-specific sequence, you begin your writing with a general statement and then provide facts or examples to develop and support that statement. For example, if you begin a report with the general statement "Companies that diversify their products or services are more successful than those that do not," the remainder of the report would offer examples and statistics that prove to your reader that companies that diversify are, in fact, more successful than companies that do not.

    A memo or report organized in a general-to-specific sequence discusses only one point. All other information in the memo or report supports the general statement (Figures 2–18 and 2–19 on page 50). Examples and data that support the general statements are frequently accompanied by charts and graphs, providing further data to support your general point.

◆ *For guidelines for creating and presenting charts, tables, and other visuals, see pages 220–256 in Chapter 7, Designing Effective Documents and Visuals.*

Memo

To: Tawana Shaw, Director, Human Resources Department
From: Frank W. Russo, Chief, Claims Department *FWR*
Date: November 12, 2010
Subject: Selection of Chief of the Claims Processing Section

This memorandum summarizes my assessments of three candidates for the position of chief of the Claims Processing Section. The assessments are based on an evaluation of each candidate's application for the position, work history, and a personal interview.

Memo begins with most important information (strongest candidate) and includes reasons why

The most qualified candidate for chief of the Claims Processing Section is April Jackson, who is at present acting chief of the Claims Processing Section. In her 12 years in the Claims Department, Ms. Jackson has gained wide experience in all facets of the department's operations. She has maintained a consistently high production record and has demonstrated the skills and knowledge that are required for the supervisory duties she is now handling in an acting capacity. Another consideration is that she has continually been rated "outstanding" in all categories of her job-performance appraisals. However, her supervisory experience is limited to her present three-month tenure as acting chief of the section, and she lacks the college degree required by the job description.

Third and fourth paragraphs rank and evaluate other candidates

Michael Bastick, claims coordinator, my second choice, also has strong potential for the position. An able administrator, he has been with the company for seven years. Further, he is currently enrolled in a management-training course at Belmont University. He is ranked second because he lacks supervisory experience and because his most recent work has been with the department's maintenance and supply components. He would be the best person to take over many of April Jackson's responsibilities if she should be made chief of the Claims Processing Section.

Jane Fine, my third-ranked candidate, has shown herself to be a skilled administrator in her three years with the Claims Processing Section. Despite her obvious potential, she doesn't yet have the breadth of experience in claims processing that would be required of someone responsible for managing the Claims Processing Section. Jane Fine also lacks on-the-job supervisory experience.

Figure 2–15   Memo Organized by Decreasing Order of Importance

OUTLINE

   I. Staffing problem
     A. Too few qualified electronics technicians
     B. New recruiting program necessary
  II. Apprentice program
     A. Providing insufficient numbers
     B. Enlistment bonuses are attracting the attention of high school graduates
 III. Technical school
     A. Enrollment at area and regional technical schools up, but fewer students studying electronics
     B. Keen competition from the military for technical school graduates
 IV. Military veterans
     A. Relied heavily on veterans in the past
     B. Military reenlistment incentives and extended active duty assignments have affected this source
  V. Strategy to compete with the military

Figure 2–16 Outline for Information Organized by Increasing Order of Importance

To: Phillip Ting, Vice President, Operations
From: Harry Mathews, Human Resources Department
Date: May 19, 2010
Subject: Recruiting Qualified Electronics Technicians

As our company continues to expand, and with the planned opening of the Lakeland Facility late next year, we need to increase and refocus our recruiting program to keep our company staffed with qualified electronics technicians. In the past five years, we have relied on our in-house apprentice program and on local and regional technical schools to fill our needs.

Although our in-house apprentice program provided a qualified pool of employees in the past, the military is doing a more effective job of strengthening its recruitment efforts with bonuses. Thus graduating high school seniors continue to join a branch of the military services rather than join our apprentice program or attend technical schools. The military often sends graduating high school students to a technical school free of charge while they are in the service. Even our most vigorous Career Day recruiting at the technical schools has yielded disappointing results.

We have also in the past relied on recruiting skilled veterans from all branches of the military. With the military now offering very attractive reenlistment incentives and extending active duty assignments, however, this source of technicians has been greatly reduced.

I would like to meet with you soon to devise a strategy for competing with the military's current practices.

The point-by-point description of the dilemma leads the reader to the urgency of the conclusion

Final paragraph states the e-mail's most important message

Figure 2–17 E-mail Organized by Increasing Order of Importance

OUTLINE

The company needs to locate additional suppliers of computer chips because of several related events.

    I. The current supplier is reducing output.
   II. Domestic demand for our laptop computers continues to increase.
 III. We are expanding into the international market.

Figure 2–18   Outline for Information Organized from General to Specific (Excerpt)

Specific to General

When you organize information in a specific-to-general pattern, you begin with specific information and build to a general conclusion. The examples, facts, and statistics that you present in your writing support the conclusion that comes at the end. For example, if your subject were highway safety, you might begin with details of a specific highway accident, go on to generalize about how that accident was similar to many others, and then present recommendations for reducing the probability of such accidents. If your purpose is to persuade a skeptical audience by providing specific details, this pattern is useful because it suspends the general point until your case has been made. This pattern of organization is somewhat like increasing order of importance in that you carefully build your case and reach your conclusion at the end, as shown in Figures 2–20 and 2–21.

General statement

LOCATING COMPUTER-CHIP SUPPLIERS

On the basis of information presented at the supply meeting on April 14, we recommend that the company locate additional suppliers of computer chips. Several related events make such action necessary.

Supporting information includes specific details

Our current supplier, ABC Electronics, is reducing its output. Specifically, we can expect a reduction of between 800 and 1,000 units per month for the remainder of this fiscal year. The number of units should stabilize at 15,000 units per month thereafter.

Domestic demand for our computers continues to grow. Demand during the current fiscal year is up 25,000 units over the last fiscal year. Sales Department projections for the next five years show that demand should peak next year at 50,000 units and then remain at that figure for at least the following four years.

Finally, our expansion into Eastern Europe will require additional shipments of 5,000 units per quarter to each country for the remainder of this fiscal year. Sales Department projections put computer sales for each country at double this rate, or 40,000 units in a fiscal year, for the next five years.

Figure 2–19   Document Organized from General to Specific (Excerpt)

OUTLINE

    I. Study of 4,500 accidents involving nearly 7,200 adult front-seat passengers showed only 20 percent of the vehicles equipped with passenger-side air bags

    II. Study shows adult front-seat passengers in vehicles without air bags twice as likely to be killed as those in vehicles with air bags

       A. Children riding as front-seat passengers can be killed by deployment of air bags

       B. Children should ride in the backseat

    III. Estimated 40 percent of adult front-seat passenger vehicle deaths could be prevented if passenger-side air bags were installed

---

Figure 2–20   Outline for Information Organized from Specific to General

Comparison

When you use comparison as a pattern of development, you evaluate the relative merits of the items you are considering. Comparison works well in determining which of two or more items is most suitable for some specific purpose, such as selecting the best color printer for digital photographs, determining the most cost-effective messenger service for your company, or choosing the most qualified applicant for your job opening. Showing such information in tables often facilitates item-to-item comparisons when you have more than a few options to consider, as in Table 2–2. The advantage of a table is that it provides a quick reference, allowing readers to see and compare all the information at once. The disadvantage is that a table cannot convey as much related detailed information as a narrative description.

ON THE WEB

For more examples of comparison, go to Model Documents Gallery, bedfordstmartins.com/writingthatworks

---

FACTS ABOUT AIR BAGS

Recently, a government agency studied the use of passenger-side air bags in 4,500 accidents involving nearly 7,200 front-seat passengers. Nearly all these accidents occurred on routes that had a speed limit of at least 40 mph. Only 20 percent of the adult front-seat passengers were riding in vehicles equipped with passenger-side air bags. Those not riding in vehicles equipped with passenger-side air bags were more than twice as likely to be killed as passengers riding in vehicles that were so equipped.

A conservative estimate is that 40 percent of the adult front-seat passenger vehicle deaths could be prevented if all vehicles came equipped with passenger-side air bags. Children, however, should always ride in the backseat because other studies have indicated that a child can be killed by the deployment of an air bag. If you are an adult front-seat passenger in an accident, your chances of survival are far greater if the vehicle in which you are riding is equipped with a passenger-side air bag.

Statistical details build the case for the final paragraph

General conclusion

Figure 2–21   Document Organized from Specific to General (Excerpt)

TABLE 2–2   Table Layout for a Comparison

Comparison of Woodworking Glues				
	White Glue	*Aliphatic Resin Glue*	*Plastic Resin Glue*	*Contact Cement*
Bonding strength	Low	Moderate	High	High
Moisture resistance	Low	Moderate	High	High
Setting time	30 minutes	30 minutes	4 to 6 hours	Bonds on contact
Common uses	Light construction	General purpose	General purpose	Bond laminate and veneer to wood

Types of glue ———

Characteristics

◆ *For a discussion of tables, see pages 224–228 in Chapter 7, Designing Effective Documents and Visuals.*

To be sure that your choice will be the best one, you must determine the basis (or bases) for making your comparison. For example, if you were comparing the features commonly used to evaluate woodworking glues, you could organize them as shown in Table 2–2.

Once you decide on the bases important to your comparison, you can determine the most effective way to structure your comparison: whole by whole or part by part.

- In the *whole-by-whole pattern*, all the relevant characteristics of one item are discussed before those of the next item are considered.

- In the *part-by-part pattern*, the relevant features of each item are compared one by one.

Hearing aids, for example, may be compared in a variety of ways: style, size, correction range, control features, and more. To help consumers comparing hearing-aid options, the whole-by-whole pattern would allow them to consider each type in turn. The outline shown in Figure 2–22 and the discussion in Figure 2–23 on page 54, comparing types of hearing aids are organized according to the whole-by-whole pattern. The writer describes each type according to its size and placement, features, and drawbacks before going on to the next type.

As is often the case when the whole-by-whole pattern is used, the purpose of this comparison is to weigh the advantages and disadvantages of each type of device against the others. However, if your purpose were to compare, one at a time, the major *functions* of hearing aids, the information might be arranged according to the part-by-part pattern (Figures 2–24 and 2–25 on page 56). Note that this pattern emphasizes the specific characteristics of the hearing aids rather than the different types of hearing aids. The features being compared can be further highlighted by word order and by mechanical highlighting (*italic*, **boldface**, or <u>underlining</u>), as in the narratives comparing hearing aids in Figures 2–24 and 2–25 on page 56.

OUTLINE: Common Types of Hearing Aids

   I. Completely in the canal
      A. Size and placement
      B. Special considerations
         1. Correction range
         2. Volume control . . .
      C. Potential problems
         1. Acoustic feedback
         2. Ear-wax maintenance . . .
  II. In the canal (partial)
      A. Size and placement
      B. Special considerations
         1. Correction range
         2. Volume control . . .
      C. Potential problems
         1. Acoustic feedback
         2. Wind noise . . .
 III. In the ear
      A. Size and placement
      B. Special considerations
         1. Correction range
         2. Amplification range . . .
      C. Potential problems
         1. Acoustic feedback
         2. Ear-wax maintenance . . .
 IV. Behind the ear
      A. Size and placement
      B. Special considerations
         1. Correction range
         2. Volume control . . .
      C. Potential problems
         1. Cosmetic appeal
         2. Acoustic feedback . . .

Figure 2–22   Outline for a Whole-by-Whole Comparison (Excerpt)

COMMON TYPES OF HEARING AIDS

Hearing aids are tiny instruments worn in or behind the ear that amplify sounds for people with hearing loss. The following comparison describes the most common types of hearing aids and their advantages and disadvantages. Figure 1 illustrates their placements.

Types of hearing aids being compared

Behind the Ear   In the Ear   In the Canal   Completely in the Canal

Figure 1. Common Hearing Aids and Their Placement
Source: American Academy of Audiology (<www.audiology.org>)

Completely in the Canal

Completely in the canal (CIC) hearing aids are the smallest type of hearing aid manufactured. They are custom fitted for insertion into the ear canal next to the eardrum and are virtually invisible when worn, which makes them cosmetically appealing. They require no outside wires or tubes and are removed by the wearer with a transparent wire. The CIC hearing aids are especially effective for mild-to-severe hearing loss; they are not designed for profound hearing loss. . . .

The advantage in size of the CIC hearing aid does result in certain kinds of problems that can impede the effectiveness of the hearing aid. Its small size often limits its power and the range of frequencies it picks up. It can make manipulating the controls and changing the tiny batteries challenging, too. Acoustic feedback (whistling) can occur because the microphone is close to the speaker in this model.

Detailed descriptions of advantages and disadvantages provide basis for comparison

In the Canal (Partial)

The in the canal (ITC) style is larger than the CIC model, but it is still small and discreet. Although partially visible when worn, it too affords the wearer cosmetic appeal. Like the CIC model, the ITC hearing aid is effective for mild-to-severe hearing loss; it is not effective for profound hearing loss.

Figure 2–23 **Whole-by-Whole Comparison (Excerpt)** (continued)

This model offers additional control functions compared with the CIC model, like the capability to hold a telecoil for telephone conversations and a directional microphone. . . .

Problems impeding effectiveness include its size, which requires manual dexterity to manipulate its controls and change the battery. Without frequent cleaning, it can be damaged by ear wax. . . .

In the Ear

The in the ear (ITE) style is larger than the full or partial ITC models and is fully visible when worn. It is custom made to fit the contours of the outer ear and fits just outside the opening to the ear canal. The ITE devices are effective for mild-to-severe hearing loss but not for profound hearing loss.

Because of their size, ITE devices afford a wide array of user-controlled features, such as directional microphones, tone control, and a telecoil to enhance hearing during telephone conversations. . . .

Certain models can be damaged by ear wax, so they require frequent cleaning. . . .

Behind the Ear

The behind the ear (BTE) style is the largest of the common models. It fits snugly behind one or both ears and can be fully or partially hidden, depending on the wearer's hairstyle. The BTE device is connected to a plastic ear mold inside the outer ear. It can also be attached to eyeglasses. It is designed for severe-to-profound hearing loss. Its size and placement minimize the likelihood of acoustic feedback and make manipulating the controls and changing the battery easier than in the smaller models.

The BTE devices can be connected to a variety of external sound sources, such as television sets and infrared listening devices that make targeted sounds, such as speakers in a classroom or an auditorium, easier to hear. . . .

This type of device cannot be worn by those with deformed or missing outer ears. Eyeglass wearers require a special adaptation to wear this style. The BTE devices are prone to acoustic feedback (whistling) if poorly fitted. Finally, their size and location reduce their cosmetic appeal.

Figure 2–23 Whole-by-Whole Comparison (Excerpt) (continued)

OUTLINE: Evaluating Hearing-Aid Characteristics

I. Size and Placement
   A. Completely in the canal
   B. In the canal (partial)
   C. In the ear
   D. Behind the ear
II. Special Considerations
   A. Hearing-correction range
      1. Mild to moderate
      2. Moderate to severe
      3. Severe to profound
   B. Special features
      1. Volume control
      2. Telecoil for phone use
      3. Connection to external sound source
      4. Amplification range . . .
III. Potential Problems
   A. Acoustic feedback
   B. Ear-wax maintenance
   C. Wind noise
   D. Cosmetic appeal

Figure 2–24   Outline for a Part-by-Part Comparison (Excerpt)

EVALUATING HEARING-AID OPTIONS

Hearing aids are tiny instruments worn in or behind the ear that amplify sounds for people with hearing loss. The following comparison describes the features that consumers in need of hearing aids should evaluate in selecting the model most appropriate to their hearing loss and ease of use.

Size and Placement

Characteristics that distinguish different kinds of hearing aids

The most common types of hearing aids are classified according to their size and location in or behind the ear. *Completely in the canal* (CIC) hearing aids, the smallest type manufactured, are worn deep inside the ear canal, next to the eardrum. *In the canal* (partial) (ITC) hearing aids, although larger than the CIC devices, are small and discreet. *In the ear* (ITE) hearing aids are worn in the contour of the outer ear, just outside the opening to the ear canal. *Behind the ear* (BTE) models fit snugly behind the ear and are the largest of the common models.

Comparison of features organized by topics important to consumers

Correction Range and Special Features

Hearing loss is categorized from mild to profound. Mild-to-severe hearing loss can be helped with CIC, ITC, and ITE hearing aids. Severe-to-profound hearing loss can be helped with BTE hearing aids.

Figure 2–25   Part-by-Part Comparison (Excerpt) (continued)

Hearing aids provide a variety of features to improve the user's quality of hearing. All models offer on/off capability, volume control, and circuitry to limit maximum volume of sound to tolerable levels. The ITC and ITE models can hold a telecoil. The BTE model can be connected to external sound sources, such as TV sets, radios, and infrared listening devices. . . .

Potential Problems

Acoustic feedback (whistling) is most often a problem for the smallest models because of the close proximity of the microphone to the speaker. Except for the BTE model, the others can be damaged by ear wax. The BTE hearing aid is the least cosmetically appealing because of its size. . . .

Figure 2–25   Part-by-Part Comparison (Excerpt)   (continued)

CONSIDERING AUDIENCE AND PURPOSE

Organizing Information

Organize your writing from the perspective of your audience and purpose. Keep in mind that some types of writing lend themselves logically to only one kind of organization and will best convey information to your reader by that pattern.

- **Sequential** organization takes your reader step by step through the stages of a process in the order in which the process occurs (example: instructions in a user's manual).

- **Chronological** organization takes your reader step by step through the stages of an activity or event as it occurs *in time* from beginning to end (example: a trip report).

- **Spatial** organization describes physical objects, areas, and phenomena at the level of detail necessary for your reader to envision their appearance or how they occurred (example: an accident report).

- **Division** is a way of organizing information about a complex whole by breaking it into smaller units for your reader, making it easier to understand (example: a description of the parts of a desktop computer).

- **Classification** is a way of organizing information that groups disparate units into categories recognizable to your audience (example: a description of different types of vacation packages).

- **Decreasing order of importance** introduces your reader to your main, or most important, points at the beginning of your writing, followed by background information that supports your main points (example: a news story or formal report for busy readers).

- **Increasing order of importance** leads your reader through the thought process and details that support conclusions you reach at the end of your writing (example: a persuasive presentation).

(continued)

▶ **CONSIDERING AUDIENCE AND PURPOSE**

(continued)

- **General-to-specific** organization introduces your reader to the main, or general, point you wish to make at the beginning of your writing and leads your reader through the facts and other supporting information that describes how you reached your general point (example: a memo or proposal that begins with a recommendation).

- **Specific-to-general** sequence leads your reader through the facts and other supporting information you use to build your case for reaching the conclusion you state at the end of your writing (example: a report that begins by giving the details of an event).

- **Comparison** allows your reader to evaluate the relative strengths of the items that are under evaluation after you establish the basis for the comparison (example: a memo that considers a variety of options).

CHAPTER 2 SUMMARY: ORGANIZING YOUR INFORMATION

Before you begin to write, consider the following questions as you organize your information into a logical sequence.

- Will I need a brief list or a full-scale outline to organize my information?
- Will I need to circulate the outline to colleagues or superiors?
- Is the outline divided into parts and subparts that reflect the logical divisions of the topic?
- Will my word-processing software structure the outline automatically?
- Does the topic lend itself naturally to one of the following patterns of development?
  - Sequential
  - Chronological
  - Spatial
  - Division and classification
  - Decreasing order of importance
  - Increasing order of importance
  - General to specific
  - Specific to general
  - Comparison
- Does the topic need to be organized by more than one pattern of development?

ON THE WEB

For more exercises and an online quiz on organization, go to Chapter 2, bedfordstmartins.com/ writingthatworks

▦ Exercises

1. Determine for each of the following topics the best organizational method—sequential, chronological, spatial, division and classification, decreasing order of importance, increasing order of importance, general to specific, specific to general, or comparison.

- Explaining how to register for classes at your school
- Supporting an argument against smoking
- Describing different types of dogs at a dog show
- Determining the job that is right for you
- Explaining how to get the job you want
- Describing the most important room in your home
- Announcing the winners of a contest
- Describing the fire-escape route for a building
- Determining the best computer to buy
- Describing the planets in our solar system
- Explaining the changing educational system in your state
- Supporting an argument for or against specific environmental-protection laws

2. Identify the method of organization that would be most effective for each of the following topics and explain how consideration of audience and purpose might affect your decision.
- Instructions for performing CPR
- A report of the results of a police stakeout or other police activity
- A report on the different kinds of news, drama, and comedy programs on prime-time television
- A report on the differences among the major personal computer manufacturers
- Instructions for preparing a five-course meal, including recipes
- A report on the different types of media coverage of a world event
- A report on the results of a governmental election and its importance
- Instructions for buying or selling a house

3. Make a list of topics and create an outline for one of the following writing projects, organizing each *sequentially*. As your instructor directs, use the outline to write a document of assigned length.
- Preparing a household budget for clients of a financial planner
- Tuning a guitar for customers with little musical training
- Setting up a personal computer for use in a home office: parts, peripherals, and desktop configuration
- Applying for a personal loan for customers of a local bank
- Finding an apartment to rent: a guide for foreign students
- Maturing of a monarch butterfly egg to an adult for a display at a nature center
- Hosting a social event for members of a networking group
- Purchasing a product on the Internet

4. Make a list of topics and create an outline for one of the following descriptions, organizing each *spatially*. As your instructor directs, use the outline to write a description of assigned length. Without relying on illustrations, describe the topic clearly enough so that a classmate, if asked, could create an accurate drawing or diagram based on your description.
- The layout of your apartment or of a floor in your home (as it is, or as you would like it to be)
- The layout of the reference room or other area of the school or community library
- The dimensions and most significant features of a public park or building
- The layout of a garden for a home-improvement Web site

- The layout of the shop, office, or laboratory where you work for new employees
- The physical process for disinfecting a hospital room or for painting or wall-papering a room

5. Make a list of topics and create an outline for one of the following writing projects, organizing each by a *decreasing-order-of-importance* sequence. As your instructor directs, use the outline to write a document of assigned length.
   - Your job qualifications and career goal to be used in a letter of application and résumé
   - The advantages of living in a particular city or area of the country for an employee relocation guide
   - The importance of preventive care in one health-related area (diet, exercise, dental care, and so on)
   - The advantages of having paychecks directly deposited into checking accounts, of having savings automatically deducted from paychecks, or of using online banking for credit union members
   - The advantages of recycling for a city-council booklet
   - The advantages of owning life insurance for an agent training manual
   - The advantages of carpooling for an employee intranet Web site

6. Make a list of topics and create an outline for one of the following writing projects, organizing each by an *increasing-order-of-importance* sequence. As your instructor directs, use the outline to write a document of assigned length.
   - The advantages of learning to pilot a small airplane for prospective students of a flying school
   - The reasons you deserve a pay raise for a possible meeting with or a memo to your manager
   - The advantages of alternatively fueled vehicles for an environmental-resource organization
   - A proposal to change a procedure where you work for your management

7. For this exercise, use a *general-to-specific* sequence. Choose one of the following statements, then support it with pertinent facts, examples, anecdotes, and so on. As your instructor directs, outline the information to write a document of assigned length.
   - Volunteer jobs and internships provide valuable experience in the working world.
   - For families living within limited means, budgeting is essential.
   - Capable managers are willing to delegate authority.
   - Post–high school education or vocational training is essential in today's job market.
   - A sound human-resources training program pays off for companies.

8. Create a topic outline for one of the following subjects, organizing it by *division and classification*. Using the outline, write a document of assigned length as instructed.
   - Personal digital assistants (including pocket personal computers)
   - Conventional and alternative medical therapies
   - Weight-loss strategies and programs
   - Home exercise equipment
   - Bicycles (for example, racing, mountain)

- Cameras (for example, quality, convenience, price ranges)
- Cable TV channels (select a single category: for example, news, information, public access, shopping, special interest)

9. Create a topic outline for one of the following subjects, organizing it by the *comparison* method of development. Using the outline, write a document of assigned length appropriate to the topic or as your instructor directs.
   - The features of two or more social-networking Web sites (College Tonight, Facebook, MySpace, etc.)
   - U.S. intellectual property laws (for example, copyright law, trademark law, and patent law)
   - Features of at least five specialized library databases (for example, InfoTrac, Clearinghouse, Health AtoZ, Thomas Legislative Information, ZIP Code Lookup)

Collaborative Classroom Projects

ON THE WEB

For more collaborative classroom projects, go to Chapter 2, bedfordstmartins.com/ writingthatworks

1. Following is an example of a poorly developed outline. In small groups and within the allotted time frame, revise this outline, using the guidelines provided in this chapter. Select a spokesperson from your group to present your outline to the class.

   Company Sports
   I. Intercompany sports
      A. Advantages to the company
         1. Publicity
         2. Intercompany relations
      B. Disadvantages
         1. Misplaced emphasis
         2. Athletic participation not available to all employees
   II. Intracompany sports
      A. Wide participation
      B. Physical fitness
      C. Detracts from work
      D. Risks injuries

2. Bring five common tools to class (a can opener, a pencil sharpener, and so on). In small groups, outline a narrative description of one or more of the tools, keeping in mind the particular function of the tool(s). When finished, exchange papers and critique one another's outlines based on whether the outline effectively describes the tool.

3. Long-term project: In small groups, create an outline for a guide for new students who need to learn how to sign up for classes. First, consider the obvious things students have to do, like learn their student identification numbers, meet with their advisers, and go over the course catalog and class schedules. Then, evaluate the scope of signing up for classes. (Review pages 11–12 in Chapter 1, Assessing Audience and Purpose, for advice on considering scope in your writing.) Would it help to start at the very beginning—with enrollment at the university, required immunizations, and learning the locations of classroom buildings, for example?

Determine the amount of information necessary before creating the outline; be prepared to defend your choices.

ON THE WEB

For more research projects, go to Chapter 2, **bedfordstmartins** .com/writingthatworks

■ Research Projects

1. Locate a government, a business, or an industry report or an article in a professional journal. Analyze the organization of information in the report or article, and write an outline that mirrors the organization. Develop the outline to the level of detail of the outline shown in Figure 2–1 or to the level of detail specified by your instructor. Then assess the report or article for its use of the methods of organization described in this chapter, citing specific sections or paragraphs in which each method is demonstrated. Finally, describe how the organization of the report or article made it easier or more difficult to understand its content.

2. Material that will be read quickly is often organized by decreasing order of importance. Newspaper articles and news releases (announcements of upcoming events or company news created by public relations writers) are two such types of material. At a university or college, the university relations or advancement office often sends news releases about campus events to local newspapers and news stations, hoping to persuade reporters or camera crews to attend an event and write an article or present a film segment about it. Newspaper editors and television producers get many news releases a day, so they don't spend much time reading each one.
   a. Go to your university public relations office (or its link on your school's Web site) and ask for several examples of news releases about major events on your campus. You can also go to PR Newswire at <www.prnewswire.com> and look for news releases about your school. Then, in groups, analyze the order of the information in these releases. Create an outline of a news release based on your analysis.
   b. Ask someone in your university public relations office for copies of articles that were published by local newspapers based on the news releases they received. (You can also find articles in the LexisNexis database at your school's library.) In the same groups, analyze how these newspaper articles were written. Then create an outline of a newspaper article based on your analysis. Present your findings to the class.

3. Visit five or more government Web sites (.gov) and analyze the variety of ways that information is organized at each site; use specific examples to support your analysis. Write one to three paragraphs that detail the effectiveness or ineffectiveness of how information is presented at each site. Compare the sites. Write another analysis of the same length explaining how other methods of organization and the use of outlining (as discussed in this chapter) could improve each of these sites.

4. As noted in this chapter, writers should not overstate claims they make about a product or service, nor should they speak negatively or disparagingly about a competitor. Search the Web for products that are usually marketed with a large degree of hype, like diet products, sports drinks, weight-loss products, or home electronics.

a. Print out several examples of online advertisements or Web pages for a particular type of product. First look at the visual persuasive strategies that the graphics and Web designers have chosen to use. (*Note*: Before you begin, read about graphics and design in Chapter 7, Designing Effective Documents and Visuals.) Describe the pictures on the pages, the colors used, and the fonts and blinking images used. What do the visuals say about these products?

b. Examine the sites' persuasive writing strategies. Do they include action words? repetitious use of certain words? lots of exclamation points?

c. Write your findings in a memo to the class. How have the visual and rhetorical strategies added to or subtracted from the designers' and writers' persuasiveness?

3 Writing the Draft

AT A GLANCE: Drafting

Once you have gathered and organized your information, you are ready to write. But how do you turn an outline into a workable document? This chapter describes and illustrates several well-established strategies for preparing a first draft.

- Managing your time / 65
- Focusing on audience / 67
  - Writing from your reader's perspective / 68
  - Considering different kinds of audiences / 68
  - Establishing your voice / 71
- Applying strategies for conveying information / 75
  - Explaining a process / 76
  - Describing information / 77
  - Defining terms and concepts / 79
  - Explaining cause and effect / 82
- Crafting effective openings / 84
- Creating persuasive closings / 86

This chapter describes proven techniques for successfully writing your draft as well as staying connected to your audience and developing your topic as you do so. It also guides you through the process of writing effective openings and closings and continues the development of the Lifemaker brochure introduced in Chapter 2, Organizing Your Information.

The most effective way to start and to keep going is to use a good outline as a springboard and a map for your writing. The outline also serves to group related facts and details. Once these facts are grouped, you are ready to construct unified and coherent paragraphs—the major building blocks of any piece of writing. Keep in mind, however, that first drafts are necessarily rough and unpolished. Writing and revising are two very different tasks. Trying to write something perfectly the first time puts undue pressure on you that can become self-defeating. In fact, any attempt to correct or polish your writing as you create the first draft only stimulates your internal critic and undermines your ability to complete your draft. When you write the draft, your goal is to transcribe and expand the notes from your outline into paragraphs without worrying about grammar, refinements of language, or spelling. Experienced writers use the tactics described in this chapter to start, keep moving, and get the job done; you will discover which ones are the most helpful to you.

Time-Management Tactics

Because on-the-job writers must work not only under constant deadlines but also with several assignments at once, managing time is an essential part of the writing process. You may not feel inspired to begin, but you will gain confidence as you continue writing. Use positive motivation: Remember that your goal at this point is to write a draft, not a polished final product.

WRITER'S CHECKLIST
Developing Confidence

✔ Nothing builds a writer's confidence more than adequate preparation.

✔ Remember past writing projects—you have completed something before, and you will this time.

✔ Don't wait for inspiration to write the rough draft—treat writing the draft as you would any on-the-job task.

✔ Think of writing a rough draft as simply transcribing and expanding the notes from your outline into paragraphs.

✔ Don't worry about creating a good opening—that can wait until you've constructed your paragraphs.

✔ Concentrate on ideas without attempting to polish or revise. Don't worry about precise word choices, usage, syntax, grammar, or spelling.

✔ Keep writing quickly to achieve unity, coherence, and proportion.

✔ Don't criticize yourself for not being able to write a smooth, readable sentence the first time; it is natural for first drafts to be clumsy and long-winded.

✔ Remind yourself that you are beginning a *draft* that no one else will read.

VOICES IN THE WORKPLACE
Thinking About Writing Deadlines

Debra Canale, a competitive intelligence manager at Roadway Express, consciously organizes her work space and schedule to keep writing requirements on track despite routine interruptions: "Organizing your thoughts and your work space is essential to writing for business. I find it helps to keep to-do lists and date-due lists and to re-prioritize my writing responsibilities on a daily basis in order to accommodate interruptions, emergencies, and ever-changing business priorities."

Allocating Your Time

Keep a calendar on your desk or computer that indicates various deadlines for projects, appointments for interviews, and time periods for gathering information. Your daily calendar should also include "writing appointments," times set

◆ For detailed advice on outlining ideas before drafting, review Chapter 2, Organizing Your Information.

◆ For a detailed explanation of the revision process, see Chapter 4, Revising the Draft.

◆ For editing guidelines, see Part Four, Revision Guide.

ON THE WEB
For online resources for drafting, go to Chapter 3, bedfordstmartins.com/ writingthatworks

◆ For tips on practicing freewriting to get your ideas down quickly, see page 66, Digital Tips: Drafting on Your Computer.

◆ *For guidelines on writing three types of time-sensitive documents, see*
• *Meeting the Deadline: The Time-Sensitive Message on pages 293–295*
• *Meeting the Deadline: The Time-Sensitive Proposal on pages 488–490*
• *Meeting the Deadline: The Time-Sensitive Presentation on pages 519–523*

aside for writing that you must keep (without interruptions) as if you had an appointment with another person.

Begin small. Within the deadlines set by teachers, managers, and others, set your own short-term, manageable deadlines for completing sections of a draft and other tasks. Concentrating on such small goals can help you meet the overall deadline, and it can also relieve some of the pressure of writing the draft. Some professional writers think of the completion of small goals as building a draft one brick at a time.

List these goals, together with your other job tasks; then schedule each task for a specific time. As you set your schedule, remember that time-management experts advise working on the most difficult or unpleasant tasks during the time of day when your mind is keenest.

Preparing Your Work Environment

Another useful time-management strategy is to prepare your writing environment and assemble your materials before you begin. Find an isolated place or a method of isolating yourself for writing the draft, then hang the "Do Not Disturb" sign. Especially when a deadline is in jeopardy, finding a quiet area away from phones and meetings can be effective. Put order into your writing environment by arranging your materials and supplies. Use whatever writing technology (pen and pad, computer, or tape recorder) is most comfortable for you. You may even discover that certain props will help you get started. Sitting in a favorite chair, opening computer files, or placing a reference book on your desk may symbolize your commitment to yourself and your work.

Remaining Flexible

Start with your outline as a guide, but remember that it is not cast in concrete. Feel free to improve your organization as you work. Consider starting with the easiest or most interesting part to get moving and build some momentum. You may find that just writing a statement of your purpose will help you get started. Once you

---

@ DIGITAL TIPS: Drafting on Your Computer

■ Try freewriting to overcome writer's block. Turn off the monitor and write your thoughts as quickly as possible without stopping to correct mistakes, to complete sentences, or to polish your writing. After you finish, you can turn the monitor back on and review, revise, and reorganize as appropriate.

■ If a difficult section hinders your progress, use the highlighting or comment feature to make note of it and move on.

■ Save each draft separately so that you can return to earlier versions if necessary, but do not create separate drafts for minor corrections.

■ Use a consistent naming pattern for multiple drafts, such as course abbreviation, assignment number, and draft number or date.

are rolling, keep going. You may wish to write comments to yourself while you are writing the rough draft if that tactic keeps you moving. When you reach landmarks (such as the small goals within the deadlines set by others, as described earlier) or feel powerfully tempted to start revising, you may need to take a break. When you do, leave a signpost, such as a printout of an unfinished section or a note in the outline recording the date and time you stopped, so you will not waste time searching for your place when you resume work. When you finish a section, reward yourself with a cup of coffee, a short walk, or another small diversion. Physical activity serves as an excellent break for writers. If possible, avoid immersing yourself in another mental activity while you are on your break. If you are not under mental pressure, you may discover a solution to a nagging writing problem.

When you resume, reread what you have written so that you can recall your frame of mind. Some writers also like to change their writing tools or environment when they resume writing the draft.

◆ *For more on statements of purpose, see page 5 in Chapter 1, Assessing Audience and Purpose.*

WRITER'S CHECKLIST
Writing a Rough Draft

✔ Set up a quiet writing area with the necessary equipment and materials; then hang the "Do Not Disturb" sign.

✔ Start with the section that seems easiest or most interesting to you.

✔ The first rule of good writing is to help your audience by communicating clearly. Write in a plain and direct style that is comfortable and natural for both you and your audience.

✔ To make your writing more direct and conversational, imagine a typical reader sitting across the desk from you as you explain your topic.

✔ If you are writing instructions or procedures, visualize your readers actually performing the actions you are describing. This will help you envision the necessary steps and ensure that you provide adequate information in the right sequence and level of detail.

✔ If you are writing a sales letter, think of your arguments from the reader's point of view. Imagine how the features you describe can best be translated into benefits for a prospective customer.

✔ Give yourself a 10- or 15-minute time limit in which you write continually, regardless of how good or bad your writing seems to you. The point is to keep moving.

✔ Stop writing when you've finished a section (or before you're completely exhausted) and give yourself a small reward.

✔ Reread what you have written when you return to your writing. Often, seeing what you have written will trigger the frame of mind that was productive.

■ Keeping Your Audience in Mind

When writing the draft, focus on communicating with your readers. Think of your subject from your readers' perspective. Ask: "What does my reader probably know?" and "What are my reader's feelings about the subject—sympathetic? hostile? neutral?" These questions will always help improve the effort required to

◆ *For detailed advice on analyzing an audience, see pages 6–7 in Chapter 1, Assessing Audience and Purpose.*

think about them. For international readers, keep language and cultural differences in mind and consult someone from the target audience for guidance if possible. For persuasive writing, support your ideas convincingly, acknowledge opposing points of view, and use the appropriate medium for your message. In all your writing, adopt the tone of voice—formal, authoritative, conversational—appropriate to your audience and purpose.

Writing from the Audience's Point of View

Whether your reader is a coworker, customer, or company president, he or she is interested in the problem you are addressing more from his or her point of view than from yours. Imagine yourself in your reader's position, perhaps by visualizing your reader performing a set of activities or taking certain actions based on your writing. Taken together with what you know about your reader's background, this picture will help you predict your reader's needs and reactions and ensure that you clearly provide all the information your reader needs. For instance, suppose you work for a bicycle manufacturer and you need to write assembly instructions so that people who buy the new model 1050J can get from opening the carton to riding the bicycle with a minimum of frustration. You would break down the assembly process into a sensible series of easy-to-follow steps. You would avoid technical language and anticipate questions that your audience would be likely to have, making it unnecessary for them to consult other sources to follow your directions. You would also include assembly diagrams, a list of parts, and a list of the tools necessary for assembly. You would not explain the engineering theory that is responsible for the bicycle's unique design. You would approach the situation differently if you were preparing assembly instructions for a bicycle dealer. You could use standard technical terms without defining them, and you would probably combine related steps because the dealer would be familiar with bicycle assembly and able to follow a more sophisticated set of instructions. Your audience would not need a list of tools required for assembly; the shop would no doubt have all the necessary tools, and the dealer would know which ones to use. You might well, in a separate section, include some theoretical detail, too. The dealer could possibly use this information to explain to customers the advantages of your bicycle over a competitor's.

Accommodating Multiple Audiences

When you write for readers similar in background and knowledge—all sales associates, for example, or all security officers—picture a typical representative of that group and write directly to that person. Occasionally, however, you may need to write for readers with widely different work environments, technical backgrounds, or professional positions. For example, if you were to write a technical report that would be used by company executives, field-service engineers, and sales associates, you might address each audience separately in clearly identified sections of your document: an executive summary for the executives, the body of the document for the sales associates, and an appendix for the service engineers. When you cannot segment your writing this way, determine who your primary audience is, and make certain that you meet all of that audience's needs. Then try to meet the needs of other readers—only if you can do so without placing a burden on your primary audience.

Figures 3–1 and 3–2 are from a technical-assessment report that describes to an organization the advantages of acquiring media-streaming technology. The first part of the report (Figure 3–1) provides an overview of the topic for policy makers who may be unfamiliar with this technology and its uses. The second part (Figure 3–2) is targeted at technical experts who must understand the hardware and software requirements for the system.

◆ *For an explanation of how the different parts of a formal report address the needs of different audiences, see Chapter 11, Writing Formal Reports.*

INTRODUCTION

This report demonstrates how the Office of the Chief Information Officer can improve the distribution of agency information and enhance communications with the staff, the nuclear industry, other federal agencies, the media, and the public by using media-streaming technology (MST). This report explains this technology and its advantages to our organization, details the resources necessary to deploy it, and recommends a course of action to achieve these goals.

Overview and purpose of report

Media streaming is the receipt of audio and video broadcast media over the Internet at one's desktop or laptop computer. The advantages of providing this capability to the agency are threefold:

Definition of a key term

- It enhances the agency's ability to collaborate with the nuclear industry, the states, other federal agencies, the public, and other agency stakeholders.
- It provides desktop and laptop delivery of training, commission meetings, public meetings at remote locations, staff safety programs, nuclear industry standards, and much else.
- It builds partnerships with government and private-sector organizations.

List of high-level advantages to organization

This report provides no single solution to deploying MST. Agency requirements are not static and will require alternative configurations over time at headquarters and the regional offices. Accordingly, the coverage includes necessary background information for decision makers in the following areas:

Statement defines intended audience (decision makers)

- Business requirements for and cost of supporting MST
- Technology cost alternatives based on a variety of agency program requirements
- A new internal Web site focusing on MST to assist management and staff in determining how the technology can be used to improve agency programs and customer relations

Statement of scope of report

Figure 3–1 Introduction to a Report (for a General Audience)

ARCHITECTURE OF THE REAL SYSTEM

Real System G2 is a client-server application that delivers live and on-demand MST content across TCP/IP networks. The Real System architecture has three main components: Real Server, Real Player, and content publishing tools. Real Server streams live and on-demand Real Audio, Real Video, Real Flash animation, Real Pix (GIF and JPEG images), and Real Text content across the Internet and NGN. Real System G2 supports most other existing media file formats, such as ASF, AVI, JPEG, MPEG, VIV, and WAV. The Real Player is used on client workstations to play the MST content. Real System publishing tools, such as the Real Producer and Real System G2 Authoring Tool, are used to create MST content.

Technical vocabulary and abbreviations for expert audience

Figure 3–2   Subsection of a Report (for a Technical Audience)

ON THE WEB

Intercultural Press (interculturalpress .com) provides publications aimed at specific cultures and that cover a wide variety of subjects from cross-cultural theory to international business. For links to other resources for global communication, go to Chapter 3, bedfordstmartins.com/ writingthatworks

◆ *For a fuller discussion of cultural differences, see pages 343 and 346–351 of Chapter 9, Writing Business Correspondence, and, for presentations, see pages 515–516 of Chapter 14, Giving Presentations and Conducting Meetings.*

Writing for an International Audience

The prevalence of global communication technology, international trade agreements, and the emergence of Europe as a single market have made communicating with audiences from varied cultural backgrounds an essential skill. Language differences, of course, create the biggest obstacle to writing for readers whose primary language is not English.

The communications habits and expectations of audiences whose primary language is not English often will differ from those common in the United States and Canada. Organizational patterns, forms of courtesy, and ideas about efficiency can vary significantly from culture to culture. What might seem direct and efficient in the United States, for example, could be seen as blunt and even impolite in other cultures.

Cultural differences and the reasons behind them are often so subtle that only someone who is very familiar with a culture can explain the effect those differences may have on others from the culture. For that reason, consult with someone from your intended reader's culture before writing a draft or preparing a presentation for an international audience. The reasons behind these differing attitudes are complex and have given rise to important studies because of their significance to international business.

Persuading Your Audience

ON THE WEB

To see a draft of a persuasive letter with a peer editor's suggestions, go to Model Documents Gallery, bedfordstmartins.com/ writingthatworks

Suppose you and a friend are arguing over whether the capital of Maine is Portland or Augusta. The issue is a simple question of fact that easily can be checked in an almanac or atlas. (It's Augusta.) Now suppose you are trying to convince management at your company that it ought to adopt flexible working hours for its employees or to upgrade software to improve communications with its customers. A quick look in a reference book will not settle the issue. You will have to persuade management that your idea is a good one. In all on-the-job writing, strive to keep your reader's needs, as well as your own, clearly in mind. Doing so is especially important in persuasive writing, in which your purpose may often be to ask your reader to change working procedures or habits. You may think that most people would automatically accept a recommendation for an improvement in the workplace, but people tend to resist change. Your proposed idea may be a threat to a staff member's pet project or it may make the accumulated knowledge and experience of a veteran employee seem out of date. To overcome resistance, you'll have to establish the need for your recommendation and support it with convincing, objective evidence.

The memo in Figure 3–3 was written by an MIS (management information systems) administrator to persuade her staff to accept and participate in a change to a new computer system. Notice that not everything in this memo is presented in a positive light. Change brings disruption, and the writer acknowledges that fact.

For persuasive communications outside the company, you must take equal if not greater care in the way you present information. In the letter in Figure 3–4 on page 73, the writer is disappointed with the response to a request, but she attempts to persuade her audience to reconsider. Instead of responding with anger or sarcasm ("Your fee is highway robbery!"), the writer thanks the publisher and gets quickly to the point: her concern for the high fee and her wish to have it reduced. Throughout, her tone and language are courteous and respectful.

ETHICS NOTE

When writing to persuade your audience, do not overlook opposing points of view. Most issues have more than one side, and you should acknowledge them, as does the writer proposing a disruptive change in Figure 3–3. By anticipating and bringing up opposing views *before* your readers do, you gain several advantages:

- You show that you are honest enough to recognize opposing views when they exist.
- You demonstrate the advantage of your viewpoint over those of others.
- You may be able to anticipate some or all of your readers' objections.

Finally, use the appropriate medium for communicating with your audience. The writer of the memo in Figure 3–3 recognized that a brief e-mail message was not the appropriate means to present her call for cooperation in the face of disruptive change. Her staff needed the formality and readability that a memo offers. As you plan your writing and prepare the draft, consider how you want to package your finished communication.

◆ *For more on persuasive writing, see pages 452–454 in Chapter 13, Writing Proposals.*

◆ *For a description of options available to help you make this decision, see pages 277–280 in Chapter 8, Understanding the Principles of Business Communication.*

Establishing Your Role and Voice as the Writer

Writers must also assume roles. As an on-the-job writer, for example, you may need to assume the role of a teacher who guides the audience through the process of learning a new task. In this case, you must do more than explain or persuade — you must also anticipate your audience's reactions and growing understanding of

Memo

TO: Engineering Sales Staff

FROM: Bernadine Kovak, MIS Administrator *BK*

DATE: April 10, 2010

SUBJECT: Plans for Changeover to NRT/R4 System

As you all know, our workload has jumped by 30 percent in the past month. It has increased because our customer base and resulting technical support services have grown dramatically. This growth is a result, in part, of our recent merger with Datacom. This growth has meant that we have all experienced the difficulty of providing our customers with up-to-date technical information when they need it. In the next few months, we anticipate that the workload will increase another 20 percent. Even a staff as experienced as ours cannot handle such a workload without help.

To cope with that expansion, in the next month we will be installing the NRT/R4 server and QCS enterprise software with Web-based applications and a global sales and service network. The system will speed processing significantly as well as give us access to all relevant companywide databases. It should enable us to access the information both we and our customers need.

The new system, unfortunately, will cause some disruption at first. We will need to transfer many of our existing programs and software applications to the new format. And all of us need to learn to navigate in the R4 and QCS environments. However, once we have made those adjustments, I believe we will welcome the changes.

I would like to put your knowledge and experience to work in getting the new system into operation. Let's meet in my office to discuss the improvements on Friday, April 17, at 1:30 p.m. I will have details of the plan, including a training schedule, to discuss with you. I'm also eager to get your comments, suggestions, and—most of all—your cooperation.

Writer's handwritten initials for printed memo

Background of problem

Statement of problem

Statement of solution

Candid acknowledgment of disruption

Call for cooperation

Figure 3–3 Persuasive Memo (Sent on Paper)

the subject. You must be alert to questions that readers might ask, such as "Why do I need to read this document?" "How much time must I spend to learn this subject?" and "Where can I find a quick answer to my problem?" By anticipating that the audience will ask such questions, you will be more likely to answer them in your draft.

You may discover that an audience's interests do not always coincide with its needs. Some readers, for example, would prefer not to read your document at all;

Commuter Aircraft Corporation
7328 Wellington Drive
Partridge, Ohio 45424
commair.com

March 8, 2010

Adele Chu, Permissions Editor
Poet's Press, Inc.
One Plaza Way, Suite 3
Boston, MA 02116

Dear Ms. Chu:

Thank you for responding so quickly to my request for permission to reprint the poem "Flight" in the pilot's manual for our new Aerosoar 100 Commuter.

Complimentary and courteous opening

I am writing to express concern about the fee you have requested for the use of this selection. It is much higher than we expected. Because the manual is an instructional booklet distributed to pilots free of charge, the budget for this project is strictly limited, particularly for nontechnical, ancillary materials such as poetry. We continue to feel that the poem would interest and even inspire our readers, however, and we would like to ask you to consider lowering your fee to make this possible. To meet the demands of our budget, we are able to pay no more than $300 for each selection in the manual—considerably less than the $900 you have requested.

Statement of problem, its basis, and counteroffer

I hope you understand our position and that you will consider reducing your fee for the use of this material. Thank you for considering my request. I look forward to hearing from you.

Restatement of request and respectful closing

Sincerely,

J. T. Walters

J. T. Walters
Publications Manager

cc: Legal Department

(890) 321-1231
Fax (890) 321-5116
jtw@commair.com

Figure 3–4   Persuasive Letter

however, they are interested in completing a task or solving a problem as quickly as possible. You must demonstrate how your document links the readers' interests with their need to read the document.

As you write the draft, consider which voice your audience should hear. Should it be authoritative or friendly, formal or accessible, provocative or reassuring—or somewhere in between? Determine the voice you adopt by considering what is appropriate to your specific purpose. The guidelines shown in Figure 3–5 are intended for respiratory-care therapists who assess patients to develop a plan of care. The writer's voice is slightly formal (the guidance is in the imperative mood) yet caring in tone, as befits the subject.

Authoritative voice instructs, yet reassures

RESPIRATORY-CARE PLAN

1. Let the patient know exactly what is being done.
2. Maintain a good rapport; answer questions the patient may ask to allay fear.
3. Maintain the privacy and dignity of the patient at all times.
4. Be prepared. A stethoscope, a watch with a sweep second hand or a stopwatch, and a pen are basic items essential to this process.
5. Document your findings as soon as time permits; otherwise, you may forget important points.

Figure 3–5   Formal Voice (in Medical Instructions)

◆ *For guidance on writing for users averse to reading instructions, see Chapter 12, Writing Instructions.*

◆ *For guidance on whether to use the first or third person in your writing, see page 107 in Chapter 4, Revising the Draft.*

By contrast, newsletter readers may expect a voice that is friendly, fast-paced, and conversational. Consider the attention-getting approach used in the opening of an article in a professional association newsletter (Figure 3–6).

Conversational voice directly engages audience

OVERCOMING WRITER'S BLOCK

Um, er, I would have delivered this article earlier, perhaps even on time, but, er, you see, I had writer's block!

Has this ever happened to you? Hah! Of course it has. It happens when you're writing to your Aunt Hattie to thank her for the butterfly book she gave you for your birthday as easily as when you're writing a crucial report to your boss or looking for a different way of presenting a procedure. Nobody is immune; it happens to us all at various times. November's meeting . . . dealt with how three successful writers cope with this near universal problem.

Source: Capital Letter, Society for Technical Communications (December 1999).

Figure 3–6   Conversational Voice (in a Professional Association Newsletter)

CONSIDERING AUDIENCE AND PURPOSE

Preparing to Write a Draft

When preparing to write a draft, ask yourself the following questions:

■ What is my purpose in writing this document? What action do I want my readers to take after reading it?

■ Who are my primary readers? Is there a secondary audience? What do my readers know and how do they feel about the subject I'm addressing or the idea I'm proposing?

■ Does my audience include international clients or colleagues?

■ Why do my readers need to read this document or e-mail message? (Do they need to perform a task? to obtain basic information? to investigate a problem? to make a decision?)

■ How much information will my readers need to understand the subject or to be persuaded or informed by my idea? What is the best way to clearly present this material?

■ What objections might my readers have to the subject or proposed idea?

■ What medium would be most appropriate? (Should I use e-mail? memo? Web posting?)

■ What voice would best convey my message? (Should it be authoritative? friendly? provocative? reassuring?)

ETHICS NOTE

Keep in mind that the way you present your ideas is as important as the ideas themselves. Respect your audience's needs and feelings by applying some basic manners in your writing. Avoid sarcasm or any other hostile tone that may offend your audience. Also avoid exaggerating or being overly enthusiastic. Your audience may interpret such an attitude as insincere or presumptuous. Of course, you should not conceal genuine enthusiasm; just be careful not to overdo it.

Development Strategies

The following strategies for developing your ideas will help you to convey information and to present evidence persuasively:

• **Explaining a process**: tells how something works or how something happened

• **Describing information**: explains how something looks or is planned to look

- **Defining terms and concepts**: clarifies the meanings of ideas crucial to your topic
- **Explaining cause and effect**: analyzes why something happened

Although this section focuses on each method separately, the methods are often used in combination. For investigative and accident reports, for example, the writer must state exactly what happened (explaining a process), which may also require the writer to describe the physical appearance of people, places, or equipment (describing information), and to explain terminology or ideas that the audience may not understand (defining terms and concepts). Finally, the writer must try to explain why the event or accident happened (analyzing cause and effect). A skillful integration of these methods to present evidence will do much to convince your audience that your findings and recommendations are accurate and appropriate.

Explaining a Process

When you explain a process, you tell your audience how something works, how it happened, or how it is done. The process you explain might be an event that occurs in nature (the tidal pull of the moon), a function that requires human effort (conducting a marketing survey), or an activity in which people maintain machinery to produce goods or services (robotic assembly-line production).

The explanation of a process is composed of steps and may also include illustrations that show the process from beginning to end. As in all on-the-job writing, you must aim your writing at a level appropriate to your audience's background and be as clear, accurate, and complete as possible. Beginners require more basic information and less technical vocabulary than do experienced workers.

In your opening paragraph, tell your readers why it is important for them to become familiar with the process you are explaining. Before you explain the steps necessary to form a corporation, for example, you could cite the tax savings that incorporation would permit. To give your audience a framework for the details that will follow, you might present a brief overview of the process. Finally, you might describe how the process works in relation to a larger whole of which it is a part. In explaining the air-brake system of a large dump truck, for example, you might note that the braking system is one part of the vehicle's air system, which also controls the throttle and transmission-shifting mechanisms.

A process explanation can be long or short, depending on how much detail is necessary. The passage in Figure 3–7 explains the process by which drinking water is purified. It provides essential background information in the context of a discussion of how drinking water, which may be contaminated, is then treated before distribution to homes. The information is intended for the average homeowner, but the vocabulary does assume an elementary familiarity with biological and chemical terms. The explanation is enhanced by a step-by-step illustration that

---

DRINKING WATER TREATMENT PROCESS

After it has been transported from its source to a local water system, most surface water must be processed in a treatment plant before it can be used. Some ground-water, on the other hand, is considered chemically and biologically pure enough to pass directly from a well into the distribution system that carries it to the home.
    Background to process

Although there are innumerable variations, surface water is usually treated as follows: First, it enters a storage lagoon (A) where a chemical, usually copper sulfate, is added to control algae growth. From there, water passes through one or more screens that remove large debris. Next, a coagulant, such as alum, is mixed into the water to encourage the settling of suspended particles. The water flows slowly through one or more sedimentation basins (B) so that larger particles settle to the bottom and can be removed. Water then passes through a filtration basin partially filled with sand and gravel (C) where yet more suspended particles are removed. (See Drinking Water Treatment Process illustration [Figure 3–8].)
    Overview of steps in the process

At that point in the process, the Safe Drinking Water Act has mandated an additional step for communities using surface water. . . . Water is to be filtered through activated carbon to remove any microscopic organic material and chemicals that have escaped the other processes. Activated carbon is extremely porous—one pound of the material can have a surface area of one acre. This honeycomb of minute pores attracts and traps pollutants through a process called adsorption. . . .
    Definition of key term

The final stage of water treatment is disinfection, where an agent capable of killing most biological pathogens is added to the water. Until the chlorination process was developed, devastating epidemics—such as the outbreak of typhoid and cholera that took 90,000 lives in Chicago in 1885. . . .
    Basis for importance of the process

Figure 3–7   Explanation of a Process.   *Source:* S. Coffel and K. Feiden, *Indoor Pollution* (1990). Reprinted by permission of Ballantine Books, a division of Random House, Inc.

complements the pattern of the writing by providing an overview image (first panel in Figure 3–8) and then three more detailed drawings of the water-treatment process (remaining three panels of Figure 3–8).

Describing Information

When you give your audience information about an object's size, shape, construction, or other features of its appearance, you are describing it. The kinds of description you write will vary—engineers must describe products they design according to technical specifications, marketing professionals must describe the products they are marketing to potential customers, software developers face the daunting task of describing something the audience cannot see, police must describe accident scenes, and so on. Your description may be of something concrete, such as a machine, or of something abstract, such as computer software. The key to writing an effective description is to present details accurately. To select appropriate details, determine what your audience will use the description for—to identify something? to assemble or repair the object being described?

Overview of steps in a process

Detailed steps

Figure 3–8   **Illustration for Explanation of a Process.**   *Source:*
S. Coffel and K. Feiden, *Indoor Pollution* (1990). Reprinted by permission of Ballantine Books, a division of Random House, Inc.

Descriptions can be brief and simple or they can be highly complex, but they
should always be clear and specific. Simple descriptions usually require only a
listing of key features. A purchase order, shown in Figure 3–9, is a typical example
of simple descriptive writing. Notice that even an order for something as ordinary
as trash-compactor bags needs (in addition to the part number) four specific descriptive details to ensure accuracy.

Complex descriptions, of course, require more detail than simple ones. The
details you select should accurately and vividly convey what you are describing. If
it is useful for your audience to visualize an object, for instance, include details—

Product specifications

PURCHASE ORDER		
Part No.	Description	Quantity
GL/020	Trash-compactor bags, 31″ × 50″ tubular, nontransparent, 5-mil thickness, including 100 tie wraps per carton	5 cartons @ 100 per carton

Figure 3–9   **Simple Description**

such as color and shape—that appeal to the sense of sight. Sometimes you may want to describe the physical characteristics of an object and, at the same time, itemize the parts that go into its makeup. To describe a piece of machinery, for example, you would probably find this approach, called the *whole-to-parts method*, the most useful for your purpose. You would first present a general description of the device as a frame of reference for the more specific details that follow—physical description of the various parts and the location and function of each in relation to the whole. The description would conclude with an explanation of how the parts work together.

Illustrations can be powerful aids in descriptive writing, especially when they show details too intricate to explain completely in words. Do not hesitate to use an illustration with a complex description if doing so creates a clearer image. Figure 3–10 describes a body harness and includes an illustration for occupational safety officials who must assess such devices as they seek ways to protect worker health and safety on the job. Figure 3–11 on page 81 illustrates a storm-shutter installation that small businesses can use to protect windows from windborne debris damage. The illustration, with callouts highlighting important features, largely eliminates the need for extensive written details to describe their relationship to one another and their function.

◆ *For detailed instructions on the use of illustrations, see Chapter 7, Designing Effective Documents and Visuals.*

Defining Terms and Concepts

Accurate definitions are crucial to many kinds of writing, especially for an audience unfamiliar with your subject. Depending on your audience's needs, your definition can be formal, informal, or extended.

A *formal definition* places a term in a class of related objects or ideas and shows how it differs from other members of the same class. (An auction is a public sale in which property passes to the highest bidder through successive increased offers.) An *informal definition* uses a familiar word or phrase as a synonym for an unfamiliar word or phrase. (Plants live in a symbiotic, or mutually beneficial, relationship with certain kinds of bacteria.) Informal definitions permit you to explain the meaning of a term with a minimum of interruption in the flow of your writing.

When more than a phrase or a sentence is needed to explain an idea, use an *extended definition*, which explores a number of qualities of the item being defined. How an extended definition is developed depends on your readers' needs and on the complexity of the subject. Readers familiar with a topic might be able to handle a long, fairly complex definition, whereas readers less familiar with a topic might require simpler language and more basic information.

Perhaps the easiest way to define a term is to give specific examples of it. Listing examples gives readers easy-to-picture details that help them see and thus understand the term being defined. To clarify the abstract term *metadata*, the definition in Figure 3–12 on page 81 provides specific examples of how metadata is used to identify subject matter on Web sites.

Approximately 50 ironworkers fall to their deaths each year in the United States. The latest fall-protection system may change all this. The following illustration shows a system that protects ironworkers from falls without interfering with their work. This system complies with the Occupational Safety and Health Administration's strict fall-protection requirements.

Known as the Beamwalker, the system consists of two stanchions that clamp to a standard I-beam. A 40-foot line, to which workers can attach their lifelines, runs between the stanchions. The Beamwalker is installed while the beam is on the ground.

The Beamwalker

Figure 3–10   Illustration to Aid Description

Another way to define a difficult concept, especially when you are writing for nonspecialists, is to use an analogy to link the unfamiliar concept with a simpler or more familiar one. An analogy can help the reader understand an unfamiliar term by showing its similarities to a more familiar term. In Figure 3–13 on page 82, the writer uses analogy to define *management by objective.*

Sometimes it is useful to point out what something is *not* to clarify what it *is.* A what-it-is-not definition is effective only when the reader is familiar with the

Protect Windows and Doors

Protecting windows and doors is one of the most effective actions you can take to reduce your risk of wind damage. High winds and windborne debris can easily break unprotected windows and cause doors to fail. Once wind enters a building, the likelihood of severe structural damage increases, and the contents of the building will be exposed to the elements.

The most reliable method of protecting windows and doors is installing permanent storm shutters. Alternatives include using temporary plywood covers, replacing existing glass with impact-resistant glass, and covering existing glass with a protective film.

Permanent

ROLLDOWN SHUTTER PERMANENTLY ATTACHED TO BUILDING

SHUTTER IS HELD BY GUIDE TRACKS ALONG SIDES OF WINDOW

SHUTTER IS SECURED BY LATCH AT BASE OF GUIDE TRACK

storm shutters are usually made of aluminum or steel and are attached to a building in such a way that they can be closed quickly before a storm arrives. One type is the "rolldown" shutter (as shown here), which is contained in a housing mounted above the window and lowered when necessary. Manually operated and motor-operated models are available.

Description concentrates on the types of shutters available and their function

Illustration appears next to or immediately after the text that discusses it

Figure 3–11   Detailed Description (with Illustration).   *Source:* Federal Emergency Management Agency (<www.fema.gov>).

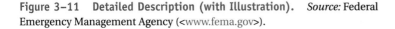

Metadata. Literally, "data about data." Examples of metadata include the author's name, creation date, content category, content type, intended audience, and access control properties. Metadata can be used to generate automated content directories, drive dynamic behavior, and support site measurement. . . .

Figure 3–12   Extended Definition, Using Examples.   *Source:* Gartner, Inc., *Dealing in Web Currency* (2001).

> Management by objective has been quite popular, but it is important to remember that carefully selecting objectives is the key to successfully applying this principle. Think, for example, of a golfer who wishes to improve by hitting the ball farther. The golfer sets a goal of hitting every drive as far as possible. Every decision the golfer makes is governed by that goal—hitting the ball as far as possible. The golfer would then be managing his or her game by objective. However, the golfer is shortsighted because golf is as much a game of accuracy as it is of hitting balls for distance. Some of the decisions the golfer makes to hit the ball farther, therefore, might well be counterproductive to achieving the larger goal of obtaining the lowest possible score. In the same way, when a company decides to use a management-by-objective strategy, it must be certain that the objective is appropriate for achieving the desired results.

Figure 3–13   Extended Definition, Using Analogy

item with which the defined item is contrasted. If you say *x* is not *y*, your audience must understand the meaning of *y* for the explanation to make sense. In a crane operator's manual, for instance, a "negative definition" is used to show that, for safety reasons, a hydraulic crane cannot be operated in the same manner as a lattice boom crane (Figure 3–14).

> A hydraulic crane is not like a lattice boom crane [a friction machine] in one very important way. In most cases, the safe lifting capacity of a lattice boom crane is based on the weight needed to tip the machine. Therefore, operators of friction machines sometimes depend on signs that the machine might tip to warn them of impending danger. This practice is very dangerous with a hydraulic crane. . . .

Figure 3–14   Negative Definition.   *Source: Operator's Manual* (Model W-180), Harnischfeger Corporation.

Explaining Cause and Effect

When your purpose is to explain why something happened or why you think something will happen, cause-and-effect analysis is a useful writing strategy. For instance, if you were asked to report on why the accident rate for the company truck fleet rose by 30 percent, you would use cause-and-effect analysis to work from an effect (higher accident rate) to its cause (bad driving weather, inexperienced drivers, poor truck maintenance, and so on). If you were to report on the possible effects that switching to a four-day workweek (ten hours per day) would have on the office staff, you would also use cause-and-effect analysis—but this time you would start with cause (the new work schedule) and look for possible effects (changes in morale, in productivity, in absenteeism, and the like).

The goal of cause-and-effect analysis is to make as plausible as possible the relationship between a situation and either its cause or its effect. The conclusions you draw about the relationship should be based on the evidence you have gathered. Because not all facts and arguments will be of equal value to you as you draw conclusions, it's a good idea to keep the following guidelines in mind.

- *Evidence should be relevant to your topic.* Be careful not to draw a conclusion that your evidence does not lead to or support. You may have researched some statistics, for example, that show that an increasing number of Americans are licensed to fly small airplanes. You cannot use that information as evidence for a decrease in new car sales in the United States—the evidence does not lead to that conclusion.

- *Evidence should be adequate.* Incomplete evidence can lead to false conclusions. If, for example, you know two people who completed driver-training classes but later crashed their cars, you do not have sufficient evidence to conclude that driver-training classes do not help prevent automobile accidents. A thorough investigation of the usefulness of driver-training classes in keeping down the accident rate would require more than one or two examples; it would also require a comparison of the driving records of those who had completed training with the driving records of those who had not.

- *Evidence should be representative.* If you conduct a survey to obtain your evidence, do not solicit responses only from individuals or groups whose views are identical to yours; be sure you obtain a representative sampling. A survey of backpackers in a national park on whether the park ought to be open to off-road vehicles would more than likely show them overwhelmingly against the idea. Such a survey should include opinions from more than one interested group.

- *Evidence should be demonstrable.* Two events that occur close to each other in time or place may or may not be causally related. For example, that new traffic signs were placed at an intersection and the next day an accident occurred does not necessarily prove that the signs caused the accident. You must demonstrate the relationship with pertinent facts and arguments.

To show a true relationship between a cause and an effect, you must demonstrate that the existence of the one *requires* the existence of the other. It is often difficult to establish beyond any doubt that one event was the cause of another event. More often, a result will have more than one cause. As you research your subject, your task is to determine which cause or causes are most plausible. When several probable causes are equally valid, report your findings accordingly, as in Figure 3–15. The paragraph is an excerpt from an article on the use of a furnace-vent damper, an energy-saving device that can be dangerous if it fails to work properly. The investigator located more than one cause of damper malfunctions and reported on them. Without such a thorough account, recommendations to prevent similar malfunctions would be based on incomplete evidence.

> One damper was sold without proper installation instructions, and another was wired incorrectly. Two of the units had slow-opening dampers (15 seconds) that prevented the [furnace] burner from firing. And one damper jammed when exposed to a simulated fuel temperature of more than 700 degrees.

Figure 3–15   Paragraph Linking Cause and Effect.   *Source:* Don DeBat, "Save Energy But Save Your Life, Too." *Family Safety.*

■ Writing an Opening

As discussed earlier in this chapter, you do not need to begin your draft by writing the opening; however, understanding the purposes of an opening and the strategies for writing one can help you start the draft. The opening statement of your writing should (1) identify your subject, (2) provide any necessary context for the subject, and (3) catch the interest of your audience.

The title of your report or the subject line of the memo or e-mail message will announce the subject. The first paragraph of the opening should describe the context for why you are writing—the "story" behind the document. It should state what series of events led to your need to write: to answer a request for information, to recommend a new process to accomplish a goal, to propose that a new employee be hired, or to pass on information to someone.

Most audiences of on-the-job writing are preoccupied with other business when they begin to read a memo, a letter, a report, or even an e-mail message. To catch your audience's interest, you first must know your audience's needs. An awareness of those needs will help you determine which details your audience will find important and thus interesting. Consider the opening from a memo written by a human resources manager to her supervisor (Figure 3–16). This opening not only states the subject of the report (its context) but also promises that the writer will offer solutions to a specific problem. Solutions to problems are always of interest to audiences.

◆ *For a discussion of assessing an audience's needs, see pages 6–7 in Chapter 1, Assessing Audience and Purpose.*

◆ *For examples of openings for special types of writing, such as application letters, complaint letters, and formal reports, refer to specific entries in the Index.*

For most types of writing done in offices, shops, and laboratories, openings that simply get to the point are more effective than those that provide detailed background information. Furthermore, the subject line of a memo or the title of a report is often, by itself, enough to catch the audience's interest. The openings in Figures 3–17 and 3–18 on page 86 are typical; however, do not feel that you must slavishly follow these patterns. Rather, always first consider the purpose of your writing and the needs of your audience and then tailor your opening accordingly. Notice that these openings do not introduce irrelevant subjects or include unnecessary details. They give the audience exactly what they need to focus their attention on what is to follow. As direct as they are, they establish context by noting the background for the communication (an error was made, a solution is proposed, a rewiring program is under way).

Memo

To: Paul Route, Corporate Relations Director
From: Sondra L. Rivera, Human Resources Manager   *SLR*
Date: November 1, 2010
Subject: Decreasing Applications from Local College Graduates

This year, only 12 local college graduates have applied for jobs at
Securex. Last year, over 30 graduates applied; the year before, 50 applied. This decline in applications is occurring despite increasing en-
rollments at local schools. After talking with several college counselors,
I am confident that we can solve the problem of decreasing applications from local colleges.

First, we could resume our advertisements in local student newspapers. . . .

*Concise statement
of a problem sets the
stage for a proposed
solution*

Figure 3–16   Opening of a Memo

PENROSE FIRST INVESTOR'S BANK
12 Powell Square
Penrose, Maine 04291
penrosefib.com

March 3, 2010

Mr. George Whittier
12 Nautical Drive
Penrose, ME 04291

Dear Mr. Whittier:

You will be happy to know that we have corrected the error in your
bank balance. The new balance shows . . .

Figure 3–17   Opening of a Letter

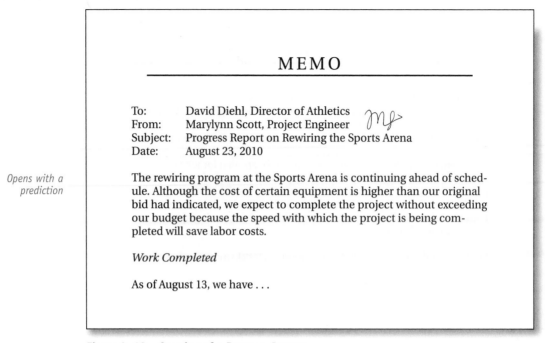

MEMO

To: David Diehl, Director of Athletics
From: Marylynn Scott, Project Engineer
Subject: Progress Report on Rewiring the Sports Arena
Date: August 23, 2010

Opens with a prediction

The rewiring program at the Sports Arena is continuing ahead of schedule. Although the cost of certain equipment is higher than our original bid had indicated, we expect to complete the project without exceeding our budget because the speed with which the project is being completed will save labor costs.

Work Completed

As of August 13, we have . . .

Figure 3–18   Opening of a Progress Report

■ Writing a Closing

A good closing is concise and ends your writing emphatically. It can tie your points together in a number of ways: recommending a course of action, offering a value judgment, speculating on the implications of your ideas, making a prediction, or summarizing your main points. Even if your closing only states, "If I can be of further help, please call me" or "I would appreciate your comments," you end in a co-operative spirit.

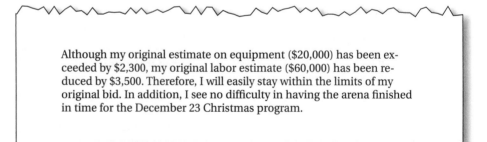

Ends with a summary of costs and a final prediction

Although my original estimate on equipment ($20,000) has been exceeded by $2,300, my original labor estimate ($60,000) has been reduced by $3,500. Therefore, I will easily stay within the limits of my original bid. In addition, I see no difficulty in having the arena finished in time for the December 23 Christmas program.

Figure 3–19   Closing of a Progress Report

The way you close depends on the purpose of your writing and the needs of your audience. For example, a committee report about possible locations for a new production facility might end with a recommendation that is realistic given the options available; a lengthy sales proposal might conclude persuasively with a summary of the proposal's salient points and the company's main strong points; or the closing of a company's annual report might offer a judgment about why sales are up (or down). A report for a retail department store about consumer buying trends could end by speculating on the implications of these trends, perhaps even suggesting new product lines that the store might carry in the future. Figures 3–19 and 3–20 illustrate typical closings.

I recommend that ABO, Inc., participate in the corporate membership program at Aero Fitness Clubs, Inc., by subsidizing employee memberships. Implementing this program will help ABO reduce its health-care costs while building stronger employee relations by offering employees a desirable benefit. If this proposal is adopted, I have some additional thoughts about publicizing the program to encourage employee participation. I look forward to discussing the details of this proposal with you and answering any questions you may have.

Ends with a recommendation and an offer to discuss the proposal in more detail

Figure 3–20   Closing of a Company Internal Proposal

Finally, do not introduce a new topic in your closing. A closing should always relate to and reinforce the ideas presented in the opening and body of your writing. Closings with recommendations or predictions, in particular, must grow out of the discussion that preceded them.

■ Case Study: Drafting the Lifemaker Brochure

The techniques for drafting discussed in this chapter can be applied to any kind of workplace document. Figure 3–21 shows the rough draft of a sales brochure meant to persuade consumers to purchase the Lifemaker home gym. It follows the gist of the writer's initial outline and uses many of the drafting skills and development strategies discussed in this chapter.

The draft is quite rough—loosely organized, lacking in transitions and punctuation, ungrammatical, inconsistent in uppercase and lowercase letters and point of view, and cluttered with jargon and unnecessary phrases. Still, as drafts go, this one reflects a strong start for the writer. Not only has she followed the basic organization of her outline, but she has managed also to work through so-called writer's blocks and to jot down the new idea of emphasizing financial incentives.

◆ *For an outline of this brochure, see Figure 2–2.*

◆ *For a marked-up version of a later draft of this memo, along with the final version, see Figures 4–2 and 4–3.*

****DRAFT****

LIFEMAKER: The Compact Exercise System You Can Afford

Tentative cause-and-effect linkage

For opening—say something about how owning a Lifemaker will give you healthy bones and teeth, straighten your hair, improve your love life . . . no . . . Whether you are young or young at heart, male or female, developing well-conditioned muscles will help your body perform better, look better, and help you maintain an ideal level of fitness (Needs work!! Keep going, go back to it later. Get to the muscle of the matter.)

Tentative description of system compared with competitors' systems

(*Description*) The Lifemaker design more compact than leading competitor's, eliminates hassle and expense of going to health club to work out. The Lifemaker fits easily into small space—4 × 7 ft living room can accommodate the Lifemaker with more ease than many home gym systems, offers more stations and more exercises because of its multiple stations. What's the point I'm making? More compact than many fancy systems, offers 40+ exercises, more than most systems priced at a comparable level—comparably priced and sized systems. OK OK, don't compromise your exercise needs with an overpriced or ineffective system. The integration of an exercise program to suit your lifestyle and budget is possible with Lifemaker. (I'm writing all over the place—too loose and unfocused. Needs headings like you used in outline.)

Cast-Iron Weight Stack

Physical description

Dual weight stacks total 200 pounds of cast-iron plates. You can arrange stacks to offer a resistance range of 10 to 150 pounds and they are adjustable in 10-pound increments.

Adjustable Cables

Combined process and physical description

Resistance can be increased—no—The unique cable system is engineered to increase resistance at the stations that work the strongest muscle groups. The cables can quickly be redesigned—restructured—reconfigured without taking apart the entire system. Just pulling the center rod permits adding or removing as many plates as needed.

Process description

The cable tension is also adjustable within sets to make sure that your muscles get the most resistance from each exercise for maximum efficiency and results.

(*Closing*) Heading? Low Maintenance—Easily Affordable

Best of all, no it's not best of all, (think later about transition. . . .) The Lifemaker is easy to assemble and requires little maintenance. And at $999.99, it is priced lower than the leading competitor.

***Need to emphasize financial perks—mention low-interest monthly payment plan. Lifemaker will fit your back and your budget.

Figure 3–21 Draft of a Sales Brochure (with Writer's Notes)

She can now go on to write a second draft, develop an opening and a closing that will help her tighten her focus, and then revise the entire document by using the techniques covered in Chapter 4, Revising the Draft.

CHAPTER 3 SUMMARY: WRITING THE DRAFT

Gathering the details you need (see Chapter 1, Assessing Audience and Purpose) and grouping them in an outline (see Chapter 2, Organizing Your Information) will enable you to write a good rough draft. When writing the draft, remember that your task is to produce only a working document, not a polished piece of writing. Polish will come with revision (see Chapter 4, Revising the Draft). Use the following guidelines as you write the draft:

- Concentrate solely on getting your draft written.
- Do not confuse writing with revising; they are different tasks, and each requires a different frame of mind.
- Avoid revising as you write—do not worry about perfection at this point in the writing process. Focus on *what* you are writing, not on *how* you are writing.
- Allocate your time efficiently.
- Prepare a comfortable work environment.
- Sustain momentum once you begin writing.
- Take brief breaks after reaching milestones.
- Keep your intended readers actively in mind, visualizing them if possible, and address your topic from their point of view.
- Consider the voice your readers should hear—concerned, neutral, or authoritative.
- Be persuasive.
  - Take your readers' feelings into account.
  - Appeal to your readers' good sense.
  - Acknowledge other points of view where an issue is controversial.

Consider the following kinds of writing:

- Explain a process.
  - Introduce the process with information about its purpose and significance.
  - Divide the process into steps.
  - Present each step in its proper sequence.
  - Illustrate steps and procedures when this aids clarity.
  - Present the information at a level appropriate to your readers' background.
  - Write concisely.
- Describe information.
  - Select details carefully, based on what use your readers will make of the description.
  - Provide a brief explanation of the function of any physical objects you describe, such as equipment.
  - Do not overwhelm your readers with unnecessary details.
  - Include illustrations where they add clarity.

■ Define terms and concepts.

■ Explain cause and effect.

- Establish a plausible relationship between an event and its cause.
- Evaluate evidence for the relationship carefully: Is it pertinent? sufficient? representative? plausible?
- Do not overstate conclusions.

■ Write an opening that identifies your subject to focus your readers' attention.

■ Get to the point first, even when providing essential background information in the opening.

■ Create closings that reinforce, summarize, or tie together the ideas in the body of your writing.

■ Do not introduce ideas in the closing that have not been discussed elsewhere in your writing.

ON THE WEB

For an online quiz on drafting, go to Chapter 3, bedfordstmartins .com/writingthatworks

ON THE WEB

For a detailed free-writing assignment, go to Chapter 3, bedfordstmartins.com/ writingthatworks

■ Exercises

1. Write an opening paragraph for one or two of the following purposes and the audiences specified, as directed by your instructor:

- The instructor from whom I learned the most (for a letter nominating him or her for a teaching award)
- Ways to improve employee participation in a blood donation (or similar) program (to the president or head of the organization that employs you)
- Ways to improve student use of the career counseling office at your school (to the dean of students or someone in an equivalent position)
- What to look for in housing in your area (for a guide for transferred employees)
- Important features to consider when purchasing a new automobile, cellular phone, or personal computer (for a consumer guide)
- The advantages of setting up a budget or checking account on a personal computer (for an informational handout at a senior center or for students seeking help at your college mentoring center)

2. Building on Exercise 1, write a closing for the same topics and audiences.

3. Using the Lifemaker compact exercise system as your topic (see Figure 3–21), write three different opening paragraphs for a Lifemaker System 40 sales brochure geared toward each of the following audiences (one paragraph for each):

- College students
- Retired persons
- Industry executives

4. Based on Exercise 3, write three different closing paragraphs for a Lifemaker System 40 sales brochure geared toward each of the following audiences (one paragraph for each):

- College students
- Retired persons
- Industry executives

5. Summarize in a list all of the differences you had to be aware of when writing for different audiences and for different purposes in Exercises 3 and 4 (for example, time constraints, mobility constraints, and so forth).

6. Write a letter to a high school guidance counselor who wants to inform students about your chosen course of study. With your audience and purpose in mind, draft a letter that includes an effective opening, specifies important elements of the program and other relevant details in the body, and uses an appropriate closing. Use correct business-letter format when preparing your letter. For guidelines on format, see Chapter 8, Understanding the Principles of Business Communication.

7. Assume that the administration of your college or university is contemplating creating a learning center that will offer math and English tutoring. To implement this program, offices will need to be created from classroom space, tutors will need to be paid from the Student Services program, and a director will need to be hired. Reaction to this center is mixed. As the president of a student organization, you have been asked to write a letter to the administration about your organization's position on the creation of the center.

   a. Make a list of several possible points of view on this center. (Consider, for example, the perspectives of the admissions office, computing services, maintenance, faculty, and students.) Realize that different audiences may share both supportive and unsupportive views on the same topic for different reasons.

   b. Based on the points of view you have listed, draft an outline of a letter that supports creating the center, supports it with conditions, or opposes it.

   c. Write a letter to the administration, explaining your organization's point of view on the creation of the learning center. Be sure you have addressed the potential multiple points of view in your letter. If you are for the center, offer strategies to address the concerns of those who are unsupportive; if you are against the center, address the concerns of those who believe such a center is needed.

■ Collaborative Classroom Projects

1. Building on Exercise 7, form a small group and read each other's letters. Choose a spokesperson from your group to contact the director of your school's real learning center (if your school has one) for an interview. Select two or three people from your group to interview this person about the creation of the center. Ask questions about the many points of view and concerns that had to be addressed regarding funding, staffing, location, and so on. You can also interview faculty and staff about their experiences related to the creation of the center. (You should read the section on interviewing in Chapter 6, Researching Your Subject, first.) Are there similarities between your letters in Exercise 7 and what happened in the creation of a real center? If your school does not have a learning center, interview someone in administration about creating one. What concerns does the administration have about such a project? In either case, write a memo to the class about your group's findings.

2. In small groups, design a draft of a brochure that helps volunteer relief workers put together a personal supplies kit. (You might refer to Chapter 7, Designing

ON THE WEB

For more collaborative classroom projects, go to Chapter 3, bedfordstmartins.com/ writingthatworks

Effective Documents and Visuals.) This brochure should detail items the workers should bring with them when they travel to the site of an earthquake, a hurricane, or a similar natural disaster—for example, alcohol-based hand sanitizer, toilet paper, sunblock, insect repellent, soap, shampoo, lightweight clothing, boots, rain gear, rubber gloves, flashlights, and a cell phone. What kinds of clip art or photos would you use to represent different categories of supplies? Be ready to share your ideas with the class.

ON THE WEB

For extra research projects, go to Chapter 3, bedfordstmartins .com/writingthatworks

▓ Research Projects

1. Assume that the brochure that you prepared for Collaborative Classroom Project 2 created a surge of interest in the fields of relief work, outdoor rescue, and survival skills. Research businesses that offer courses and products related to wilderness medicine. Based on your findings, write a rough draft of an informal report for a local volunteer group. (For guidance, see Chapter 10, Writing Informal Reports.) Be sure to define what wilderness medicine is, what kinds of courses are offered, and whether there are certifications or degrees in the field. Also, describe what kind of products these companies sell for rescue work. Support your findings with examples. Be sure to locate and discuss information that is supportive as well as critical of the field, schools, and products.

2. Research a business or technological advancement that you are curious about. Narrow your topic to one particular aspect of that field and write an informal report entitled "Recent Breakthroughs in _____ [a particular field]: _____ [specific breakthrough]." (Again, for guidance, see Chapter 10, Writing Informal Reports.) Analyze the topic and support your analysis with information that you've researched. For example, if you decided to write about a new medical procedure, your analysis might be that the risks do or do not outweigh the benefits; you would then support your opinion with the findings that persuaded you.
   a. Submit a four- to five-page draft with an outline to your instructor.
   b. Meet with your instructor to discuss his or her suggestions for revision.
   c. Conduct further research if necessary.
   d. Revise your draft.

3. Locate at least three companies on the Web that hire business or technical writers. For example, what companies in the area of medicine, technology, or environmental engineering hire writers? What kinds of documents or other materials do writers for these companies produce? (Search the companies' Web sites for documents produced by their professional writers.) How would the information covered in this chapter apply to the writing required by these companies? Prepare a brief draft of your reply.

4. Many companies have offices overseas and need to prepare their employees for traveling and living abroad. Imagine that you are in charge of an orientation program for several employees who will be going on tours of major cities in Africa, the Near East, East Asia and the Pacific, or South Asia. Outline and draft a memo that will begin with general information on traveling overseas, followed by specific advice on traveling to one of these regions. After you conduct your research, you will need to decide how to organize the information for each major category.

a. Begin by researching general information on traveling overseas, such as visa and passport requirements, immunizations, and security issues. (Two good sources of information for Americans traveling overseas are the U.S. State Department and the Centers for Disease Control and Prevention (CDC); see <www.state.gov/travel/> and <www.cdc.gov/travel/>.) Make a list of topics you'll want to address in the general travel information section of your memo. Put these in your outline.

b. Pick three to five countries in the four regions listed above that you imagine employees will visit and research the major cities in each. (The U.S. State Department has links to information about these four regions at <www.state.gov/r/pa/ei/bgn/>; another good source is the Library of Congress's Country Studies page at <http://lcweb2.loc.gov/frd/cs/cshome.html>.) Make a list of topics to address and put them in your outline.

c. Following your outline, draft a memo to the employees who will be traveling to one of the regions. Refer to the Writing a Rough Draft checklist on page 67 as needed.

d. Have your classmates review your draft. Make necessary changes and present your outline, drafting strategies, and travel information to the class.

4 Revising the Draft

AT A GLANCE: Revision

Have you ever found after writing a first draft that you knew you could do better, but you did not know how to improve it? If your answer is yes, you are not alone. All writers—including professional writers—have the same problem at some time or another. This chapter introduces the elements essential to effective revision.

- Ensuring completeness of coverage and clarity of organization / 96
- Unifying and linking ideas / 97
- Emphasizing key content / 101
- Establishing the writer's point of view / 106
- Ensuring that the language throughout is precise, concise, unbiased, and free of affectation / 107
- Editing and proofreading your draft / 115
- Checking your draft for appropriate physical appearance / 116

One of the enduring legends of U.S. history is that President Abraham Lincoln wrote the Gettysburg Address as he made the train trip from Washington, D.C., to Gettysburg, Pennsylvania. The address is a remarkable accomplishment, even for a writer as gifted as Lincoln. It is the eloquent testimony of a leader with a powerful intellect and a compassionate heart.

The facts of how the Gettysburg Address was composed do not support the legend, however. Lincoln actually worked on the address for weeks and revised the draft many times.[1] What Lincoln was doing on the train to Gettysburg was nothing more than what any of us must do before our writing is finally acceptable: he was revising. What is remarkable about the address is that Lincoln made so many revisions of a speech of well under 300 words. Obviously, he wanted it to fit the occasion for which it was intended, and he knew that something written hastily and without reflection would not satisfy his purpose and audience.

This principle is as true for anyone who writes on the job (which, of course, is what the president was doing) as it was for Lincoln. Unlike the Gettysburg Address, however, most on-the-job writing should not strive for oratorical elegance; the more natural writing sounds, the more ef-

---

[1] Tom Burnam, *The Dictionary of Misinformation* (New York: Perennial Library, 1986), pp. 93–94.

fort the writer has probably put into revising it. Revising requires a different frame of mind than writing the draft does. Immediately after you write a rough draft, ideas are so fresh in your mind that you cannot read the words, sentences, and paragraphs objectively. You must detach yourself from them to be able to look at the writing critically. Do not allow yourself to think, "Because my ideas are good, the way I've expressed them must also be good." The first step of revision is to develop a critical frame of mind—to become objective.

During revision, be hard on yourself for the benefit of your readers. Read and evaluate the draft as if you were a reader seeing it for the first time. The techniques used by experienced writers, and listed in the following Writer's Checklist (Revision Strategies), can help you achieve this mindset. Adopt the techniques most effective for you as you revise your draft.

ON THE WEB

For online resources for revising, go to Chapter 4, bedfordstmartins.com/writingthatworks

VOICES IN THE WORKPLACE

Thinking About Revision

As chief of Voluntary Services, U.S. Department of Veterans Affairs, Togus, Maine, Steven Hurd writes for diverse audiences and knows the importance of revision to tailor his communications: "I often have to write multiple drafts, depending on the intended reader. Sometimes we have drafts reviewed by people in the field who will give us smart, honest feedback. When writing for a potential donor in particular, I have to choose my tone and words carefully."

WRITER'S CHECKLIST
Revision Strategies

✔ Allow for a cooling period. Wait a day or two (or even a few hours) between writing a rough draft and revising it—you will be able to look at the writing itself more objectively.

✔ Pretend that a stranger has written your draft. When you can look at your writing and ask, "How could I have written that?" you are in the right frame of mind to revise.

✔ Revise your draft in multiple passes. Don't try to improve everything all at once. Concentrate first on larger issues, such as content and organization; then turn to improving emphasis and polishing your language. Save mechanical corrections, like spelling and punctuation, for later proofreading.

✔ Be alert for your most frequent problems. Be sure that you are aware of the errors you typically make, and watch for them as you revise.

✔ Read your draft aloud. Listening to sentences aloud often enables you to detect flawed word order or other problems.

✔ Ask someone else to read and critique your draft. Someone unfamiliar with your draft can see it objectively and identify problems that you need to address as you revise.

■ Content and Organization

Once you have put yourself in a frame of mind to view your work objectively, what should you look for? Begin with the whole-text tasks that involve your purpose and organization. Then in separate passes look for the accuracy of your content. Do you need to add content to clarify meaning or to delete redundant information? Are your recommendations adequately supported by your conclusions? Ensure, too, that topics mentioned in the introduction are not left out of the summary or conclusion. The easiest way to test the soundness of your organization is to write an outline of your rough draft—a technique most useful for longer drafts but helpful with smaller ones, too. The advantage of creating an outline of your first draft is that it breaks down blocks of text to essential ideas and makes the sequence of points easy to evaluate; it enables you to experiment with sequences and to lay out the most direct route to achieving your purpose. Does the outline of your draft conform to your planning outline? It may not because you may have rethought some ideas or added or deleted information as you wrote. If you find a problem with the logic of the sequence or with the amount or type of information included or omitted, revise the outline—and then your draft—to reflect the solution.

In revising your draft for completeness, you may also think of new information that you failed to include when you were preparing and writing your outline. This is the time to insert any missing facts or ideas. Always carefully consider such new information in the context of your audience and purpose. If the information will help satisfy your audience's need and accomplish your purpose, by all means add it now. However, if the information—no matter how interesting—does not serve these ends, it has no place in your document.

ESL Tips
Supporting an Argument

■ Remember that your goal is to persuade your audience—and that most North American readers expect arguments to be supported with concrete evidence, not general analogies or traditional wisdom.

■ Support arguments, opinions, recommendations, and conclusions with specific facts and examples.

■ Be direct and straightforward, rather than subtle or suggestive.

WRITER'S CHECKLIST
Evaluating Your Draft

✔ Is the purpose of the document clear?

✔ Is the information organized in the most effective sequence?

✔ Does each section follow logically from the one that precedes it?

✔ Is the scope of coverage adequate? Is there too little or too much information?

✔   Are all the facts, details, and examples relevant to the stated purpose?

✔   Is the draft written at the appropriate level for the reader?

✔   Are the main points obvious? Are subordinate points related to main points?

✔   Are contradictory statements resolved or eliminated?

✔   Do the descriptions and illustrations aid clarity? Are there enough illustrations?

✔   Are any recommendations adequately supported by the conclusions?

✔   Are any topics mentioned in the introduction and text also addressed in the conclusions?

A review of the relevant information in Chapters 1, 2, and 3 will be especially helpful as you reassess the effectiveness of your draft when it comes to these larger issues. Review in Chapter 1, Assessing Audience and Purpose, the sections titled Establishing Your Scope (page 11) and Organizing Your Ideas (page 12). Further evaluate the logic of your organization by reviewing the material in Chapter 2, Organizing Your Information, on outlining (pages 26–33). See Chapter 3, Writing the Draft, for guidance on ensuring that you address the right audience in the right voice (pages 71–74). Once you complete this review, you are ready to tackle the smaller, more detailed steps of the process described in the remainder of this chapter.

Coherence

Writing is coherent when the relationship between ideas is clear to your audience. Each idea should relate clearly to the others, with one idea flowing smoothly to the next. Coherence must be tested after writing. As you revise, ask "Can my reader move from this sentence or from this paragraph to the next without feeling a break in meaning?" If there is a break, add a transitional phrase or sentence to explain it.

The basic building blocks of a coherent draft are paragraphs. Effective paragraphs must be unified around a central idea so that every sentence is related to that idea. Paragraphs must also be coherent, with all ideas arranged in a logical order and with transitional devices linking sentences and paragraphs throughout the draft so that the audience can follow your reasoning from sentence to sentence and from paragraph to paragraph.

Paragraph Unity

When every sentence in a paragraph contributes to developing one central idea, the paragraph has unity. If a paragraph contains sentences that do not develop the central idea, it lacks unity.

The most effective way to make sure that your paragraph has unity is to provide a topic sentence that clearly states the central idea of that paragraph and double-check that every sentence directly relates to the topic sentence. Consider the following example, from a report evaluating possible locations for a company's new distribution center:

▶ *Probably the greatest advantage of Chicago as the location for our new distribution center is its excellent transportation facilities.* The city is served by three major railroads. In fact, Chicago was at one time the hub of cross-country rail transportation. Chicago is also a major center of the trucking industry, and most of the nation's large freight carriers have terminals there. We are concerned, however, about the delivery problems that we've had with several truck carriers. We've had far fewer problems with air freight. Both domestic and international air-cargo services are available at O'Hare International Airport. Finally, except in the winter months when the Great Lakes are frozen, Chicago is a seaport, accessible through the St. Lawrence Seaway.

Although the paragraph opens with a clearly stated topic sentence (in *italics*) about the advantages of Chicago's transportation facilities, three sentences do not develop that central idea. The sentence about Chicago as the former hub of railroad transportation, although historically accurate, is not relevant to the company's assessment; the two sentences about the relative merits of truck and air-carrier delivery are not relevant here. Stripped of these digressions, the paragraph becomes unified:

▶ *Probably the greatest advantage of Chicago as the location for our new distribution center is its excellent transportation facilities.* The city is served by three major railroads. Chicago is also a major center of the trucking industry, and most of the nation's large freight carriers have terminals there. Both domestic and international air-cargo services are available at O'Hare International Airport. Finally, except in the winter months when the Great Lakes are frozen, Chicago is a seaport, accessible through the St. Lawrence Seaway.

For workplace writing, it's best to place a topic sentence at the beginning of a paragraph. In this position, the reader knows immediately what the paragraph is about because the opening sentence states the central idea. This placement also allows the writer to more easily construct a unified paragraph because every sentence supports the topic sentence and the central idea it expresses.

A paragraph should be just long enough to deal adequately with the central idea stated in its topic sentence. Begin a new paragraph whenever you change the subject significantly. Keep in mind that long paragraphs can intimidate your reader by failing to provide manageable subdivisions of thought. Overly short paragraphs have a disadvantage, too: They may make it difficult to adequately develop the point stated in the topic sentence. A series of short paragraphs can also sacrifice unity by breaking a single idea into several pieces.

Transitions

Effective paragraphs take the reader logically from one idea to the next. Providing transitions will help you achieve a smooth flow of ideas from sentence to sentence, paragraph to paragraph, and subject to subject. Transition is a two-way indicator of what you have said and what you are about to say; it provides readers with guideposts for linking ideas and clarifying the relationship between them.

Transitions Between Sentences

Within a paragraph, transitional expressions clarify and smooth the movement from idea to idea. The words and phrases in Table 4–1 commonly function as transitional devices. Some transitional words and phrases in this table are nearly synonymous but imply somewhat different logical connections. Be sure that the transitional words and phrases you choose convey the precise meaning you intend.

Table 4–1   Common Transitions

To add information			
also	besides	moreover	furthermore
in addition	finally	next	additionally
first, second, etc.	last		
To give an example or to illustrate a point			
for example	for instance	to illustrate	specifically
in particular	in this case	to demonstrate	notably
To compare or contrast			
on the other hand	on the contrary	likewise	however
although	similarly	nevertheless	meanwhile
whereas			
To prove			
because	therefore	thus	hence
To show time			
initially	eventually	during	thereafter
finally	then	later	previously
formerly	first, second, etc.	next	afterward
at last	before	at the same time	currently
To show sequence			
next	now	finally	simultaneously
first, second, etc.	after	concurrently	
To conclude			
in conclusion	to summarize	finally	as a result
all in all			
Conjunctions			
and	or	nor	so
yet	for	but	

You can achieve effective transitions between sentences by repeating key words or key ideas from preceding sentences and by using pronouns that refer to antecedents in previous sentences. Consider the following short paragraph, which uses both of those means:

▷   Over the past several months, I have heard complaints about the Merit Award *Program.* Specifically, many employees feel that this *program* should be linked to annual *salary increases.* They believe that *salary increases* would provide a much better incentive than the current $1,000 and $1,500 *cash awards* for exceptional service. In addition, these *employees* believe that their supervisors consider the *cash awards* a satisfactory alternative to *salary increases.* Although I don't think this practice is widespread, the fact that the *employees* believe that it is justifies a reevaluation of the Merit Award *Program.*

Transitions Between Paragraphs

Transitional language between paragraphs serves the same function as it does between sentences: It signals the relationship between one paragraph and the next. For paragraphs, however, longer transitional elements are often necessary. One technique is to begin a new paragraph with a sentence that summarizes the preceding paragraph, as in the following excerpt from an environmental report:

▹   Each year, forest fires in our region cause significant environmental and economic damage. For example, wood ashes washed into streams after a fire often kill large numbers of fish. In addition, the destruction of the vegetation along stream banks causes water temperatures to rise, making the streams unfit for several varieties of cold-water fish. Forest fires, moreover, hurt the tourist and recreation business because vacationers are not likely to visit flame-blackened areas.
      These losses, and many other indirect losses caused by forest fires, damage not only the quality of life but also the economy of our region. They also represent a huge drain on the resources and personnel of the Department of Natural Resources. For example, our financial investment last year in fighting forest fires . . .

If used sparingly, another effective transitional device between paragraphs is to ask a question at the end of one paragraph and answer it at the beginning of the next.

▹   New workplace technology has always been feared because it has at times displaced some jobs. However, it invariably creates many more jobs than it eliminates. Almost always, the jobs eliminated by technological advances have been menial, unskilled jobs, and workers who have been displaced have been forced to increase their skills, which resulted in better and higher-paying jobs for them. *In view of these facts, is new workplace technology really bad?*
      Certainly technology has given us unparalleled access to information and created many new roles for employees. . . .

When you use this transitional device, make sure that the second paragraph does, in fact, answer the question posed in the first.

WRITER'S CHECKLIST
Creating Effective Paragraphs

✔   Unify the paragraph around a central idea.

✔   Ensure that every sentence relates to the topic sentence.

✔ Arrange ideas (and sentences) in a logical order.

✔ Use transitions to help readers follow the sequence of your ideas.

Emphasis

Effective writing is emphatic writing—it highlights the facts and ideas that the writer considers most important and subordinates those of less importance. By focusing the reader's attention on key elements, emphatic writing enables the reader to determine how one fact or idea in a sentence is related to another. You can achieve emphasis by using any number of the techniques described in this section.

Active and Passive Voice

A sentence is in the active voice if the subject of the sentence acts; it is in the passive voice if the subject is acted on.

ACTIVE
Rajesh Patel prepared the design for the new pump.
[The subject—*Rajesh Patel*—acts on *the design*—the direct object.]

PASSIVE
The design for the new pump was prepared by Rajesh Patel.
[The subject—*the design*—receives the action.]

In workplace writing, it is often important to emphasize who or what performs an action. Because the active voice is generally more direct, more concise, and easier for readers to understand, use the active voice unless the passive voice is more appropriate. Doing so allows your audience to move quickly and easily from the actor (the subject) to the action performed (the verb) to the receiver of the action (the direct object).

The passive voice, however, can be useful, too. For example, when the doer of the action is less important than the receiver of the action, the writer can emphasize the receiver by making it the subject of the sentence.

EFFECTIVE
PASSIVE
Sharon Gleason was appointed chief pathologist of Pine Cone County Hospital by the hospital's board of directors.

The important person in this sentence is Sharon Gleason, not the board of directors who made the appointment. To give her—the receiver of the action—the needed emphasis, the sentence makes sense in the passive voice. The same principle holds true in the sciences for situations where the data are more important than the scientist collecting that data. Laboratory or test reports are good examples of the proper use of the passive voice.

EFFECTIVE
PASSIVE
The test was conducted to identify the soil pH levels at the site.

Finally, the passive voice is also useful when the performer of the action either is not known or is not important.

| EFFECTIVE | The wheel was invented thousands of years ago. |
| PASSIVE | [Who invented it is not known.] |

As you revise, select the voice, active (usually) or passive (occasionally), appropriate to your purpose and topic.

ETHICS NOTE

Do not use the passive voice to avoid responsibility for an action or to obscure an issue, as in the following examples: "Several mistakes were made in the processing of your claim" (Who made the mistakes?) and "It has been decided that annual bonuses will be discontinued this year" (Who has decided?). Although writers sometimes need to use the passive voice or they use it unintentionally, their attempts to evade responsibility for a problem or future commitment clearly involve an ethical choice.

ESL Tips

Choosing Voice

Different languages place different values on active-voice and passive-voice constructions. In some languages, the passive is used frequently; in others, hardly at all. As a nonnative speaker of English, you may have a tendency to follow the pattern of your native language. But remember that even though business writing may sometimes require the passive voice, active verbs are highly valued in English.

Subordination

First drafts are often plagued by an overabundance of short, staccato-like sentences. Read the following passage, for example:

▷ The landscape design firm submitted its proposal. It was extensively illustrated. It was ten pages long.

The passage is monotonous because every sentence has the same subject-verb structure; it is unemphatic because each idea is given equal weight. The key to transforming a series of repetitive, unemphatic sentences is *subordination*, a technique in which a fact or an idea is shown to be secondary to another fact or idea in the same sentence. You can subordinate an element in a sentence by making it a dependent clause, a phrase, or a single modifier.

| DEPENDENT CLAUSE | The landscape design firm's proposal, *which covered ten pages*, was extensively illustrated. |
| PHRASE | The landscape design firm's proposal, *covering ten pages*, was extensively illustrated. |

SINGLE MODIFIER	The landscape design firm's *ten-page* proposal was extensively illustrated.

You can also shift the focus from one idea to another by its placement in a sentence. If you wish to highlight an item, place it either at the beginning or at the end of the sentence; if you wish to subordinate an item, place it in the middle of the sentence.

WITHOUT SUBORDINATION	Poison ivy grows throughout the United States except in Alaska, Hawaii, and parts of the West Coast. It can grow as a vine or a shrub.
EMPHASIZES GEOGRAPHICAL RANGE	Poison ivy, which can grow as a vine or shrub, can be found throughout the United States except in Alaska, Hawaii, and parts of the West Coast.
EMPHASIZES PLANT TYPE	Poison ivy, found throughout the United States except in Alaska, Hawaii, and parts of the West Coast, can grow as a vine or a shrub.

Although subordination can help you to write clear and readable sentences, it can be overdone. Be careful not to pile one subordinating clause on top of another—doing so will force your reader to work harder than necessary to understand what you are saying. The following sentence is hard to read because the bottleneck of subordinate clauses prevents the reader from moving easily from one idea to the next.

TOO MUCH SUBORDINATION	When the two technicians, who had been trained to repair Maurita printers, explained to Erin that the new Maurita 5090 printer, which she had told them was not working properly, needed a new fuser drum, she decided that until the part arrived, the department would have its sales letters reproduced by an independent printing supplier.
EFFECTIVE SUBORDINATION	Erin told the two Maurita technicians that the new Maurita 5090 printer was not working properly. The technicians examined the printer and explained to her that it needed a new fuser drum. She decided that until the part arrived, the department would have its sales letters reproduced by an independent printing supplier.

ETHICS NOTE

Highlighting advantages of a product or service in a document is appropriate, but subordinating or failing to mention related disadvantages could easily mislead the audience. Even making a bulleted list of advantages, where they stand out, and then burying a disadvantage in the middle of a paragraph could unfairly mislead the target audience. You might also be tempted to dramatically highlight a feature or service that your audience would find attractive but that may be available only with some models of a product or at extra cost. In that case, the audience could justifiably object that you have given them a false impression in order to sell a product or service, especially if any extra cost was also deemphasized.

Parallel Structure

Parallelism can produce an economy of language, clarify meaning, and indicate the equality of related ideas. It promotes emphatic writing by linking ideas in a recognizable pattern. A reader who has sensed the pattern of a sentence can go from one idea to another more quickly and confidently.

Parallel structure requires that sentence elements—words, phrases, and clauses—that are alike in function be alike in structure as well. The wording you choose to make a sentence parallel depends on the degree of emphasis you wish to create: Words produce some emphasis, phrases produce more emphasis, and clauses produce the most emphasis.

WORDS	Customer-service trainees must be *punctual, courteous,* and *conscientious.*
PHRASES	Customer-service trainees must recognize the importance *of punctuality, of courtesy,* and *of conscientiousness.*
CLAUSES	Customer-service trainees *must arrive punctually, they must behave courteously,* and *they must study conscientiously.*

To make the relationship among parallel units clear, repeat the word (or words) that introduces the first unit.

▷ The advantage is not in the pay but ^in^ the greater opportunity.

▷ The study of electronics is a necessity and ^a^ challenge to the trainees.

Lists

Lists can save readers time by allowing them to see at a glance specific items, questions, or directions. Lists also help readers by breaking up complex statements and by allowing key ideas to stand out. When you use a list of phrases or short sentences, be sure to keep all elements parallel, as in the following example:

▷ Please note the following policy changes:

- Do not use company phones for personal long-distance calls.
- Use low-grade yellow paper rather than bond for any written copy that is not to go out of the office.
- Make double-sided copies rather than one-sided photocopies of all internal correspondence.

To make sure a list fits with the surrounding sentences, provide adequate transition before and after it. Introduce each list with a sentence or phrase that puts it in context. Otherwise, readers may have to guess why it's there. And although lists help focus reader attention, their overuse can confuse readers. When a document consists almost entirely of lists, the audience is unable to distinguish their relative importance or understand how they are related to one another.

WRITER'S CHECKLIST
Using Lists

✔ List only comparable items.

✔ Use parallel structure throughout.

✔ Use only words, phrases, or short sentences.

✔ Provide context by introducing lists with complete sentences, followed by a colon.

✔ Provide adequate transitions before and after lists.

✔ Use numbers when rank or sequence is important.

✔ Use bullets when rank or sequence is not important.

✔ Do not overuse lists.

Other Ways to Achieve Emphasis

You can create a feeling of anticipation in your audience by arranging a series of facts or ideas in order of importance. Begin such a series with the least important or lowest impact idea and end it with the most important or highest impact one.

▷ The hostile takeover of the company will result in some employees being relocated to different cities, some being downgraded, and some being let go.

The writer leads the audience step by step from the lowest potential impact on employees to the highest: (1) employee relocation, (2) downgraded jobs, and (3) the loss of jobs. Note how the sentence presents these three potential outcomes in parallel structure.

An abrupt change in sentence length can also highlight an important point.

▷ We have already reviewed the problems that the accounting department identified during the past year. We could continue to examine the causes of our problems and point an accusing finger at all the elements beyond our control, but in the end it all leads to one simple conclusion: *We must cut costs.*

Sometimes, simply labeling ideas as important creates emphasis.

▷ *But most important,* we can do everything in our power to make sure that we are producing the best communication equipment on the market.

If you don't overuse them, direct statements such as *most important* should make your audience notice what follows.

Important information may also be brought to the audience's attention by a special format—the material may be boxed, for instance—or by attention-getting

◆ *For additional high-lighting devices, see pages 213–219 in Chapter 7, Designing Effective Documents and Visuals.*

devices such as dashes, ALL-CAPITAL letters, <u>underlined words</u>, or a distinctive typeface, such as **boldface** or *italic* type. These features can be used to emphasize important words and phrases in warnings. Overuse of such typographical devices may cancel their effectiveness, however. Readers quickly learn to gloss over these devices if they are used for subordinate as well as truly important material.

WARNING

DO NOT proceed to the next instruction until you have unplugged the equipment. The electrical power generated by this equipment can kill!

WRITER'S CHECKLIST
Achieving Emphasis

✔ Use the active voice, as appropriate.

✔ Subordinate secondary ideas.

✔ Use parallel structure to focus attention on how ideas are related.

✔ Use lists to highlight ideas by setting them apart from surrounding text.

✔ Arrange ideas in least important to most important order.

✔ Label key ideas as important.

✔ Selectively use typographical devices such as ALL-CAPITAL LETTERS, *italic* type, **boldface** type, or <u>underlined text</u>.

■ Point of View

Point of view shows the writer's relation to the information presented. First-person point of view indicates that the writer is a participant or an observer. Second- and third-person points of view indicate that the writer is giving directions, instructions, or advice or is writing about other people or something impersonal.

FIRST PERSON   *I* scrolled down to find the Settings option.

SECOND PERSON   Scroll down to find the Settings option and double-click. [*You* is understood.]

THIRD PERSON   *He* scrolled down to find the Settings option.

Many people think they should avoid the pronoun *I* in their workplace writing. Doing so, however, often leads to inappropriate passive constructions or to awkward sentences in which writers refer to themselves as *one* or as *the writer* instead of as *I*.

▷ ~~It is regrettable~~ that the equipment shipped on the 12th ~~is unacceptable~~.
I regret   we cannot accept

▷ ~~One~~ can only conclude that the bond rate is too low.
I

Do not use the personal point of view, however, when you need to emphasize the subject matter over the writer or the reader. In the following example, the use of *I* communicates no useful information and is less tactful than the impersonal version.

PERSONAL   I received objections to my proposal from several of your managers.

IMPERSONAL   Several managers have raised objections to the proposal.

Whether you adopt a personal or an impersonal point of view depends on your purpose and readers. In an informal e-mail to an associate, for example, you would most likely adopt a personal point of view because you know the recipient. However, in a report to a large group, you would probably emphasize the subject by using an impersonal point of view.

ETHICS NOTE

In correspondence on company stationery, use of the pronoun *we* may be interpreted as reflecting company policy, whereas *I* clearly reflects personal opinion. Use the appropriate pronoun according to whether the matter discussed in the letter is a corporate or an individual concern.

▷   *I* understand your frustration with the price increase, but *we* must now include the cost of the recent import tax in our pricing.

ESL Tips

Stating an Opinion

In some cultures, stating an opinion in writing is considered impolite or unnecessary, but in the United States and Canada, readers expect to see a writer's opinion stated clearly and explicitly. The opinion should be followed by specific examples to help the reader understand the writer's point of view.

■ Language

The words you use matter. Focus on them carefully as you revise. Ensure that you use the right word in the right context throughout and that your writing is economical by eliminating redundant or otherwise needless language. Now is also the time to evaluate your draft for any stated or implied bias toward people or groups. Finally, consider whether you need to use technical, legal, or other specialized vocabulary that may be inappropriate for some members of your audience. The plainer your language, the more time and effort you will usually save your readers.

Context and Word Choice

As Mark Twain once said, "The difference between the right word and almost the right word is the difference between 'lightning' and 'lightning bug.'" Precision requires that you choose the right word.

Be alert to the effect that a word may have on your audience—and try to avoid words that might, by the implications they carry, confuse, distract, or offend your audience. For example, in describing a piece of machinery that your company recently bought, you might refer to the item as cheap—meaning inexpensive. However, because "cheap" often suggests "of poor quality" or "shoddily made," your audience may picture the new piece of equipment as already falling apart and in need of repairs.

In selecting the appropriate word, you will want to keep in mind the *context*—the setting in which the word appears. Suppose instead of "cheap" you call the new machine "inexpensive." But the use of the word will depend on the context. While a $1,000 desktop laser printer might be overpriced, an audience unfamiliar with the cost of printing machinery might be surprised to learn that an $80,000 printing press is a good buy. It is up to you, the writer, to provide your readers with a context—to let them know, in this case, the relative costs of printing equipment.

The context will also determine whether a word you choose is specific enough. When you use the word *machine*, for instance, you might be thinking of an automobile, a lathe, a robot, or a laboratory centrifuge. *Machine* is an imprecise word that must be qualified, or explained, unless you want to refer to every item included in the general category *machine*. If you have a particular kind of machine in mind, you must use more precise language. Conversely, to include

---

REDUCING MOBILE EMISSIONS

Automobiles, trucks, and buses have been identified as significant sources of both ozone and particulate matter in the region, with their emissions accounting for over 30 percent of the smog precursors emitted countywide. In response, Gillette County has adopted a "technology neutral" plan to use all available technologies that provide the least amount of emissions, while conserving natural resources until a completely sustainable transportation source is discovered. While both compressed natural gas and diesel technologies were already a part of the county fleet, both hybrid sedans and buses have been added, including four hybrid vehicles used by the Department of Environmental Services. . . . *These vehicles include a Saturn Vue (XR V6) sport utility vehicle (SUV), a Ford Escape (XLT V6) small SUV, a Chevrolet Tahoe (LT V8) large SUV, and a Saturn Aura Hybrid (XE 4 cyl) 4-door sedan.*

Figure 4–1   Information Too Detailed for Audience and Context printer model numbers in a company's annual report, a detailed parts list in a sales brochure, or highly technical language in a memo to the accounting department would, of course, be inappropriate. In Figure 4–1, for example, the specific automobile models (in italics) listed in an annual report on an organization's environmental protection practices are an inappropriate level of detail for an overview aimed at the report's general readers.

In all the writing you do, you must determine your purpose and your intended audience, and then select terms that are neither too general nor too specific for the context.

ETHICS NOTE

Use words correctly and appropriately. Consider the company document that stated, "A *nominal* charge will be assessed for using our facilities." When clients objected that the charge was actually very large, the writer pointed out that the word *nominal* means "the named amount" as well as "very small." In this situation, the audience had a strong case in charging that the company was attempting to deceive. In other circumstances, various abstract words, technical or legal jargon, and euphemisms— when used to mislead an audience or to hide a serious or dangerous situation—are unethical, even though technical or legal experts could interpret the language as accurate.

Appropriate overview

Inappropriate level of detail

Conciseness

As you revise, focus on removing unnecessary words, phrases, clauses, and sentences from your writing. Wordiness, as well as stilted or pretentious language, can place a barrier between you and your audience by obscuring your essential meaning. Be particularly alert for two types of wordiness: redundancy and padded phrases.

Redundancy

Modifiers—whether adjectives, adverbs, prepositional phrases, or subordinate clauses—make the words they describe accurate and specific. However, avoid modifiers that simply repeat the idea contained in the word they modify, such as the expressions in the following list:

blue in color	plan ahead
resume again	basic essentials
square in shape	attach together
brief in duration	visible to the eye
completely finished	present status
final outcome	round circle

Padded Phrases

A padded phrase expresses in several words an idea that could easily be expressed in a word. *Due to the fact that* is a wordy way of saying *because*. Examine your work for padded language, often composed of the following words: *case, fact, field, factor, manner,* and *nature.*

Sometimes, however, longer wording or phrasing clarifies meaning.

▶ *In terms of* gross sales, the year has been successful; *in terms of* net income, however, it has been discouraging.

Instead of being redundant, the phrase *in terms of* balances the sentence and highlights the contrast in meaning. Expressions such as these must be evaluated individually. If the expression does not contribute to the meaning of the sentence, use its simpler substitute.

Bias

Biased words and expressions offend because they make inappropriate assumptions or stereotypes about gender, ethnicity, physical or mental disability, age, or sexual orientation.

ETHICS NOTE

The easiest way to avoid bias is simply not to mention differences among people unless the differences are relevant to the discussion. Keep current with accepted usage, and, if you are unsure of the appropriateness of an expression or the tone of a passage, have several classmates or colleagues review the material and give you their honest assessment.

Sexist Language

Sexist language can be an outgrowth of sexism, the arbitrary stereotyping of men and women. It can breed and reinforce inequality. To avoid sexism in your writing, treat men and women equally, and do not make assumptions about traditional or occupational roles. Accordingly, use nonsexist occupational descriptions in your writing.

Instead of	**Consider**
chairman	chair *or* chairperson
foreman	supervisor
manpower	staff, personnel, *or* workers
policeman *or* policewoman	police officer
salesman *or* saleswoman	salesperson
male nurse	nurse
female chemist	chemist

Use comparable terms to describe men and women.

Instead of	Consider
man and wife	husband and wife
Ms. Jones and Bernard Weiss	Ms. Jones and Mr. Weiss *or* Mary Jones and Bernard Weiss
ladies and men	ladies and gentlemen *or* women and men

Unintended sexism can creep into your writing by the unthinking use of male pronouns where a reference could apply equally to a man and a woman. One way to avoid such usage is to rewrite the sentence in the plural.

> *All employees*   *their managers*   *their travel vouchers.*
▷ ~~Every employee~~ will have ~~his manager~~ sign ~~his travel voucher.~~

Other possible solutions are to use *his or her* instead of *his* alone or to omit the pronoun completely if it is not essential to the meaning of the sentence.

>   *an*
▷ Everyone must submit ~~his~~ expense report by Monday.

He or she can become monotonous when repeated frequently, and a pronoun cannot always be omitted without changing the meaning of a sentence. Another solution is to omit troublesome pronouns by using the imperative mood whenever possible.

>   *Submit all*
▷ ~~Everyone must submit his or her~~ expense reports by Monday.

Other Types of Biased Language

Identifying people by racial, ethnic, or religious categories is simply not relevant in most workplace writing. Telling readers that an engineer is Native American or that a professor is African American almost never conveys useful information. Similarly, linking a profession or a characteristic to race or ethnicity reinforces stereotypes, implying that it is rare or expected for a person of a particular background to have achieved a certain position.

Consider how you refer to people with disabilities. If you refer to "a disabled employee," you imply that the part (*disabled*) is as significant as the whole (*employee*). Use "an employee with a disability" instead. Similarly, the preferred usage is "a person who uses a wheelchair" rather than "a wheelchair-bound person"; the latter expression inappropriately equates the wheelchair with the person. Likewise, references to a person's age can also be inappropriate, as in expressions like "middle-aged manager" or "young Web designer."

In most workplace writing, such issues are simply not relevant. Of course, in some contexts race, ethnicity, religion, disability, or age should be identified. For example, if you are writing an Equal Employment Opportunity Commission report about your firm's hiring practices, the racial and gender composition of the workforce is relevant. In such cases, you need to present the information in ways that are accurate and that respect the individuals or groups to which you refer.

Plain Language

ON THE WEB

For background information about plain-language laws and practices, go to Chapter 4, bedfordstmartins .com/writingthatworks, and select *Web Links*.

Strive to communicate with your audience in language that is both uncomplicated and accurate. Even with the best of intentions, however, you cannot always avoid using specialized terms and concepts. This section will help you sort out the difference between writing that is plain and accurate and writing that is either too complicated or too simplistic.

ETHICS NOTE

Many states have created plain-language laws, which require that documents be written in clear, understandable language. The federal government also now requires that all its new regulations be written in plain language.

Affectation

Do not use language that is more formal, technical, or showy than it needs to be to communicate information to your reader. Such inflated language creates a smoke screen that the audience must penetrate to discover your meaning. Consider the following example, in which a company needs to tell employees about its policy for personal phone calls.

INFLATED   It is the policy of the company to provide the proper telephonic apparatus to enable each employee to conduct the interoffice and intra-business communication necessary to discharge his or her responsibilities; however, it is contrary to company policy to permit telephones to be utilized for personal employee communications.

PLAIN   Your telephone is provided for company business; do not use it for personal calls.

Most people would have to read the first version of the policy several times before deciphering its message. The meaning of the revised version, which uses direct, simple, and precise language, is evident at a glance.

Another common type of affectation is adding prefixes and suffixes to simple words. For example, *analyzation, summarization,* and *notation* are simply fancy-sounding versions of *analysis, summary,* and *note.* The extra syllables tacked on such words do not make them mean anything more precise; they make them incorrect and longer.

Understanding the possible reasons for affectation is the first step toward avoiding it. Review and revise your writing if you recognize any of the following tendencies:

- *Impression.* Some writers use pretentious language in an attempt to impress others. Evidence and logic will create a much more positive impression, whether you are a student trying to impress a teacher or an employee trying to impress a superior or customer.

- *Insecurity.* If you are unsure of your facts, conclusions, or arguments, don't try to cover these gaps with a smoke screen of pretentious language. Continue to research the topic until you are certain of what to say.

- *Imprecision.* Avoid opaque and ambiguous language in descriptions that appears to finesse troublesome situations. Precise language is especially important in health and safety communications, but it is also crucial to investment and financial planning guidance because the information involves financial risk.

- *Imitation.* Avoid the tendency to imitate the poor writing you see around you. For example, maybe everyone in your company refers to himself or herself as *the writer* rather than *I* in letters and memos. These practices are frequently simply bad habits thoughtlessly repeated rather than formal company policy. At least find out your company's policy before falling into the habit with everyone else.

- *Initiation.* If you just completed your education or training for an occupation, it's natural to feel that one way to prove your professional standing is to use technical terminology and jargon as much as possible. Although this impulse usually passes with time, be especially careful to avoid it in your writing for senior officials and customers. These readers are much less likely to be as technically knowledgeable as you.

- *Intimidation.* A few writers, consciously or subconsciously, try to overwhelm their readers with pretentious language. Their reasons for doing so can vary; regardless of why, the practice obscures meaning.

WRITER'S CHECKLIST
Avoiding Affectation

✔ Do not refer to yourself as *the writer* or *one*; use the first person (*I*).

✔ Choose simple words that say exactly what you mean—do not substitute big, imprecise, or unusual words for well-thought-out, precise language.

✔ Avoid trying to impress your reader with pretentious language—such as *discharge responsibilities, aforesaid, hereto*—or with vague or trendy language—such as *calendarize, synopsize, monetize, locavore, solution* (in the sense of product or service).

✔ Be certain of your facts, conclusions, and arguments. Insecurity in these areas can lead to inflated language.

✔ As you revise, identify wording that should be replaced with clearer, shorter, more common words and phrases.

Technical Terminology

Technical terms are standard, universally recognized words used in a particular field to refer to specific principles, processes, or devices. Unlike inflated language, technical terms are useful and often essential in communicating accurately and concisely. For example, the term *divestiture* has a specific meaning for audiences familiar with management strategies. Similarly, the term *logic gate* would be understood by an audience who studied computer science or electrical engineering.

If you are certain that your audience (and potential audience) will understand a technical term, use it to ensure precision. If you are at all uncertain, however, define the term in plain language when you first use it. If your audience is likely to be confused by a concept, explain it, perhaps including an easy-to-understand example. Digressing into an explanation, though less efficient than using a technical term, is sometimes required to make your writing easily understandable—your ultimate goal.

WRITER'S CHECKLIST
Revising for Clarity

✔ Organize your writing logically.

✔ Use effective transitions between sentences, paragraphs, and sections.

✔ Be consistent in your point of view toward your topic.

✔ Emphasize key ideas and subordinate ancillary ideas.

✔ Choose precise language to ensure accuracy and to eliminate vagueness and ambiguity.

✔ Strive for conciseness by eliminating words, phrases, and sentences that are not necessary to your subject, purpose, and audience.

Jargon

Jargon is highly specialized technical slang that is unique to an occupational group. If you are addressing a particular occupational group, jargon (like technical terminology) may provide a time-saving and an efficient means of communicating with them. For example, human-resource professionals adopted the term *headhunters* to describe the specialists who recruit professional and executive personnel. Such terms should be used only in the appropriate context. Technical shorthand is not a satisfactory substitute for everyday language outside the field in which it is standard.

Another type of jargon is used to define occupations euphemistically. Tactfulness dictates that if you are writing to an undertaker and must refer to his or her occupation, you should use the term *funeral director*. For similar reasons, a trash collector is frequently called a *sanitation worker*.

◆ *For guidance on how to define terms accurately and incorporate them smoothly into your writing, see pages 79–82 in Chapter 3, Writing the Draft.*

When jargon becomes so specialized that it applies only to one company or subgroup of an occupation, it is referred to as "shop talk." For example, an automobile manufacturer might produce a "pollution-control valve—Model LV-20." In the department where the device is built, it may be referred to as an "LV-20." Obviously, shop talk is appropriate only for those familiar with its special vocabulary and should be reserved for speech, informal memos, and e-mail messages within a company.

Proofreading

Proofreading is your final opportunity to review your content for accuracy and for sentence-level corrections in grammar, punctuation, mechanics, and spelling. Even though you are familiar with your content at this point, inadvertent errors can remain unless you methodically examine the draft for them.

Above all, your information must be accurate. Although accuracy is important in all types of writing, it takes on special significance when you write on the job. One misplaced decimal point, for example, can create a staggering financial error. Incorrect or imprecise instructions can cause injury to a worker. At the very least, if your writing is not accurate, you will quickly lose the confidence of your readers. They will be confused, for example, if a figure or fact in your text differs from one in a chart or graph. These kinds of inaccuracies are easily overlooked as you write a first draft, so you must correct them during revision.

◆ *For an easy-access reference to grammar, punctuation, mechanics, and spelling while revising, see Part Four, Revision Guide.*

Whether the material you examine is your own writing or that of someone else, consider editing and proofreading in several stages. Although you need to tailor the stages to the specific document and to your own problem areas, the Proofreading in Stages writer's checklist that follows provides a useful starting point for proofreading.

@   DIGITAL TIPS: Grammar Checkers and Spell Checkers

Do not rely entirely on computer grammar checkers and spell checkers. They may help with proofreading, but they can make writers overconfident. If a typographical error results in a legitimate English word (for example, *coarse* instead of *course*), the spell checker will not flag the misspelling. Moreover, spell checkers will not be familiar with proper names, technical terminology, and non-English expressions. Because grammar checkers cannot anticipate the meaning of your sentences, they have a tendency to flag proper usage as incorrect and to suggest inappropriate revisions. Therefore, you still must proofread your work carefully—both on your monitor and on paper.

WRITER'S CHECKLIST
Proofreading in Stages

First-Stage Review
- ✔ Appropriate format, as for reports or correspondence
- ✔ Typographical consistency (headings, spacing, fonts)

Second-Stage Review
- ✔ Specific grammar and usage problems
- ✔ Appropriate punctuation
- ✔ Correct abbreviations and capitalization
- ✔ Correct spelling (especially names and places)

✔ Complete Web or e-mail addresses and the like

✔ Accurate figures and consistent units of measurement in tables and lists

✔ Cut-and-paste errors; for example, a result of moved or deleted text and numbers

Final-Stage Review

✔ Final check of your goals: readers' needs and purpose

✔ Appearance of the document (see pages 210–220 in Chapter 7, Designing Effective Documents and Visuals)

✔ Review by colleague for crucial documents

Use the standard proofreaders' marks shown on page 624, especially for proofreading someone else's document.

Physical Appearance

The most thoughtfully prepared, carefully written, and conscientiously revised writing will quickly lose its effect if it has a poor physical appearance. In the classroom or on the job, a sloppy document will invariably lead your reader to assume that the work that went into preparing it was also sloppy. In the classroom, that carelessness will reflect on you; on the job, it can reflect on your employer as well. Unless your instructor provides other specific instructions, use the following guidelines for preparing your document:

◆ *For format guidelines for letters and memos, see Chapter 8, Understanding the Principles of Business Communication.*

◆ *For guidance for formal reports, see Chapter 11, Writing Formal Reports.*

◆ *For guidance on page design, see Chapter 7, Designing Effective Documents and Visuals.*

- Use good-quality, white paper.
- Check that your printer produces a clear, dark image.
- Use at least one-inch margins on all sides of the page.
- Number all pages.
- Leave ample white space to separate sections.

@ **DIGITAL TIPS: Proofreading for Format Consistency**

An effective way to check formatting, spacing, and typographical consistency as well as general appearance of documents is to view the whole page on-screen in your word-processing program. You may also wish to view two pages side by side to compare their layout. For more on this topic, see <bedfordstmartins.com/writingthatworks> and select *Digital Tips*.

ON THE WEB

For samples of an original and a revised draft of a persuasive letter, go to the Model Documents Gallery, bedfordstmartins.com/writingthatworks

Case Study: Revising the Lifemaker Brochure

A variety of the revision techniques discussed in this chapter apply to the Lifemaker sales brochure that was outlined and drafted in Chapters 2 and 3. In Figure 4–2, the writer has taken her second draft and, after allowing for a cooling-off period,

The Lifemaker System 40—DRAFT
The Compact, Affordable Home Gym
Designed for Maximum Fitness Conditioning

Home gyms were designed to eliminate the hassle and expense of going to a health club to work out, but most of them are too bulky and awkward to fit either your budget or your wallet. The Lifemaker System 40 is designed for (limped) living space, a modest budget, and maximum fitness needs.
sp

Compact Design

too much jargon

The Lifemaker's multiple stations provide a technologically sophisticated strength training program, (and is) architecturally configured for minimal space and maximal efficiency. (At 4 (fett) wide and 7 feet long,) your living room can (easily) accommodate the Lifemaker with more (ease) than other home systems. At the same time, the Lifemaker offers more stations and more exercises. ——— *faulty comparison*

missing pronoun

misplaced modifier

sp

redundant

point of view

move this ¶ to intro- duction

(One) need not compromise (your) exercise needs with an (overside) or ineffective system. Our home gym lets you integrate a complete home exercise system into your available space and your budget.
sp

Cast-Iron Weight Stack

need direct object "of plates"

too vague "can be adjusted in 5, 10, 15 pound incre- ments"

agreement

The dual cast-iron weight stacks totals 200 lbs. Which can be arranged to offer a resistance range of 10 to 150 pounds. In addition, Lifemaker offers the only weight system on the market that can be adjusted in (multiplied) increments.
sp

not true!!

Adjustable Cables

missing subject- verb agreement

The Lifemaker's unique cable system (allows) quick (reconfiguring) of the weight stacks without taking apart the entire system. Just pulling the center rod and one can add or remove as many plates as you need.

verb agreement; point of view

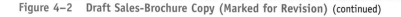

Figure 4–2   Draft Sales-Brochure Copy (Marked for Revision) (continued)

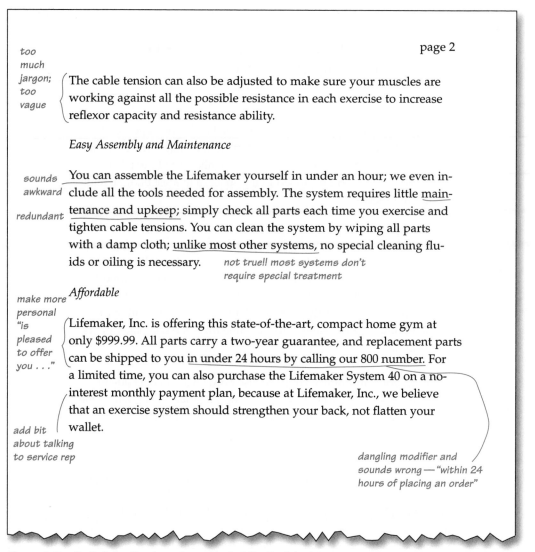

too much jargon; too vague

{ The cable tension can also be adjusted to make sure your muscles are working against all the possible resistance in each exercise to increase reflexor capacity and resistance ability.

Easy Assembly and Maintenance

sounds awkward

redundant

You can assemble the Lifemaker yourself in under an hour; we even in-clude all the tools needed for assembly. The system requires little main-tenance and upkeep; simply check all parts each time you exercise and tighten cable tensions. You can clean the system by wiping all parts with a damp cloth; unlike most other systems, no special cleaning flu-ids or oiling is necessary.   *not true!! most systems don't require special treatment*

make more personal "is pleased to offer you . . ."

Affordable

{ Lifemaker, Inc. is offering this state-of-the-art, compact home gym at only $999.99. All parts carry a two-year guarantee, and replacement parts can be shipped to you in under 24 hours by calling our 800 number. For a limited time, you can also purchase the Lifemaker System 40 on a no-interest monthly payment plan, because at Lifemaker, Inc., we believe that an exercise system should strengthen your back, not flatten your wallet.

add bit about talking to service rep

dangling modifier and sounds wrong — "within 24 hours of placing an order"

Figure 4–2   Draft Sales-Brochure Copy (Marked for Revision) (continued)

critiqued her work, using the main points covered in this chapter as her guide. Figure 4–3 shows a revised version of the draft. Notice that the writer has not sim-ply made mechanical, sentence-level corrections to her work; she used her marginal comments to revise the structure and organization as well as its sentences.

The Lifemaker System 40
The Compact, Affordable Home Gym
Designed for Maximum Fitness Conditioning

Home gym systems are designed to eliminate the hassle and expense of working out at a health club, but most systems take up too much space and can injure both your budget and your back. The Lifemaker System 40 offers a solution to the problem of oversized, overpriced, and ineffective home gyms, because Lifemaker is designed to fit a limited living space, a modest budget, and maximum fitness requirements. Purchasing a Lifemaker System 40 will let you integrate a complete weight-and-cable exercise system into your living space and your budget.

Introduces major benefits from Figure 2–2

Compact Design

The Lifemaker's comprehensive strength-training program is designed to occupy minimal space. The system offers more than 40 exercise combinations, but because it measures only 4 feet wide and 7 feet long, Lifemaker will fit easily into almost any room.

Headings make brochure inviting to readers

Multiple Stations

Three workout stations let you move through your conditioning program as efficiently as if you owned a roomful of weight-and-cable machines. In addition, the multiple stations are designed so that two people can work out at the same time.

Cast-Iron Weights

The Lifemaker features dual weight stacks, totaling more than 200 pounds of cast-iron plates. The dual stacks offer a resistance range of 10 to 150 pounds; resistance can be adjusted in 5-, 10-, or 15-pound increments.

Expands equipment, fitness, maintenance, and affordability benefits from introductory paragraph

Adjustable Cables

A unique cable system allows you to reconfigure the dual weight stacks without taking apart the entire system. Simply pull the rod located between the stacks and you can add or remove as many plates as you need for a particular exercise. The cable tension can also be adjusted to increase or decrease the amount of resistance within exercise sets.

Easy Assembly, Easy Maintenance

The Lifemaker System 40 can be assembled in less than an hour; no special tools are needed for assembly. You can maintain the Lifemaker in good condition simply by wiping down the system with a damp cloth; no oiling or scrubbing of parts is ever necessary. All parts carry a two-year guarantee and can be shipped to you within 24 hours of your placing an order.

Affordable

Lifemaker, Inc., is pleased to offer you this state-of-the-art, compact home gym for only $999.99. You can also purchase the Lifemaker on a low-interest monthly payment plan. Call (800) 554-1234 and we will be happy to arrange a plan that works with your financial needs. At Lifemaker, Inc., we believe that owning a home-gym system should strengthen your back, not flatten your wallet.

Figure 4–3 Final Sales-Brochure Copy

@ DIGITAL TIPS: Revising Your Draft

- Print a double-spaced copy of your draft. Write notes and revisions on paper before returning to the computer to enter changes and corrections.
- Move blocks of text as needed.
- Use the Find command to locate inappropriate diction such as *a lot*; padded phrases such as *that is, there are, the fact that,* and *to be*; jargon that needs to be eliminated or technical terms that may need further explanation; and your most commonly misused words, such as *affect* for *effect*.
- Use spell checkers and grammar checkers carefully, and reread the text for accuracy.

CHAPTER 4 SUMMARY: REVISING THE DRAFT

ON THE WEB

For an online quiz on revision, go to Chapter 4, bedfordstmartins .com/writingthatworks

Use the following checklist to help you remember the various aspects of revision covered in this chapter. Refer to this list both before and after you write the final draft of any document; fix any problems before your reader sees them.

- Have I allowed a cooling period?
- Have I included all the information my readers need?
- Is the writing organized logically?
- Do any potential ethical problems need to be resolved?
- Does each paragraph have a topic sentence?
- Are the sentences in each paragraph related to the paragraph's central idea?
- Have I included enough transitions, so readers can follow the logical relationships among ideas?
- Are active and passive voices used appropriately?
- Are secondary ideas subordinated to primary ideas?
- Are ideas of equal importance written in grammatically parallel structure?
- Are other highlighting devices used appropriately?
- Is the point of view appropriate and consistent?
- Does the language accurately and precisely suit the topic and the audience?
- Is the writing concise?
- Is the writing free of actual or implied bias?
- Does the vocabulary avoid unnecessary technical terminology and jargon?
- Have all errors—grammatical and factual—been corrected during proofreading?
- Is the document appropriately formatted?
- Is the document's appearance crisp and clean?

Exercises

ON THE WEB

For additional exercises, go to Chapter 4, bedfordstmartins.com/ writingthatworks

1. Well-constructed paragraphs enable readers to quickly understand their content and writers to achieve their purpose. Read the following paragraph and then (a) underline its topic sentence and (b) cross out any sentences that do not contribute to paragraph unity.

   ▶ Frequently, department managers and supervisors recruit applicants without working through our corporate human-resources office. Our human-resources departments at all of our locations across the country have experienced this problem. Recently, the manager of our tool-design department met with a recent industrial-design graduate to discuss an opening for a tool designer. The graduate was sent to the human-resources department, where she was told that no such position existed. When the tool-design manager asked the director of human resources about the matter, the manager learned that the company president had ordered a hiring freeze for two months. I'm sure that our general employment situation will get better. As a result of the manager's failure to work through proper channels, the applicant was not only disappointed but bitter.

2. The sentences in the following paragraph have been purposely placed in the wrong order. Examine key terms and transitional devices, and then rearrange the sentences so that the paragraph moves smoothly and logically from one sentence to the next. Indicate the correct order of the sentences by placing the sentence numbers in the order in which the sentences should appear.

   ▶ (1) If such improvements could be achieved, the consequences would be significant for many different applications. (2) However, the most challenging technical problem is to achieve substantial increases in the quantities of electrical energy that can be stored per unit weight of the battery. (3) The overall process yields about 70 percent of the electricity originally put into the battery. (4) A storage battery is a relatively efficient way of storing energy.

3. Each of the following pairs of sentences lacks a transition from the first sentence to the second. From the list of transitional devices in Table 4–1, select the most appropriate one for each sentence pair. Then rewrite the sentences as necessary.

   a. The Doctors Clinic was able to attain its fund-raising goal on time this year. Mercer Street Hospital was forced to extend its fund-raising deadline for three months.

   b. When instructing the new tellers, the branch manager explained how to deal with impatient customers. The personal-banking assistant told the new employees that they should consult her if they had difficulty handling those customers.

   c. A car may skid on ice for several reasons. The driver may be going faster than road conditions warrant.

   d. Unit sales dropped 12 percent between the first and second quarters. Revenue increased by 6 percent.

4. Bring to class or submit online a document that you have written either in this (or another) class or at your job. Under the direction of your instructor, take the following steps:

   a. Create a rough outline of your document by writing a one-sentence summary of each paragraph in the order that the paragraphs appear.

  b. Determine whether your sequence of points is logical and effective.
  c. Make a note of any information that you could have added or deleted to make the document more effective.
  d. If you find a problem with the logic of the sequence or with the amount or type of information included or omitted in your paper, revise the outline and then your draft.

5. Bring to class or submit online a document that you have written either in this (or another) class or at your job. (You may use the same document you examined for Exercise 4 if you wish.) Under the direction of your instructor, take the following steps:

  a. Circle all the words or phrases that provide transition between sentences.
  b. If you find two sentences that do not have adequate transition, place an X in the space between them.
  c. For sentences that seem not to have adequate transition, insert a word, phrase, or clause that will improve the transition.

6. To persuade readers to take a specific course of action, successful workplace writers support their suggestions with evidence. When such details are missing in a first draft, they must be added at the revision stage. Referring to the opening and closing paragraphs you wrote for Exercises 1 and 2 in Chapter 3, outline and draft a letter that takes into account the following questions:

  a. What concrete details can you include in your letter to persuade your audience?
  b. What specific examples, facts, and statistics will you include as evidence?
  c. What point of view (first person, second person, or third person) would be most effective for your purpose?

7. Rewrite the following sentences to eliminate excessive subordination.

  a. The duty officer who was on duty at 3:30 a.m. was the one who took the call that there was a malfunction in the Number 3 generator that had been repaired at approximately 9:00 a.m. the previous morning.
  b. I have referred your letter that you wrote to us on June 20 to our staff attorney who reviewed it in the light of corporate policy that is pertinent to the issue that you raise.

8. Each of the following sentences contains a redundant word, phrase, or clause. Rewrite the sentences to eliminate the redundant elements.

  a. We began the project in the month of April.
  b. He opened the conversation with a reference to the subject of inflation.
  c. The field of engineering is a profession that offers great opportunities.
  d. The human-resources manager spoke to the printing-plant supervisor with regard to the scheduling of employee vacations.
  e. Our experienced salespeople, who have many years of work behind them, will plan an aggressive advertising campaign to sell the new product.

9. The following passages contain unnecessary jargon, padded phrases, and affectation. Revise the passages.

  a. I hereby designate Mr. Samson, who has been holding the position and serving in the capacity of assistant technical supervisor, to be named and appointed to the position and function of deputy director of customer relations. In his newly elevated position Mr. Samson will report, in the first instance, directly to the department director — that is, to me.

b. Purchasers of the enclosed substance should carefully and thoroughly follow the instructions provided herein for the use of the substance, and should in no case whatsoever consume, or otherwise partake of, said substance without proceeding in the manner set forth on the accompanying circular of instructions.

10. Some of the following sentences violate the principles of parallel structure. Identify the incorrect sentences and revise to make them parallel. The sentences may be correctly changed in more than one way.

a. We expected to be disappointed and that we would reject the proposal.
b. Etiquette is important in social life, and you need it in business too.
c. To type fast is one thing, but typing accurately is another.
d. Do you prefer filing, typing, or balancing the budget?
e. Is your home well-heated and with adequate ventilation?
f. The mailing notation should not only appear on the original but also on the copies.
g. The office has not only been cleaned but also newly decorated.
h. Our friends enjoy winter sports like hockey, skiing, and to skate.
i. Ms. Jory either wants Anna or me to proofread the galleys for our annual report.
j. The desk was neither the correct size nor the right model.
k. You may either send a check or a money order.
l. We are afraid that either the package is lost or stolen.

Collaborative Classroom Projects

ON THE WEB

For more collaborative classroom projects, go to Chapter 4, bedfordstmartins.com/ writingthatworks

1. Affected language can confuse both native and nonnative speakers. During the next 15 minutes, in groups try to figure out common proverbs buried in these overwritten substitutes. Then, translate these proverbs and put them into regular sentences that might appear in a business-oriented document. When finished, exchange papers with members of your group to evaluate the results.

EXAMPLE   Everything that coruscates with effulgence is not ipso facto aureous.

TRANSLATION   Everything that glitters is not gold.

REWRITE   Sometimes things that appear valuable are not as valuable as they seem: "Despite the large amount of advertising and public relations that went into the shoe company's new product line, the design of its new athletic shoes is really not appealing to consumers."

a. Never calculate the possible number of juvenile poultry until the usual period of incubation has been accomplished.
b. People who reside in transparent domiciles should not cast geological specimens.
c. The warm-blooded, feathered, egg-laying vertebrate animal that is among the first invariably comes in the possession of a small, legless crawling invertebrate animal.

   d. Where there is gaseous evidence of flammable matter, there is an indicated insinuation of incendiary pyrotechnic.

   e. Ornithological specimens of identical plumage tend to congregate in close proximity.

   f. Do not utter loud or passionate vocal expressions because of the accidental overturning of a receptacle containing a whitish nutritive liquid.

   g. Do not traverse a structure erected to afford passage over a waterway prior to the time of drawing nigh to the same.

   h. Hemoglobin is incapable of being extracted from the edible root of brassica rapa.

2. Rewrite each of the following sentences so that the verb is in the active voice. Whenever a potential subject is not given in a sentence, supply one as you write. When you have finished your sentences, divide into groups to share and discuss them. Is there much variation in the wording of your sentences? Is the meaning of the sentence affected by the differences in wording? Is a different tone implied?

   a. The entire building was spray-painted by Charles and his brother.

   b. It was assumed by the superintendent that the trip was postponed until next Tuesday.

   c. The completed form should be submitted to Tim Hagen by the 15th of every month.

   d. The fluid should be applied sparingly and should be allowed to dry for eight to ten seconds.

   e. The metropolitan area was defined as groups of counties related by commuting patterns by the researchers.

ON THE WEB

For extra research projects, go to Chapter 4, bedfordstmartins.com/writingthatworks

▦ Research Projects

1. As discussed in this chapter, affected language is very hard to read. In small groups, visit the U.S. government's Plain Language Web site at <www.plainlanguage.gov>, which has as its purpose "to promote the use of plain language for all government communications." Divide the work so that each person does one of the following tasks: researches the history of Plain Language, describes what it is, examines samples of government documents written before and in Plain Language style, or makes a list of ways to use Plain Language. Write a draft of your findings and be ready to submit them to the class for peer review. See Project 3 for more topics.

2. Find a document (instructions, direct-mail advertising, or other sample) or Web site that you believe demonstrates one or more of the ethical problems discussed in this chapter: using language that attempts to evade responsibility, to mislead the audience, to deemphasize or suppress important information, or to emphasize misleading or incorrect information. As your instructor directs, (a) report what ethical problems you see and describe how the document might be revised to eliminate those problems, and (b) rewrite the samples to eliminate the ethical problems.

3. Following up on Research Project 1, in your groups go to at least two federal or state government agency Web sites and review their Plain Language guidelines. You can find them by typing "Plain Language Initiative" into a search engine. What

are these government agencies, and what is the purpose of their communication with U.S. citizens? What guidelines are these agencies implementing? What are the agencies' goals in implementing these guidelines as they relate to U.S. citizens reading their material? Take your findings and add them to the draft of the document you wrote earlier about Plain Language. Have another group proofread your work, using the Proofreading in Stages checklist on page 116. (Your instructor can determine if your work should be peer reviewed in stages by different groups.) Distribute your final document or present your findings to the class, as your instructor directs. (You may want to review Chapter 14, Giving Presentations and Conducting Meetings.)

4. Consider that you work for an employment agency that specializes in recruiting nursing staff for major hospitals. Your company needs to hire a variety of different types of nurses (prenatal, triage, and so on) in the coming months, and you are part of a committee that is working to find the best candidates. The lead recruiter is concerned because this is a competitive market and your company's online ads have not been attracting the most qualified candidates. For example, one of the ads reads: "Desperately need hospital nurses for multiple locations and shifts. We offer lots of benefits like daily pay, 401(k), and uniform programs!"

   a. You have been asked to review the ads of local hospitals and competing employment agencies to see why their recruitment efforts are more successful. Go to the Web sites of several local hospitals and nursing employment agencies and make notes about their nursing ads (be careful to note what kind of nurse each ad refers to) and compare them to one another.

   b. In a memo to the lead recruiter, discuss the lack of content in your company's ad. Based on your research, revise this ad for a particular type of nurse so that it attracts the right candidates and persuades them to contact your employment agency. As you prepare your recommendation, refer to the section on Content and Organization on pages 96–97.

PART 2

Essential Skills: Collaboration, Research, and Design

Chapter 5
Collaborative Writing, 129

Chapter 6
Researching Your Subject, 148

Chapter 7
Designing Effective Documents and Visuals, 209

While Part One discussed the general principles that apply to all on-the-job writing, Part Two focuses on skills that you will need to approach more complex projects requiring collaboration, research, and design. The following chapters will help you prepare for the specific writing and communicating presented in Part Three—such as writing correspondence, reports, and proposals, and developing presentations.

◆ **Collaboration.** Chapter 5 discusses the importance of writing strategies learned in Chapters 1 through 4 to collaborative writing projects on the job, whether you are a member of a collaborative writing team or the team leader.

◆ **Research.** Chapter 6 provides extensive treatment of gathering information for your subject, including using the Internet and library, interviewing, using questionnaires, and making firsthand observations. You will also find advice for using the APA (American Psychological Association) and MLA (Modern Language Association) styles of documenting your research.

◆ **Design.** Chapter 7 gives detailed advice on designing effective documents— printed and electronic; developing informative and uncluttered illustrations, charts, and graphs; and successfully integrating them into your text. Attention to format and design is crucial to your success in creating instructions, reports, proposals, presentations, and other communications that are clear and appealing to your audience.

5 | Collaborative Writing

AT A GLANCE: Collaboration

Workplace writing is often collaborative writing—working with other people on a team to produce a single document. Like any team project, it requires the cooperation of people with different personalities and backgrounds working toward a common goal. Achieving the goal can be stressful but rewarding. This chapter describes the following classroom- and workplace-tested process for successful collaboration:

- Assessing the advantages and disadvantages of collaborative writing / 130
- Functioning as a collaborative writing team / 131
- Managing conflict / 137
- Leading a collaborative writing team / 139
- Collaborating with other departments / 141

On the job or in the classroom, no one works in a vacuum. To some degree, everyone must rely on the help of others to do his or her job. No matter what you write or how often you write, you will likely have to collaborate with other people. Collaborative writing occurs when two or more people work together, as a team, to produce a single document, with each team member contributing to the planning, designing, and writing. The teams that collaborate best are composed of people who are professionally competent, who have mutual respect for the abilities of the other members, and who are compatible enough to work together harmoniously toward a common goal. It also involves sharing equal responsibility for the end product.

Collaborative writing is generally done for one of three reasons:

1. The project requires expertise or specialization in more than one subject area.
2. The project will benefit from merging different perspectives into a unified perspective.
3. The size of the project, time constraints, or importance of the project to your organization requires a team effort.

The larger and more important the document, the more likely it is to be produced collaboratively. Sales proposals, for example, often require contributions from many different types of experts (financial specialists, sales managers, systems analysts, engineers, lawyers, and so on). Formal reports and technical specifications are among other documents that are commonly written by teams. For collaborative writing projects, the writing process varies only by the

ON THE WEB

For online resources for writing collaboratively, go to Chapter 5, bedfordstmartins.com/ writingthatworks

addition of a team-review step; otherwise, the process itself is no different, consisting of planning, researching, writing, reviewing, and revising. Typically, one person edits the final draft to unify the writing style and manages the reproduction and distribution of the finished document.

VOICES IN THE WORKPLACE

Collaboration as a Fact of Life in the Workplace

In "Groupwork and Collaborative Writing," Brian Connery and John Vohs of the University of California, Davis, note the central role of collaborative writing in the workplace: "While we give lip service to the value of the rugged individual . . . the social reality is that for most of us the bulk of our professional lives will be spent working in cooperation and collaboration with others within committees, research teams, departments, professional societies, or corporations." They conclude emphatically by asserting, "Group work is here to stay. Get used to it."

From "Group Work and Collaborative Writing" cited from <http://dhc.ucdavis.edu/ vohs/index.html>.

Advantages and Disadvantages of Collaborative Writing

Collaborative writing offers many benefits.

- *Many minds are better than one.* Collaborative teams usually produce work that is considerably better than the work produced by any one member. Team members stimulate each other to consider ideas and perspectives different from those they would have explored individually.

- *Team members provide immediate feedback.* Collaborating is like having your own set of critics who have a personal stake in helping you do a good job. Even if it is sometimes contested and debated, feedback is one of the great advantages of collaborative writing. Fellow team members may detect problems with organization, clarity, logic, and substance— and point them out during review. Receiving multiple responses also makes criticism easier to take; if all team members make the same point, you can more readily accept its validity.

- *Team members play devil's advocate for each other.* That is, they take contrary points of view in an attempt to make certain that all important points are covered and that all potential problems have been exposed and resolved.

- *Team members help each other past the frustrations and stress of writing.* When one team member needs to make a decision, someone is always available to talk it through.

- *Team members write more confidently.* Knowing that peers are depending on your contribution and will offer constructive criticism—not to find fault but to make the end product better—reduces anxiety.

- *Team members develop a greater tolerance of and respect for the opinions of others.* Team members become more aware of and involved in the planning of a document than if they were working alone. The same is true of reviews and revisions.

The primary disadvantages of collaborative writing include the demand it can place on your time, energy, and ego as a writer. Conflicts can also arise when not all team members participate or share equally in the team's work. And unless the final document is edited for clarity and consistency, it will be difficult to read and possibly incorrect. These stresses are discussed on pages 137–138.

Functions of a Collaborative Writing Team

Writing teams collaborate on every facet of the writing process:

- Planning the document
- Researching the subject
- Writing the draft
- Reviewing the drafts of other team members
- Revising the draft on the basis of comments from all team members

Planning

The team collectively identifies the readers, purpose, and scope of the project. Collaborators work together to create a broad outline of the document to be produced, divide the work into segments, and assign each segment to individual team members, usually on the basis of their expertise.

In the preliminary planning stage, the team also produces a schedule for each stage of the project. The agreed-on schedule should include due dates for drafts, for team reviews of drafts, and for revisions. (Individual team members must plan how they will meet their assigned responsibilities.) The other team members will have the opportunity to comment on drafts and suggest improvements. A deadline missed by one person may hold up the work of the entire team, so all members must be familiar with the schedule and submit their drafts and revisions on time.

As part of the planning process, the team should also agree on a standard reference guide for style and format, such as the *Publication Manual of the American Psychological Association* or the *Chicago Manual of Style*. Because different members of the team are producing separate sections of the same document, the guidelines should provide for uniformity and consistency of style. Lacking a standard guide, the team should establish project style guidelines that address the following issues:

- Levels of headings and their style: all-capital letters, all underlined, first letter capitalized, boldfaced, italicized, or some combination of these
- Spacing and margin guidelines
- Research sources that must be cited and those that need not be cited
- Use of the active voice, the present tense, and the imperative mood
- Format for References or Works Cited (if they are used)
- Capitalization of words in the text (A.M. versus a.m.)
- Abbreviations, acronyms, and symbols
- Standards for terms that should be written as one word, two words, or hyphenated (*on site/onsite, e-mail/email, on-line/online*)
- Number standards (when to spell out or use numerals)
- Format and wording of disclaimers (to satisfy legal or policy requirements)

◆ *Read pages 523–533 in Chapter 14, Giving Presentations and Conducting Meetings, before calling your first meeting.*

ON THE WEB

For a list of standard reference guides, go to Chapter 5, bedfordstmartins.com/ writingthatworks

◆ *The revision strategies outlined in Chapter 4, Revising the Draft, work well for most collaborative work.*

To achieve consistency, consider using word-processing style templates to automate document layout and format. (For additional information, see Digital Tips: Designing Documents with a Word Processor, page 214, and Creating Styles and Templates, page 364.)

In addition, the team must agree on the format and handling of digital project files. The most efficient means of sharing drafts electronically is for everyone to use the same collaborative writing software. (For an overview of collaborative writing software, see Digital Tips: Using Collaborative Writing Software on page 133.) If that's not possible, the team must decide on an effective alternative. (To set up and share a document for electronic review, refer to Digital Tips: Using Word Processing to Review Collaborative Documents, page 136, and Using E-mail for Collaborative Writing, page 137.)

WRITER'S CHECKLIST
Planning a Collaborative Writing Project

✔ Establish guidelines to ensure that all team members are working toward the same goal and moving in the same direction.

✔ Agree on a standard reference guide for matters of style and format.

✔ Make sure that work assignments are appropriate to each person's particular talents.

✔ Establish a schedule that includes due dates for drafts, for team reviews of drafts, and for revisions.

✔ Agree on how to exchange digital project files and whether to use collaborative writing software.

@

DIGITAL TIPS: Using Collaborative Writing Software

Collaborative writing software helps teams of students, employees, researchers, and others work together on a common writing task. It allows collaboration on a task whether team members are in the same office building or in different countries—as long as they have access to the collaborative writing site. Like a word processor, collaborative writing software permits team members to draft, review, edit, and comment on their collective work, but it also enables live text chat for brainstorming ideas, collaborative editing in real time, version tracking ("Am I commenting on the third or fourth draft?"), calendars to alert users of due dates, and spreadsheets to track work schedules. Some systems give real-time alerts about content changes. The finished documents can be exported to word-processing file formats.

Some collaborative writing software is Web-based and some is located only on a corporate, university, or government-agency network. Free and fee-based systems are also available. For links to additional information about collaborative writing software, see <bedfordstmartins.com/writingthatworks> and select *Digital Tips*, "Collaborative Writing Software Links."

Wikis, a related collaborative writing technology, are Web sites that host collaborative writing projects. They too may be public access (e.g., Wikipedia) or private only, such as those maintained on a company intranet. For detailed advice about creating and editing documents in a wiki, see <bedfordstmartins .com/writingthatworks> and select *Digital Tips*, "Using Wikis for Collaborative Work."

Research and Writing

The planning stage is followed by the research and writing stages. These are periods of intense independent activity by the individual team members. At this point, you gather and research information for your assigned segment of the document, create a master outline of the segment, flesh out the outline by providing the necessary details, and produce a first draft.

Collaboration requires flexibility. The team should not insist that individual members rigidly follow an agreed-on outline if it proves to be inadequate or faulty in one or more areas. For instance, a writer may find that the general outline for his or her segment was based on insufficient knowledge and is not appropriate, or even accurate, as written. During the research process, in particular, a writer may discover highly relevant information that is not covered in the team's working outline. In such cases, the writer must have the freedom to alter the outline. If the deviation is great enough, or will change other parts of the document, the writer should consult with the other team members before proceeding.

Revise your draft until it is as good as you can make it. Then, by the deadline established, send copies of the draft to all other team members for their review. You may circulate the draft by distributing hard copy, by sending an attachment through e-mail, or by sharing files in a collaborative writing system.

◆ *For guidelines on planning and writing a rough draft, see Chapters 2, Organizing Your Information, and Chapter 3, Writing the Draft.*

◆ *For a detailed explanation of the research process, see Chapter 6, Researching Your Subject.*

Review and Revision

During the review stage, team members try to address any questions that might arise for a given reader—a customer, a senior official in the organization, or the board of directors, for example. Each team member reviews the work of the other team members carefully and critically (but also with sensitivity to the person whose work is being reviewed), checking for problems in content, organization, and style. A good reviewer evaluates a document in terms of audience, purpose, coherence, emphasis, and accuracy. (For a discussion of interacting productively with other members, see pages 137–138.) For a document intended for an international audience, this is the stage to have it reviewed by someone familiar with the country or culture of that audience.

The review stage may lead to additional planning. If, for example, a review of the first draft reveals that the original organization for a section was not adequate or correct or if new information becomes available, the team must return to the planning stage for that segment of the document to incorporate the newer knowledge and understanding.

Figures 5–1 and 5–2 represent one section of a proposal that was written by Brady Associates to persuade a prospective client to merge a company's profit-sharing plans. Two people collaborated to prepare the document; Figure 5–1 shows one team member's initial draft with the other's review comments, while Figure 5–2 on page 136 shows the revised section, addressing those draft comments. The proposal describes the merger process and shows its associated costs. Because the final report will be submitted to a company president whose time is limited and who has only a general knowledge of profit-sharing plans and mergers, the reviewer carefully noted any parts of the proposal that were not appropriate for a nonexpert reader.

Revising collaborative writing is much like revising any other type of writing: The writer considers suggested changes, checks questionable facts, and reworks the draft as appropriate. At this point, you, as a writer, must be careful not to let your ego get in the way of good judgment. You must consider each suggestion objectively on the basis of its merit, rather than reacting negatively to criticism of your writing. Writers who are able to accept criticism and use it to craft a better draft participate in the most productive kind of collaboration.

◆ *For a discussion of writing for international audiences, see page 70 of Chapter 3, Writing the Draft, and pages 343–351 of Chapter 9, Writing Business Correspondence.*

ON THE WEB

For a sample of a reviewer's handwritten comments on a draft, go to Model Documents Gallery, bedfordstmartins.com/ writingthatworks

WRITER'S CHECKLIST
Reviewing Drafts by Other Writers

✔   Does the draft meet the established purpose of the document?

✔   Does the draft meet the needs of the target audience?

✔   Does the material fall within the predetermined scope of coverage?

✔   Does the draft generally follow the agreed-on outline?

✔   Is the content complete?

✔   Does the draft contain technical errors? Does anything seem technically questionable?

✔   Do details and examples support the main points?

****DRAFT****

Part II. Merger of Plans/Amending and Restating Plans/Applications for Determination Letters

Comment [EMK1]: Title is too technical—"Costs/Benefits of Merging"?

We can no longer test the Oakite product services 401(k) Profit Sharing

Plan separately for coverage and nondiscrimination because combined,

Oakite products and Oakley services have fewer than 50 employees.

The merger of the 401(k) Profit Sharing Plans takes care of this problem

while reducing the implementation and audit costs. We will need to amend

and restate the new plan to bring it into compliance with tax law 409921-65.

Comment [WO2]: This is covered in Part I (make this into transition).

Comment [WO3]: sp

Comment [WO4]: #

The cost of merging, amending, restating, and redesigning the surviving

401(k) Profit Sharing Plan and for filing of notices 54-90 and 36-98 and

applications 56-98 and 45-98 would be between $18,000 and $25,000.

Comment [EMK5]: Too technical and you need to emphasize benefits.

Comment [WO6]: Cost reduction over 2 years

Team members comment on need to clarify title, eliminate redundancy, and sharpen focus on topic.

Additional Comments: Team Member #2 (B. Reisner, Sales Development)

Information sounds correct, but the prospective client will need definitions and explanations for many terms and names (notices 54-90 and 36-98). Also I suggest noting in your opening that Part I explains the problems associated with maintaining separate plans. Doing so will give you a better lead into your section than you've got at this point.

Further, break down specific financial costs and benefits that will result from the merger. Don't go into detail here; remember, Part III describes the details of the merger process. Simply note specific costs for specific services in a table, and give an estimate of the client's projected financial gain. NOTE: The range for costs is $19,000 to $26,000, not $18,000 to $25,000. CHECK: Can client deduct merger costs from gross profit?

Finally, I think it would be good to promote our services with more vigor. You're not simply re-porting information so that Mr. B. can phone up another company to do the merger—you're talking him into working with Brady Associates.

Figure 5–1 Draft Section of a Proposal, with Comments of a Team Member

Note new title

Introduction sharpens focus on problem and proposed solution

PART II. BENEFITS AND COSTS OF MERGING CURRENT PROFIT-SHARING PLANS

As Part I of this report explains, the separate profit-sharing plans for your two companies, Oakite Products and Oakley Services, can no longer ensure that each employee is assigned the correct number of shares and the correct employer contribution. In addition, administrative costs for maintaining separate plans are high. If you commissioned Brady Associates to merge the plans, however, adequate tests could be performed to ensure accuracy, and administrative costs would be greatly reduced. Further, although a merger would require you to make certain changes to your current profit-sharing procedures, Brady Associates would help you amend and restate the new plan so that it complies with the most recent tax legislation.

Second paragraph revised to clarify additional advantages of merging plans

Brady Associates will also prepare and file necessary merger documents with the Departments of Taxation and Labor. The estimated cost for merging, amending, and refiling the profit-sharing plans would be between $19,000 and $26,000. Please see Table 1 for a breakdown of specific costs.

Strengthens case for Brady's services by including specific expenses and savings

Because of reduced administrative costs, you would in reality incur no cost if Brady Associates merged your profit-sharing plans. According to our estimates, the merger would give you a yearly net reduction of $36,000 in administrative costs. Thus, you would save approximately $11,000 during the first year of administering the plan and at least $36,000 annually after the first year. See Table 2 for a breakdown of net reductions in administrative costs.

Figure 5–2   Revised Section of Draft Proposal in Figure 5–1

DIGITAL TIPS: Using Word Processing to Review Collaborative Documents

Adobe Acrobat and many word-processing packages have options for providing feedback on the drafts of collaborators' documents. You can add text or voice annotations to the text, allowing your readers to read or hear your comments; you can also add track changes in your text and allow readers to accept or reject each change. In Acrobat, you can use a drawing tool to input traditional proofreaders' marks. For more on this topic, see <bedfordstmartins.com/writingthatworks> and select *Digital Tips*, "Reviewing Collaborative Documents."

VOICES IN THE WORKPLACE

Collaboration in a Global Economy

Ulrike Mueller, a senior information developer in Germany, comments on the complexities of international collaborative work in her management of a team of technical writers based in Ireland: "In our case, working for a global player, you might have to deal with different time zones, different cultures, and different mentalities and work ethics. All this creates a need for more coordination. . . . Toward the end of the project, more time needs to be spent on aligning the different parts [of the document] and making it coherent in style."

> **@ DIGITAL TIPS: Using E-mail for Collaborative Writing**
>
> - E-mail encourages members of a collaborative writing team to communicate with each other often, share information, ask questions, and solve problems.
> - A draft sent as an attachment enables collaborative team members to solicit feedback electronically and revise the original draft based on comments received.
> - Individual team members can solicit feedback and revise accordingly until all sections are in final form and ready for consolidation into the master copy maintained by the team leader.
> - The team leader should rename each draft with the revision number (for example, "merger proposal—rev 3") so that team members know they are working on the latest version.
> - Although e-mail can reduce the frequency of face-to-face communication, it does not eliminate the need for a group to meet in person when possible, especially during project planning periods.

The Role of Conflict in Collaborative Writing

It is critically important to the quality of any team-written document that all contributors' viewpoints be considered. However, when writers collaborate, conflicts occur. These may range from a relatively minor difference over a grammatical point (such as whether to split an infinitive) to a major conflict over the basic approach to a document (such as how much detail is necessary). Regardless of the severity of a conflict, it must be worked through to a conclusion or compromise that all team members can accept, even though all might not entirely agree. When a group can tolerate some disharmony and work through conflicting opinions to reach a consensus, the final document benefits.

Although mutual respect among team members is necessary, too much deference can inhibit challenges—and that reduces the team's creativity. You have to be willing to challenge another team member's work while still being sensitive to that person's ego. The same rule applies to collaborative writing that applies whenever critical give-and-take occurs: Focus on the problem and how to solve it rather than on the person.

Conflicts over valid issues almost always generate more innovative and creative work than does passive acceptance. However, even though the result of conflict in a peer-writing team is usually positive, it can sometimes produce doubt about yourself or your team members. Remember that conflict is a natural part of group work. Learn to harness it and turn it into a positive force.

To maximize the benefits and minimize the negative effects of conflict, the team members should emphasize areas of agreement. They then should identify differences of opinion and ask why they exist. If differences occur over facts, simply determine which are or are not correct. If there is a problem of differing goals, review the project's purpose statement to ensure common understanding. When conflict arises for other reasons, define the problem, describe or brainstorm possible solutions, and select the one solution—or compromise—that best satisfies the views of each team member and of the overall team.

The following suggestions can help you manage conflict:

- Avoid taking a win-or-lose stand, which gains one person's victory at another person's expense. This approach is not constructive because, by definition, there must be a loser. Most conflicts don't start out this way, but when a team member faces personal defeat, reaching a productive compromise is almost impossible.

- Avoid accusations, threats, or disparaging comments. Instead, emphasize common interests and mutual goals, bearing in mind that conciliation fosters cooperation. Expressing a desire for harmonious relations can have a very disarming effect on an aggressive personality in the group.

- Support your position with facts. Show how your position is consistent with precedent, prevailing norms, or accepted standards (if true, of course). Point out the ways that your position could benefit the team's ultimate goal and tactfully point out any disadvantages or logic errors in the other person's point of view. Again, focus on the problem and its solution, not on the person.

- Use bargaining strategies to arrive at an exchange of concessions until a compromise is reached. Both parties win through a compromise. Even if you settle for less than you initially wanted, you don't risk losing out altogether as in a win-or-lose struggle. A successful compromise satisfies each participant's minimum needs.

Used well, collaboration resolves conflicts. Each team member must accept the group's goals, and all must work to achieve the best outcome for the team. A flexible, exploratory attitude is a prerequisite for collaboration; always strive to understand each other's points of view and meet the group's needs.

WRITER'S CHECKLIST
Working in a Collaborative Group

✔ Know the people on your team and establish a good working rapport with them.

✔ Put the interests of your team ahead of your own.

✔ Think collectively, as a group, but respect the views of members with subject-area expertise.

✔ Participate constructively in group meetings.

✔ Be an effective listener (see pages 516–519 in Chapter 14, Giving Presentations and Conducting Meetings).

✔ Be receptive to constructive criticism.

✔ Provide constructive feedback to your team members.

✔ Meet your established deadlines.

▪ Leading a Collaborative Writing Team

Although the team may designate one person as its leader, that person shares decision-making authority with the others while assuming the responsibility for coordinating the team's activities, organizing the project, and producing the final product. Leadership can be granted by mutual agreement to one team member or it can be rotated if the team produces many documents over time.

On a practical level, the team leader's responsibilities include scheduling and leading meetings, writing and distributing minutes of meetings, and maintaining the master copy of the document during all stages of its development. To make these activities as efficient as possible, the leader should prepare and distribute forms to track the project's status. These forms should include style guidelines mutually agreed to in the project planning meeting (covering the issues listed on page 132), a project schedule, and transmittal sheets to record the status of reviews. Collaborative writing software systems usually include a calendar for posting due dates and tracking the status of writing projects.

Schedule

All team members must know not only what is expected of them but when it is expected. The schedule provides this information. Schedules come in different formats. Figure 5–3, for example, shows a schedule used for a team project for a business-writing class. Figure 5–4 on page 140 shows a bar-chart schedule for the production of a software user's manual that required coordination among the

Project due dates

Project Schedule

January 4:	Assignments
	Introduction—Raveen
	Theory section—Jeff
	Methods section—Carina
February 1:	Sections to coauthors for review
February 15:	Sections returned to coauthors for revision
March 1:	Sections to instructor
March 1:	Assignments
	Tutorial—Raveen
	Parts list—Jeff
	Appendix—Carina
March 15:	Sections to coauthors for review
April 1:	Sections returned to coauthors for revision
April 15:	Sections to instructor

Project members and assignments

Figure 5–3   Project Schedule (Class Project)

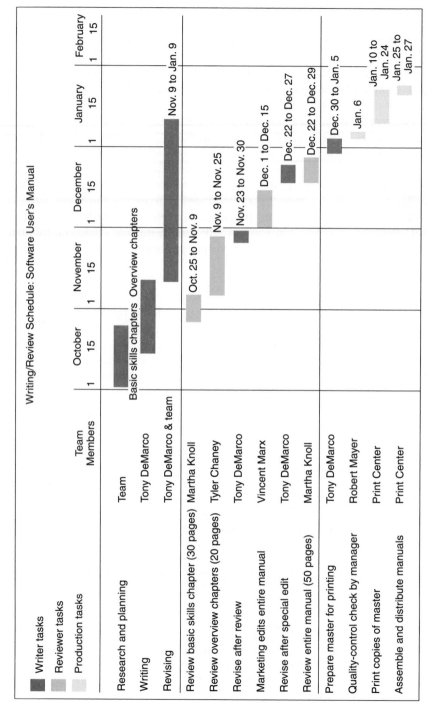

Figure 5–4   Project Schedule Presented as a Bar Chart (Workplace Project)

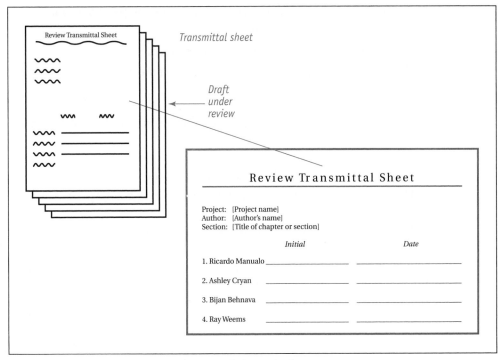

Transmittal sheet

Draft under review

Review Transmittal Sheet

Project: [Project name]
Author: [Author's name]
Section: [Title of chapter or section]

	Initial	Date
1. Ricardo Manualo		
2. Ashley Cryan		
3. Bijan Behnava		
4. Ray Weems		

Figure 5–5   Review Transmittal Sheet Attached to a Draft

writing, review, and production staffs over a five-month period. Regardless of the format, the schedule must state explicitly who is responsible for what and when the draft of each section is due.

Review Transmittal Sheet

If drafts will be circulated on paper, the team leader should provide review transmittal sheets. Writers attach the sheets to their drafts or to a file folder or an envelope that holds the draft. Each reviewer signs off after reviewing the draft, then distributes it to the next reviewer on the list. The review transmittal sheet shows at a glance where the project is in its progression through the review cycle. It also lists in order those who must review the draft, as shown in Figure 5–5.

▩ Collaborating with Other Departments

In some work settings, writing-team leaders also arrange for the cooperation of different departments within the organization in the creation or publication of final documents. For example, the team leader may need to meet with art, media, or Web production staff to do the following:

- Plan for the creation of graphs, charts, drawings, maps, and so on.
- Plan for the document's cover.
- Arrange for photographs to be taken or scanned.
- Determine the date and file format for posting the document to the organization's Web site.

The team leader may also meet with print production staff or the off-site printer to do the following:

- Inform the staff or the printer when to expect the manuscript.
- Discuss any special printing requirements, such as color, special binding, document size, foldout pages, and so on.
- Ensure that the publication date meets the project deadline.

◆ *For guidance on posting documents to Web sites, see pages 554–555 in Chapter 15, Writing for the Web.*

In addition, the team leader may need to obtain reviews and approval from other departments, such as the sales and legal departments. (In the classroom, your instructor or group team leader may take these roles.)

CHAPTER 5 SUMMARY: COLLABORATIVE WRITING

Form a collaborative writing team when:

- Your project requires specialists in more than one subject area.
- Your project would benefit from the merging of different perspectives.
- Your project's size, importance, or deadline requires a team effort.

As a member of a collaborative writing team, you are expected to:

- Work with others as a team of peers to plan, design, and write a single document.
- Ensure that all important points are discussed and that all problems are addressed.
- Research the topics of your assigned section.
- Write your draft.
- Review the work of other team members.
- Revise your draft based on comments from other team members.
- Maintain the project schedule.
- Share equal responsibility for the end product.
- Respect the opinions of others.

As a team leader, you are expected to:

- Share decision-making authority with other team members.
- Coordinate the activity of team members.
- Maintain the project schedule.
- Coordinate the production of the final product.

ON THE WEB

For an online quiz on collaborative writing, go to Chapter 5, bedfordstmartins.com/ writingthatworks

▨ Exercises

ON THE WEB

For additional exercises, go to Chapter 5, bedfordstmartins.com/writingthatworks

1. a. Draft a 300-word summary of a news article related to a professional or technical development, then exchange it with a study partner by e-mail. Review each other's work, make suggestions for revision, and return the file by e-mail. Refer to Digital Tips: Using Collaborative Writing Software, page 133, and Using E-mail for Collaborative Writing, page 137. Together decide which method you will use to mark the files. Also review the Reviewing Drafts by Other Writers checklist on page 134.
    b. Bring a hard-copy draft of your writing assignment to class and exchange it with another student or share it with another student if taking an online course. Each student makes comments and suggestions for revision and returns the draft for rewriting.

2. Schedule a telephone, an e-mail, or a personal interview with a health-care, a business, a technology, or an industry representative who is part of a collaborative writing team. Before the interview, review this chapter to help you prepare a list of questions to ask about details of the collaborative writing style used by his or her group or company. Keep your interview to no more than 20 to 30 minutes. Consider asking about planning meetings and how they are conducted, collaboration with other specialists or peer reviews, preparing drafts of documents and how they are circulated and commented on for revision, and any positive or negative experiences your interviewee found most helpful during the collaborative writing process. After the interview, prepare an outline, a draft, and a final report on your findings. Be ready to share your interview report with your classmates, and send the person you interviewed a thank-you letter.

3. Assume that a group of you work as staff in your school's career-development center and you are concerned about some students not getting interviews. You call various recruiters and find out that they are turned off by the students' use of emoticons and silly addresses in their e-mail messages. Collaborate with classmates to develop a memo that could be sent to all students, advising them of proper e-mail etiquette. (You may want to review Structuring Effective Correspondence on pages 283–293 in Chapter 8, Understanding the Principles of Business Communication.)

4. Form a collaborative writing team with your classmates based on common occupational interests, such as agriculture, communications, early childhood education, or engineering. Assume that you have been asked by your university's recruiting staff to create a document based on your experience as a student, explaining why your campus is a great place to prepare for the occupational interest you and your team have chosen. In your group, appoint a team leader and a team recorder, and decide how to organize and write this assignment so that recruiters can use your material to persuade students to attend your university.

5. Write a brief narrative explaining why collaborative writing experiences are (or are not) a productive part of learning business-writing skills. Review this chapter before you begin your draft, then use your own academic and on-the-job collaborative writing experiences as a basis for your conclusions.

6. Collaborate with a classmate to develop a process that your class can follow to review and comment on each other's written work. Before you begin, review this

chapter. Then create an outline and a rough draft for a plan that facilitates peer feedback. Highlight the specific benefits of your plan and be ready to share your plan with the rest of the class.

7. Form a collaborative group of no more than six members in which both genders are represented equally. Appoint a group leader and a group recorder. Based on your personal experiences, brainstorm as a group to create a list of gender-related issues that you have encountered as college students, such as the stereotyping of women and men with regard to verbal or mathematical abilities or technological skills. Use your collaborative lists to generate a brief report about these campus gender issues for your college's Office of Diversity (or comparable unit) that includes the ideas of each group member. Be ready to share your report with the rest of the class or write an individual report, summarizing the personal interactions of your group during your meetings.

ON THE WEB

For more collaborative classroom projects, go to Chapter 5, bedfordstmartins.com/ writingthatworks

▓ Collaborative Classroom Projects

1. An important stage of the collaborative writing process is the planning stage, during which time all members of the team need to work toward the same goal, select a reference guide, set up a schedule, and agree on how to enforce the standards that have been established. Assume that your manager has given you a collaborative writing assignment on a topic specific to the company's main product. In groups of five or fewer, take the next 30 minutes to do the following:

   a. Become acquainted with one another's expertise by asking each person to talk about his or her background for two minutes or less.
   b. Select a team leader.
   c. Decide the schedule for making initial assignments and submitting drafts, coauthor reviews, and revisions.
   d. Decide what method you will use to enforce the time line.
   e. Decide what other guidelines are necessary to ensure the group's success. Keep in mind that unstated policies can lead to confusion about responsibilities. Therefore, when your group has discussed project guidelines, the team leader will summarize these policies in a list.

2. Using the same group you selected for Collaborative Classroom Project 1, experiment with positive conflict, which almost always generates more innovative and creative work than does passive acceptance. Assuming that half of the members of your team have young children and half do not, as a team write a recommendation on whether your company should provide space for on-site day care. The parents on the team claim that an unused storage room in the building is large enough to accommodate a day-care center, while those without young children feel it would be more productive to convert the space into an employee lounge. As a team, spend 45 minutes developing an outline of the pros and cons for both sides of the issue.

   a. Quickly establish who is a parent of young children and who is not.
   b. Appoint a team leader.
   c. Brainstorm your list of pros and cons for first one side of the issue and then the other.

d. During the next 15 minutes, quickly draft your collaborative outline and be ready to share it with the class.

3. Imagine that several of you have been hired as a collaborative writing team for a national home décor and architecture magazine. This magazine has won awards for its high-end presentation of celebrity homes and parties, but its senior editor and upper management have recently been lured away by a competing publication. The last two issues have suffered as new hires and interns struggle to come up with successful story ideas, coordinate celebrity interviews and photo shoots, get error-free copy from advertisers and freelance writers on time, coordinate with the graphics department so that the issues are laid out properly, and meet the printer's deadlines. The magazine publisher is very worried about the upcoming holiday issue, which is usually popular with readers and advertisers.

Magazines typically have a six-month lead time. For example, December magazine articles are assigned to writers in July. Choose someone to be team leader, then using Figures 5–3, 5–4, and 5–5, create a schedule and transmittal sheets for the holiday issue. Decide on the final production deadline (when everything is ready to go to the printer) and then individual production deadlines for the following:

a. Help the editorial staff determine all of the copy (written material) that will be included in the issue, the dates freelance and staff writers need to start writing the copy, and the copy deadlines (make them due at least six weeks before the production due date). Don't forget the time the editorial staff will need to edit the copy and fact-check it. Create a Review Transmittal Sheet (see Figure 5–5) to ensure that all the editors, proofreaders, and fact-checkers have reviewed the drafts.

b. Help advertising staff determine the number of ads for this issue and make them due at least seven weeks before the production due date. Then help the graphics staff determine when they need to have the artwork for the ads (display artwork) completed (no more than a week or two after the ads come in). Remember to have the artwork and ads proofread by members of the editorial staff.

c. Help the graphics staff schedule the time needed to lay out the entire magazine and then have it proofread by members of the editorial staff to make sure that everything was included in the issue and that copy or ads weren't accidentally forgotten.

Research Projects

ON THE WEB

For extra research projects, go to Chapter 5, bedfordstmartins .com/writingthatworks

1. Form a collaborative writing team to research and write a major report for a department manager, recommending the purchase of laptop computers for traveling staff. In your proposal, identify the type and brand of computer you will be evaluating, as well as how and where you will gather information on the product (in person at a retail location, on the Internet, and so on).

a. Decide on a team leader and an evaluation board, then do the following:
   • Write a memo requesting your instructor's approval for your team to undertake the project and to evaluate specific computer brands and models.

- Create biweekly progress reports, to start as soon as your team has received project approval and to continue for the duration of the project.

b. Have the team leader delegate research responsibilities so that members are able to collect information that answers why the computers are needed and how many are needed; describe the specific features the portable computers should have (such as memory size, operating speed, and compatibility with personal computers already installed at the company); describe the types of software that should be installed; define what the total cost will be and whether an educational discount or a quantity discount is available; and explain how the computers should be kept secure and how borrowing them would be controlled.

c. Decide collaboratively on dates for submission of the proposal, progress reports (every two weeks from project approval), the final report, and the final presentation.

d. Present an oral description of your research to the other team members, as well as a report on the results of your preliminary evaluation. Each team member should do the same.

e. Have the team leader present the final results of the project and the recommendations to an evaluation board.

f. Finally, (1) prepare and submit a joint (single) copy of the proposal, progress reports, and formal report, and (2) make group oral presentations. Provide handouts of any printed information you have obtained or of any important text from your proposal (see page 511 in Chapter 14, Giving Presentations and Conducting Meetings). As a team, consider how much the visual appearance of your report will influence whether your recommendations receive approval. If the department manager likes what he or she reads, your report may be attached to his or her budget request to demonstrate why the computers are needed (this is commonly known as "the justification"). Consequently, the quality of your report, both in appearance and in content, can help convince those readers who will approve the expenditure for your request. Your instructor will award a group mark for each assignment, which all team members will receive.[1]

2. Teamwork is used in corporations around the globe. On your own or with a collaborative writing team, research at least two different countries' perspectives on the need for teamwork in the workplace. Compare your findings to the American perspective on teamwork in the workplace. Present your findings to the class. As your instructor directs, use some of the strategies from earlier collaborative assignments.

3. One of the major experts in teamwork and corporate success is W. E. Deming, who created total quality management (TQM). Form a collaborative group. Then research and write a report about Deming and TQM. The presentation should consist of an introduction and a conclusion and the following three parts that form the middle of the report:

---

[1]This project is adapted, with permission, from "An Integrated Collaborative Writing Project" by Ron S. Blicq, in *Collaborative Technical Writing: Theory and Practice*, ed. Richard Louth and Martin Scott (Hammond, La.: Association of Teachers of Technical Writing, n.d.), pp. 57–60.

    a. A definition and an explanation of TQM, with background on the history of TQM and its creator.

    b. An explanation of TQM's 14 principles and how TQM supports teamwork. Give examples of why companies like General Motors have used or continue to use TQM.

    c. An explanation of both the positive and the negative issues that need to be addressed regarding TQM or other teamwork programs. One might be that people from different cultures may have different problems adapting to teamwork. For example, many Amesricans value individualism, which may at times conflict with teamwork principles.

4. Many successful companies encourage collaborative writing on the job. Search the Web to learn how such companies advertise their team approach when hiring. You might explore the job listings on Web sites for companies such as Saturn and the Kimberly-Clark Corporation, as well as the job descriptions on career sites such as Monster.com and HotJobs.com. Outline the kinds of collaborative writing assignments that a writer at a particular company might encounter. Your outline should cover areas such as product information, warranty information, employment training, management styles, and so on.

6 Researching Your Subject

AT A GLANCE: Research

This chapter discusses tools, strategies, and resources for researchers of various levels of expertise.

- Conducting primary research / 149
  - Drawing on your experience / 150
  - Conducting interviews / 150
  - Making firsthand observations / 152
  - Drafting questionnaires / 152
- Conducting secondary research / 157
  - Developing a search strategy / 157
  - Using the library / 158
  - Searching the Internet / 166
- Evaluating, recording, and acknowledging sources / 171
  - Evaluating print or online sources / 171
  - Taking notes / 174
  - Quoting sources / 176
  - Paraphrasing sources / 178
  - Summarizing sources / 179
  - Avoiding plagiarism / 180
- Documenting sources, including guidelines and model citations / 181
  - The American Psychological Association (APA) style / 182
  - The Modern Language Association (MLA) style / 193
  - Other style manuals / 203

Tom Cabines, production manager of Nebel Desktop Publishers, received a memo from Alice Enklend, purchasing director, asking him how many copies of an employee manual a corporate customer had commissioned the firm to print. Tom probably had the answer at his fingertips or was able to find it after a quick look at his computer's production-scheduling spreadsheet. Tom's *research*—or tracking down of information on the topic—would be minimal.

Suppose, instead, that Tom were asked to write a market-research report for the president of Nebel about developing a Web publishing division. How would he go about obtaining the necessary information? For this task, he would have to do some extensive work, which could involve primary research—conducting interviews or collecting questionnaire responses on the topic—or secondary research—gathering information from the Internet, the library, or both.

ON THE WEB

For online resources for conducting research, go to Chapter 6, bedfordstmartins .com/writingthatworks

VOICES IN THE WORKPLACE

Using the Internet for Legal Research

Susan Ladwig, associate attorney in the Employee Benefits Department at Reinhard Boerner Van Deuren in Milwaukee, Wisconsin, notes that legal research is essential to her job: "The Internet has become a basic research tool for attorneys who must quickly access the most up-to-date information on law changes, corporations, court decisions, and various legal subjects. Learning how to critically evaluate and efficiently gather key data from the Internet is an important skill."

■ Conducting Primary Research: Experience, Interviews, Observations, and Questionnaires

Primary research is the gathering of raw data from such sources as firsthand experience, interviews, direct observations, and questionnaires. In fact, direct observation and interaction are the only ways to obtain certain kinds of information, such as human and animal behavior, natural phenomena, and the operation of systems and equipment. For example, you might use primary research to test the usability of instructions you have created to submit quarterly financial data to an updated spreadsheet system.

◆ *For more on usability testing, see pages 442–443 in Chapter 12, Writing Instructions.*

In college, you may talk about resources with your peers, your instructors, and especially a research librarian. On the job, you may rely on your own knowledge and experience and that of your colleagues. In business, the most important sources of information may include market research, questionnaires and surveys, focus groups, public meetings, shareholder meetings, and the like. In this setting, begin by brainstorming with colleagues about what sources will be most useful for your project and how you can track them down.

ETHICS NOTE

If you are conducting an observation or distributing a questionnaire at your university or college, ask your instructor whether you need to file an application with your school's Institutional Review Board (IRB). (An IRB reviews all research studies that involve human subjects and animals.) This may be necessary if you plan to present or publish the results of your research, but it may not be required for an in-class project.

Beginning with Experience

If your research topic deals with something familiar (a hobby or an area of inter-est, for example) or relates to an occupation you are in or hope to be in, you may already know enough to get started. In addition, you can check your home or of-fice files for any materials you have acquired on the subject. Based on this back-ground, make a rough outline—it will tell you how much you know about the topic. Your own experience is a starting point from which you can expand your knowledge by finding and using other sources discussed in this chapter.

◆ *For detailed advice on using outlines, see pages 26–34 in Chap-ter 2, Organizing Your Information.*

Interviewing for Information

To learn from the experience of others, you may be able to do some of your re-search by interviewing someone who is an expert on the subject. This process includes determining the proper person to interview, preparing for the inter-view, conducting the interview, and expanding your notes immediately after the interview.

Determining Whom to Interview

Many times, your subject or purpose logically points to the proper person to in-terview for information. If, for instance, you were writing about how to use the Web to market a software-development business, the logical experts to interview would include someone with extensive experience in Web marketing and some-one who has built a successful business developing software. The following sources can help you identify an appropriate person to interview: (1) workplace colleagues or faculty in relevant academic departments, (2) a local firm or orga-nization whose staff includes experts on your subject, (3) information from Internet research, (4) local chapters or Web sites of professional societies, and (5) Yellow or business pages of the local telephone directory.

@

DIGITAL TIPS: Using E-mail to Ask Questions

Even if geography or scheduling prevents you from interviewing an expert in per-son, you may be able to ask some questions through e-mail. To locate an expert's e-mail address, check company, organization, or university Web sites, which often include staff directories with contact information. Many scholarly publications, par-ticularly in the sciences, include the author's e-mail address; these addresses are often available in specialized library databases.

When sending questions by e-mail, be as concise and informative as possible in the Subject line. Send the request from your school or work e-mail account to avoid the impression that your request is spam, and do not include any attachments. In the body of your message, briefly describe your quest, write out a few questions, and ask your expert for a referral if he or she is unable to respond. (See also pages 321–324 in Chapter 9, Writing Business Correspondence.) Above all, remember that the person you're writing to is not obligated to answer your e-mail. To improve your chances of a reply, be brief, clear, and respectful.

Preparing for the Interview

Once you have selected the person or persons you would like to interview, learn as much as possible about each person and the organization for which he or she works. When you contact the prospective interviewee, explain who you are, why you would like to interview him or her, the subject and purpose of the interview, and how much time it will take.

After you have made the appointment, prepare a list of questions to ask your interviewee. Avoid vague, general questions such as "What do you think of the Internet?" Instead, ask specific but open-ended questions such as "How do you use your Web site to help clients?" and "Do your Web site's usage statistics help focus your organization's customer communications?" Such questions prompt interviewees to provide specific information. Organize your questions so that you begin with the least complex aspects of the topic, then move to the more complex aspects.

ETHICS NOTE

Aim for accuracy as you take notes to avoid misrepresenting or misquoting your source. If you plan to record the interview, obtain the interviewee's permission to do so beforehand. Also let your interviewee know that you will allow him or her to review your draft if possible given your deadline.

Conducting the Interview

Arrive for your interview on time and be prepared to guide the discussion. Once you've introduced yourself, take a few minutes to chat informally — this will help both you and your interviewee to relax. During the interview, follow the guidelines listed in the Writer's Checklist: Interviewing Successfully.

◆ *See also pages 516–519 in Chapter 14, Giving Presentations and Conducting Meetings.*

WRITER'S CHECKLIST
Interviewing Successfully

✔ Be pleasant but purposeful. You are there to get information, so don't be timid about asking leading questions on the subject.

✔ Use the list of questions you have prepared, starting with the less complex or controversial aspects of the topic to get the conversation started and then going on to the more complex or controversial aspects.

✔ Let your interviewee do most of the talking. Remember that he or she is the expert.

✔ Be objective. Don't offer your opinions on the subject. You are there to get information, not to debate.

✔ Some answers prompt additional questions; ask them as they arise.

✔ Stay on track. If the interviewee strays too far from the subject, ask a specific question to redirect the conversation.

✔ Be flexible. If a prepared question is no longer suitable, move to the next question.

✔ Do not let a tape recorder lull you into relaxing so that you neglect to ask crucial questions.

✔ As the interview comes to a close, take a few minutes to skim your notes. If time allows, ask the interviewee to clarify anything that is ambiguous. After thanking the interviewee, ask if you can telephone or e-mail with a follow-up query to clarify a point or two as you complete your interview notes.

Expanding Your Notes After the Interview

Immediately after leaving the interview, use your memory-jogging notes to help you mentally go over the interview and record your detailed notes. Review your notes, fill in any material that is obviously missing, and summarize the speaker's remarks. Do not postpone this step. No matter how good your memory is, you will forget some important points if you do not do this at once. As soon as possible, convert the notes to complete sentences. Select the important information you need and transfer it to your outline or working draft.

A day or two after the interview, thank the interviewee in a brief letter or e-mail.

Observing Firsthand

Visiting a location and conducting firsthand observations may provide valuable information about how a process or procedure works or how a group interacts. If you are planning research that involves observation, choose your sites and times carefully, and be sure to obtain permission in advance. During your observations, remain as unobtrusive as possible and keep accurate, complete records that indicate date, time of day, duration of the observation, and so on. Save interpretations of your observations for future analysis.

Using a Questionnaire

Consider expanding the number of people you gather information from beyond those you've interviewed by using a questionnaire. A questionnaire—a series of questions on a particular topic, sent out to a number of people—is an interview on paper. It has several advantages over the personal interview, and several disadvantages.

Advantages
- You can gather information from more people more quickly than you could through personal interviews.
- You can obtain responses from people who are hard to reach or who are in scattered geographical locations.
- Respondents have more time to think through their answers than they would under the pressure of composing thoughtful and complete answers in an interview.
- The questionnaire may yield more objective data because it reduces the possibility that the interviewer's tone of voice or facial expressions might influence an answer.

- The cost of distributing and tabulating a questionnaire is lower than the cost of conducting numerous personal interviews.

Disadvantages

- The results of a questionnaire may be slanted in favor of those people who have strong opinions on a subject because they are more likely to respond than those with only moderate views.

- Even if a questionnaire is designed to let one question lead logically to another, the questionnaire does not allow specific follow-up to answers.

- Distributing questionnaires and waiting for replies may take considerably longer than conducting a personal interview.

Selecting Questionnaire Recipients

Selecting the proper recipients for your questionnaire is crucial if you are to gather representative and usable data. If you wanted to survey the opinions of large groups in the general population—for example, all medical technologists working in private laboratories or all independent garage owners—your task would not be easy. Because you cannot include everybody in your survey, you need to choose a representative cross section—for example, include enough people from around the country, of both genders, and with varied educational training. Only then could you make a generalized statement based on your findings from the sample. (The best sources of information on sampling techniques are marketing-research and statistics texts.)

ON THE WEB

For online resources related to marketing, marketing research, and more, go to Chapter 6, bedfordstmartins .com/writingthatworks, and select *Web Links*.

Preparing and Designing Your Questionnaire

A key goal in designing a questionnaire is to keep it as brief as possible. The longer it is, the less likely the recipient will be to complete and return it. Next, the questions should be easy to understand. A confusing question will yield confusing results, whereas a carefully worded question will be easy to answer. Ideally, recipients should be able to answer most questions with a "yes" or "no" or by checking or circling a choice among several options. Such answers are simple to tabulate and require minimum effort on the part of the respondent, thus increasing your chances of obtaining a response.

▶ Do you recommend that the flextime program be made permanent?

❏ Strongly agree   ❏ Agree   ❏ No opinion   ❏ Disagree   ❏ Strongly disagree

If you need more information than such questions produce, provide an appropriate range of answers, as in the following example:

▶ How many hours of overtime would you be willing to work each week?

❏ 4 hours   ❏ 8 hours   ❏ Over 10 hours
❏ 6 hours   ❏ 10 hours   ❏ No overtime

Questions should be neutral; their wording should not lead respondents to give a particular answer, which can result in inaccurate or skewed data.

SLANTED   Would you prefer the freedom of a four-day workweek?

NEUTRAL   Would you choose to work a four-day workweek, ten hours a day, with every Friday off?

ETHICS NOTE

Follow your company's policy or applicable laws in requesting information about the respondent's age, gender, occupation, or other privacy information. Include such information only if it will be of value in interpreting the answers. Also be clear about whether the respondent's identity and any information the respondent provides will be kept confidential.

The sample cover memo and questionnaire in Figures 6–1 and 6–2 were sent to employees who had participated in a large organization's six-month pilot program of flexible working hours.

Luxwear Products Corporation
Memo

To: All Company Employees
From: Nelson Barrett, Human Resources Director
Date: October 18, 2010
Subject: Review of Flexible Working Hours Program

Please complete and return the questionnaire enclosed regarding Luxwear's trial program of flexible working hours. Your answers will help us decide whether we should make the program permanent.

Return the completed questionnaire to Ken Rose, Mail Code 12B (Fax 212-936-8358), by October 28. Your signature on the questionnaire is not necessary. All responses will be confidential and given serious consideration. Feel free to raise additional issues pertaining to the program.

If you want to discuss any item in the questionnaire, call Pam Peters in the Human Resources Department at extension 8812, or send her an e-mail at pp1@lpc.com.

Enclosure: Questionnaire

Figure 6–1   Questionnaire Cover Memo

Flexible Working Hours Program
Questionnaire

1. What kind of position do you occupy?

   ☐ Supervisory
   ☐ Nonsupervisory

2. Indicate to the nearest quarter of an hour when you begin work under flextime.

   ☐ 7:00 a.m.   ☐ 8:15 a.m.
   ☐ 7:15 a.m.   ☐ 8:30 a.m.
   ☐ 7:30 a.m.   ☐ 8:45 a.m.
   ☐ 7:45 a.m.   ☐ 9:00 a.m.
   ☐ 8:00 a.m.   ☐ Other (specify)

3. Where do you live?

   ☐ Talbot County   ☐ Greene County
   ☐ Montgomery County   ☐ Other (specify)

4. How do you usually travel to work?

   ☐ Drive alone   ☐ Walk
   ☐ Bus   ☐ Carpool
   ☐ Train   ☐ Motorcycle
   ☐ Bicycle   ☐ Other (specify)

5. How has flextime affected your commuting time?

   ☐ Increase: Approximate number of minutes
   ☐ Decrease: Approximate number of minutes
   ☐ No change

6. If you drive alone or in a carpool, has flextime increased or decreased the amount of time it takes you to find a parking space?

   ☐ Increased   ☐ Decreased   ☐ No change

7. How has flextime affected your productivity?

   a. Quality of work
      ☐ Increased   ☐ Decreased   ☐ No change

   b. Accuracy of work
      ☐ Increased   ☐ Decreased   ☐ No change

   c. Quiet time for uninterrupted work
      ☐ Increased   ☐ Decreased   ☐ No change

8. Have you had difficulty getting in touch with coworkers who are on different work schedules from yours?

   ☐ Yes   ☐ No

Figure 6–2   Questionnaire (continued)

9. Have you had trouble scheduling meetings within flexible starting and quitting times?

   ☐ Yes   ☐ No

10. Has flextime affected the way you feel about your job?

    ☐ Yes   ☐ No

    If yes, please answer (a) or (b):

    a. Feel better about job
       ☐ Slightly   ☐ Considerably

    b. Feel worse about job
       ☐ Slightly   ☐ Considerably

11. How important is it for you to have flexibility in your working hours?

    ☐ Very   ☐ Not very   ☐ Somewhat   ☐ Not at all

12. Has flextime allowed you more time to be with your family?

    ☐ Yes   ☐ No

13. If you are responsible for the care of a young child or children, has flextime made it easier or more difficult for you to arrange babysitting or day-care services?

    ☐ Easier   ☐ More difficult   ☐ No change

14. Do you recommend that the flextime program be made permanent?

    ☐ Yes   ☐ No

15. Please describe below or on a separate page any major changes you recommend for the program.

Thank you for your assistance.

Figure 6–2   Questionnaire (continued)

Creating a Questionnaire

✔ Prepare a cover letter, a memo (if the questionnaire is to be circulated within an organization), or an e-mail explaining who you are, the questionnaire's purpose, the date by which you need a response, and how and where to send the completed questionnaire. Include your contact information (mailing address, phone number, and e-mail address).

✔ Include a stamped, self-addressed envelope if you are using regular mail.

✔ Construct as many questions as possible that can be quickly answered with "yes," "no," or a check mark.

✔ Include a section for additional comments, where respondents may clarify their overall attitude toward the subject.

✔ Consider offering some tangible appreciation to those who answer the questionnaire by a specific date, such as a copy of the results or, for a marketing questionnaire, a gift certificate.

Conducting Secondary Research: The Library and the Internet

Secondary research sources are evaluations or compilations of primary sources. Secondary sources include books and articles, as well as reports, Web documents, online discussion forums, audio and video recordings, podcasts, business letters, minutes of meetings, operating manuals, brochures, and so forth. To find these materials, you will need to conduct research using your library and the Internet.

Developing a Search Strategy

Developing an effective search strategy entails considering what you already know and ferreting out further questions about the topic. Early stages may have dead ends and enticing side trips as you begin to focus your topic. Start your research with a question or purpose statement. If your topic is unfamiliar, try to find background information about it through general Internet sources, such as online encyclopedias, reference sites, or other sources that summarize the history of the topic. Familiarizing yourself with the issues surrounding your topic will help you clarify a preliminary question or purpose statement.

When you have a general understanding of the topic, focus on sources of information specific to your needs. For example, if you need the latest data on obesity-prevention programs, you might start by checking your library's subject directory to current medical and statistical sources. For additional information, you could then search a database—such as Academic Search Premier—for recent journal articles on the subject. Do you want to include opinions about the impact of a smoking ban in the workplace? Search a newspaper database or a business database. For an overview of a subject, check your library's reference materials. For in-depth or historical discussions, the best resources are books and periodicals.

Finally, consider limiting the scope of your search. Do you need to describe why the topic is important? Will the chronology of changes in the topic strengthen your argument? Once you have clearly defined the focus of your search, sum up your research question or thesis statement in two or three key terms. What words might you use to conduct keyword or key subject searches? If you are using an American academic library, consider checking the subject headings issued by the Library of Congress at <www.loc.gov> for categories relevant to your topic. Public libraries most often use the older Dewey Decimal system for classifying information in their collections.

Review the Writer's Checklist: Developing a Search Strategy to analyze your assignment and consider the type, quantity, and format of information you need.

WRITER'S CHECKLIST
Developing a Search Strategy

Your answers to the following questions will help to narrow your focus and determine where you should look.

✔ Who is your audience, and what is the purpose of the assignment?

✔ What is the scope of your project? Is it a 5-minute oral presentation? a 20-page research paper? a combined group presentation?

✔ How much information is needed? Is currency a factor?

✔ What kinds of sources (newspapers, signed encyclopedia articles, scholarly journal articles, books, Web sites) are appropriate?

✔ What formats (visual images, audio, print, or electronic) are needed?

✔ Do you need others' opinions or points of view?

✔ What are your deadlines?

As you look for sources, keep in mind that in many cases the more recent the information, the better. Articles in periodicals and newspapers provide current sources. Academic (.edu), organizational (.org), and government (.gov) Web sites may include recent research, works in progress, interviews, articles, papers, and conference proceedings.

When a resource seems useful, consider its authorship and other aspects of a text or document as outlined in Evaluating Sources (page 171). Then read the material carefully and take notes that include any additional questions about your topic. Some of your questions may eventually be clarified in other sources; questions that remain unanswered may point to future research projects.

Library Research

Libraries provide organized paths into scholarship, information, and the ever-expanding Internet. Library resources include (1) online catalogs useful for locating books, videos, and government documents; (2) licensed online databases and indexes of scholarly articles; (3) specialized tools; and (4) subject directories for using the Web. Start with your college or university library. As a student or an affiliate of the school, you will have access to resources not otherwise available to you, such as subscription-only databases of recently published journal articles. Although you may be able to find listings or abstracts of such articles on your personal computer, you can only access the full article text through your school's library, which has already purchased a subscription to the database.

One of the most valuable resources in the library isn't a book or reference tool but the librarians who work there. They can tell you where to begin, how to refine your search strategy, and how to find research materials related to your topic. They can also interpret your questions and guide your search toward the best print or online resources for your topic, often saving you time. A brief conversation may help to focus your research and alert you to the most productive information sources. In addition to providing help in person and on the phone, an increasing number of libraries now offer e-mail or live chat access for answering reference questions and giving research support. Use your school library's home page, like the one shown in Figure 6–3 on page 160, to access this feature as well as the library catalog, article databases, Web directories, and more.

ON THE WEB

For glossaries of common library and Internet research terms, go to Chapter 6, bedfordstmartins.com/ writingthatworks

Using Library Catalogs to Locate Books

A library's catalog—Figure 6–3 shows a typical catalog dialogue box—allows you to search a library's books, journals, and videos; tells you an item's location and availability; and may even permit you to search the holdings of other libraries in the region or around the world. (Check with the library staff or the library home page for interlibrary loan policies and requirements.)

ON THE WEB

To find library catalogs or home pages online, go to Chapter 6, bedfordstmartins.com/ writingthatworks, and select *Web Links*.

Methods for searching library catalogs vary. Typically, you can search by author, title, subject, or keyword. Become familiar with the way your library's catalog works. If you are at the library, ask a reference librarian to give you a brief tour of the catalog; otherwise, check for guidelines or FAQs (Frequently Asked Questions). Help screens, like the author search screen in Figure 6–4 on page 161, can be particularly useful in learning the best strategies for locating appropriate materials. Knowing how to use a few basic tools will prepare you to start your research and will often help you streamline the search process.

Follow these basic steps to search a library catalog:

- *Consider multiple search terms.* Unlike a search engine for Web sites, library catalogs don't search the full text of books; instead, they categorize the main subject of the book as a whole. If your initial search doesn't find anything about your specific topic, broaden your search terms.

- *Skim subject headings.* Librarians use consistent terminology when they describe the subject of a book. If you find a listing for one book that looks useful, the subject headings on the screen may lead you to other relevant sources. You'll have the best results if you search using the same terms catalogers do.

- *Browse the shelves.* In addition to categorizing books by subject, librarians shelve related books together. Combine searching the catalog with browsing the shelves.

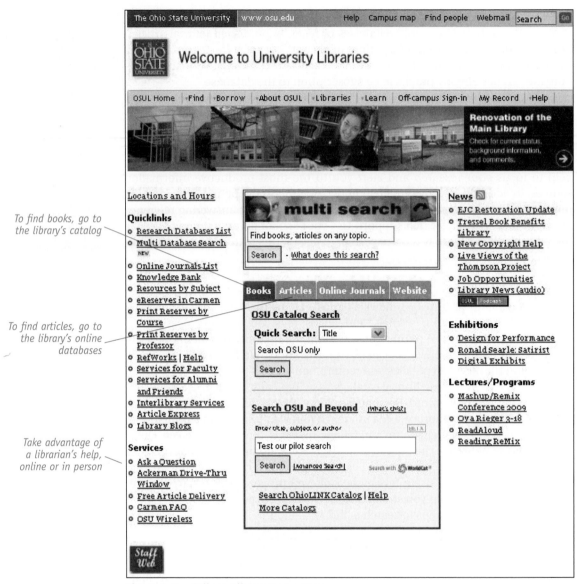

To find books, go to the library's catalog

To find articles, go to the library's online databases

Take advantage of a librarian's help, online or in person

Figure 6–3   College Library Home Page

ON THE WEB

For access to online library catalogs, go to Chapter 6, bedfordstmartins.com/ writingthatworks, and select *Web Links*.

- *Don't overlook reference books.* Reference books offer valuable nuggets of information and authoritative overviews of topics. However, it can be hard to know which specialized reference book will cover your specific topic. The quickest way to find the most helpful reference books is to ask a librarian for suggestions.

Provides examples of search items

Figure 6–4   Online Catalog Help Screen (for Author Search)

ON THE WEB

For online tours of the Library of Congress and Dewey Decimal organizing systems, go to Chapter 6, bedfordstmartins.com/ writingthatworks, and select *Web Links*.

- *Set search limits.* If your search turns up too many results, narrow it by using the "limit search" or "advanced search" option offered by many catalogs. Using the "advanced search" page, you can limit your search by language, date range, or media type. An example of an advanced search by keyword is shown in Figure 6–5.

Using Databases to Locate Articles

Libraries subscribe to databases that provide citations for print resources and electronic collections of full-text articles; they can be searched within the library building or through remote access available to registered students, faculty, and staff. Figure 6–6 is an example of a library home page that provides access to articles in journals organized by subject area. A library's database and index subscriptions might include any or all of the following:

- *EBSCOhost's Academic Search Premier*: a large multidisciplinary database, which provides full text for nearly 4,500 magazines and scholarly publications, including full text for more than 3,700 peer-reviewed journals. Some libraries have an even larger database: Academic Search Complete.

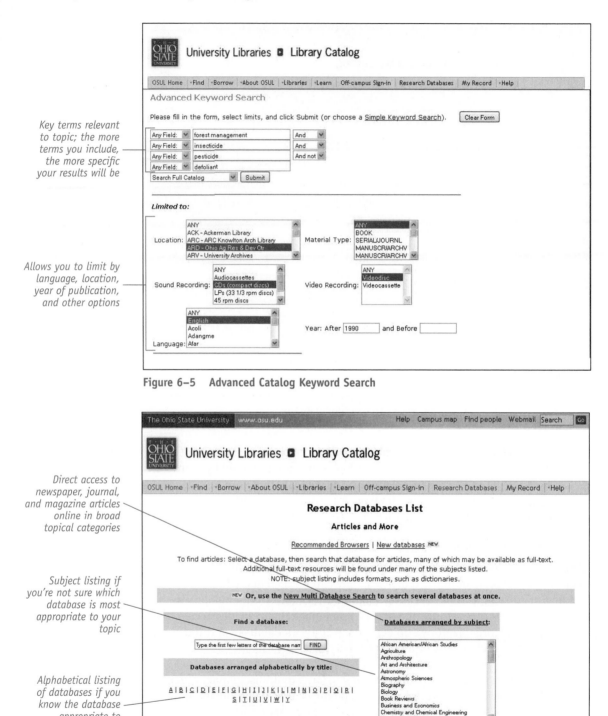

Key terms relevant to topic; the more terms you include, the more specific your results will be

Allows you to limit by language, location, year of publication, and other options

Figure 6–5   Advanced Catalog Keyword Search

Direct access to newspaper, journal, and magazine articles online in broad topical categories

Subject listing if you're not sure which database is most appropriate to your topic

Alphabetical listing of databases if you know the database appropriate to your topic

Figure 6–6   College Library Database Page

- *Expanded Academic ASAP*: another enormous database, covering general-interest and scholarly journals, plus business, law, and health-care publications (many in full text). Some libraries offer Academic OneFile, an even larger database.

- *ERIC (Education Resources Information Center)*: a U.S. Department of Education database providing access to journals and reports in education

- *JSTOR*: a full-text, archival collection of journals in the humanities, social sciences, and sciences

- *LexisNexis Academic*: a collection of databases that is particularly strong for news, business, legal, and corporate and financial information (most articles in full text), as well as congressional, statistical, and governmental resources

These databases are excellent resources for articles published within the last 10 to 20 years. Some include descriptive abstracts and full texts of articles. To find older articles, you may need to consult a print index, such as the *Readers' Guide to Periodical Literature* and the *New York Times Index*.

To locate articles within a particular database, conduct a keyword search. If your search turns up too many results, narrow your search by connecting two search terms with *AND*— "business writing AND employment"— or use other options offered by the database, such as a limited, a modified, or an advanced search, as shown in Figure 6–7.

@ DIGITAL TIPS: Storing Search Results

Databases offer various ways to save your results. You may be able to save your searches and results within the database itself by creating a personal account, send selected references and full-text articles to an e-mail account, or export them to citation-management software such as RefWorks, Endnote, or Zotero. These programs allow you to build your own database of references from multiple sources, sort them into folders, and generate bibliographies in the format of your choice. Database search tools and citation-management software will vary from library to library, so contact a reference librarian for usage guidance at your library.

Using Reference Works to Locate Facts and Topic Overviews

In addition to articles and books, you may want to consult reference works such as specialized encyclopedias and dictionaries for a brief overview of your subject. Ask your reference librarian to recommend reference works that are most relevant to your topic. Many are located online and can be accessed through your library's home page.

Encyclopedias. Encyclopedias are comprehensive, multivolume collections of articles arranged alphabetically. Some, such as the *Encyclopaedia Britannica*, cover a wide range of subjects, while others, such as *The Encyclopedia of Careers*

Area to specify keyword search —

Search results can be limited to full text only

Search results can be limited to scholarly or peer-reviewed journals only

More options for focusing your search by publication date, publication type, or document type

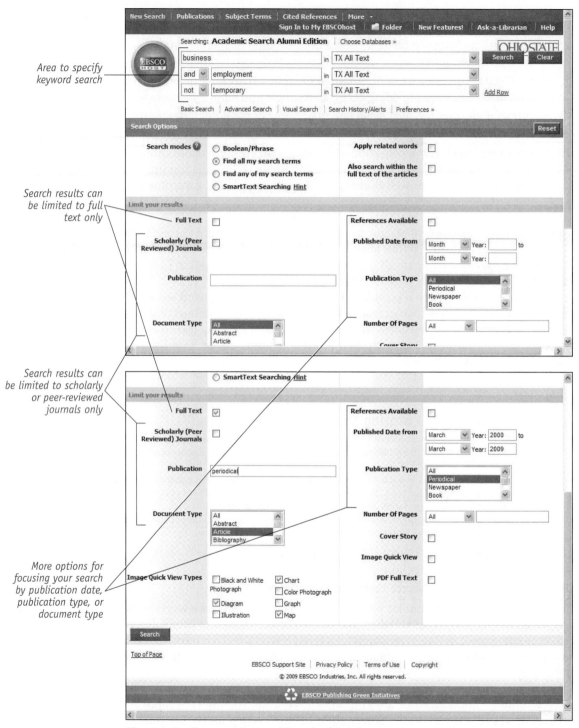

Figure 6–7   Narrowed Keyword Search of Database

and Vocational Guidance, 13th ed., edited by William Hopke (Chicago: Ferguson, 2005), and the *McGraw-Hill Encyclopedia of Science and Technology*, 10th ed. (New York: McGraw-Hill, 2007), are dedicated to specific subjects. For almost every academic discipline, there is at least one specialized encyclopedia with its entries written by noted scholars in the field. The free online encyclopedia *Wikipedia* (<www.wikipedia.org>) should be used only as a starting point for a topic overview because site users continually update entries, with only varying degrees of editorial filtering.

Dictionaries.   General and specialized dictionaries are available in print and online. General dictionaries can be compact or comprehensive, unabridged publications. Specialized dictionaries define terms used in a particular field, such as engineering, computer science, architecture, or consumer affairs, and offer detailed definitions of field-specific terms, usually written in straightforward language.

Handbooks and Manuals.   Handbooks and manuals are typically one-volume compilations of frequently used information in a particular field. They offer brief definitions of terms or concepts, standards for presenting information, procedures for documenting sources, and visuals such as graphs and tables.

Other Library Resources

Many libraries offer special kinds of research information. For example, a library may provide access to data that can be downloaded into statistical packages, such as SPSS (statistical package for the social sciences), for manipulation. Others offer GIS (geographic information systems) software that links data to spatial information, allowing the researcher to create detailed maps that show factors such as income, ethnicity, or purchasing habits.

WRITER'S GLOSSARY
Using Common Library Terms

✔ *Abstract*: a brief version of a long document that gives the reader the document's main points.

✔ *Bibliographic information*: the author, title, and publication information needed to locate an item in a journal article or book.

✔ *Bibliography*: (1) a listing of sources used in the writing of a document; (2) in the MLA format, it is called a works-cited page; in the APA format, it is called the references page.

✔ *Bound periodical*: several issues of a journal or magazine that are secured together in book form.

✔ *Call number*: the number assigned to every item in the library to help locate the item.

✔ *Circulation desk*: the desk where a patron can check out, return, and renew library materials.

✔ *Database*: a searchable electronic catalog of articles from journals, newspapers, and magazines accessible by subscription only.

✔ *Interlibrary loan*: material requested from another library and sent to the patron's library for use.

✔ *Journal*: a periodical containing scholarly articles written by experts in a particular subject area.

✔ *Peer review*: the journal publishing practice in which experts review articles for accuracy, completion, and adherence to the highest research standards prior to publication.

✔ *Magazine*: a popular periodical meant for the general public; articles are written by paid journalists.

✔ *Microform*: older books, journal articles, government documents, and more in film or fiche (i.e., greatly reduced) format that must be viewed in the library on a magnifying device.

✔ *Periodical*: a publication issued regularly, such as a newspaper, magazine, or journal.

Internet Research

Although the Internet contains a wealth of information, it has no one indexing scheme, no single catalog that brings the information together for browsing or easy access, unlike the information in a library. However, search engines and Web directories can streamline your Internet search.

Using Search Engines and Web Subject Directories

A search engine locates information based on words or combinations of words that you specify. It finds documents or files that contain one or more of these words in their titles, descriptions, or text. Most search engines provide "advanced search" options that can help you narrow your results. Figure 6–8 shows an advanced search conducted on Google for information about remote sensing, forest management, and pesticides.

Search-engine results are based on a number of different strategies. Some sites base relevance on how high on the given page your search term appears, on the number of appearances of your term in previous searches, or on the number of other sites that link to the page (a technique called *relevance ranking*). Be aware that the first items in the search results may not be the most relevant to your search.

Your best strategy is to investigate how your favorite search engines work; nearly all provide detailed instructions on their help pages. Although search engines vary in what and how they search, you can use some of the basic strategies in Digital Tips: Using Search Engines (page 170).

A subject directory organizes information by broad subject categories (business, entertainment, health, sports) and related subtopics (marketing, finance, investing). Many college and university libraries produce their own Web directories like the one shown in Figure 6–9 on page 168; check your library's home page. A subject-directory search eventually produces a list of specific sites that contain information about the topics you request. Once you locate a site of interest that you want to revisit, you can bookmark it.

Specify key terms and number of results desired per page

Limit your search to a specific domain (for example, .org, .edu, .com)

Figure 6–8   Advanced Google Search

Most major search engines, such as Google and Yahoo!, also offer directories. The following search engines and subject directories are among the most widely used on the Web.

Search Engines

Google (<www.google.com>). The largest and most popular search engine, Google features several specialized search tools, including the following:

Blogs (<www.google.com/blogsearch>)

Books (<http://books.google.com>)

Finance (<www.google.com/finance>)

Geography (<http://earth.google.com>)

Images (<http://images.google.com>)

Maps (<http://maps.google.com>)

News (<http://news.google.com>)

Scholarly publications (<http://scholar.google.com>)

Yahoo! (<yahoo.com>). Yahoo! is another popular search engine, directory, and portal.

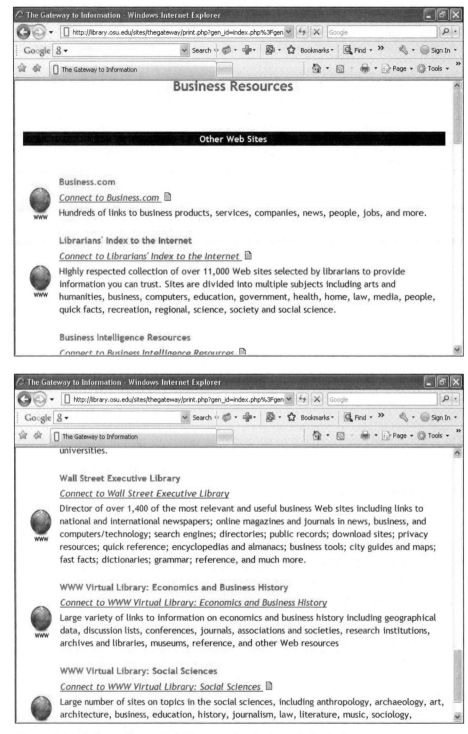

Each site provides detailed sources of information about the broad topic it covers

Figure 6–9   College Library Web Directory for Business Information

Subject Directories

The following Web directories offer access to sites selected for their quality. They are a good way to find useful sites when a search engine produces too many results.

GlobalEDGE (<http://globaledge.msu.edu/>). A directory of sites of particular interest to international business professionals.

Infomine (<http://infomine.ucr.edu/>). A Web directory specializing in scholarly Internet resources of interest to academics and scholars.

Internet Public Library (<www.ipl.org>). A collection of over 45,000 links handpicked, organized, and described by librarians and library students.

Internet Scout Project (<http://scout.wisc.edu/>). Published continually since 1994, Internet Scout presents the efforts of librarians and educators at the University of Wisconsin–Madison, who have selected and annotated more than 10,000 academically useful Web sites.

Librarians' Internet Index (<www.lii.org>). A searchable, annotated directory of continually updated Internet resources that are evaluated and annotated by research librarians.

Scirus (<www.scirus.com/>). A search engine that focuses on scientific information.

WWW Virtual Library (<www.vlib.org>). This collection of subject directories was started when the Web was new and continues to be updated.

Metasearch Engines

These programs search other search engines for information about your query and list relevant results.

Dogpile (<www.dogpile.com>). Dogpile searches other search engines for responses to your query and sifts the findings.

Metacrawler (<www.metacrawler.com>). Metacrawler searches Yahoo!, Google, and other search engines for responses to your query, lists the search engines where relevant sites were found, and allows you to e-mail the results. Try <www.metafind.com> if you are searching for a business.

ON THE WEB

For information on evaluating search engines, see Chapter 6, bedfordstmartins.com/ writingthatworks

Web-Based Tools

A growing number of Web-based applications are available to enhance your research, such as the following examples.

- **Create your own maps.** Find maps or create your own customized maps using Google Maps (<http://maps.google.com>) or the National Atlas (<http://nationalatlas.gov/>) .

- **Get the latest blog postings automatically.** Keep up to date with changes on news sites and blogs by using RSS (really simple syndication). To do so,

◆ *For a discussion about creating blogs, see pages 558–562 in Chapter 15, Writing for the Web.*

you can either add feeds to your browser toolbar or use a feed aggregator such as Bloglines (<http://bloglines.com>) or Google Reader (<www.google.com/reader>).

- **Create graphic representations** of ideas or visualize data using tools such as Mindomo (<www.mindomo.com/>).

@

DIGITAL TIPS: Using Search Engines

■ *Think small.* Enter words and phrases that are as specific to your topic as possible. For example, if you are looking for information about *nuclear power* and enter only the term *nuclear*, the search will also yield listings for *nuclear family*, *nuclear medicine*, and *nuclear winter*.

■ *Use Boolean operators (AND, OR, NOT) to narrow your search.* For example, if you are searching for information on breast cancer and are finding references to nothing but prostate cancer, try "breast AND cancer NOT prostate." Consider conducting an advanced search (see Figure 6–8) to further narrow your search.

■ *Put phrases in quotation marks to limit results.* For example, searching for "usability testing" will return only pages that have the full phrase.

■ *Pay attention to a site's domain name.* Sites ending in .gov are official government sites and tend to be carefully edited. Sites ending in .com or .biz are commercial sites, and sites ending in .edu are college or university sites.

■ *Use the search box on an organization's or agency's home page.* If you know an organization or agency is likely to have reliable information on its Web site, use the search tool there.

■ *Try a variety of search engines and consider how well they provide relevant information.* You may want to stick to using your favorite search engine, but you will get more varied results if you use more than one.

■ *To obtain as many hits as possible, consider using a metasearch engine, such as Dogpile (<www.dogpile.com>) and Metacrawler (<www.metacrawler.com>).*

Locating Business and Government Sites

The Web includes numerous sites devoted to specific subject areas. Following are some suggested resources for researching business topics.

Business Resources

Business Internet Resources (www.pace.edu/library/links/links.html>)

Business Reference Services: Science, Technology, and Business Division (<www.loc.gov/rr/business/>). This site is developed and maintained by the Library of Congress. See the Subject Guide to Internet Resources.

Google Directory: Business (<www.google.com/Top/Business/>)

Yahoo! Directory: Business and Economy (<http://dir.yahoo.com/Business_and_Economy/>)

Government Resources

Government Documents and Reports

- Congressional Budget Office (<www.cbo.gov/>)
- Congressional Research Service Reports (<www.opencrs.com/>)
- Government Accountability Office (<www.gao.gov/>)
- GPO Access (<www.gpoaccess.gov/>)

Sites for Statistics

- Government Sources
  - American Factfinder (<http://factfinder.census.gov>)
  - Bureau of Economic Analysis (<www.bea.gov/>)
  - Bureau of Justice Statistics (<www.ojp.usdoj.gov/bjs/>)
  - Bureau of Labor Statistics (<www.bls.gov/>)
  - Fedstats (<www.fedstats.gov/>)
  - National Center for Education Statistics (<http://nces.ed.gov/>)
  - National Center for Health Statistics (<www.cdc.gov/nchs/>)
  - United Nations Statistics Division (<http://unstats.un.org/unsd/>)
  - U.S. Census Bureau (<www.census.gov/>)
- Opinion Polls
  - Pew Global Attitudes Project (<http://pewglobal.org/>)
  - World Public Opinion (<www.worldpublicopinion.org/>)

▪ Evaluating, Recording, and Acknowledging Research Sources

As you research your topic, weigh the merits of your sources carefully. Once you've decided which materials to use, you will need to record information from each source so that you can accurately quote, paraphrase, and summarize it in your paper or report. Recording your sources is especially important so that you can acknowledge where your information came from, thereby avoiding plagiarism.

Evaluating Sources

After you have located a number of promising books, articles, and Web resources, you need to decide which ones to continue to use in your research. As you interview for information or work with print or online material, evaluate each source by asking yourself the following questions:

- Is the information accurate and up to date?
- Is the speaker or author reputable and qualified?
- Is the publisher or sponsoring organization well-established and respected in the field?

Evaluate the usefulness of information on the Internet with the same standards that you use to evaluate information from other sources. These standards apply for printed material, for people you interview, or for any other source.

The easiest way to ensure that information is valid is to obtain it from a reputable source. For example, data from the Bureau of Labor Statistics, the Securities and Exchange Commission, and the Bureau of the Census are widely used by U.S. businesses. Likewise, online versions of established, reputable journals in medicine, engineering, computer software, and other fields merit the same level of trust as the printed versions. However, as you move away from established, reputable sites, exercise more caution. Be especially wary of blogs, unmoderated online discussion groups, and public wikis. Remember that anyone with access can place information on the Internet, so for many sources there are no editorial checks and balances in place. Treat information obtained from these sources cautiously.

Keep in mind the following four criteria when evaluating any source, whether print or online: authority, accuracy, bias, and currency.[1]

Authority

Consider the author's reputation: Is the writer an authority in the field? Has he or she written other, highly regarded books or articles? If you don't know, ask a librarian, an instructor, or an expert who is familiar with the subject area whether the author of a book or an article has an established reputation.

Because anyone can publish on the Web, it is sometimes difficult to determine authorship of a document, and frequently a person's qualifications for speaking on a topic are absent or questionable. If you do not recognize the author or the organization sponsoring the site as well-known and respected in the field, check the site's "about us" page or mission statement if available. This information should give you a sense of the site's purpose and perspective. Ask the following questions to help you determine the authority of a site or document:

- Is the author's document listed in or linked from a reliable source or document?
- Is the author referenced or mentioned positively by another author or organization whose authority you trust?
- Does the document give ample biographical information about the author so that you can evaluate his or her credentials, or can you get this information by linking to another document?

If the publisher or sponsor is an organization, you can usually assume that the document meets the standards and aims of the group. Consider also the following:

- The suitability of the organization to address this topic.

---

[1]Adapted from Leigh Ryan, *The Bedford Guide for Writing Tutors*, 4th ed. (Boston: Bedford/St. Martin's, 2006).

- Whether this organization or agency is recognized and respected in the field.
- The relationship of the author to the publisher or sponsor. (Does the document tell you something about the author's expertise or qualifications?)

Accuracy

Criteria for evaluating accuracy would include the following:

- Other sources that the document relies on are reputable and cited or linked.
- Background information can be verified.
- Methodology is appropriate for the topic.
- With a research project, data that were gathered include explanations of research methods and interpretations.
- The graphs and visuals are free of distortion.
- The site is modified or updated regularly.

Bias

To determine bias, consider how the context reveals the author's knowledge of the subject and his or her stance on the topic. Check for the following:

- The publication or site identifies its audience.
- The book, article, or site was published or developed by a recognized academic institution; government agency; or national, international, or commercial organization with an established reputation in the subject area.
- The author shows knowledge of theories, techniques, or schools of thought usually related to the topic.
- The author shows knowledge of related sources and attributes them properly.
- The author discusses the value and limitations of the approach if it is new.
- The author acknowledges that the subject itself or his or her treatment of it is controversial if you know that to be the case.

Currency

If currency is important, consider whether the document has a publication or "last updated" date or includes date of copyright, gives dates showing when information was gathered, or gives information about new material when appropriate.

WRITER'S CHECKLIST
Evaluating Print Resources

For a Book

✔ Is the text up to date and relevant to your topic?

✔ Who is the author? Does the preface or introduction indicate the author's purpose or credentials?

✔ Does the author present information in an objective way? Are the language, tone, and style unbiased?

✔ Does the table of contents relate to your topic? Does the index contain terms related to your topic? Does the text contain a bibliography, reference list, or footnotes?

✔ Are the chapters useful? (Skim through one that seems related to your topic — notice especially the introduction, headings, and closing.)

✔ Does the book contain informative diagrams or other visuals?

For an Article

✔ Is the article up to date and relevant to your topic?

✔ Who is the author?

✔ Is the publisher of the magazine or other periodical well known? Who is the publication's main audience? (Is it the mainstream public? a small group of specialists?)

✔ Does the publication target or show bias toward a particular audience?

✔ What is the article's purpose? (For a journal article, read the abstract; for a newspaper article, read the headline and the lead sentences.)

✔ Does the article contain informative diagrams or other visuals that indicate its scope?

WRITER'S CHECKLIST
Evaluating Online Resources

✔ *Who* is the author? Why should that author be trusted?

✔ *What* is the main focus of the page? Does it make sense?

✔ *Where* does the site originate? Is it put out by an organization, an individual, or an institution?

✔ *When* was the site put online? Is it updated regularly?

✔ *Why* does that page exist? Can you find a purpose statement or an "about us" page? Is there a particular bias?

✔ *Does* the information available compare favorably with at least two other reputable online sources?

ON THE WEB

For more resources for evaluating Web content, go to Chapter 6, **bedfordstmartins** **.com/writingthatworks**

Taking Notes

Taking notes enables you to condense and record information from books, articles, Web sites, and other sources. The notes you take will furnish much of the material for your outline and final written work.

Document the following information about any book that you decide to include in your research:

Call number
Author (if the author is an organization, indicate that fact)
Title
City of publication
Publisher's name
Year of publication

For an article, record the following information:

Author
Title of the article
Name of the journal in which the article appears
Journal volume and issue numbers
Date of publication
Page numbers of the article
Database (if you found the article's full text in a library database)
Digital object identifier (DOI; for full-text articles found online)

For online sources, you can print out the search screen containing the full bibliographic citation, download the citation from an online database to your hard drive, or e-mail the citation to yourself. See Digital Tips: Storing Search Results (page 163) for more information on recording online search results.

When working with paper sources (books and journals), you can photocopy material and highlight important passages with a highlighter, jot notes on index cards, or keyboard them into your laptop or desktop computer. If you are using Internet sources, you can highlight passages and cut and paste them into a word-processing file, in addition to taking notes. When you cut and paste information from the Internet, be very careful: Consider changing the font or color of the text so that you can easily distinguish borrowed material from your own notes; at the very least, put quotation marks around the material. Always include the source to provide proper credit in your final work. Otherwise, you will be plagiarizing from the source. If the source is copyrighted, you may also be guilty of copyright infringement. (A full discussion of avoiding plagiarism begins on page 180.)

Whichever method you use, identify the source of the information and include the author's last name (also include first name or initials if you have two authors with the same last name) and the page number or numbers on which the material appears in the original source. If you have consulted more than one book or article by an author, include the title as well; for long titles, you may use a shortened form.

◆ *For a sample list of research topics, see Christine Thomas's notes on page 13.*

As you take notes, make a list of the topics you will cover in your research. Identify your notes as appropriate with these topics (sometimes called *tags*). When you arrange the index cards or word-processing notes by topic in preparation for creating an outline, you can use the tags as a guide in organizing your material.

For the sake of accuracy and correctness, be careful to distinguish whether you are quoting directly from your source, paraphrasing (restating the text you're using in your own words), or summarizing (writing down a condensed version of the text). If you are a beginning researcher, you should probably stick to writing down direct quotations. Then, when you turn to actually writing your research paper, you can decide whether you want to quote directly, paraphrase, or summarize.

Quoting from Your Sources

When you quote directly from another source, use only the information you need to make your point. The following section describes long-standing techniques to help you do so and to credit your information sources.

Direct Quotations

A direct quotation is a word-for-word copy of the text of an original source. Choose direct quotations (which can be of a word, a phrase, a sentence, or, occasionally, a paragraph) carefully and use them sparingly. Enclose direct quotations in quotation marks and separate them from the rest of the sentence by a comma or colon. The initial capital letter of a quotation is retained if the quoted material originally began with a capital letter.

▶   The economist stated, "Regulation cannot supply the dynamic stimulus that in other industries is supplied by competition."

When a quotation is divided, the material that interrupts the quotation is set off, before and after, by commas, and quotation marks are used around each part of the quotation.

▶   "Regulation," he said in a recent interview, "cannot supply the dynamic stimulus that in other industries is supplied by competition."

Indirect Quotations

An indirect quotation is a paraphrased version of an original text. It is usually introduced by the word *that* and is not set off from the rest of the sentence by punctuation marks.

▶   In a recent interview he said that regulation does not stimulate the industry as well as competition does.

Deletions or Omissions

Deletions or omissions from quoted material are indicated by three ellipsis points (. . .) within a sentence and a period plus three ellipsis points (. . . .) at the end of a sentence.

▸ "If monopolies could be made to respond . . . we would be able to enjoy the benefits of . . . large-scale efficiency. . . ."

When a quoted passage begins in the middle of a sentence rather than at the beginning, ellipsis points are not necessary; the fact that the first letter of the quoted material is not capitalized tells the reader that the quotation begins in mid-sentence.

▸ Rivero goes on to conclude that "coordination may lessen competition within a region."

Regardless of where the ellipsis points appear, be careful to retain the accuracy and grammatical consistency of the original passage.

Inserting Material into Quotations

When it is necessary to insert a clarifying comment within quoted material, use brackets.

▸ "The industry is an integrated system that serves an extensive [geographic] area, with divisions existing as islands within the larger system's sphere of influence."

When quoted material contains an obvious error or might be questioned in some other way, the expression *sic* (Latin for "thus"), in italic type and enclosed in brackets, follows the questionable material to indicate that the writer has quoted the material exactly as it appeared in the original.

▸ The company considers the Baker Foundation to be a "guilt-edged [*sic*] investment."

ETHICS NOTE

When you are quoting, do not make any changes or omissions in the quoted material unless you clearly indicate what you have done. For further information on incorporating quoted material and inserting comments, see Avoiding Plagiarism and Copyright Violations on page 180 and Incorporating Quotations into Text below.

Incorporating Quotations into Text

Quote word for word only when your source concisely sums up a great deal of information or reinforces a point you are making. Quotations must also relate logically, grammatically, and syntactically to the rest of the sentence and surrounding text.

Depending on the length, there are two methods of handling quotations in your text. For MLA style, a quotation of no more than four lines is incorporated into the text and enclosed in quotation marks. For APA style, a quotation of fewer than 40 words is incorporated into the text and enclosed in quotation marks.

Material that runs longer than four lines (MLA style) or at least 40 words (APA style) is usually set off from the body of the text by being indented from the left margin one inch (MLA style) or one-half inch (APA style). The quoted passage is spaced the same as the surrounding text and is not enclosed in quotation marks, as shown in the following example, which uses MLA style. If you are not following a specific style manual, you may block indent one inch from both the left and right margins for reports and other documents.

▶ After reviewing a large number of works in business and technical communication, Alred sees an inevitable connection between theory, practice, and pedagogy:

> Therefore, theory is necessary to prevent us from being overwhelmed by what is local, particular, and temporal. In turn, pedagogy both mediates practice and transforms our theory. Indeed, one reason I find this work rewarding is that I sense it puts me at the intersection of theory, practice, and pedagogy as they are involved with writing in the workplace. (ix–x)

The use of the Web today has reinforced this connection because it calls on the Web-page designer to engage in a teaching function as well as reflect on the practice of Web design. For example, the widespread use of . . .

Notice that the quotation blends with the content of the surrounding text, which uses transitions to introduce and comment on the quotation. At the end of the document, the following entry appears in the MLA-style list of works cited as the source of the quotation in the example.

Alred, Gerald J., Charles T. Brusaw, and Walter E. Oliu. *The Business Writer's Handbook*. 9th ed. Boston: Bedford/St. Martin's, 2009.

Do not rely too heavily on the use of quotations in the final version of your document. Generally, avoid quoting anything that is more than one paragraph.

Paraphrasing

Paraphrasing is restating or rewriting in your own words the essential ideas of another writer. Because the paraphrase does not quote the source word for word, quotation marks are not necessary. However, paraphrased material should be credited because the *ideas* are taken from someone else. The following example is an original passage explaining the concept of object blur. The paraphrased version restates the essential information of the passage in a form appropriate for a report.

ORIGINAL   One of the major visual cues used by pilots in maintaining precision ground reference during low-level flight is that of object blur. We are acquainted with the object-blur phenomenon experienced when driving an automobile. Objects in the foreground appear to be rushing toward us, while objects in the background appear to recede slightly.
                —Wesley E. Woodson and Donald W. Conover, *Human Engineering Guide for Equipment Designers*

PARAPHRASED   Object blur is an optical illusion that affects people in fast-moving vehicles: nearby objects seem to rush toward the observer, while distant objects seem to move away slightly (Woodson and Conover).

Strive to put the original ideas into your words without distorting them.

Summarizing

A summary is a condensed version, in the researcher's own words, of an original passage. Summaries present only the essential ideas or conclusions of the original and are considerably shorter than paraphrases of the same passage. As with directly quoted and paraphrased material, the source of summarized information must be credited in a footnote.

Following this passage is a brief summary of its content.

ORIGINAL   Now that we have learned something about the nature of elements and molecules, what are fuels? Fuels are those substances that will burn when heat is applied to them. Some elements, in themselves, are fuels. Carbon, hydrogen, sulfur, magnesium, titanium, and some other metals are examples of elements that can burn. Coal, charcoal, and coke, for example, are almost pure carbon; hydrogen, another element, is a highly flammable gas. But the most familiar combustible materials are not pure elements; they are compounds and mixtures. Wood, paper, and grass are principally composed of molecules of cellulose, a flammable substance. If we examine the chemical makeup of this compound, we will discover what elements form the basic fuels in most solid materials. The cellulose molecule contains twenty-one atoms: six carbon, ten hydrogen, and five oxygen atoms: $C_6H_{10}O_5$. Since oxygen is not flammable . . . , it follows that the carbon and hydrogen found in most common combustible solids are the elements that burn. This conclusion becomes even stronger when we look at common flammable liquids. Gasoline, kerosene, fuel oils, and other petroleum compounds are composed of only carbon and hydrogen atoms, in varying amounts. These compounds, called hydrocarbons (hydrogen + carbon), will all burn.
                —James H. Meidl, *Flammable Hazardous Materials*

SUMMARIZED   The chemical makeup of a substance determines whether it is flammable. Carbon and hydrogen are highly flammable elements, so material made up largely of these elements, called hydrocarbons, are good fuels (Meidl 8–9).

Summarize a source to remind yourself of the substance of a research source. Summarized information can also be useful to your reader because it condenses passages that give more details than the reader needs.

Avoiding Plagiarism and Copyright Violations

Plagiarism is the use of someone else's ideas without acknowledgment or the use of someone else's exact words without quotation marks and appropriate credit. Plagiarism is considered to be the theft of someone else's creative and intellectual property and is unacceptable in any field. If you intend to publish, reproduce, or distribute material that includes quotations from published works, including Web sites, you may need to obtain written permission from the copyright holders of those works.

Acknowledging Your Sources

The gold standard for avoiding ethical and legal problems is to carefully document your sources of information. This standard applies both in the classroom and on the job, regardless of whether your primary audience is your instructor, your company management, or the readers of a publication or Web site. (Details regarding commonly used systems for documenting sources begin on page 181.)

Quoting a passage—including cutting and pasting a passage from an Internet source into your work—is permissible only if you enclose the passage in quotation marks and properly cite the source. Likewise, you may paraphrase the words and ideas of another *if you document your source*. Although you do not enclose paraphrased ideas or materials in quotation marks, you must document their sources. Paraphrasing a passage without citing the source is permissible only when the information paraphrased is common knowledge.

Common Knowledge

Common knowledge generally refers to information that is widely known and readily available in handbooks, manuals, atlases, and other references. For example, the distances between two cities, the names of routes, and the geographic features of an area found on virtually every travel map qualify as common knowledge. You need not document the source of such information. Common knowledge also refers to information within a specific field that is generally known and understood by most others in that field—even though it may not be widely known by those outside the field. For example, the fact that the 1918 Spanish Flu pandemic killed millions of Americans is common knowledge among public health officials, epidemiologists, and historians. The source for this information need not be documented. However, the number of deaths caused by the 1918 flu among members of the U.S. military or among the population of a North American city would not be common knowledge and would require a citation. An indication that something is common knowledge is whether it is repeated in multiple sources without citation. If you are in any doubt about whether information meets this standard, document its source.

Copyright

Most published material—written or visual—is copyrighted. In workplace writing, you must obtain prior approval to reproduce virtually all copyrighted information and cite the source of that information in your final work. However, small amounts of material from a copyrighted source may be used, especially for educational purposes, without permission or payment as long as you indicate that it is someone else's material and your use satisfies the "fair use" criteria of the U.S. Copyright Office.

ON THE WEB

The "fair use" criteria are described on the Web site of the U.S. Copyright Office at <www.copyright.gov/>.

To seek permission to reproduce copyrighted material, write to the copyright holder. In some cases, it is the author; in other cases, it is the editor or publisher of the work. For Web sites, read the site's "terms-of-use" information (if available) and e-mail your request to the appropriate party. State specifically which portion of the work you wish to reproduce and how you plan to use it. The copyright holder has the right to charge a fee and specify conditions and limits of use.

Public-Domain Materials

Works created by or for U.S. government agencies are in the public domain—that is, they are not copyrighted and can be reproduced without permission. Some older written works may also be in the public domain because their copyright has lapsed; the rules governing copyright can be complex, however, so it's generally wise to assume that any work not created by the U.S. government is protected. As with other material you use in your own work, you must give appropriate credit to the source. (See the next section, Documenting Sources.)

In-House Materials

ON THE WEB

For a tutorial on using sources correctly, see bedfordstmartins.com/ writingthatworks and select *Tutorials*, "The St. Martin's Tutorial on Avoiding Plagiarism." For links to other helpful resources, select *Web Links*.

In the workplace, employees often repurpose text, financial and statistical data, and visuals from in-house manuals, reports, and other company documents and Web sites. Because the company is considered the author of works prepared by its employees on the job, there is no need to acknowledge such sources because the information is simply being used in a different setting by the organization to which it already belongs.

ETHICS NOTE
In the classroom, borrowing published and Web-based information is necessary and acceptable, whether quoted or paraphrased, *but you must document the source*.

Documenting Sources

By documenting your sources, you identify where you obtained the facts, ideas, quotations, and paraphrases you used in preparing your content. This information can come from books; newspaper, magazine, or trade-journal articles; manuals; proposals; investigative reports; interviews; e-mail; the Internet; and other sources. Documenting sources achieves three important purposes:

- It allows readers to locate and consult the sources used and to find further information on the subject.
- It enables writers to support and lend credibility to their assertions and arguments.
- It helps writers to give proper credit to others and thus avoid plagiarism by identifying the sources of facts, ideas, quotations, and paraphrases.

This section shows citation models and sample pages for two principal documentation systems: APA and MLA.

> American Psychological Association. *Publication Manual of the American Psychological Association.* 5th ed. Washington, DC: American Psychological Association, 2001. See also <www.apastyle.org>.
>
> *APA Style Guide to Electronic References.* Washington, DC: American Psychological Association, 2007.

The APA system of citation is often used in the social sciences. It is referred to as an author-date method of documentation because parenthetical in-text citations and a reference list (at the end of the paper) emphasize the author(s) and date of publication so that the currency of the research is clear.

> Joseph Gibaldi. *MLA Handbook for Writers of Research Papers.* 7th ed. New York: Modern Language Association of America, 2009. See also <www.mla.org>.

The MLA system is used in the humanities. This style uses parenthetical citations and a list of works cited (at the end of the paper), and it places greater importance on the pages on which cited information can be found than on the publication date.

APA Style

APA In-Text Citations

To document direct quotations in text, give the author's last name, the year of publication, and the page number in parentheses. APA style requires that you use the past or past perfect tenses only for introducing cited material; *Hanley claimed* or *Hanley has claimed*, not *Hanley claims*.

▶ Environmental groups battling global warming need to convince the public that "a low-impact lifestyle" is both worthwhile and doable (Sylvan, 2009, p. 42).

The page number is optional for paraphrased information and ideas.

▶ Despite its gains, the environmental movement has struggled to keep pace with the problems of globalization (Sylvan, 2009).

If the author's name is mentioned in the text, give only the year of publication and the page number in parentheses.

▷   According to Sylvan (2009), environmental groups are working hard to sell the "low-impact
    lifestyle" to the public (p. 42).

Include no more information than is necessary to enable readers to find the corresponding entry in the reference list. If the author's name and the year of publication are mentioned in the text, give only the page number for direct quotations.

▷   As Sylvan pointed out in his 2009 volume, "sadly, natural disasters may be the best way to
    draw attention to the problem of global warming" (p. 184).

Omit parenthetical information for paraphrased material.

▷   In his 2009 volume, Sylvan pointed out the attention-getting impact of natural disasters.

If the citation follows a block quotation, place the citation after the final punctuation mark, as shown in Figure 6–10 on page 191. Use the spacing shown in the examples. Within the citation itself, separate the name, date, and page number with commas. Allow one space after each comma. Use the abbreviation *p.* or *pp.* before page numbers.

If your reference list includes more than one work by the same author published in the same year, list the works alphabetically by title and add the lowercase letters *a*, *b*, *c*, and so forth, to the year in both the reference-list entries and the text citations: (Ostro, 1999b, p. 347). When a work has two authors, cite both names joined by an ampersand: (Maddie & Khoshaba, 2008). For the first citation of a work with three, four, or five authors, include all names.

▷   As Burns, Brooks, and MacNeil (2009) argued . . .

For subsequent citations, include only the name of the first author followed by *et al.* (not italicized).

▷   Burns et al. (2009) put forth the alternate theory . . .

For a work with six or more authors, use the name of the first author followed by *et al.* in all citations.

▷   Their findings led to a burgeoning interest in the new theories of child development (Hargrove
    et al., 2009, p. 21).

When two or more works by different authors are cited in the same parentheses, list the citations alphabetically and use semicolons to separate the citations: (Loftus, 2008; Testerman, Kuegler, & Dowling, 2004; Van Gremergen, 2006).

If you are citing a source created by a corporation or an organization, use its name as the author.

▶ However, high employment rates in the Midwest affected this trend considerably (U.S. Department of Labor, 2009).

If you are quoting a source by an unknown author, use a brief version of the title in your citation.

▶ Textile manufacture had replaced the local maritime trade well before the mid-nineteenth century ("A Short History," p. 19).

If two or more sources have authors with the same last name, use first initials in your citation: (J. Kellogg, p. 414). When citing e-mail, phone calls, or personal interviews, use the words *personal communication* in your parenthetical citation.

▶ Linda Waters (personal communication, November 28, 2008), an executive at CorTex, stated the case succinctly. . . .

To refer to an entire Web site (not just to a particular article or document at that site), include the URL in your parenthetical citation.

▶ The U.S. Department of Commerce provides current statistics on international trade at the Bureau of Economic Analysis Web site (http://www.bea.doc.gov/bea/rels.htm).

However, do not cite the entire Web site in your reference list. To cite a specific document from a Web site, follow the format that you would for a print document (citing the author, year, and page or paragraph number).

▶ Sokol (2009) argued that funding for technical assistance must keep pace with the needs of local communities (para. 8).

If there are no page or paragraph numbers in the online document, include just the author and the year in your parenthetical citation (you will provide further details in the reference list).

▶ In his previous address to the group, he expressed his belief in the value of using technology in the classroom (Maxwell, 2008).

APA Citation Format for a References List

Begin the references list on the first new page following the end of the text and title it "References." Begin each new entry at the left margin, and indent the second and subsequent lines one-half inch from the left margin. (Your instructor may require you to use a paragraph indent instead. If so, begin at a paragraph indent, with subsequent lines continuing at the left margin.) Double-space within and between entries.

Include full page numbers when citing a range of pages for articles (119–124, not 119–24) and indicate with a comma if the page flow of an article is interrupted (119–124, 128–132). Use the abbreviation *p.* or *pp.* only with articles in newspapers (not in magazines or other sources), chapters in edited books, or proceedings.

Include only sources that were essential to the preparation of your document; do not include background reading. Do not include forms of personal communication, such as letters, e-mail, messages from electronic bulletin boards, personal interviews, and telephone conversations. Cite these sources only in the text.

The following listing specifies the APA format and order of elements in a reference list.

Author

- Alphabetize the list by author's last name and initials.
- List multiple works by the same author in publication date order, from earliest to latest. Give each a separate entry.
- For works by corporations or government agencies, alphabetize by organizational name.
- When no author is given, alphabetize by the first significant word in the title.
- For works by multiple authors, list the authors in the order in which they appear on the title page of the work, last name first. Separate author names with commas and insert an ampersand (&) before the last author's name. If there are more than six authors, as there may be on some research articles, provide the first six names and "et al." (*and others*).

Publication Date

- Enclose in parentheses.
- For journals and books, give only the year.
- For periodicals other than journals, give the year, comma, and month or day.

Title

- Capitalize the first word of the title and subtitle of books, articles, or chapters.
- Lowercase all other words except proper nouns.
- Italicize the titles of books.
- Do not use quotation marks or italics for titles of articles or chapters from books.
- End titles with a period.

Multiple Volume or Series Publications

- List the series number following the title, enclosed in parentheses.
- List the volume number following the title, enclosed in parentheses.
- List the edition number following the title, if it is not the first, enclosed in parentheses.

Publishing Information

- List the publishing information last for citations to books, pamphlets, and conference proceedings.
- Show a shortened form of the publisher's name.
- Include the publisher's city and state, unless the publisher's city is well known (e.g., New York).
- Abbreviate the state name using the postal code.
- Omit terms like Publisher, Co., and Inc.
- Do not abbreviate the words *Books* and *Press*.

Periodicals

- Show the title of a journal, magazine, or newspaper in uppercase and lowercase letters.
- List the volume and page numbers after the title.
- Italicize the title and volume numbers.
- Separate elements with commas and end with a period.
- If a journal article has been assigned a digital object identifier (DOI), insert it after the page numbers.

Online Sources

- Review the specific models for citing electronic sources on pages 188–190.

Figure 6–11 on page 192 shows a sample APA-style references page.

APA Documentation Models

Books

Single Author

Stewart, M. (2009). *The management myth: Management consulting past, present, and largely bogus.* New York: Norton.

Multiple Authors

Rosenberger, L. E., & Nash, J. (2009). *The deciding factor: The power of analytics to make every decision a winner.* San Francisco: Jossey-Bass.

Corporate Author

Standard and Poor's. (2009). *Standard and Poor's 500 guide, 2009 edition*. New York: McGraw-Hill.

Edition Other Than First

Sowell, T. (2007). *Basic economics: A common sense guide to the economy* (3rd ed.). New York:
    Basic Books.

Multivolume Work

Edgar, C., & Padgett, R. (Eds.). (2007). *Educating the imagination: Essays and ideas for teachers and
    writers* (Vols. 1–2). New York: Teachers & Writers Collaborative.

Work in an Edited Collection

Eagly, A. H., & Sczesny, S. (2008). Stereotypes about women, men, and leaders: Have times
    changed? In M. Barreto, M. K. Ryan, & M. T. Schmitt (Eds.), *The glass ceiling in the 21st
    century: Understanding barriers to gender equality* (pp. 21–48). Washington, DC: American
    Psychological Association.

Encyclopedia or Dictionary Entry

Wah, B. W. (Ed.). (2009). Agent technology. In *Wiley Encyclopedia of Computer Science and
    Engineering*. Boston: Wiley.

*Articles in Periodicals (*See also *Electronic Sources)*

Magazine Article

Cufone, M. (2008, December). Ocean fish farms and public-resource privatization. *The American
    Prospect, 19*(12), A16–A18.

Journal Article

Jordan, J. (2009). A social cognition framework for examining moral awareness in managers and
    academics. *Journal of Business Ethics, 84*(2), 237–258.

Newspaper Article

Spors, K. K. (2008, October 13). Top small businesses 2008. *Wall Street Journal*, p. R1.

Article with Unknown Author

The battle for the smart-phone's soul. (2008, November 22–28). *The Economist*, pp. 76–77.

APA

Electronic Sources

The APA recommends that a reference to a Web source should provide a document title or description, a date of publication or retrieval, an address (URL) that links directly to the document or section, and an individual or a corporate author, whenever possible. If the document has a fixed publication date, the date of retrieval is not necessary. On the rare occasion that you need to cite multiple pages of a Web site (or the entire site), provide a URL that links to the site's home page. If a document has a DOI, omit the database name; if it does not have a DOI, provide the exact URL; and if the document is accessible by subscription only, provide the URL of the home page.

Document on a Web Site, with an Author

Dubinsky, J. M. (2007). *The future of the ABC: A five-year strategic plan proposal.* Retrieved September 20, 2009, from http://www.businesscommunication.org/about/history/history.html

Document on a Web Site, with a Corporate or an Organizational Author

Boeing. (n.d.). *The shared heritage.* Retrieved May 2, 2009, from http://www.boeing.com/history/narrative/n001intro.html

Document on a Web Site, with an Unknown Author

Vaccine safety: The facts. (2008). Retrieved February 23, 2009, from http://www.cispimmunize.org/pro/pdf/VaccineSafety_parenthandout.pdf

Article with a DOI

Hilbert, T. S., and Renkl, A. (2009). Learning how to use a computer-based concept-mapping tool. *Computers in Human Behavior, 25*(2), 267–274. doi:10.1016/j.chb.2008.12.006

Article or Other Work from a Database

Henderson, S. J. (2009, January). Assessment of personal goals: An online tool for personal counseling, coaching, and business consulting. *Measurement and Evaluation in Counseling and Development, 41*(4), 244–249.

Article in an Online Periodical

Wang, P. (2008, December 12). Fixing the 401(k). *CNNMoney.com.* Retrieved from http://money.cnn.com/2008/12/10/retirement/fixing_401k.moneymag/index.htm

Online Book

Maltoni, V. (2009). *Marketing in 2009.* Available from http://conversationagent.typepad.com/Marketingin2009.pdf

E-mail

Personal communications (including e-mail and messages from discussion groups and electronic bulletin boards) are not cited in an APA references list. They can be cited in the text as follows: "According to J. D. Kahl (personal communication, October 2, 2009), Web pages need to reflect . . ."

Entry in a Wiki

Learning theory. (n.d.). Retrieved February 9, 2009, from EduTech Wiki:
　　http://edutechwiki.unige.ch/en/Learning_theory

Message Posted to a Newsgroup, an Online Forum, or a Discussion Board

proftext. (2008, August 3). Re: Surviving the job search [Reply 165]. Message posted to Chronicle
　　Forums, archived at http://chronicle.com/forums/index.php/topic,40486.165.html

Blog Post

Aula, A., & Rodden, K. (2009, February 6). Eye-tracking studies: More than meets the eye. Message
　　posted to http://googleblog.blogspot.com/2009/02/eye-tracking-studies-more-than-meets.html

Publication on CD-ROM

Tapscott, D., & Williams, A. D. (2007). *Wikinomics: How mass collaboration changes everything*
　　[CD-ROM]. Old Saybrook, CT: Tantor.

Multimedia Sources

Map or Chart

China. (2009). [Map]. Retrieved February 12, 2009, from https://www.cia.gov/library/publications/
　　the-world-factbook/geos/ch.html

Wisconsin. (2007). [Map]. Chicago: Rand.

Film or Video

Fripp, P. (Host), & Jeffreys, M. (Director). (2007). *Super sales presentations: How to captivate your
　　prospects in a distracted, preoccupied world* [DVD]. Waterford, MI: Seminars on DVD.

Iowa Public Television. (2008, December 12). *National debt impact on national security* [Video file].
　　Video posted to http://www.youtube.com/watch?v=hW1UCvqWY2E

Radio or Television Program

Neary, L. (Host). (2009, February 11). Battle brewing over electronic books. *All things considered*
　　[Radio broadcast]. Boston: WGBH. Retrieved February 12, 2009, from http://www.npr.org/
　　templates/story/story.php?storyId=100584020

Koppel, T. (Host). (2009, February 28). The fast lane. *Koppel: People's Republic of Capitalism* [Television broadcast]. Washington, DC: Discovery Channel.

Podcast

Hirsch, P. (2009, February 10). Write-downs. *APM: Marketplace Whiteboard.* Podcast retrieved from http://marketplace.publicradio.org/RSS/

Other Sources

Published Interview

Pitney, J. (2008, January). Q & A [Interview]. *Automobile, 22*, 66.

Personal Interview and Letters

Personal communications (including telephone conversations) are not cited in a reference list. They can be cited in the text as follows: "According to J. D. Kahl (personal communication, October 2, 2009), Web pages need to reflect . . ."

Brochure or Pamphlet

Library of Congress. U.S. Copyright Office. (2007). *Copyright basics* [Brochure]. Washington, DC: U.S. Government Printing Office.

Government Document

U.S. Department of Labor, Bureau of Labor Statistics. (2008). *Women in the labor force: A databook.* Washington, DC: U.S. Government Printing Office.

Report Published in a Collection

Rude, C. D. (2002). Legal and ethical issues in editing. In K. J. Harty (Ed.), *Strategies for business and technical writing*, 5th ed. (pp. 367–378). New York: Pearson.

Report Published Separately

Pew Forum on Religion & Public Life. (2009). *How the faithful voted.* Washington, DC: Author.

Unpublished Data

Kavsan, G., & Hersom, P. (2008). [Oregon small business statistics, by county]. Unpublished raw data.

APA Sample Pages

14   Ethics Cases

This report examines the nature and disposition of the 3,458 ethics cases handled companywide by CGF's ethics officers and managers during 2008. The purpose of such reports is to provide the Ethics and Business Conduct Committee with the information necessary for assessing the effectiveness of the first year of CGF's Ethics Program (Davis, Marks, & Tegge, 2001). According to Matthias Jonas (2004), recommendations are given for consideration "in planning for the second year of the Ethics Program" (p. 152).

The CGF Aircraft Corporation takes its commitment to an ethical work environment seriously. Throughout its 64-year history, CGF has fostered high ethical standards in its relations with its customers, suppliers, and employees. The size, diversity, and decentralized locations of our workforce make it imperative that CGF's ethical commitment — both in principle and in practice — be formalized.

The Office of Ethics and Business Conduct was created to administer the Ethics Program. The director of the Office of Ethics and Business Conduct, along with seven ethics officers throughout CGF, was given the responsibility for the following objectives, as described by Rossouw (1997):

> Communicate the values, standards, and goals of CGF's Program to employees. Provide companywide channels for employee education and guidance in resolving ethics concerns. Implement companywide programs in ethics awareness and recognition. Employee accessibility to ethics information and guidance is the immediate goal of the Office of Business Conduct in its first year. (p. 1543)

The purpose of the Ethics Program, established by the Committee, is to "promote ethical business conduct through open communication and compliance with company ethics standards" (Jonas, 2001, p. 89). To accomplish this purpose, any ethics policy must ensure confidentiality and anonymity for employees who raise genuine ethics concerns. The procedure developed at CGF guarantees appropriate

Shortened title and page number

One-inch margins; text double-spaced

Long quote indented one-half inch, double-spaced, without quotation marks

In-text citation gives name, date, and page number

Figure 6–10   APA Sample Page

APA

Ethics Cases   21

References

Davis, W. C., Marks, R., & Tegge, D. (2001). *Working in the system: Five new manage-*
  ment principles. New York: St. Martin's.

Jonas, M. (2001). Ethics in organizational communication: A review of the literature. *Journal of Ethics and Communication, 29,* 79–99.

Jonas, M. (2004). The Internet and ethical communication: Toward a new paradigm. *Journal of Ethics and Communication, 27,* 147–177.

Lehrer, J. (Host). (2006). *NewsHour business ethics anthology* [DVD]. Encino, CA:
  Business Training Media.

Library of Congress. U.S. Copyright Office. (2008). *Copyright registration for online*
  works [Brochure]. Washington, DC: U.S. Government Printing Office.

Rossouw, G. J. (1997). Business ethics in South Africa. *Journal of Business Ethics, 16,*
  1539–1547.

Schipper, F. (2007). Transparency and integrity: Contrary concepts? In K. Homann,
  P. Koslowski, & C. Luetge (Eds.), *Globalisation and business ethics* (pp. 101–118).
  Burlington, VT: Ashgate.

*Heading
centered*

*List alphabetized by
authors' last names
and double-spaced*

*Hanging-indent style
used for entries*

Figure 6–11   APA Sample List of References

MLA Style

MLA In-Text Citations

When you cite a source in text, give only the author's last name and the page number or numbers in parentheses.

▷ Preparing a videotape of measurement methods is cost-effective and can expedite training (Peterson 151).

If the author's name is mentioned in the text, give only the page number of the source in parentheses.

▷ Peterson summarized the results of these measurements in a series of tables (183–91).

If two or more sources have authors with the same last name, include their initials (or first names if their names begin with the same letter) to avoid confusion.

▷ These results were summarized 40 years ago (R. Peterson 183–91). S. Peterson has recently suggested the reevaluation of these findings (29).

Include no more information than is necessary to enable readers to find the corresponding entry in the list of works cited. To cite an entire work rather than a particular page in a work, mention the author's name in the text and omit the parenthetical citation.

Place a parenthetical citation in the text between the closing quotation mark or the last word of the sentence (or clause) and the end punctuation mark (usually a period). Use the spacing shown in the examples.

▷ The results of these studies have led even the most conservative managers to adopt technologies that will "catapult the industry forward" (Peterson 183–84).

If the parenthetical citation refers to an indented quotation, however, place it outside the last sentence of the quotation, as shown in Figure 6–12 on page 201.

If you are citing a page or pages of a multivolume work, give the volume number, followed by a colon, a space, and the page number(s): (Jones 2: 53–56). If the entire volume is being cited, identify the author and the volume: (Smith, vol. 3).

For more than one work by the same author, give the title of the work (or a shortened version if the title is long) in the parenthetical citation, unless you mention it in the text. If, for example, your list of works cited includes more than one work by Thomas J. Peters, the citation for his book *The Pursuit of Wow: Every Person's Guide to Topsy-Turvy Times* would appear as (Peters, *Pursuit* 93). Use only one space between the title and the page number.

To cite a source written by two or three authors, include all of the names in your parenthetical citation: (Rotherson and Peters 467–75); to cite a source written by four or more authors, include the first author's name followed by the phrase *et al.* ("and others," not italicized) or give all the authors' last names (depending on the style used in the works-cited list). To cite a source in which a separate work is quoted, provide the name of the person being quoted.

▶ According to Billings, there is "a greater potential for a small business to succeed in an urban area" (qtd. in Kooper et al. 421).

To quote a source written by a corporation or an organization, use that name as the author.

▶ However, many declining industries that fueled the economy of the 1950s are now being faced with a government mandate to clean up and preserve the environment (Environmental Protection Agency 16–17).

To quote a source by an unknown author, use a brief version of the title in your citation. (Put titles of articles in quotation marks and titles of books in italics.)

▶ The benefits of this treatment have been known since the early 1980s ("Audio Therapy" 56).

For a sentence that refers to two separate sources, include both in your parenthetical citation, separating them with a semicolon.

▶ Some analysts believe that the impact of electronic commerce caused the extreme market fluctuations of the late 1990s (Jones 174; Dragonetti 267).

To cite electronic sources, follow the same rules that you would for print sources, including as much identifying information as available (e.g., names and page numbers).

▶ As pointed out in a recent *Slate.com* article, America's poor are more numerous but less visible than ever (Connors).

If no names are indicated in the electronic source, use the title (full or shortened) in your citation; if no page numbers are indicated, do not cite any numbers, unless there are paragraph or section numbers. In this case, use the abbreviation *par.* or *sec.* Do not include URLs in your parenthetical citations or in your works-cited list.

▶ According to one online article, the organization's stated mission is to connect North American exporters with appropriate markets in Eastern Europe ("Business to Go," par. 18).

MLA Citation Format for a List of Works Cited

Begin the list of works cited on the first new page following the end of the text. Each new entry should begin at the left margin, with the second and subsequent lines within an entry indented one-half inch from the left margin. Double-space within and between entries. The correct format for dates is as follows: day, month, year, with no commas (19 Jan. 2009). Abbreviate all months except May, June, and July.

The following listing specifies the format of the elements in a list of works cited.

Author

- Alphabetize the list by the author's last name for a single author and by the last name of the first author for works with more than one author.
- List multiple works by the same author in alphabetical order by first significant word in the title. Put three hyphens and a period in place of the author's name for the second and subsequent titles.
- When a corporation or government agency is the author, alphabetize by organizational name, followed by a period.
- When no author is given, alphabetize by the first significant word in the title.
- For edited works, follow the editor's name with a comma and *ed.* or *eds.* (for more than one editor).

Title

- Capitalize the first word in the title and subtitle and all significant words thereafter.
- Italicize the title of a book or pamphlet.
- Put quotation marks around the titles of articles in periodicals, essays in collections, or papers in proceedings.
- End titles with a period.

Multiple Volume or Series Publications

- Specify the edition, if not the first, after the title.
- Give the name of the series and series number after the publication information.
- When you cite one volume, include the volume number after the title and the total number of volumes at the end of the entry; otherwise, include the total number of volumes before the publication information.

Publication Information

- List the place of publication, publisher's name, and date of publication.
- Use a shortened form of the publisher's name.
- When publication information cannot be found, use *n.p.* (no publication place), *n.p.* (no publisher), and *n.d.* (no date).
- For familiar reference works, list only the edition and year of publication.

Medium Consulted

- Include the medium of the work you consulted: *Print, Web, MP3 file, DVD, Lecture, MS* (for a handwritten manuscript or letter), *TS* (for a typescript or typed letter).
- In most cases, the medium is listed at the end of the entry.
- For online entries, the medium is listed before the date of access.

See the documentation models for placement of the medium.

Periodicals

- For journal articles, list the volume number and issue number, date, and page numbers after the title of the periodical.
- For an article in a magazine or newspaper, omit the volume and issue numbers.
- For a newspaper, give the edition and page number(s).
- For a magazine article, give the page number(s).

Online Sources

Standards continue to evolve for citations of online and electronic sources. When citing online information, the two primary goals are to give credit to the author and to enable readers to retrieve the source. The MLA no longer requires the use of URLs but instead assumes readers will be able to find a source by entering the author, title, and other relevant information in a search engine or database.

Review the following guidelines for citing online sources:

- Begin with the author, the title of the work, and, if the work also appears in a printed version, the print publication information.
- Italicize the name of the Web site and follow it with the sponsor or publisher of the Web site. (The sponsor can usually be found in the site's copyright notice.) Then list the date of publication or most recent update, the medium (*Web*), and the date of access.
- For works accessed through a library database, insert the name of the database (in italics) after any print publication information. After the database name, list the medium (*Web*) and the date of access.
- For specific works found online, such as podcasts, wikis, postings to a discussion group, consult the models in the following section.

See Figure 6–13 (page 202) for a sample list of works cited in MLA style.

MLA Documentation Models

Books

Single Author

Duggan, William. *Strategic Intuition: The Creative Spark in Human Achievement.* New York: Columbia
UP, 2007. Print.

Multiple Authors

Scarborough, Norman M., Thomas W. Zimmerer, and Doug Wilson. *Effective Small Business
Management.* 9th ed. New York: Prentice, 2008. Print.

Corporate Author

Microsoft Corporation. *Windows Vista: The New Experience.* Redmond, WA: Microsoft Press, 2007. Print.

Edition Other Than First

Moran, Robert T., Philip R. Harris, and Sarah V. Moran. *Managing Cultural Differences: Global
Leadership Strategies for the 21st Century.* 7th ed. Boston: Butterworths, 2007. Print.

Multivolume Work

Standard and Poor. *2008 Standard and Poor's Register of Corporations, Directors and Executives.*
2 vols. New York: McGraw, 2008. Print.

Work in an Edited Collection

Obriadina, Anna. "Designer Diagnostic Reagents and Allergens." *Medicinal Protein Engineering.*
Ed. Yury E. Khudyakov. Boca Raton: CRC, 2008. Print.

Encyclopedia or Dictionary Entry

"Agent Technology." *Wiley Encyclopedia of Computer Science and Engineering.* Ed. Benjamin W. Wah.
2009 ed. Print.

Articles in Periodicals (See also *Electronic Sources)*

Magazine Article

Surowiecki, James. "Nice Work If You Can Get It." *New Yorker* 2 Mar. 2009: 23. Print.

Journal Article

Thorne, Debbie M., and Beverly T. Venable. "Governance Theory and Practice for Nonprofit
Organisations." *International Journal of Business Governance* 4.2 (2008): 148–65. Print.

Newspaper Article

Zweig, Jason. "1930s Lessons: Brother, Can You Spare a Stock?" *Wall Street Journal* 14 Feb. 2009:
B1. Print.

Article with Unknown Author

"Hard Sell, Hard Times: Shopping in the Recession." *Economist (US)* 13 Dec. 2008: 42. Print.

Electronic Sources

Entire Web Site

Association for Business Communication. Assn. for Business Communication, 2002. Web. 20 Sept.
2008.

Short Work from a Web Site, with an Author

Dubinsky, James M. "The Future of ABC: A Five-Year Strategic Plan Proposal." *Association for
Business Communication*. Assn. for Business Communication, Dec. 2007. Web. 20 Sept. 2008.

Short Work from a Web Site, with a Corporate Author

Kraft Foods. "Measuring Our Environmental Efforts, Making Steady Progress." *Kraft Foods*. Kraft
Foods, 2008. Web. 14 Oct. 2008.

Short Work from a Web Site, with an Unknown Author

"Timeline: World Trade Center Chronology." *American Experience*. PBS Online, 22 Aug. 2003. Web. 26
Sept. 2008.

Article from a Database (Subscription)

Stewart, Nikita. "Officials Want Probe of Lead-Study Paper: WASA's Involvement Also Questioned."
Washington Post. 14 Feb. 2009: B1. *General Reference Center Gold*. Web. 2 Mar. 2009.

Article in an Online Magazine

Manjoo, Farhad. "Jurassic Web: The Internet of 1996 Is Almost Unrecognizable Compared with What
We Have Today." *Slate*. Washington Post. Newsweek Interactive, 24 Feb. 2009. Web. 15 Mar. 2009.

Article in an Online Newspaper

Abate, Tom. "Technology as a Lens to Ponder Imperfect Future." *SFGate.com*. Hearst Communications,
29 Sept. 2008. Web. 12 Jan. 2009.

Online Book

Keynes, John Maynard. *The General Theory of Employment, Interest, and Money*. San Diego: Harcourt,
1964. *Google Books*. Web. 12 Jan. 2009.

Publication on CD-ROM

Tapscott, Don, and Anthony D. Williams. *Wikinomics: How Mass Collaboration Changes Everything.*
CD-ROM. Old Saybrook, CT: Tantor, 2007.

E-mail Message

Kahl, Jonathan D. "Re: Web page." Message to the author. 2 Oct. 2008. E-mail.

Blog

Pham, Alex. *Technology: The Business and Culture of Our Digital Lives.* Los Angeles Times, 9 Mar. 2009.
Web. 20 Mar. 2009.

Entry or Comment on a Blog

Pham, Alex. "Amazon App Lets iPhone Users Read Kindle e-Books." *Technology: The Business and
Culture of Our Digital Lives.* Los Angeles Times, 4 Mar. 2009. Web. 20 Mar. 2009.

Posting to an Online Discussion Group

Viv92. "Laptop Linux and Vista Installation." *Linux: Laptop and Netbook Forum.* LinuxQuestions.org,
LQConsulting, 1 Mar. 2009. Web. 15 Apr. 2009.

Entry in a Wiki

"Category: Organic Farming." *Appropedia.org.* Appropedia, 19 Dec. 2008. Web. 25 Feb. 2009.

Multimedia Sources

Map or Chart

Wisconsin. Map. Chicago: Rand, 2007. Print.

"Grand Canyon National Park." Map. *Google Maps.* Google, 2009. Web. 20 Apr. 2009.

Film or Video

Accident Investigation. Dir. Gordon Massingham. Emergency Film Group, 2002. DVD.

Beuchler, Tina. "Conducting the Job Interview: Hiring a New Employee." *expertvillage.com.* Demand
Media, 2009. Web. 18 Jan. 2009.

Radio or Television Program

"Why Won't Carmakers Buy American?" *Lou Dobbs Tonight.* Host Lou Dobbs. CNN. 30 Dec. 2008.
Television.

"Video Gaming Industry Finds Itself Recession-Proof." *All Things Considered.* Host Robert Siegel.
Natl. Public Radio. *NPR.org.* Web. 14 Jan. 2009.

Television Interview

Woodruff, Bob. "A Conversation with Bob Woodruff, ABC News." Interview by Charlie Rose. *The Charlie Rose Show*. PBS. WGBH, Boston. 5 Aug. 2008. Television.

Podcast

"Cuomo, Goodwin, Holzer, Beschloss, McPherson Discuss Lincoln." Host Tom Keene. *Best of On the Economy*. Bloomberg Radio, 18 Feb. 2009. MP3 file. 22 Mar. 2009.

Other Sources

Published Interview

Clinton, Hillary. "A Common Experience." Interview by Suzanne Smalley. *Newsweek* 17 Mar. 2008: 44. Print.

Personal Interview

Sariolgholam, Mahmood. Personal interview. 29 Nov. 2008.

Personal Letter

Pascatore, Monica. Letter to the author. 10 Apr. 2009. TS.

Brochure or Pamphlet

United States. US Copyright Office. *Copyright Registration for Online Works*. Washington: GPO, 2008. Print.

Government Document

United States. Cong. Congressional Budget Office. *Policy Options for Reducing Carbon Dioxide Emissions*. Washington: GPO, 2008. Print.

Lecture or Speech

Isaacson, Walter. "Einstein, Franklin, and the Role of Creativity in Today's World." Princeton U. 18 Nov. 2008. Lecture.

MLA Sample Pages

Marks 14

This report examines the nature and disposition of the 3,458 ethics cases handled companywide by CGF's ethics officers and managers during 2008. The purpose of such reports is to provide the Ethics and Business Conduct Committee with the information necessary for assessing the effectiveness of the first year of CGF's Ethics Program (Davis, Marks, and Tegge 142). According to Matthias Jonas, recommendations are given for consideration "in planning for the second year of the Ethics Program" ("Internet" 152).

The CGF Aircraft Corporation takes its commitment to an ethical work environment seriously. Throughout its 64-year history, CGF has fostered high ethical standards in its relations with its customers, suppliers, and employees. The size, diversity, and decentralized locations of our workforce make it imperative that CGF's ethical commitment — both in principle and in practice — be formalized.

The Office of Ethics and Business Conduct was created to administer the Ethics Program. The director of the Office of Ethics and Business Conduct, along with seven ethics officers throughout CGF, was given the responsibility for the following objectives, as described by Rossouw:

> Communicate the values, standards, and goals of CGF's Program to employees. Provide companywide channels for employee education and guidance in resolving ethics concerns. Implement companywide programs in ethics awareness and recognition. Employee accessibility to ethics information and guidance is the immediate goal of the Office of Business Conduct in its first year. (1543)

The purpose of the Ethics Program, according to Jonas, is to "promote ethical business conduct through open communication and compliance with company ethics standards" ("Ethics" 89). To accomplish this purpose, any ethics policy must ensure confidentiality and anonymity for employees who raise genuine ethics concerns. The procedure developed at CGF guarantees appropriate discipline, up to and

Author's last name and page number

One-inch margins; text double-spaced

Long quote indented one inch, double-spaced, without quotation marks

In-text citations give author name and page number; title used when multiple works by same author cited

Figure 6–12   MLA Sample Page

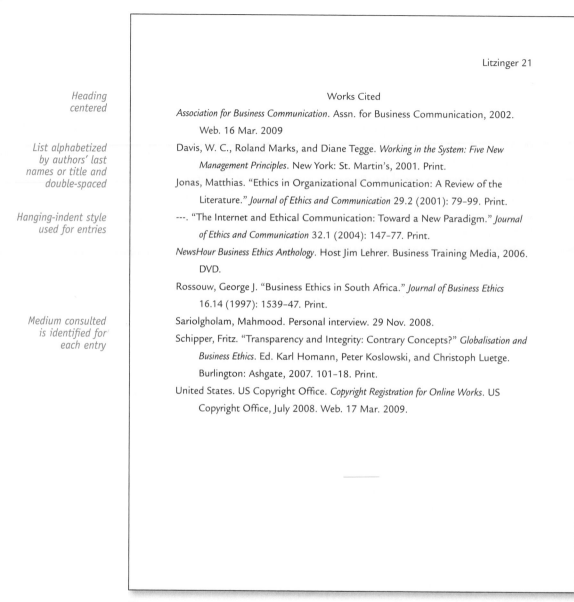

Heading centered

List alphabetized by authors' last names or title and double-spaced

Hanging-indent style used for entries

Medium consulted is identified for each entry

Litzinger 21

Works Cited

Association for Business Communication. Assn. for Business Communication, 2002. Web. 16 Mar. 2009

Davis, W. C., Roland Marks, and Diane Tegge. *Working in the System: Five New Management Principles.* New York: St. Martin's, 2001. Print.

Jonas, Matthias. "Ethics in Organizational Communication: A Review of the Literature." *Journal of Ethics and Communication* 29.2 (2001): 79–99. Print.

---. "The Internet and Ethical Communication: Toward a New Paradigm." *Journal of Ethics and Communication* 32.1 (2004): 147–77. Print.

NewsHour Business Ethics Anthology. Host Jim Lehrer. Business Training Media, 2006. DVD.

Rossouw, George J. "Business Ethics in South Africa." *Journal of Business Ethics* 16.14 (1997): 1539–47. Print.

Sariolgholam, Mahmood. Personal interview. 29 Nov. 2008.

Schipper, Fritz. "Transparency and Integrity: Contrary Concepts?" *Globalisation and Business Ethics.* Ed. Karl Homann, Peter Koslowski, and Christoph Luetge. Burlington: Ashgate, 2007. 101–18. Print.

United States. US Copyright Office. *Copyright Registration for Online Works.* US Copyright Office, July 2008. Web. 17 Mar. 2009.

Figure 6–13   MLA Sample List of Works Cited

Other Style Manuals

Many professional societies, publishing companies, and other organizations publish manuals that prescribe bibliographic reference formats for their publications or for publications in their fields. In addition, several general style manuals are well known and widely used.

Biology

> Council of Science Editors. *Scientific Style and Format: The CSE Manual for Authors, Editors, and Publishers.* 7th ed. Reston: Council of Science Editors, 2006. Print.
>
> See also <councilscienceeditors.org>.

Chemistry

> Dodd, Janet S., ed. *ACS Style Guide: A Manual for Authors and Editors.* 2nd ed. Washington: Amer. Chemical Soc., 1997. Print.
>
> See also <www.acs.org>.

Government Documents

> United States Government Printing Office. *Style Manual.* Washington: GPO, 2000. Print.
>
> See also <www.gpo.gov>.

Journalism

> Christian, Darrell, Sally Jacobson, and David Minthorn, eds. *Associated Press Stylebook and Briefing on Media Law.* Rev. ed. New York: Associated Press, 2008. Print.
>
> See also <www.apstylebook.com>.

Law

> Harvard Law Review et al. *The Bluebook: A Uniform System of Citation.* 18th ed. Cambridge: Harvard Law Rev. Assn., 2005. Print.
>
> See also <www.legalbluebook.com>.

Medicine

> Iverson, Cheryl, et al. *American Medical Association Manual of Style: A Guide for Authors and Editors.* 9th ed. Baltimore: Williams, 1998. Print.
>
> See also <www.ama-assn.org>.

Political Science

> American Political Science Association. *Style Manual for Political Science.* Rev. ed. Washington: APSA, 2001. Print.
>
> See also <www.apsanet.org>.

Social Work

National Association of Social Workers. *Writing for the NASW Press: Information for Authors.* National Association of Social Workers. Web. <www.naswpress.org/resources/tools/01-write/guidelines_toc.htm>.

CHAPTER 6 SUMMARY: RESEARCHING YOUR SUBJECT

Information sources available to you as you research job-related topics include firsthand observations that you gather directly and the results of research published by others that is available in print or online.

- Firsthand observations and experiments are essential to gather information about behavior, natural phenomena, and the functions of processes or equipment. To gather observational information:
  - Choose sites and times carefully and, as necessary, request permission in advance.
  - Keep complete, accurate records and note dates, times, durations, and other details.
  - Remain as unobtrusive as possible to not interfere with the process under observation.
- Interview yourself. Your own knowledge, training, and experience may provide essential information.
- Personal interviews with subject-matter experts can provide up-to-date information not readily available elsewhere, but interviews require thoughtful preparation.
  - Select the subject-matter expert most likely to be helpful.
  - Prepare specific questions before the interview.
  - Take careful notes during the interview.
  - Review and summarize your notes immediately after the interview.
- Questionnaires permit you to obtain the views of groups of people without the time and expense necessary for conducting numerous personal interviews.
  - Design the questionnaire to gather as much information as you need with as little effort as possible on behalf of those answering the questions.
  - Formulate questions so that the answers can be readily tabulated.
  - Carefully select respondents to ensure that their responses represent a cross section of the population to which you wish to generalize your results.
- Libraries provide organized access to a wealth of information in their print, audio-visual, and digitized collections. Researchers can access the information through
  - Library catalogs
  - Databases
  - Reference works
- The Internet provides online access to immense amounts of information, although its lack of a coherent organization makes locating salient information a challenge. To increase the odds of locating what you need, use search engines, subject directories, and metasearch engines.
  - Evaluate print and online sources of information for their relevance, timeliness, and accuracy.

- Review the information source for its depth and breadth of coverage of your topic.
- Ensure that the source is reputable.
- Evaluate the information for any evidence of bias.
- Keep detailed records of these sources for your bibliography.

- Take notes that accurately summarize the information relevant to your topic.
- Avoid plagiarism by giving complete and accurate credit to all your information sources, which will do the following:
  - Allow readers to locate the source of the information given.
  - Establish your credibility by supporting your work with information from existing sources.
  - Give proper credit to your sources.
- Document the information that you quote, paraphrase, or summarize in your text:
  - In brief *parenthetical citations* in text, with full information in an alphabetical list of works cited
  - In *numbered references* in text that refer to full information in a reference section, where citations are listed numerically in the order of their first citation in text.
  - In *notes* that appear either at the bottoms of text pages (footnotes) or in a separate section at the end of a chapter or section (endnotes).
- Document the information that you quote.
- Follow the guidelines of a documentation system like APA or MLA, or another system for a specific field.

ON THE WEB

For an online quiz on research, go to Chapter 6, bedfordstmartins .com/writingthatworks

Exercises

ON THE WEB

For additional exercises, go to Chapter 6, bedfordstmartins.com/ writingthatworks

1. Review the online catalog search in this chapter (illustrated in Figures 6–4 through 6–6 on pages 161 and 162). Choose a topic related to your area of study and conduct a step-by-step online catalog search by keyword. What three to five books would you consider using, and why?

2. For each sentence in the following passage, decide whether it is necessary to add quotation marks or cite a source. Explain your reasoning.

   ▶ Many people have made money investing in real estate in the past couple of years. However, what goes up, comes back down (1). EZHomeBuilders, a corporation that builds luxury homes, announced that falling real estate values are causing them to scale back some projects and cancel others (2). After they announced this, shares of EZHomeBuilders fell 50% on the New York Stock Exchange, closing at $27.14 per share (3). Shares of other major builders fell as well (4).

   My aunt, Shelly Maughn, who is a residential real estate broker, says she thinks the market will return to the way it was about a decade ago, with prices increasing more slowly (5). She also used to work in retail sales and sold furnishings and appliances for homes where she watched sales go up and down with the housing market (6). When business for home builders slowed, business slowed for us, she says (7).

   I worked as an intern in Aunt Shelly's real estate office last summer and I really enjoyed it (8). One day, I hope to become a residential real estate broker and investor even though real estate can be a challenging career (9).

3. Prepare an MLA-style works-cited list or an APA-style reference list, as directed by your instructor, using the following list of sources:

- Allen, R. C. Guiding Change Journeys. New York: John Wiley & Sons, Inc., 2002
- Eula Bingham, Barbara Cohrssen, Charles H. Powell, Editors. Patty's Toxicology: Hydrocarbons/Organic Nitrogen Compounds, Volume four. Fifth edition, John Wiley & Sons, New York, 2001
- Kuhn, Thomas S. The Structure of Scientific Revolutions. 3rd edition, University of Chicago Press, Chicago, Illinois, 1996
- Richard Saul Wurman, Information Anxiety 2, Que, Indianapolis, Indiana, 2001
- Highsmith's Complete School & Library Catalog. Highsmith Inc., Fort Atkinson, WI, 1998
- Jeanine Wornisse Turner, Jean A. Grube, Catherine H. Tinsley, Cynthia Lee, and Cheryl O'Pell. Exploring the Dominant Media: How Does Media Use Reflect Organizational Norms and Affect Performance? Journal of Business Communication, volume 43, number 3, pages 220–250, 2006.
- Bob Boiko, Content Management Bible, Hungry Minds, New York, NY, 2002
- Edward R. Tufte, Beautiful Evidence. Graphics Press, Cheshire, Connecticut, 2006.
- Karen A. Schriver, Dynamics in Document Design. John Wiley & Sons, New York, NY, 1997.
- Wayne Applehans, Alden Globe, and Greg Laugero. Managing Knowledge: A Practical Web-based Approach, Addison-Wesley Information Technology Series. Reading, Mass., Addison-Wesley Longman. 1999.
- Lisa Scherzer, Clearing Emotional Hurdles Leads to More Profits. SmartMoney.com, December 6, 2007, accessed December 17, 2008.
- Thomas Sowell, Basic Economics: A Common Sense Guide to the Economy. Third edition. Basic Books, New York, NY, 2007. Google Books, accessed March 20, 2009.

4. Use one of your library's online periodical databases (such as Academic Search Elite) to find articles related to a recent discovery or an important trend in your field. Write a three-page report of your findings, using the APA or MLA style of documentation. Cite your sources within your text and include an APA-style reference list or an MLA-style list of works cited.

5. Paraphrase the following passage. Then summarize the information. Identify the topic of the passage for each version.

> To keep pipes from freezing, wrap the pipes in insulation made especially for water pipes or in layers of old newspaper, lapping the ends and tying them around the pipes. Cover the newspaper with plastic to keep out moisture. When it is extremely cold and there is real danger of freezing, let the faucets drip a little. Although this wastes water, it may prevent freezing damage. Know where the valve for shutting off the water coming into the house or apartment is located. You may as a last resort have to shut off this main valve and drain all the pipes to keep them from freezing and bursting.

6. For Research Project 2 in Chapter 1, you interviewed instructors about how they prepare their class lectures for their different groups of students. Go back to your interview transcripts and incorporate at least two direct quotes and two paraphrases of your interviewees' comments into your written findings.

7. The use of cell phones, laptop computers, and digital cameras has created a grow-ing need for the recycling of portable rechargeable batteries. Many retail stores are promoting goodwill with their customers and helping to preserve the environ-ment by shipping spent battery packs to recycling centers. Create a questionnaire designed to determine if people are aware of the need to recycle portable rechargeable batteries and how people feel about companies that provide recy-cling programs. Give the questionnaire to at least 20 people, tally your results, and present your findings to the class.

Collaborative Classroom Projects

1. Bring to class information related to your area of study from three Web sites. Print out relevant pages from each site and draft a brief synopsis of the resources pro-vided there. Form groups with three to five students who share your major. Review the guidelines in this chapter for evaluating a Web site and draft a list of questions to consider when evaluating a Web site as a research resource specific to your field. Evaluate and compare each of the sites that your group members have found and decide which sites would be the most valuable for your research. Write a brief group summary of your findings to share with the class.

2. Using the online sources that you brought to class for Collaborative Classroom Project 1, work in a group of three to five students to create an MLA-style list of works cited and an APA-style list of references from your collective online sources. (Refer to the Documenting Sources section of this chapter as needed.)

ON THE WEB

For extra collaborative and research projects, go to Chapter 6, bedfordstmartins.com/ writingthatworks

Research Projects

1. Prepare to interview someone who is now in the career you seek. You can find someone in your field through the campus career development office, local pro-fessional organizations related to your field, or even through relatives and friends. Submit the name and position of the individual as well as a list of questions you plan to ask to your instructor for approval. Write a short report in which you incor-porate the information you gathered at your interview and document the inter-view in MLA or APA style. Submit to your instructor your organized notes of the in-terview and the letter or e-mail that you sent to request the interview.

2. Imagine that you have decided to expand the story in Exercise 2 for publication in a local newspaper. Your goal is to explore trends in your local real estate market over the last three years, using primary sources (interviews and questionnaires, for example) and research published by others.

   a. Begin researching your state's real estate data by going to industry-specific Web sites (such as the Media Center of the Florida Association of Realtors at <http://media.living.net/releases/archive.htm>) and national government sites (like FedStats at <www.fedstats.gov/>).

   b. Use newspaper databases such as LexisNexis (available through your school's library) to locate relevant newspaper articles. NewsLink at (<http://newslink .org/news.html>) lists newspapers and their Web sites in all states.

c. After you have reviewed your notes and have a good idea of local real estate market trends, conduct primary or firsthand research by interviewing a real estate agent or broker from your market, or someone who researches real estate for his or her job—an economics or a statistics professor, for example. Your goal is to include quotes from qualified sources in your story.

Write a story incorporating all of your research. Be sure you paraphrase, quote, and cite your sources correctly.

3. Assume you are a manager at a small manufacturing firm (you may choose the product that your company produces). Because of a rising national concern about the environment and land use, the board of directors has asked your department to develop a policy statement outlining your corporation's views on the conservation of natural resources. Use your library's Web subject directory to locate information about how government environmental policy affects your business. Submit your list of at least five sites with your notes, describing the information contained at each site and giving reasons why you chose these sites. Include with your notes an APA-style reference list or an MLA-style list of works cited.

4. Imagine that you work in public relations at an engineering college and your department is hosting a "brain teaser" competition for local high school students as a strategy to get more of them interested in the sciences and especially in your university. Many engineering professors and consultants will be in the audience. You decide to create a list of questions about space shuttles and go to several sites to research their history, height, wingspan, which three are still in service, and the missions they have flown. You also decide to include quotes from former and current crew members. It is very important not only that you have accurate answers for your questions but also that you have credible sources in case someone doubts your answers.

7 Designing Effective Documents and Visuals

AT A GLANCE: Design

Workplace—and classroom—communications require more than words. They often require tables, drawings, photos, maps, graphs, and charts, elements that must be integrated with text into a unified whole. The integration of text and images takes careful thought to blend these components effectively to advance your purpose and to meet your audience's needs. This chapter describes ways to plan, create, and integrate these nontext elements by doing the following:

- Designing special-purpose documents to make them easy for readers to understand / 210

- Creating or locating the most appropriate visuals to accurately depict data and ideas / 220

- Creating or selecting accurate and culturally sensitive images for international audiences / 250

This chapter is divided into two main parts: The first, Designing Documents, offers detailed information for document layout and design; the second, Creating Visuals, provides guidelines and models for designing illustrations, for integrating them with text, and for using graphics to communicate with an international audience.

Clarity and consistency are important not only for good writing but also for the design and layout of any document—especially one that includes visuals—and for the creation and use of the visuals themselves. Effectively designed documents help readers locate the information they need and grasp how the parts of the document fit together. The Designing Documents section describes how to achieve these goals by providing your readers with carefully selected visual cues. Whether you are creating a memo, a report, or a newsletter, everything from your choice of type size and style to the arrangement of text and visuals on each page contributes to your reader's comprehension.

The Creating Visuals section of this chapter focuses on how to use visual aids to increase your reader's understanding of your topic. Tables, graphs, drawings, charts, maps, and photographs—often collectively called *visuals*—can express ideas or convey information that words alone cannot. Clear, concise visuals support your text and help your readers focus on key points. By allowing readers to understand and interpret data at a glance, visuals can encourage faster decision-making and be used to persuade your audience.

■ Designing Documents

Most memos, letters, meeting minutes, progress reports, and other routine communications are formatted according to a predetermined set of standards. Business-correspondence formats, for example, are discussed in Chapter 8, Understanding the Principles of Business Communication; formal-report formats are discussed in Chapter 11, Writing Formal Reports. However, certain high-visibility, complex, or special-purpose documents, such as those aimed at customers, stockholders, or clients, require special layout-and-design consideration.

This section introduces you to the document layout-and-design principles for such nonroutine materials. Thoughtfully applied, these principles will make even the most complex information look accessible and give readers a favorable impression of the organization that produced it. To accomplish these goals, any document's design should do the following:

- Offer a simple, uncluttered presentation of the topic.
- Highlight the content's structure, hierarchy, and order.
- Help readers find information easily.
- Reinforce an organization's image.

The same content can read differently with and without a well-designed page layout. Figure 7–1, for example, is a sample page from a software instruction manual without any conscious design devices. Note the effort necessary to follow the logic of the instructions—the words and sentences run together without any breaks or pointers to the content's organization and logic. Figure 7–2 shows the

---

Reference numbers have three parts: the basic reference number, a transposition check digit (TCD) that helps verify correct entry of the number, and a suffix that lets the system link related reference numbers such as an incoming message and the reply to that message. The system adds hyphens to longer reference numbers to make them easier to read. Parts of a reference number: in the sequence 123-456789-B123, 123-456789 is the basic reference umber, B is the TCD, and 123 is the suffix.

System messages are informational, advisory, or error messages that appear on screens. Simple messages appear on the last line of any screen. Multiple messages appear on the Message Screen, which is accessed by pressing MESSAGE. The start of the message indicates the message type. Information Message is a confirmation that the system accepts your transaction. ⊠ Important: The most important informational message is TRANSACTION ACCEPTED AND POSTED TO FILES, which indicates the transaction has been successfully completed and is now part of the record for that account, instrument, or instruction. Look for this message as you post each message.

Figure 7–1   Page without Layout or Design

8   System messages — *Header with rule*

Reference numbers — Reference numbers have three parts: the basic reference number, a *transposition check digit* (TCD) that helps verify correct entry of the number, and a *suffix* that lets the system link related reference numbers such as an incoming message and the reply to that message. — *Two-column design*

The system adds hyphens to longer reference numbers to make them easier to read.

Parts of a reference number

— *Boxed figure with caption*

Parts of a reference number: TCD → 123-456789-B123, basic reference number, suffix

System messages — System messages are informational, advisory, or error messages that appear on screens. — *Headings*

Where do the messages appear? — Single messages appear on the last line of any screen. Multiple messages appear on the Message screen, which is accessed by pressing **MESSAGE**.

Message types — The start of each message indicates the message type:

    Informational Message — a confirmation that the system accepts your transaction.

    ▷ **Important**: The most important informational message is TRANSACTION ACCEPTED AND POSTED TO FILES, which indicates the transaction has been successfully completed and is now part of the record for that account, instrument, or instruction. Look for this message as you post each transaction. — *White space / Icon and boldface*

— *Rule and footer*

Figure 7–2   Page Illustrating Design and Layout Choices

same information with a layout that both highlights the content's sequence and cues the reader to the location of this material within the manual.

Effective design is based on visual simplicity and harmony, such as using compatible fonts and the same highlighting device for similar items. Design should reveal hierarchy by signaling the difference between topics and subtopics, between primary and secondary information, and between general points and examples that support those points. Writers can achieve these goals by intentionally selecting fonts, choosing devices to highlight information, and arranging text and visual components on a page. In addition to making information easy to find, the design should project the appropriate image of an organization. For example, if clients are paying a high fee for consulting services, they may expect a sophisticated, polished design; if employees inside an organization expect management

ON THE WEB

For more information on designing effective documents and visuals, go to Chapter 7, bedfordstmartins.com/ writingthatworks to be frugal, they may accept — even expect — economical and standard company design.

Typography

Typography refers to the style and arrangement of type on a printed page. A complete set of all the letters, numbers, and symbols available in one typeface (or style) is called a *font*.

Typeface

Ideal type sizes for presentation slides and Web sites are discussed in Chapter 14, Giving Presentations and Conducting Meetings, and Chapter 15, Writing for the Web.

For most on-the-job writing, select a typeface primarily for its simplicity and legibility. Avoid typefaces that may distract readers with contrasts in thickness or with odd-looking features, as is often the case with script and cursive typefaces. One major distinction among typefaces is the presence or absence of serifs. Serifs are the small projections at the end of each stroke in a letter. The text of this book is set in Utopia, a serif typeface, and all headings are in Officina Sans, a sans serif (without serifs) typeface. Serif type is easier to read, especially in the smaller sizes, and it works better for main text than sans serif. Sans serif type, however, works well for headings (like the ones in this book). The simpler design of sans serif letters also makes them ideal for use with text on Web sites and for use in other documents read on-screen. Choose popular typefaces with which readers are familiar, such as Times New Roman, or any of the following:

Baskerville	Century	Gill Sans	Palatino
Bodoni	Garamond	Helvetica	Univers

Do not use more than two or three typefaces in a single document — using too many typefaces will create visual disharmony in your document. To create a dramatic contrast between headings and text, as in a newsletter, use a typeface for the heading that is distinctively different from that of the text. You can also use a noticeably different typeface within a graphic element. In any case, experiment before making your final decision. (Keep in mind that not all fonts have the same assortment of symbols and other characters that you may need for your graphics.)

Type Size

Ensure that your text is easily readable. Small print can cause eyestrain and make the text look crammed and intimidating. Six-point type, for example, is too small for almost anything other than classified ads. Likewise, large type makes reading difficult for a general audience, although it may be suitable for readers with visual impairment. Ideal point sizes for text in paper documents range from 10 to 12 points. For documents that will be read from a distance or that are geared toward visually impaired readers, use large type sizes. Figure 7–3 illustrates a range of type sizes.

6 pt. This size might be used for dating a source.
8 pt. This size might be used for footnotes.
10 pt. This size might be used for headers and footers.
12 pt. This size might be used for main text and figure captions.
14 pt. This size might be used for section headings.
18 pt. This size might be used for chapter titles.

Figure 7–3   Samples of 6- to 18-Point Type Sizes

Highlighting Devices

Highlighting devices can give a document a visual logic and organization. For example, rules and boxes can set off steps and illustrations from surrounding explanations. However, be selective about how you use typographical devices and special graphics; too many design devices clutter a page and interfere with comprehension. And consistency is important: Use the same technique to highlight a particular feature throughout your document. Writers use a number of methods to emphasize important words, passages, and sections within documents:

- Typographical devices
- Headings and captions
- Headers and footers
- Rules, icons, and color

Look at Figure 7–2 again to see a variety of highlighting devices.

◆ *For additional guidance on highlighting facts and ideas, see pages 101–106 in Chapter 4, Revising the Draft.*

Typographical Devices

When used sparingly, **boldface**, *italics*, and ALL-CAPITAL LETTERS can help you achieve emphasis.

- Use **boldface** type for headings or short passages of text to which you would like to draw attention.
- Use *italics* to highlight a key term or phrase or to slow readers, as in cautions or warnings.
- Use ALL-CAPITAL LETTERS for headings (with or without boldface) or to alert readers to crucial steps in a process, as in instructions, or to indicate danger, such as in a caution or warning message.

Headings and Captions

Headings—titles and subtitles within the body of a document—divide material into comprehensible segments by highlighting the main topics and signaling

@ DIGITAL TIPS: Designing Documents with a Word Processor

A variety of word-processing features can help you adhere to the requirements of your instructor or employer or to customize the text layout and other elements affecting the appearance of your document.

■ *Page margins.* Page margins, usually preset at one or one-and-a-quarter inches on all sides of a page, can be changed for an entire document, for a given page, or for blocks of text within a page.

■ *Columns.* Lines of text can be arranged to run across the page from left to right or to run in two or more columns. The columns feature can also be used for data in tables, membership lists, financial statements, rosters, and the like.

■ *Margin alignment.* Headings, columns, blocks of text, and visuals can be centered, aligned solely on the left margin, or aligned on both left and right margins.

■ *Centering.* Words. Lines of text and blocks of text can be centered between the right and left margins, a feature useful for creating titles, letterheads on stationery, and captions for tables and figures.

■ *Line, word, and letter spacing.* The space between lines of text can be adjusted (single-, double-, triple-spaced, and so on), and unnecessary space between words and letters on a line can be eliminated.

■ *Headers, footers, and page numbers.* Headers (titles at the top of a page), footers (titles at the bottom of a page), and page numbers can be inserted automatically on each page.

■ *Type fonts.* The text for letters, reports, manuals, and other types of documents can be printed with a variety of type fonts that you deem appropriate to your purpose and readers. (A *font* is a complete set of letters, numbers, and other type characters with a distinctive and uniform design.)

■ *Type style.* The text may also be printed using a variety of type styles within the basic font chosen. Type-style options include **boldface**, *italic*, and <u>underlining</u> to highlight or otherwise create distinctive text.

■ *Preview mode.* Preview mode allows you to view a full page or facing pages of your document on-screen exactly as it will look when it is printed. Save time and paper by evaluating the overall look of a page and adjusting it if necessary before you print.

■ *File type.* To preserve the format of a document you send by e-mail, you can create it as a word-processing file and send that as an attachment, scan and save the document as a graphic file, or convert it to PDF format using Adobe Acrobat software. Whichever format you use, confirm in advance that your recipient can open the file you send.

■ *Style sheets and templates.* For multiple documents that need a uniform look, create and save format specifications as a separate file. The file can be called up and automatically applied to subsequent versions of the same kind of document.

For a tutorial on these options, see <bedfordstmartins.com/writingthatworks> and select *Tutorials,* "Designing Documents with a Word Processor." For step-by-step instructions for setting margins, alignment, columns, and other design elements, select *Digital Tips,* "Laying Out a Page."

topic changes. They indicate the hierarchy within a document and help readers decide which sections they need to read. Captions—titles that highlight or describe illustrations or blocks of text—often appear below figures, above tables, and in the left or right margins next to blocks of text. Note the captions used to describe the figures and tables throughout this book.

Headings appear in many typeface variations (**boldface** being most common) and often use sans serif typefaces. The most common positions for headings and subheadings are centered, flush left, indented, or by themselves in a wide left margin. Insert an additional line of space above a heading to emphasize the division on the page. Major section or chapter headings normally appear at the top of a new page. Never leave a heading as the final line on a page—the heading will be disconnected from its text and thus ineffective. Instead, move the heading to the start of the next page. A heading that appears near the end of a page should be followed by at least two lines of text.

◆ *For detailed advice on using and formatting headings in formal reports, see pages 403–409 in Chapter 11, Writing Formal Reports.*

Headers and Footers

A header is identifying information carried at the top of each page; a footer is similar information at the bottom of each page. They help readers pinpoint their location within a document. (The header at the top of the next page reads "Chapter 7 ◆ Designing Effective Documents and Visuals," and includes the page number.) Document pages may have headers or footers or both. They carry such information as the topic or subtopic of a section, the section number, the date the document was written, the page number, the document name, or the section title. Although headers and footers are important reference devices, limit the amount of information in them to avoid visual clutter. Headers and footers are usually in a smaller type size than the main text.

Rules, Icons, and Color

Rules are vertical or horizontal lines used to divide one area of the page from another or to create boxes; used in moderation, rules isolate and highlight important information for ease of reading. Figure 7–2 illustrates the effective use of rules to separate the header and footer from the main text.

An icon is a pictorial representation of an idea; it can be used to identify specific actions, objects, or sections of a document. Commonly used icons include the small envelopes on Web pages to symbolize e-mail links and paper clips to denote attachments to an e-mail. Because they convey ideas without words, they are especially useful in communications with international audiences. To be effective, however, icons must be simple and easily recognizable to your reader. Figures 7–36 and 7–37 on pages 254–255, for example, illustrate internationally recognized icons (also called symbols).

Color and screening (or shading) can distinguish one part of a document from another or unify a series of documents. Color and screening can set off sections within a document, highlight examples, or emphasize warnings. These devices are especially useful in graphs, maps, and drawings to differentiate boundaries and to depict the actual colors of geological and biological samples. In tables, you can use screening to highlight column titles or sets of data to which you want to draw the reader's attention. Figure 7–13 on page 233, for example, uses screening to differentiate the data between January to June from data for the year.

Page Design

◆ *For information about using graphics and typography on Web sites, see pages 550–552 in Chapter 15, Writing for the Web.*

Page design is the process of combining the various elements on a page to make a coherent whole. The flexibility of your design is based on the capabilities of your software, how the document will be reproduced, and your budget. (High-quality offset color printing, for example, is far more expensive and time-consuming than black-and-white printing.)

Thumbnail Sketches

Before you spend time positioning text and visuals on a page, you may want to create a thumbnail sketch, in which blocks indicate the placement of elements. Thumbnails are usually sketched by hand on a lined tablet or graph paper, although some software programs make sample layout and design easy to experiment with on-screen. Your sketches need not be formal or even neat. They are simply a way to brainstorm design options before you begin the actual layout of a report, newsletter, brochure, or other document. Figure 7–4 shows thumbnail sketches of designs for an 8 1/2-by-11-inch report with two columns per page and for an 8 1/2-by-11-inch newsletter with three columns per page. You can go further by roughly assembling all the thumbnail pages, showing size, shape, form, and general style of a large document. Such a mock-up, called a *dummy*, allows you to see how a finished document will look. As you work with elements on the page, experiment with different layouts to make sure that your ideas work in practice.

ON THE WEB

For examples of well-designed newsletters and brochures, go to Model Documents Gallery, bedfordstmartins.com/writingthatworks

Columns

As you design pages, consider the size and number of columns. A single-column format works well with larger typefaces, double-spacing, and left-justified margins. For smaller typefaces and single-spaced lines, the two-column structure enhances legibility by keeping text columns narrow enough so that readers need not scan back and forth across the width of the entire page for every line. Check and correct your document for single words or parts of words that appear alone as first or last lines of your columns. Figure 7–5 on page 218 shows a report formatted in two columns.

White Space

White space (the area on the page or screen free of text or design elements) visually frames information and breaks it into manageable chunks. For example, white space between paragraphs helps readers see the information in the paragraphs as units. White space between sections is also a visual cue that one section is ending and another is beginning. You need not have access to sophisticated equipment to

Figure 7–4 Thumbnail Sketches for a Report (*top*) and a Newsletter (*bottom*)

Left-justified columns

Nonuniform right-margin line endings

Optical and Handwritten Character Recognition Software: Recent Developments

Since the inception of computers, programmers have been teaching them to mimic humans. One such task that humans often take for granted is literacy. The process of reading printed text with a computer is called Optical Character Recognition (OCR). This method is optical because it uses a scanner to measure the reflected light off a piece of paper much like a copy machine does (Srihari and Lam 1–4). Along with OCR technology came handwriting recognition. Handwriting recognition occurs when the computer identifies each character the user writes with an electronic pen. Both OCR and handwriting recognition currently allow the computer almost 100 percent accuracy in understanding the writing of its human counterpart ("Looking Forward" 213).

What Are the Practical Applications?
OCR and handwriting recognition are used daily for such tasks as reading your tax forms and checking your passport at customs. The IRS, for example, receives about 200 million tax forms every year. So OCR is an important technology in processing tax forms because of OCR's speed and accuracy compared with manual interpreta-

to 45,000 pieces of mail an hour (Srihari and Lam 12). . . .

How Does Scanning Work?
When the computer scans a page of text it does so graphically. All the computer sees at first is a grid of many small dots where each dot is either black or white. A typical scanner reads 300 of these dots per square inch.

The Letter R as printed (*left*) and as scanned into a matrix of dots (*right*).

In the first step of processing a page of text, the computer looks at the whole document and decides which regions contain text, and within those regions it searches for individual

---

Full-justified columns

Uniform right-margin line endings

Optical and Handwritten Character Recognition Software: Recent Developments

Since the inception of computers, programmers have been teaching them to mimic humans. One such task that humans often take for granted is literacy. The process of reading printed text with a computer is called Optical Character Recognition (OCR). This method is optical because it uses a scanner to measure the reflected light off a piece of paper much like a copy machine does (Srihari and Lam 1–4). Along with OCR technology came handwriting recognition. Handwriting recognition occurs when the computer identifies each character the user writes with an electronic pen. Both OCR and handwriting recognition currently allow the computer almost 100 percent accuracy in understanding the writing of its human counterpart ("Looking Forward" 213).

What Are the Practical Applications?
OCR and handwriting recognition are used daily for such tasks as reading your tax forms and checking your passport at customs. The IRS, for example, receives about 200 million tax forms every year. So OCR is an important technology in processing tax forms because of OCR's speed and accuracy compared with manual interpretation

to 45,000 pieces of mail an hour (Srihari and Lam 12). . . .

How Does Scanning Work?
When the computer scans a page of text it does so graphically. All the computer sees at first is a grid of many small dots where each dot is either black or white. A typical scanner reads 300 of these dots per square inch.

The Letter R as printed (*left*) and as scanned into a matrix of dots (*right*).

In the first step of processing a page of text, the computer looks at the whole document and decides which regions contain text, and within those regions it searches for individual letters

Figure 7–5   Left-Justified (*top*) and Full-Justified (*bottom*) Text Columns make good use of white space. Use the default-margin setting on your word processor (usually 1 or 1¼ inches), but allow extra space at the left margin for the binding if your document will be three-hole punched for binders.

Left- or Full-Justified Margins

Pages with left-justified margins are generally easier to read than pages with full-justified margins because the uneven contour of the right margin (or "ragged" right) allows the spacing within and between words to be more uniform. Full justification causes word-processing software to insert irregular-sized spaces between words, producing unwanted gaps or unevenness in blocks of text, often making your document more difficult to read. Full-justified text is more appropriate for publications such as corporate annual reports, consumer booklets, sales brochures, and other documents aimed at a broad readership that expects a more formal, polished appearance. Full justification is often useful with multiple-column formats because the spaces between the columns (alleys) need the definition that full justification provides. Figure 7–5 shows the same document with left-justified (*top*) and full-justified (*bottom*) columns.

Lists

Lists are an effective way to highlight words, phrases, and short sentences. Further, they are easy to read. Lists are particularly useful for certain types of information:

- Steps in sequence
- Materials or parts needed
- Items to remember
- Criteria for evaluation
- Concluding points
- Recommendations

Avoid both too many lists and too many items in lists.

ON THE WEB

For advice on using word-processing software to lay out your document, go to Chapter 7, **bedfordstmartins .com/writingthatworks**

◆ *For more information about using lists effectively, see page 105 in Chapter 4, Revising the Draft.*

Illustrations

Readers notice illustrations, especially large ones, before they notice text. Therefore, choose the size of an illustration according to its relative importance within your document. For newsletter articles and publications aimed at wide audiences, consider especially the proportion of the illustration to the text. In magazine design, for example, page layout is more dramatic and appealing when the major illustration (photograph, drawing, and so on) occupies three-fifths rather than half the available space. The same principle can be used to enhance the visual appeal of a report. Although aesthetic considerations are important, it's most important that your document is clear and useful. For example, placing illustrations at the end of a report usually makes the writer's task easier, but placing them in the text closer to their accompanying explanations gives readers more convenient access to them and provides visual breaks from blocks of text. (Creating visuals and integrating them with text is discussed in the next section.)

> ## DESIGNING YOUR DOCUMENT
> ### Laying Out the Page
> ▪ Select typefaces for legibility in style and size, not simply for variety.
> ▪ Emphasize important information with consistent typographical and design devices, using the following:
> - All-capital, italic, and boldface type styles selectively
> - Headings (in boldface or italic type) to denote major sections and topic changes
> - Captions to identify figures and tables, and to emphasize boxed information
> - Headers and footers to orient readers at the page level
> - Rules, icons, and color to highlight crucial information
> ▪ Integrate the typographical and page-level design elements into a consistent, coherent whole.
> - Experiment with the positions of text and visuals on a variety of thumbnail sketches to evaluate how the elements look together.
> - Create a mock-up copy, or dummy, of the whole document by assembling the thumbnail sketches for review.
> - Experiment with one- and two-column text layouts.
> - Allow adequate white space between paragraphs and around visuals and text boxes.
> - Use lists to highlight comparable types of information by setting them off from the surrounding text.
> - Position visuals in proportion to their importance and set them off with adequate white space.

▪ Creating Visuals

Visuals can express ideas or convey information in ways that words alone cannot. For example, tables allow readers to easily compare large numbers of statistics that would be difficult to understand in sentence form. Graphs make trends and mathematical relationships immediately evident. Drawings, photographs, charts, and maps render shapes and spatial relationships more concisely and efficiently than text can. By allowing the reader to interpret data at a glance, visuals not only encourage faster decision-making but may add to the persuasiveness of your document or Web site. The guidelines in Table 7–1 can help you select the most appropriate visuals based on their purpose and special features.

Designing and Integrating Visuals with Text

When using tables, graphs, or illustrations, consider your purpose and your reader carefully. For example, a drawing of the major regions of the brain for a high school science class would be different from an illustration provided for research

TO SHOW OBJECTS AND SPATIAL RELATIONSHIPS

DRAWINGS CAN . . .

- Depict real objects difficult to photograph
- Depict imaginary objects
- Highlight only parts viewers need to see
- Show internal parts of equipment in cutaway views
- Show how equipment parts fit together in exploded views
- Communicate to international audiences more effectively than text alone

PHOTOGRAPHS CAN . . .

- Show actual physical images of subjects
- Record an event in progress
- Record the development of phenomena over time
- Record the as-found condition of a setting for an investigation
- Show the colors essential to the accuracy of information in medical, chemical, forensic, botanical, and other fields

TO DISPLAY GEOGRAPHIC INFORMATION

MAPS CAN . . .

- Show specific geographic features of an area
- Show distance, routes, or locations of sites
- Show the geographic distribution of information (e.g., populations by region)

TO SHOW NUMERICAL AND OTHER RELATIONSHIPS

TABLES CAN . . .

- Organize numerical and nonnumerical information systematically in rows and columns
- Present large numerical quantities concisely
- Facilitate item-to-item comparisons more easily than if embedded in text
- Clarify trends and other graphical information with precise data

BAR AND COLUMN GRAPHS CAN . . .

- Depict data in vertical bars and horizontal columns for comparison
- Show quantities that make up a whole
- Visually represent data shown in tables

LINE GRAPHS CAN . . .

- Show trends over time in amounts, sizes, rates, and other measurements
- Give an at-a-glance impression of trends, forecasts, and extrapolations of data

TABLE 7–1 Choosing Appropriate Visuals (continued)

LINE GRAPHS CAN . . .	• Compare more than one kind of data over the same time period
	• Visually represent data shown in tables
PICTURE GRAPHS CAN . . .	• Use recognizable images to represent specific quantities
	• Add visual appeal to help nonexpert readers grasp the information
	• Visually represent data shown in tables
PIE GRAPHS CAN . . .	• Show quantities that make up a whole
	• Give an immediate visual impression of the parts in proportion to one another
	• Visually represent data shown in tables or lists

TO SHOW STEPS IN A PROCESS OR RELATIONSHIPS IN A SYSTEM

FLOWCHARTS CAN . . .	• Show how the parts or steps in a process or system interact from beginning to end
	• Show the stages of an actual or a hypothetical process in the correct direction, including recursive steps
SCHEMATIC DIAGRAMS CAN . . .	• Show how the components in electronic, chemical, electrical, and mechanical systems interact and are interrelated
	• Use standardized symbolic representations rather than realistic depictions of system components

TO SHOW RELATIONSHIPS IN A HIERARCHY

ORGANIZATION CHARTS CAN . . .	• Give an overview of an organization's departmental components
	• Show how the components relate to one another
	• Depict lines of authority within an organization: who reports to whom

TO SUPPLEMENT OR REPLACE WORDS

SYMBOLS OR ICONS CAN . . .	• Convey ideas without words
	• Save space and add visual appeal
	• Transcend individual languages to communicate ideas effectively for international readers
	• Communicate culturally neutral images

TABLE 7–1 Choosing Appropriate Visuals (continued)

VOICES IN THE WORKPLACE

Tailoring Visuals for the Target Audience

As an information analyst at Compuware Corporation, Howard Ellis relies heavily on visuals to reach a diverse audience: "Visuals play a significant role in the work I do; it would be impossible for me to write effectively about technology without them. . . . For a highly technical audience, I may present detailed visuals from some aspect of a project, including tables, screen shots, and possibly graphs. For another audience, such as a group of executives, I'll pare back the details."

scientists studying brain abnormalities. Be aware, though, that even the best visual only enhances, or supports, the text. It is your writing that must carry the burden of providing context for the visual and pointing out its significance.

To make the most effective use of visuals and to integrate them smoothly with the text of your document, consider your graphics requirements even before you begin to write. Plan your visuals—tables, graphs, drawings, charts, maps, or photographs—when you're planning the scope and organization of your final work, whether it's a report, newsletter, brochure, presentation, or Web site. Make graphics an integral part of your outline, noting approximately where each should appear throughout the text. At each place where you plan to include a visual, either make a rough sketch of the visual or write "illustration of . . ." and enclose each suggestion in a box in your outline. If you are working on your computer, you can copy and paste graphics directly into your outline at the appropriate places, using your computer's clipboard feature. Like other information in a working outline, these boxes and sketches can be moved, revised, or deleted as required.

The following guidelines will help you create your visual materials and incorporate them into your documents effectively. (If you have an international audience, be sure to read Using Visuals to Communicate Internationally on pages 250–256.)

◆ *For guidance on preparing presentation graphics, see pages 504–511 in Chapter 14, Giving Presentations and Conducting Meetings.*

- **Why include your visual?** Explain in the text why you've included the illustration. The description for each visual will vary with its complexity and its importance. Consider your audience: Nonexperts require lengthier explanations than experts do, as a rule.

- **Is the information in your visual accurate?** Gather the information from reliable sources.

- **Is your visual focused and free of clutter?** Include only information necessary to the discussion in the text and eliminate unnecessary parts and components as well as labels, arrows, boxes, and lines.

- **Are terms and symbols in your visual defined and consistent?** Define all acronyms in the text, figure, or table. If any symbols are not self-explanatory, include a listing (known as a *key*) that defines them. Keep terminology consistent. Do not refer to the same data as a "proportion" in the text and as a "percentage" in the illustration.

- **Does your visual specify measurements and distances?** Specify the units of measurement used, when appropriate. Ensure that relative sizes are clear or indicate distance by a scale, as on a map.
- **Is the lettering readable?** Position any explanatory text or labels horizontally for ease of reading, if possible.
- **Is the caption clear?** Give each illustration a concise caption that clearly describes its contents.
- **Is there a figure or table number?** Assign a figure or table number for documents containing five or more illustrations. The figure or table number precedes the title:

  ▷   Figure 1. Projected research budget for 2009–2013

  Note that graphics (photographs, drawings, maps, and so on) are generically labeled "figures"; tables (data organized in rows and columns) are labeled "tables."
- **Is a list of figures or tables needed?** In documents with more than five illustrations, list the illustrations in a separate section of the table of contents by title, together with figure and page numbers, or table and page numbers, following the table of contents. Title the list of figures "List of Figures" and of tables "List of Tables."
- **Are figure or table numbers referred to in your text?** Refer to each visual by its figure or table number in the text of your document.
- **Are visuals appropriately placed?** Place illustrations as close as possible and following the text where they are discussed. Place lengthy and detailed illustrations in an appendix and refer to them in the text of your document.
- **Do visuals stand out from surrounding text?** Allow adequate white space on the page around and within each illustration.

◆ *For more on evaluating sources, see pages 171–181 in Chapter 6, Researching Your Subject.*

A discussion of specific types of visuals commonly used in on-the-job writing follows. Your topic will ordinarily determine the best type of visual to use.

Tables

A table is useful for showing large numbers of specific, related data in a brief space. The data may be numerical, as in Figure 7–6 on page 226, or verbal, as in Table 7–2 on page 253. Because a table displays information in rows and columns, your readers can easily compare data and see their significance more clearly than if the data were presented in the text.

Following are the elements of a typical table, as shown in Figure 7–6, with guidelines:

- *Table number.* Number each table sequentially throughout the text.

- *Table title.* Create a title that describes concisely what the table represents; place it above the table.

- *Boxhead.* In the boxhead (beneath the title) provide column headings that are brief but descriptive. Include units of measurement either as part of the heading or enclosed in parentheses beneath it. Standard abbreviations and symbols are acceptable. When possible, avoid vertical or diagonal lettering.

- *Stub.* In the left-hand vertical column of a table, called the stub, list all the items to be shown in the body of the table.

- *Body.* Provide data in the body of your table below the column headings and to the right of the stub. (Each datum element is located in a *cell.*) Within the body, arrange columns so that the terms to be compared appear in adjacent rows and columns. Where no information exists for a specific cell, substitute a row of dots or a dash to acknowledge the gap. If you substitute the abbreviation "N/A" for missing data in a cell, add a footnote to clarify whether it means "not available" or "not applicable."

- *Rules.* Use rules (lines) to separate your table into its various parts. Include horizontal rules below the title, below the body of the table, and between the column headings and the body of the table. You may include vertical rules to separate the columns, but do not use rules to enclose the sides of the table.

- *Source line.* Below the table, include a source line to identify where you obtained the data (when appropriate). Many organizations place the source line below the footnotes.

- *Footnotes.* Include a footnote when you need to explain an item in the table. Use symbols (*, †) or lowercase letters (sometimes in parentheses) rather than numbers to make it clear that the notes are not part of the data or the main text.

- *Continuing tables.* When you must divide your table to continue it on another page, repeat the column headings and give the table number at the head of each new page with a "continued" label ("Table 3, continued"), as shown in Figure 7–7 on page 227.

ETHICS NOTE

Whether you reprint a preexisting image or use published information to create your own graph or table, you must acknowledge your borrowings in a source or credit line. Place source information below the caption for a figure and below any footnotes at the bottom of a table. (See Figure 7–6 for an example.) If you wish to use illustrations found on the Web or in printed sources, obtain written permission from the copyright holder. Material that is not copyrighted (generally limited to publications of the U.S. government) can be reproduced without permission, but you must still acknowledge the source in a credit line.

Table number

Boxhead

Stub

Rule

Footnotes

Source line

Table title

Column headings

Body

Table 1 U.S. Population, Employment, and Gross Product Projections, 1980–2010

	1980	1990	2000	2010	1980–2010*
Population (thousands)					
Total	226,549	249,402	276,241	300,431	32.6
Under 18	63,755	64,156	71,789	73,617	15.5
18–64	137,240	154,011	169,131	186,709	36.0
65 and over	25,549	31,235	35,322	40,104	57.0
Employment (thousands of jobs)					
All-industry total	113,726	138,981	157,656	176,164	54.9
Manufacturing	20,777	19,756	18,890	18,850	(9.3)[†]
Retail trade	17,853	23,020	26,402	29,450	65.0
Services	24,558	38,188	49,474	59,379	141.8
Government	18,796	21,203	23,065	24,750	31.7
Other	31,743	36,815	39,825	43,737	37.8
Gross state product (millions of 1987 dollars)					
All-industry total	3,697,140	4,888,324	6,025,600	7,219,400	95.3
Manufacturing	725,428	928,483	1,105,409	1,279,410	76.4
Retail trade	320,134	478,080	603,150	726,774	127.0
Services	609,012	869,360	1,103,812	1,371,477	125.2
Government	494,431	564,163	617,863	686,916	38.9
Other	1,548,135	2,048,238	2,595,367	3,154,824	103.8

*Represents percent change
[†]Figures in parentheses are negative
Source: U.S. Small Business Administration, Office of Advocacy, from data provided by the Bureau of Economic Analysis.

Figure 7–6   Table

To list relatively few items that would be easier for the reader to grasp in tabular form, use an informal table within the text of your document.

   The sound-intensity levels (decibels) for the three frequency bands (in hertz) were determined to be the following:

Frequency Band (Hz)	Decibels
600–1,200	68
1,200–2,400	62
2,400–4,800	53

Although you need not include titles or table numbers to identify informal tables, you do need to include headings that describe the information provided and columns and rows that are properly aligned. You may also need to acknowledge the source of the information, as discussed in the Ethics Note on page 225.

Table 4

Assessment of Electronic Media and Format Standards in Federal Agencies: Number, Percentage, and Basis for Use by Agency

Format	Agency mandated		Common agency practice		Other		None	
	Number	Percent	Number	Percent	Number	Percent	Number	Percent
Database								
Oracle	7	38.9	8	44.4	1	5.6	1	5.6
WAIS	1	4.3	21	91.3	0	0.0	0	0.0
MARC	1	33.3	1	33.3	0	0.0	0	0.0
Sybase	0	0.0	4	80.0	0	0.0	0	0.0
dBase	0	0.0	8	80.0	0	0.0	0	0.0
Other	2	4.4	21	46.7	12	26.7	9	20.0
Spreadsheet								
Lotus 1-2-3	6	25.0	9	37.5	3	12.5	5	20.8
Excel	4	11.8	24	70.6	0	0.0	4	11.8
Other	0	0.0	0	0.0	0	0.0	2	50.0
Tagged markup								
HTML	21	13.3	114	72.2	6	3.8	15	9.5
SGML	2	13.3	9	60.0	2	13.3	1	6.7
XML	0	0.0	1	33.3	0	0.0	1	33.3
Other	0	0.0	7	53.8	1	7.7	4	30.8
Image								

Table 4, continued

Assessment of Electronic Media and Format Standards in Federal Agencies: Number, Percentage, and Basis for Use by Agency

Format	Agency mandated		Common agency practice		Other		None	
	Number	Percent	Number	Percent	Number	Percent	Number	Percent
Audio								
WAV	2	15.4	8	61.5	0	0.0	2	15.4
AU	4	66.7	0	0.0	0	0.0	1	16.7
AIFF	1	50.0	0	0.0	0	0.0	0	0.0
Other	0	0.0	1	20.0	2	40.0	1	20.0
Video								
MOV	0	0.0	5	62.5	0	0.0	2	25.0
MPEG	1	10.0	5	50.0	1	10.0	2	20.0
AVI	1	20.0	3	60.0	0	0.0	0	0.0
Other	0	0.0	0	0.0	1	50.0	0	0.0
Text								
ASCII	21	13.3	87	70.7	6	4.9	15	9.5

Figure 7–7   Divided Table (Continued on a Second Page)

> **DESIGNING YOUR DOCUMENT**
> ## Presenting Information in Tables
>
> ■ Use tables to present data that you want readers to quickly evaluate and compare, but that would be difficult or tedious to present in your main text.
>
> ■ Identify each table with a concise, descriptive title and a unique table number.
>
> ■ Use horizontal lettering, if possible.
>
> ■ Do not enclose the left and right sides with vertical rules.
>
> ■ Include a source line when necessary to identify where you obtained your data.
>
> ■ For tables continued on another page, repeat the table number (followed by "continued"), title, and column headings.
>
> ■ Use informal tables—those without a title or number—when there are only a few items to categorize.

> **@**
>
> **DIGITAL TIPS: Creating Simple Tables for a Document**
>
> Word-processing programs can automate the creation of tables. They allow you to specify the number of rows and columns needed for your data, to define the style of the table elements, and to select vertical and horizontal rules. For step-by-step instructions on creating tables, see <bedfordstmartins.com/writingthatworks> and select *Digital Tips*, "Creating Tables."

Graphs

Graphs, also called charts, present numerical data in visual form, showing trends, movements, distributions, and cycles more readily than the same data in text or tables do. Although graphs present statistics in a format that is easy to understand, they are less precise than tables. For this reason, they are often accompanied by tables that give exact numbers. (Note the difference between the graph and the table showing the same data in Figure 7–8.) To solve the problem of showing only approximate data in graphs, you can include the exact data for each column—if this will not clutter your graph—giving the reader both a quick overview of the data and precise numbers. (See Figure 7–9 on page 231 and Figure 7–13 on page 233.) The most commonly used graphs are line graphs, bar graphs, pie graphs, and picture graphs, all of which you can easily render on your computer once you have entered your data into a spreadsheet or database application.

Line Graphs

The line graph shows the relationship between two or more sets of figures. The graph is composed of a vertical axis and a horizontal axis that intersect at right angles, each representing one set of data. The relationship between the two sets is

On-Time Performance - Flight Delays at a Glance

January to July

Filter Airport: All Airports
Filter Carrier: All Carriers
Filter Time: Year-To-Date
Filter Operation: Arrivals

Recalculate

More Analysis ... Delays and Causes ... Holiday Flight Delays ...

Year	Ontime Arrivals	Ontime (%)	Arrival Delays	Delayed (%)	Flights Cancelled	Cancelled (%)	Diverted	Flight Operations
1998	2,376,545	76.04%	667,769	21.37%	72,756	2.33%	8,259	3,125,329
1999	2,357,237	74.01%	716,448	22.50%	101,814	3.20%	9,397	3,184,896
2000	2,408,182	73.10%	765,408	23.23%	112,253	3.41%	8,691	3,294,534
2001	2,797,894	76.83%	732,976	20.13%	102,876	2.82%	7,934	3,641,680
2002	2,501,616	81.07%	538,633	17.45%	40,538	1.31%	5,073	3,085,860
2003	3,102,852	82.35%	597,853	15.87%	60,539	1.61%	6,562	3,767,806
2004	3,196,658	77.60%	846,282	20.54%	68,489	1.66%	8,231	4,119,660
2005	3,236,805	76.99%	876,862	20.86%	81,934	1.95%	8,644	4,204,245
2006	3,143,078	76.19%	909,668	22.05%	63,150	1.53%	9,684	4,125,580
2007	3,141,524	72.21%	1,091,378	25.09%	106,847	2.46%	10,720	4,350,469

* For purposes of this report, a flight is considered delayed if it arrived at (or departed) the gate 15 minutes or more after the scheduled arrival (departure) time as reflected in the Computerized Reservation System. ** The information is based on data submitted by reporting carriers. The number of reporting carriers varies as follows: 10 from 1997 to 1999, 11 in 2000, 12 in 2001, 10 in 2002, 18 in 2003, 19 in 2004, 20 in 2005, 21 in 2006 and 20 in 2007 (See Reporting Carriers by Year). Major Carriers 1997–Present refers to the 8 major carriers that reported for all those years. They are Alaska Airlines, American Airlines, Continental Airlines, Delta Air Lines, Northwest Airlines, Southwest Airlines, United Airlines, and US Airways. American Eagle Airlines and ATA Airlines are not included because they did not report for the full period. America West Airlines stopped reporting in 2006.

Figure 7–8   Graphs and Table Showing the Same Data.   *Source:* Bureau of Transportation Statistics, U.S. Department of Transportation.

indicated by points plotted along appropriate intersections of the two axes that are then connected to form a continuous line. The line graph's vertical axis usually represents amounts, and its horizontal axis usually represents increments of time (Figure 7–9). Line graphs with more than one plotted line allow for comparisons between two sets of data. In creating such graphs, label each plotted line, as shown in Figure 7–10. You can emphasize the difference between the two lines by shading the space that separates them. The following guidelines apply to most line graphs:

- Give your graph a title that describes the data clearly and concisely.
- Indicate the zero point (where the two axes meet). If the range of data is too large to begin at zero, insert a break in the scale (Figure 7–11 on page 232); otherwise, the graph would show a large area with no data.
- Divide the vertical axis into equal portions, from the least amount at the bottom to the greatest amount at the top. The caption for this scale may be placed at the upper left (as in Figure 7–10), or, as is more often the case, vertically along the vertical axis (as in Figure 7–11).
- Divide the horizontal axis into equal units from left to right, and label them to show what values each represents.
- Include enough points to plot the data accurately; too few data points will distort a depiction of the trends (Figure 7–12 on page 232).
- Keep grid lines to a minimum so that the curved lines stand out. Detailed grid lines are unnecessary because precise values are usually shown either on the graph or in an accompanying table.
- Include a label or a key when necessary to define symbols or visual cues to the data, such as in Figure 7–13 on page 233.
- Include a source line under the graph at the lower left, indicating where you obtained the data (see Figures 7–9, 7–10, and 7–13).
- Present all type horizontally if possible, although the type for the vertical axis caption is usually presented vertically (see Figures 7–11 and 7–12).

Be sure to proportion the vertical and horizontal scales so that they present data precisely and without visual distortion—to do otherwise is inaccurate and potentially misleading. In Figure 7–12, the graph on the left gives the appearance of a slight decline followed by a steady increase in investment returns because the scale is compressed, with some of the years selectively omitted. The graph on the right represents the trend more accurately because the years are evenly distributed without omissions.

Vertical axis shows quantity, and horizontal axis shows time increments

Changes in the import petroleum prices
index, December 2005 to December 2006

Figure 7–9   Single-Line Graph.   *Source:* Bureau of Labor Statistics, U.S. Department of Labor.

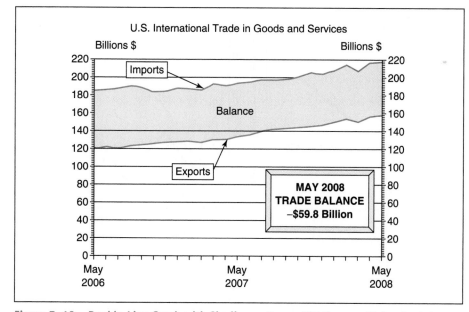

Actual data plotted with normal range shaded to highlight difference

Figure 7–10   Double-Line Graph with Shading.   *Source:* U.S. Bureau of Labor Statistics.

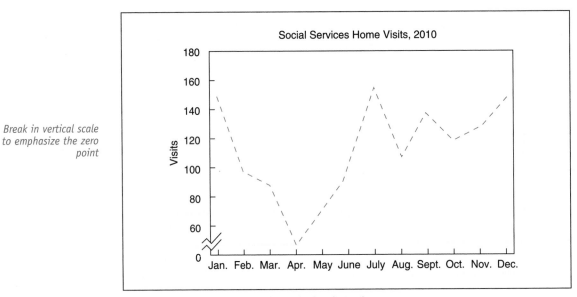

Break in vertical scale to emphasize the zero point

Figure 7–11   Line Graph with Vertical Axis Broken

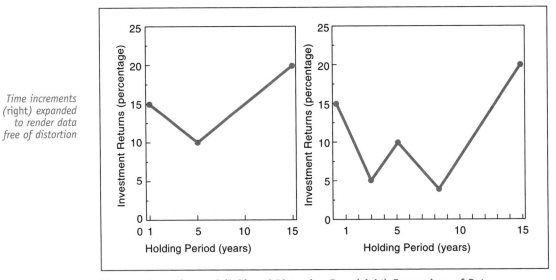

Time increments (right) expanded to render data free of distortion

Figure 7–12   Distorted (*left*) and Distortion-Free (*right*) Expressions of Data

Bar Graphs

Bar graphs consist of horizontal or vertical bars of equal width but scaled in length or height to represent some quantity. They are commonly used to show the following proportional relations:

- Different types of information during different periods of time (Figure 7–13)
- Quantities of the same kind of information at different periods of time (Figure 7–14)
- Quantities of different information during a fixed period of time (Figure 7–15)
- Quantities of the different parts that make up a whole (Figure 7–16 on page 235)

Bar graphs can also indicate what proportion of a whole the various component parts represent. In such a graph, the bar, which is theoretically equivalent to 100 percent, is divided according to the proportion of the whole that each item

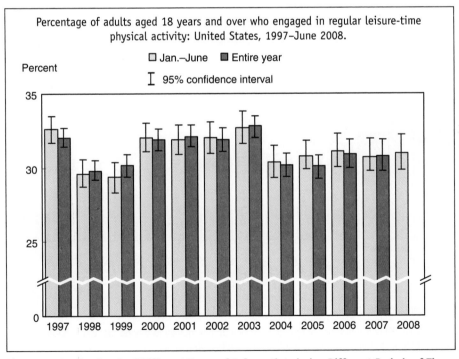

Figure 7–13 Bar Graph of Different Types of Information during Different Periods of Time. *Source:* Centers for Disease Control and Prevention.

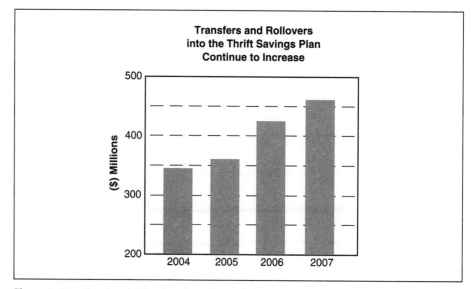

Figure 7–14 Bar Graph Showing Quantities of the Same Kind of Information at Different Periods of Time. *Source:* Thrift Savings Plan <http://www.tsp.gov/forms/tspbk08.pdf>.

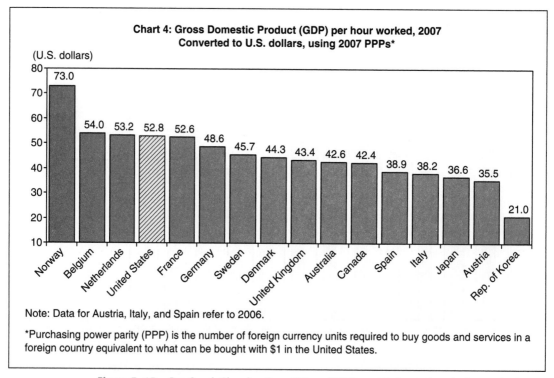

Figure 7–15 Bar Graph Showing Quantities of Different Information during a Fixed Period of Time. *Source:* Bureau of Labor Statistics, U.S. Department of Labor.

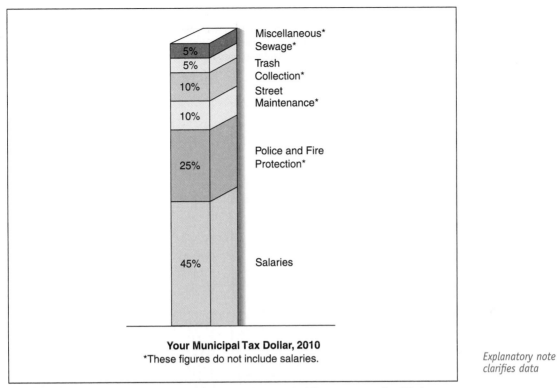

Your Municipal Tax Dollar, 2010
*These figures do not include salaries.

Explanatory note clarifies data

Figure 7–16   Bar Graph Showing Different Quantities of Different Parts of a Whole

sampled represents. (Compare the displays of the same data in Figures 7–16 and 7–18 on page 237.) In some bar graphs, the completed bar does not represent 100 percent because not all parts of the whole have been included or not all are pertinent in the sample (Figure 7–17). Bar graphs are also used to track project schedules, where each bar represents the time allotted for each task of a project. A project-tracking bar graph, also called a *time-line graph,* is shown in Figure 5–4 on page 140.

Note that in Figure 7–19 on page 238, a type of bar graph showing travel frequency, the exact quantities appear at the end of each picture column, eliminating the need to have an accompanying table giving the percentages. If the bars are not labeled, the different portions must be clearly indicated by shading, cross-hatching, or other devices. Include a key that represents the various subdivisions.

Pie Graphs

A pie graph presents data as wedge-shaped sections of a circle. The circle equals 100 percent, or the whole, of some quantity (a tax dollar, a bus fare, the hours of a working day), with the wedges representing the various parts into which the whole is divided. In Figure 7–18, for example, the circle stands for a city tax dollar

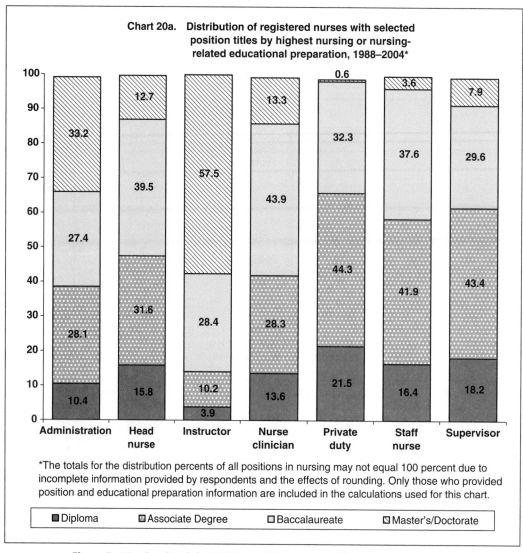

Figure 7–17   Bar Graph in Which Not All Parts of a Whole Have Been Included.   *Source:* Health Resources and Services Administration, U.S. Department of Health and Human Services.

and is divided into units equivalent to the percentages of the tax dollar spent on various city services. Note that the slice representing salaries is slightly offset (exploded) from the others to emphasize that data. This feature is commonly available on spreadsheet and database software.

The relationships among the various statistics presented in a pie graph are easy to grasp, but the information is often general. For this reason, a pie graph is often accompanied by a table that presents the actual figures on which the percentages in the graph are based.

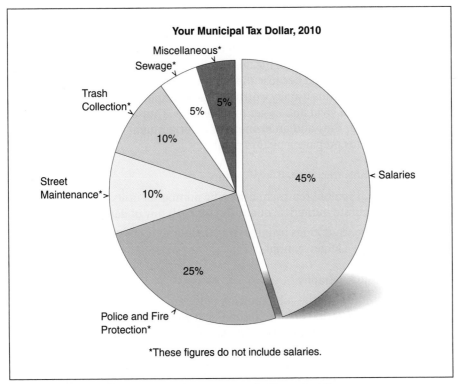

Figure 7–18   Exploded Pie Graph (Same Data as in Figure 7–16)

Following are guidelines for constructing pie graphs:

- Keep in mind that the complete 360° circle is equivalent to 100 percent.
- When possible, begin at the 12 o'clock position and sequence the wedges clockwise, from largest to smallest. (This is not always possible because the default setting for some charting software sequences the data counter-clockwise.)
- Apply a distinctive pattern or various shades of gray or different colors for each wedge.
- Keep all labels horizontal and, most important, provide the percentage value of each wedge.
- Check that all wedges and their respective percentages add up to 100 percent.

Although pie graphs have a strong visual impact, they also have drawbacks. If more than five or six items of information are presented, the graph looks cluttered and, unless percentages are labeled on each section, the reader cannot compare the values of the sections as accurately as on a bar graph.

Picture Graphs

Picture graphs (also called *pictograms*) are modified bar graphs that use picture symbols to represent the item for which data are presented. Each symbol corresponds to a specified quantity of the item, as shown in Figure 7–19. Note that exact numbers are also included because the picture symbol can indicate only approximate figures. Pictograms usually work well for nonexpert audiences because they make the data more vivid and easier to remember. They are also popular in presentations because they add an element of entertainment to the data. Consider these guidelines for preparing picture graphs:

- Use symbols that are self-explanatory.
- Have each symbol represent a specific number of units and be sure to include accurate numerical quantities for each row of data.
- Show larger quantities by increasing the number of symbols rather than by creating a larger symbol.

Dimensional-Column Graphs

Consider a common on-the-job reporting requirement—tracking a series of expenses over a given period of time. Assume that you wish to show your company's expenses over a three-month period for security, courier, mail, and custodial services. Once you enter the data for these services into a spreadsheet program, you can display them in a variety of graph styles. As you select from among the options available, keep in mind your reader's need to interpret the data accurately and quickly, so keep the graph style as simple as possible for the information shown.

Graphs that depict columns as three-dimensional pillars are popular—they give the data a solid, three-dimensional, building-block appearance. They can,

Quantity increases represented by increased number of symbols

Quantity for each symbol specified

Figure 7–19   Picture Graph

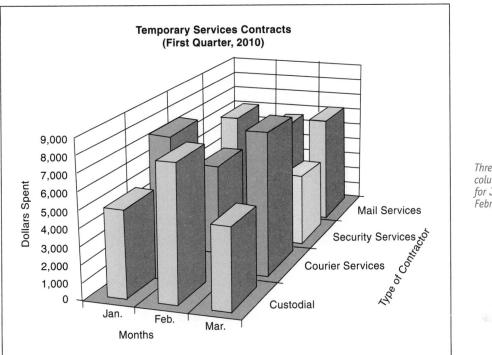

Three-dimensional columns obscure data for January and February

Figure 7–20 Three-Dimensional Column Graph

however, obscure rather than clarify the information, depending on how they are displayed. Consider the graph in Figure 7–20. Although the data are accurate, they cannot be interpreted as shown because the axis showing expenditures is too far from most columns representing the various services. The graph also obscures the columns for courier and security services. Finally, this graph style does not allow readers to spot trends for expenditures over the three-month period, which is key information to decision makers.

The graph in Figure 7–21 presents more clearly the same data as that shown in Figure 7–20. The trends of expenditures are easy to spot, and all the data are at least visible. Yet this graph is not ideal. To interpret the information, the reader would need to put a ruler on the page and align the tops of the columns with the axis showing expenditures.

The three-dimensional appearance can also cause confusion: Is the front or back of each column the correct data point? Also somewhat confusing is that, at first glance, the reader is tricked into interpreting the spaces between the column clusters as columns because they are of equal width.

The graphs in Figures 7–22 and 7–23 on page 241 would best represent the data, depending on your intent. Figure 7–22 avoids the ambiguity of the graph in Figure 7–21 by showing the data in two dimensions. It also displays the horizontal lines for expenditures on the vertical axis, thus making the data for each column

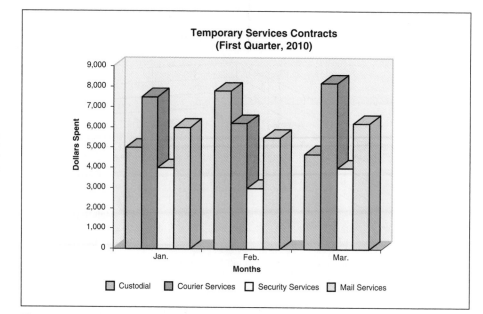

Tops of three-dimensional columns cannot be interpreted without a ruler

Figure 7–21 **Three-Dimensional Column Graph (Same Data as in Figure 7–20)**

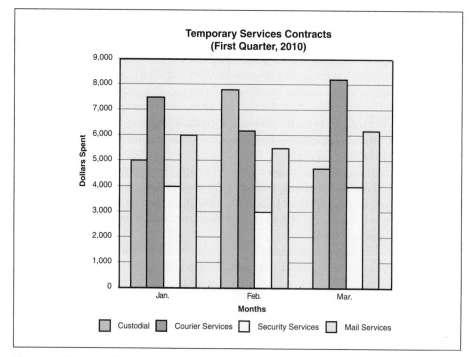

Two-dimensional columns make data easy to interpret at a glance

Figure 7–22 **Two-Dimensional Column Graph (Same Data as in Figures 7–20 and 7–21)**

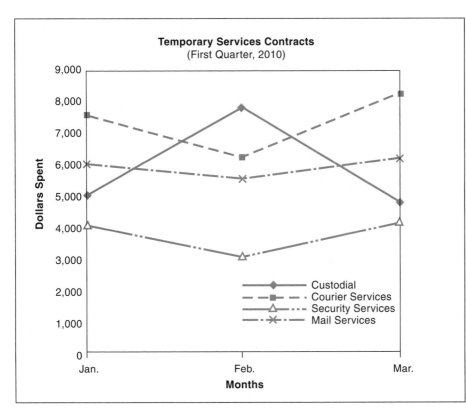

Line graph makes data trends easy to interpret at a glance

Figure 7–23   Line Graph (Same Data as in Figures 7–20 through 7–22)

easier to interpret. If you wished to show relative expenses among the four variables for a given quarter, this graph would be ideal. However, if you wished to show trends for the entire three-month period in contract expenditures at a glance, the graph in Figure 7–23 is preferable.

When precise dollar amounts for each service are equally important, you can provide a table showing that information. As Figures 7–20 through 7–23 show, the more complicated a graph looks, the harder it is to interpret. On balance, simpler is better for the reader. Use this principle when you review your computer graphics on-screen in several styles and consider your reader's needs before deciding which style to use.

Drawings

A drawing is useful when your reader needs an impression of an object's general appearance or an overview of a series of steps or directions. Note, for example, the sequence of drawings in Chapter 12 that show the steps used to install a waste disposer (Figure 12–9 on page 438). Drawings are the best choice when you need to focus on details or relationships that a photograph cannot capture. A drawing can

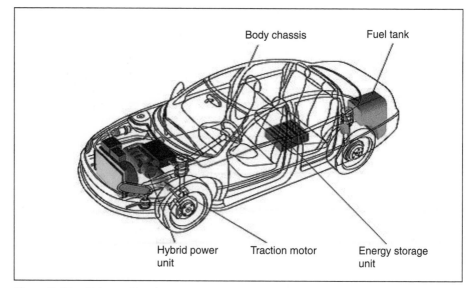

Cutaway shows internal structure of a device (hybrid car)

Figure 7–24 **Cutaway Drawing**

ON THE WEB

For another example of an exploded-view drawing, go to Model Documents Gallery, bedfordstmartins.com/writingthatworks

emphasize the significant piece of a mechanism, or its function, and omit what is not significant—for example, a cutaway drawing can show the internal parts of a piece of equipment in such a way that their relationship to the overall equipment is clear (Figure 7–24). An exploded-view drawing can show the proper sequence in which parts fit together or the details of each individual part (Figure 7–25).

Drawings are also the best option for illustrating simple objects or tasks that do not require photography (Figure 7–26 on page 244). However, if the actual appearance of an object (a dented fender) or a phenomenon (an aircraft wind-tunnel experiment) is necessary to your document, a photograph is essential. For drawings that require a high degree of accuracy and precision, seek the help of a graphics specialist.

Many organizations have their own format specifications for drawings. In the absence of such specifications, the following guidelines should be helpful:

- Show the equipment from the point of view of the person who will use it.
- When illustrating part of a system, show its relationship to the larger system of which it is a part.
- Draw the different parts of an object in proportion to one another, unless you indicate that certain parts are enlarged.
- For drawings used to illustrate a process, arrange them from left to right and from top to bottom.
- Label important parts of each drawing so that text references to them are clear and consistent.
- Depending on the complexity of what is shown, label the parts themselves—see Figure 7–25—or use a letter or number key.

Exploded view shows parts of a mechanism, packing container, and part names

Figure 7–25   Exploded-View Drawing

For general-interest images needed to illustrate newsletters, brochures, or presentation slides, use the clip-art libraries provided with word-processing programs, graphics programs, and the numerous image libraries available on the Web. These sources contain thousands of noncopyrighted symbols, shapes, and images of people, equipment, furniture, buildings, and the like. An added advantage is that you can adjust their size according to your document's layout and space requirements. Figure 7–27 shows examples of clip-art images.

ON THE WEB

For access to image libraries on the Web, go to Chapter 7, bedfordstmartins.com/writingthatworks

Prevent Repetitive-Motion Injuries

Before beginning keying and during breaks throughout the day, take time to do the stretches as shown.

Gently press the hand against a firm flat surface, stretching the fingers and wrist. Hold for five seconds.

Rest the forearm on the edge of a table. Grasp the fingers of one hand and gently bend back the wrist, stretching the hands and wrist. Hold for five seconds.

Figure 7–26   Drawing

Flowcharts

A flowchart is a diagram that shows the stages of a process from beginning to end; it presents an overview that allows readers to grasp essential steps quickly and easily. Flowcharts can illustrate a variety of processes, ranging from the steps required to process an invoice to the stages in the life cycle of the honey bee.

Flowcharts can take several forms to represent the steps in a process: labeled blocks (Figure 7–28), pictorial representations (Figure 7–29), or standardized symbols (Figure 7–30 on page 246). The items in any flowchart are always connected according to the sequence in which the steps occur. They are typically depicted

Figure 7–27   Clip-Art Images

Figure 7–28   **Flowchart Using Labeled Blocks (Depicting Electric Utility Power Restoration Process).**   *Source:* Potomac Electric Power Company.

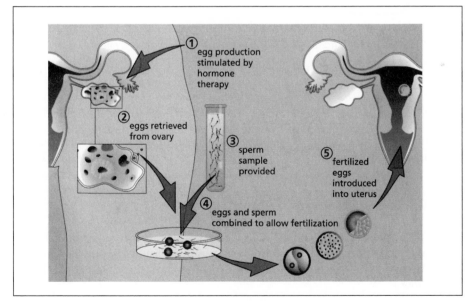

Pictorial flowchart with numbered steps and directional arrows

Figure 7–29   **Flowchart Using Pictorial Symbols**

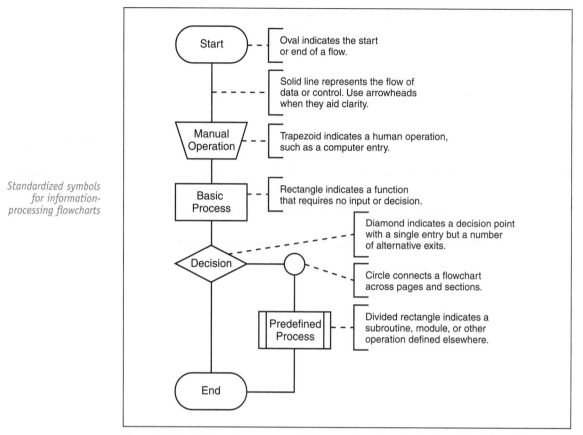

Standardized symbols for information-processing flowcharts

Figure 7–30   Information Standards Organization (ISO) Flowchart Symbols (with Annotations)

ON THE WEB

For additional examples of flowcharts, go to Model Documents Gallery, bedfordstmartins.com/writingthatworks

left to right or top to bottom. When the flow is otherwise, indicate it with arrows. Flowcharts that document computer programs and other information-processing procedures use standardized symbols set forth in *Information Processing: Documentation Symbols and Conventions for Data, Program, and System Flowcharts, Program Network Charts, and System Resources Charts* (ISO publication 1985E).

Follow these guidelines when creating a flowchart:

- With labeled blocks and standardized symbols, use arrows to show the direction of flow, especially if the flow is opposite to the normal direction. With pictorial representations, use arrows to show the direction of all flow.

- Label each step in the process or identify it with a conventional symbol. Steps can also be represented pictorially or by captioned blocks.
- Include a key if the flowchart contains symbols that your audience may not understand.
- Leave adequate white space on the page. Do not crowd the steps and directional arrows too close together.

Organizational Charts

An organizational chart shows how the various parts of an organization are related to one another. Such illustrations give readers an overview of an organization or indicate the lines of authority within an organization (Figure 7–31).

The title of each organizational part (office, section, division) is placed in a separate box. These boxes are then linked to a central authority. If useful to your readers, include the name of the person occupying the position identified in each box. As with all illustrations, place the organizational chart as close as possible following the text that refers to it.

Maps

Maps can be used to show the specific geographic or human-made features of an area (mountains, rivers, roads, dams) or to show information according to geographic distribution (population, housing, manufacturing centers, and so forth) (Figure 7–32 on page 248).

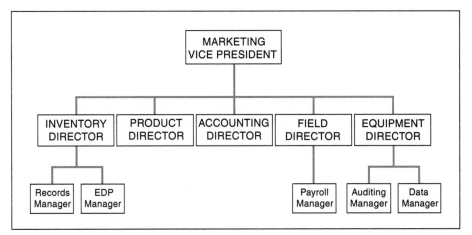

Boxes are linked to show hierarchy of and relationships among units in an organization

Figure 7–31 Organizational Chart.
Source: Cramer, Inc. Field Marketing Organization.

*Focus of map is loca-
tion of three sites
(highlighted with call-
outs and arrows)*

*Note state, reservation
and county boundaries;
highways; and scales
of distance*

Figure 7–32   Map

◆ *For more informa-
tion on researching or
creating maps, see
Chapter 6, Researching
Your Subject.*

Keep in mind the following points as you create maps for use with your text:

- Clearly identify all boundaries within your map. Eliminate those that are unnecessary to the area you want to show.
- Eliminate unnecessary information. For example, if population is the focal point, do not include mountains, roads, rivers, and so on.
- Include a scale of miles or feet, or kilometers or meters, to give your reader an indication of the map's proportions.
- Indicate which direction is north.
- Emphasize key features by using color, shading, dots, crosshatching, or appropriate symbols, and include a key telling what the different colors, shadings, or symbols represent (Figure 7–33).

Photographs

Photographs are vital to show the surface appearance of an object or to record an event or the development of a phenomenon over a period of time. Not all representations, however, call for photographs. They cannot depict the internal work-

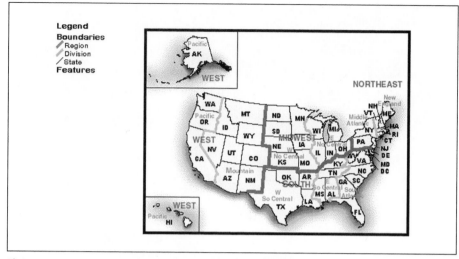

Figure 7–33   Map Showing Legend and Shading to Depict Data.
Source: U.S. Census Bureau.

ings of a mechanism or below-the-surface details of objects or structures. Such details are better shown in drawings or diagrams.

Highlighting Photographic Objects

Select important details and the camera angles that will record these details. Stand close enough to the object so that it fills your picture frame. To show the relative size of an unfamiliar object, place a familiar object—such as a ruler, a book, a tool, or a person—near the object that is to be photographed, as shown in Figure 7–34.

Ask the printer reproducing your publication for special handling requirements if you use glossy photographs. If you use digital photos, ask about the preferred resolution of the images before you shoot. The higher the resolution, the better the quality. You can digitize film photos using scanners and digital cameras, so ensure that the equipment has the necessary memory for the resolution required by the printer.

Using Color

Color is, in many cases, the only way to communicate crucial information. In medical, chemical, geological, and botanical publications, for example, readers often need to know exactly what an object or a phenomenon looks like to accurately interpret it.

Posting color images at a Web site is no more complicated or expensive than posting black-and-white images. For publications, however, preparing and printing color photographs are complex technical tasks performed by graphics and printing professionals. If you are planning to use color photographs in your

Examiner's hands illustrate relative size of specimen

Figue 7–34   Photo of Plant Tissue Examination

ON THE WEB

For information on locating photographs and other images for your documents, go to Chapter 7, bedfordstmartins.com/ writingthatworks

publication, discuss with these professionals the type, quality, and number of photographs required.

Be mindful that color reproduction is significantly more expensive than black-and-white reproduction. Color can also be tricky to reproduce accurately without losing contrast and vividness. For this reason, the original photographs must be sharply focused and rich in contrast.

Using Visuals to Communicate Internationally

More than ever, business and technical communicators use graphics to communicate with international audiences. As companies expand their markets in Saudi Arabia, China, South America, Eastern Europe, and dozens of other places, the marketplace becomes more global—a trend marked by the prevalence of multinational corporations, the international subsidiaries of many companies, multinational trade agreements, the increasing diversity of the U.S. workforce, and even increases in immigration. The audiences for these communications include clients, business partners, colleagues, and current and potential employees and customers. Even though English is rapidly becoming the global language of business and science, many people speak it as a second or third language. For this reason, graphics offer distinct advantages for communicating in a global business climate.

- Graphics can communicate a message more effectively than text, particularly in the context of safety warnings or cautions.

- Graphics can sometimes replace technical terms that are difficult to translate.

Despite their unquestionable value in communicating with international readers, symbols, images, and even colors are not free from cultural associations: How they are perceived depends on many factors—including the values and

---

@

DIGITAL TIPS: Using Graphics Software*

- *Vector graphics packages* allow you to manipulate predefined shapes (boxes, circles, arcs, lines, letters) that you then combine to produce images. Vector packages render crisp, high-resolution images that are ideal for producing complex technical graphics (isometric drawings, exploded views, and detailed line drawings), as well as basic images (flowcharts and organizational charts). These images—lines, shapes, letters—retain high-quality resolution regardless of the size at which they are produced.

- *Bitmapped* (or *raster*) *programs* allow you to manipulate individual pixels (picture elements, or dots) to produce lines, shapes, and patterns. These programs—also called *paint programs*—work best with images that have broad variations in colors, shapes, or hues, such as photos and detailed drawings. Use these programs to edit photos, create Web graphics, or modify screen shots for use in print and online publications. You can alter these images by manipulating the color and intensity of the dots. The resolution quality of the images is affected by the number of dots they contain—more dots equal higher quality. At lower resolution, the images have a fuzzy or jagged appearance.

Which program should you use? Typical vector programs include Visio, SmartDraw, MSProject, PaintShop, and Adobe Creative Suite. Among the many bitmapped programs, many students use the freeware program InfanView, which is useful for manipulating images. Select the program based on the type of image you will produce.
  Use a vector program for the following:

- Line drawings
- Blueprints
- Flow and organizational charts
- Isometric drawings
- Network and process diagrams

  Use a bitmapped program for the following:

- Photographs
- Computer screen shots
- Web graphics
- Special effects

Note that most vector programs can convert vector images to dots to create bitmap images for editing with a bitmap image editor. However, bitmap programs cannot convert bitmap images to vector images.

*Based on "An Introduction to Illustration Software" by Bryan J. Follas, *Intercom*, September/October 2001: 6–8.

@ **DIGITAL TIPS: Computer Graphics**

Creating computer graphics allows you to do the following:

- Save images for future use and update them as necessary.
- Use the same images in reports, other documents, and Web sites, where appropriate.
- Send images to presentation software programs such as Microsoft PowerPoint or Apple iWork Keynote to create printed transparencies or digital presentations for meetings.
- Communicate image files to others electronically via e-mail.
- Automate sharing and updating data in images created and maintained in different applications—spreadsheet, database, graphics, word-processing, and presentation programs.

norms of a given culture. International graphics standards exist in some fields—computer technology, airport signage, mathematics, and most scientific and engineering disciplines—but generally do not for the vast majority of other images. Writers who create documents for an international audience can avoid confusing and possibly offending their readers by understanding the following cultural connotations of visuals.

Colors

The use of a particular color can distort or even change the meaning of graphics symbols. Red commonly indicates warning or danger in North America, Europe, and Japan. In China, however, red symbolizes joy. In Europe and North America, blue generally has a positive connotation; in Japan, the color represents villainy. In Europe and North America, yellow represents caution or cowardice; in Arab countries, yellow generally means fertility or strength.

People, Parts of the Body, and Gestures

Depicting people and parts of the body in graphics can be problematic (Table 7–2). If your graphics will reach an international audience, it is better to avoid depictions of people eating or representations of bare arms and feet. Nudity in advertising, for example, generally is acceptable in Europe but not in North America or in predominantly Muslim countries. Even showing isolated body parts could lead to communication difficulties. For example, some Middle Eastern cultures regard the display of the soles of one's shoes to be disrespectful and offensive. Therefore, a technical manual that attempts to demonstrate the ease of running a software program by showing a user with his or her feet on a desk could be considered offensive to that audience.

TABLE 7–2   International Implications of Gestures and Body Language

Body Part	Gesture	Country	Interpretation
Head	Nodding up and down	Bulgaria	No
Left hand	Showing palm	Muslim countries	Dirty, unclean
Index finger	Pointing to others	Venezuela, Sri Lanka	Rude
Fingers and thumb	Circular OK	Germany, Netherlands	Rude
Ankle and leg	Crossing over knee	Indonesia, Syria	Rude
Eye	Touching finger below eye	Honduras	Caution

Consider the graphic warning weightlifters against the use of steroids in Figure 7–35. The image is appropriate for North American audiences (and others) but is highly inappropriate in cultures where the image of a partially clothed man

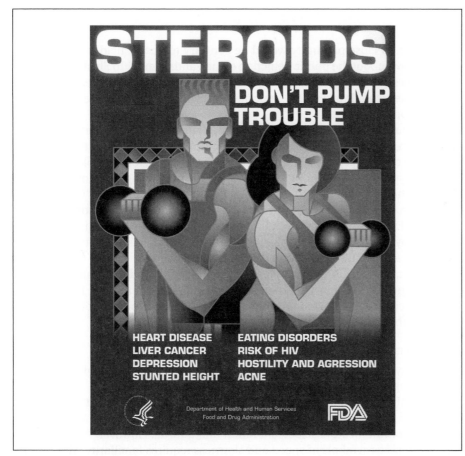

Figure 7–35   Graphic for a U.S. Audience

Figure 7–36   Graphic for a Global Audience

and woman in close proximity would be contrary to deeply held cultural beliefs and even laws about the public depiction of men and women. To illustrate the anti-steriod message, the writer could use the image in Figure 7–36, instead, depicting a weightlifter icon. It avoids the connotations associated with more realistic images of people.

Communicators producing instructions often use hand gestures such as the victory sign (✌) or the "OK" sign (👌) as positive motivators. However, the meaning of each of these gestures varies by culture. In Australia, for example, the victory sign conveys the same meaning as holding up the middle finger in North America. Similarly, the gesture that means "OK" in North America can mean "worthless" in France, can mean "money" in Japan, and is a sexual insult in many other parts of the world. Even a smile may have different connotations. In Japan, smiling can be a sign of joy or can be used to hide displeasure; in some Asian cultures, smiling may be considered a sign of weakness.

Further, a manual that contains a pointed finger to indicate "turn the page" might offend someone in Venezuela. A writer preparing a manual for export to Honduras could indicate "caution" by using a picture of a person touching a finger below the eye.

Cultural Symbols

Signs and symbols are so culturally rooted that we often lose sight of the fact that the meaning we intend may be understood only in our culture.

A Michigan manufacturer of window fans, for example, wanted to use easily understood symbols to represent the two speeds of its product: fast and slow. The technical communicators selected a rabbit and a turtle. However, recognition of these animals as symbols of speed and slowness requires familiarity with Aesop's fables—a Western tradition.

Figure 7–37   International Organization for Standardization (ISO) Symbols

Symbols that carry simultaneous religious and nonreligious meanings have long been used in North America, where it is common to use the cross as a symbol for first aid or a hospital. In Muslim countries, however, a cross solely represents Christianity; a crescent (usually green) is a symbol for first aid.

The symbols or icons we create to represent technology are also laden with cultural assumptions. If users do not have regular contact with PDAs, computers, or cell phones, technical and business communicators cannot predict how users will interpret representations of these devices. Even punctuation marks are affected by cultural expectations. For example, in English-speaking countries, the question mark generally represents the need for information or the Help function in a computer manual or program. In many countries, this symbol is not used and therefore not understood at all. To avoid confusion, when possible include a key that associates the English-language question mark with the local language's equivalent mark.

These and similar examples suggest why international groups, such as the International Organization for Standardization (ISO), have established agreed-on symbols, such as those shown in Figure 7–37, designed for public signs, guidebooks, and manuals.[1]

Reading Practices

Whether text is read right to left or left to right influences how graphics are sequenced. In the Middle East and in many parts of Asia, for example, text is read from right to left. For these audiences, you will need to alter the design and sequencing of text and graphics.

Directional Signs

The signs we use to represent direction or time are open to misinterpretation. For example, the arrow sign on shipping cartons can be interpreted to mean either that the carton should be placed with the arrow pointing up to the top of the carton, or pointing down to the carton's most stable position. Western cultures tend to indicate the future (or something positive) by pointing to the right (→) and the

ON THE WEB

For links to intercultural resources for business writers, go to Chapter 7, bedfordstmartins.com/ writingthatworks

---

[1]See Henry Dreyfuss, *Symbol Sourcebook: An Authoritative Guide to International Graphic Symbols* (Hoboken, N.J.: John Wiley and Sons, 1984).

past (or something negative) by pointing to the left (←); in the Chinese culture, left represents honor and right self-destruction.

Careful attention to the different connotations visual elements may have for an international audience makes translations easier, saves a company from potential embarrassment, and, over time, earns respect for the company and its products and services.

▶ CONSIDERING AUDIENCE AND PURPOSE

Using International Graphics

- Consult with someone from your intended audience's country or culture who will be able to recognize and explain the effects of subtle visual elements on your intended readers.

- Acknowledge diversity within your company and recognize that not everyone interprets visual information in the same way.

- Learn about the use of gestures in other cultures as a first step to learning about cultural context because the interpretation of gestures differs widely.

- Invite international and intercultural communication experts to speak to your colleagues, and contact companies in your area that may have employees who could be resources for cultural discussions.

- Be sure that the graphics you use have no unintended religious or symbolic implications.

- Use few colors in your graphics. Generally, black-and-white or gray-and-white illustrations are less problematic than color graphics.

- Create simple visuals. Simple shapes with few elements are easier to read in most cultures.

- Use outlines or neutral abstractions to represent human beings. For example, use stick figures for bodies or a circle for a head.

- Be consistent in labeling elements. Use simple, consistent signs for all visual items.

- Explain the meaning of icons or symbols. Include a glossary to explain symbols that cannot be changed (for example, company logos).

- Test icons and symbols in context with members of your target audience. Usability testing with cultural experts is critical.

- Organize visual information for intended audiences. North American readers read visuals from left to right in clockwise rotation. Middle Eastern readers read visuals from right to left in counterclockwise rotation.

CHAPTER 7 SUMMARY: DESIGNING EFFECTIVE DOCUMENTS AND VISUALS

Integrating Visuals and Text

- Have you noted in your document planning outline the approximate location of your graphics?

- Does the text preceding a table or figure make clear why the visual is there and what it shows?

- Do all graphics have clear, concise captions?
- Is the graphic located as close as possible to—but following—the text describing it? Is the language in the text consistent with the language in the graphic?
- Have you allowed adequate white space around and within the text and graphics in your documents?
- Do the layout and design of your finished document highlight the organization and hierarchy of your information?
- Have you obtained permission to reproduce copyrighted graphics in your document?

Creating Visuals

- Do your tables organize numerical or verbal information for ease of understanding?
- Are the trends depicted in your graphs free of distortions?
- Are graphs supported by precise data in tables or by exact figures on the graph?
- Are color, shading, or crosshatching patterns on graphs easy to interpret?
- Are graphs free of unnecessary details that obscure at-a-glance interpretations?
- Are drawings shown from the correct perspective and focused on the significant piece of a device or mechanism?
- Do flowcharts indicate the direction of flow?
- Are the steps in a pictorial flowchart labeled?
- Are unfamiliar symbols in a flowchart explained?
- Are maps free of details that obscure the features you wish to highlight?
- Do photographs show key objects and details from the best perspective and degree of visual clarity?

Using Visuals to Communicate Internationally

- Has someone from your audience's culture or country reviewed your visuals for appropriateness?
- Do visuals feature culturally neutral shapes and designs?
- Are important features, including icons and symbols, labeled on the visual or explained in a glossary or key?

ON THE WEB

For an online quiz on designing documents and visuals, go to Chapter 7, bedfordstmartins.com/ writingthatworks

■ Exercises

ON THE WEB

For additional exercises, go to Chapter 7, bedfordstmartins.com/ writingthatworks

1. Assume that you work for PLANET (the Professional Landcare Network), a professional association for landscape designers and contractors. You have been asked to create a table for the organization's Web site (<www.landcarenetwork.org/>) that shows the seasonal lawn-maintenance tasks landscape services or homeowners might perform over the period of one year. Use the following information to create your table:

   Mow: April to June (every two weeks), July and August (weekly), and September to October (every two weeks)
   De-thatch: April or September
   Aerate: April or September

Fertilize: March, May, July, September, November
Water: Twice a week June through September, or as needed
Apply weed killer: February, April, June, August, October

2. Assume that a survey of 100 companies resulted in the following distribution percentages by type of industry: computer-related, 32 percent; industrial equipment, 7 percent; business services, 8 percent; telecommunications, 10 percent; media and publications, 10 percent; consumer goods, 10 percent; medical and pharmaceutical, 14 percent; other, 9 percent. Prepare a pie graph showing the distribution.

3. Create a line or bar graph that compares sales in thousands of dollars among the various truck-parts divisions of the ABC Corporation for 2007, 2008, and 2009. Sales for each division are as follows:

   • Axles: 2007 ($225K), 2008 ($200K), 2009 ($75K)
   • Universal joints: 2007 ($125K), 2008 ($100K), 2009 ($35K)
   • Frames: 2007 ($125K), 2008 ($100K), 2009 ($50K)
   • Transmissions: 2007 ($75K), 2008 ($65K), 2009 ($50K)
   • Clutches: 2007 ($35K), 2008 ($30K), 2009 ($15K)
   • Gaskets and seals: 2007 ($28K), 2008 ($25K), 2009 ($20K)

4. Briefly explain whether a photograph or a line drawing would better illustrate features of the following subjects: a dry-cell battery (for an article in a general encyclopedia), a flower arrangement (in a florist's brochure), an electrical-outlet box (in a wiring instructions booklet), or the procedure for wrapping a sprained ankle (for a first-aid handbook).

5. Beginning at the main entrance and ending at the checkout desk, draw a flowchart that traces the path you follow in the process of locating and obtaining books from your library (as outlined in Chapter 6, Researching Your Subject).

6. Create an organizational chart for a campus group to which you belong or for the department in your area of study.

7. Misleading visuals are unethical and can result in a loss of credibility for you and your organization. Sometimes deceptive visuals are based on incorrect statistics; sometimes statistics are manipulated to help a person or an organization improperly achieve goals. In either case, visuals and the statistics that inform them can help or hurt specific groups. (For example, a graph that accurately shows the number of college binge drinkers could help gain support for the creation of a campus substance-abuse counseling center; visuals that inaccurately suggest a lower number of binge drinkers could be used to argue against stricter alcohol regulations on campus.) For each of five subjects from the following list, suggest a potential visual based on statistics and list ways in which that visual might be used to help or hurt the people involved:

   • Immigrants seeking asylum in the United States
   • Abused children or homeless teens
   • Elderly people who need financial assistance
   • Children with learning disabilities
   • Women who give birth in prison
   • Disabled veterans
   • Battered wives or husbands

- Infants affected by illegal drugs
- Underpaid health-care workers
- Adults on Social Security

8. Following up on Exercise 7, imagine that you are planning to create a report for local government leaders on the use and ethics of visuals and statistics as they relate to promoting social programs and public policy. Using the Designing Your Document checklist on page 220, think strategically about the layout of your pages as a means of persuading this audience. For example, how many columns will you use? What kind of font type and size would promote quick and efficient reading? How will you highlight statistics and other crucial information? (You may want to revisit Chapter 1, Assessing Audience and Purpose, for information on audience and their needs.) Use your answers to create a thumbnail sketch of your report.

9. Create a pie chart that breaks down the expense percentages in your monthly budget, including housing, food, utilities, transportation (car, bus, subway), insurance (car, life, property, medical), school, clothing, entertainment, and the like. Support your pie chart with a detailed table that specifies the exact amount you budgeted for each item.

Collaborative Classroom Projects

ON THE WEB

For more collaborative classroom projects, go to Chapter 7, bedfordstmartins.com/ writingthatworks

1. Bring to class or submit online an explanation of how something works (such as a cell phone or computer chip) that *does not* contain visuals (one good source is <http://howthingswork.virginia.edu/>). Now divide into teams of five or fewer students and choose the explanations for two different objects. Brainstorm with your team about how you would add visuals to these explanations to make them easier to understand. Be sure you have a specific audience in mind before you begin (such as prospective customers overseas, new users, or repair technicians).
   a. Search through this chapter for the types of visuals that would be best suited for this project. List them and give a brief rationale for your choice.
   b. Create thumbnail sketches of the visuals and where they would be placed in relation to the text. Give a brief explanation of your strategy.
   c. Present your work to the class and explain your strategies and why you think they would successfully help your audience to better understand the explanations. Ask for feedback on your work.
   d. As your instructor directs, use your peers' feedback to combine your thumbnail sketches with the text into handouts for the class. (If you want to use clip art or photos from the Web, be sure to review the ethics note on page 225 of this chapter and page 181 of Chapter 6, Researching Your Subject.)

2. Bring to class a set of illustrated instructions (such as assembly instructions for a bookcase or a quick-start guide for a digital video recorder) that you believe could be designed more effectively. Then do the following, as your instructor directs:
   a. Critique the design and create a list of what could be improved.
   b. Recommend specific steps for improving the instructions' clarity.
   c. Create a new set of instructions either yourself or in a group.

ON THE WEB

For extra research projects, go to Chapter 7, bedfordstmartins.com/ writingthatworks

▓ Research Projects

1. Interview someone from another country or culture about the use of visual symbols in that person's culture. Write a report of 500 to 700 words on the cultural differences in the use of visuals in his or her culture and in the United States. Consider punctuation marks, religious symbols, colors, body parts, gestures, directional signals, or technology symbols. Do not use any specific examples already discussed in this chapter.

2. Imagine that you just got hired as a graphic artist for a marketing company. Your job is to design visuals for a new promotional campaign your company is creating for a famous sneaker company. You come up with the idea for a graphic, featuring a mound of sneakers piled high to the sky. You decide to copyright your idea. You then create the sneaker graphic and register it in your name instead of the marketing company's. You later run into a friend who shows you an interesting graphic, featuring people running. The artist gave him permission to use that graphic for a project. You ask to use it, too, and your friend gives you permission. Your new boss gets wind of your activities and threatens to fire you unless you learn about copyright laws. Research the basic copyright and fair-use laws regarding graphics to find out what you did wrong. Present your findings to the class in an oral presentation.

3. Create a bar graph showing the median sales price of new single-family homes in the United States for 1980 and at five-year intervals through the most current data available at the Web site of the U.S. Census Bureau at <www.census.gov>.

4. On the Web, you can find sites that use both text and visuals to explain how things work. One source is <www.howstuffworks.com>. After reviewing the guidelines in this chapter for creating documents and integrating visuals:

   a. Choose a handheld electronic device (such as a video game or digital camera) and search the Web for an explanation of how it works. Print the explanation and evaluate it according to the criteria listed under Designing and Integrating Visuals with Text, on pages 220–224.

   b. Mark the pages of the explanation, indicating any changes you would make to improve the explanation's design. Feel free to sketch out your ideas.

   c. Draft a memo to your instructor in which you explain what does and does not work in the explanation's original design, supporting your ideas with information from this chapter. Specify how your changes would improve the document's design. Attach to your memo the marked-up printout of the explanation and any sketches you've created.

Writing @ Work

A Portfolio

In Part One of this book you learned the key steps of the process common to all types of workplace writing—planning, organizing, drafting, and revising. This section focused on the primary concepts of audience and purpose and how they help writers impart their message clearly and best address their readers' needs. In Part Two you focused on communications skills essential in today's workplace—how to collaborate with writing partners, perform and receive peer reviews, and edit documents; how to conduct primary and secondary research using reliable Web and print sources; and how to design and create effective visuals and illustrations for your print and online documents.

Now that you are familiar with the principles of good workplace writing, you are ready to start applying them. Part Three offers specific guidelines for the most common types of written and oral communications you will likely have in the workplace. It offers detailed advice on content and design for routine correspondence via e-mail, letters, and memos; informal and formal reports; instructions; proposals; presentations; and common Web documents.

Before you begin Part Three, however, it may be helpful to get a sense of the diversity of workplace writing. The portfolio that follows, "Writing @ Work," illustrates the myriad forms that writing at work can take. Some documents, like routine correspondence or presentations, may be consistent across professions, while others, like instructions or proposals, will differ considerably from profession to profession. And in many professions, you may be called upon to create a document germane to that particular field, such as a media review, press release, or scientific paper. This portfolio provides a glimpse into the kinds of documents used in professions as diverse as public relations, nursing, education, science, and engineering.

WRITING @ WORK: Nursing

Nurses write discharge instructions for patients leaving the hospital after a medical procedure. This example, from the Department of Perioperative Services at Newton-Wellesley Hospital in Massachusetts, is distributed to individuals who have just undergone a tonsillectomy or adenoidectomy, or both. The instructions begin with a brief explanation of the procedure; then they provide advice for the recuperation period, discussing possible pain, foods to eat as well as to avoid, and ways to spot potential complications. Clarity and accessibility are vitally important to such a document; an illustration and succinct bulleted lists help ensure that patients and caregivers understand postoperative instructions.

Department of Perioperative Services
617-243-5243

TONSILLECTOMY AND/OR ADENOIDECTOMY INSTRUCTIONS

What Are Tonsillectomies and Adenoidectomies?

The tonsils are two pads of tissue located on either side of the back of the throat. Tonsils can become enlarged in response to recurring tonsil infections or strep throat. A tonsillectomy is recommended when tonsil infections become frequent enough that they interfere with a patient's general health (such as airway obstruction as well as hearing). People with enlarged tonsils can also have enlarged adenoid glands, which commonly results in an adenoidectomy. The adenoids are similar to tonsils but are located in the back of the nose. If enlarged, they can compress the Eustachian tube causing fluid in the middle ear and frequent ear infections.

Anesthesia

Your child has received general anesthesia for this procedure. He/she may feel somewhat dizzy and/or sleepy after the surgery. Anesthetic agents can remain in one's body for up to 24 hours. It is important for your child to rest for the remainder of the day and be under adult supervision. Your child should not ride his/her bike or perform such activities that require coordination.

Pain

Patients tend to experience a fair amount of pain postsurgery. An earache is a common complaint among patients. The same nerve that travels to the throat is connected to the ear, so stimulation of this nerve can feel like an earache. Expect some discomfort while eating, drinking, and sleeping. This discomfort can fluctuate from mild to severe for up to 14 days.

11/2007 PS057290

NEWTON-WELLESLEY
HOSPITAL

Department of Perioperative Services
617-243-5243

Medicate as prescribed for pain. DO NOT take Aspirin, Aspergum, Advil, or Ibuprofen. Things you can do to relieve the pain:

- Ice the neck.
- Chew gum.
- Have a humidifier in the room.
- Gargle with cold water.

Eating/Drinking

Expect some discomfort when swallowing food. Many children are uninterested in eating for up to a week. **Hydration is extremely important!** *Encourage*: juice (except for drinks that are high in citrus like lemon, lime, and grapefruit). *Encourage*: jello and popsicles or ice chips. These not only help in hydration but soothe the throat. *Avoid*: milk products such as pudding, yogurt, and ice cream for the first 24 hours. Also stay away from sports drinks like Gatorade, which dry the throat. Pedialyte is okay. Stay away from foods like chips and crackers, which can scratch the back of the throat, until you see your doctor for the follow-up appointment.

Signs of Dehydration

- Dark urine
- Urinating less than two to three times a day
- Crying without tears
- Lethargy
- Dry skin
- Temp higher than 101 degrees

Breathing

Snoring and mouth breathing are normal after surgery because of swelling. Normal breathing should resume 10 to 14 days after surgery. It is normal to have liquid go up the back of your nose after an adenoidectomy. This may occur for a few days following the surgery.

Activity

Light activity for up to 10 days. Generally, children may return to school when they are eating and drinking normally, off of all pain medications, and sleeping through the night. This is 7 to 10 days on average and can be less or more, depending on the conditions. However, keep in mind that even though the patient may be feeling fine, he/she is at risk for bleeding up to 14 days after surgery. No diving into pools until after the follow-up check with the doctor.

NEWTON-WELLESLEY HOSPITAL

11/2007 PS057290

PARTNERS. HealthCare

Department of Perioperative Services
617-243-5243

Bleeding

If there is excessive bleeding (more than a little spit up) from the mouth or nose, consult your doctor immediately. If it isn't office hours, go straight to the Emergency Department. This bleeding could be a result of the scabs falling off too early and needs immediate attention. **Note**: It is not unusual to vomit old blood and gastric secretions after surgery (once or twice), but if it persists, consult the doctor. You may also notice large white patches in the back of your child's throat after surgery for up to about two weeks; this is completely normal.

Notify your doctor if the following occurs:

- Child is unable to swallow fluids.
- You notice bleeding in the back of your child's throat and/or your child is spitting up blood.
- Your child has a fever higher than 101 degrees.
- Your child is in severe pain that is not relieved by pain medicine.

11/2007 PS057290

 NEWTON-WELLESLEY
HOSPITAL

PARTNERS

WRITING @ WORK: **Radio Disc Jockey**

For some radio disc jockeys (DJs), one of the most enjoyable parts of the job is scouting out new music that listeners will enjoy. This feature, posted on a Pittsburgh radio station's Web site, details and reviews a "CD of the Week." The DJ establishes a friendly insider tone, providing both description and back-story for the highlighted band and album. For this nonprofit radio station, such features are integrally tied to fundraising efforts, which help keep the noncommercial programming on the air. A link from the "CD of the Week" page to the station's pledge page makes it easy for readers to donate online and reinforces the station's sense of community.

WRITING @ WORK: Elementary Education

Progress reports are used in elementary education to inform a parent or guardian of a child's academic and social development. For a classroom teacher, the progress report is a vital tool to maintain open communication between the home and the school, alerting parents to possible problems and acknowledging good behavior and habits. This progress report was created by a second-grade teacher; in it, she spells out her expectations for the student and how they are being met and sometimes even surpassed. She also describes current classroom work, which allows the parent to consider the report in context of the class curriculum. A document such as this would be mailed to the parent or guardian's home by the teacher or by a school administrator three or four times a year.

PROGRESS REPORT

Student: Jared Greene
Teacher: Melissa Holman
Report: December 2010

It has been a pleasure to welcome Jared to second grade. A responsible member of our classroom community, his behavior at school is respectful and appropriate, and he is a student who can be counted on to do the right thing. At all times, he works hard, takes pride in his work, and is eager to share what he has accomplished with teachers, family members, and classmates.

Reading: The reading curriculum is taught through the structure of Reading Workshop. This includes reading independently, reading with a teacher, reading with other students in a weekly reading group, and taking lessons on reading strategies and phonics. . . . Jared is an enthusiastic participant during group meetings. He likes to discuss literature, and he frequently makes text connections and predictions during group mini-lessons.

Writing and Spelling: During Writers' Workshop, instruction has focused on generating story ideas; developing one idea into a story with a beginning, a middle, and an end; "reading like a writer" to notice choices authors make in the structure and language of their published works; and expanding "small moments" into detailed stories. Jared is working on a research piece about the Wampanoag (Native American) language. Jared has a strong sense of story structure (beginning, middle, end) as well as many of the conventions of nonfiction (table of contents, index, glossary).

Mathematics: We have completed three units in our *Everyday Math* curriculum, incorporating lessons in money, telling time, addition and subtraction, place value, and "number stories" (word problems). Mathematical thinking is an area of true strength for Jared. He understands concepts of operation (addition, subtraction, etc.) and demonstrates comfort with basic and more complex math facts. He is growing increasingly limber with his use of numbers and is able to see that there are many strategies for solving any given problem.

Social Studies and Science: We are wrapping up the work of our first three Charles River research units, which focused on river geology and erosion, mapping, and the water cycle. Jared has been an active participant in our Charles River research. He is naturally inquisitive, enthusiastic about the material, and careful in his hypotheses and observations. He is able to record detailed notes and enjoys predicting the outcome of experiments and projects.

It has been wonderful to have Jared in my classroom this year. I look forward to fostering his intellectual and social development throughout the year.

WRITING @ WORK: Public Relations

Stoneham
THEATRE

FOR IMMEDIATE RELEASE
November 14, 2008

Press Contact: Liz O'Meara-Goldberg, 781.279.2200
liz@theatre.org

STONEHAM THEATRE CONTINUES HOLIDAY SHOW TRADITION WITH
IT'S A WONDERFUL LIFE

Stoneham Theatre opened its doors eight years ago, in the winter of 2000, with a holiday production of Charles Dickens' *A Christmas Carol*. Since then, the holiday show has become a tradition at the theatre. In addition to *A Christmas Carol*, they have produced *A Christmas Story*, *Miracle on 34th Street*, and this year's *It's a Wonderful Life*.

Based on the classic holiday film by Frank Capra and the short story by Philip Van Doren, *It's a Wonderful Life* tells the story of George Bailey (played by Owen Doyle, last seen on stage at Stoneham Theatre in *A Young Lady from Rwanda* and *A Prayer for Owen Meaney*), a man who retraces his life with his guardian angel Clarence Odbody (Bill Gardiner, Kris Kringle in last year's *Miracle on 34th Street*) and discovers what the small, fictional town of Bedford Falls would be without him. Along the way, we're introduced to the greedy Mr. Potter (Allan Mayo), George's wife Mary (Jessica Webb, making her Stoneham Theatre debut), brother Harry (Lucas Loyd), and children Janie (Rebecca Lerman), Tommy (Michael Sticca), and Zuzu (played at alternating performances by Grace Goddard and Molly Geaney). The production is directed by Chris Jorie.

Next year will mark Stoneham Theatre's tenth anniversary season, and they are looking for help from the community to choose next year's holiday show. If you have a holiday favorite or would like to see them bring back a classic, please e-mail marketing@stonehamtheatre.org with your suggestions.

It's a Wonderful Life runs Friday, November 28, through Sunday, December 21. Show times are Wednesdays, Thursdays, and Fridays at 7pm, Saturdays at 3pm & 7pm, and Sundays at 1pm & 5pm. Tickets are $40 (Adult), $35 (Senior), and $20 (Student). Stoneham Theatre is located at 395 Main Street in Stoneham. For tickets and information, visit or call the Box Office at 781-279-2200, open Tuesday through Saturday 1-6pm, or e-mail at www.stonehamtheatre.org.

Also, celebrate New Year's Eve with Stoneham Theatre as they present a tribute to Benny Goodman and Peggy Lee, featuring vocalist Amanda Carr and the Everett Longstreth Orchestra. Two shows on December 31 at 7pm & 10pm. All tickets $45, which includes a champagne toast.

###

Preparing press releases is an integral part of any public relations job. This press release for the Stoneham Theatre, a small professional theater in Massachusetts, announces an upcoming production of *It's a Wonderful Life*. Press releases generally announce new products, services, events, or important developments in a company and are sent to news organizations. Press releases address the essential *who*, *what*, *where*, *when*, and *why* that journalists need to know about the product, service, or event. The publicist who wrote this press release describes the upcoming play and its cast and crew; she also communicates basic information about show times, prices, and box-office information.

WRITING @ WORK: **Microbiology**

Although microbiologists and other scientists spend most of their time in the lab, publishing their data is an important step in establishing credentials as experts in their fields. This excerpt, from the introduction to a longer scientific paper, was written for possible publication in a peer-reviewed journal. In this introduction, the author explains biosensor technology and offers a brief review of the literature on this topic. The paper will go on to present findings about using a specific biosensor and how it can be used to detect herbicides and other environmental pollutants. A figure illustrates the structure of a biosensor and supports the author's definition.

DEVELOPMENT OF A NOVEL *SYNECHOCYSTIS SPP.* BIOSENSOR FOR DETECTION OF HERBICIDES, HEAVY METALS, AND ORGANIC POLLUTANTS

The evolution of industrial processes has doubtless changed the face of the environment, especially in the past century. Large-scale industrial endeavors and other anthropogenic activities have resulted in such catastrophic changes as the astronomical emission rates of methane and carbon dioxide and the introduction of a plethora of pollutants, such as polychlorinated biphenyls, insecticides, pesticides, detergents, and metals, into the environment. The growing presence of such harmful impurities necessitates fast, cost-effective methods of monitoring contamination in air, water, and soil to better understand and manage the risks posed to both humans and the environment. Biosensors are unique tools that are well-suited to the task of environmental monitoring, and researchers continue to use novel and useful applications for them in this capacity.

While there are many functional definitions, biosensors are widely understood as being self-contained systems in which biological-recognition elements interface with chemical sensors, that together reversibly respond to chemical species in a concentration-dependent fashion (Rogers, 2005). The technology started modestly in 1962 with Dr. Leland Clark's development of the oxygen electrode, still the gold standard for measuring dissolved oxygen concentrations in biomedical, environmental, and industrial applications (Liu and Ju, 2003). However, since its inception, this field has virtually exploded with functions and formats as diverse as life itself.

The past four decades have seen the evolution of a wide range of bioassay designs, which can be classed functionally by the biological element utilized. Enzyme-based biosensors were the first developed, and the focus of overwhelming attention until such advances as PCR and sequencing in the 1980s and subsequent years enabled genetic engineering. Such a format has a number of inherent advantages, including stable source of material, the ability to modify catalytic properties or specificities by genetic engineering, and catalytic amplification of biosensor response by modulation of enzyme activity (Bhattacharyya et al., 2004).

Figure 1: Structural schematic of a biosensor. Regardless of the type of biosensor, each possesses three components: a sensitive biological component, a detector element that converts the biological response to a measurable chemical effect, and a transducer that connects the two elements. (Rogers, 2005)

WRITING @ WORK: **Casting Agencies**

From: mparadice@casting.com
To: actors@casting.com
Date: January 7, 2009
Subject: Casting Call

Happy New Year!!!

We have an audition on Monday for Bettencourt Publishing. It's a CATEGORY I industrial and would pay spokes rate.

The commercial is for online textbooks; the target audience is teachers and administrators.

We are holding these auditions from 2–5 p.m. on Monday and clients will be present. Please dress in formal business attire.

Please e-mail or call me back and let me know what time slot you would like. Or to let me know you aren't available for the audition. The clients don't have a shoot date set yet, as this may become an ongoing project.

Thanks!
Melissa Paradice
Casting Director
mparadice@casting.com

Casting agencies draft commercial casting calls for their actor clients to communicate upcoming casting needs. A casting call such as this one is an informal announcement sent out to the pool of actors whose headshot and résumé are on file at the agency. The call is generally distributed by the agent or agent's assistant via a mass e-mail; its casual tone and jargon reflect the close relationship this agent's assistant has with her clients. The brief announcement contains pertinent day and time information for the audition and identifies the client, product, and target audience. It also refers to the pay range and expected duration of the project, to give the actors a sense of the project's scope.

WRITING @ WORK: Structural Engineering

Structural engineers design buildings, bridges, tunnels, highway overpasses, and other structures. During the schematic design (SD) phase of a project, a structural engineer will draft a structural narrative, such as the one excerpted here. The structural narrative describes how the space will be used, the types of structural systems that will be employed (such as the "steel frame" and "diagonal braced frames" described here), and the type of foundation to be used. It also references relevant building codes and includes size estimates and design loads. This excerpt from a structural narrative describes the plan for a performing arts and humanities building at the University of Maryland, Baltimore County.

7A – BUILDING: STRUCTURAL NARRATIVE

The complex is composed of a variety of spaces, including the three performance spaces, a scene shop, studios, classrooms, offices, and support areas. These spaces dictate a variety of column grids, floor-to-ceiling heights, and performance criteria for acoustics and vibration. The plan geometry also includes angled and curved geometry.

To respond to the variety of spatial and performance challenges, a composite structural steel frame is recommended. Floor slabs will generally be composed of two-inch 20-gauge galvanized steel deck plus 3-1/4" of lightweight concrete reinforced with WWF $6 \times 6 \times$ W2.9 $\times$ W2.9, creating a 2-tier floor system. The slab will be supported by composite steel beams, ranging in depth from 12" at 20' spans to 18" at 40' spans. In general, column spacings have been planned to allow floor beams and girders not to exceed a total structural envelope of 2'-0". This will expand slightly at some spaces such as the dance studio when a built-up floor with a damping slab and floor vibration criteria may require a slightly deeper structure.

There are six different roof elevations, and many will have rooftop units supported thereon. Roof screen frames are also required. The baseline scheme suggests the use of composite steel construction for all roofs as the concrete is necessary for noise attenuation. Future value engineering may investigate limited areas where concrete may not be required at the roof, such as at the loading dock.

Column sizes are generally W10s, although larger columns may be required at tall spaces, such as in the scene shop and theater rehearsal spaces.

The façade is a mix of metal panel and masonry. Perimeter columns are generally spaced at less than 30' to ensure spandrel beams are rigid enough to meet façade support deflection criteria without being excessively heavy or deep. There will be at least two large-scale window wall supports at the lobby café and theater rehearsal where tube steel columns will be integrated with the wall design to supplement lateral loads on the wall systems.

The performance spaces require concrete walls that are isolated from the adjoining spaces. The concrete walls will support the floor and roof framing within the performance spaces. A combination of cast-in-place concrete and steel framing will support the floors and balconies of these spaces. The roof will be composite steel construction as described above. Catwalks, tech galleries, and rigging grids will be structural steel hung from the roof framing.

The concrete walls surrounding the performance spaces will also serve as the lateral support system, resisting wind and seismic forces. As these walls are isolated from the surrounding structure for acoustic reasons, the bordering columns of the steel frame will have diagonal braced frames to stabilize the surrounding structure. Should the necessary braced frames not be consistent with architectural layouts, some moment frames along the perimeter may be introduced.

In general, the stepped and curved seating platforms for the Proscenium Theater and Concert Hall are planned cast-in-place concrete construction. The Proscenium Theater slab will be cast on grade. The Concert Hall slab will be cast above a crawlspace.

WRITING @ WORK: **Research Consulting**

PROPOSAL TO CONDUCT A MULTIYEAR EVALUATION OF PERMANENT
SUPPORTIVE HOUSING IN LOWELL COUNTY

LS Group is pleased to partner with Barton Consulting, LLC, to provide the Supportive Housing Initiative (SHI) with a proposal to evaluate State-Financed Permanent Supportive Housing (PSH) in Lowell County. LS Group's national research and technical assistance experience in homelessness, housing, and community development, complemented by Barton's expertise in housing development, finance, and operations, provides an exceptional foundation on which to help SHI and its partners execute groundbreaking research on the long-term sustainability of PSH and its effectiveness over time for the tenants housed in various PSH settings. We are very excited about this study and believe the results have the opportunity to shape state policy, local practice, and national understanding of PSH and its ongoing impact and role.

LS Group and Barton offer SHI a *"full-service" research team*, with the breadth of staff and project skills necessary to complete *all three components* of the proposed study: program and cost effectiveness, community and neighborhood impact, and project stability and quality. This comprehensive approach allows us to achieve economies of scale across the three evaluation components, enabling us to propose richer analysis and more frequent interim reports than might otherwise be feasible. Most important, the technical approach is sufficiently rigorous to yield results that can guide important decision-making about the future of PSH in Lowell County.

Our proposal is organized as follows: In Section 1, we discuss the key elements of our technical approach and design considerations, including challenges that may be encountered and strategies to mitigate these challenges, and our plan for reporting and dissemination. Section 2 details the work plan and overall project time line. Section 3 describes our management plan and organizational and staff qualifications related to this study. Appendix A presents résumés for project staff, and Appendix B contains our references. Our budget and budget narrative and writing samples are included in separate documents.

Research consultants perform a wide range of research, evaluation, and data-collection projects. They may evaluate the effectiveness of government programs, provide technical assistance and training for new policy initiatives, collect and analyze data, and conduct large-scale research programs. Their clients may include federal, state, and local government agencies and departments; private businesses and corporations; universities; and nonprofit foundations or institutions.

The proposal excerpted here, by LS Group, presents a comprehensive plan for evaluating a state-supported housing program. The introduction establishes the credentials of LS Group and its partners, outlines the scope of the evaluation, and provides an overview of the proposal's structure. The proposal's work plan is formatted as a table and itemizes in detail each task of the work being proposed. It assigns target due dates, describes the involvement of all parties, projects outcomes, and identifies deliverables (or products) for each task listed. Because the LS Group is proposing a multiyear evaluation, the detailed work plan is essential for keeping all parties on schedule.

Section 2.   Work Plan

This section presents our proposed work plan for designing and completing the required study tasks. The LS Group/Barton team has extensive experience researching and providing technical assistance on homelessness, housing development, and neighborhood redevelopment. Our technical approach and work plan is based on these perspectives, as well as extensive experience analyzing administrative data, designing and conducting site-visit interviews and cost data collection. Time lines are noted to convey the general time frames for the proposed work; however, these dates may be able to be adjusted depending on data availability. For instance, from our experience negotiating access to mainstream data on other projects, we have allotted a significant period of time to obtain mainstream data. If these data are available sooner, this work can be completed and delivered earlier. In addition, the schedule can be resequenced or adapted in other ways to better meet SHI and state legislative or programmatic deadlines.

	Properties and Neighborhoods	Tenants, PSH Involvement, PSH Outcomes	Mainstream System Use and Outcomes	Project Planning, Management, and Deliverables
Year 1				
May 2010	Assess data on properties and costs	Assess data on tenants, PSH occupancy and service use, and outcomes	Assess mainstream system data availability and access	Opening meeting
June 2010	Analyze inventory and prepare description of properties Select Samples A, B, and C	Work with SHI on a strategy to obtain data (SHI will assume lead role in data acquisition)	Agree upon target data sets and plan for obtaining data	Develop work plan based on assessment of data types and availability Draft and deliver work plan
July 2010	Develop/refine cost templates and cost specs related to development cost data Use GIS to analyze neighborhood characteristics and appropriateness	Develop protocols for assessing tenant satisfaction Define specifications for data needs re: tenants, service use, and outcomes	Develop data use agreement template and mainstream table shells to inform mainstream data request(s)	Prepare data collection and analysis plan (DCAP) Deliver data collection and analysis plan (DCAP)

PART 3

Writing at Work:
From Principle to Practice

Chapter 8
**Understanding the Principles
of Business Communication, 275**

Chapter 9
Writing Business Correspondence, 320

Chapter 10
Writing Informal Reports, 358

Chapter 11
Writing Formal Reports, 385

Chapter 12
Writing Instructions, 422

Chapter 13
Writing Proposals, 448

Chapter 14
Giving Presentations and Conducting Meetings, 498

Chapter 15
Writing for the Web: Rhetorical Principles, 539

Chapter 16
Finding the Right Job, 570

Parts One and Two discuss the principles of effective writing that apply to all on-the-job writing tasks; Part Three focuses on the practical applications of these principles. Chapters 8 through 15 provide explicit guidelines for writing the most common types of work-related communications and offer plenty of examples: e-mail messages, memos, business letters, instructions, proposals, a variety of formal and informal reports, and content for Web sites, including blogs, wikis, FAQs, and podcasts. Part Three ends with a chapter that puts everything you have learned in this text to its first practical test: finding a job appropriate to your education and abilities.

8 Understanding the Principles of Business Communication

AT A GLANCE: Communication Principles

Most jobs involve at least some written communication—with coworkers, supervisors, staff, clients, vendors, and customers. You can achieve your goals and convey a professional image by using appropriate tone and style in your writing and adhering to expected formats. This chapter covers the following skills essential to successful business communication:

- Selecting the appropriate medium for your message / 277
- Developing style and tone / 280
- Structuring effective correspondence / 283
- Working under the pressure of deadlines / 293
- Sending e-mail and instant messages / 295
- Designing memos / 303
- Designing letters / 306

Business communication, especially the correspondence among people within an organization or between those people and their clients or customers, is essential to the success of individuals and businesses. Because of their importance, such communications should be well-written; those that are not waste time and money. For example, the poorly written letter shown in Figure 8–1 was actually sent to a law firm (the names have been changed). Imagine you received this letter from a client. What does that client want? What impression do you get of that sender? The staff at the law firm could not understand it, even though a number of attorneys, paralegals, and assistants were familiar with the case. Staff members exchanged e-mail messages and phone calls with Ralph Madison and others at his company to try to clarify the request but without success. This letter wasted the time of a high-paid staff—and caused a delay in legal services to Ralph Madison's company. Such carelessly written letters or e-mail messages also project a poor image of the writer and can result in other kinds of losses. A reader's negative reaction to an unclear or unprofessional message, for example, can cost a firm its reputation and future business—and can even cost an employee his or her job.

February 16, 2010

Mr. Stewart R. Cassidy
Fiorello and Cooke, Attorneys at Law
1212 Broadway
Hartford, CT 06119

Dear Mr. Cassidy:

Omitted words

Unclear reference

In regard to claim on Account #5-861 see enclosed copy of letter received and copy of delivery receipt regarding same. There had been a claim which was disallowed and debtor withheld payment on the bill, and the one we referred to your office for collection, as no pro was mentioned but the one the claim was on was referred to the bill is still open and they still owe Universal, please review and advise.

Confusing, run-on sentence filled with grammatical errors

Sincerely,

Ralph Madison

Ralph Madison
Account Manager

Figure 8–1   Poorly Written Letter

This chapter focuses on the most common forms of written correspondence—business letters, memos, e-mail messages, and instant messages—and covers many of the steps that go into most other on-the-job writing tasks:

1. Establishing your purpose, your reader's needs, and your scope.
2. Outlining key points or jotting down the points you wish to make and the order in which you wish to make them for a short e-mail, a memo, or a letter (see Chapter 2, Organizing Your Information).
3. Writing a rough draft from the outline (see Chapter 3, Writing the Draft).
4. Allowing a cooling period (see Chapter 4, Revising the Draft), especially when a letter or an e-mail responds to a problem. Even a lunch-hour break can give you a chance to remove any inappropriate statements made in the heat of the situation.

◆ *For an overview of the writing process at work, see Chapter 1, Assessing Audience and Purpose.*

5. Revising the rough draft by checking for logic and development as well as for grammar, spelling, and punctuation (see Chapter 4, Revising the Draft, and Part Four, Revision Guide).

6. Formatting the message, especially the arrangement and spacing of letter parts (see pages 303–313), and printing a copy for review and proofing before signing it.

7. Assuming final responsibility: As the author of a letter or memo, you are responsible for its accuracy and appearance.

ON THE WEB

For more resources on writing and formatting business correspondence, go to Chapter 8, bedfordstmartins.com/ writingthatworks

Selecting the Appropriate Medium

Important as they are, e-mail messages and letters are not the only means of communication in the workplace. The possibilities include e-mail, instant messaging, faxing, voice mail, and videoconferencing in addition to more traditional means of communication, such as letters and memos, telephone calls, and face-to-face meetings. With so many means of communication available, how do organizations and individuals decide which is preferable in a given situation?

In selecting the appropriate medium (or *channel*, as it is sometimes called), first consider your audience, your purpose, and the context of the communication. For example, when you need to solve an urgent problem, a written message (even one sent electronically) can take too long or create confusion. In such a case, a telephone call is the more efficient choice. When you need precise wording and you and your reader need a permanent record of the information exchanged, a written message (letter, memo, or e-mail) is best. When you wish to establish close rapport with someone in the interest of developing a long-term working relationship, a face-to-face meeting is indispensable. The following primary methods of communicating are all currently in use because each communicates certain kinds of information better than the others, even though the advantages overlap in some cases.

E-mail

E-mail (or *email*) is a primary medium to communicate messages and share electronic files with colleagues, clients, and customers. These messages should follow the writing strategy and style for business correspondence described later in this chapter. Because e-mail recipients can easily forward messages and attachments to others and because e-mail messages are subject to legal disclosure, writers must review them carefully before clicking the Send button.

Instant Messages

Instant messaging (IM) is a text-based communication medium that fills a niche between telephone calls and e-mail messages. It allows both real-time communication, like a phone call, and the transfer of text or other files, like an e-mail message, on computers, cell phones, or portable digital assistants (PDAs). It can help people collaborate from multiple work sites, functioning like an abbreviated Internet chat-room discussion. Instant messaging might be useful when a workplace Web site is down, for example, and staff located in Europe or Asia must communicate to repair it immediately.

Memos

Memos on printed company stationery or attached to an e-mail message are appropriate for internal communications among members of an organization, especially when offices are geographically separated. Printed memos may be used in manufacturing or service industries, for example, where employees do not have easy access to e-mail. In such cases, memos can be used to instruct employees, announce policies, report results, disseminate information, and delegate responsibilities.

Letters

Letters are most appropriate for initial contacts with business associates or customers, as well as for other official business communications outside a company or an organization. Stationery with an organization's printed letterhead and the writer's handwritten signature communicates formality, respect, and authority. A written promise, conveyed above the signature of an employee who has the authority to act on behalf of an organization, ensures that the information is accurate and that the sender will honor it. For example, a formal letter is often used to summarize the terms and conditions of a proposed business relationship.

Faxes

A fax (facsimile transmission) is most useful when speed is essential and when graphic information—a drawing or signed contract, for example—must be viewed in its original form. Faxes are useful when the recipient does not have access to e-mail or when graphic material has not been scanned or converted into electronic form. When an original is also needed, the paper copy can be sent separately by overnight or regular mail. Faxed material should be sent with a cover sheet (available as a word-processing template) or a commercially prepared fax stick-on label. Be aware that fax machines in offices are often located in shared areas, so alert the intended recipient before you send confidential or sensitive messages.

Telephone and Conference Calls

Telephone calls are best used for exchanges that require substantial interaction and the need for participants to interpret each other's tone of voice. Phone calls are useful for discussing sensitive issues and quickly resolving misunderstandings, although they do not provide the visual cues possible during face-to-face meetings. Cell (or *mobile*) phones are useful for communicating away from an office, but users should follow appropriate etiquette, such as speaking in an appropriate tone and switching off the ringer or setting the ringer to vibrate during meetings.*

Conference calls are useful among three or more participants. They are a less expensive alternative to a face-to-face meeting that would require the participants to travel to a central meeting place. They also provide a setting for the immediate resolution of issues.

Such calls are more efficient if the person setting up the call works from an agenda shared by all the participants. That person must be prepared to direct the discussion as though he or she were leading a meeting. The participants should also take notes on any key points or decisions made during the call. Of course, the call must be planned to ensure that everyone is available at the same time. Timing is especially important when participants are located in different time zones—especially for international calls.

◆ *For further information on preparing agendas and leading conference calls, see pages 525–526 in Chapter 14, Giving Presentations and Conducting Meetings.*

Voice-Mail Messages

Voice-mail systems are common in and out of the workplace. Anticipate what you will say if you reach a voice-mail recording instead of the person you've called. Speak clearly and leave your name, phone number, the date and time of the call, and a succinct message ("Call me about the deadline for the new project" or "I got the package from RTL, so you don't need to call the distributor"). If the message is complicated or contains numerous details, use another medium, such as an e-mail message, to ensure that the information is communicated accurately. If you want to discuss a subject at length, let the recipient know the subject so that he or she can prepare a response before returning your call.

Face-to-Face Meetings

Face-to-face meetings are most appropriate for initial or early contacts with business associates and customers with whom you intend to develop an important long-term relationship or with whom you need to establish rapport. Meetings are also the best medium for exchanges in which you need to solve a serious problem. The most productive meetings occur when all participants come prepared to contribute to a collective effort toward a well-defined objective.

◆ *For a more detailed discussion on how to conduct effective meetings and record the meeting discussions and decisions, see pages 523–533 in Chapter 14, Giving Presentations and Conducting Meetings.*

Videoconferences

Videoconferences are particularly useful for meetings where travel is impractical or too expensive. Unlike telephone conference calls, videoconferences have the advantage of allowing participants to see as well as to hear one another. Videoconferences work best with participants who are at ease in front of a camera.

---

*Based on LetsTalk.com's cell-phone etiquette survey and resulting guidelines at <www.letstalk.com/promo/unclecell/unclecell2.htm>.

Web Communication

A public Internet or company intranet Web site is ideal for posting announcements or policies as well as for making available or exchanging documents and files with others. Your Web site can serve not only as a home base for resources but also as a place where ideas can be developed through, for example, discussion boards, blogs, and wikis. See Chapter 15, Writing for the Web, pages 539–569.

WRITER'S CHECKLIST
Selecting the Medium

✔ Consider your audience, purpose, and what is typical or expected in your organization. In general, use written forms and messages for precise wording; use telephone, videoconference, and in-person communication when you need, for example, to resolve a misunderstanding.

✔ Use e-mail to send messages and electronic documents, maintain professional relationships, elicit discussions, and collect opinions from distant as well as wide audiences.

✔ Use instant messaging when you need to communicate and share files with one or more people in multiple locations who do not have convenient access to e-mail at their current locations.

✔ Use letters on organizational stationery for outside business communications; printed letterhead on quality paper communicates formality, respect, and authority.

✔ Use memos (printed and electronic) for in-house business communications—from policy announcements to short reports.

✔ Use faxes when the exact image of nondigital documents or signed documents must be viewed and when speed matters.

✔ Use telephone and conference calls when give-and-take or tone of voice is important; conference calls, when carefully planned, are a less expensive alternative to a face-to-face meeting for participants in distant locations.

✔ Use voice mail for short, uncomplicated messages.

✔ Use face-to-face meetings for early contacts with business associates and customers or when solving problems.

✔ Use videoconferencing as a substitute for face-to-face meetings when travel is impractical.

✔ Use Web sites for company or group postings as well as for making available or exchanging documents and files with others.

▦ Developing Style and Tone

Corresponding with others in the workplace enables you to establish or maintain a positive working relationship with your readers and to convey a professional image of yourself and your organization. Your attitude toward the reader (tone) and the way you express yourself (style) determine how readers react to you and your organization.

VOICES IN THE WORKPLACE

The Importance of Electronic Communications in the Workplace

Robert Demers, software engineer at Philips Medical Systems, discusses how central e-mail, instant messaging, and other electronic communication are in his workplace: "Almost all of my everyday communication is now electronic. We use e-mail, instant messaging, online meetings, company Web sites, and the telephone—almost all accessible from anywhere, anytime. . . . Review your message. Try to get spelling, capitalization, and sentence structure correct and make sure your message is clear. Your recipients will appreciate it and it will reflect well on you."

Audience and Writing Style

Effective correspondence uses an appropriate conversational style. To achieve that style, imagine your reader sitting across from you and write to the reader as if you were talking face to face. Anticipate your reader's needs and feelings. Ask yourself, "How might I feel if I received this letter or e-mail?" and then tailor your message accordingly. Remember, an impersonal and unfriendly message to a customer or client can tarnish the image of you and your business, but a thoughtful and sincere one can enhance it.

Whether you use a formal or an informal writing style depends on your reader, your purpose, and the context. You might use an informal (or a casual) style, for example, with a colleague you know well and a formal (or restrained) style with a client you do not know.

CASUAL   It worked! The new process is better than we had dreamed.

RESTRAINED   You will be pleased to know that the new process is more effective than we had expected.

You will probably find yourself using the restrained style more frequently than the casual style. Remember that an overdone attempt to sound casual or friendly can sound insincere. However, do not adopt a style so formal that your writing reads like a legal contract. Affectation not only will irritate and baffle readers but also can waste time and produce costly errors.

AFFECTED   Per our dialogue yesterday, we no longer possess an original copy of the brochure requested. Please be advised that a PDF copy is attached to this correspondence.

IMPROVED   We are out of original copies of the brochure we discussed yesterday, so I am attaching a PDF copy to this e-mail.

◆ For detailed advice about adopting an appropriate style in your writing, see pages 108–114 in Chapter 4, Revising the Draft.

The improved version is not only clearer and less stuffy but also more concise.

Goodwill and the "You" Viewpoint

Write concisely, but do not be so blunt that you risk losing the reader's goodwill. Responding to a vague written request with "Your request was unclear" or "I don't understand" could offend your reader. Instead, establish goodwill to encourage your reader to provide the information you need.

▶   I will be glad to help, but I need more information to find the report you requested. Specifically, can you give me the report's title, release date, or number?

Although this version is a bit longer, it is more tactful and will elicit a faster response.

You can also build goodwill by emphasizing the reader's needs or benefits. Suppose you received a refund request from a customer who forgot to enclose the receipt. In a response to that customer, you might write the following:

WEAK   We must receive the sales receipt before we can process a refund. [The writer's needs are emphasized: "*We* must."]

If you consider how you might keep the customer's goodwill, you could word the request this way:

IMPROVED   Please mail or fax the sales receipt so that we can process your refund. [This is polite, but the writer's needs are still emphasized: "so that *we* can process."]

You can put the reader's needs and interests foremost by writing from the reader's perspective. Often, doing so means using the words *you* and *your* rather than *we*, *our*, *I*, and *mine*—a technique called the "you" viewpoint. Consider the following revision:

EFFECTIVE   So that you can receive your refund promptly, please mail or fax the sales receipt. [The reader's needs are emphasized with *you* and *your*.]

This revision stresses the reader's benefit and interest and will be more likely to accomplish its purpose: to get the reader to act.

If overdone, however, goodwill and the "you" viewpoint can produce writing that is fawning and insincere. Messages that are full of excessive praise and inflated language may be ignored—or even resented—by the reader.

EXCESSIVE PRAISE   You are just the kind of astute client that deserves the finest service that we can offer—and you deserve our best deal. Knowing how carefully you make decisions, I know you'll think about the advantages of using our consulting service.

REASONABLE   From our earlier correspondence, I understand your need for reliable service. We strive to give all our priority clients our full attention, and after you have reviewed our proposal, I am confident you will appreciate our "five-star" consulting option.

WRITER'S CHECKLIST
Using Tone to Build Goodwill

Use the following guidelines to achieve a tone that builds goodwill with your recipients.

✔ Be respectful, not demanding.

| DEMANDING | Submit your answer in one week. |
| RESPECTFUL | I would appreciate your answer within one week. |

✔ Be modest, not arrogant.

| ARROGANT | My attached report is thorough, and I'm sure that it will be essential. |
| MODEST | The attached report contains details of the refinancing options that I hope you will find useful. |

✔ Be polite, not sarcastic.

| SARCASTIC | I just now received the shipment we ordered six months ago. I'm sending it back—we can't use it now. Thanks a lot! |
| POLITE | I am returning the shipment we ordered on March 12. Unfortunately, it arrived too late for us to be able to use it. |

✔ Be positive and tactful, not negative and condescending.

| NEGATIVE | Your complaint about our prices is way off target. Our prices are definitely not any higher than those of our competitors. |
| TACTFUL | Thank you for your suggestion concerning our prices. We believe, however, that our prices are comparable to or lower than those of our competitors. |

■ Structuring Effective Correspondence

Correspondence needs to be structured to meet the readers' needs. This section covers organizational patterns and elements that will help you accomplish your purposes in writing.

Direct and Indirect Patterns

The direct pattern is effective in workplace correspondence because readers appreciate messages that present the main point early—at the outset, if at all possible. Called the direct pattern, this approach begins with the main point, follows with an explanation of details, and provides a goodwill closing that builds a positive relationship with the recipient that may also accomplish the tasks described on pages 276–277:

Direct Pattern

1. Main point of message
2. Explanation of details or facts
3. Goodwill closing

Figure 8–2 shows an example of a reader-focused letter using the direct pattern. By presenting the main point first, you save the reader time, increase the likelihood that the reader will pay careful attention to the supporting details, and generally achieve goodwill from the start.

The direct pattern is especially appropriate for presenting good news, as shown in Figure 8–3 on page 286. This message presents the good news in the opening (the main point), follows with an explanation of facts, and closes by looking toward the future (goodwill).

The indirect pattern is effective when you need to present negative messages in correspondence. Research has shown that people form their impressions and attitudes very early when reading correspondence. For this reason, presenting bad news, refusals, or sensitive messages *indirectly* is often more effective than presenting them directly, especially if the stakes are high.*

As with any type of writing, imagine how your audience will react to your message. Consider the thoughtlessness in the job rejection that follows:

▷   Dear Ms. Mauer:

Your application for the position of Records Administrator at Southtown Dental Center has been rejected. We have found someone more qualified than you.

Sincerely,

◆ *For more guidance on organizing information, see Chapter 2, Organizing Your Information.*

Although the letter is concise and uses the pronouns *you* and *your*, the writer has not considered how the recipient will feel as she reads the letter. The letter is, in short, rude. The pattern of this letter is (1) bad news, (2) curt explanation, (3) close.

The indirect pattern for such bad-news correspondence allows the explanation or details to lead logically and tactfully to the negative message, as in the following:

◆ *For more examples, see pages 303–343 in Chapter 9, Writing Business Correspondence, and pages 70–73 in Chapter 3, Writing the Draft.*

1. Context (or "buffer")

2. Explanation or details

3. Bad news or negative message

4. Goodwill closing

ON THE WEB

For more examples of well-written bad-news letters, go to Model Documents Gallery, bedfordstmartins.com/ writingthatworks

The opening (often called a "buffer") should provide a context for the subject and establish a professional tone. It must not, however, mislead the reader to believe that good news may follow.†

---

*Gerald J. Alred, "'We Regret to Inform You': Toward a New Theory of Negative Messages," in *Studies in Technical Communication*, ed. Brenda R. Sims (Denton: University of North Texas and NCTE, 1993), 17–36.

†Kitty O. Locker, "Factors in Reader Responses to Negative Letters: Experimental Evidence for Changing What We Teach," in *Journal of Business and Technical Communication* 13:1 (January 1999), 29.

July 28, 2010
Mr. James Longo
Longo's Café and Deli
157 Adams Drive
Trumbull, TN 37802

Dear Mr. Longo:

Would you be willing to share your personal history with the Trumbull Historical Society? Mary Tran recommended you as somebody we should talk to because of your long commitment to neighborhood improvement.

Main point

As you may have heard, Historical Society volunteers are interviewing people whose experiences illustrate Trumbull's rich and varied cultural fabric. The oral history project aims both to document local traditions and to demonstrate that Trumbull is a vibrant neighborhood with strong community ties. At the same time, by sharing oral histories at public forums, the Historical Society hopes to replace negative stereotypes with a truer picture of what the community means to its residents.

Explanation

We would like to add your voice to the official history of Trumbull. If you choose to participate, you will be asked to recall events, experiences, personal or family memories, and cultural traditions that are important to you. You won't be pressed to discuss anything you're not comfortable with, and you will determine the focus of the conversation. Interviews take about an hour and are scheduled at your convenience.

I hope I've piqued your interest. I'll call you in the next couple of weeks to discuss the project, but do feel free to contact me before then if I can answer any questions.

Closing

Thank you,

Margaret Schweinhurt

Margaret Schweinhurt
Project Coordinator
Trumbull Oral History Project
611.999.9999
oralhistory@mas.com

Figure 8–2   Reader-Focused Request Letter

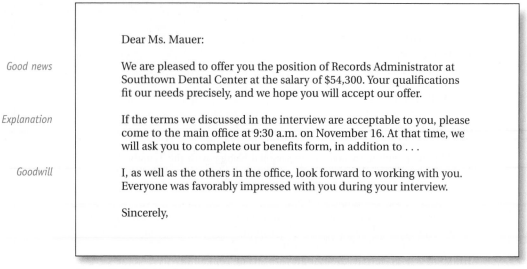

Good news

Explanation

Goodwill

Dear Ms. Mauer:

We are pleased to offer you the position of Records Administrator at Southtown Dental Center at the salary of $54,300. Your qualifications fit our needs precisely, and we hope you will accept our offer.

If the terms we discussed in the interview are acceptable to you, please come to the main office at 9:30 a.m. on November 16. At that time, we will ask you to complete our benefits form, in addition to . . .

I, as well as the others in the office, look forward to working with you. Everyone was favorably impressed with you during your interview.

Sincerely,

Figure 8–3   A Good-News Message

The body should provide an explanation by reviewing the details or facts that lead to a negative decision or refusal. Give the negative message simply, based on the facts; do not belabor the bad news or provide an inappropriate apology. Neither the details nor an overdone apology can turn bad news into something positive. Your goal should be to establish for the reader that the writer or organization has been *reasonable* given the circumstances. To accomplish this goal, you need to organize the explanation carefully and logically.

The closing should establish or reestablish a positive relationship through goodwill or helpful information. Consider, for example, the revised bad-news letter, shown in Figure 8–4. This letter carries the same disappointing news as the letter on page 284, but the writer of this letter begins by not only introducing the subject but also thanking the reader for her time and effort. Then the writer explains why Ms. Mauer was not accepted for the job and offers her encouragement by looking toward a potential future opportunity. Bad news is never pleasant; however, information that either puts the bad news in perspective or makes the bad news seem reasonable maintains respect between the writer and the reader. The goodwill closing is intended to reestablish an amicable professional relationship.

The indirect pattern can also be used in relatively short e-mail messages and memos. Consider the unintended secondary message a manager conveys in the following notice:

WEAK   It has been decided that the office will be open the day after
               Thanksgiving.

"It has been decided" not only sounds impersonal but also communicates an authoritarian, management-versus-employee tone. The passive voice also suggests

November 9, 2010

Ms. Barbara L. Mauer
157 Beach Drive
San Diego, CA 92113

Dear Ms. Mauer:

Thank you for your time and effort in applying for the position of
Records Administrator at Southtown Dental Center.

*Context (or
buffer) opening*

Because we need someone who can assume the duties here with
a minimum of training, we have selected an applicant with several
years of experience.

*Explanation leading
to bad news*

Your college record is excellent, and I encourage you to apply for
another position with us in the future.

Goodwill closing

Sincerely,

Mary Hernandez
Office Manager

Figure 8–4   Courteous Bad-News Letter

that the decision maker does not want to say "I have decided" and thus accept responsibility for the decision. One solution is to remove the first part of the sentence.

IMPROVED   The office will be open the day after Thanksgiving.

The best solution, however, would be to suggest both that there is a good reason
for the decision and that employees are privy to (if not a part of) the decision-
making process.

EFFECTIVE   Because we must meet the December 15 deadline for submitting the
                Bradley Foundation proposal, the office will be open the day after
                Thanksgiving.

By describing the context of the bad news first (the need to meet the deadline), the
writer focuses on the reasoning behind the decision to work. Employees may not

necessarily like the message, but they will at least understand that the decision is not arbitrary and is tied to an important deadline.

Openings

Openings are crucial because readers in the workplace are busy meeting deadlines and coping with dozens of messages every day. Openings should identify the subject, its relevance to your readers, and often the main point of the message.

E-MAIL	Attached is the final installation report, which I hope you can review by Monday, December 6. You will notice that the report includes . . .
MEMO	ACM Electronics has asked us to prepare a comprehensive set of brochures for its Milwaukee office by August 9. We have worked with similar firms in the past. . . .
LETTER	Enclosed with this letter is your refund check for the defective compressor, number AJ50172. I have also enclosed a catalog of our latest . . .

Even if your opening gives the essential background of a problem, state the main point early in the first paragraph.

BACKGROUND	Last year we did not hire new staff because of the freeze on hiring. As a result of the increased workload described in this memo, we need to hire two additional application support specialists this year.

When the reader is not familiar with the subject or with the background of a problem, provide an introductory paragraph before stating the main point (shown in italics in the following example) of the memo. Doing so is especially important in correspondence that serves as a record for crucial information months or years later.

MAIN IDEA	ACM Electronics has asked us to prepare a comprehensive brochure for its Milwaukee office by August 9, 2010. We have worked with electronics firms in the past, so this job should not cause significant problems. I estimate that it will take two months to complete. Ted Harris has requested time and cost estimates for the project, Fred Moore in production will prepare the cost estimates, and *I would like you to prepare a tentative schedule for the project.*

Generally, longer or complex subjects benefit most from more thorough introductions. However, even when you are writing a short message about a familiar subject, remind readers of the context. In the following examples, words that provide context are shown in italics.

▶ *As we discussed after yesterday's meeting*, we need to set new guidelines for . . .

▶ *As Maria recommended*, I reviewed the office reorganization plan. I like most of the features; however, the location of the receptionist and administrative assistant . . .

Do not state the main point first when (1) readers are likely to be highly skeptical or (2) key readers, such as managers or clients, may disagree with your position. In those cases, a more persuasive tactic is to state the problem or issue first, then present the specific points supporting your final recommendation, as discussed in the earlier section on negative messages.

Because business messages are often more personal than reports and other formal documents, an opening must also establish an appropriate tone that achieves your purpose.

◆ *For more information on openings and closings, see pages 84–87 in Chapter 3, Writing the Draft.*

▷ I'm seeking advice about organizational communication, and several people have suggested that you are an authority on the subject.

The tone of respect in this opening is not only appropriate but also persuasive because it appeals to the reader's pride. Other openings might appeal to the reader's curiosity or personal interests, as in the following:

▷ I have a problem you may be interested in helping me solve.

▷ Mr. Walter Jenkens has given us your name as a reference for his company's services. I hope you'll be willing to help us by answering some specific questions about his company.

Closings

An effective closing can accomplish many important tasks, such as building positive relationships with readers, encouraging colleagues and employees, and letting recipients know what you will do or what you expect of them and, if necessary, when an assignment is due.

▷ I will discuss the problem with the marketing consultant and let you know by Wednesday (August 4) what we are able to change.

Closings can also provide an incentive for the reader to act, as in the following:

▷ Please consider the highlighted changes on the contract and return it to me with the additional material in the preaddressed envelope. If I can receive your approval by Tuesday, May 4, I can have the amended contract ready for your signature by the end of the week.

Although routine statements are sometimes unavoidable ("If you have further questions, please let me know"), try to make your closing work for you by providing specific prompts to which the reader can respond.

◆ *For more examples of openings and closings in various types of correspondence, review the figures in Chapter 9, Writing Business Correspondence.*

▷ Thanks again for the report, and let me know if you want me to send you a copy of the test results.

▷ If you would like further information, such as a copy of the questionnaire we used, please e-mail me at delgado@prn.com.

Clarity and Emphasis

To produce a clear message—one that emphasizes your main points and adequately develops them—be as specific as possible. Adequate development is crucial to the clarity of any message, as in the following example.

VAGUE	Be more careful on the loading dock.
DEVELOPED	To prevent accidents on the loading dock, follow these procedures:
	1. Check to make sure . . .
	2. Load only items that are rated . . .
	3. Replace any defective parts . . .

◆ *To review the out-lining process, see Chapter 2, Organizing Your Information.*

Although the first version is concise, it is not as clear and specific as the "developed" revision. Do not assume your readers will know what you mean: Vague messages are easily misinterpreted. Readers may be pressed for time and misinterpret your message if it is vague.

Lists

Vertically stacked words, phrases, and other items with numbers or bullets can effectively highlight such information as steps in a sequence, materials or parts needed, key or concluding points, and recommendations. A particularly useful type of list is one that helps define goals.

> I recommend we focus on the following tasks in our meeting:
> - Identifying and analyzing the audiences for our business plan
> - Refining our goals for convincing potential investors to provide financing
> - Assessing the profitability and goals for our new business venture

As described on pages 108–109 in Chapter 4, Revising the Draft, make sure you provide context so that the reader can understand the purpose of the list. Be careful not to overuse lists—a message that consists almost entirely of lists is difficult to understand because it forces readers to connect separate and disjointed items. Further, lists lose their impact when they are overused.

Headings

Another attention-getting device, particularly in long messages, is the use of headings. Headings have a number of advantages:

- They divide material into manageable segments.

- They call attention to main topics.

◆ *For additional guid-ance on using lists, see the Using Lists checklist on page 105 of Chap-ter 4, Revising the Draft.*

- They signal a shift in topic.

Especially for messages to several readers, headings allow each reader to scan them and read only the section or sections appropriate to his or her needs. Notice the use of both a list and headings in Figure 8–8 on page 304. See also pages 403–408 in Chapter 11, Writing Formal Reports.

Subject Lines

Although they may seem simple, subject lines for e-mails, memos, and some letters require careful preparation for important reasons:

- They announce the topic and focus of the correspondence.
- They enable recipients to decide at a glance how the message is related to their needs.
- They are important aids to filing and later retrieval.

As these functions suggest, each e-mail or memo should address one subject (as illustrated in Figure 8–6 on page 300 and Figure 8–8 on page 304). If you need to cover two subjects, write two messages. Multisubject e-mails and memos are not only difficult to file (thus easily lost) but also confusing to a hurried reader.

Subject lines should be concise yet complete, specific, and accurate to achieve their goals.

VAGUE	Subject: Tuition Reimbursement
VAGUE	Subject: Time-Management Seminar
SPECIFIC	Subject: Tuition Reimbursement for Time-Management Seminar

Capitalize all major words in a subject line except articles, prepositions, and conjunctions with fewer than five letters (unless they are the first or last words). Remember that the subject line should not substitute for an opening that provides context for the message.

Observing Protocol

The decision to send a message as a letter or memo on paper, attached to an e-mail message, or within an e-mail depends on the organizational practice and the purpose of the communication. Some organizations may prefer the printed memo for announcements and other official messages, while reserving e-mail for informal communications. Others may use e-mail almost exclusively, not only because of its speed but also because it fosters the easy exchange of information. Even when e-mail substitutes for printed memos, some recipients print copies of important e-mails to highlight sections or to save a hard copy for their records.

Organizational Rank

Pay attention to the practices of your school or workplace regarding communications by letter, paper memo, or e-mail attachment. Although practices vary, be alert to expectations in your organization for who writes and receives certain types of communications. Learn your organization's practices for internal communications. Small businesses and organizations, for example, may not need formal guidelines for internal communications, so their expectations and practices will differ from those of large organizations. In corporations and governmental agencies, however, protocol for internal communications is usually based on lines of authority. For example, staff members at large companies seldom send recommendations directly to senior executives beyond their immediate manager. Doing so could put the sender's immediate supervisor in an awkward position.

Consider also the order in which addressees should be named on the "To" line—senior managers, for example, usually take precedence over junior managers. An employer's organizational chart determines the lines of authority and channels in which internal communications travel.

Organizational policy may specify whether internal paper communications are signed or initialed by the sender. In many organizations, the sender's typed name in the "From" line indicates approval of and responsibility for a document's content; in other organizations, the sender's signature or initials next to the typed name verifies the writer's approval. Signatures or initials are unnecessary for memos sent as or attached to e-mail messages.

Copy Protocol

The person listed on the memo or e-mail's "To" line is the primary recipient. To share the same message with others, the sender provides each of them a separate or courtesy copy (cc:) of the message. This notation (cc: Jane Doe) appears in the memo or e-mail heading and informs all the recipients of who else has received the message.

Courtesy copies are usually sent on a for-your-information basis. While the primary recipient may have to act on a request in the memo (for example, approve hiring a new employee), the courtesy-copy recipients are included because they need to know that the request was made.

ETHICS NOTE

The blind-copy (bcc:) function allows writers to send copies of an e-mail message to someone without the primary receiver's knowledge. For printed letters and memos, the bcc: notation serves the same function and thus appears only on the copy, not on the original.* The blind-copy function may be used ethically for e-mails to protect the privacy of the e-mail addresses for a large group of recipients. Use the bcc: notation with great care. Sending sensitive or confidential information to a third party without the original recipient's knowledge is unethical, as is the use of a blind copy to play office politics.

*The abbreviation "bcc:" originally referred to the term *blind carbon copy* when copies of letters could only be produced on a typewriter using carbon paper. The bcc: notation (*bcc: Dr. Brenda Shelton*) was separately typed on only the copied pages. Even though technology changed, the abbreviation bcc: was retained but is often defined as "blind courtesy copy."

Send courtesy copies only to those who need the information, especially when the message contains confidential personnel, medical, or financial information. Unnecessary copies also clog up in-boxes with unwanted information.

Also be aware of lines of authority when you copy recipients. If you send a memo or an e-mail to your immediate supervisor about a pet project, for example, do not copy your supervisor's manager unless you are instructed to do so.

■ MEETING THE DEADLINE: The Time-Sensitive Message

More than once in your career you will be asked to do a seemingly impossible task—write an important memo, a crucial e-mail, or a relatively high-profile letter that requires some research—all in less than an hour! These messages are often written for the signature of someone else who is higher up in the organization. When you get such an assignment, do not panic. Instead, use the following straightforward principles drawn from this book to focus your energies on the task at hand.

Understand the Assignment

Nothing could be worse than to waste time under a short deadline by misunderstanding the purpose or intended reader of such a writing task. Ask the person giving you the assignment to be as explicit as possible about the following:

- The topic
- The reader(s) and the reader's background
- The purpose and intended outcome
- The key points that must be covered
- The person who will sign or send the document

Gather Information

The essential background information for your research can almost always be located within your company or organization. Sources include previous letters, memos, e-mails, press releases, contracts, budget data, handbooks, speeches by senior officials, legal opinions, and the like. Be careful to gather *only* the information pertinent to the correspondence. The person assigning the job will usually provide essential background information or tell you where to find it. If the information is not readily available, be sure to ask for it.

As long as the information originated in your organization, fits your context, and is accurate and well-written, use as much of it as you need without citation. If necessary, revise such material for consistency of content, style, and format as you prepare the draft. When using information from other sources, make sure you avoid plagiarism and any violation of copyright (see pages 180–181 in Chapter 6, Researching Your Subject).

On the job, you will have another source of information that you may not always have in the classroom—your experience. In fact, one reason you may receive such an assignment is because of your knowledge of the subject, reader, organization, or professional area. Brainstorming using your own knowledge, as discussed on pages 9–10, will prepare you to draw the most benefit from your experience when you are under pressure.

Organize Your Thoughts

Do not overlook this important step. Your message should have an opening, a middle (body), and a closing. Organizing the information into this structure does not have to be a formal process—you won't have time to create a full-blown outline, nor should one be necessary. Jot down the points you need to make in a sequence that makes sense. Keep it simple. In some cases, you will organize by classifying and dividing your subject matter, presenting the information on one subject before going on to another subject. Sometimes a problem-and-solution order makes sense. At other times, a chronological, sequential, or general-to-specific order will be appropriate.

◆ *For typical organizing strategies, see pages 34–58 in Chapter 2, Organizing Your Information.*

Write the Draft

With the right information and a structure for organizing it, the writing will not be difficult. Stick to your plan—your rough outline—and begin. Make the structure easy for you and your reader to follow. Cover only one subject in each paragraph. After a topic sentence, provide essential supporting information—facts, examples, policy, procedures, guidelines.

Write a quick draft first; you can polish it after it is on the screen or paper. Write without worrying about grammar, sentence structure, or spelling. Given the limited time available, your main focus should be on getting your ideas down.

Polish the Draft

You will not have much time left, but discipline yourself to read the draft several times, concentrating on different elements each time.

First, concentrate on larger issues. Is the information accurate? Is it complete? Have you made all your points? Are your points organized in the right sequence? Have you provided too much information? Revise accordingly.

Next, focus on polishing at the sentence and word level. Aim for simple sentences in the active voice. Include some longer sentences to avoid the monotony of too many simple sentences strung together. Structure longer sentences so that subjects and verbs agree and primary ideas are distinct from subordinate ideas.

Use parallel structure to convey matching ideas. Use lists where possible. Don't forget to review punctuation. A misplaced comma or semicolon can change the meaning of a sentence. In this situation, you do not have time for a cooling period, so watch for any emotionally charged language.

As a final review, use your spell checker, but don't rely on it to catch all of your spelling errors. Make sure you read through a paper version of the final draft at least once to catch any remaining errors. If you have time, ask a second reader to help.

Take a Well-Deserved Break

After your draft is written, you may e-mail it to a superior for review before you prepare the final form for signature and distribution. Now sit back and enjoy the sense of professional pride you have earned from a job well done under pressure!

Writing E-mail and Instant Messages

E-mail (or *email*) and instant messaging in the workplace function as a medium to exchange information and share electronic files with colleagues, clients, and customers. Among their many functions, e-mail messages are particularly useful for facilitating discussions and collecting opinions. They enable a collaborative writing team, for example, to exchange multiple drafts to produce a final document. Although e-mail may take the form of informal notes, you should follow the writing strategy and style described earlier in this chapter because e-mail messages often function as traditional business letters to those outside your organization and as memos to those within your organization. Of course, digital files of memos and letters can also be attached to e-mails.

Review and Confidentiality Implications

Avoid the temptation to send a draft of your message before you review it. As with other workplace correspondence, maintain a high level of professionalism when you send e-mail: A message should be grammatically and factually correct, with no ambiguities or unintended implications.

Be especially careful when sending messages to superiors in your organization or to people outside the organization. Spending extra time reviewing your e-mail before you click "Send" can save you the embarrassment of errors and misunderstandings caused by a carelessly written message. One helpful strategy is to write the draft and revise your message before filling in the "To" line with the address of your recipient. Be careful as well to follow the rules of netiquette, discussed in the next section.

ETHICS NOTE

Keep in mind that e-mail (as well as instant messages) can be intercepted by someone other than the intended recipient and that your messages are never truly deleted. Most companies back up and save all their e-mail messages and are legally entitled to monitor e-mail use. Companies can be compelled, depending on circumstances, to provide electronic files and message logs in a court of law. Consider the content of all your messages in the light of these possibilities, and carefully review your text before you click Send.

Observing Netiquette

To maintain a high level of professionalism in workplace e-mail and instant messages, observe the rules of netiquette (*Internet* + *etiquette*):

- Review your organization's policy regarding the appropriate use of e-mail.
- Maintain a high level of professionalism in your use of e-mail.
  - Do not forward jokes or spam, discuss office gossip, or use biased language.
  - Do not send flames (e-mails that contain abusive, obscene, or derogatory language) to attack someone.
  - Do not use an e-mail account with a clever or hobby-related address (*yogalover@gja.com*); e-mail addresses based on your last name are more professional (*jones23@gja.com*).
- Provide a subject line that describes the topic and focus of your message (as described on page 291) to help recipients manage their e-mail.
- When forwarding messages, revise the subject line to reflect the current content and delete irrelevant previous text, based on your purpose and context.
- Use the "cc:" (courtesy copy) and "bcc:" (blind courtesy copy) address lines thoughtfully and consider your organization's practices or protocol, as discussed on page 292. See also the ethics note on the use of blind copies on page 292.
- Include a cover (or *transmittal*) message for all e-mail messages with attachments ("Attached is a copy of the TeraTech report for your review. . . ."). Be aware that e-mails with attachments and no message may be deleted or routed to a "spam" or "junk mail" folder.
- Send a "courtesy response" informing someone when you need a few days or longer to reply to a request.
- Do not write in ALL-UPPERCASE LETTERS (called *shouting*) or in all lowercase letters.
- Avoid e-mail abbreviations (BTW for *by the way*, for example) often used in personal e-mail, chat rooms, and instant messaging.

- Do not use emoticons (keyboard characters used to create sideways faces conveying emotions) for business and professional e-mail.
- Always sign the e-mail or use a signature block (see pages 298–299) or both; doing so not only is polite but also avoids possible confusion.

@

DIGITAL TIPS: Sending an Attachment

Large graphics and other files attached to e-mails can slow the transmission speed of messages, and the recipient's software or Internet provider may not be able to accept large attachments. Consider using a compression software utility such as WinZip at <http://winzip.com>, which can reduce the file size by 80 percent or more. **Caution:** Viruses can be embedded in e-mail attachments, so regularly update your virus-scanning software and do not open attachments from anyone you do not know. For more on this topic, see <bedfordstmartins.com/writingthatworks> and select *Digital Tips*, "Sending an Attachment."

Design Considerations

Although some e-mail systems allow you to use typographical features, such as various fonts and bullets, these options increase your e-mail file size and may display unpredictably in other e-mail systems. Unless you are sure your recipient's software will display your formatted message correctly, set your e-mail software to send messages in "plain text" and use alternative highlighting devices. For example, capital letters or asterisks, used sparingly, can substitute for boldface, italics, and underlines as emphasis.

▷ Dr. Wilhoit's suggestions benefit doctors AND patients.

▷ Although the proposal is sound in *theory*, it may not work in *practice*.

Dilbert

Intermittent underlining can replace solid underlining or italics when referring to published works in an e-mail message.

▷   My report follows the format given in _The Business Writer's Handbook_.

If you find that you need many such substitutions, consider preparing a document that you attach to an e-mail. Doing so will allow you to use formatted elements, such as bulleted lists and tables, that do not transmit well in e-mail messages.

Keep in mind the following additional design considerations when sending e-mail:

- Break the text into short paragraphs to avoid dense blocks of text.
- Consider providing an overview in a brief paragraph at the top for messages that run longer than a screen of text.
- Place your response to someone else's message at the beginning (or top) of the e-mail window so that recipients can see it immediately.
- When replying to a message, quote only relevant parts. If your system does not distinguish the quoted text, note it with a greater-than symbol (>).

Salutations, Closings, and Signature Blocks

An e-mail can function as a letter, memo, or personal note; therefore, you must adapt your salutation and complimentary closing to your audience. Unless your employer requires certain forms, use the following guidelines:

- When your e-mail functions as a traditional letter, use the standard letter salutation (*Dear Ms. Tucker:* or *Dear Docuform Customer:*) and closing (*Sincerely,* or *Best wishes,*).
- When you send e-mail messages to individuals or small groups inside an organization, you may wish to adopt a more personal greeting (*Dear Andy,* or *Dear Project Colleagues,*).
- When an e-mail functions as a personal note to a friend or close colleague, you can use an informal greeting or only a first name (*Hi Mike,* or *Hello Jenny,* or *Bill,*) and a closing (*Take care,* or *Best,*).

◆ *For guidelines applicable to writing e-mail messages for an international audience, see pages 343, 346–351.*

Of course, you may wish to use some combination of these approaches, depending on your relationship with the recipients and the practice of your e-mail correspondents. Be aware that business correspondents do not use first names as quickly in some cultures as they do in the United States. See examples of inappropriate and appropriate e-mail messages in Figures 8–5 and 8–6 (page 300), respectively.

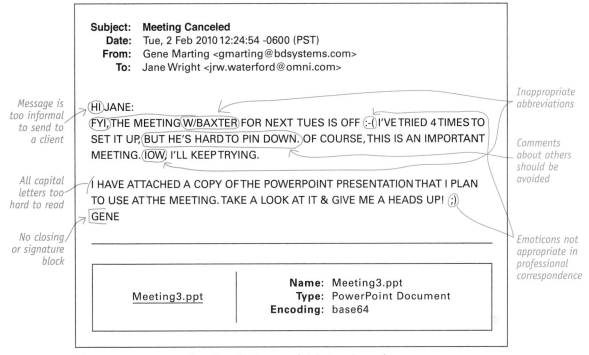

Figure 8–5   Inappropriate E-mail Message (with Attachment)

Because e-mail does not provide letterhead with standard addresses and contact information, many companies and individual writers include signature blocks (also called *signatures*) at the bottom of their messages. Signature blocks, which writers can set to appear on every e-mail they send, supply information that company letterhead usually provides as well as appropriate links to Web sites. If your organization requires a certain format, adhere to that standard. Otherwise, use the pattern shown in Figure 8–6. For signature blocks, consider as well the following guidelines:

- Keep line length to 60 characters or fewer to avoid unpredictable line wraps.
- Test your signature block in plain-text e-mail systems to verify your format.
- Use highlighting cues, such as hyphens, equal signs, and white space, to separate the signature from the message.
- Avoid using quotations, aphorisms, or sayings from popular culture, religion, or poetry in signatures to maintain a professional image.

Subject: **Baxter Meeting Canceled**
Date: Tue, 2 Feb 2010 12:24:54 -0600 (PST)
From: Gene Marting <gmarting@secsystems.com>
To: Jane Wright <jrw.waterford@omni.com>

Jane:

I need to cancel the meeting with Thomas Baxter for next Friday (Feb 12). I will work to schedule another meeting because we need to meet with him.

I have attached a copy of the PowerPoint presentation that I'd like to use at the meeting. Let me know if you see possible improvements.

Thanks,

Gene

=================================
Signature block separated from message
Gene Marting, Manager
Sales Division, Building Systems, Inc.
3555 South 47th Street, Boise, ID 83703
Off: 208-719-6620 Fax: 208-719-5500
http://www.building/sys/com
e-mail: gmarting@secsystems.com
=================================

Meeting3.ppt

Name: Meeting3.ppt
Type: PowerPoint Document
Encoding: base64

Figure 8–6　Revised, Appropriate E-mail Message (with Attachment)

@　**DIGITAL TIPS: Leaving an Away-from-Desk Message**

Many e-mail systems allow you to create an automatic response to incoming e-mails when you are away from your desk or unavailable for any period of time. Your message should inform senders when you are expected back and, if necessary, whom they can contact in your absence. To learn how to set up an automatic response, see <bedfordstmartins.com/writingthatworks> and select *Digital Tips*, "Leaving an Away-from-Desk Message."

WRITER'S CHECKLIST
Managing Your E-mail and Reducing Overload

Given the high volume of e-mail in business, you need to manage your e-mail strategically.* Avoid becoming involved in an e-mail exchange if a phone call or meeting would be more efficient.

✔ Consider whether your e-mail message could prompt an unnecessary response from the recipient and make clear if you expect a response.

✔ Send a copy (cc:) of an e-mail only when the person copied needs or wants the information.

✔ Review all messages on a subject before responding to avoid dealing with issues that are no longer relevant.

✔ Set priorities for reading e-mail by skimming sender names and subject lines as well as where you appear in a "cc:" (courtesy copy) and "bcc:" (blind courtesy copy) address line.

✔ Check e-mail addresses before sending an e-mail and keep your addresses current.

✔ Check your in-box regularly and try to clear it by the end of each day.

✔ Create e-mail folders using key topics and personal names to file messages.

✔ Copy yourself or save sent copies of important e-mail messages in your topic folders.

✔ Use the search command to find particular subjects and personal names.

✔ Print copies of messages or attachments that you need for meetings, files, or similar purposes.

---

*For understanding the causes of e-mail overload, see Gail Fann Thomas and Cynthia L. King, "Reconceptualizing E-mail Overload," *Journal of Business and Technical Communication* 20, no. 3 (July 2006): 252–287.

Writing and Managing Instant Messages

Instant messaging is a text-based communications medium that fills a niche between telephone calls and e-mail messages. It allows both real-time communications, like a phone call, and the transfer of text or other files, like an e-mail message. It is especially useful to cell-phone users who are working at sites without access to e-mail.

To set up routine IM exchanges, add to your contact list the user names of those with whom you regularly exchange messages. Choose a screen name that your colleagues will recognize. If you use IM routinely as part of your job, create an away message that signals when you are not available for IM interactions.

When writing instant messages, keep them simple and to the point, covering only one subject in each message, to prevent confusion and inappropriate responses. Because screen space is often limited and speed is essential, many who send instant messages use abbreviations and shortened spellings ("u" for "you" and "L8R" for "later"). Be sure that your reader will understand such abbreviations; when in doubt, avoid them.[†]

[†]Many online sites, such as <www.netlingo.com>, define IM and other such abbreviations.

In Figure 8–7, the manager of a software-development company in Maine ("Diane") is exchanging instant messages with a business partner in the Netherlands ("Andre"). Notice that the correspondents use an informal style that includes personal and professional abbreviations with which both are familiar ("NP" for "no problem"; "FYI" for "for your information"; and "QSG" for Quick Start Guide). These messages demonstrate how instant messaging can not only help exchange information quickly but also build rapport among distant colleagues and team members. The exchange also demonstrates why IM is not generally appropriate for many complex messages or for more formal circumstances, such as when establishing new professional relationships.

ON THE WEB

For a detailed list of abbreviations used in IM exchanges and their definitions, go to Chapter 8, bedfordstmartins .com/writingthatworks

> ● ● ●   **Instant Message with "Andre"**
>
> **Andre**
> Last message received at: 09:04:09 AM
>
> Andre (08:58:06 AM): Hi Diane!
> Diane (08:58:36 AM): good morning
> Andre (09:00:04 AM): Time for a quick question?
> Diane (09:00:37 AM): NP!
> Andre (09:00:58 AM): How is it going with the QSG?
> Andre (09:01:02 AM): Will you be finished soon?
> Diane (09:01:49 AM): I am working on it.
> Diane (09:01:59 AM): I am targeting Friday
> Andre (09:02:16 AM): If you are not quite finished, send me what you have.
> Diane (09:02:58 AM): I would recommend finishing the QSG before we focus on user guide.
> Andre (09:03:09 AM): good idea
> Andre (09:03:47 AM): ok, I won't keep you any longer
> Andre (09:03:57 AM): bye
> Diane (09:04:09 AM): Talk to you later.
>
> Impact   14   **B** *I* U   A▼ A▼   ▼   Link   ☺▼   ❖
>
> |
>
> Block... Warn...   Add   Get Info   Send

Figure 8–7 Instant-Message Exchange

ETHICS NOTE

Be sure to follow your employer's IM policies, such as any limitations on sending personal messages during work hours or requirements concerning confidentiality. If no specific policy exists, assume that personal use of IM is not appropriate in your workplace.

DIGITAL TIPS: **IM Privacy and Security**

- Organize your contact lists to separate workplace contacts from family and friends so that you do not inadvertently send personal messages to professional associates and vice versa. Consider restricting contact lists on professional IM accounts to business associates.

- Learn the options, capabilities, and security limitations of your IM system and set the preferences that best suit your use of the system.

- Be especially alert to the possibilities of virus infections and security risks with messages, attachments, contact lists, and other privacy issues.

- Save significant IM exchanges (or logs) for your future reference.

- Be aware that instant messages can be saved by your recipients and may be archived by your employer. (See the Ethics Note on page 296.)

- Do not use professional IM for gossip or inappropriate exchanges.

Designing Memos

Memos are documents that use a standard form (*To: From: Date: Subject:*) whether sent on paper or as attachments to e-mail messages. They are used within organizations to announce policies, report results, instruct employees, disseminate information, and delegate responsibilities.

Even in organizations where e-mail messages have largely taken the function of memos, a printed or an attached memo with organizational letterhead can communicate with formality and authority with its full range of word-processing features. Paper memos are also useful in manufacturing and service industries, as well as in other businesses where employees do not have easy access to e-mail.

Memo Format and Parts

The memo shown in Figure 8–8 illustrates that the memo format can be used not only for routine messages but also for short reports, proposals, and other internal documents.

Although the level of detail or specific content may vary, the format in Figure 8–8 is typical. As this example also illustrates, headings and lists often foster clarity and provide emphasis in memos. For a discussion of subject lines, see page 291.

Standard memo heading

Handwritten initials if sent in printed form

Introduction

Headings signal shift in topics

Closing

Additional recipients

Enclosed material

Professional Publishing Services

MEMORANDUM

TO:	Barbara Smith, Publications Manager
FROM:	Hannah Kaufman, Vice President *HK*
DATE:	April 14, 2010
SUBJECT:	Schedule for ACM Electronics Brochures

ACM Electronics has asked us to prepare a comprehensive set of brochures for its Milwaukee office by August 9, 2010. We have worked with similar firms in the past, so this job should be relatively easy to prepare. My guess is that the job will take nearly two months. Ted Harris has requested time and cost estimates for the project. Fred Moore in production will prepare the cost estimates, and I would like you to prepare a tentative schedule for the project.

Additional Personnel
In preparing the schedule, check the status of the following:
- Production schedule for all staff writers
- Availability of freelance writers
- Availability of dependable graphic designers

Ordinarily, we would not need to depend on outside personnel; however, because our bid for the *Wall Street Journal* special project is still under consideration, we could be short of staff in June and July. Further, we have to consider vacations that have already been approved.

Time Estimates
Please give me time estimates by April 16. A successful job done on time will give us a good chance to obtain the contract to do ACM Electronics' annual report for its stockholders' meeting this fall.

I have enclosed several brochures that may be helpful.

cc: Ted Harris, President
    Fred Moore, Production Editor

Enclosures: Sample Brochures

Figure 8–8 Typical Memo Format (Printed with Sender's Handwritten Initials)

As with e-mail, be alert to the practices of addressing and distributing memos in your organization, as discussed on pages 291–292. Consider who should receive or needs to be copied on a memo and in what order — senior managers, for example, take precedence over junior managers. If rank does not apply, alphabetizing recipients by last name is safe.

Some organizations ask writers to initial by hand or sign printed memos to verify that the writer accepts responsibility for a memo's contents. Electronic copies of memos do not need simulated initials.

Additional Pages

When memos require more than one page, use a second-page header and always carry at least two lines of the body text over to that page. The header should include either the recipient's name or an abbreviated subject line (if there are too many names to fit), the page number, and the date. Place the header in the upper left-hand corner or across the page, as shown in Figure 8–9.

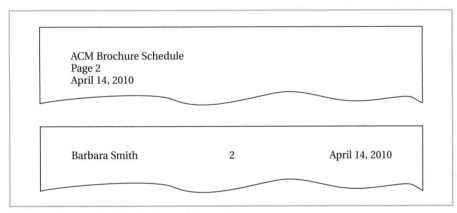

ACM Brochure Schedule
Page 2
April 14, 2010

Barbara Smith   2   April 14, 2010

Figure 8–9   Headers for the Second Page of Memos

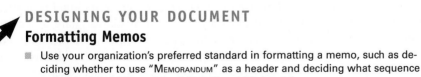

DESIGNING YOUR DOCUMENT
Formatting Memos

- Use your organization's preferred standard in formatting a memo, such as deciding whether to use "MEMORANDUM" as a header and deciding what sequence to list the "To:," "From:," "cc:," Date:," and "Subject:"

- Use headings and lists to highlight important information.

- Review your memo for its general professional appearance before you send, initial, or sign it, depending on your organization's practice.

■ Designing Letters

Letters printed on organizational letterhead communicate formality, respect, and authority. Just as the clothes you wear to job interviews play a part in the first impression you make on potential employers, the appearance of a business letter may be crucial in influencing a recipient who has never seen you. A neat appearance alone will not improve a poorly written letter, but a sloppy appearance will detract from a well-written one. Business letters—normally written for those outside an organization—are often the most appropriate choice for formal communications with professional associates or customers.

If you use express or overnight deliveries for letters and other documents, phone or send an e-mail message ahead to alert the recipient that the material has been sent. If speed is essential and the situation requires a signed document, you can fax it and follow up by mailing the original.

Although word-processing software provides templates for correspondence, it may not always provide appropriate dimensions and spacing. To achieve a professional appearance, use the following guidelines:

- Center the letter with equal margins at the top and bottom of the page.
- Use 1- or 1¼-inch margins, the default standard in many word-processing programs.
- When you use organizational stationery, treat the bottom of the letterhead as the top edge of the paper and make the right margin approximately as wide as the left margin.
- For very short letters, increase both side margins to about an inch and a half.
- Use your computer's full-page or print-preview feature to check for proportion of text to the blank space that surrounds it.

If your employer or instructor requires a particular format, use it. Otherwise, follow the design guidelines shown in Figures 8–10 and 8–11 (page 308).

The two most common styles for business letters are the full-block style shown in Figure 8–10 and the modified-block style shown in Figure 8–11. In the full-block style, which should be used with letterhead, the entire letter is aligned at the left margin. In the modified-block style, the return address, date, and complimentary close begin at the center of the page and the other elements are aligned at the left margin. All other letter styles are variations of the full-block and modified-block styles. Of course, not every letter requires all the elements shown. Include only what's necessary.

Heading

The heading is the writer's full return address—street or post office box, city and state, zip code—or printed letterhead and the date. Do not include the writer's

2"

520 Niagara Street, Braintree, MA 02184

Phone: (781) 787-1175
Fax: (781) 787-1213
E-mail: info@evans.com

EVANS
and Associates

Transportation Engineers

Letterhead

——————————— 3 lines

May 14, 2010

——————————— 2–6 lines

Mr. George W. Nagel
Director of Operations
Boston Transit Authority
57 West City Avenue
Boston, MA 02210

Inside address aligned with left margin

1" or 1¼"

——————————— 2 lines

Dear Mr. Nagel:

Salutation

——————————— 2 lines

Begin at left margin

Enclosed is our final report evaluating the safety measures for the Boston Intercity Transit System.

Single-space within paragraphs

Body text is flush left

We believe that the report covers the issues you raised in our last meeting and that you will be pleased with the results. However, if you have any further questions, we would be happy to meet with you again at your convenience.

Double-space between paragraphs

1" or 1¼"

We would also like to express our appreciation to Bob Sullivan of your committee for his generous help during our trips to Boston.

——————————— 2 lines

Sincerely,

Complimentary close is flush left

——————————— 4 lines

Handwritten signature followed by signature block

Carolyn Brown, Ph.D.
Director of Research

——————————— 2 lines

cbrown@evans.com
CB/ls
Enclosure: Final Safety Report
cc: ITS Safety Committee Members

End notations

Figure 8–10   Format for a Letter with Letterhead (Full-Block Style)

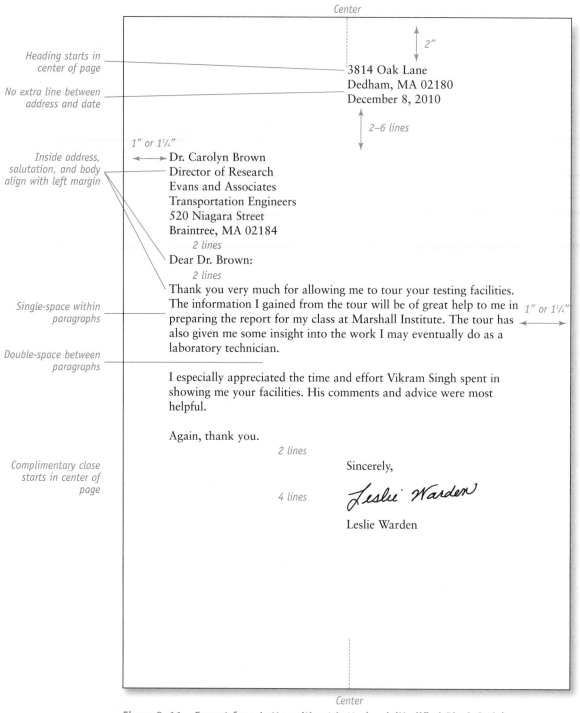

Figure 8–11   Format for a Letter without Letterhead (Modified-Block Style)

name in the heading (unless it is part of a printed letterhead) because it appears at the end of the letter. In giving your address, do not use abbreviations for words such as Street, Avenue, First, or West (as part of a street or city name). You may either spell out the name of the state in full or use the standard U.S. Postal Service abbreviations available at <usps.com/ncsc/lookups/abbreviations.html>. The date usually goes three lines below the letterhead or directly beneath the last line of the address when there is no letterhead. Do not abbreviate the name of the month.

> 1638 Parkhill Drive East
> Great Falls, MT 59407
> April 9, 2010

Begin the heading about two inches from the top of the page. If you are using company letterhead that gives the address, enter only the date three lines below the last line of printed copy.

Inside Address

The inside address is the recipient's full name, title, and address.

> Ms. Gail Smith
> Production Manager
> Docuform Printing Company
> 14 President Street
> Sarasota, FL 33546

Place the inside address two to six lines below the date, depending on the length of the letter. The inside address should be aligned with the left margin, which should be at least one inch wide.

Salutation

Place the salutation, or greeting, two lines below the inside address and align it with the left margin. In most business letters, the salutation contains the recipient's personal title (such as *Mr., Ms., Dr.*) and last name, followed by a colon. If you are on a first-name basis with the recipient, use only the first name in the salutation.

> Dear Dr. Smith:

> Dear Captain Smith:

> Dear Professor Smith: [Note that titles such as Captain and Professor are not abbreviated.]

> Dear Gail: [if you are on a first-name basis]

For a recipient who does not have a professional title, use Mr. or Ms. (if a woman has expressed a preference for Miss or Mrs. instead, honor her preference). When you do not know the name of the recipient, you may need to use a title appropriate to the context of the letter, such as the following:

▶ Dear Customer:

▶ Dear Homeowner:

▶ Dear Service Manager:

When a person's first name could be either feminine or masculine, one solution is to use both the first and last names in the salutation (*Dear Pat Smith:*). Avoid "To Whom It May Concern" because it is impersonal and dated.

For multiple recipients, the following salutations are appropriate:

▶ Dear Professor Allen and Dr. Rivera: [two recipients]

▶ Dear Ms. Becham, Ms. Moore, and Mr. Stein: [three recipients]

▶ Dear Colleagues: [*Members*, or other suitable collective term]

If you are writing to a large company and do not know the name or title of the recipient, you may address a letter to an appropriate department or identify the subject in a subject line and use no salutation. (For information on creating subject lines, see page 291.)

▶ National Medical Supply Group
501 West National Avenue
Minneapolis, MN 55407

Attention: Customer Service Department

or

Subject: Defective Cardio-100 Stethoscopes

I am returning six stethoscopes with damaged diaphragms that . . .

Body

The body of the letter should begin two lines below the salutation (or any element that precedes the body, such as a subject or an attention line). Single-space within and double-space between block paragraphs, as shown in Figures 8–10 and 8–11. To provide a fuller appearance to a very short letter, you can increase the side margins or increase the font size. You can also insert extra space above the inside address, the typed (signature) name, and the initials of the person typing the letter—but do not exceed twice the recommended space for each of these elements.

Complimentary Closing

Type the complimentary closing two spaces below the body. Use a standard expression such as *Sincerely*, *Sincerely yours*, or *Yours truly*. (If the recipient is a friend as well as a business associate, you can use a less formal closing, such as *Best wishes* or *Best regards* or, simply, *Best*.) Capitalize only the initial letter of the first word, and follow the expression with a comma.

Writer's Signature Block

Type your full name four lines below and aligned with the complimentary closing. On the next line include your business title, if appropriate. The following lines may contain your individual contact information, such as a telephone number or an e-mail address, if not included in the letterhead or the body of your letter. Sign the letter in the space between the complimentary closing and your name, as shown in Figures 8–10 and 8–11.

Continuing Pages

If a letter requires a second page (or, in rare cases, more), always carry at least two lines of the body text over to that page. Use plain (nonletterhead) paper of quality equivalent to that of the letterhead stationery for the second page. It should have a header with the recipient's name, the page number, and the date. Place the header in the upper left-hand corner or across the page, as shown in Figure 8–12, and resume the body of the letter two to three lines below the header.

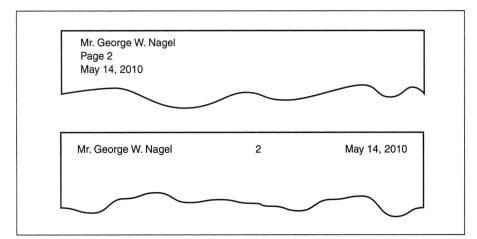

Figure 8–12   Headers for the Second Page of a Letter

End Notations

Business letters sometimes require additional information that is placed at the left margin, two spaces below the typed name and title of the writer in a long letter, four spaces below in a short letter.

Reference initials show the letter writer's initials in capital letters, followed by a slash mark (or colon), and then the initials of the person typing the letter in lowercase letters, as shown in Figure 8–13. When the writer is also the person typing the letter, no initials are needed.

Sincerely yours,

Jane T. Rogers

Typist's initials — Jane T. Rogers
Enclosure notation — Manager

cc: appears on — JTR/pst
all copies — Enclosure: Preliminary proposal
cc: Ms. Marlene Brier
bcc: appears only on — bcc: Dr. Brenda Shelton
the letter to the blind-
copy recipient

Figure 8–13   Closing with Initials, Enclosure Notation, and Copy Notations

Enclosure notations indicate that the writer is sending material along with the letter (an invoice, an article, and so on). You should mention the enclosure in the body of the letter. These notations may or may not specify the enclosure by name, as shown below.

▷ Enclosure: Final Safety Report

▷ Enclosures (2)

▷ Enc. *or* Encs.

Copy notation (*cc:*) tells the reader that a copy of the letter is being sent to the named recipient(s) (see Figure 8–13). A blind courtesy copy notation (*bcc:*) is used when the sender does not want the addressee to know that a copy is being sent to one or more other recipients. That means the blind-copy notation must not appear on the original letter, only on the letter to the blind-copy recipient, as shown in Figure 8–13. For a discussion of protocol for sending copies and blind copies to others, see page 292 and the ethics note on page 292.*

---

*For additional details on letter formats and design, you may wish to consult a guide such as *The Gregg Reference Manual,* 10th edition, by William A. Sabin (New York: McGraw, 2005).

DESIGNING YOUR DOCUMENT
Formatting Letters

- Use good-quality white paper and envelopes of standard size.
- Center the letter with equal margins at the top and bottom of the page.
- Place the date three lines below the letterhead or directly below the address line when there is no letterhead.
- Place the inside address two to six lines below the date, aligned with the left margin, which should be at least one inch wide.
- Use full-block style with letterhead stationery; use a modified-block style on blank paper.
- Place the salutation two lines below the inside address, also aligned with the left margin.
- Begin the body of the letter two lines below the salutation.
- Single-space within paragraphs and double-space between paragraphs.
- Start the complimentary close two lines below the body of your letter.
- If a letter requires a second page, always carry at least two lines of the body over to page two.
- After you have finished writing a letter, check the arrangement and spacing of its parts before you sign it.
- Review Figures 8–10 and 8–11 and adapt the design to your content.

CHAPTER 8 SUMMARY: UNDERSTANDING THE PRINCIPLES OF BUSINESS COMMUNICATION

Selecting the Appropriate Medium

- E-mail and instant messages
  - To communicate and share electronic files with colleagues, clients, and customers
  - To collaborate with colleagues when e-mail is not available
- Memos
  - To circulate information within your organization
  - To communicate with those who need print communication
- Letters on your organization's stationery
  - To represent a commitment to the recipient outside your organization
  - To formalize a business relationship
- Faxes
  - To transmit a document not available in electronic format
  - To transmit a document that must be viewed in its original form (for instance, a letter with a signature or an official seal)
- Telephone and conference calls
  - To resolve misunderstandings more quickly than in writing
  - To provide an alternative to a face-to-face meeting

▧ Voice-mail messages
- • To record brief messages for later retrieval

▧ Face-to-face meetings
- • To make initial or early contacts with associates and customers
- • To plan a project or facilitate group decisions about specific objectives

▧ Videoconferences
- • To save money on the travel costs of face-to-face meetings
- • To enable participants to hear and see one another

▧ Web sites
- • To post announcements, policies, and documents
- • To allow collaboration using communication software

Developing Style and Tone

▧ Focus on a positive relationship and professional image.

▧ Choose a writing style appropriate to the topic and audience.

▧ Use goodwill and the "you" viewpoint.

Structuring Effective Correspondence

▧ Use the direct pattern for goodwill and positive messages:
1. Main point or good news
2. Explanation of details or facts
3. Goodwill closing

▧ Use the indirect pattern for some negative messages:
1. Context (or buffer)
2. Explanation or details
3. Bad news or negative message
4. Goodwill closing

▧ Organize your ideas into an opening, body, and closing.

▧ Use lists and headings for clarity and appropriate emphasis.

▧ Construct a subject line that is complete and helpful, yet concise.

▧ Observe protocol for ranking recipients and copying messages.

Meeting the Deadline: The Time-Sensitive Message

▧ Make sure that you understand the assignment.

▧ Gather pertinent background information.

▧ Organize your major points into a sequence that makes sense.

▧ Write the draft quickly, covering only one subject in each paragraph.

▧ Polish the draft—focus on content and organization before revising at the sentence and word level.

Writing E-mail and Instant Messages

▧ Use an appropriate and clear writing style that conveys a professional image.

▧ Review e-mail carefully for appropriate content and for any issues of privacy or confidentiality.

▧ Observe the rules of netiquette.

- Consider the format and design needs of e-mail messages.
- Create an appropriate salutation, closing, and signature block.
- Manage your e-mail by prioritizing, using folders, and reviewing messages.
- Keep IM communications brief.
- Cover only one topic in each IM.
- Use only IM abbreviations your recipients understand.
- Maintain accurate and current contact lists.

Designing Memos
- Use an appropriate format.
- Include a continuing page header, if needed.
- Determine if the memo should be printed or attached as an e-mail transmittal.

Designing Letters
- Determine if a letter printed on organizational letterhead is appropriate.
- Follow the letter format appropriate to the context or required by your employer.
- Prepare a heading or use printed letterhead.
- Provide an inside address.
- Create an appropriate salutation, body, and complimentary close.
- Include a continuing page header, if needed.
- Add end notations as required.

ON THE WEB

For an online quiz on communication principles, go to Chapter 8, bedfordstmartins.com/writingthatworks

Exercises

ON THE WEB

For additional exercises, go to Chapter 8, bedfordstmartins.com/writingthatworks

1. You are the manager of accounting for a company that sells computer-software packages. You have just received word from the comptroller that there has been a change in the expense allowances for employees using their own cars on business. Previously, one rate was applied to all employees, but now there will be different allowance rates for regular and nonregular drivers. Effective immediately, regular drivers will receive $1.00 per mile for the first 650 miles driven per month, and 25¢ for each additional mile; nonregular drivers will receive 80¢ per mile for the first 150 miles per month, and 25¢ for each additional mile. Regular drivers are those who use their own cars frequently on the job to drive to their sales territories. Nonregular drivers are those employees—such as home-office personnel—who only occasionally use their cars on business. To ensure that these categories are used properly, you have requested that the manager of each department notify Accounts Payable, in writing, which employees in his or her department should be classified as regular drivers. Accounts Payable will reimburse those employees not identified by the letter according to the nonregular-driver formula. Prepare a memo or an e-mail message to communicate this information to all employees.

2. Complete this assignment either on your own or as part of a collaborative team.

   a. You are director of corporate communications for a nationwide insurance company called The Provider Group. Management has asked you to design a letterhead that reflects a "modern, yet responsible image." For this project, collect as many samples of letterhead stationery as you can. Then, using word-processing software with graphics capability, design a letterhead for The Provider Group (using a local address, phone number, and any other appropriate details). As you design, consider the image and personality your design will project, as well as the amount of information you should provide.

b. Survey three or four organizations in your area (including your college) to determine the standard letter formats they use (full block, modified block, and so on). Evaluate the formats using the guidelines provided in this chapter and in Chapter 7, Designing Effective Documents and Visuals.

c. Using the results in parts a and b, determine the best format for letters sent to clients by The Provider Group.

3. Briefly describe a work- or school-related e-mail message that you have received that was inappropriate, using specific points from the netiquette and e-mail guidelines in this chapter.

4. Rewrite the following statements, improving them as indicated.

a. Make the following statement more positive and less blunt:

▷ I will not pay you because you have not sent the final software upgrade. If you do not send the right one immediately, I will not pay you at all.

b. Make the following passage more friendly:

▷ I wrote for the Music Collection you advertised on TV, and, not only did it take six weeks to get here, but it was the wrong set of CDs. Can't you get anything right? I'm canceling payment on my check and sending this set of CDs back!

c. Make the following passage clear and unpretentious:

▷ With reference to your recent automobile accident, I have been unable to contact you due to the fact that I have been in Chicago working day and night on a proposal—a biggie. I should be back in the office in the neighborhood of the 15th or so. In the unforeseen and unlikely event that I should be delayed, you can utilize Mr. Strawman, of my office, who will also endeavor in your behalf.

5. Imagine that you work for a company where many of the new hires have been using text messaging to pass on confidential material to each other or relay emergency information. This greatly concerns the chief executive officer (CEO), who especially has a problem with employees using business IM names like "Sexyguy2010" and "Squirrelgirl42." Draft a company memo, to be sent by the CEO, detailing proper IM etiquette.

6. Based on your own experience as a student, write a memo to your instructor on one of the following topics in less than one hour.

a. Should student tickets to athletic events on campus be included with the price of tuition?

b. Should the library add a coffee kiosk in the reserve room?

c. Should the college offer more (or fewer) Internet-access courses?

Be sure to cover the points you feel must be included to support your conclusion.

7. You work for Smith Consultants, and your manager has asked you to draft a complaint letter to the software-supply company that developed your new customer-service database—the level of service and technical support to date has not met your manager's expectations. Include the following points:

a. Telephone calls from your employees to the software help department are often not returned in a timely fashion. Sometimes they are not returned at all.

b. Software-assistance personnel often blame your hardware for the problem; however, when consulted, the hardware representative reports that the problem is with the software.

c. Promised monthly four-hour in-service training sessions have not been scheduled for the past three months.

You must also mention that your company is considering not paying the software provider the remaining 30 percent of the purchase amount. However, this is a very delicate matter because Smith Consultants has already invested thousands of dollars in the software system and would like to resolve the problem without losing the investment. Following the principles of business correspondence offered in this chapter, submit your draft in correct business-letter format to your instructor.

8. Explore the templates offered by your word-processing software. Most word-processing packages offer several styles of business-document templates, both contemporary and traditional. (Check your software's "help" menu for "templates.") Use a template for letters offered by your software to format a letter you have composed. Print out the letter and submit it to your instructor with a memo that addresses the following questions:

a. Why did you choose this particular template?

b. Did the template make writing your letter easier? Why or why not?

c. Why might businesses request that their employees use a template when formatting business letters?

d. What are the drawbacks, if any, of using templates?

Collaborative Classroom Projects

ON THE WEB

For more collaborative classroom projects, go to Chapter 8, bedfordstmartins.com/ writingthatworks

1. Divide into small groups (three or four students) and elect a group leader. As a writing team, draft a letter explaining the changes in shipping charges to customers of your wholesale office-supply company.

   For more than five years, your company has been able to offer online customers a flat shipping rate of $5.95 for any order under $300. This has been a strong advertising point for the company. However, profits have fallen steadily in the past two years, so the president of your company has announced that shipping charges will increase in two months. Shipping will be $12.95 for orders over $300 and will increase by $3 for each additional $100 worth of product.

   Your writing team must inform your existing customers of the change—a difficult task because the customers have been conditioned by your marketing representatives to expect "the industry's most reasonable" shipping charges. The letter should provide the context and an explanation of the charges, the bad news, and a goodwill close. Follow the guidelines in this chapter for reference.

2. Imagine that members of your group work as interns for a new local nonprofit organization that works with parents to teach expressive skills to autistic toddlers. The organization has received several financial and automobile donations in response to a recent fund-raising drive, and it needs to send a form letter to donors

that thanks them for their generosity and subtly encourages them to give again in the future. Because some donors have asked how they can write off their car donations, the organization has decided to supplement the letter with an information sheet that explains how to deduct noncash contributions from their income taxes. Create a thank-you letter and an information sheet as follows:

a. For the letter:
- Create a name and letterhead for the charity.
- Begin with the donor's inside address and a salutation with the donor's name.
- Write the letter using a "we" or "I" viewpoint.
- Thank the donor for the contribution to your charity and detail the amount donated.
- Describe the good works of the charity (who is helped by the charity and how).
- Let donors know that because no goods or services were exchanged, the donation is tax-deductible and they should keep this letter for their tax records.
- Provide a contact name and number.
- The director of the charity should sign the letter.

b. For the information sheet, use the following information paraphrased from the IRS Web site. Be sure to organize it logically and attractively (see Chapter 7, Designing Effective Documents and Visuals) and use the "you" viewpoint.
- If a donor claims a deduction on his or her return of over $500 for all contributed property, the donor must attach a Form 8283 (PDF), *Noncash Charitable Contributions*, to the return.
- If a donor claims a total deduction of $5,000 or less for all contributed property, the donor need complete only Section A of Form 8283.
- If a donor claims a deduction of more than $5,000 for an item or a group of similar items, the donor generally needs to complete Section B of Form 8283, which usually requires a qualified appraiser to appraise the vehicle and its value.
- The donor will need to keep records of the donation and substantiate the car's current fair market value. The charity will need to provide written acknowledgment (a description of the car and whether the charity provided any goods or services in exchange, including their value) if the donor is claiming a deduction of $250 or more for the car.

3. Divide into two groups of equal numbers. One group represents the local electric company's consumers, and the other group represents the company's marketing representatives. If you are in the consumer group, write a letter as a team to the utility commissioner asking that the rate increase requested by the electric company not be granted. If you are in the marketing group, write a letter as a team asking the utility commissioner to grant your rate-increase request. Each group has 30 minutes to write the letter, which should address the following issues:

a. Dependability of service of the utility
b. Need for a rate increase
c. Ability of customers to pay for the increase

   Trade letters and, during the next 30 minutes, work as a group to write bad-news response letters from the utility commissioner's office. If you are writing to the consumers, break the bad news that the rate increase will be necessary. If you are writing to the electric company's marketing representatives, break the bad news that a rate increase will not be granted. Remember to provide a context, an explanation, the bad news, and a goodwill close when drafting your replies.

Research Projects

1. Imagine that several administrative assistants in your company have been sending sales letters to female customers randomly using *Ms.* and *Mrs.* as titles. Research the history of the title *Ms.* and write a memo to the assistants detailing when the term was coined and for what reasons and explaining the conventions they should use when addressing women in their written correspondence.

2. Search newspaper Web sites for three recent articles about e-mail etiquette. Write a brief analysis in which you compare and contrast the content of the articles. E-mail your analysis to your instructor and include links to the articles analyzed.

ON THE WEB

For extra research projects, go to Chapter 8, bedfordstmartins.com/ writingthatworks

9 Writing Business Correspondence

AT A GLANCE: Routine, Positive, and Negative Messages

There are almost as many types of workplace correspondence as there are reasons for writing. This chapter discusses some of the most frequently written types, including international correspondence, focusing in particular on the style and tone suitable to each type.

▨ Routine and Positive Messages / 321
- Covers (or transmittals) / 321
- Acknowledgments / 321
- Inquiries / 321
- Responses to inquiries / 325
- Sales and promotions / 325

▨ Sensitive and Negative Messages / 330
- Refusals / 330
- Complaints / 331
- Adjustments / 336
- Collections / 339

▨ International Correspondence / 343

For each of these types, you must also determine what form—such as letter, memo, or e-mail—is best. Keep in mind any company or organizational practices regarding the form for specific types of messages.

This chapter applies the principles described in Chapter 8 to widely used types of workplace correspondence. Much of this correspondence involves routine information exchanges, but even straightforward communications provide opportunities to benefit you and your recipient. Equally important is correspondence that promotes a positive image of your organization's product or service. Finally, and most challenging, is correspondence that communicates sensitive or negative information.

Routine and Positive Messages

The types of correspondence discussed in this section provide the opportunity to build goodwill with readers and to create a positive image of your organization.

Covers (or Transmittals)

When you send a formal report, proposal, brochure, or similar material, you should include a short message, often called a cover (or transmittal) letter, to identify what you are sending. An e-mail message used to send an electronic attachment also serves this purpose, as does a memo sent within an organization. The cover message also provides you with a record of when and to whom you sent the material.

Keep your remarks brief. Your opening should explain what is being sent and why. A cover letter that accompanies a report, for example, may identify the report's title, briefly describe its contents, state its purpose, and note who requested it. In an optional second paragraph, you might summarize the information or point out any sections of particular interest to the reader. This paragraph could mention the conditions under which the material was prepared, such as limitations of time or budget. Your closing paragraph should contain acknowledgments of help received, offer more assistance, or express the hope that the material will fulfill its purpose. If your letter accompanies a proposal, you could mention a key point or two as to why your firm is the best one to do the job.

Figure 9–1 is an example of a cover letter that is brief and to the point. Figure 9–2 on page 323 shows a cover letter that is a bit more detailed, touching on the manner in which the information was gathered.

Acknowledgments

One way to build goodwill with colleagues and clients is to let them know that you have received something they sent and to express thanks. A letter, an e-mail message, or a memo that serves these functions is usually a short, polite note. The example shown in Figure 9–3 on page 324 is typical and could be sent as a letter or an e-mail.

Inquiries

An inquiry letter or e-mail message can be as simple as a request for a free brochure or as complex as asking a consultant to define specific requirements for a usability testing lab.

The two broad categories of inquiries include those that benefit the recipient and those that benefit the writer. Inquiries of obvious benefit to the recipient include requests for information about a recently advertised product. Inquiries that primarily benefit the writer include, for example, a request to a professional association to send demographic information about its members. If your inquiry is of

◆ *For information on formatting letters and memos, see pages 303–313 in Chapter 8, Understanding the Principles of Business Communication.*

◆ *For advice on proposal cover letters and a sample, see pages 470 and 478 in Chapter 13, Writing Proposals.*

◆ *For advice on selecting the form (or medium) most appropriate for your purpose and audience, see Chapter 8, pages 277–280.*

◆ *For job applications, another type of inquiry letter, see Chapter 16, Finding the Right Job.*

ECOLOGY SYSTEMS AND SERVICES

39 Beacon Street, Boston, Massachusetts 02106
(617) 351-1223 • Fax: (617) 351-2121
ecologysystems.com

May 24, 2010

Mario Espinoza, Chief Engineer
Louisiana Chemical Products
3452 River View Road
Baton Rouge, LA 70893

Dear Mr. Espinoza:

Identification of enclosure —— Enclosed is the final report on our installation of pollution-control
equipment at Eastern Chemical Company, which we send with
Eastern's permission. Please call me (ext. 1206) or e-mail me at the
Offer of assistance —— address below if I can answer any questions.

Sincerely,

Susan Wong

Susan Wong, Ph.D.
Technical Services Manager
swong@ecologysystems.com

SW/ls
Enclosure: Report

Figure 9–1 Brief Cover Letter (for a Report)

the second kind, be particularly considerate of your reader's needs. Your objective
will probably be to obtain, within a reasonable time, answers to specific questions. You will be more likely to receive a prompt, helpful reply if you follow the
guidelines listed in Considering Audience and Purpose: Writing Inquiries on page
325 and illustrated in Figure 9–4 on page 324.

WATERFORD PAPER PRODUCTS
P.O. Box 413
WATERFORD, WI 53474

Phone: (414) 738-2191 • Fax: (414) 738-9122
waterfordpaper.com

January 15, 2010

Mr. Roger Hammersmith
Ecology Systems, Inc.
1015 Clarke Street
Chicago, IL 60615

Dear Mr. Hammersmith:

Enclosed is the report estimating our energy needs for the year, as requested by John Brenan, Vice President, on September 10.

Identification of enclosure

The report is a result of several meetings with the manager of plant operations and her staff and an extensive survey of all our employees. The survey was delayed by the transfer of key staff in Building A. We believe, however, that the report will provide the information you need in order to furnish us with a cost estimate for the installation of your Mark II Energy Saving System.

Background and purpose of report

We would like to thank Diana Biel of ESI for her assistance in preparing the survey. If you need any more information, please let me know.

Acknowledgment of help

Sincerely,

James G. Evans
New Projects Office
jge@waterfordpaper.com

Enclosure

Figure 9–2   Cover Letter (with Background Information)

> **From:**   Wilbur Kohn <kohn@kohns.com>
> **To:**   Marsha Stein <stein39@macrofoods.com>
> **Sent:**   Friday, February 26, 2010 5:52 PM
> **Subject:** Checkout Reporting System
>
> Dear Ms. Stein:
>
> *Acknowledgment*
>
> I received your comprehensive report today. When I finish studying it in detail, I'll send you our cost estimate for the installation of the Checkout Reporting System.
>
> *Thanks to writer*
>
> Thank you for preparing such a thorough analysis.
>
> Regards,
>
> Wilbur Kohn

Figure 9–3   Acknowledgment Letter (Sent as an E-mail Message)

> **From:**   Kathryn J. Parsons <kparsons@fly.ud.edu>
> **To:**   Jane E. Metcalf <metcalf@mvpc.org>
> **Sent:**   16 March 2010 09:23:45 -0500 (EST)
> **Subject:** Inquiry on Heating Systems
>
> Dear Ms. Metcalf:
>
> *Reason for request*
>
> I am an architecture student at the University of Dayton working with a team of students to design an energy-efficient house for a class project. I am writing to request information on heating systems based on the specifications of our design. We would appreciate any information you could provide.
>
> The house we are designing contains 2,000 square feet of living space (17,600 cubic feet) and meets all the requirements in your brochure "Insulating for Efficiency." We need the following information, based on the southern Ohio climate:
>
> *List of questions*
>
> • the proper-size heat pump for such a home
> • the wattage of the supplemental electrical heating units required
> • the estimated power consumption and rates for those units for one year
>
> *Offer to share results and contact information*
>
> We will be happy to send you our preliminary design report. If you have questions or suggestions, please contact me at kparsons@fly.ud.edu or call 513-229-4598.
>
> Thank you for your help.
>
> Kathryn Parsons

Figure 9–4   Inquiry (Sent as an E-mail Message)

CONSIDERING AUDIENCE AND PURPOSE

Writing Inquiries

- Make your questions specific, clear, and concise. Phrase your questions so that the reader will know immediately the type of information you are seeking, why you need it, and how you will use it.

- If possible, present your questions in a list to make it easy for your reader to address them.

- Keep the number of questions to a minimum to improve your chances of receiving a prompt response.

- Offer some inducement for the reader to respond, such as promising to share the results of what you are doing.

- Promise to keep responses confidential, if appropriate.

- Close by thanking the reader for taking the time to respond. Provide contact information, such as a phone number or an e-mail address, to simplify a reply.

Responses to Inquiries

When you receive an inquiry, read it quickly to determine whether you have both the information and the authority to respond. If you do, reply as promptly as you can, answering every question asked. Adjust the length of your response to the questions and the information provided by the writer. Even if the writer has asked a question that seems silly or has what you feel is an obvious answer, respond courteously and as completely as you can. You may tactfully point out that the writer has omitted or misunderstood something.

If you feel you cannot answer an inquiry, find out who can and forward the inquiry to that person. Notify the writer that you have forwarded the inquiry, as shown in Figure 9–5. If you reply to a forwarded inquiry, state in the first paragraph why someone else is answering, as shown in Figure 9–6 on page 327.

Sales and Promotions

A sales letter or promotional message requires a thorough understanding of the product, service, or business and the potential customer's needs. For this reason, many businesses (such as major retailers) employ specialists to compose their sales letters and other promotional material. However, if you work in a small business or are self-employed, you may need to write sales letters yourself. An effective sales message accomplishes the goals described in the Writing Effective Sales Messages checklist on page 330.

Your first task is to identify your audience: those who should receive your letter or other material. If you do not select your recipients carefully, your message will likely be dismissed as junk mail or spam (if sent by e-mail). Appropriate recipients may include existing customers, people who have purchased a product or

*Acknowledgment
of inquiry*

*Notification
of forwarding*

Subject: **Report Received**
Date: Mon, 22 March 2010 11:42:25 -0500 (EST)
From: Jane E. Metcalf <metcalf@mvpc.org>
To: Kathryn J. Parsons <kparsons@fly.ud.edu>

Dear Kathryn Parsons:

Thank you for inquiring about the heating system we recommend for homes designed according to the specifications in our brochure "Insulating for Efficiency."

Because I cannot answer your specific questions, I have forwarded your inquiry to
Michael Wang, Engineering Assistant in our Development Group. He should be able
to answer your questions, and you should hear from him shortly.

Best wishes,

Jane E. Metcalf

=================================
Jane E. Metcalf, Director of Public Information
Miami Valley Power Company
P.O. Box 1444 ~ Miamitown, OH 45733
Office 513-264-4800 ~ Fax 513-264-4889
Web ~ mvpc.org
=================================

Figure 9–5   Acknowledgment of an Inquiry (Indicating That the Request Has Been Forwarded)

service from you and may do so again. You also might want to seek new customers who may be interested in certain products or services. Companies that specialize in marketing techniques compile and sell such lists of members of professional, fraternal, and religious organizations, trade-show attendees, and the like. Because these lists tend to be expensive, select them with care.

Once you decide on those who should receive your sales letter, learn as much as you can about their age, gender, vocation, geographical location, educational level, financial status, and interests. You must be aware of your readers' needs so that you can effectively tell them how your product or service will satisfy those needs.

Analyze your product or service carefully to determine your strongest psycho-logical sales points—the product's intangible benefits rather than its physical fea-tures—and build your sales letter around those points. Begin by identifying how your product or service will make your reader's job easier, status higher, personal life more pleasant, and so on. Then in the body of the letter, show how your prod-uct or service can satisfy the need or desire identified in your opening. Describe the physical features of your product in terms of their benefit to your reader. Help your reader imagine using your product or service—and enjoying its benefits.

If the price of your product or service is especially competitive, you may de-cide to emphasize the cost. However, if your product or service is relatively costly (even if priced competitively), you may be able to emphasize its high quality, reli-

---

Subject: RE: Inquiry on Heating Systems
Date: 29 March 2010 16:09:22 -0500 (EST)
From: Michael Wang <mwang@mvpc.org>
To: Kathryn J. Parsons <kparsons@fly.ud.edu>

Dear Ms. Parsons:

Jane Metcalf forwarded to me your inquiry of March 16 about the house that your architecture team is designing. I can estimate the heating requirements of a typical home of 17,600 cubic feet as follows:

- For such a home, we would generally recommend a heat pump capable of delivering 40,000 BTUs, such as our model AL-42 (17 kilowatts).
- With the AL-42's efficiency, you don't need supplemental heating units.
- Depending on usage, the AL-42 unit averages between 1,000 and 1,500 kilowatt-hours from December through March. To determine the current rate for such usage, check with Dayton Power and Light Company.

I can give you an answer that would apply specifically to your house based on its particular design (such as number of stories, windows, and entrances). If you send me more details, I will be happy to provide more precise figures for your interesting project.

Sincerely,

Michael Wang

Engineering Assistant
mwang@mvpc.org

Acknowledgment of inquiry

Responses to list of questions

Offer of further help

Figure 9–6   Response to an Inquiry (Sent as an E-mail Message)

ability, or special benefits. If you feel a need to minimize the negative effect of price, you might state the cost in terms of a unit rather than a set ($20 per item instead of $600 per set); identify the daily, the monthly, or even the yearly cost based on the estimated life of the product; suggest a series of payments rather than the total; or compare the cost with that of something the reader accepts readily ("costs the same as a movie and a dinner out").

ETHICS NOTE

Be certain that any claim you make in a sales message is valid. To claim that a product is safe guarantees its absolute safety; therefore, say the product is safe "provided that normal safety precautions are taken." Further, do not exaggerate or speak negatively about a competitor. For further ethical and legal guidelines, visit the Direct Marketing Association at <www.the-dma.org>. See also the ethics note on page 104 in Chapter 4, Revising the Draft.

Notice the informal, friendly tone of the typical sales letter, as shown in Figure 9–7—an approach frequently used by small, local businesses to make the reader feel comfortable about coming to them. The signature line of sales letters often shows the name of the company rather than the name of an individual, as is the case in this example. The e-mailed sales message in Figure 9–8 also uses an informal but professional tone, appealing to the readers' interests while instilling confidence in the company's ability to provide timely information.

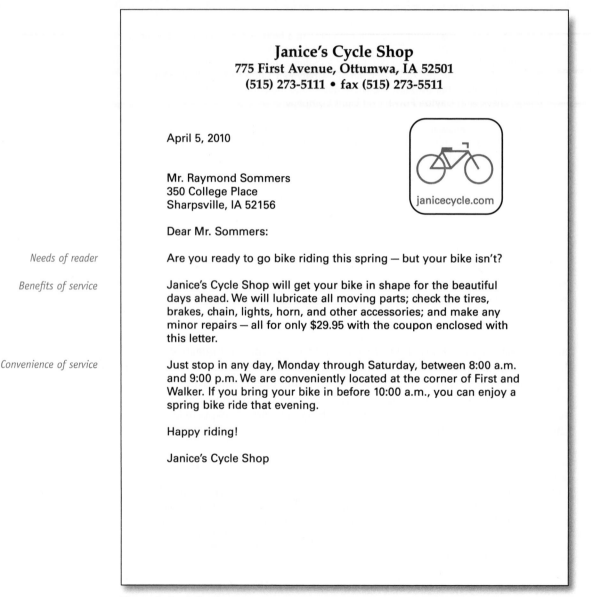

Figure 9–7   Sales Letter

From: contact_us@cartoonbank.com
Sent: Wednesday, April 07, 2010 3:27 PM
To: Mary Hughes
Subject: A Gift for Registering

Welcome Mary Hughes!

Thanks for registering at Cartoonbank.com, your premier source for New Yorker cartoons and cover prints. *——— Acknowledgment of customer relationship*

As a special gift for becoming a member, we want to give you an exclusive coupon. Use the coupon code "WELCOME1" on your next purchase of $100 or more and receive 10% off. *——— Incentive for customer to return*

Almost every cartoon that has ever appeared in the New Yorker is available from The Cartoon Bank as a framed or matted print or a T-shirt or sweatshirt.

www.cartoonbank.com *——— Link for easy response*

New Yorker cartoons are also a great way to get your message across in a PowerPoint presentation or lighten up your company newsletter or corporate annual report. Learn more about our licensing benefits by going here: *Benefits of product described with a business audience in mind*

www.cartoonbank.com/licensing.asp

The Cartoon Bank is also home to the New Yorker's Vintage Cover Collection (1925–1992). Over 60 years of illustrated cover art available as large museum-quality prints. *Description of other products written to a general audience*

www.cartoonbank.com/covers.asp

Find all this and more at Cartoonbank.com, including Limited-Edition Signed Cover Lithographs, New Yorker Desk Diaries, cartoon books, and more!

And remember, use "WELCOME1" and save 10% on your next purchase!

If you need any help at all, please don't hesitate to contact us by e-mail (mailto:toon@cartoonbank.com) or phone (1-800-897-TOON, 1-800-897-8666). You can also chat online with a live customer service representative by clicking on the green button located on the upper left of every page in Cartoonbank.com. *——— Customer service contact information and friendly close*

Yours in good humor,

Bob Mankoff
President

Figure 9–8   Sales E-mail

Writing Effective Sales Messages

✔ Develop your letter to accomplish three basic goals.

  – Open by attracting your reader's attention and arousing his or her interest.

  – Describe features of the product or service that would appeal strongly to your reader's wants or needs.

  – Suggest ways that the reader can immediately use the product or service.

✔ If sending an e-mail message, create a subject line that encourages recipients to read the message ("Special Offer When You Respond to This Message").

✔ Be certain that any claim you make in a sales letter is truthful, not an overstatement.

✔ Present evidence to convince your reader that your product or service is everything you claim it to be.

✔ Don't exaggerate, make unreasonable claims, speak negatively of a competitor, or use other unfair tactics. You can build confidence with a money-back guarantee, a free trial offer, testimonials, or case histories.

✔ Make the customer's response easy and worthwhile. You might include a map to your store, a discount coupon, instructions for phone-in orders and free delivery, or a Web address for more information, special discounts, and online orders.

■ Sensitive and Negative Messages

Writing sensitive or negative messages requires careful thought. You must decide, for example, how direct or indirect your message should be and then choose words that maintain a professional relationship with a correspondent despite any difficult circumstances.

Refusals

When you receive a request to which you must give a negative reply, you may need to write a refusal message containing bad news—something that a reader does not want to receive. Opening with the bad news can affect your reader negatively. The ideal refusal says *no* in such a way that you not only avoid antagonizing your reader but also maintain goodwill. To do so, you must convince your reader that the reasons for refusing are logical or understandable before you present the bad news. The following pattern effectively deals with this problem:

1. *Context.* In the opening (or *buffer*), introduce the subject and establish a professional tone.

2. *Explanation.* Review the facts that lead logically to the bad news, but try to see things from your reader's point of view.

3. *Bad news.* State your refusal, based on the facts, concisely and without apology.

4. *Goodwill.* In the closing, establish or reestablish a positive relationship by providing an option, assure the reader of your high opinion of his or her product or service, offer a friendly remark, or merely wish the reader success.

In the case of a rejected proposal, such as that in Figure 9–9, express appropriate and genuine appreciation for the reader's time, effort, and interest. Thoroughly detail the reasons for the refusal with the goal of convincing the reader that the conclusion is reasonable. State the negative message concisely, clearly, and as positively as possible. Close by working to reestablish goodwill and avoid rehashing the bad news. (Do not write, "Again, we're sorry we can't use your idea.")

Refusals often vary with what is at stake for the writer or the reader. The refusal in Figure 9–10 on page 333 declines an invitation to speak at a meeting, and the stakes for the writer are relatively low; however, the writer wishes to acknowledge the honor of being asked. Figure 9–11 on page 334 shows a letter rejecting a job applicant in which the stakes are higher. Finally, Figure 9–12 on page 335 shows a refusal sent to a supplier whose product was not selected, yet the writer wishes to maintain a harmonious relationship.

VOICES IN THE WORKPLACE

Considering Bad News from the Reader's Point of View

A mechanical engineer who designs customized products for municipal construction projects, Robert Repetto is careful to inform clients of any potential problems.

"When I have to tell customers something unpleasant, I always try to look at the situation from their point of view. It can be tempting to lay blame or say, 'I told you so,' but it's much more effective to explain what the problem is and focus on how it can be solved. Delivering the bad news in writing keeps the relationship professional and helps to prevent miscommunication, which is important when you're trying to stay on schedule."

Complaints

By the time you need to write a complaint letter (sometimes called a *claim letter*), you may be irritated and angry. If you write a letter that reflects only your annoyance and anger, you may simply seem petty and irrational. The best complaint letters — the ones taken most seriously — do not sound complaining. Remember, too, that the person who receives your complaint may not be the one who was directly responsible for the situation. An effective letter should assume that the recipient will conscientiously correct the problem. However, anticipate reader reactions or rebuttals.

◆ *See also Goodwill and the "You" Viewpoint on pages 282–283, Direct and Indirect Patterns on pages 283–288, and Sending a Resignation Letter on pages 615–617.*

◆ *For advice about writing resignation and job-refusal letters, see Chapter 16, Finding the Right Job.*

▶   I reviewed my user manual's "safe operating guidelines" carefully before I installed the device. [Assures readers you followed instructions.]

Memo

To: Darrell Munro
From: Amelia Jackson, Screening Procedures Committee   *AJ*
Date: May 17, 2010
Subject: Response to Proposed Security-Clearance Procedures

Context and thanks

The Screening Procedures Committee appreciates the time and effort you spent on your proposal for a new security-clearance procedure.

Explanation with logical reasons

We reviewed the potential effects of implementing your proposed security-clearance procedure companywide. We not only asked the Security Systems Department to review the data but also surveyed industry practices, sought the views of senior management, and submitted the idea to our legal staff. As a result of this process, we have reached the following conclusions:

- The cost savings you project are correct only if the procedure could be required throughout the company.
- The components of your procedure are legal, but most are not widely accepted by our industry.
- Based on our survey, some components could alienate employees who would perceive them as violating an individual's rights.
- Enforcing companywide use would prove costly and impractical.

Refusal

For these reasons, the committee recommends that divisions continue their current security-screening procedures.

Goodwill closing with option

Because some components of your procedure may apply in certain circumstances, we would like to feature your ideas in the next issue of *The Guardian*. I have asked the editor to contact you next week. On behalf of the committee, thank you for the thoughtful proposal.

Figure 9–9   Memo Rejecting an Internal Proposal

From: Ralph Morgan <rpmorgan@wec.com>
To: Javier Lopez <jlopez@tnco.com>
Date: Wednesday, March 24, 2010
Subject: Speaking Invitation

Dear Mr. Lopez:

I am honored to have been invited to address your regional meeting in St. Louis on May 17. That you would consider me as a potential contributor to such a gathering of experts is indeed flattering.

Positive context

On checking my schedule, I find that I will be attending the annual meeting of our parent corporation's Board of Directors on that date. Therefore, as much as I would enjoy addressing your members, I must decline.

Review of facts and refusal

I have been very favorably impressed over the years with your organization's contributions to the engineering profession, and I would welcome the opportunity to participate in a future meeting.

Goodwill closing with option

Sincerely,

Ralph P. Morgan

```
==============================
Ralph P. Morgan
Research Director
Watashaw Engineering Company
301 Industrial Lane
Decatur, IL 62525
Phone: (708) 222-3700
Fax: (708) 222-3707
wec.com
==============================
```

Figure 9–10   E-mail Refusing a Speaking Invitation

Without such explanations, readers may be tempted to dismiss your complaint. Although the circumstances and severity of the problem may vary, effective complaint letters (or e-mails) should generally follow this pattern:

1. Identify the problem or faulty item(s) and include relevant information, such as invoice numbers, part names, and dates, as well as a copy of the receipt, bill, or contract, being sure to keep the original for your records.
2. Explain logically, clearly, and specifically what went wrong—especially for a problem with a service. (Avoid speculating about why you think a problem occurred.)
3. State what you expect the reader to do to solve the problem to your satisfaction.

Liberty Associates
3553 West Marshall Road
San Diego, California 92101

Liberty
Associates | FINANCIAL
CONSULTANTS

Phone (619) 555-1001
Fax (619) 555-0110

January 19, 2010

Ms. Sonja Yadgar
2289 South 63rd Street
Hartford, CT 06101

Dear Ms. Yadgar:

Positive context

Thank you for your interest in financial counseling at Liberty Associates. I respect your investment experience and professionalism, and I enjoyed our conversation.

Review of facts and refusal

Shortly after our meeting, an especially appropriate, well-qualified internal candidate applied for the position, and we have decided to offer the job to that individual. I say in all honesty that the decision was very difficult. Both Nancy Linh and I were impressed with your qualifications and believe that you have a great deal to offer our profession.

Goodwill closing

Please do stay in touch. Best wishes for the future.

Sincerely,

Meike Künkel
Vice President
Director of Development

www.libertyassociates.com

Figure 9–11   Letter Rejecting a Job Applicant

MARTINI BANKING AND DATA SYSTEMS

251 West 57th Street
New York, New York 10019
Phone (212) 555-1221   Fax (212) 555-2112
martinisystems.com

February 11, 2010

Mr. Henry Coleman
Abbott Office Products, Inc.
P.O. Box 544
Detroit, MI 48206

Dear Mr. Coleman:

Thank you for your cooperation and your patience with us as we struggled to reach a decision in selecting a check-sorting system. We believe our long involvement with your company indicates our confidence in your products.   *Positive context*

Based on our research, we found that the Winton Check Sorter has all the features that your sorter offers and, in fact, has two additional features that your sorter does not. The more important one is a backup feature that retains totals in its memory, even if the power fails. The second additional feature is stacked pockets, which are less space-consuming than the linear pockets on your sorter. After much deliberation, therefore, we have decided to purchase the Winton Check Sorter.   *Review of facts*

Refusal

Although we did not select your sorter, we were very favorably impressed with your system and your people. Perhaps we will be able to use other Abbott products in the future.   *Goodwill closing*

Sincerely,

Muriel Johnson

Muriel Johnson
Business Manager

Figure 9–12   Letter Rejecting a Sales Proposal

To reach someone who can help you in a large organization, first check its Web site or call its main office so that you can address your letter to the appropriate department (often Customer Service, Consumer Affairs, or Adjustments). In smaller organizations, you might write to a vice president in charge of sales or service. For very small businesses, write directly to the owner. As a last resort, you may find that sending copies of a complaint letter to more than one person in the company will get fast results. Each employee who receives the letter will know (because of the notation at the bottom of the page) that others, possibly higher in the organization, have received the letter and will take note of whether the problem is solved. Figure 9–13 shows a typical complaint letter.

Adjustments

An adjustment letter or e-mail responds to a complaint and tells a customer or client what your organization intends to do about the complaint or problem. You should settle such matters quickly and courteously, always trying to satisfy the customer at a reasonable cost to your company. An effective adjustment letter actually builds goodwill as it both repairs any damage that has been done and restores the customer's confidence in your company.

Open your letter with what the reader will consider good news.

- Grant the adjustment, if appropriate, for uncomplicated situations ("Enclosed is a replacement for the damaged part").

- Reveal that you intend to grant the adjustment by admitting that the customer was right ("Yes, you were incorrectly billed for the delivery"). Then explain the specific details of the adjustment. This method is good for adjustments that require detailed explanations.

- Apologize for the error ("Please accept our apologies for not acting sooner to correct your account"). This method is effective when the customer's inconvenience is as much an issue as money.

- Use a combination of these techniques. Often, situations that require an adjustment also require flexibility.

The tone of your correspondence is critical. Grant adjustments graciously; a settlement made grudgingly will do more harm than good. No matter how unreasonable the complaint, your response should be positive and respectful, focusing not on the unfortunate situation but on what you are doing to correct it. Not only must you be gracious, but you must also acknowledge the error in such a way that the customer or client will not lose confidence in your organization.

Before granting an adjustment to a claim for which your company is at fault, as illustrated in Figure 9–14 on page 338, you must determine what happened and what you can do to satisfy the customer. Be certain that you are familiar with your company's adjustment policy—and be careful with word choice:

▶   We have just received your letter of May 7 about our ~~defective~~ gas grill.

BAKER HEALTHCARE SYSTEMS

Purchasing Department
501 Main Street
Springfield, OH 45321
(513) 683-8100
Fax (513) 683-8000

September 22, 2010

Manager, Customer Relations
Medical Solutions, Inc.
521 West 23rd Street
New York, NY 10011

Subject: ST3 Diagnostic Scanners

On July 9, I ordered nine ST3 Diagnostic Scanners (order # ST3-1179R). The scanners were ordered from your customer Web site.

On August 3, I received seven HL monitors from your parts warehouse in Newark, New Jersey. I immediately returned those monitors with a note indicating that a mistake had been made. However, not only have I failed to receive the ST3 scanners that I ordered, but I have also been billed repeatedly for the seven monitors.

Explanation of error

I have enclosed a copy of my confirmation e-mail, the shipping form, and the most recent bill. If you cannot send me the scanners I ordered by November 1, please cancel my order.

Enclosures substantiating complaint
Request for solution

Sincerely,

Paul Denlinger

Paul Denlinger
Manager
pld@baker.org

Enclosures

www.baker.org

Figure 9–13   Complaint Letter

INTERNET SERVICES CORPORATION
10876 Crispen Way
Chicago, Illinois 60601

May 11, 2010

Mr. Jason Brandon
4319 Anglewood Street
Tacoma, WA 98402

Dear Mr. Brandon:

Gracious tone

We are sorry that your experience with our customer support help line did not go smoothly. We are eager to restore your confidence in our ability to provide dependable, high-quality service. Your next three months of Internet access will be complimentary as our sincere apology for your unpleasant experience.

Adjustment

Providing dependable service is what is expected of us, and when our staff doesn't provide quality service, it is easy to understand our customers' disappointment. I truly wish we had performed better in our guidance for setup and log-on procedures and that your experience had been a positive one. To prevent similar problems in the future, we plan to use your letter in training sessions with customer support personnel.

Positive closing

We appreciate your taking the time to write us. It helps to receive comments such as yours, and we conscientiously follow through to be sure that proper procedures are being met.

Yours truly,

Inez Carlson

Inez Carlson, Vice President
Customer Support Services

www.isc.com

Figure 9–14   Adjustment Letter (Company Takes Responsibility)

Saying something is "defective" could be ruled in a court of law as an admission that the product is in fact defective. When you are in doubt about the appropriate language, seek legal advice. Treat every claim individually, and lean toward giving the customer the benefit of the doubt.

Sometimes you may decide to grant a partial adjustment to regain the customer's lost goodwill, even though the claim is not really justified, as in Figure 9–15.

You also might need to educate your reader about the use of your product or service. Customers sometimes submit unjustified claims honestly believing them to be fair (for example, a problem resulting from a customer not following maintenance instructions properly). You would grant such a claim only to build goodwill. When you write a letter of adjustment in such a situation, give the explanation before granting the claim—otherwise, your reader may never get to the explanation. If your explanation establishes customer responsibility, do so tactfully, as Figure 9–16 on page 341 illustrates.

ON THE WEB

For additional examples of adjustment letters, go to Model Documents Gallery, bedfordstmartins.com/writingthatworks

WRITER'S CHECKLIST
Writing Tactful Adjustment Letters

✔ Address your reader respectfully, whether you apologize, explain, educate, or offer an adjustment.

✔ Explain what caused the problem if such an explanation will help restore your reader's confidence or goodwill.

✔ Explain specifically how you intend to make the adjustment if it is not obvious in your opening.

✔ Express appreciation to the customer for calling your attention to the situation, explaining that this helps your firm keep the quality of its product or service high.

✔ Point out any steps you may be taking to prevent a recurrence of whatever went wrong, giving the customer as much credit as the facts allow.

✔ Avoid recalling the problem in your closing. (Do not say, "Again, we apologize. . . .") Close positively, looking forward, not back.

Collections

Collection letters serve two purposes: (1) to collect the overdue bill and (2) to preserve the customer relationship. In some states, collection letters should be prepared by attorneys because certain language and requirements must be followed to demand payment. However, even if you never need to write a collection letter, understanding the principles behind such letters offers important insights into the strategies of sensitive correspondence.

Most companies use a series of collection letters in which the letters become increasingly demanding and urgent. The series usually proceeds in three stages, each of which may include several letters as well as follow-up phone calls. All letters should be courteous and show a genuine interest in the customer and whatever problems may be preventing prompt payment.

Computer Solutions, Inc.
521 West 23rd Street
New York, NY 10011

Customer Relations
Phone (212) 574-3894
Fax (212) 574-3899
ssiegel@compsol.com

September 28, 2010

Mr. Fred J. Swesky
7811 Ranchero Drive
Tucson, AZ 85761

Dear Mr. Swesky:

Thank you for your letter requesting the replacement of your CS5 Laptop Computer.

Explanation of customer responsibility

You said in your letter that you used the unit on an open deck. As our service representative pointed out, this model is not designed to operate in extreme heat. As the instruction manual accompanying your new CS5 states, such exposure can produce irreparable damage. Because your unit was used in such extreme heat conditions, we cannot honor the warranty.

However, we are enclosing a certificate entitling you to a trade-in allowance equal to your local CSI dealer's markup for the unit. This means you can purchase a new unit at wholesale, provided you return your original unit to your local dealer.

Partial adjustment

Sincerely yours,

Susan Siegel

Susan Siegel
Assistant Director

SS/mr
Enclosure

CSI.com

Figure 9–15   Partial Adjustment Letter (Customer Is Responsible)

9025 North Main Street
Butte, MT 59702

Phone (800) 233-5656
Fax (800) 233-3010

August 26, 2010

Mr. Carlos Ortiz
638 McSwaney Drive
Butte, MT 59702

Dear Mr. Ortiz:

Enclosed is your SWELCO Coffeemaker, which you sent to us on August 17.

In various parts of the country, tap water may have a high mineral content. If you fill your SWELCO Coffeemaker with water for breakfast coffee before going to bed, a mineral scale will build up on the inner wall of the water tube—as explained on page 2 of your SWELCO Instruction Booklet. *Education of customer*

We have removed the mineral scale from the water tube of your coffeemaker and thoroughly cleaned the entire unit. To ensure the best service from your coffeemaker in the future, clean it once a month by operating it with four ounces of white vinegar and eight cups of water. To rinse out the vinegar taste, operate the unit twice with clear water. *Adjustment and instruction*

With proper care, your SWELCO Coffeemaker will serve you faithfully and well for many years to come. *Positive closing*

Sincerely,

Helen Upham

Helen Upham
Customer Services

HU/mo
Enclosure

swelco.com

Figure 9-16 Educational Adjustment Letter

The first stage consists of reminders stamped on the invoice ("overdue"), form letters, or brief personal notes. These early reminders should maintain a friendly tone that emphasizes the customer's good credit record. They should remind the customer of the debt and may even solicit more business by including promotional material for new items. As in the example in Figure 9–17, you might suggest that nonpayment may be a result of a simple error or oversight.

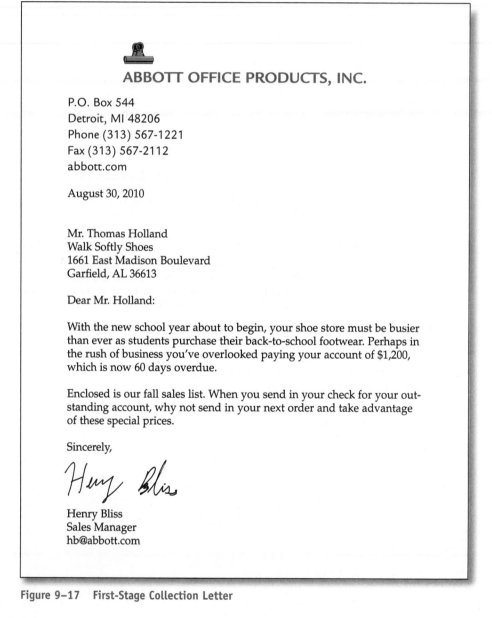

ABBOTT OFFICE PRODUCTS, INC.

P.O. Box 544
Detroit, MI 48206
Phone (313) 567-1221
Fax (313) 567-2112
abbott.com

August 30, 2010

Mr. Thomas Holland
Walk Softly Shoes
1661 East Madison Boulevard
Garfield, AL 36613

Dear Mr. Holland:

Tactful reminder

With the new school year about to begin, your shoe store must be busier than ever as students purchase their back-to-school footwear. Perhaps in the rush of business you've overlooked paying your account of $1,200, which is now 60 days overdue.

Enclosure seeks future business

Enclosed is our fall sales list. When you send in your check for your outstanding account, why not send in your next order and take advantage of these special prices.

Sincerely,

Henry Bliss
Sales Manager
hb@abbott.com

Figure 9–17   First-Stage Collection Letter

In the second stage, the collection letters are more than just reminders. You now assume that some circumstances are preventing payment. Ask directly for payment, and inquire about possible problems, perhaps inviting the customer to discuss the matter with you. You might suggest an optional installment payment plan if you are able to offer one. Mention the importance of good credit, appealing to the customer's pride, self-esteem, and sense of fairness. Remind the customer that he or she has always received good value from you. Make it easy to respond with a return envelope, a telephone or fax number, or a Web address where the payment can be made. At this stage, your tone should be firmer and more direct than in the early stage, but it should never be rude, sarcastic, or threatening. Notice how the second-stage letter shown in Figure 9–18 is more direct than the first-stage letter but no less polite.

Third-stage collection letters reflect a sense of urgency, for the customer has not responded to your previous letters. Although your tone should remain courteous, make your demand for payment explicit. Point out how reasonable you have been, and urge the customer to pay at once to avoid legal action. Again, make it easy to respond by providing a return envelope, a telephone or fax number, or a Web address, as shown in Figure 9–19 on page 345.

Writing International Correspondence

With so many companies operating globally, you may need to write letters, memos, or e-mail messages to readers from other cultures. Because English is widely taught and used in international business, you will be able to send most international correspondence in English. If you must use a translator, however, be sure that the translator understands the purpose of your correspondence. It is also prudent to let your reader know (in the letter itself or in a postscript) that a translator helped write the letter. For first-time contacts, consider sending both the English version and a translation in the reader's native language. If at all possible, have someone from your intended reader's culture or with appropriate expertise review your draft before you complete your final proofreading.

Culture and Business-Writing Style

U.S. business-writing style has changed over time, and ideas about appropriate business-writing style vary from culture to culture. Be alert to the needs and expectations of readers from different cultural and linguistic backgrounds. For example, in the United States, direct, concise writing demonstrates courtesy by not wasting another person's time; in other countries (such as Spain and India), such directness and brevity suggest that the writer dislikes the reader so much that he or she wishes to make the communication as brief as possible. Whereas a U.S. business writer might consider one brief letter sufficient to communicate a request, a writer in another culture may expect an exchange of three or four longer letters to pave the way for action.

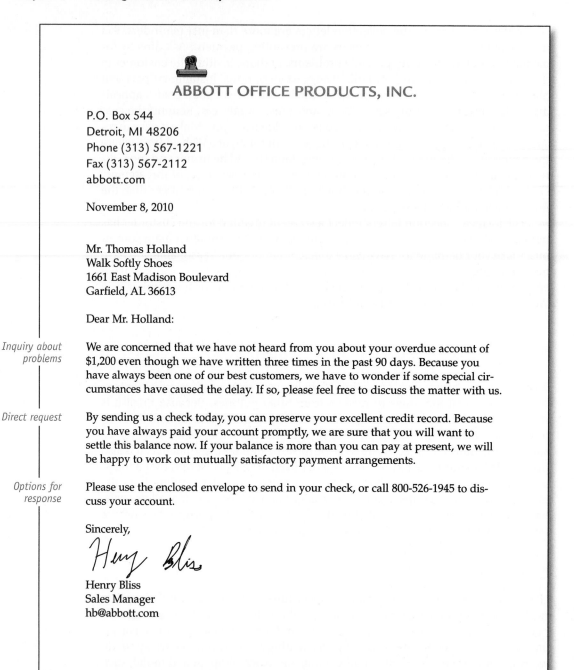

ABBOTT OFFICE PRODUCTS, INC.

P.O. Box 544
Detroit, MI 48206
Phone (313) 567-1221
Fax (313) 567-2112
abbott.com

November 8, 2010

Mr. Thomas Holland
Walk Softly Shoes
1661 East Madison Boulevard
Garfield, AL 36613

Dear Mr. Holland:

Inquiry about problems

We are concerned that we have not heard from you about your overdue account of $1,200 even though we have written three times in the past 90 days. Because you have always been one of our best customers, we have to wonder if some special circumstances have caused the delay. If so, please feel free to discuss the matter with us.

Direct request

By sending us a check today, you can preserve your excellent credit record. Because you have always paid your account promptly, we are sure that you will want to settle this balance now. If your balance is more than you can pay at present, we will be happy to work out mutually satisfactory payment arrangements.

Options for response

Please use the enclosed envelope to send in your check, or call 800-526-1945 to discuss your account.

Sincerely,

Henry Bliss
Sales Manager
hb@abbott.com

Figure 9–18   Second-Stage Collection Letter

ABBOTT OFFICE PRODUCTS, INC.

P.O. Box 544
Detroit, MI 48206
Phone (313) 567-1221
Fax (313) 567-2112
abbott.com

December 28, 2010

Mr. Thomas Holland
Walk Softly Shoes
1661 East Madison Boulevard
Garfield, AL 36613

Dear Mr. Holland:

Your account in the amount of $1,200 is now 180 days overdue. You have already received a generous extension of time and, in fairness to our other customers, we cannot permit a further delay in payment.

Urgent request

Because you have not responded to any of our letters, we must turn your account over to our attorney for collection if we do not receive payment immediately. Such action, of course, will damage your previously fine credit rating.

Explicit demand

Why not avoid this unpleasant situation by sending your check in the enclosed return envelope within 10 days or by calling 800-526-1945 to discuss payment.

Options for response

Sincerely,

Henry Bliss

Henry Bliss
Sales Manager
hb@abbott.com

Figure 9–19   Third-Stage Collection Letter

Japanese business writers, as another example, often use traditional openings that reflect on the season, compliment the reader's success, and offer hopes for the reader's continued prosperity. These traditional openings may strike some U.S. readers as being overly elaborate, literary, or even insincere. Likewise, Japanese business writers express negative messages and refusal letters indirectly to avoid embarrassing the recipient or causing a loss of face.

In U.S. business correspondence, traditional salutations such as *Dear* and complimentary closings such as *Yours truly* have, through custom and long use, acquired meanings distinct from their dictionary definitions. Understanding the unspoken meanings of these forms and using them naturally is routine for those who are a part of U.S. business culture. Likewise, people in many cultures are slower to use an individual's first name in communications than are most Americans. In fact, in some cultures, first names are never used in business settings — even if the individuals have worked together for years. Such customs vary from culture to culture and even within cultures. Therefore, when you read correspondence from businesspeople in other cultures or countries, be alert to these differences and consider how you should address them and your own colleagues in correspondence.

The first step in avoiding misunderstandings is to be aware that differences exist and to learn how they affect communication. To learn more about this subject, use the term *intercultural communication* to search library and reliable Internet sources.

Language and Usage

Take special care in international correspondence to avoid American idioms ("touching base," "give a heads-up," and the like), unusual figures of speech, and allusions to events or attitudes particular to American life. Such expressions could easily confuse your reader. Avoid humor, irony, and sarcasm because they are easily misunderstood outside their cultural context.

Pretentious or overly ornate writing will also impede the reader's understanding. Moreover, if you plan to use jargon or technical terminology, check whether the words you choose might be found in the abbreviated English language dictionary that your reader would likely be using.

Write clear and complete sentences. Unusual word order or rambling sentences will frustrate and confuse a nonnative reader of English. Read your writing aloud to identify overly long sentences and to eliminate any misplaced modifiers or awkwardness. Long sentences that contain more information than the reader can comfortably absorb should be divided into two or more sentences. Also avoid using an overly simplified storybook style. A reader who has studied English as a second language might be insulted by a condescending tone and childish language.

Finally, proofread your correspondence carefully; a misspelled word such as *there* for *their* or *discreet* for *discrete* will be particularly troublesome for a nonna-

---

ON THE WEB

Google's International Business and Trade Directory provides an excellent starting point for searching the Web for information related to customs, communications, and international standards.

◆ *For advice on using appropriate language in business writing, see pages 108–115 in Chapter 4, Revising the Draft.*

tive reader of English—especially if that reader turns to a dictionary for help and cannot find the word because it is misspelled.

Dates, Time, and Measurement

Countries differ in their use of formats to represent dates, time, and other kinds of measurement. To represent dates, most countries typically write the day before the month and year. For example, 1/11/10 means 1 November 2010 in most parts of the world; in the United States, it means January 11, 2010. To avoid uncertainty, write out the name of the month to make the entire date immediately clear to all international readers.

Clock time poses similar problems, so you may need to specify time zones or refer to international standards, such as Greenwich Mean Time (GMT) or Universal Coordinated Time (UCT), for clarity. In Europe and the U.S. military, the 24-hour system is used for clock time. The hours between midnight and noon are numbered 1 to 12, and the hours between noon and midnight are numbered 13 to 24. In this system, four o'clock in the afternoon (4:00 p.m.) is 1600, and 30 minutes later (4:30 p.m.) is 1630. Do not separate the hour and minute with a period or colon. Using this system in letters and e-mail messages will avoid confusion for European correspondents.

Using other international standards, such as commas for decimal points and the metric system (standard in most countries except the United States and the United Kingdom), will also help your reader. For up-to-date information about accepted conventions for numbers and symbols in chemical, electrical, data-processing, pharmaceutical, and other fields, consult guides and manuals specific to the subject matter.

◆ *For a list of subject-specific style guides and manuals, see page 182.*

Cross-Cultural Examples

When you write for international readers, rethink the ingrained habits that define how you express yourself, learn as much as you can about the cultural expectations of others, and focus on politeness strategies that demonstrate your respect for your readers. Doing so will help you achieve clarity and mutual understanding.

Consider the two versions of a letter written by a U.S. businessman to a Japanese businessman in Figure 9–20 and Figure 9–21 on pages 350–351. The opening and closing of the draft in Figure 9–20 do not include enough of the politeness strategies that are important in Japanese culture, and the informal salutation inappropriately uses the recipient's first name (*Dear Ichiro:*). This draft also contains idioms (*drop us a quick . . . , fruits of your labor*), jargon (*skycap*), contractions (*I'm, don't*), informal language (*just drop us a quick e-mail or fax, Cheers, get your stuff*), and humor and allusion (*the powers that be, his limited capacity*).

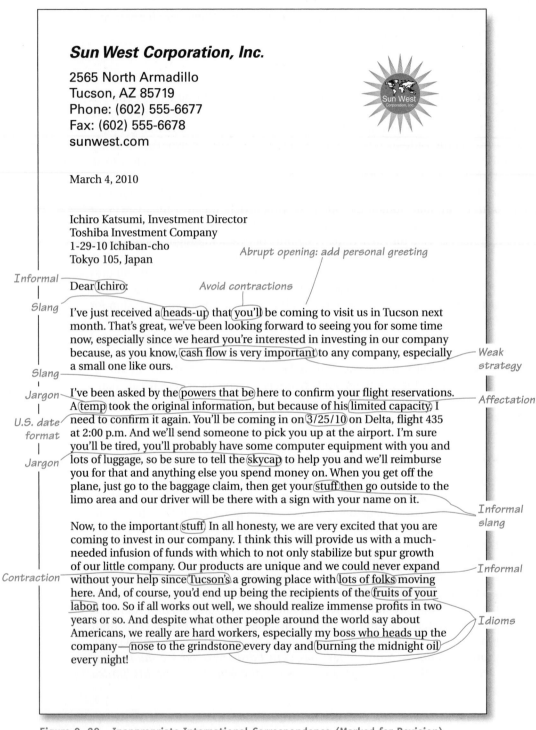

Sun West Corporation, Inc.

2565 North Armadillo
Tucson, AZ 85719
Phone: (602) 555-6677
Fax: (602) 555-6678
sunwest.com

March 4, 2010

Ichiro Katsumi, Investment Director
Toshiba Investment Company
1-29-10 Ichiban-cho
Tokyo 105, Japan

Abrupt opening: add personal greeting

Informal

Dear Ichiro: *Avoid contractions*

Slang

I've just received a heads-up that you'll be coming to visit us in Tucson next
month. That's great, we've been looking forward to seeing you for some time
now, especially since we heard you're interested in investing in our company
because, as you know, cash flow is very important to any company, especially   *Weak strategy*
a small one like ours.

Slang

Jargon   I've been asked by the powers that be here to confirm your flight reservations.   *Affectation*
A temp took the original information, but because of his limited capacity, I
U.S. date   need to confirm it again. You'll be coming in on 3/25/10 on Delta, flight 435
format   at 2:00 p.m. And we'll send someone to pick you up at the airport. I'm sure
you'll be tired, you'll probably have some computer equipment with you and
Jargon   lots of luggage, so be sure to tell the skycap to help you and we'll reimburse
you for that and anything else you spend money on. When you get off the
plane, just go to the baggage claim, then get your stuff then go outside to the
limo area and our driver will be there with a sign with your name on it.   *Informal slang*

Now, to the important stuff. In all honesty, we are very excited that you are
coming to invest in our company. I think this will provide us with a much-
needed infusion of funds with which to not only stabilize but spur growth
of our little company. Our products are unique and we could never expand   *Informal*
Contraction   without your help since Tucson's a growing place with lots of folks moving
here. And, of course, you'd end up being the recipients of the fruits of your
labor, too. So if all works out well, we should realize immense profits in two
years or so. And despite what other people around the world say about   *Idioms*
Americans, we really are hard workers, especially my boss who heads up the
company—nose to the grindstone every day and burning the midnight oil
every night!

Figure 9–20   Inappropriate International Correspondence (Marked for Revision)
(continued)

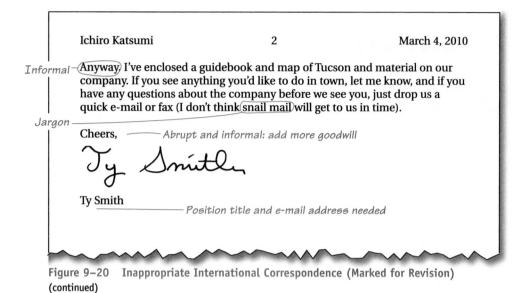

Figure 9–20   Inappropriate International Correspondence (Marked for Revision)
(continued)

Compare that letter to the one in Figure 9–21, which is written in language that is courteous, literal, and specific. This revised letter begins with concern about the recipient's family and prosperity because that opening honors traditional Japanese patterns in business correspondence. The letter is free of slang, idioms, and jargon. The sentences are shorter than in the draft, bulleted lists break up the paragraphs, contractions are avoided, and months are spelled out.

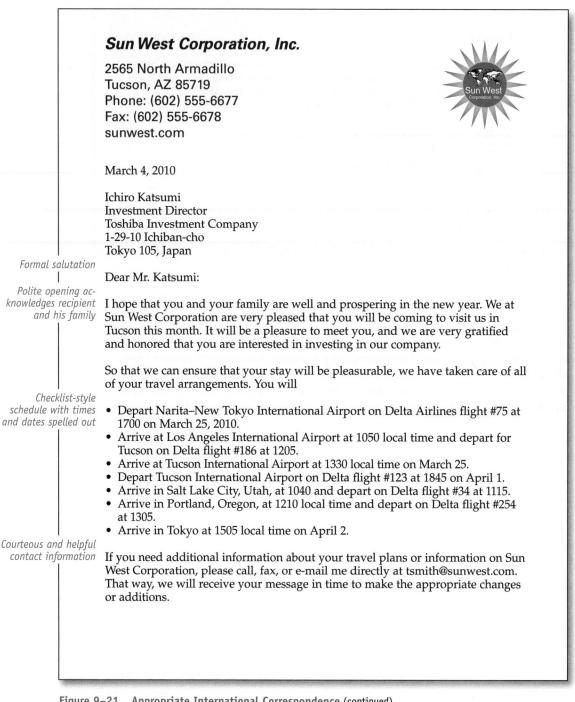

Sun West Corporation, Inc.

2565 North Armadillo
Tucson, AZ 85719
Phone: (602) 555-6677
Fax: (602) 555-6678
sunwest.com

March 4, 2010

Ichiro Katsumi
Investment Director
Toshiba Investment Company
1-29-10 Ichiban-cho
Tokyo 105, Japan

Formal salutation

Dear Mr. Katsumi:

Polite opening ac-knowledges recipient and his family

I hope that you and your family are well and prospering in the new year. We at Sun West Corporation are very pleased that you will be coming to visit us in Tucson this month. It will be a pleasure to meet you, and we are very gratified and honored that you are interested in investing in our company.

So that we can ensure that your stay will be pleasurable, we have taken care of all of your travel arrangements. You will

Checklist-style schedule with times and dates spelled out

- Depart Narita–New Tokyo International Airport on Delta Airlines flight #75 at 1700 on March 25, 2010.
- Arrive at Los Angeles International Airport at 1050 local time and depart for Tucson on Delta flight #186 at 1205.
- Arrive at Tucson International Airport at 1330 local time on March 25.
- Depart Tucson International Airport on Delta flight #123 at 1845 on April 1.
- Arrive in Salt Lake City, Utah, at 1040 and depart on Delta flight #34 at 1115.
- Arrive in Portland, Oregon, at 1210 local time and depart on Delta flight #254 at 1305.
- Arrive in Tokyo at 1505 local time on April 2.

Courteous and helpful contact information

If you need additional information about your travel plans or information on Sun West Corporation, please call, fax, or e-mail me directly at tsmith@sunwest.com. That way, we will receive your message in time to make the appropriate changes or additions.

Figure 9–21   Appropriate International Correspondence (continued)

Mr. Ichiro Katsumi   2   March 4, 2010

After you arrive in Tucson, a chauffeur from Skyline Limousines will be waiting   *Specific arrival plans*
for you at Gate 12. He or she will be carrying a card with your name, will help
you collect your luggage from the baggage claim area, and will then drive you
to the Loewes Ventana Canyon Resort. This resort is one of the most prestigious
in Tucson, with spectacular desert views, high-quality amenities, and one of the
best golf courses in the city. The next day, the chauffeur will be back at the
Ventana at 0900 to drive you to Sun West Corporation.

We at Sun West Corporation are very excited to meet you and introduce you to
all the staff members of our hardworking and growing company. After you meet
everyone, you will enjoy a catered breakfast in our conference room. At that
time, you will receive a schedule of events planned for the remainder of your
trip. Events include presentations from the president of the company and from
departmental directors on

- the history of Sun West Corporation
- the uniqueness of our products and current success in the marketplace
- demographic information and the benefits of being located in Tucson   *Specific trip event*
- the potential for considerable profits for both our companies with your   *plans*
  company's investment

We encourage you to read through the enclosed guidebook and map of Tucson.
In addition to events planned at Sun West Corporation, you will find many natural wonders and historical sites to see in Tucson and in Arizona in general. If
you see any particular event or place that you would like to visit, please let us
know. We will be happy to show you our city and all it has to offer.

Again, we are very honored that you will be visiting us, and we look forward to   *Polite closing*
a successful business relationship between our two companies.

Sincerely,

Ty Smith

Ty Smith
Vice President
tsmith@sunwest.com

Enclosures (2)

Figure 9–21   **Appropriate International Correspondence** (continued)

CHAPTER 9 SUMMARY: WRITING BUSINESS CORRESPONDENCE

Routine and Positive Messages

- *Cover* (or *transmittal*) messages accompany material sent to a recipient, identify what is being sent, and explain why it is being sent.

- *Acknowledgments* build goodwill with colleagues and clients by confirming the arrival of something they sent and expressing thanks.

- *Inquiries and responses* state clearly the information wanted, who wants it, and why. Answer inquiries by responding to all the questions or forwarding the inquiry to someone who can.

- Sales and promotions attract the reader's attention to a product, service, or business by arousing interest, emphasizing benefits, and inviting a response.

Sensitive and Negative Messages

- *Refusals* deny requests or give negative replies while working to maintain goodwill.

- *Complaints* use a professional tone to describe a problem and how you expect it to be corrected.

- *Adjustments* tell customers how your company intends to redress a complaint and apologize if the company is at fault.

- *Collections* work to preserve the customer relationship while collecting payment on an overdue account.

Writing International Correspondence

- Determine whether to use English only or include a translated version.

- Adjust for cultural preferences in pacing and organizing ideas.

- Consider the decision-making style of your recipient's culture.

- Avoid using humor and slang.

- Read the letter aloud for ambiguity and confusing sentence structure.

- Check for appropriate forms of dates, times, and measurements.

ON THE WEB

For an online quiz on writing business correspondence, go to Chapter 9, bedfordstmartins.com/ writingthatworks

ON THE WEB

For additional exercises, go to Chapter 9, bedfordstmartins.com/ writingthatworks

Exercises

1. Find an article on the importance of workplace communication and either photocopy it or attach it to an e-mail to your instructor. Write a cover letter or an e-mail message to your instructor that describes why the article is interesting or helpful to you. Review both cover letters, in this chapter, and e-mail, in Chapter 8, Understanding the Principles of Business Communication, before you send the message.

2. The following situations require different types of correspondence. Read *a* through *e*, and then write the letters, memos, or e-mail messages assigned by your instructor, using the proper format for each.

   a. You are writing a letter requesting a free booklet that explains how college students can apply for scholarships to study abroad. Address the letter to Nancy

Reibold, the executive director of the Global Initiative Center at 1012 Third Avenue, New York, NY 10021. You learned about this booklet when you were surfing the Web and came upon the Global Initiative Center Web site.

b. Assume that you are Nancy Reibold and you received the request for the booklet. You are out of copies at the moment, however, because you have received more requests than anticipated. You expect to receive more copies within two weeks. Write a response to the inquiry, explaining these circumstances. Tell the reader that you will send the booklet, titled "Study Abroad," as soon as you can—and offer the alternative of downloading a document that you will make available at your Web site.

c. You are Nancy Reibold's assistant at the Global Initiative Center, and you are both angry. You have just received 10,000 copies of the booklet from the Jones Printing Company, 105 East Summit Street, New Brunswick, NJ 08910. When you opened the carton, you discovered each booklet is missing several pages. This is the second printing mistake made by Jones Printing, and the shipment is late as well, even though Robert Mason, the sales representative, had promised that you would have no problems this time. Nancy Reibold wants to "get this problem corrected immediately." Write a complaint letter to Robert Mason for Ms. Reibold to sign.

d. Assume that you are Robert Mason. You have received the complaint letter about the printing mistake. After checking, you discover that the booklets sent to the Global Initiative Center had been subcontracted to another printing firm (ILM Printing Company) because of the backlog at Jones. You know that Jones Printing will not be billed for the booklets if you return them to ILM Printing within five working days. You decide that you must write an adjustment letter to Ms. Reibold quickly, asking her to return the booklets.

e. Assume that you are Robert Mason. Send a convincing, detailed memo to J. R. Jones, your boss and president of Jones Printing, recommending that ILM Printing Company not be used for future subcontracting work.

3. You manage Sunny River Resort. Charles James, director of the Sunny River Business League, has requested the free use of your lodge for a two-day staff meeting. You'd like the business league to use your meeting room, but you have a problem: You charge any group $1,500 per day to use the room. You can't afford to give it away. The room has a number of fixed and variable costs required to clean, pay for lighting and air-conditioning, and supply and repair equipment. Also, what might happen if others knew you had provided the room at no cost? Write a letter to Mr. James selling him on the idea of using your lodge while holding to the $1,500 fee. Use tact, a positive tone, and persuasive details.

4. You are the manager of Hamon's Fine Clothing. Dr. Klaus Müller, a busy cardiac surgeon, has purchased two suits (total $1,578) from you and is six months overdue in paying for them despite several standard form notices. You'll now need to start a series of collection letters, but you want to make the pace slow. Dr. Müller is highly respected in the community. Write a series of collection letters, spacing them appropriately (date the first letter January 4).

5. You are the membership director of a fitness center that caters to professional women. You decide to bring in additional revenue by offering personal training sessions at $90 per hour and hire three fitness instructors who have been certified as personal trainers by the Aerobics and Fitness Association of America.

Unfortunately, clients have been slow to sign up. Write a sales letter to existing members, announcing your fitness center's personal training program. In addition to convincing your readers of the benefits of personal training, the letter should introduce the trainers, describe their backgrounds and interests, and emphasize the extensive training they received in their certification workshops. Their training includes the following:

- Anatomy and kinesiology
- Fitness-assessment testing procedures (including skin-fold caliper measuring and sit-up, reach, and abdominal strength tests)
- Weight management and nutrition for the average person as well as those with special medical needs
- Motivation

6. Imagine that the sales letter in Exercise 5 worked well and many people signed up with the three trainers, especially C. J., who really knows how to motivate people. However, a rumor spreads through the fitness center that she isn't certified, and members begin to complain about paying $90 an hour for an uncertified trainer. You check with a source at the Aerobics and Fitness Association of America who confirms that C. J. never completed the certification workshop. Write an adjustment letter to the members who scheduled personal training sessions with C. J. You'll want to consider that C. J. has a loyal following, but your fitness center's credibility is at risk. What solution can you offer that might appease C. J.'s clients and keep your fitness center's credibility intact?

7. You are Mr. Henry Coleman of Abbott Office Products, who received the letter in Figure 9–12. Write a memo to R. P. McMurphy, vice president of engineering (with a copy to Pat Smith, director of marketing), recommending improvements in the check sorter (or another office system of your choice). Collect facts by visiting a local office-systems store or examining its catalog.

8. You have recently purchased a local high-end camera store and wish to build your business. You have a mailing list of former customers, but many of them were unhappy with the previous owner's products and service. You would like to win them back. You specialize in the highest-quality digital and single-lens reflex (SLR) cameras as well as accessories. The shop is also an authorized repair service for Nikon and Sony cameras and lenses. Your partner is highly qualified as a photographer and is an expert in digital imaging for commercial and Web applications. The community you serve is relatively affluent, but the former owner's reputation included overcharging customers and refusing to service what he sold. Your store is located on East Capitol Drive near a variety of appliance stores and restaurants, and a chain electronics store that sells cameras but is not known for quality service. You believe that satisfied customers will improve your business. Write a sales letter, addressed to former customers, effectively promoting your services. Plan this letter as the basis for other promotional materials.

9. Eight years ago, you opened Tiny Tots Day Care with six children, and it has grown to a capacity of 65 children. Its reputation is so high that there is a waiting list of 78 children. As the director and owner of the center, you now face a problem that you have never before encountered. You must expel a child from the center. You need to write a letter to Mr. and Mrs. Brady, telling them that their four-year-old son, Brett, is being expelled from Tiny Tots. Since Brett entered your center, things

haven't been the same. This child is not able to get along with other children. In his two months at Tiny Tots, he has bitten six children (causing one child to require stitches); kicked a teacher; and regularly scratched, hit, and pulled hair. Several parents have threatened to pull their children out of your center if Brett does not leave. Despite several conferences with Brett's parents, who seem reasonable and concerned about their son, you have observed no changes in his behavior. Write the letter to the Bradys, following the pointers for a refusal letter. Remember that this is the Bradys' only child, and choose your words carefully.

10. Prepare an e-mail message to inform a group of international customers of the following: Your company's newsletter will now be delivered electronically, by e-mail, and will be updated monthly instead of bimonthly. Customers who wish to receive the print version of the newsletter will be charged an annual handling fee of $30. New items listed in the newsletter can be ordered at your company's Web site at a 10 percent discount. Customers need to inform the company if they wish to cancel their subscriptions to the newsletter. Be sure to present these changes positively—with your customers' point of view in mind. Refer to Chapter 8, Writing E-mail and Instant Messages (page 295), and Writing International Correspondence (page 343) in this chapter.

11. Draft an inquiry letter to Mr. José Espinosa of the Spanish Tourist Bureau in Madrid, Spain, asking for information about work opportunities in Spain. Explain that you are interested in relocating to Spain after you graduate. To draft the letter, first gather information about both the proper protocol and the format of the letter. With the approval of your instructor, ask an instructor at your college who teaches Spanish (and would understand the form and protocol of such a letter) to comment on the appropriateness of the letter you have drafted.

Collaborative Classroom Projects

ON THE WEB

For more collaborative classroom projects, go to Chapter 9, bedfordstmartins.com/ writingthatworks

1. Form groups of five or fewer members. Your company, an office-supply business, has just mistakenly sent a letter to all your customers offering a 20 percent discount off the total of their next order. The letter was supposed to have offered a 20 percent discount off the most expensive item in their next order. After receiving input from all appropriate departments, the company president has decided the business cannot afford to grant the overall 20 percent discount. You have been instructed to draft a letter to your customers explaining the mistake and clarifying that they will be allowed to take 20 percent off only the most expensive item, not the entire order. Your company president asks that you appeal to your customers' vested interest in your company's ability to keep prices competitive and advises you to ask for their understanding of the error. Appoint a team leader and, as a group, take no more than 20 minutes to brainstorm the points you want to include in the letter. During the next 20 minutes, draft your letters individually. As a group, select one letter that best represents your group's ideas.

2. Your class has been asked to organize a three-hour workshop on business writing for your university's continuing-education department. As a class, you have discussed this workshop with your instructor and decided that because of your course loads, your jobs, and other outside responsibilities you are unable to

volunteer to conduct a successful workshop at this time. Appoint a class leader or facilitator and a class recorder. As a group, draft a letter to the Department of Continuing Education explaining why your class cannot help. Brainstorm to develop a list of points to include in your letter. Open the letter with an explanation of the context, introducing the subject and establishing the tone. Then explain the facts, lead logically to your refusal, and conclude with goodwill to retain a positive relationship with the department. (Keep in mind that your class's refusal creates a sensitive situation for your instructor, who will be working again with the Department of Continuing Education.) After you have completed your letter, your instructor may want to give the class feedback.

ON THE WEB

For extra research projects, go to Chapter 9, **bedfordstmartins** **.com/writingthatworks**

■ Research Projects

1. Choose one of the following topics:
   - How to write effective sales letters (or, generally, how to write persuasively)
   - How to write effective refusal letters ("bad news" or "negative messages")
   - How to write effective complaint letters
   - How to respond to complaint letters

   Find at least three recent articles on your topic in an academic journal or periodical, such as the *Journal of Business Communication* or *Business Communication Quarterly*. (Your reference librarian can suggest indexes or abstracting services that will help you find articles.) Write a brief critical analysis of what you find. Compare and contrast the articles and, in conclusion, give your opinion on the article with the most helpful advice. Support your analysis with examples from the articles.

2. Assume you work for a company that is expanding to include several international branches. Research and write an informal investigative report on cultural differences in workplace communication: slang expressions and technical jargon, methods of addressing people, punctuation marks, colors, references to body parts, physical gestures, technology symbols, cultural symbols, or other aspects of written communication. You may choose one culture to compare to the United States in great detail or more than one culture to compare on different points. Before beginning your research and writing, determine your audience, your purpose, and the scope of your report.

3. Imagine that your company is eager to sell its new nonlinear video editing system internationally, starting in Canada, then moving on to Switzerland. Your marketing director, who is very industrious, has already created business cards, brochures, and other marketing materials and planned a public relations campaign that will launch in six weeks. Unfortunately, she did not do enough research into Canadian business practices to know that the country is officially bilingual and the province of Quebec requires that there be a French translation for all promotional materials. You suspect there may be similar issues with the Swiss campaign. Address the situation by doing the following:
   a. Research official language requirements and business etiquette in Canada and Switzerland. A good starting point is Executive Planet at <www.executiveplanet .com/>.

b. Search the Web for professional translation services and find a rough estimate for the cost of translating an eight-page brochure into French on a rush basis. Find out also what additional translations for the Swiss campaign might cost.

c. Write a memo that commends the marketing director for working hard on the project but also describes the current translation issue. Being aware of your tone, advise the director of the need to thoroughly research any countries the system will be marketed in before creating final material, and give two or three examples of other issues she may find with regard to doing business in Canada and Switzerland. Advise the director to quickly have the materials translated into French by a professional translating service and describe how much money will be allocated from the marketing department's budget for this service and why (again, be aware of your tone). Conclude your memo with a form of goodwill that encourages the director to be as industrious as she has been, but to also be aware of cultural differences and the impact they can have on companies trying to do business internationally.

4. You work for a small, budget-conscious company of fewer than 50 employees. Your supervisor has asked you to investigate one of the items listed below for possible purchase by your company. Your supervisor's primary consideration is cost. Using the Web, review information provided by at least three online vendors about the product or service you are interested in. E-mail the vendors to obtain any further information you may need. Which vendor offers the best value? Write a persuasive memo to your supervisor that explains your recommendation for the product or service. Include key points from your research, and support your recommendation with specific details. Possible products and services to investigate include the following:

- A wireless communication system
- A company vehicle (for purchase or lease)
- A computer software package
- A security system
- An accounting or another business-related service

10 | Writing Informal Reports

AT A GLANCE: Informal Reports

The successful operation of many organizations depends on reports that are either circulated within the organization or submitted to customers, clients, and others. This chapter discusses report-writing strategies (see pages 358–360) and the most common types of informal reports:

- Progress and periodic reports / 361
- Investigative reports / 365
- Trouble reports / 370
- Trip reports / 373
- Test reports / 374

What is a report? Although the term is used to refer to hundreds of different types of written communications, it can be defined as an organized presentation of factual information prepared for a specific audience.

Reports fall into two broad categories: formal and informal. Formal reports, described in detail in Chapter 11, Writing Formal Reports, generally grow out of projects that require many months of work, large sums of money, and the collaboration of many people. They may run several hundred pages and usually include a table of contents and other devices to aid the reader because of their length and scope of coverage. Informal reports, however, generally run from a few paragraphs to a few pages and include only the essential elements of a report: an introduction, a body, conclusions, and, when appropriate, recommendations. Because of their brevity and limited scope, informal reports are customarily written as letters (for recipients outside a company) or as memos, e-mails, or intranet postings (for recipients within an organization).

▇ Planning and Writing Informal Reports

Informal reports often describe specific incidents, note the progress of ongoing activities or projects, or summarize the results of a completed project or investigation. They may also recommend follow-up work that should be performed based on the conditions described.

Considering Audience

As with all workplace writing, first consider the makeup of your audience. An informal report is almost always written for a specific small group of readers (or a single reader)—usually at their request. As a result, readers will likely be familiar with the subject of the report, making it easier for you to determine how much background information to provide and how much specialized or technical language to use. Note, for example, that the writer of the trouble report in Figure 10–4 on page 371 assumes that the reader is familiar with "circle of safety" checks. Without such knowledge, the reader would be unable to interpret the writer's recommendations.

◆ For additional guidance on audience analysis, see pages 6–7 in Chapter 1, Assessing Audience and Purpose.

Collecting Information

For a report to be effective, you need to include all the information that will meet your objective (such as describing the status of an office remodeling project or explaining the need to upgrade a staff training program) and address your reader's needs (such as keeping a project on schedule or having enough data to make a decision). To achieve these goals, keep notes through every stage of the activity on which you will be reporting. Otherwise, you may have trouble obtaining or trying to remember information when the time comes to write the report.

◆ For more on note-taking, see pages 174–176 in Chapter 6, Researching Your Subject.

◆ For more on organizing information, see Chapter 2, Organizing Your Information.

The purpose of taking notes is to record, in an abbreviated form, the background information that will go into your report. Be careful, however, not to make your notes so brief that you forget what you intended when you wrote them. Once you have prepared and gathered your notes, organize them into a sequence that makes sense from the perspective of your objective and audience. When you are working with an outline, add your notes to the appropriate places to flesh it out.

ON THE WEB

For more help with writing informal reports, see Chapter 10, bedfordstmartins.com/ writingthatworks

▶ CONSIDERING AUDIENCE AND PURPOSE

Planning and Evaluating Informal Reports

- Who is the audience for your report?
- What specifically have your readers requested?
- How knowledgeable are your readers about the topic?
- Have you selected the right format—e-mail, memo, or letter—for your readers?
- Have you framed the topic for your audience and provided any necessary background information in your introduction?
- Do your graphics depict the findings accurately and clearly for your intended audience?
- Does the body of the report present an organized account of the topic? Is it sufficient in scope so that your audience can understand and interpret your findings, conclusions, and recommendations?

Parts of the Informal Report

Most informal reports have three or four main parts: the introduction, the body, conclusions, and recommendations. For routine reports, the introduction may be replaced by an opening that simply announces the subject—"Monthly Customer Services, June 2010." Likewise, the conclusion may consist of a closing statement or sentence signaling the end of the report—"If you wish to discuss the summary of sales prospects for June, please contact me directly."

Introduction

The introduction announces the subject of the report, explains its purpose, and, when appropriate, names anybody who assisted with or provided information for the report. It may describe the scope of information covered, any limitations of the topic, or the reason for the amount of detail presented. A trip report, for example, could note the facilities or customers visited, the reason for the visits, and an explanation for any delays or problems encountered. It may also provide any essential background information about the subject of the report. The introduction may also concisely preview any conclusions, findings, or recommendations made in the report. An overview is useful because it saves your readers time by providing essential information at a glance and helps focus their thinking for the discussion that follows.

◆ *For a discussion of openings and closings, see pages 84–87 in Chapter 3, Writing the Draft.*

Body

The body presents a clearly organized account of the report's subject—the results of a market survey, the findings of a test carried out, the status of a construction project, and so on. The amount of detail you include in the body depends on your objective, the complexity of your subject, and your readers' familiarity with the subject. This information is frequently supported by tables, graphs, drawings, and other visuals to clarify ideas and concepts in ways that words alone cannot, as well as to save space.

◆ *For detailed advice on creating and using visuals, see Chapter 7, Designing Effective Documents and Visuals.*

Conclusions and Recommendations

The conclusion summarizes your findings and tells readers what you think the significance of those findings may be. The conclusion may make a judgment or prediction, issue a call for action, or suggest ideas for further action. It should not go outside the scope of topics discussed in the report.

Recommendations, when included, are sometimes combined with conclusions in one section at the end of the report. In this section, you recommend a course of action that you believe is warranted by your findings. Recommendations can cover a broad range of options, from suggesting new safety procedures based on findings about an accident, to developing new products or marketing campaigns based on consumer surveys, to hiring new employees as a result of growing business.

VOICES IN THE WORKPLACE

Focusing on Accuracy to Avoid Costly and Dangerous Mistakes

David Noyes, a project manager at HLM Design–Heely International architecture firm, writes informal reports frequently and approaches them systematically:

"First, I include the title of the project; the date; and the names, titles, and contact information of the participants. Next, I summarize the information as clearly and concisely as possible—if my reports were to be misunderstood, they could lead to potentially expensive and dangerous mistakes. I also make sure that my technical points are absolutely accurate. Finally, I edit my reports so that they are never longer than two or three pages—otherwise, people won't take the time to read them!"

Types of Informal Reports

Because there are so many different types of informal reports and because the categories sometimes overlap (a trip report, for example, might also be a progress report), it would be unrealistic to attempt to study or try to itemize every type. However, it is possible to become familiar with report writing in general and to examine some of the most frequently written kinds of informal reports in the workplace:

- Progress reports
- Periodic reports
- Investigative reports
- Trouble reports
- Trip reports
- Test reports

Progress and Periodic Reports

Both progress reports and periodic reports are written to inform decision makers about the status of work performed over the course of an ongoing project. The chief difference between them is when they are written. The progress report is issued at certain milestones during a project. Construction and manufacturing projects, for example, must be done in stages: Whether the project involves adding a sunroom to a private residence or building a deep-sea oil-drilling rig, it follows a coordinated sequence. *Progress reports* describe in detail the status of activities at each stage in the sequence: work in progress, work completed, special problems or delays, costs, worker availability, and anything else that affects the schedule for completing the project. *Periodic reports*, sometimes called status reports, detail the status of an ongoing project at regular intervals—weekly, monthly, quarterly. Both types of reports may be required for work being performed within an organization or by an outside contractor or consultant.

Progress Reports

The purpose of a progress report is to keep others—usually management or a client—informed of the status of a project. In answering various questions (Is the project on schedule? running smoothly? within its budget?), the report lets readers know precisely what work has been completed, what work remains to be done, and the reasons for any possible delays. Often the report will include recommendations for changes in procedure or will propose new courses of action. Progress reports are generally prepared when a particular stage of a project is reached. For a companywide computer-network upgrade, for example, the significant stages could include after the electrical power enhancements have been completed, the hardware and software have been installed and tested, and the employees trained.

The projects most likely to generate progress reports are long-term and fairly complex. The construction of a building, the development of a new product, the opening of a branch office in another part of town, and a major redesign of a company's Web site are examples of such projects. Progress reports are frequently required in the contract for a project that will take weeks, months, or longer to complete.

Progress reports allow managers and clients to keep track of the project and to make any necessary adjustments in assignments, schedules, and budget allocations while the project is under way. Progress reports can make it easier for management to schedule the arrival of equipment and supplies so that the right personnel are available when needed. Such reports can, on occasion, avert crises. If a hospital had planned to open a new wing in February, for instance, but a shortage of wallboard caused a two-month lag in construction, a progress report would alert hospital managers to the delay in time for them to make alternative plans.

Many projects, of course, require more than one progress report. In general, the more complicated the project, the more frequently management will want to review it. All reports issued during the life of a project should be submitted in the same format to make it easier for readers to recognize at a glance where they need to focus their attention. Progress reports sent outside the company are normally prepared as letters (Figure 10–1); those circulated within a company can be written as memos.

The first in a series of reports should identify the project in detail and specify what materials will be used and what procedures will be followed throughout the project. Later reports in the series contain only a transitional introduction that briefly reviews the work discussed in the previous report. The body of the reports should describe in detail the current status of the project. Every report should end with any conclusions or recommendations—for instance, alterations in schedule, materials, or procedures.

Hobard Construction Company
9032 Salem Avenue
Lubbock, TX 79406

www.hobardcc.com
Phone (808) 769-0832
Fax (808) 769-5327

August 16, 2010

Walter M. Wazuski
County Administrator
109 Grand Avenue
Manchester, NH 03103

Subject: Progress Report for July 31, 2010

Subject line identi-fies topic

Dear Mr. Wazuski:

The renovation of the County Courthouse is progressing on schedule and within budget. Although the cost of certain materials is higher than our original bid indicated, we expect to complete the project without exceeding the estimated costs because the speed with which the project is being completed will reduce overall labor expenses.

Project status summary

Costs

Materials used to date have cost $178,600, and labor costs have been $258,000 (including some subcontracted plumbing). Our estimate for the remainder of the materials is $59,000; remaining labor costs should not exceed $400,000.

Work Completed

Detailed status of project

As of July 31, we finished installation of the circuit-breaker panels and meters, level-one service outlets, and all subfloor wiring. The upgrading of the courtroom, the upgrading of the records-storage room, and the replacement of the air-conditioning units are in the preliminary stages.

Work Schedule

We have scheduled the upgrading of the courtroom to take place from August 27 to October 5, the upgrading of the records-storage room from October 6 to November 12, and the replacement of the air-conditioning units from November 15 to December 17. We see no difficulty in having the job finished by the scheduled date of December 21.

Sincerely yours,

Tran Nuguélen

Tran Nuguélen, Project Engineer
<ntran@hobardcc.com>

Figure 10–1   Progress Report (Letter to a Client)

In the example shown in Figure 10–1, a contractor reports to the county administrator on progress in renovating the county courthouse. Notice that the emphasis is on meeting specified costs and schedules.

@

DIGITAL TIPS: Creating Styles and Templates

In most word-processing programs, you can create styles—sets of formatting characteristics for text elements such as headings, paragraphs, and lists—that allow you to automate much of the work of formatting your report. Once you have specified your styles, save them as a template and use it each time you create a report.

For step-by-step instructions, see bedfordstmartins.com/writingthatworks and select *Digital Tips*, Creating Styles and Templates.

Periodic Reports

Periodic reports are issued at regular intervals—daily, weekly, monthly, quarterly, annually—rather than at the stages of a project where significant milestones were reached. Employees routinely submit status reports (also called *activity reports*) to their supervisors about their ongoing projects.

Quarterly and annual reports, because of their scope, are usually presented as formal reports. Most other kinds of periodic reports seldom run longer than a page or two. Like progress reports, these shorter reports are most often written as memos or e-mail messages within an organization and as letters when sent to clients and customers outside an organization.

Many kinds of routine information that must be reported periodically—and that do not require a narrative explanation—can be recorded on forms, entered into networked computer databases or spreadsheets, or printed as graphs or tables in the body of a written report. Examples include human resources, accounting, and inventory records; production and distribution figures; sales numbers; and travel and task logs.

DESIGNING YOUR DOCUMENT
Formatting Progress and Periodic Reports

- For internal distribution, format the report as a memo or an e-mail message.
- If the report will be sent to clients or others outside your organization, format it as a letter.
- Use headings to organize the contents of your report.
- Keep narrative information brief and easy to skim.
- Present routine and numerical data in tables or graphs.
- Create a template and use the same format—headings, tables, organization, and so on—for each consecutive report in a series.

One- and two-page periodic reports can be organized in a variety of ways. The standard sequence of introduction, body, and conclusions and recommendations may serve your needs. Otherwise, modify the organizational pattern to suit your reader's reporting requirements. Once you have established a format and an organization, create a template and use it consistently for each consecutive report.

The sample periodic report shown in Figure 10–2 on pages 366–367 is sent monthly from a company's district sales manager to the regional sales manager either with a brief cover memo or as an attachment to a brief e-mail message. Notice that there is no traditional opening and closing, both of which are superfluous because the report is routine; that is, the report goes to the same person every month and covers the same topics. It also goes to a high-level manager who receives many such reports each month, so he or she does not have time to read unnecessary narrative. Because this report is written to someone completely familiar with the background details of the projects discussed, the district sales manager can write a spare narrative with many shorthand references to equipment, customers, and project status. For example, the writer mentions a "best and final" presentation to Watsorg rather than writing that Rockport, his company, has presented its final sales proposal to Watsorg, Inc., for equipment and services. The writer need not describe the details of the project because the regional sales manager is already familiar with them. Such an abbreviated narrative is appropriate for the intended reader.

For a discussion of the scope and format of formal reports, see Chapter 11, Writing Formal Reports.

Investigative Reports

Investigative reports are most often written in response to a request for information. You might be asked, for instance, to check the range of prices that companies charge for a particular item or service, to conduct an opinion survey among customers, to study alternative procedures for performing a specific operation, to review business trends in your line of work, and so on. You would then present your findings in an investigative report. In law enforcement, investigative reports result from the analysis of traffic accidents, crimes, and related activities.

Investigative reports are usually prepared as *memos* if written within an organization and as *letters* if written by an outside consultant. They may also be written in the narrative section of routine forms.

The results of long, complex investigations are usually written as formal reports. For memo and letter reports, open with a brief introductory summary of the information you were seeking, any relevant background as to why the investigation was necessary, and who requested it. Then, in the body of the memo or letter, describe the extent of or method used for your investigation. Finally, state your findings and any recommendations based on the findings.

For guidance on writing and formatting letters and memos, see Chapter 8, Understanding the Principles of Business Communication.

In the example shown in Figure 10–3 on pages 368–369, a store manager has investigated three alternative ways of reducing shoplifting in his store and recommended the one most suitable for the store's size and budget.

For formal reports, see Chapter 11, Writing Formal Reports.

Rockport
Customer Services
Monthly Report
June 2010

*Frequency
of report*

Mid-Atlantic District

*Standardized
heading*

Current personnel:	13
Changes this month:	None
Awards/relocations/promotions:	• Alonzo Berg attended the Field Business Conference.
	• Dawon Washington was honored by his peers for superior customer satisfaction at Southwest Utility.
Human resources issues:	None

*Routine categories
of information—
narrative introduc-
tion unnecessary*

*Project status
grouped into
standard categories*

Product Revenue

*Numerical infor-
mation formatted
as a table*

Customer	Equipment	Maint. $	Notes
Southwest Utility	6650–200	$6,200/mo	None
Demeter, Inc.	SVR	$800/mo	Installing a new SVR in February
Barg Aerospace	6650–900	$10,000	Installation charge
Barg Aerospace	6650–900	$9,000/mo	New monthly maintenance (2 years)

Top Prospects

Customer	Service	Revenue	Odds	Comments
Herndon Bank	PPR	$5,600	100%	LAR Services
Southwest Utility	PPR	$10,000	100%	Configuration
MacDonalds	PPR	$10,000	100%	Maintenance
MacDonalds	PPR	$6,900	100%	Conversion
Reece Corp.	PPR	$13,000	100%	Upgrades
Reece Corp.	PPR	$2,300	100%	Maintenance
Gabbard Mfg.	PPR	$25,000	80%	Cynergy Installation
Gabbard Mfg.	ERCAR	$95,000	50%	ERCAR Upgrades

Competitive Customer or Marketplace News

• Cynergy, Inc.'s new maintenance offering is not going over well with some customers. We should be able to take advantage of this.

• Watsorg's decision will be announced July 26–31. This is for $18 to $20 million, going either to us or to Cynergy. The problem is that we finished our "best and final" presentation in the first week of February, and Watsorg gave Cynergy an

Figure 10–2 Periodic Report (continued)

Monthly Report, Mid-Atlantic District   June 2010

extension to the end of the month. Dragging this out increases Cynergy's odds of winning. However, the last word is that the negotiations are not going well with Cynergy, so we are keeping our fingers crossed.

- AREDOT is installing the largest Saki tape library system in the world. The sales rep said that Saki had been working with a company to develop a "virtual tape system" when Embry was sold to Jordan. This resulted in Jordan not getting the contract.

- Charlestown Customer Services met with a CARL team director from Columbus, Ohio, to discuss future services with CARL. He is considering Rockport as the prime contractor for all necessary services in Charlestown. He will base his decision on the cost analysis.

Significant Wins and Accomplishments

- Hector Martinez convinced Barg Aerospace to acquire two additional 6650A–900s from us on a rental basis with a two-year maintenance contract worth $9,000 per month per machine. The installation team has installed the second 900 and will install the third in the coming weeks.

- Charlestown Customer Services completed installation of a Cynergy 2063 and a Rockport 1006 at Ft. Lee, Virginia. We partnered with Rathbone Corporation to win the business.

Product Issues

Secard performance issues have continued from last month. We applied new code with high hopes, but no improvement was noted by the customer. Currently, ERT traces are running to gather more information. The customer is getting very concerned with this issue, and they are our only Secard customer in Charlestown.

2

Figure 10–2   Periodic Report (continued)

Green Department Stores
Memo

To: William Bernardi, Regional Manager
From: Julius Chernoff, Department Manager *JC*
Date: September 24, 2010
Subject: Shoplifting at Store E-5150

Introduction and background

As we have discussed over the last several months, shoplifting at Store E-5150 has increased since the store opened one year ago this month. Although we have budgeted $30,000 a year for shoplifting losses, our monthly inventory check shows that we have lost $47,800 in merchandise this year. The loss was especially evident during the summer months. It is time to take action to reverse this trend.

Section heading and overview of options

Proposed Solutions

My staff and I have researched several options for minimizing shoplifting in our store. They include hiring security guards, using strategically placed security cameras in the store, and using undercover employees. In investigating options available to us, we considered effectiveness, convenience, and cost.

Security Guards

First option investigated, with findings

We first considered hiring security guards. I met with the president of Hall Security on July 26. Hall Security is a local company that has been in business ten years. I also talked to other store managers in the area who have contracts with Hall Security—all are very pleased with the service and its effectiveness. They believe that the presence of uniformed security guards in their stores discourages theft. The managers surveyed report shoplifting reduction rates of from 50 to 70 percent. I can provide you with detailed data from these interviews at your request.

If we decide to have one security guard on duty during all store hours, we would pay a flat monthly rate of $4,300. One guard on duty from 4 p.m. until 10 p.m. daily, our busiest hours, would cost $2,100 a month. We are not considering the option of a night guard because we have not had any problems with break-in burglaries after hours.

Security Cameras

Second option investigated, with findings

We next considered the use of security cameras. The cameras provide a record of thefts in progress and make prosecuting shoplifters much easier once they're caught. The technicians from TSC, Inc., a camera service company, visited our store on August 6. They studied the floor plan to determine the most effective placement of cameras throughout the store. They recommend six cameras placed so that we have a view of the whole store at all times. We would need to purchase a single

Figure 10–3   Investigative Report (Memo with Recommendations) (continued)

William Bernardi   2   September 24, 2010

monitor that would display each camera's view on a rotational basis every ten seconds. The monitor would be located in the store manager's office where I or, in my absence, someone I designate, can observe activity throughout the store's retail space. The videotapes can be kept for a week and then recorded over.

TSC, Inc., would install the system and train our employees to operate it. TSC, Inc., also provides a five-year on-site service warranty for the cameras and monitor. They make service calls to the store during business hours within four hours of being called. Total cost, including installation, will be $7,500. We were impressed with the knowledge, experience, and professionalism of the TSC representatives. They provided data for stores comparable to ours that showed an average 60 to 75 percent drop in the incidence of shoplifting after cameras were installed. I called several store managers where the cameras are in use, and they verified these results.

Impressions of second option

Undercover Employees

The third option examined is the use of undercover employees. This option involves having store employees who pose as customers as they stroll through the store monitoring customers for shoplifting. We estimate that this option would require two employees each shift. They would alternate between their regular duties, such as stocking shelves, and performing inventory-control tasks. If we also employ security guards, these two units could work in conjunction to help discourage theft.

Third option investigated, with findings

However, the option has some risks associated with it. It would require that our employees receive training in the legal rights of customers and could potentially put our employees at risk in encounters with criminals. Hall Security can provide training over a one-week period at a cost of $1,500 per employee.

Risks associated with option

Recommendations

Section heading and recommendations based on findings

After completing our research on these possibilities for theft prevention, my staff and I believe that the best option is the installation of security cameras. After comparing the cost of the system with the amount of merchandise we are losing, we believe that the expense is worth the investment. Once the system is installed, there will be negligible expense in its use and maintenance. Our research shows that theft has declined in more than 90 percent of the stores that have had security cameras installed. Pending our approval, TSC, Inc., can install the system in four days. Once it is installed, we would evaluate the effectiveness of the system on a monthly basis, and I would provide you with a monthly status report. I look forward to your assessment of this recommendation.

Figure 10–3   Investigative Report (Memo with Recommendations) (continued)

Trouble Reports

Incidents involving personal injuries, accidents, and work stoppages (those caused by equipment failures, worker illnesses, and so on) occur in many industrial and construction settings. Problematic episodes may also occur in health-care, social-work, and criminal-justice settings. Every such incident must be reported so that management can determine its cause and take any necessary steps to prevent or reduce the impact of a recurrence. A trouble report—also called an accident report or an incident report, depending on the situation—is the record of an accident, mechanical breakdown, medical emergency, or personnel confrontation in an institution. The report may be used by the police or by a court of law in establishing guilt or liability.

The trouble report is usually a written memo by the person in charge of the site where the incident occurred, addressed to his or her superior. (Some organizations have printed forms for specific types of trouble reports, which include a section for the writer to describe in detail what happened.) Figure 10–4 shows a trouble report written by a safety officer after interviewing all the people involved in a work-site accident.

ON THE WEB

To access guidelines and forms for incident reports prepared by the Occupational Safety and Health Administration (OSHA), go to Chapter 10, bedfordstmartins.com/ writingthatworks

ETHICS NOTE

Because insurance claims, workers' compensation awards, and even lawsuits may hinge on the information contained in a trouble report, be sure to include precise times, dates, locations, treatment of injuries, names of any witnesses, and any other crucial information. Be thorough and accurate in your analysis of the problem and support any judgments or conclusions with facts. Be objective: Always use a neutral tone and avoid assigning blame. If you speculate about the cause of the problem, make clear to your reader that you are speculating.

Consolidated Energy, Inc.

To: Marvin Lundquist, Vice President
        Administrative Services
From: Kalo Katarlan, Safety Officer   *KK*
        Field Service Operations
Date: August 29, 2010
Subject: Field Service Employee Accident on August 9, 2010

An Accident Review was conducted on Wednesday, August 18, 2010, at the Reed Service Center. The attendees were as follows:

Injured Representative:	John Markley
Union Representative:	Harry Hartsock
Employee's Supervisor:	Carl Timmerinski
Safety Officer:	Kalo Katarlan
Safety Officer, Field Service Operations:	Marie Sonora
Date of Accident:	August 9, 2010
Days of Lost Time:	2

How accident was evaluated—employee interviews

Accident Summary

While John Markley loaded branches into the bed of the truck at the site of a rewiring job on German Road, a piece broke off in his right hand and struck his right eye. Following is a description of the accident.

What happened, who was involved, what injury resulted

Accident Details

1. Prior to the accident, Chico Ruiz was stringing new wire at the site, and John checked with Chico about the materials he wanted for framing a pole. Some trees had been trimmed in the area, and John offered to help remove some of the debris by loading it into his pickup truck.
2. John's right eye was struck by a piece of tree branch. John had just undergone laser surgery on his right eye on Friday, August 6, to reattach his cornea. At the time of the accident, he was not wearing protective eyeware.
3. John immediately covered his right eye with his hand, and Chico Ruiz gave him a paper towel with ice to cover his eye and help ease the pain.
4. After the initial pain subsided, John got into his truck and began to back up to return to the Service Center. Chico reminded John about the pole trailer parked behind his truck and then returned to the crews he was supervising. John continued backing up, but did not see the trailer behind him because his visibility was blocked by the tree debris in his truck bed.

Events listed in order of occurrence

Figure 10–4   Trouble Report (Memo with Recommendations) (continued)

Lundquist   2   August 29, 2010

5. When John struck the trailer, his head struck the back window of the truck, shattering the glass. He was not wearing a safety helmet.

6. John returned to the Service Center to report the accident to his supervisor. However, because he had pieces of glass inside his clothes and on his neck, he decided to go home to shower and change clothes. He also used eyedrops prescribed to him after his surgery to thoroughly wash his injured right eye.

7. The next day, August 10, John went to Downtown Worker's Care because he was experiencing headaches. He was diagnosed with a bruised eyeball and eyelid. The headaches were caused by the impact to his head when it hit the rear window of his truck.

8. On Friday, August 13, John returned to his eye surgeon. Although bruised, his eye was not damaged, and the surgically implanted lens was still in place.

Preventive Measures

To prevent a recurrence of such an accident, the Safety Department will require the following actions in the future:

List of corrective actions

• When working around and moving debris such as tree limbs or branches, all service-crew employees must wear helmets and safety eyewear with side shields.

• Service-crew employees must always consider the possibility of shock for an injured employee. If crew members cannot leave the job site to care for the injured employee, someone on the crew must call for assistance from the Service Center. An injured employee should never be allowed to drive immediately after an accident. The Service Center phone number is printed in each service-crew member's handbook.

• All service-crew employees must conduct a "circle of safety" check around any vehicle before moving it.

Figure 10–4   Trouble Report (Memo with Recommendations) (continued)

WRITER'S CHECKLIST

Writing a Trouble Report

✔ On the *subject line* of your memo, state what you are reporting:

▶ SUBJECT: Personal-Injury Accident in Section A-40.

✔ Write a brief *introductory summary* of the incident.

✔ In the *body* of your memo:

- State exactly when and where the accident, breakdown, emergency, or conflict took place.

- Describe any physical injury or any property damage that occurred.

- Itemize any expenses that resulted from the incident (for example, an injured employee may have missed a number of workdays or an equipment failure may have caused a disruption in service to the company's customers).

- Include precise data on times, dates, location, treatment of injuries, names of any witnesses, and any other crucial information.

✔ In your *conclusion*, provide a detailed analysis of what you believe caused the trouble.

- Avoid condemnation or blame; be thorough, exact, and objective, and support any opinion you offer with facts.

- Mention what was or will be done to correct the conditions that may have led to the incident.

✔ Include your *recommendations* for preventing further incidents (such as increased safety precautions, improved equipment, or the establishment of training programs). If you are speculating on the cause of the accident, make sure that this is clear to the reader.

Evaluating and Revising a Trouble Report

✔ Who is the audience for the report?

✔ Do you need to interview workers or others about the accident or incident?

✔ Are your notes thorough enough to accurately summarize the accident or incident?

✔ Have you organized your thoughts into a concise outline to guide your writing?

✔ Does the introduction state the subject and purpose of the report?

✔ Does the body include sufficient detail to lead the reader to the same findings and conclusions that you present?

✔ Do the findings and conclusions logically follow from the details described in the body?

✔ Do the recommendations make sense based on your conclusions?

Trip Reports

Many companies require or encourage employees to prepare reports on their business trips. A trip report not only provides a permanent record of a business trip and its accomplishments but also enables many employees to benefit from the information that one employee has gained.

A trip report is normally written as a memo or an e-mail message and addressed to an immediate supervisor, as shown in Figure 10–5. On the subject line, give the destination (or purpose) and dates of the trip. Explain the purpose of the trip in a brief introductory summary and note whom or where you visited and what you accomplished. The report should devote a brief section to each major event and may include a heading for each section (you needn't give equal space to each event; instead, elaborate on the more important events). End the report with any appropriate conclusions and recommendations. Finally, if required, attach a record of expenses to the trip report.

ON THE WEB

For an example of an extended trip report, go to Model Documents Gallery, bedfordstmartins.com/ writingthatworks

Test Reports

Test reports, also called laboratory reports when tests are performed in laboratories, record the results of tests and experiments. Normally, those who write test reports do so as a routine part of their work. Tests that form the basis of reports are not limited to any particular occupation; they commonly occur in many fields, from chemistry to fire science, from metallurgy to medical technology, and include studies on cars, blood, mercury thermometers, pudding mixes, smoke detectors—the list goes on. Information collected in testing may be used to upgrade or abandon products or to streamline testing or manufacturing procedures.

Because accuracy is the essential goal of a test report, be sure to take careful notes while you are performing the test. Then state your findings in clear, straightforward language. Use tables, graphs, or illustrations if they will help your readers interpret the findings. Because a test report should be objective, it is one of the few writing formats in which the passive voice is usually more suitable than the active voice. As with other reports, the format in which test reports are prepared depends on the intended audience: letters for customers outside your organization and memos, e-mails, or intranet postings for employees within your organization.

On the subject line, identify the test you are reporting. If the purpose of the test is not obvious to your reader, explain it in the body of the report. Then, if it is helpful to your reader, specify the testing procedures or methodology. You need not give a detailed explanation of how the test was performed, but a summary is usually expected for your reader to have a general idea of the testing methods. Next, present the data—the results of the test. If an interpretation of the results would be useful to your reader, furnish such an analysis in your conclusion. Close the report with any recommendations you are making as a result of the test.

◆ *For guidance in preparing visuals, see Chapter 7, Designing Effective Documents and Visuals.*

◆ *For a discussion of the use of active versus passive voice, see pages 101–102, Chapter 4, Revising the Draft.*

Figure 10–6 on page 377 shows a test report that notes briefly how the test was conducted. Figure 10–7 on page 378 shows a test report that explains in detail how the tests were performed and describes the federal standards on which the testing was based.

Watson Engines

Memorandum

June 14, 2010

To: Jacob Stein, International Service Manager
From: Wilhelm Kurtz, Engine Specialist
Subject: Trouble-Shooting Trip to Garcia Tractor Company, Caracas, Venezuela,
         June 8–11, 2010

Subject line with destination and trip dates

The Problem

Headings separate sections of the report

I visited the Garcia Tractor Company's dealership in Caracas to determine the cause of severe overheating and the loss of power in one of their tractors.

Purpose of the trip

Action Taken

I inspected the tractor's engine to find the cause of the problem and determined that the cooling water in the tractor's Watson engine (serial number L94847U) contained minerals that solidified when the engine temperature exceeded 65°C (149°F), thereby creating a layer of mineral deposits on the walls of the cooling spaces and rendering the engine incapable of rejecting heat. The ultimate result of this problem was the engine's loss of power because of overheating.

Summary of actions

I further inspected the engine to determine whether other parts may have been harmed and discovered that the following lubricated moving parts were damaged.

- The crankshaft and all bearing contact surfaces showed signs of extensive wear, which could have been caused either by breakdown of the lubricating oil's viscosity or by contaminated lubricating oil.

- The engine block was damaged on the seating surface of the number three bearing, which could have been caused by either oil acidification or water condensation.

- The number five main bearing cap was also damaged because of either oil acidification or water condensation.

Recommendations based on actions

- On the rear half of the left camshaft, the lobe that operated the number eight fuel injection pump showed signs of aggravated wear.

- Twenty-one of the twenty-four pushrods were damaged on the surface where they make contact with the cam followers. This damage could have been caused by the breakdown in viscosity of the lubricating oil or by lack of scheduled maintenance.

Figure 10–5   Trip Report (Memo) (continued)   *Source:* Adapted with permission from a report prepared by Johan De Beer of Mitsubishi Engines, N.A.

Page Two   Jacob Stein   June 14, 2010

- Three of the twenty-four cam followers were damaged on the inside cup where they support the pushrods.

Recommendations

I recommend that the following actions be taken:

- The crankshaft should be machined down 0.25 millimeters for the connecting rods and the mains.
- The block and the main bearings should be machined and line bored.
- The damaged camshaft lobe should be sleeved and the damaged part of the camshaft replaced.
- The damaged pushrods and cam followers should be replaced.
- The vibration damper should be remanufactured to prevent heat developed by the engine from solidifying the viscous oil and nullifying the damping action.

I requested a sample of used oil from the engine, but the oil had been drained and discarded before my arrival. I recommend that the oil viscosity be tested after the engine has been operated for several hours.

Suggested Follow-Up

Because Garcia Motors uses many additional Watson engines that potentially could also be damaged, I strongly recommend sending a detailed report of these problems to the client and commissioning a set of Spanish-language maintenance guides for current and future customers in Venezuela.

Figure 10–5   Trip Report (Memo)   (continued)

BIOSPHERICS
Inc.

4928 Wyaconda Road
Rockville, MD 20852
Phone (301) 492-3331
Fax (301) 492-1832
biosphericsinc.com

March 15, 2010

Mr. Luigi Sebastiani, General Manager
Midtown Development Corporation
114 West Jefferson Street
Milwaukee, WI 53201

SUBJECT: Results of Analysis of Soil Samples for Arsenic

Dear Mr. Sebastiani:

The results of our analysis of your soil samples for arsenic showed considerable variation; a high iron content in some of the samples may account for these differences.

Following are the results of the analysis of eight soil samples. The arsenic values listed are based on a wet-weight determination. The moisture content of the soil is also given to allow conversion of the results to a dry-weight basis if desired.

Hole	Depth	Moisture (%)	Arsenic Total (ppm)
1	12"	19.0	312.0
2	Surface	11.2	737.0
3	12"	12.7	9.5
4	12"	10.8	865.0
5	12"	17.1	4.1
6	12"	14.2	6.1
7	12"	24.2	2,540.0
8	Surface	13.6	460.0

I noticed that some of the samples contained large amounts of metallic iron coated with rust. Arsenic tends to be absorbed into soils high in iron, aluminum, and calcium oxides. The large amount of iron present in some of these soil samples is probably responsible for retaining high levels of arsenic. The soils highest in iron, aluminum, and calcium oxides should also show the highest levels of arsenic, provided the soils have had approximately equal levels of arsenic exposure.

If I can be of further assistance, please do not hesitate to contact me.

Yours truly,

Gunther Gottfried

Gunther Gottfried, Chemist
<ggottfried@biosphericsinc.com>

Report in letter format for a customer

Test identified in subject line

Testing methodology

Table of areas tested and findings

Interpretation of test findings

Figure 10–6   Test Report (Letter to Customer)

BIOSPHERICS
Inc.

4928 Wyaconda Road
Rockville, MD 20852
Phone (301) 492-3331
Fax (301) 492-1832
biosphericsinc.com

April 5, 2010

*Report in letter format
for a customer*

Mr. Leon Hite, Administrator
The Angle Company, Inc.
1869 Slauson Boulevard
Waynesville, VA 23927

Dear Mr. Hite:

Scope of test

On March 22, Biospherics Inc. performed asbestos-in-air monitoring at your Route 66 construction site, near Front Royal, Virginia. Six persons and three construction areas were monitored.

Testing methodology

All monitoring and analyses were performed in accordance with "Occupational Exposure to Asbestos," U.S. Department of Health and Human Services, Public Health Service, National Institute for Occupational Safety and Health, 1995. Each worker or area was fitted with a battery-powered personal sampler pump, operating at a flow rate of approximately two liters per minute. The airborne asbestos was collected on a 37-mm Millipore-type AA filter mounted in an open-face filter holder. Samples were collected over an eight-hour period.

Test findings

In all cases, the workers and areas monitored were exposed to levels of asbestos fibers well below the standard set by the Occupational Safety and Health Administration. The highest exposure found was that of a driller exposed to 0.21 fibers per cubic centimeter. The driller's samples were analyzed by scanning electron microscopy followed by energy-dispersive X-ray techniques that identify the chemical nature of each fiber, to identify the fibers as asbestos or other fiber types. Results from these analyses show that the fibers present are tremolite asbestos. No nonasbestos fibers were found.

Yours truly,

Allison Jones

Allison Jones, Chemist
AJ/jrm

Figure 10–7 Test Report with Methodology Explained (Letter to Customer)

CHAPTER 10 SUMMARY: WRITING INFORMAL REPORTS

Check informal reports to make sure the following is done:

- The introduction states the subject and purpose and summarizes conclusions and recommendations.
- The body presents a detailed account of the work reported on.
- The conclusion summarizes findings and indicates their significance.
- The recommendations of actions you believe should be taken are based on the conclusions.

The following types of informal reports are typical:

- Progress and periodic reports
  - Inform the reader of the status of an ongoing project either at certain stages (progress) or at regular intervals (periodic).
  - Alert readers to any necessary adjustments in scheduling, budgeting, and work assignments.
- Investigative reports
  - Open with a statement of the information the writer has sought.
  - Define the extent of the investigation.
  - Present the findings, interpretations, conclusions, and, when appropriate, recommendations.
- Trouble reports
  - Identify the precise details, such as time and place of an accident or other incident.
  - Indicate any injuries or property damage.
  - State a likely cause of the accident or incident.
  - Specify what is being done to prevent a recurrence, if that's possible.
- Trip reports
  - Include the destination and dates of the trip.
  - Explain why the trip was made, who was visited, and what was accomplished.
  - State any findings or recommendations based on the purpose of the trip.
- Test reports
  - State the purpose of the test and indicate the procedures used to conduct the test.
  - Indicate the results of the test or experiment and any interpretations helpful to the reader.

ON THE WEB

For an online quiz on informal reports, go to Chapter 10, bedfordstmartins.com/writingthatworks

Exercises

1. Assume that you are the traffic manager of a trucking company that has had four highway accidents within a one-week period. Using the following facts, write a trouble report to your company president, Michael Spangler.
   - Your company operates in your state.

ON THE WEB

For additional exercises, go to Chapter 10, bedfordstmartins.com/writingthatworks

- The four accidents occurred in different parts of the state and on different dates (specify the date and location of each).
- Each accident resulted in damage not only to the truck (specify the dollar amount of the damage) but to the cargo (specify the type of cargo and the dollar amount of the damage).
- Only one of the accidents involved another vehicle (a company truck swerved into a parked car when a tire blew out). Give the make and year of the damaged car and its owner's name.
- Only one of the accidents involved injury to a company driver (give the name).
- Your maintenance division traced all four of the accidents to faulty tires, all the same brand (identify the brand), and all purchased at the same time and place (identify the place and date).
- The tires have now been replaced, and your insurance company, Acme Underwriters, has brought suit against the tire manufacturer to recover damages, including lost business while the four trucks were being repaired (specify the dollar amount of the lost business).

2. Worker's compensation allows employees who are injured on the job to receive benefits like medical expenses and lost wages, depending on when the injury happened, how the injury happened, and the severity of the injury. Imagine that you work for a human-resources manager of a large online retailer. Most of your company's workers spend their days packing books, DVDs, and other products into mailing boxes, then lifting the boxes and putting them onto carts and pulling the carts to the mailing rooms. Your manager asks you to draft an investigative end-of-the-year report in the form of a memo that details the most common type of employee injury and other yearly information. Your research uncovers the following:

- Back injuries are the most common, occurring mostly in the warehouse.
- In 2009–2010, 956 injuries occurred.
- The total cost of the injuries was $3.5 million.
- There is still a cost of $8.2 million for all open claims.
- This information reflects a significant loss in productivity.

Be sure to open your memo with a brief introductory summary that details the information you were seeking, why the investigation was necessary, and who requested it. In the body of the memo or letter, describe the extent of or method used for your investigation. Then state your findings and any recommendations based on the findings.

3. As the medical staff administrative assistant at a hospital, write a progress report to the director of the hospital outlining the current status of the annual reappointment of committees. Use the following facts to write the report:

- A total of ten committees must be staffed.
- The chief of staff has telephoned each person selected to chair a committee, and you have sent each of them a follow-up letter of thanks from the chief.
- You have written letters to all physicians who are currently on committees but are not being reappointed, informing them of the fact.
- You have written letters to all physicians being asked to serve on committees.
- You expect to receive replies from those physicians declining the appointment by the 15th of the following month.
- Once committee assignments have been completed, you will type the membership lists of all committees and distribute them to the complete medical staff.

4. You are a field-service engineer for a company that markets diesel-powered emergency generators. Based on the following information, write a trip report.

   You have just visited five cities to inspect the installation of your company's auxiliary power units in hospitals, and you need to report to your manager about your findings. You visited the following hospitals and cities:

   - May 17: Our Lady of Mercy Hospital in San Antonio
   - May 18: Dallas Presbyterian Hospital in Dallas
   - May 19: St. Elizabeth Hospital in Oklahoma City
   - May 20: New Orleans General Hospital in New Orleans
   - May 21: Jefferson Davis Memorial Hospital in Atlanta

   You found that each installation was properly done. With the cooperation of the administrators, you switched each hospital to auxiliary power for a one-hour trial run. All went well. You held a brief training session for the maintenance staff at each hospital, teaching them how to start the engine and how to regulate its speed to produce 220 volts of electricity from the generator at 60 hertz. You want to commend your company's sales staff and field personnel for creating a positive image of your company in the minds of all five customers you visited.

5. Locate a laboratory report prepared by a private or government agency on the Web, as directed by your instructor. Compare elements of the report to the guidelines in this chapter. To what extent does the actual laboratory report match the chapter guidelines, and how could they help to improve the report? Comment on any differences you see based on the context of the report and the organization that produced it. Submit your report in memo form to your instructor.

6. Each of the following topics presents a situation in which a company plans a significant change that could threaten its existing customer base. Select one of the following topics (or create your own topic based on your area of study and professional interest) and write a memo in which you offer your recommendations for ensuring that the change that your company proposes will not jeopardize its existing customer base. With your customers in mind, make specific suggestions for facilitating as smooth and positive a transition as possible.

   a. Assume that you are part of the management team of a fast-food restaurant with a "burgers only" identity—and a loyal customer base—that wants to add distinctive and healthful menu items.

   b. Assume that you are part of the management team for an apparel manufacturing firm known for its conservative fashions. Your firm is about to introduce a new line of clothing with a distinctly contemporary appeal.

   c. Assume that you work for a small medical insurance company concerned with the rising number of medical claims being submitted by your customers. To combat this, your company has initiated a campaign designed to entice your customers to adopt healthier lifestyles and has begun sending brochures and personalized letters to customers. Some customers have expressed concern that this is an indication that the company will become more reluctant to pay their claims.

7. Imagine that you are a security consultant and have been hired by a company that creates security systems for the average homeowner. The company has hired you to test its new wireless camera—one that promises to work in low light and transmit pictures up to 100 meters—in a real-world environment. You decide to take several of the cameras home and place them within reception range under the

eaves of the garage, in the baby's room, overlooking your front door, and in the yard near the pool. Although you appreciate the ease with which you could set up the system, it becomes apparent over the course of your week of testing that the picture and sound quality were negatively impacted by the interference of other electrical equipment in the house, such as the baby monitor, the microwave oven, and the cordless phone. Static noises and jumping lines made it nearly impossible to understand the sound and picture. Write a test report to the security systems corporation detailing your findings.

ON THE WEB

For more collaborative classroom projects, go to Chapter 10, bedfordstmartins.com/ writingthatworks

▓ Collaborative Classroom Projects

1. In Collaborative Classroom Project 3 in Chapter 8, Understanding the Principles of Business Communication, your class broke into two groups, the local electric company's consumers and the company's marketing representatives. Both sides wrote letters asking that a rate increase be rejected or accepted, respectively. Now assume that before the marketing representatives wrote their letter, they had investigated the company's need for a rate increase to build a fourth natural gas–fired generating unit. The investigation uncovered the following information:[1]

   - The electric company supplies electricity to three cities and over 1.65 million customers.
   - Population growth is beginning to add strain to an already overloaded system (the company currently generates power using nuclear, coal, natural gas, and oil plants at 12 different sites).
   - Customers set two peak records for summer usage in 2010: They used approximately 8,992 megawatt-hours (MWh) of electricity on July 16 between 4:00 and 5:00 p.m., and approximately 9,027 MWh on July 19 in the same time period.
   - Despite the summer heat, peak energy use occurs during the winter: the highest demand (10,142 MWh) was recorded on January 15, 2010.
   - Company engineers report that a new natural gas–fired generating unit would add approximately 500 megawatts of capacity, which could generate electricity for about 320,000 additional consumers.

   Rewrite your group's marketing representatives' letter to include the research. When you are finished, exchange letters for peer reviews. Comment on the level of persuasion that these letters now contain with the added details and facts.

2. As a class, plan to visit a lab or learning center on campus, preferably one outside your department. Determine as a group which lab you would like to visit and the specific purposes of your visit. The lab may be a science lab, a computer lab, an engineering lab, or a writing center. After an explanation of the lab's procedures and a tour of the lab or center, your class will reconvene in your own classroom and write a trip report about the visit. Include the date of the visit, your destination, the purpose of your trip, and an explanation of what you learned during the visit.

---

[1]Adapted from Florida Power's Web site <www.progress-energy.com/aboutus/news/article.asp?id =12022>.

Research Projects

ON THE WEB

For extra research projects, go to Chapter 10, bedfordstmartins.com/ writingthatworks

1. The use of cell phones, laptops, and digital cameras has created a growing need for the recycling of portable rechargeable batteries. Many retail stores are helping to preserve the environment by shipping spent battery packs to recycling centers. In Chapter 6, Researching Your Subject, Exercise 7, you created a questionnaire designed to determine if people are aware of the need to recycle portable rechargeable batteries and how people feel about companies that provide recycling programs. Expand your investigation and write an investigative report on the recycling of portable rechargeable batteries. In this report, be sure you do the following:

   a. Define the many different types of rechargeable batteries being used today (like nickel cadmium and lithium ion).
   b. Explain how the recycling is accomplished.
   c. List the local businesses in your city that participate in recycling programs.
   d. Include the findings from your questionnaire.

2. You have been asked to determine for your campus organization where members can volunteer 10 to 12 hours a week for local community service.

   a. Begin by investigating at least three organizations that accept volunteers, such as nursing homes, hospitals, political and civic groups, or schools. Detail the type of volunteer help needed, the hours and days when the help is needed, whether any training is required, and to whom you'll report. Also be sure to find out if volunteers do hands-on work with people—such as playing games with children or adults or bathing, lifting, or turning those who aren't mobile—or if volunteers work behind the scenes, making solicitation calls, addressing envelopes, stocking supplies, and so on.
   b. Then write an eight- to ten-page investigative report in which you evaluate each of the three organizations given the criteria above, as well as from the point of view of your own background, experience, and future vocational goals that are similar to those members of your organization.
   c. Finish by selecting the one that is most suitable for members of your organization and explain the reasons for your selection.

3. Assume that you work for a small business and the company president has asked you to gather information from the Small Business Administration (SBA) that will benefit your company, such as opportunities for government contracts, or special programs or training available through the SBA. Visit the SBA Web site at <www .sba.gov> and prepare an investigative report of 300 to 500 words to be submitted to your instructor.

4. Many large international companies target sections of their Web sites to the different world markets where their products are sold. For example, McDonald's <www.McDonalds.com> includes customized pages for each of the fifty-plus countries where its restaurants are established. Assume that you work for a company that is considering expanding its Web site for international markets. You have been assigned to investigate and report your findings on the differences and similarities between the regional sections of other companies' sites. To research your report, examine the Web sites of at least three international corporations. You

might visit, for example, McDonald's American and European sites, or Sony's Asian and Eastern European sites. Note the translations of the company's slogan, the colors and graphics used on the sites, the presentation of products, and so on. (You may want to revisit the sections on international correspondence in Chapter 8, Understanding the Principles of Business Communication; on using graphics to communicate to global audiences in Chapter 7, Designing Effective Documents and Visuals; and on considering international Web users in Chapter 15, Writing for the Web.

AT A GLANCE: Formal Reports

This chapter discusses the parts of formal reports, the information they should include, and how best to organize them into an effective final product. Depending on the subject, objective, and scope, a formal report is typically divided into three major parts—front matter, body, and back matter—and contains the following elements:

▪ Transmittal letter or memo (precedes front matter) / 388
▪ Front matter / 389
  • Title page / 389
  • Abstract / 390
  • Table of contents / 394
  • List of figures / 394
  • List of tables / 394
  • Foreword / 395
  • Preface / 396
  • List of abbreviations and symbols / 396
▪ Body / 396
  • Executive summary / 398
  • Introduction / 400
  • Text (Body) / 403
  • Conclusions / 410
  • Recommendations / 410
  • Works cited (or references) / 411
▪ Back matter / 414
  • Bibliography / 414
  • Appendixes / 415
  • Glossary / 415
  • Index / 415

Formal reports are written accounts of major projects. Such projects include research into new developments in a field, explorations of the feasibility of a new product or a new service, or an organization's end-of-year review. Because of the variety of purposes they serve, formal reports can be called by many different names: feasibility study, annual report, investigative report, research report, analytical report, and the like. The purpose, scope, and complexity of the project will determine which components will be included and how those components are organized. Most formal reports require signposts that point to the material in the report. A table of contents, a list of figures, and an abstract (a brief summary of the report), for example, make the information in the report more easily accessible. Creating a formal topic outline, which lists the report's major facts and ideas and indicates their relationship to one another, should help you to write a well-organized report.

The components in formal reports are organized to address the needs of more than one audience. These audiences will occupy a variety of positions, have different levels of knowledge about your topic, and be responsible for reading and responding to different parts of the report. Few in the audience will read the entire report, so the executive summary and abstract must make sense independently of the rest of the report. Although everybody will skim the table of contents, managers and other decision makers will focus on the executive summary because it concisely summarizes the report in full. These readers need to know the "bottom line" quickly for its potential impact on their staffing, organizational, and budget decisions. They may also need to refer to the report's glossary for definitions of special terms. Technical experts, however, will be responsible for implementing the report's recommendations, so they need to understand in detail how the conclusions and recommendations were reached. General readers whose needs are less immediate may read only the abstract to decide whether to read the whole report. Therefore, overlapping content is appropriate in the introduction, executive summary, abstract, and conclusions and recommendations.

As you read this chapter, keep in mind all that you've learned about the process of drafting and revising on-the-job writing tasks because careful planning, drafting, and revising, as much as using the organizational frameworks covered in this chapter, form the basis for a successful formal report. Formal-report preparation involves *researching* and generating a substantial amount of information, which you will need to evaluate, select, and organize before you begin the drafting process. The research required for a formal report can be extensive, so *brainstorming* and refining the scope of the topic are essential.

In addition, *outlining* is an important step in preparing your report: Prepare one outline as an overview of the whole project and smaller, more specific outlines for individual sections. Breaking the work into parts can make the daunting task of pulling together a long report more manageable.

Revising the report (several times) and *evaluating* each draft for coherence, clarity, and correctness are critical. *Reviewing* the drafts is essential to see whether the individual sections of the report connect smoothly and logically, whether sources are used correctly and consistently, and whether visuals—drawings, tables, graphs, charts, photographs, and maps—are well designed and correctly positioned. Collaborative reviews of your work will help you immensely; colleagues, fellow students, or instructors may offer valuable suggestions to improve your organization, coverage, and language.

In the workplace, formal reports are often written by a team of specialists assembled for that purpose. Each member of the team is selected to contribute material based on his or her specialty or background and collaborates on every facet of the writing process:

- Planning the report
- Researching the subject and writing a chapter or section of the report
- Reviewing the drafts of other team members
- Revising their drafts on the basis of comments from the team members

A team leader usually coordinates the team's work by setting a schedule for the work, leading the effort to plan the report, assigning responsibilities, coordinating all content reviews, editing the final draft, and overseeing production and distribution of the final report. The team leader also performs the essential task of controlling the master draft to ensure that it is current and accurate and that no parts are confused with earlier drafts that have been revised and superseded.

VOICES IN THE WORKPLACE

Reaching Multiple Audiences

As a writing staff team leader at Los Alamos National Laboratory (LANL), Judy Prono notes that her readers range from technical experts and elected officials to public interest groups and the general public. To reach such a diverse readership, her staff will "begin by explaining the 'what' and 'so what' of the research to nonexpert readers and add technical details as the report progresses. . . . We may also tell two stories, one in the text and one in the accompanying graphics, captions, and sidebars. The two become complementary explanations . . . that tell the full story together but capture its highlights if readers have time only for the 'pictures.'"

@

DIGITAL TIPS: Automating Report Formatting

In most word-processing programs, you can create styles—sets of formatting characteristics for text elements such as headings, paragraphs, and lists—that allow you to automate much of the work of formatting your report. Once you have specified your styles, save them as a template and use it each time you create a formal report. Creating a template allows you to automate the following:

- Fonts and font sizes for text, headings, titles, footnotes, headers, and footers
- Paragraph formats, including indentation and margins
- Lists, including indentation from the margin and spacing
- Number of columns
- The table of contents based on a report's headings and subheadings
- For step-by-step instructions, see <bedfordstmartins.com/writingthatworks> and select Digital Tips, Automating Report Formatting.

ON THE WEB

For more help with writing formal reports, go to Chapter 11, bedfordstmartins.com/writingthatworks

◆ *For guidance on conducting research, see Chapter 6, Researching Your Subject.*

◆ *For brainstorming strategies, see Chapter 1, Assessing Audience and Purpose.*

◆ *For outlining, see Chapter 2, Organizing Your Information.*

◆ *For advice on planning, creating, and integrating visuals, see Chapter 7, Designing Effective Documents and Visuals.*

◆ *For a description of the collaborative review process, see Chapter 5, Collaborative Writing.*

◆ *For a review of revising strategies, see Chapter 4, Revising the Draft.*

◆ *Examples of transmittal letters are also shown in Figures 9–1 and 9–2.*

▨ Transmittal Letter or Memo

When you submit a formal report, include with it a brief transmittal (or cover) letter or memo that identifies the report topic and explains why the report was prepared. Written in the form of a standard business letter or memo, the transmittal most often opens with a brief paragraph (one or two sentences) explaining what is being sent and why. The next paragraph briefly summarizes the report's contents or stresses some feature that would be important to the audience. This section may also mention any special conditions under which the material was prepared (limitations of time or money, for instance). The closing paragraph may acknowledge any help received in preparing the report or may express the hope that the information fulfills its purpose.

Typically, transmittal letters and memos are brief—usually one page. Figure 11–1 shows a sample transmittal memo.

CGF Aircraft Corporation
Memo

Addressed to recipients designed by the program

To: Members of the Ethics and Business Conduct Committee
From: Susan Litzinger, Director of Ethics and Business Conduct SL
Date: March 3, 2010
Subject: Reported Ethics Cases 2009

Brief opening describes the enclosure

Enclosed is "Reported Ethics Cases: 2009 Annual Report." This report, required by CGF Policy CGF-EP-01, contains a review of the ethics cases handled by CGF ethics officers and managers during 2009, the first year of our Ethics Program.

Brief summary of report contents

The ethics cases reported are analyzed according to two categories: (1) major ethics cases, or those potentially involving serious violations of company policy or illegal conduct, and (2) minor ethics cases, or those that do not involve serious policy violations or illegal conduct. The report also examines the mode of contact in all of the reported cases and the disposition of the substantiated major ethics cases.

Closing with offer of additional support

It is my hope that this report will provide the committee with the information needed to assess the effectiveness of the first year of CGF's Ethics Program and to plan for the coming year. Please let me know if you have any questions about this report or if you need further information. I may be reached at (555) 211-2121 and by e-mail at sl@cgf.com.

Enclosure notation

Enc.

Figure 11–1   Transmittal Memo for a Formal Report.   *Source:* Reprinted and adapted by permission of Susan Litzinger, a student at Pennsylvania State University, Altoona.

▨ Front Matter

The front matter, which includes all the elements that precede the body of the report, serves several purposes: (1) It explains the topic, organization, and purpose of the report; (2) it indicates whether the report contains the kind of information that the audience is looking for; and (3) it lists where in the report the audience can find specific chapters, headings, illustrations, and tables. Not all formal reports require every one of these elements. A title page and table of contents are usually mandatory, but whether the remaining items are included will depend on the scope of the report and its intended audience. Scientific and technical reports, for example, often include a separate listing of abbreviations and symbols; in most business reports, such lists are unnecessary. The front-matter pages are numbered with lowercase Roman numerals. Throughout the report, page numbers are often centered either near the bottom or near the top of each page.

ON THE WEB

For additional formal reports, go to Model Documents Gallery, bedfordstmartins.com/ writingthatworks

Title Page

Although the formats of title pages vary, the page could include the following information: (1) the full title of the report; (2) the name(s) of the writers, principal investigators, or compilers who prepared it; (3) the date the report was issued; (4) the name of the organization for which the writer(s) works; and (5) the name of the organization or person to whom the report is submitted.

1. *Full title of the report.* The title should reflect the topic as well as the scope and objective of the report. Titles often provide the only basis on which audiences can decide whether to read a report. Aim for accuracy and conciseness: Titles too vague or too long not only hinder the audience but can prevent efficient filing and later retrieval of the report. Follow these guidelines when creating the title:

   - Focus on the subject matter of the report. Avoid titles that begin "Notes on," "Studies on," "A Report on," or "Observations on." These phrases are often redundant and state the obvious. However, phrases such as "Annual Report" or "Feasibility Study" should be used in a title or subtitle because they help define the purpose and scope of the document.
   - Avoid using abbreviations in the title. Use them only when the report is intended for an audience familiar enough with the topic that the abbreviation will be understood.
   - Do not include the period covered by a report in the title; include that information in a subtitle:

     ▶ EFFECTS OF PROPOSED HIGHWAY CONSTRUCTION ON PROPERTY VALUES
     Tri-State Regional District
     Annual Report, 2010

2. *Names of the writers, principal investigators, or compilers, as appropriate.* Frequently, contributors simply list their names. Sometimes they identify themselves by their job titles in the organization (Jane R. Lihn, Cost Analyst; Rodrigo Sánchez, Head, Research and Development). They also identify themselves by their tasks in contributing to the report (Antoine Baume, Compiler; Wanda Landowska, Principal Investigator).

3. *Date or dates of the report.* For one-time reports, list the date when the report is to be distributed. For periodic reports, which may be issued monthly or quarterly, list the period that the present report covers in a subtitle, as well as the date when the report is to be distributed.

4. *Name of the organization for which the writer works.*

5. *Name of the organization or individual to whom the report is being submitted*, if the work is being done for an organization other than your own.

These categories are standard on most title pages. Some organizations may require additional information. A sample title page appears in Figure 11–2.

The title page, although unnumbered, is considered page i (small Roman numeral one). The back of the title page, which is blank and unnumbered, is considered page ii, and the abstract then falls on page iii so that it appears on a right-hand (that is, an odd-numbered) page. For reports with printing on both sides of each sheet of paper, it is a long-standing printer's convention that right-hand pages are always odd-numbered and left-hand pages are always even-numbered. (Note the pagination in this book.) New sections and chapters of reports typically begin on a new right-hand page. Reports with printing on only one side of each sheet can be numbered consecutively regardless of where new sections begin.

Abstract

An abstract is a condensed version of a longer work that summarizes and highlights its major points. Abstracts enable prospective readers to decide quickly whether to read the report. Usually 200 to 250 words long, abstracts must make sense independently of the work they summarize because they may appear in databases or online in citations to the full report. Depending on the kind of information they contain, abstracts are usually classified as either descriptive or informative.

A descriptive abstract includes information about the purpose, scope, and methods used to arrive at the findings contained in the report. It is thus a slightly expanded table of contents in paragraph form. Provided that it adequately summarizes the information, a descriptive abstract need not be longer than several sentences (Figure 11–3, page 392).

An informative abstract is an expanded version of the descriptive abstract. In addition to information about the purpose, scope, and research methods of the original report, the informative abstract includes the results, conclusions, and

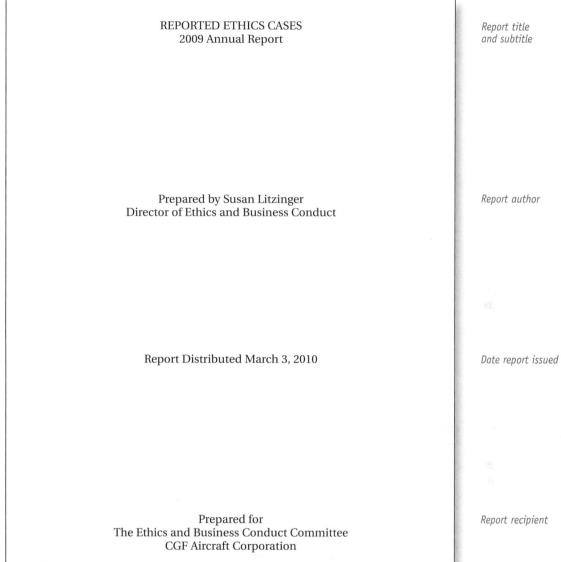

REPORTED ETHICS CASES
2009 Annual Report

*Report title
and subtitle*

Prepared by Susan Litzinger
Director of Ethics and Business Conduct

Report author

Report Distributed March 3, 2010

Date report issued

Prepared for
The Ethics and Business Conduct Committee
CGF Aircraft Corporation

Report recipient

Figure 11–2   Title Page of a Formal Report

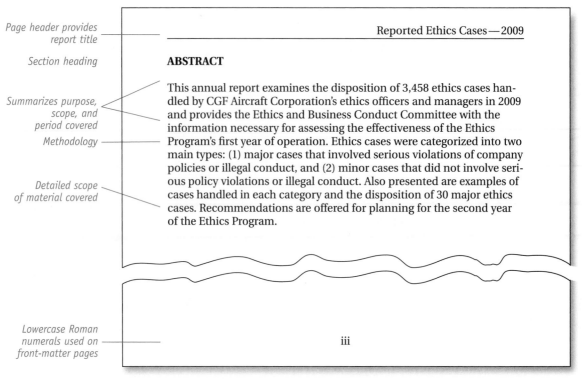

Page header provides report title

Section heading

Summarizes purpose, scope, and period covered

Methodology

Detailed scope of material covered

Lowercase Roman numerals used on front-matter pages

Reported Ethics Cases—2009

ABSTRACT

This annual report examines the disposition of 3,458 ethics cases handled by CGF Aircraft Corporation's ethics officers and managers in 2009 and provides the Ethics and Business Conduct Committee with the information necessary for assessing the effectiveness of the Ethics Program's first year of operation. Ethics cases were categorized into two main types: (1) major cases that involved serious violations of company policies or illegal conduct, and (2) minor cases that did not involve serious policy violations or illegal conduct. Also presented are examples of cases handled in each category and the disposition of 30 major ethics cases. Recommendations are offered for planning for the second year of the Ethics Program.

iii

Figure 11–3   Descriptive Abstract of a Formal Report

recommendations, if any. The informative abstract thus retains the tone and essential scope of the report while omitting its details (Figure 11–4).

Which of the two types of abstract should you write? The answer depends on your employer. If there is a policy, comply with it. Otherwise, aim to satisfy the needs of the principal readers of your report. Informative abstracts satisfy the needs of the widest possible audience, but descriptive abstracts are preferable for information surveys, progress reports that combine information from more than one project, and any report that compiles a variety of information. For these types of reports, conclusions and recommendations either do not exist in the original or are too numerous to include in an abstract. Typically, an abstract follows the title page and is numbered page iii.

Write the abstract after finishing your report. Otherwise, your abstract may not accurately reflect the final version. Begin with a topic sentence that announces the subject and scope of the report. Then, using the major and minor heads of your table of contents to distinguish primary from secondary ideas, decide what material is relevant to your abstract. Write clearly and concisely, eliminating unnecessary words and ideas, but do not omit articles (*a, an, the*) and im-

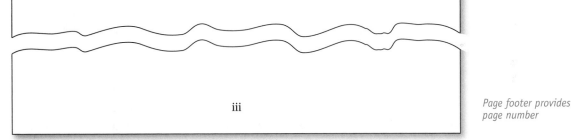

Reported Ethics Cases—2009

Page header provides report title

ABSTRACT

Section heading

This annual report examines the disposition of 3,458 ethics cases handled by CGF Aircraft Corporation's ethics officers and managers in 2009 and provides the Ethics and Business Conduct Committee with the information necessary for assessing the effectiveness of the Ethics Program's first year of operation. Ethics cases were categorized into two main types: (1) major cases that involved serious violations of company policies or illegal conduct, and (2) minor cases that did not involve serious policy violations or illegal conduct. Also presented are examples of cases handled in each category and the disposition of 30 major ethics cases.

Purpose and scope

Methodology

The effectiveness of CGF's Ethics Program during the first year of implementation is most evidenced by (1) the active participation of employees regarding ethics concerns, and (2) the action taken in the cases they reported. Disseminating information about the disposition of ethics cases sends a message to employees that unethical or illegal conduct will not be tolerated.

Conclusions

Recommendations for planning for the second year of the Ethics Program are (1) continuing the channels of communication now available in the Ethics Program, (2) increasing financial and technical support for the Ethics Hotline, (3) disseminating the annual ethics report to employees to ensure their awareness of CGF's commitment to uphold its Ethics Policy and Procedures, and (4) implementing measures to promote ethical behavior and reward ethical conduct.

Recommendations

iii

Page footer provides page number

Figure 11–4   Informative Abstract of a Formal Report

◆ *For additional advice, review pages 179–180 in Chapter 6, Researching Your Subject.*

portant transitional words and phrases (*however, therefore, but, in summary*). Write complete sentences, but avoid stringing a group of short sentences end to end; instead, combine ideas by using subordination and parallel structure. As a rule, spell out most acronyms and all but the most common abbreviations (°C, °F, mph). Finally, as you summarize, keep the tone and emphasis consistent with the original report.

WRITER'S CHECKLIST
Writing Abstracts

Include the following information:

✔ Subject

✔ Scope

✔ Purpose

✔ Methods used

✔ Results obtained (informative abstract only)

✔ Recommendations made, if any (informative abstract only)

Do not include the following kinds of information:

✔ Detailed discussion or explanation of the methods used

✔ Administrative details about how the research was undertaken, who funded it, who worked on it, and the like, unless such details have a bearing on the document's purpose

✔ Illustrations, tables, charts, maps, and bibliographic references

✔ Any information that does not appear in the original document

Table of Contents

A table of contents lists all the headings of the report in their order of appearance, along with their page numbers. It includes a listing of all front matter and back matter except the title page and the table of contents itself. The table of contents begins on a new right-hand page. Note that in Figure 11–5 the table of contents is numbered page v because it follows the abstract (page iii), and because page iv is blank.

Along with the abstract, a table of contents gives your audience an overview of the scope of information covered and how it is organized. It also aids a reader who may want to look only at certain sections of the report. For this reason, the wording of chapter and section titles in the table of contents should always be identical to those in the text.

Sometimes, the table of contents is followed by lists of figures and tables contained in the report. These lists should always be presented separately, and a page number should be given for each figure and table listed.

List of Figures

When a report contains more than five figures, list them by title, along with their page numbers, in a separate section beginning on a new page and immediately following the table of contents. Number figures consecutively with Arabic numbers.

List of Tables

When a report contains more than five tables, list them, along with their titles and page numbers, in a separate section immediately following the list of figures (if there is one). Number tables consecutively with Arabic numbers.

TABLE OF CONTENTS

ABSTRACT iii

PREFACE vii

EXECUTIVE SUMMARY 1

INTRODUCTION 2

      Ethics and Business Conduct Policy and Procedures 2
      Confidentiality Issues 2
      Documentation of Ethics Cases 3
      Major/Minor Category Definition and Examples 3

ANALYSIS OF REPORTED ETHICS CASES 4

      Reported Ethics Cases by Major/Minor Category 4
      Major Ethics Cases 4
      Minor Ethics Cases 6
      Mode of Contact 6

CONCLUSIONS AND RECOMMENDATIONS 8

WORKS CITED 10

v

The marginal annotations read:

Header provides report title

Major and subordinate headings differentiated by typeface and indentations

Page number for each section

Footer provides page number

Figure 11–5   Table of Contents of a Formal Report

Foreword

A foreword is an optional introductory statement written by someone other than the author. It generally provides background information about the publication's significance and places it in the context of other works in the field. The author of the foreword is usually an authority in the field or an executive of the company. The author's name and affiliation and the date the foreword was written appear on a separate line below the foreword.

Preface

A preface is an optional introductory statement written by the author to announce the purpose, background, or scope of the report. Sometimes a preface specifies the audience for whom the report is intended, and it may also highlight the relationship of the report to a given project or program. A preface may contain acknowledgments of help received during the course of the project or in the preparation of the report, and, finally, it may cite permission obtained for the use of copyrighted works. If a preface is not included, place this type of information, if essential, in the introduction (discussed later in this chapter). Figure 11–6 shows a sample preface.

The preface follows the table of contents (and the lists of figures and tables and the foreword, if these are present). It begins on a separate page, is numbered with Roman numerals, and is titled "Preface."

List of Abbreviations and Symbols

When the abbreviations and symbols used in a report are numerous, and when there is a chance that the audience will not be able to interpret them, the front matter should include a list of all abbreviations and symbols and what they stand for in the report. Such a list, which follows the preface, is particularly appropriate for technical reports whose audience is not restricted to technical specialists.

Figure 11–7 on page 398 shows an example of a list of symbols that appear in a report as part of equations that calculate the transfer of heat and water vapor from the surface of cooling ponds at industrial sites. The author assumes that the report readers have a technical education, however, because BTU (British thermal unit), Hg (chemical symbol for mercury), and similar terms are not defined.

▧ Body

◆ *For guidance about page-level layout and design elements—typography, margins, columns, headers and footers, and the like— see pages 212–220 in Chapter 7, Designing Effective Documents and Visuals.*

The body is the section of the report that describes in detail the methods and procedures used to generate the report, demonstrates how results were obtained, describes the results, draws conclusions, and, if appropriate, makes recommendations. It usually includes the following components:

- Executive summary
- Introduction
- Text (including headings, tables, illustrations, and references)
- Conclusions and recommendations

Number the first page of the body page 1 in Arabic rather than Roman numerals.

Reported Ethics Cases — 2009

PREFACE

The CGF Aircraft Corporation takes its commitment to an ethical work environment seriously. Throughout its 64-year history, CGF has fostered high ethical standards in its relations with its customers, suppliers, and employees. The size, diversity, and decentralized locations of our workforce make it imperative that CGF's ethical commitment — both in principle and in practice — be formalized. To this end, the CGF Aircraft Corporation established a corporation-wide ethics program in August 2008. The goal of the program is to "promote a positive work environment that encourages open communication regarding ethics and compliance issues and concerns."

The Office of Ethics and Business Conduct (OEBC) was created to implement and administer the program. The director of the OEBC and seven ethics officers from throughout the corporation are responsible for the following program objectives:

- Communicate the values and standards for CGF's Ethics Program to employees.
- Inform employees about company policies regarding ethical business conduct.
- Establish companywide channels for employees to obtain information and guidance in resolving ethics concerns.
- Implement companywide ethics-awareness and education programs.

This report examines the nature and disposition of the ethics cases handled by the OEBC in 2009, the first year of operation. The report was compiled to provide the corporation's Ethics and Business Committee of the OEBC with the information necessary to assess the effectiveness of the first year of CGF's ethics program.

This report represents the efforts of the dedicated staff of the OEBC, the ethics officers, and the many managers and employees throughout CGF. We wish to acknowledge their active support and contributions to this report and to the program.

vii

Header provides report title

Section heading

Background and purpose of program

Program background

Bulleted list makes objectives easy to read

Purpose and scope of report

Audience for report

Acknowledgment of help in preparation of report

Footer provides page number

Figure 11–6   Preface of a Formal Report

SYMBOLS

A	Pond surface area, ft^2 or acres
A_0	One-half the daily insulation, BTU/ft^2
A_n	Surface area of nth segment of the plugflow model, ft^2
C	Cloud cover in tenths of the total sky obscured
C_1	Bowen's ratio, 0.26 mmHg/°F
C_P	Heat capacity of water, BTU/lb/°F
E_1, E_2	Estimation of equilibrium temperatures using data from off-site and on-site records, respectively, °F
$E(x)$	Estimation of equilibrium temperature using monthly average meteorologic data, °F
e_a	Saturation pressure of air above pond surface, mmHg
e_s	Saturation pressure of air at surface temperature, T_s, mmHg
g	Skew coefficient
H	Heat content, BTU

Figure 11–7   List of Symbols for a Technical Report

Executive Summary

The body begins with an executive summary that provides a more complete overview of the report than the abstract does. The summary states the purpose of the investigation and gives major findings; provides background; states the scope; provides conclusions; and, if any are made, gives recommendations. It also describes the procedures or methodology used to conduct the study. Executive summaries are optional, but they are strongly recommended for reports with multiple readers with different levels of knowledge about the topic of a report.

Although more complete than an abstract, the executive summary should not contain a detailed description of the work on which the findings, conclusions, and recommendations were based. The length of the summary is proportional to the length of the report; typically, the summary should be approximately ten percent of the length of the report. The executive summary must reflect the report's final contents accurately, so it, like the abstract, should be written after the report is finished.

Some executive summaries follow the organization of the report. Others highlight the findings, conclusions, and recommendations by summarizing them first, before going on to discuss procedures or methodology.

Like the abstract, the executive summary should be written so that it can be read independently of the report. It must not refer by number to figures, tables, or references contained elsewhere in the report. Because executive summaries are frequently read in place of the full report, all uncommon symbols, abbreviations, and acronyms must be spelled out.

Figure 11–8 shows an executive summary of the report on the Ethics Program at CGF Aircraft Corporation.

Reported Ethics Cases—2009

EXECUTIVE SUMMARY

This report examines the nature and disposition of the 3,458 ethics cases handled *Purpose*
by the CGF Aircraft Corporation's ethics officers and managers during 2009.
The purpose of this report is to provide CGF's Ethics and Business Conduct Committee with the information necessary for assessing the effectiveness of the first
year of the company's Ethics Program.

Ethics information and guidance were available to employees through managers, ethics officers, and an ethics hotline.

Major ethics cases—defined as those situations potentially involving serious vio-   *Scope*
lations of company policies or illegal conduct—included cover-up of defective
workmanship or use of defective parts in products; discrimination in hiring and
promotion; involvement in monetary or other kickbacks; sexual harassment;
disclosure of proprietary or company information; theft; and use of corporate
Internet resources for inappropriate purposes, such as for conducting personal
business, gambling, or access to pornography.

Minor ethics cases—all reported concerns not classified as major ethics cases—   *Scope*
included informational queries from employees, situations involving coworkers,
and situations involving management.

The effectiveness of CGF's Ethics Program during the first year of implemen-   *Conclusions*
tation is most evidenced by (1) the active participation of employees in the
program and the 3,458 contacts employees made regarding ethics concerns
through the various channels available to them, and (2) the action taken in the
cases reported by employees, particularly the disposition of the 30 substantiated
major ethics cases.

Based on these conclusions, recommendations for planning the second year   *Recommendations*
of the Ethics Program are (1) continuing the channels of communication now
available in the Ethics Program, (2) increasing financial and technical support
for the Ethics Hotline, the most used mode of contact in the ethics cases reported in 2009, (3) disseminating this report in some form to employees to
ensure their awareness of CGF's commitment to uphold its Ethics Policy and
Procedures, and (4) implementing some measure of recognition for ethical
behavior, such as an "Ethics Employee of the Month" award to promote and
reward ethical conduct.

Figure 11–8   Executive Summary of a Formal Report

WRITER'S CHECKLIST
Writing Executive Summaries

✔ Write the executive summary after you have completed the original document.

✔ Avoid using terminology that may not be familiar to your readers.

✔ Spell out all uncommon symbols, abbreviations, and acronyms.

✔ Do not refer by number to figures, tables, or references contained elsewhere in the report.

✔ Make the summary concise, but do not omit transitional words and phrases (such as *however, moreover, therefore, for example,* and *in summary*).

✔ Include only information discussed in the original document.

Introduction

The introduction provides your audience with any general information—such as why the report has been written—required to understand the details of the rest of the report. State the subject, the purpose, the scope, and the way you plan to develop the topic. You may also describe how the report will be organized, but, as with the descriptive abstract, exclude specific findings, conclusions, and recommendations. Figure 11–9 shows the introduction to the report on the CGF Ethics Program. Note that the contents of the introduction and the contents of the preface may overlap in some cases.

Introducing the Subject

The introduction should state the subject of the report. To provide context for the audience, it should also include a summary of background information on the definition, history, or theory of the report's subject.

Stating the Purpose

The statement of the purpose in your introduction should function as a topic sentence does in a paragraph. It should make your audience aware of your goal as they read your supporting statements and examples and tell them whether your material provides a new perspective or clarifies an existing perspective.

Stating the Scope

The statement of the scope tells the audience how much or how little detail to expect. Does your report present a broad survey of the topic, or does it concentrate on one part of the topic? Once you state your scope broadly, stop. Save the details for the main body of the report.

Previewing How the Topic Will Be Developed

In a long report, state how you plan to develop or organize your topic. Is the report an analysis of the component parts of some whole? Is it an analysis of selected parts (or samples) of a whole? Is the material presented in chronological order? Does it move from details to general conclusions or from a general statement to

Reported Ethics Cases—2009

Header provides report title

INTRODUCTION

This annual report examines the disposition of the 3,458 reported ethics cases in 2009 and provides the Ethics and Business Conduct Committee with the information necessary for assessing the effectiveness of the first year of CGF's Ethics Program. Recommendations are given for planning the second year of the Ethics Program.

Purpose

Ethics and Business Conduct Policy and Procedures

Subheading signals shift in topic

Effective January 1, 2009, the Ethics and Business Conduct Committee implemented Policy CGF-EP-01 and Procedure CGF-EP-02 for the administration of CGF's new Ethics Program. The purpose of the Ethics Program is to "promote ethical business conduct through open communication and compliance with company ethics standards" (CGF "Ethical Business Conduct").

Background

The Office of Ethics and Business Conduct (OEBC) administers the Ethics Program. The director of the OEBC, along with seven ethics officers throughout CGF, is responsible for the following objectives:

- Communicate the values, standards, and goals of CGF's Ethics Program to employees.
- Inform employees about company ethics policies.
- Provide channels for employee education and guidance in resolving ethics concerns.
- Implement companywide programs in ethics awareness, education, and recognition.

Bulleted list makes information easy to read

Employee accessibility to ethics information and guidance became the immediate goal of the OEBC in its first year of operation. The following channels were set up in 2009:

Background

- Managers throughout CGF received intensive ethics training, and employees were encouraged to go to their managers as the first point of contact.
- Ethics officers were available to employees and managers through face-to-face or telephone contact, through the Ethics Hotline, and by e-mail.
- The Ethics Hotline was available to all employees, 24 hours a day, 7 days a week, to report ethics concerns anonymously.

Confidentiality Issues

Subheading signals shift in topic

CGF's Ethics Policy ensures confidentiality and anonymity for employees who raise genuine ethics concerns. Procedure CGF-EP-02 guarantees appropriate discipline, including dismissal, for retaliation or retribution against any employee who reports any genuine ethics concern.

Footer provides page number

Figure 11–9   Introduction to a Formal Report (continued)

Reported Ethics Cases—2009

Subheading

Documentation of Ethics Cases

Methodology

The following requirements were established by the director of the Office of Ethics and Business Conduct as uniform guidelines for the documentation by managers and ethics officers of all reported ethics cases:

Bulleted list high-lights guidelines

- Name, position, and department of the individual initiating contact, if available
- Date, time, and mode of contact
- Name, position, and department of the person contacted
- Category and resolution of ethics case

Managers and ethics officers entered the required information in each reported ethics case into an ACCESS database file, enabling efficient retrieval and analysis of the data.

Subheading

Major/Minor Category Definition and Examples

Methodology

Major ethics cases were defined as those situations potentially involving serious violations of company policies or illegal conduct. Procedure CGF-EP-02 requires notification of the Internal Audit and the Law departments in serious ethics cases. The staffs of the Internal Audit and the Law departments assume primary responsibility for managing major ethics cases and for working with the employees, ethics officers, and managers involved in each case.

Examples of situations categorized as major ethics cases:

Bulleted list high-lights examples

- Cover-up of defective workmanship or use of defective parts in products
- Discrimination in hiring and promotion
- Involvement in monetary or other kickbacks from customers for preferred orders
- Sexual harassment
- Disclosure of proprietary customer or company information
- Theft
- Use of corporate Internet resources for inappropriate purposes

Minor ethics cases were defined as including all reported concerns not classified as major ethics cases. Minor ethics cases were classified as follows:

- Informational queries from employees
- Situations involving coworkers or management

Page footer pro-vides page number

Figure 11–9   Introduction to a Formal Report (continued) the details that verify the statement? Does it set out to show whether a hypothesis is correct or incorrect? Stating your topic allows your audience to anticipate how the subject will be presented and gives them a basis for evaluating how you arrived at your conclusions or recommendations.

Text (Body)

Generally the longest section of the report, the text (or body) presents the details of how the topic was investigated, how the problem was solved, how the best choice from among alternatives was selected, or whatever else the report covers. This information is often clarified and further developed by the use of illustrations and tables and may be supported by references to other studies.

Most formal reports have no single best organization—the organization of the report will depend on the topic and on how you have investigated it. The text is ordinarily divided into several major sections, comparable to the chapters in a book. These sections are then subdivided to reflect logical divisions within your main sections. The sample table of contents (see Figure 11–5, page 395) indicates how the text was organized for the report on the Ethics Program at the CGF Aircraft Corporation. Figure 11–10 on pages 404–407 shows the body of the same report.

Headings

Headings (or heads) are the titles or subtitles of sections within the body of the report. They make the report more accessible to the audience by (1) dividing the body into manageable segments, (2) calling attention to the main topics, and (3) signaling changes of topics. Especially for long and complicated reports, you may need several levels of headings to indicate major divisions and subdivisions of the topic. Make headings most effective by following these guidelines:

- Use headings to signal a new topic or, if it is a lower-level heading, a new subtopic within the larger topic.
- Avoid too many or too few headings or levels of headings; too many clutter a document and too few fail to provide a recognizable structure.
- Use varying type styles and formatting conventions to distinguish among levels of headings (see Figure 11–11 on page 408 and Designing Your Document on page 409).
- Ensure that headings at the same level are of relatively equal importance and follow parallel grammatical structure.
- Subdivide sections only as needed; not every section requires lower-level headings.
- When subdividing a section, always use two or more headings (a topic cannot logically be divided into fewer than two parts).
- Do not allow a heading to substitute for discussion; the text should read as if the heading were not there.
- Do not leave a heading as the final line of a page. If two lines of text cannot fit below a heading, start the section at the top of the next page.

Header provides report title

Heading

Figure labeled and cross-referenced in text (cross-reference precedes figure)

Figure boxed and set off by white space above and below

Heading signals shift in topic

Cross-reference precedes figure

Page footer provides page number

ANALYSIS OF REPORTED ETHICS CASES

Reported Ethics Cases by Major/Minor Category

CGF ethics officers and managers companywide handled a total of 3,458 ethics situations during 2009. Of these cases, only 172, or 5 percent, involved reported concerns of a serious enough nature to be classified as major ethics cases (see Figure 1). Major ethics cases were defined as those situations potentially involving serious violations of company policy or illegal conduct.

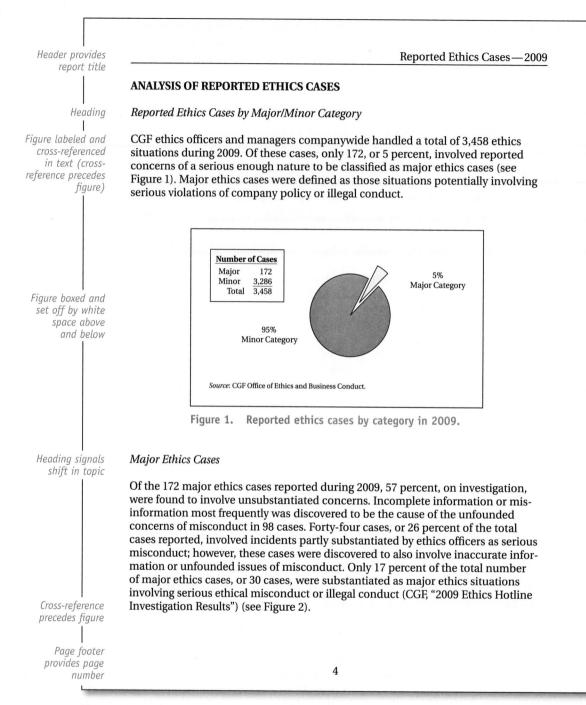

Figure 1. Reported ethics cases by category in 2009.

Major Ethics Cases

Of the 172 major ethics cases reported during 2009, 57 percent, on investigation, were found to involve unsubstantiated concerns. Incomplete information or misinformation most frequently was discovered to be the cause of the unfounded concerns of misconduct in 98 cases. Forty-four cases, or 26 percent of the total cases reported, involved incidents partly substantiated by ethics officers as serious misconduct; however, these cases were discovered to also involve inaccurate information or unfounded issues of misconduct. Only 17 percent of the total number of major ethics cases, or 30 cases, were substantiated as major ethics situations involving serious ethical misconduct or illegal conduct (CGF, "2009 Ethics Hotline Investigation Results") (see Figure 2).

Figure 11–10 **Body of a Formal Report** (continued)

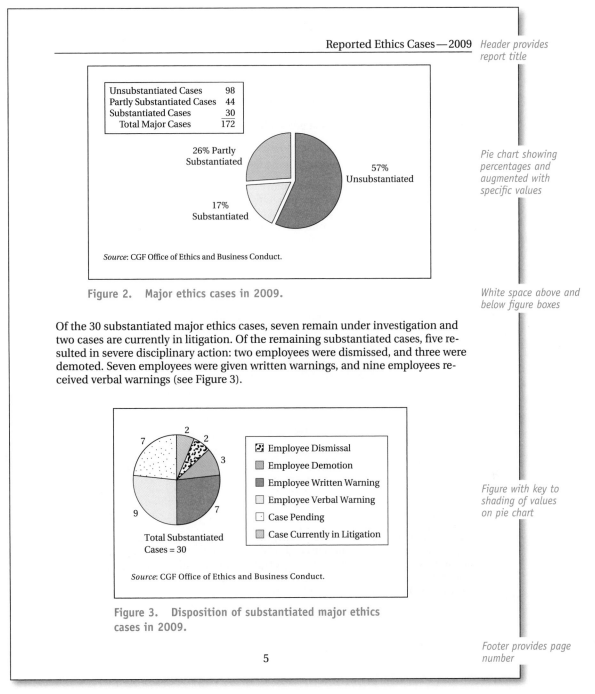

Header provides report title

Unsubstantiated Cases	98
Partly Substantiated Cases	44
Substantiated Cases	30
Total Major Cases	172

26% Partly Substantiated

57% Unsubstantiated

17% Substantiated

Source: CGF Office of Ethics and Business Conduct.

Pie chart showing percentages and augmented with specific values

Figure 2.   Major ethics cases in 2009.

White space above and below figure boxes

Of the 30 substantiated major ethics cases, seven remain under investigation and two cases are currently in litigation. Of the remaining substantiated cases, five resulted in severe disciplinary action: two employees were dismissed, and three were demoted. Seven employees were given written warnings, and nine employees received verbal warnings (see Figure 3).

7   2   2
        3

9   7

Total Substantiated
Cases = 30

☒ Employee Dismissal
▨ Employee Demotion
▨ Employee Written Warning
☐ Employee Verbal Warning
⊡ Case Pending
▨ Case Currently in Litigation

Source: CGF Office of Ethics and Business Conduct.

Figure with key to shading of values on pie chart

Figure 3.   Disposition of substantiated major ethics cases in 2009.

Footer provides page number

Figure 11–10   Body of a Formal Report (continued)

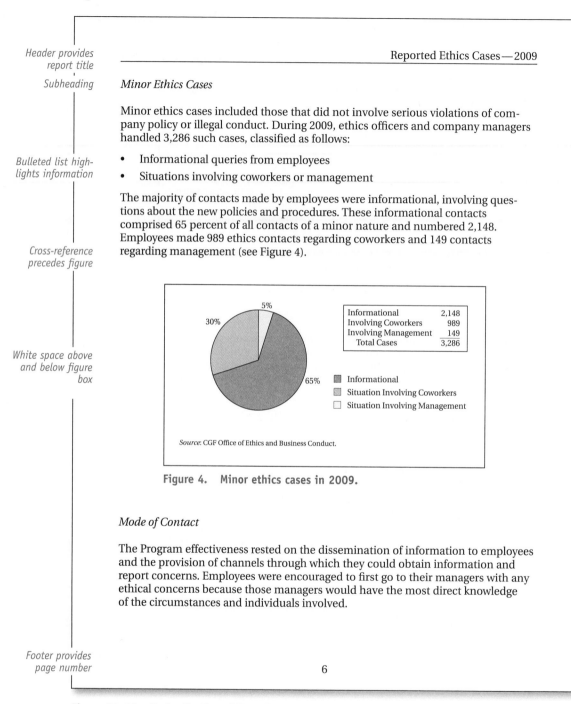

Header provides report title

Subheading

Bulleted list highlights information

Cross-reference precedes figure

White space above and below figure box

Footer provides page number

Reported Ethics Cases—2009

Minor Ethics Cases

Minor ethics cases included those that did not involve serious violations of company policy or illegal conduct. During 2009, ethics officers and company managers handled 3,286 such cases, classified as follows:

• Informational queries from employees
• Situations involving coworkers or management

The majority of contacts made by employees were informational, involving questions about the new policies and procedures. These informational contacts comprised 65 percent of all contacts of a minor nature and numbered 2,148. Employees made 989 ethics contacts regarding coworkers and 149 contacts regarding management (see Figure 4).

Informational	2,148
Involving Coworkers	989
Involving Management	149
Total Cases	3,286

■ Informational
▨ Situation Involving Coworkers
☐ Situation Involving Management

Source: CGF Office of Ethics and Business Conduct.

Figure 4.   Minor ethics cases in 2009.

Mode of Contact

The Program effectiveness rested on the dissemination of information to employees and the provision of channels through which they could obtain information and report concerns. Employees were encouraged to first go to their managers with any ethical concerns because those managers would have the most direct knowledge of the circumstances and individuals involved.

6

Figure 11–10   Body of a Formal Report (continued)

*Header provides
report title*

Other options were available, however, for employees who did not feel able to go to their manager. The ethics officers were available to employees through telephone conversations, face-to-face meetings, and e-mail messages. Ethics officers also served as contact points for managers in need of support and assistance in handling the ethics concerns reported to them by their subordinates.

The Ethics Hotline, operational in mid-January 2009, offered employees anonymity and confidentiality. It was accessible to all employees on a 24-hour, 7-day-a-week basis. Ethics officers handled calls reported through the hotline on a rotational basis.

In summary, ethics information and guidance were available to all employees during 2009 through the following channels:

- Employee to manager
- Employee telephone, face-to-face, and e-mail contact with ethics officers
- Manager to ethics officer
- Ethics Hotline

Bulleted lists summarize parallel information in parallel form

The mode of contact in the 3,458 reported ethics cases was as follows (see Figure 5):

Cross-reference precedes figure

- In 19 percent, or 657, of the reported cases, employees went to managers with concerns.
- In 9 percent, or 311, of the reported cases, employees contacted an ethics officer.
- In 5 percent, or 173, of the reported cases, managers sought assistance from ethics officers.
- In 67 percent, or 2,317, of the reported cases, employees used the Ethics Hotline.

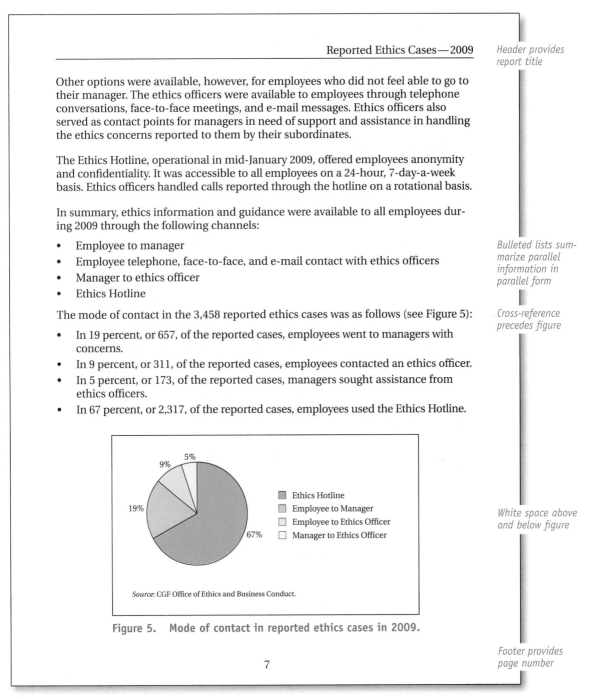

White space above and below figure

Figure 5.   Mode of contact in reported ethics cases in 2009.

*Footer provides
page number*

Figure 11–10   Body of a Formal Report (continued)

FIRST-LEVEL HEADING

The text of the document begins here.

SECOND-LEVEL HEADING

The text of the document begins here.

Third-Level Heading

The text of the document begins here.

Fourth-Level Heading

The text of the document begins here.

Fifth-level heading. The text of the document begins here and continues normally to the next line of the page.

Figure 11–11   Common Type Style for Headings

The decimal numbering system uses a combination of numbers and decimal points to subordinate levels of headings in a report. The system is used primarily for scientific and technical reports. The outline in Figure 11–12 shows the correspondence between different levels of headings and the decimal numbers used. (Note that although the second-, third-, and fourth-level headings are indented in an outline or a table of contents, as headings they are flush with the left margin in the body of the report.)

```
1.       MAJOR IDEA
1.1      Supporting idea for 1
1.2      Supporting idea for 1
1.2.1    Example or illustration of 1.2
1.2.2    Example or illustration of 1.2
1.2.2.1  Detail for 1.2.2
1.2.2.2  Detail for 1.2.2
1.3      Supporting idea for 1
2.       MAJOR IDEA
```

Figure 11–12   Decimal Numbering System for Headings

Explanatory Notes

Occasionally, reports contain notes that amplify terms or points for some readers that would be a distraction for others. This type of explanation is generally placed at the foot of the page on which the idea appears.

> ## DESIGNING YOUR DOCUMENT
> ### Heading Styles
>
> Although various systems exist, the following guidelines for formatting up to five levels of headings are common:
>
> *First-Level Head*
> - All capital letters underlined or in 18-point boldface type
> - Centered or flush left on a line by itself
> - Two spaces above and one below
>
> *Second-Level Head*
> - All capital letters or in 14-point boldface type
> - Flush left on a line by itself
> - One space above and one space below
>
> *Third-Level Head*
> - Capital and lowercase letters underlined or in boldface type
> - Flush left on a line by itself
> - One space above and one space below
>
> *Fourth-Level Head*
> - Capital and lowercase letters *not* underlined or in boldface type
> - One space above and one space below
>
> *Fifth-Level Head*
> - Indented as a paragraph on the same line as the first line of material it introduces
> - Underlined or in italic type
> - First letter capitalized; all others lowercase except proper nouns
> - Ends with a period
> - One space above the heading
>
> Figure 11–11 illustrates this system.

▷ A description of the 76 variables identified for inclusion in the regression equations, together with their method of construction, data, source, means, and ranges, is given in Appendix A. The following discussion elaborates on those variables that proved most important in explaining housing-price variations.[1]

---

[1]The number in parentheses in the following discussion refers to the variable number as used in regression equations.

◆ *For additional guidance on the purpose of these notes, see Chapter 6, Researching Your Subject.*

If such comments are very long, or if offering them as footnotes would crowd the pages of the report body, they may appear in a separate "Notes" page at the end of the section, chapter, or report.

Graphic and Tabular Matter

Formal reports often contain illustrations and tables that clarify and support the text. These materials may be numbered and sequenced in varying ways. If your employer has a preferred system, use it. If not, the following guidelines offer a typical system for numbering and smoothly integrating such materials into the text.

Identify each figure with a title and a number, in Arabic numerals, above or below the figure. For fairly short reports, number figures sequentially throughout the report (Figure 1, Figure 2, and so forth). For long reports, number figures by chapter or by section. According to this system, the first figure in Chapter 1 would be Figure 1.1 (or Figure 1–1), and the second figure would be Figure 1.2 (or Figure 1–2). In Chapter 2, the first figure would be Figure 2.1 (or Figure 2–1), and so on.

In the text, refer to figures by number rather than by location ("Figure 2.1" [or Figure 2–1] rather than "the figure below"). When the report is laid out and printed, the figures may not fall exactly where you originally expected. The figure or table should always be placed *after* its first mention in the text.

Identify each table with a title and a number, centering both of these lines above the table. For fairly short reports, number the tables sequentially throughout the report (Table 1, Table 2, and so on). For long reports, number tables by chapter or by section, according to the system described for figure numbering. As with figures, refer to tables in the text by number rather than by location ("Table 4.1" [or Table 4–1] rather than "the above table").

◆ *For a full discussion of creating and using illustrations, see Chapter 7, Designing Effective Documents and Visuals.*

Conclusions

The conclusions section of a report pulls together the report's results or findings and interprets them in the light of its purpose and methods. Consequently, this section is the focal point of the work, the reason for the report in the first place. The conclusions must grow out of the findings discussed in the body of the report; moreover, they must be consistent with the purpose stated in the introduction and with the report's methodology. For instance, if the introduction states that the report's objective is to assess the market for a new product, then the conclusion should focus on the requirements of the market examined and on how appropriate the new product is for that market.

Recommendations

Recommendations, which are sometimes combined with the conclusions, suggest a course of action that should be taken based on the results of the study. (Decide whether the report should make recommendations when the report is being planned.) What consulting group should the firm hire for a special project? With which Web-page designer should the company sign a contract? What new and emerging markets should the firm target? Which make of delivery van should the company purchase to replace the existing fleet? The recommendations section says, in effect, "I think we should purchase this, or do that, or hire them."

The emphasis here is on the verb *should.* Recommendations advise the audience on the best course of action based on the researcher's findings. In general, a decision maker in the organization, or a customer or client, makes the final decision about whether to accept the recommendations.

Figure 11–13 on pages 412–413 shows the conclusions and recommendations from the report on the CGF Ethics Program.

ETHICS NOTE

Formal reports frequently appear at the issuing organization's Web site. When a report is both printed and posted to the Web site, both versions should be identical in content. If the printed version is shortened or revised for Web posting, the Web version should be marked accordingly so that readers know how it differs from the original.

The Web version should also be reviewed before posting to ensure the following:

■ It complies with the organization's guidelines for release of information to the public.

■ Its content is consistent with the organization's current policies.

■ It does not contain proprietary, classified, or privacy information.

■ It has been granted permission to publish copyrighted text, tables, or images.

Works Cited (or References)

If you refer to material in, or quote directly from, a published work or other research source, you must cite those sources in the body of the text and provide a list of references in a separate section. Citing sources and listing references allows readers to locate and consult your sources and to find further information about the subject; the practice also enables you to avoid plagiarism while supporting your assertions and arguments with expert opinion and valid data. If your instructor or employer has a preferred reference style, follow it; otherwise, use the MLA or APA documentation guidelines shown in Chapter 6, Researching Your Subject. (*Note*: If you use MLA style, the list is titled "Works Cited"; in APA style, it is titled "References.") For a relatively short report, place the references at the end of the body of the report, as shown in Figure 11–14 on page 414. For a report with a number of sections or chapters, place the references at the end of each major section or chapter. In either case, title the reference or works-cited section as such and begin it on a new page. If a particular reference appears in more than one section or chapter, repeat it in full in each appropriate reference section.

◆ *For detailed guidance for documenting sources and avoiding plagiarism, see pages 180–204 in Chapter 6, Researching Your Subject.*

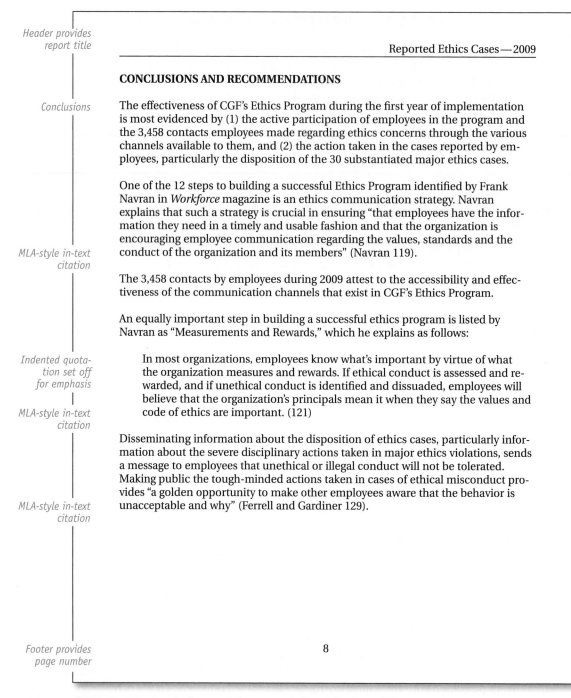

CONCLUSIONS AND RECOMMENDATIONS

Conclusions

The effectiveness of CGF's Ethics Program during the first year of implementation is most evidenced by (1) the active participation of employees in the program and the 3,458 contacts employees made regarding ethics concerns through the various channels available to them, and (2) the action taken in the cases reported by employees, particularly the disposition of the 30 substantiated major ethics cases.

One of the 12 steps to building a successful Ethics Program identified by Frank Navran in *Workforce* magazine is an ethics communication strategy. Navran explains that such a strategy is crucial in ensuring "that employees have the information they need in a timely and usable fashion and that the organization is encouraging employee communication regarding the values, standards and the conduct of the organization and its members" (Navran 119).

MLA-style in-text citation

The 3,458 contacts by employees during 2009 attest to the accessibility and effectiveness of the communication channels that exist in CGF's Ethics Program.

An equally important step in building a successful ethics program is listed by Navran as "Measurements and Rewards," which he explains as follows:

Indented quotation set off for emphasis

> In most organizations, employees know what's important by virtue of what the organization measures and rewards. If ethical conduct is assessed and rewarded, and if unethical conduct is identified and dissuaded, employees will believe that the organization's principals mean it when they say the values and code of ethics are important. (121)

MLA-style in-text citation

Disseminating information about the disposition of ethics cases, particularly information about the severe disciplinary actions taken in major ethics violations, sends a message to employees that unethical or illegal conduct will not be tolerated. Making public the tough-minded actions taken in cases of ethical misconduct provides "a golden opportunity to make other employees aware that the behavior is unacceptable and why" (Ferrell and Gardiner 129).

MLA-style in-text citation

Header provides report title

MLA-style in-text citation

Footer provides page number

8

Figure 11–13   Conclusions and Recommendations of a Formal Report (continued)

Reported Ethics Cases—2009

With these two points in mind, I offer the following recommendations for planning the Ethics Program's second year:

- Continue the channels of communication now available in the Ethics Program.
- Increase financial and technical support for the Ethics Hotline, the most highly used mode of contact in the reported ethics cases in 2009.
- Disseminate this report in some form to employees to ensure employees' awareness of CGF's commitment to uphold its Ethics Policy and Procedures.
- Implement some measure of recognition for ethical behavior, such as an "Ethics Employee of the Month," to promote and reward ethical conduct.

*Bulleted list high-
lights information*

To ensure that employees see the value of their continued participation in the Ethics Program, feedback is essential. The information in this annual review, in some form, should be provided to employees. Knowing that the concerns they reported were taken seriously and resulted in appropriate action by Ethics Program administrators would reinforce employee involvement in the program. While the negative consequences of ethical misconduct contained in this report send a powerful message, a means of communicating the *positive* rewards of ethical conduct at CGF should be implemented. Various options for recognizing employees who exemplify ethical conduct should be considered and approved.

Recommendations

Continuation of the Ethics Program's successful 2009 operations, with the implementation of the above recommendations, should ensure the continued pursuit of the Ethics Program's purpose: "to promote a positive work environment that encourages open communication regarding ethics and compliance issues and concerns."

*Footer provides
page number*

Figure 11–13   Conclusions and Recommendations of a Formal Report (continued)

Header provides report title

Works-cited listing follows MLA format

Footer provides page number

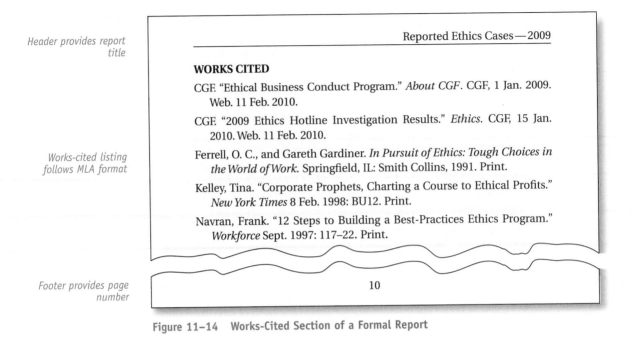

Reported Ethics Cases—2009

WORKS CITED

CGF. "Ethical Business Conduct Program." *About CGF*. CGF, 1 Jan. 2009. Web. 11 Feb. 2010.

CGF. "2009 Ethics Hotline Investigation Results." *Ethics*. CGF, 15 Jan. 2010. Web. 11 Feb. 2010.

Ferrell, O. C., and Gareth Gardiner. *In Pursuit of Ethics: Tough Choices in the World of Work*. Springfield, IL: Smith Collins, 1991. Print.

Kelley, Tina. "Corporate Prophets, Charting a Course to Ethical Profits." *New York Times* 8 Feb. 1998: BU12. Print.

Navran, Frank. "12 Steps to Building a Best-Practices Ethics Program." *Workforce* Sept. 1997: 117–22. Print.

10

Figure 11–14   Works-Cited Section of a Formal Report

ETHICS NOTE

Always identify the sources of any facts, ideas, quotations, and paraphrases you include in a report. Plagiarism—even if unintentional—is unethical and in some cases illegal. Plagiarism in a college course may result in formal academic misconduct charges; on the job, it can get you fired. Avoid trouble by giving proper credit to others.

■ Back Matter

The back matter of a formal report contains supplementary material, such as where to find additional information about the topic (bibliography), and expands on certain subjects (appendixes). Other back-matter elements define the terms used (glossary) and provide information on how to easily locate information in the report (index). For very long formal reports, back-matter sections may be individually numbered.

Bibliography

The bibliography is an alphabetical listing of all the sources you consulted to prepare the report—not just the ones you cite specifically—and suggests additional resources readers might want to consult. Accordingly, the bibliography may be longer than the works-cited section. A bibliography is not necessary if the Works

Cited (or References) page contains a complete list of sources. Like other elements in the front and back matter, the bibliography starts on a new page and is labeled by name.

Appendixes

An appendix clarifies or supplements the body with information that is too detailed or lengthy for the primary audience but that is relevant to secondary audiences. Appendixes might provide long charts and supplementary graphs or tables, copies of questionnaires and other material used in gathering information, texts of interviews, pertinent correspondence, and explanations too long for explanatory footnotes. Generally, each appendix contains one type of material. For example, a report may have one appendix presenting a questionnaire and a second appendix presenting a detailed computer printout tabulating questionnaire results.

Place the first appendix on a new page directly after the bibliography; each additional appendix also begins on a new page. Identify each appendix with a label and a title. Appendixes are ordinarily labeled Appendix A, Appendix B, and so on. If your report has only one appendix, label it "Appendix," followed by the title. To call it Appendix A implies that an Appendix B will follow.

If a report has only one appendix, the pages are generally numbered 1, 2, 3, and so forth. If it has more than one appendix, the pages are double-numbered according to the letter of each appendix (for example, the first page of Appendix B would be numbered B–1).

Glossary

A glossary is an alphabetical list of definitions of terms used in a formal report. If you are writing a report that will go to readers unfamiliar with many of the terms you use, include a glossary. If you do, keep the entries concise and be sure they are written in plain language to improve reader understanding.

> ▷ *Capital gain*: The difference between an asset's purchase price and selling price, when the difference is positive.

Arrange the terms alphabetically, with each entry beginning on a new line. The definitions then follow the terms, dictionary style. In a formal report, the glossary appears as a separate section after the appendix(es) and bibliography, and it begins on a new page.

Regardless of whether you include a glossary, you must define any specialized terms when they are first mentioned in the text.

Index

An index is an alphabetical list of all the major topics and subtopics found in the report. It cites the pages where each topic can be found and allows readers to find information on particular topics quickly and easily, as shown in Figure 11–15.

```
monitoring programs, 27–44  ───────────────  Main entry
    ☐ aquatic, 42
    ☐ ecological, 40
    ☐ meteorological, 37                          Subentries
    ☐ ☐ operational, 39
    ☐ ☐ preoperational, 37                        Sub-subentries
    ☐ radiological, 30
    ☐ terrestrial, 41, 43–44
    ☐ thermal, 27                                 Subentries
```

Figure 11–15 Index Entry (with Main Entry, Subentries, and Sub-subentries)

Indexes are especially useful for reports that will serve as reference documents in a subject area for at least several years. The index always comes at the very end of the report.

Do not attempt to compile an index until the final manuscript is completed because terminology and page numbers will not be accurate before then. The key to a useful index is selectivity. Instead of listing every possible reference to a topic, select references to passages where the topic is discussed fully or where a significant point is made about it. Use the words or phrases that best represent a topic—those that a reader would most likely look for in an index. For example, the key terms in a reference to the development of legislation about environmental impact statements would probably be *legislation* and *environmental impact statement*.

@ DIGITAL TIPS: Creating an Index

Word-processing software can help you save time when creating an index for your report.

▦ Review the document to identify entries (the words, phrases, figure captions, or symbols that you wish to index).

▦ Following your software's instructions, highlight and code these entries. (In Microsoft Word, for example, you can mark a keyword, and the software can automatically mark all other instances of the word.)

▦ The software sorts the coded entries, eliminates duplications, and arranges the entries alphabetically with their page numbers in a separate section at the end of the document.

▦ If you wish, create headings for each alphabetical grouping of the index (A, B, C, and so on).

▦ Your draft index will still need careful review and revisions, but using the software to create the first draft can certainly save time. Review for what might be missing as well as for what is there.

For further instructions, see bedfordstmartins.com/writingthatworks and select *Digital Tips*, Creating an Index.

An index entry can consist solely of a main entry and its page number; it can also include a main entry, subentries, and even sub-subentries, as shown in Figure 11–15. The first word of an entry should be the principal word because the reader will look for topics alphabetically by their main words. An index entry should be written as a noun or a noun phrase rather than as an adjective alone.

When you have compiled a list of key terms and cross-references for the entire work, sort the main entries alphabetically, then sort all subentries and sub-subentries alphabetically beneath their main entries.

ON THE WEB

The American Society of Indexers lists software available for indexing at its Web site, **www.asindexing.org**

CHAPTER 11 SUMMARY: WRITING FORMAL REPORTS

Formal reports require thoughtful planning because of their varied audiences, purposes, scope, and complexity. To ensure that your formal reports are adequately planned and written, review the following summary checklist.

- Who is the principal audience for the report? Who is the secondary audience?
- Is the transmittal letter or memo necessary and addressed to the principal audience?
- Are the elements that make up the front matter, body, and back matter of the report organized correctly?
- Does the title page include the report title, date, preparer, and recipient?
- Does the abstract highlight the report's major points?
- Does the table of contents list section titles exactly as they appear throughout the report?
- Does the executive summary describe the purpose, major findings, conclusions, recommendations, and methodology used to reach the findings? Can it be read independently of the report?
- Does the introduction state the purpose of the report, the scope of material it covers, how you plan to develop the topic, and how the report will be organized?
- Does the body of the report enable the principal audience to interpret your findings, conclusions, and recommendations?
- Is the body of the report organized into logically divided sections that best represent how the topic was developed to reach its findings, conclusions, and recommendations?
- Do the conclusions grow logically from the report's findings?
- Do the recommendations advise the audience on the appropriate course of action to take based on the findings?
- Do the works cited or references provide enough information to permit a reader to locate a source of interest?
- Is the material in the appendixes of sufficient importance to be included but so voluminous or ancillary that its presence in the body of the report would impede the reader?
- Does the report include a large number of technical terms that should be defined for your audience in an alphabetically arranged glossary?
- Are the index terms sufficiently selective that they allow the audience to locate key topics throughout the report quickly and accurately?

ON THE WEB

For an online quiz on formal reports, go to Chapter 11, bedfordstmartins.com/ writingthatworks

ON THE WEB

For additional exercises on writing formal reports, go to Chapter 11, bedfordstmartins.com/writingthatworks

Exercises

1. Write a brief analysis identifying different purposes of formal reports and list different situations in which each might be used.

2. Prepare a statement that defines the scope of a formal report, covering the benefits, risks, and costs of establishing an on-site fitness center at a local business with more than 200 employees.

3. The following is an audience-profile questionnaire for the fitness-center report in Exercise 2 or for a hypothetical research, an investigative, or an annual report that you have been asked to prepare. Briefly explain the topic of your formal report before answering the questions:

   a. Who is your audience? (Write a 75- to 100-word description.)
   b. What does your audience already know about the subject?
   c. What do you want your audience to know?
   d. What might be your readers' attitude toward the topic? (Explore several alternatives.)
   e. Why will your audience be reading the report?
   f. How will your readers' perception of the report affect the project?

4. Keeping in mind that design is an important part of a formal report, prepare a title page for the fitness-center report in Exercises 2 and 3 or for a hypothetical research, investigative, or annual report that you have been asked to prepare and bring it to class. Refer to pages 389–390 for guidelines as you design your title page.

5. Considering your audience and purpose, determine what elements you would need to include in the fitness-center or hypothetical report from Exercises 2, 3, and 4. Then prepare a table of contents that details the materials the final report would include.

6. Write a brief explanation of why you think either the executive summary or the abstract is the most important single piece of a formal report. Refer to the report included in this chapter or to another sample report to support your conclusions.

7. Assume you are starting a business of your own. First, determine what type of business you would start, depending on your knowledge or experience. Based on what you know about such a business, write an introduction for a formal report, explaining what your business will be and identifying what city would be the best location for your business and why. Assume that you are preparing this report to attach to a request for funding from the Small Business Administration. Submit an outline to your instructor before you begin your draft.

8. Assume that you work in the corporate office of a high-end automotive manufacturer and that you are coordinating a report that analyzes the effectiveness of new management initiatives that have gone into effect in the last year. Two of the people on your team, who have been lax in meeting periodic deadlines, submit hastily written drafts on the day before the entire report must be printed. To your dismay, you realize that each of them has peppered his section with abbreviations for trendy managerial phrases, such as "JIT" for "Just-in-Time" delivery and "CSR" for "Corporate Social Responsibility." There is no time left to revise these sections, but you know that several of the report's readers will not understand the abbreviations. Using the following terms, create a List of Abbreviations for the report to

explain what phrases they stand for and what those phrases mean. (You may have to do a little research to learn what the abbreviations stand for and what business concepts they refer to.)

ALF	BID	KAS
ALO	CSR	KISS
ASK	FMCG	MOP
ATNA	JIT	SONTTAP

9. Using the guidelines on pages 415–417, create an index for the sample formal report reprinted in Figures 11–9, 11–10, 11–13, and 11–14. As your instructor directs, exchange your index with that of another student and make a list of terms that differ in the indexes. Write a brief note for each distinctive index entry, evaluating whether you think it would be good to add to your index.

Collaborative Classroom Projects

ON THE WEB

For more collaborative classroom projects, go to Chapter 11, bedfordstmartins.com/writingthatworks

1. Bring to class or post online in a discussion forum a sample abstract for a journal article related to your major field of study. Divide into teams with classmates who share a similar major area of study. Appoint a group leader and a recorder. As a group, review the abstracts and answer the following questions about each:

   a. How many words are in the abstract?
   b. Is the abstract descriptive or informative? How do you know?
   c. What is the abstract's purpose? What is its scope?
   d. Is the abstract clear and concise?
   e. Does the abstract encourage you to read the rest of the report?
   f. How would you improve the abstract?

2. As a class, discuss the executive summary shown in Figure 11–8. Assume that the audience is, for example, the board of directors of CGF Aircraft Corporation. Consider the following questions:

   a. How does the executive summary introduce the report? Does it include the appropriate information?
   b. Is the background information sufficient?
   c. What is the purpose of the report?
   d. What is the scope of the report?
   e. Are costs an important concern of this report?
   f. Are the conclusions effective?
   g. How long would you expect the report to be?

Research Projects

ON THE WEB

For extra research projects, go to Chapter 11, bedfordstmartins.com/writingthatworks

1. Imagine that you work for a consulting firm that specializes in attractions, such as theme parks, aquariums, and zoos. Your firm has been hired by TRC, Inc., a company that owns several theme parks in the United States and is now interested in opening a new park in your state.

a. Write an investigative report for TRC, Inc., that includes the following (as directed by your instructor):

- An introduction
- A short history of theme parks
- The current state of the theme-park industry across the country and in your state
- An analysis of what makes theme parks successful (like popular themes that appeal to families, cutting-edge rides, quality service and cleanliness, and acceptable admissions prices)
- The local audience for theme parks (demographics) and what appeals to them
- A description of the competition in the area and their strong and weak points
- Developing trends in theme parks (what the theme park of the future will look like and offer to the public)
- Conclusions
- Recommendations
- Works cited

b. Include the following visuals in your report (be sure to cite them and label them as described in Chapter 7, Designing Effective Documents and Visuals):

- A line graph of attendance at theme parks across the country during the last five years
- A chart of services and offerings that make theme parks successful and the national theme parks that offer all or some of those services and offerings
- A pie graph of tourism in your state, broken down by the popularity of each kind of tourist activity (for example, theme parks, nature activities, museums, and so on)
- Photographs of local theme parks

2. Conduct research to prepare an analytical formal report that compares two possible courses of action. Imagine you work for a small company that has revenues of about $100 million in sales (and profits of about $4 million a year). Your company's sales force numbers 20 members who collectively travel approximately 1,000 miles a week. Your company now needs a new fleet of cars, all the same make and model, for the sales force. The cars should be economical but large enough to accommodate the samples (of equipment, books, and so on). You have been asked to determine whether the fleet should be purchased or leased.

Begin by developing a profile of your company so that you understand its needs and resources. Next, select three or four makes and models of cars. Choose specific features of the cars that you can compare. Analyze these features to determine (1) which car is the most cost-effective and the most suitable choice for your company and (2) whether to purchase or lease a fleet of these cars. In your report, clearly define, justify, and explain your findings:

- State the purpose of your report and your findings.
- Inform readers of how and where you gathered information.
- Define the criteria on which you based your research, given your company and its needs.
- Compare and contrast available options.
- Explain your conclusions and recommendations.

3. Using the *Occupational Outlook Handbook* at the Bureau of Labor Statistics Web site at <www.bls.gov/oco/home.htm>, write a formal report in which you analyze two different job positions in your major area of study. Include in your report the required background, working conditions, pay scale, geographic expectations, and job outlook. Prepare your report as if you are trying to decide objectively between two occupations, and include a conclusion and recommendations section.

4. The Federal Highway Administration (FHWA) of the U.S. Department of Transportation (DOT) works with states to conduct studies that explore the funding and feasibility of highway projects. According to the FHWA's Procedural Guidelines for Highway Feasibility Studies, six to nine tasks must occur within studies. See <www.fhwa.dot.gov/hep10/corbor/feastudy.html>. Only the last two steps of each case involve drafting the report; the first steps involve gathering and analyzing data.

   a. Write an abstract of the FHWA's Procedural Guidelines. Include a breakdown of the tasks required for (1) "improving an existing facility" or (2) "making major improvements to . . . a multi-State transportation corridor."

   b. Visit your state's DOT Web site and find a link to current construction projects. You can also research a project that local citizens and government officials are exploring, like monorail service.

   c. Imagine that you work for your state's DOT and you've been asked to draft an outline of a feasibility study for one or two current or future construction projects to get funding from the FHWA. Consider how you would address each task leading to the final report. Describe what kind of information you would try to put in each task and from where you would get these data. Sources could include the public affairs office of the local DOT, local newspapers, and the U.S. DOT's Web-site links to transportation information regarding each state. Create a transmittal memo directed to the secretary of transportation for your state.

12 Writing Instructions

AT A GLANCE: Instructions

When you tell someone how to perform a procedure or task, you are giving instructions. Instructions may describe how to carry out a particular task in the workplace (send a file to a digital copier); perform a procedure (process a Medicare form); operate equipment (use a spray-paint gun); or assemble, repair, or maintain equipment (replace a seal on a high-pressure pump).

This chapter provides guidance for the following:

- Planning instructions / 423
- Writing instructions / 432
- Illustrating instructions / 436
- Testing the effectiveness of instructions / 442

How many times have you heard people complain about instructions being unclear, inaccurate, or poorly illustrated? Poor instructions can cause miscommunication and delays in an important project or, worse, be directly responsible for an injury, which could result in damage claims and lawsuits. If your instructions are based on clear thinking and careful planning, they should enable your audience to carry out the procedure or task successfully. Clear, easy-to-follow instructions can also build goodwill for your company. Keep in mind that the most effective instructions often combine written elements and visual elements that reinforce each other. Finally, consider testing your instructions with someone unfamiliar with them and record and evaluate their behavior as they perform a task.

VOICES IN THE WORKPLACE

Reader-Focused Instructions in Words and Pictures

As an occupational therapist at St. Joseph's Hospital in Nashua, New Hampshire, Beth Blazon develops instructions for use at home when her patients are discharged: "I make my instructions simple, taking into account any language or cognitive barriers the patient may have [and] keep my instructions as basic as possible, using as few words as possible. I've found the use of pictures helps a lot, especially when demonstrating exercises."

Planning Instructions

To write effective instructions, first learn how the operation is performed and organize the instructions in the proper sequence. If possible, perform the operation yourself and record the details for each step as you perform it. Then assess your audience. Are they fellow employees within your firm, North American customers for your company's products, or non-English readers? Adapt your language and the design features of your instructions—their layout and packaging—for your target audience. After writing an introduction, listing or describing any essential tools or materials, as necessary, organize the instructions in the sequence and exact number of steps necessary to perform the task.

ON THE WEB

For more help with writing instructions, go to Chapter 12, bedfordstmartins.com/ writingthatworks

Learn to Perform the Operation Yourself

To write accurate and easily understood instructions, you must thoroughly understand the task you are describing. Otherwise, your instructions could be inaccurate or even dangerous. For example, the container of a brand-name drain cleaner directs the user to do the following:

▶   Fill sink with 1 to 2 inches of water, then close off drain opening.

Users would find it difficult to raise the water level in the sink *before* closing the drain! The writer of these instructions did not carefully observe the actual sequence of steps required to use the product. In this case, users simply ignored the instructions and performed the task according to common sense, so no harm was done. Suppose such confusing instructions were given for administering an intravenous fluid or for assembling high-voltage electrical equipment. The results of such inaccurate instructions could be both dangerous and costly.

The writer of the drain-cleaning instructions undoubtedly knew better and was just careless. Sometimes, though, a writer may be asked to write instructions for a procedure that he or she does not understand adequately. Don't let that happen to you. If you cannot perform a task yourself, request permission to watch someone else do it. As you watch, take careful notes and ask questions about any step that is not clear to you. Direct observation should enable you to write instructions that are exact, complete, and clear. Also make certain that you know the reason for the procedure, the materials and tools required, and the end result of the task.

Once you understand the procedure, you must determine the most effective way to present it to your audience.

Assess Your Audience and Purpose

In the workplace, you may need to prepare instructions for coworkers, domestic and international customers, or other users of your company's products or services. Start by determining who will use your instructions. Remember that you and your readers share a common purpose: the successful completion of a task or procedure after reading your instructions. To write instructions that best meet readers' requirements, learn as much as you can about your audience. You and your coworkers, for example, share a large amount of knowledge already. For customers and others outside the company, begin by learning their level of knowledge and experience, and try to put yourself in their position as they follow your instructions. Is the audience skilled in the kind of task for which you are writing instructions? If they are knowledgeable about the subject, use the specialized vocabulary and abbreviations appropriate to the subject. If they have little or no knowledge of the subject, use plain language or include a glossary that defines specialized terms in plain language. For international readers, learn about their proficiency in English and tailor the language accordingly.

◆ *For advice on creating a glossary, see Chapter 11, Writing Formal Reports.*

Coworkers

Employees write many kinds of informal, nontechnical instructions to coworkers every day. The advantage of communicating with coworkers is that they share your familiarity with the company's organization and hierarchy, job titles, products, customers, and numerous other details that need not be spelled out. In the e-mail instructions in Figure 12–1, for example, a budget analyst requests data about an office's copier use to plan for the upcoming fiscal year's budget. Note that this guidance is sent annually to the office manager, so both the sender and the recipient are familiar with the process. The scope of the request, its language ("seven-year life cycle"), and their shared access to an online form require no special explanations.

More detailed instructions to coworkers may describe how to perform routine workplace activities. The instructions in Figure 12–2 on page 426 address the crucial corporate responsibility of responding to consumer correspondence in a timely and responsible manner. They lay out the steps from the point when the correspondence is received until the company's response is sent. Note the use of headings, the step-by-step organization of the required tasks, and the uncomplicated language of the memo. These instructions assume that all recipients are familiar with the company's departments and job titles.

@   DIGITAL TIPS: Organizing and Highlighting Instructions

When writing instructions, use the following features of your word-processing software to organize and highlight information:

■ Font size and boldface

■ Outlining feature

■ Numbered-list feature

■ Bulleted-list feature

■ Icons, symbols, and up-to-date clip-art images

From: Carol Quenten <cquenten@techquest.com>
To: Gene Carruthers <gcarruthers@techquest.com>
Sent: March 1, 2010 09:27:42
Subject: Planning Call for FY 2011 Budget

Gene,

We are planning the 2011 budget cycle, and I'll need the following information about copier use in our headquarters' office.

Please gather and enter the following data on the budget form located on the shared S:\ drive at S:\OCIOO\IMD\copiers:

- Current and projected monthly maintenance charges for each copier and the totals
- Any indication of projected maintenance increases from our vendors
- The number of copiers we lease and the number we own
- The number of copiers we need to replace based on a seven-year life cycle per machine
- The projected costs for replacing our current copiers with networked copiers

Do not project toner and paper costs at this time.

The information is due for my review on 4/5/2010. Thanks.

===============================
Carol Quenten, Budget Analyst
Office of the Chief Financial Officer
TechQuest Inc.
119 Trowbridge Rd., Minneapolis, MN 55401
(507) 333-3333 Fax: (507) 333-3334
cquenten@techquest.com
techquest.com
===============================

Bulleted list for ease of reading and response

Qualifying guidance

Details on submitting answers

Figure 12–1   Informal Employee-to-Employee Instructions

Consumers

Some instructions are intended to help customers assemble and maintain products. The instructions can range in scope from directions for assembling a model ship to guidance for installing and testing software on the computer network of a multibranch commercial bank. These instructions tend to be formally written and carefully reviewed for accuracy and for their adherence to policy and legal requirements before they are used. The requirements common to all consumer instructions are that they be accurate, written in language appropriate to the audience, illustrated in sufficient detail (if necessary), and packaged in the medium most useful to the customer—brochure, print manual, compact disk.

Assess your customers carefully to meet these requirements. Consider their familiarity with your product based on their previous knowledge or experience,

Proctor Electronic Corporation

Consumer Response Department
Procedures for Handling Correspondence

Instructions arranged in sequential order

1. **Intake**

   When the Customer Response Department receives a written consumer query or comment, the department assistant

Bullets identify tasks within each major step

   - Logs the correspondence into the electronic tracking system.
   - Makes a paper copy.
   - Gives the copy to the section analyst for review.
   - Retains the original in the section tracking folder.

Boldface headings identify major steps

2. **Content Review**

   The department analyst

   - Reviews the content.
   - Meets with the department chief to discuss response strategy, staff assigned to respond, and date due to the department supervisor.

   The due date is two working days before the response is due to the vice president for consumer affairs.

3. **Staff Assignment**

   The department analyst

   - Informs the department assistant of who will respond and the due date.
   - Meets with the assistant and provides any necessary background for the reply.

4. **Staff Response**

   - The respondent e-mails the draft reply to the department assistant on or before the due date.
   - The department assistant logs the draft into the database and forwards it to the department analyst for review.

5. **Response Review**

   The department chief and department analyst jointly

   - Make any necessary revisions to the draft.
   - Forward the draft to the department assistant for incorporation into the final draft.

   The department assistant

   - Enters the final draft into the company electronic document database.
   - Maintains a record of concurrences on the final draft.
   - Prepares a paper correspondence package for signature.

6. **Approval**

   - The department supervisor approves the correspondence package.
   - The department assistant forwards the correspondence package to the vice president for consumer affairs for review and signature.

Figure 12–2　Coworker Instructions for Processing Correspondence

how broad your audience is (Is it a narrow group of specialists or a large cross-section of the population?), and the medium most useful to your audience. Also consider your audience's motivation for reading your instructions. Although instructions are essential to the successful use of consumer products, many readers ignore them. To increase the likelihood that readers will look at your instructions, see "Design for Ease of Use," page 438. Figure 12–3 shows a set of instructions in a customer booklet for maintaining a propane gas outdoor grill. Note that safety precautions appear at the beginning of the instructions.

Cleaning the Inside of the Grill

1. Disconnect the igniter wire from the igniter before cleaning the grill. Do not mistake the brown and black accumulation of grease and smoke for paint. The interiors of gas grills are not painted at the factory (and should never be painted).
2. Remove the grill lid, cooking grate, grease cup, and Drip VapoRISER Bar. Discard old lava rocks or briquettes. Attach the grease cup to the grease hanger and empty it after each use.
3. Using a scrub brush, apply a strong solution of detergent and water or grill cleaner to the insides of the grill lid and the bottom. Rinse and allow the equipment to air dry completely.

Instructions written in imperative mood

Instructions organized into numbered steps

Figure 12–3   Product-Maintenance Instructions

International Readers

Language differences create the biggest obstacle to writing instructions for readers whose primary language is not English. When you must write instructions for such an audience, find out as much as possible about their English-language proficiency and adjust your writing accordingly. If your text will be translated into another language, write to the extent possible in plain language and define specialized terms or abbreviations in a glossary. Help your audience by becoming familiar with their terminology for important concepts or even the names of commonly used objects. Consider, for example, the following passage from a computer-printer service manual that was translated from Japanese to English for American field engineers.

▷   Remove cover panel with great care, using plus driver to remove screws. Inside control box, wires are held in place with different screws. Take minus driver and loosen screws to remove wire from red and green terminals.

The terms "plus driver" and "minus driver" refer to a Philips-head screwdriver and a flat-head screwdriver. The Japanese translator apparently did not know the appropriate American terminology for the tools, so he used what seemed logical descriptions of them. (The Philips-head screwdriver looks like a plus sign; the flat-head screwdriver looks like a minus sign.) The result was a lot of confusion by English-speaking readers over what these terms could mean.

Well-illustrated instructions are effective in clarifying directions for international readers. In fact, instructions for many kinds of devices that require assembly are completely visual, such as the laminated cards aboard airplanes that illustrate how to evacuate the plane in an emergency. Using visual instructions is especially effective for international audiences because they avoid the pitfalls common when information is translated from one language to another. The instructions in Figure 12–4 illustrate how to install a box shelf on drywall. The product, manufactured in China, is sold internationally. The instructions show images of all parts provided and the tools needed to complete installation. They convey important image-only information about the shelving like the weight, capacity, placement, and positioning. If visual-only instructions are not possible, consult with someone from your intended audience's country as you plan and draft your instructions.

◆ *For a fuller discussion of writing for international readers, see page 70, in Chapter 3, Writing the Draft; pages 250–256, in Chapter 7, Designing Effective Documents and Visuals; and Writing International Correspondence, pages 343, 346–351, in Chapter 9, Writing Business Correspondence.*

The need for cross-cultural understanding of commonly used concepts led the International Organization for Standardization (ISO) to develop agreed-on symbols like those shown in Figure 7–37 on page 255 for use in public signs, guidebooks, and manuals.

Organize the Instructions

To make your instructions easy to follow, divide them into short, simple steps, and arrange the steps in the correct sequence. The steps can be given in either of two ways. You can label each step with a sequential number, as follows:

▷   1. Connect each black cable wire to a brass terminal.
       2. Attach one 4-inch green jumper wire to the back.
       3. Connect both jumper wires to the bare cable wires.

Or, you can use words that indicate time or sequence, as follows:

▷   *First*, assess the problem that the customer reports to you. *Next*, observe and test the system in operation. *At that time*, question the customer until you understand the problem completely. *Then*, test the following. . . .

Think ahead for your reader. If the instructions in step 2 will affect a process in step 9, say so in step 2. Sometimes your instructions have to make clear that two operations must be performed simultaneously. Either state that fact in an introduction to the specific instructions or include both operations in the same step.

CONFUSING   1. Hold the Control key down.
               2. Press the Delete key before releasing the Control key.

CLEAR   1. While holding the Control key down, press the Delete key.

If your instructions involve many steps, break them into stages, each with a separate heading so that each stage begins with step 1. Using headings as dividers

Product parts, tools needed, and width of holes

Icon of weight capacity for shelf

Placement of brackets in predrilled holes

How to mark wall for bracket holes

Sequence for installing drywall anchor and screw to wall

How to position shelf on brackets against wall

Figure 12–4   Visual Instructions Created for International Customers.   *Source:* Rubbermaid Frame Shelf Kit Product Packaging.

is especially important if your reader is likely to be performing the operation as he or she reads the instructions. Many instructions for product assembly are organized into four parts: Introduction, Required Equipment and Materials, Procedure, and Conclusion.

1. *Introduction.* Use an introduction to provide any needed background information, to state the purpose of the procedure, or to offer a theory of operation to help your audience understand why the product works the way it does. Figure 12–5 shows an excerpt from the introduction to a manual for the setup and operation of a DVD system. The excerpt describes the scope of the manual and the meaning of symbols used throughout.

2. *Required Equipment and Materials.* If special equipment, tools, or materials are needed to follow your instructions, provide a well-labeled section that tells your audience clearly what they need before they begin the procedure—

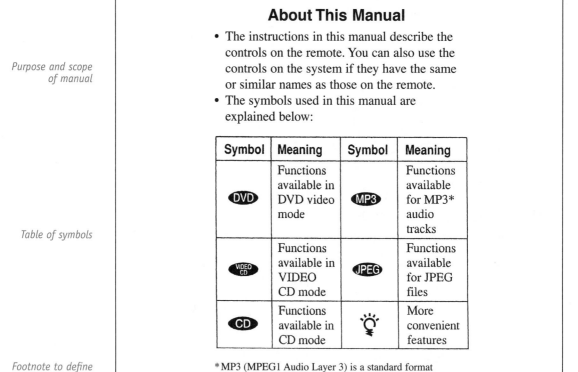

Purpose and scope of manual

Table of symbols

Footnote to define standard audio format

Figure 12–5 Introduction for Instructions. *Source:* "Home Theater System," Courtesy of Sony Corporation, 2003.

don't let them get well into the procedure before you tell them about such requirements.

3. *Procedure.* The procedure consists of the sequential steps required to complete the task. For a full discussion of this method of development, review the section on sequential organization on pages 34–36 in Chapter 2, Organizing Your Information.

4. *Conclusion.* Brief instructions can simply end with the last step in the procedure. For longer and more complex instructions, add a conclusion section that satisfies your audience's sense of confidence about completing the job successfully.

> ▷   Congratulations on successfully assembling your gas grill. With proper care, it will serve you well for many years to come.

Many instructions are organized into sections similar to this structure but are titled to more specifically describe the process. The instructions for installing a ceramic countertop in a kitchen or bathroom, for example, are organized into the following sections:

> ▷
> 1. Introduction
> 2. Tools Needed
> 3. Surface Preparation
>   • Choosing the Edge Trim
>   • Selecting the Sink
> 4. Planning the Layout
> 5. Setting the Tile
> 6. Applying Grout
> 7. Caulking and Sealing the Grout

▷ CONSIDERING AUDIENCE AND PURPOSE

Planning to Write Instructions

■ Can you perform or carefully observe others perform the task you are describing?

■ Will someone unfamiliar with the task you are describing be able to follow your instructions?

■ What vocabulary is appropriate to your audience?

■ Are your instructions to coworkers sufficiently specific to ensure that the task can be completed accurately and within the allotted schedule?

■ Have you organized the instructions in the proper sequence for the task?

■ Did you take into account your customers' level of knowledge about your product before you began writing?

■ Are your instructions written and illustrated appropriately for international readers?

■ Writing Instructions

Effective instructional writing follows a precise pattern dictated by the instruction writer's goal: telling someone how to perform a task. The most direct way of doing so is to word the instructions as commands, using the imperative mood: (1) Perform step 1. (2) Wait 5 minutes and perform step 2, and so on.

Assume that the reader will not be familiar with the task or procedure described. For that reason, use the plainest language possible to communicate with the broadest audience.

Finally, you are obligated to warn the audience explicitly of any potential risks or hazards associated with the task being explained. These warnings must be clearly spelled out, stand out from the surrounding text, and, if possible, illustrated. (This topic is discussed in more detail under "Include Warnings and Cautions" on page 433.)

Write Directly to Your Reader

The clearest and simplest instructions are written as commands. Addressing each sentence directly to your audience in the imperative mood and the active voice makes your instructions easier to follow and less wordy than if you were to write them in the passive voice.

PASSIVE	The access lid should be closed by the operator.
ACTIVE/IMPERATIVE	Close the access lid.

Although instructions should be concise, do not try to achieve conciseness by leaving out needed words such as articles (*a, an, the*), pronouns (*you, this, these*), and verbs. Doing so will certainly shorten sentences, but sentences shortened this way usually have to be read more than once to be understood—defeating the purpose of brevity. The following instruction for cleaning a power punch press assembly (a machine that punches holes and other patterns into materials), for example, is not easily understood at first reading.

UNCLEAR	Pass brush through punch area for debris.

The meaning of the phrase *for debris* needs to be made clearer. Revised, the instruction is readily understandable.

CLEAR	Pass a brush through the punch area to clear away any debris.

In any operation, certain steps must be performed with more exactness than others. Anyone who has boiled a three-minute egg for four minutes understands this all too well. Alert your audience to the steps that require exact timing or measurement.

VAGUE	Let the liquid cool.
PRECISE	Let the liquid cool for 30 minutes at room temperature.

◆ *See also pages 108–115 in Chapter 4, Revising the Draft.*

WRITER'S CHECKLIST
Writing Instructions in Plain Language

✔   Identify and write to your average reader.

✔   Keep in mind your average reader's level of technical knowledge.

✔   Avoid unnecessary jargon.

✔   Avoid confusing terms and constructions; for example,

　– Do not include undefined abbreviations and acronyms.

　– Do not use two different words for the same thing.

　– Do not give an obscure meaning to a word.

✔   Write in the imperative mood.

✔   Use the active voice.

　– It makes clear who is supposed to do what.

　– It uses fewer words.

✔   Use *you* and other pronouns.

　– Pronouns allow you to write directly to the reader rather than to a group.

　– Pronouns pull the reader into the writing and make the writing relevant to the reader.

✔   Write short sentences.

　– Aim for one message in each sentence.

　– Break up information into smaller, easier-to-understand units.

✔   Use simple tenses; use the present tense as much as possible.

✔   Select word placement carefully.

　– Keep subjects and objects close to their verbs.

　– Put *only*, *always*, and other conditional words next to the words they modify.

　– Put *if* phrases after the main clauses to which they apply, not before.

ON THE WEB

For background information about plain-language laws and practices, go to Chapter 4, bedfordstmartins.com/ writingthatworks and select *Web Links*.

Include Warnings and Cautions

Warnings and cautions are essential to instructions involving potentially hazardous equipment or materials. Many processes in industrial, medical, law enforcement, and other settings involve the use of potentially dangerous equipment, chemicals, and explosives. Instruction writers have legal and ethical reasons for ensuring that warnings and cautions are included with such instructions. Even instructions for tasks not overtly hazardous may require cautionary statements. In either case, you may need legal guidance on the appropriate language to use.

ETHICS NOTE

Product liability laws require a manufacturer to warn potential users of (1) dangers in the *normal use* of the product and (2) dangers in the *foreseeable misuse* of the product. A manufacturer, however, need not warn of *open and obvious* dangers. Hence, instructions for an electric knife need not warn the user not to use the knife for shaving a beard—an obvious danger that is also neither "normal use" nor "foreseeable" by the manufacturer. Instructions for an electric knife would need to warn users to take care when holding food to be sliced because a slip of the hand could result in injury—a danger in normal use. Even if the danger is open and obvious, the manufacturer may have a duty to warn users who may not be aware of the extent or degree of danger. If the likelihood of injury is serious, the manufacturer is also required to display a warning on the product itself.

Language of Warnings

In general, all instructions for the proper use of a product should be *clear, readable*, and *understandable*. However, readers must also be warned specifically of dangers that they might expect and dangers that they might not. Remember, a danger that is obvious to you as the writer of the instructions may not be obvious to the user. Instructions not only must warn of all risks and hazards but also must warn *adequately*. An adequate warning must do three things:

- Identify the hazard and the potential seriousness of the risk.
- Give the likely results of ignoring the warning.
- Describe how to avoid the hazard and thus the injury.

To ensure that a warning is adequate, the language in it must be clear and explicit.

VAGUE   Failure to disengage the blades may result in bodily harm.

EXPLICIT   If you do not disengage the blades, they can amputate your fingers.

Avoid words that are open to interpretation or need further defining: *proper, excessive, frequently, often, seldom, may, might, could, recommended, occasionally*. Instead, include specific time references (*every 90 days*) and use definitive verbs (*should, must*). If potential users are diverse, consider their familiarity (if any) with the product, level of literacy, and nationality.

Visual Symbols and Signal Words

Alert your readers to any potentially hazardous materials or actions before they reach the step for which the material is needed or the action will be performed. Caution readers handling hazardous materials about any requirements for special clothing, tools, equipment, and other safety measures. Highlight warnings, cautions, and precautions to make them stand out visually from the surrounding text—use an open, uncrowded format so that they do not blend in with the instructions. A clear border of heavy lines or white space adds visual emphasis to

ON THE WEB
For more guidelines on the use of terminology, colors, and symbols in instructions and labeling, visit the American National Standards Institute at <www.ansi.org/> and the International Organization for Standardization at <www.iso.org/>.

warnings. You can also place warning notices in all uppercase letters, in large and distinctive fonts, or in color.

Use symbols and icons in the text to reinforce warnings, as illustrated in Figure 12–6. Use line drawings of products that depict the physical sources of hazards and, if possible, the nature of the hazard. Cartoons can be especially helpful in instructions or warnings for adolescents and children. The Mr. Yuk image, intended to warn children away from poisonous substances, is now commonplace

Icons depict types of hazards

Source: Children's Hospital of Pittsburgh

Figure 12–6   Typical Warning Icons with Text

on product labels. Another common feature of warnings is a picture of what *not* to do, typically a slash (/) through the image, as shown in Figure 12–7.

Warning words, symbols, icons, and labels are increasingly becoming standardized, although industry practices do vary. Certain signal words in boldface and their corresponding colors are becoming standards in North America:

DANGER (red): hazard or unsafe practice that *will* result in severe injury or death

WARNING (orange): *could* result in severe injury or death

CAUTION (yellow): could result in *minor* injury or property damage

NOTICE (blue): information unrelated to safety

The hazard-alert symbol—an international standard—should appear with the signal word:

Figure 12–7   Icon Depicting a Prohibited Activity

Use cautions and warnings only when necessary, however. Too many may cause your audience to ignore those that are essential.

■ Using Illustrations and Design Principles

Well-thought-out illustrations can make even the most complex instructions easier to understand. In addition to demonstrating the steps of your instructions, line art, photographs, diagrams, and even cartoon-style drawings can help your audience identify parts and the relationships between them. In fact, some instructions, including those for international audiences, use only illustrations (see Figure 12–4 on page 429).

Consider the layout and design of your instructions to most effectively integrate text and visuals. Highlight important visuals, like warnings, by making them stand out from the surrounding text. Consider using boxes and boldface or distinctive headings. Experiment with font style, size, and color to determine which devices are most effective. If you use color, be aware that certain colors (red, green, and yellow, for example) have well-established meanings in North America but may be interpreted differently in other countries.

◆ *For a discussion of cultural differences in the use of color, see page 252 in Chapter 7, Designing Effective Documents and Visuals.*

Illustrate for Clarity

The value of illustrations will depend on your audience's needs and on the nature of the project. In general, instructions for inexperienced readers should be more thoroughly illustrated than those for experienced readers. Enhance the value of the illustration by referring to it in the instructions to explain what it shows, and use labels on the illustration to further clarify its purpose.

Ensure that step-by-step instructions are placed next to the steps illustrated or that illustrations are labeled with step numbers so that the audience immediately recognizes the connection between the two. Figure 12–8 shows instructions that guide a medical lab technician through the steps of streaking a saucer-sized disk of material (called *agar*) used to grow bacterial colonies for laboratory examination. In this case, the purpose is to thin out the original specimen (the *inoculum*) so that bacteria will grow in small, isolated colonies. When necessary or advisable, illustrate each step in your instructions (Figure 12–9), making certain that the illustration represents the current model of the equipment.

A technique especially useful for inexperienced readers is to show a close-up of a portion of a larger image, as in Figure 12–10 on page 439, which illustrates installation of a shower floor drain. The "magnified" image can show essential details impossible to see in a larger picture. Linking the two images visually puts the close-up in context for the reader.

◆ *For a complete discussion of how to create and use effective illustrations, see Chapter 7, Designing Effective Documents and Visuals.*

STREAKING AN AGAR PLATE

Distribute the inoculum over the surface of the agar in the following manner:

Step 1. After sterilizing the loop in an open flame, beginning at one edge of the saucer, thin the inoculum by streaking back and forth over the same area several times, sweeping across the agar surface until approximately one quarter of the surface has been covered. *Sterilize the loop.*

Step 2. Streak at right angles to the originally inoculated area, carrying the inoculum out from the streaked areas onto the sterile surface with only the first stroke of the wire. Cover half of the remaining sterile agar surface. *Sterilize the loop.*

Step 3. Repeat as described in step 2, covering the remaining sterile agar surface.

Single illustration shows a three-step process

Labels on the illustration link it to the steps in the instructions

Plate enlarged to emphasize the pattern and sequence of strokes

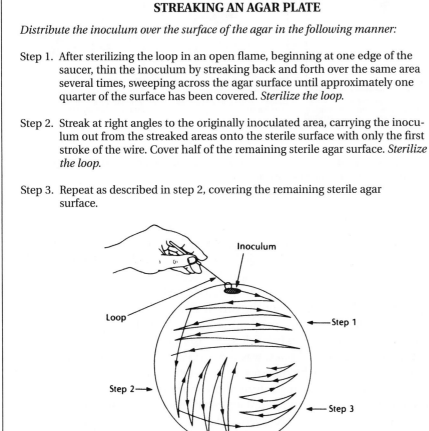

Figure 12–8   Step-by-Step Instructions with Illustration

Each step of a process is illustrated separately

Instructions are written in the imperative mood

Steps are labeled by letter to indicate sequence

HERE IS WHAT TO DO IF YOU ARE INSTALLING YOUR SINK'S FIRST DISPOSER.

EXTENSION TUBE

A.
Use a pipe wrench to loosen the nut at the top of the drain trap.

B.
Next, remove the nut at the top of the sink strainer and remove the extension tube.

C.
Now, remove the large nut at the base of the sink strainer by placing the tip of your screwdriver on the edge of the nut. (There are usually ridges to hold your screwdriver.) Then strike the head of the screwdriver with a hammer in a counterclockwise direction.

D.
Loosen the nut until you can spin it off by hand.

E.
Now, push the strainer up through the sink hole and remove it.

Figure 12–9   Illustrating Each Step in a Set of Instructions.   *Source:* "Installation of Kenmore Waste Disposers," Courtesy of Sears, Roebuck and Company, 1997, Hoffman Estates, Illinois.

Design for Ease of Use

Even clear, well-illustrated instructions are of no value if no one reads them. Customers want to use a new device as soon as they receive it. However, if the product comes with a thick user's manual of dense, legalistic text, they will avoid it. This attitude can lead to accidents, increased calls to customer help lines, dissatisfied customers, and lost time and productivity.

To address this problem, many firms have adopted a two-tier approach in their instructions. In addition to a full-scale user's manual, essential for products such as automobiles, cell phones, washers, dryers, or ovens, companies also produce a quick-start guide with pictures, easy-to-follow diagrams, and minimal text. The owner's manual contains information important to customers, like warranties, maintenance recommendations, service locations, and troubleshooting guides. However, when users are given a choice between a 200-page owner's manual and an 8-page glossy color booklet, they opt for the booklet. In another approach, many companies now provide quick-setup posters with few words and large photographs that are often color coded to parts on the equipment, as shown

Figure 12–10   Close-up of an Image to Illustrate Details

in Figure 12–11 on pages 440–441. Other firms produce booklets with indexed tabs and FAQ (frequently asked questions) sections that permit readers to find at a glance what they are looking for—the correct air pressure for tires, how to set an oven timer, and the like, as shown in Figure 12–12 on page 442. Other options include 3-x-5–inch laminated cards (for phone use), stickers (warning of poisons and providing information about emergency treatment), and even magnets. To create

QUICK SETUP

Features and configurations vary by model.
Some cables and adapters may not be included and are sold separately.

INSTALLATION RAPIDE

Les fonctionnalités et les configurations varient en fonction du modèle.
Certains câbles et adaptateurs peuvent ne pas être inclus et sont vendus séparément.

Wired option.
Match the colors.

Option câblée.
Faire correspondre
les couleurs.

USB   or
       ou   PS2

USB   or
       ou   PS2

Wireless option.
Refer to the setup instructions located in your keyboard box.
NOTE: The same receiver controls both the keyboard and mouse.

Option sans fil.
Consultez les instructions de configuration qui se trouvent dans l'emballage du clavier.
REMARQUE : le récepteur assure le fonctionnement du clavier et de la souris.

1

Refer to the setup instructions that
came with your monitor.

Monitors may be sold separately.

Consulter la notice d'installation
livrée avec votre moniteur.

Les moniteurs peuvent être vendus
séparément.

VGA   or   VGA-DVI   or   DVI   or   HDMI-DVI   or   HDMI
       ou   ou   ou   ou

2

Refer to the setup instructions that
came with your speakers.

Speakers may be sold separately.

Consulter la notice d'installation
livrée avec les haut-parleurs.

Les haut-parleurs peuvent être vendus
séparément.

or
ou

3

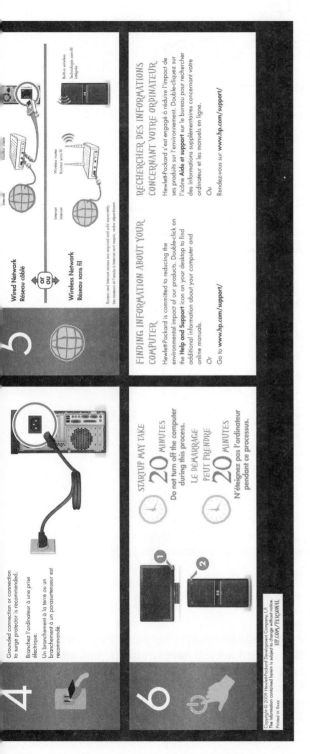

Figure 12–11   Poster of Illustrated Instructions

Spiral binding so that open guide lies flat

5 1/2"

3 1/2"

Quick Tips

Tabbed directory of contents

Illustrated instructions of equipment features and operation

Figure 12–12   Laminated Pocket-Size Owner's Guide

◆ *For more infor-mation about blogs, podcasts, and FAQs, see pages 559–565 in Chapter 15, Writing for the Web.*

instructions for complex procedures, consider using the two-tier approach. (Many other options exist for providing customers with product help, such as CD-ROMs, Web sites, help lines, instructor-led classes, blogs, podcasts, and FAQs.)

Testing for Usability

To test the accuracy and clarity of your instructions, ask someone who is not familiar with the operation to use the instructions you have written to perform the task or procedure. A first-time user of your instructions can spot missing steps or point out passages that should be worded more clearly. As you watch your tester follow your instructions, note any steps that seem especially puzzling or confusing and revise them for clarity.

Usability test participants typically are members of the actual target audience for the product or procedure. If the participants encounter problems, it is likely that actual users will experience similar problems. For example, if instructions for filling out a section of a tax form are unclear to test participants, they are likely to be confusing to most taxpayers.

Usability tests can rely on one or more of the following methods:

- *User testing.* Testers observe and record the actions of test participants who perform real tasks using the instructions.

- *Protocols.* Test participants comment aloud as they follow the instructions and perform the tasks described to reveal their thought processes, attitudes, and reasons for decision-making.

- *Comprehension tests.* Users complete tests to determine whether they understand and can recall the information, such as visuals or tables.

- *Surveys and interviews.* Testers interview users both before and after they read the instructions to determine their comprehension and attitudes and the clarity of what they have read.

ON THE WEB

For more help planning and conducting usability tests, go to Chapter 12, bedfordstmartins.com/ writingthatworks and select *Links Library*, Usability Testing.

Analyzing the results of those test methods can help instructional specialists detect and resolve problems before the instructions are put to use. If test participants have trouble understanding the instructions, the language and organization, as well as layout and design, may need to be revised. Although usability testing can be time-consuming, the extra time can pay off in greater safety, improved efficiency, and fewer customer complaints.

CHAPTER 12 SUMMARY: WRITING INSTRUCTIONS

Planning Instructions

- Make sure that you understand the task thoroughly. (For technical instructions to accompany products, learn to perform the operation yourself or carefully observe others performing the operation.)
- Learn the needs and experience level of your audience.
- Organize the task into short, simple steps.
- Present each step in the correct sequence.

Writing Instructions

- Write directly to your readers, using the active, imperative voice.
- Write clearly and concisely—short sentences are best.
- In an introduction at the beginning of your instructions,
  - Mention any necessary details, background information, and preparation.
  - List all required equipment and materials.
- Use plain language (avoid technical jargon).
- Within procedural steps, include necessary warnings and cautions.

Using Illustrations and Design Principles

▨ Use visuals to illustrate steps and procedures where needed.

▨ Create visuals at the level of detail appropriate to your audience.

▨ If you are creating instructions for users averse to reading manuals, consider creating a quick-start guide with images, easy-to-follow diagrams, and minimal text.

Testing for Usability

▨ Test the readability and effectiveness of your instructions by having someone unfamiliar with the task test them while you observe.

▨ Analyze the results of your observations to improve the instructions.

▨ Revise the instructions as necessary.

ON THE WEB

For an online quiz on writing instructions, go to Chapter 12, bedfordstmartins.com/ writingthatworks

ON THE WEB

For additional exercises, go to Chapter 12, bedfordstmartins.com/ writingthatworks

▨ Exercises

1. Write a set of instructions for either of the following topics. Assume that your audience has no knowledge of the subject. Use illustrations where they would be helpful to your audience.

   a. How to program your TiVo to record a television show that will be broadcast in several hours from the time you programmed your machine

   b. How to incorporate a visual into a text document

2. Create a set of interview questions that you could rely on as a means of checking the usability of the instructions you created in Exercise 1. Remember that you would interview users both before and after they read the instructions to determine their comprehension and attitudes and the clarity of what they have read.

3. Collect examples of instructions written in the passive voice and rewrite them using the active voice.

4. As this chapter describes, most firms have developed a two-tier approach for instructions because consumers will gravitate toward illustrated quick-start guides, easy-to-follow diagrams, and booklets instead of 200-plus-page instruction manuals. Locate a large instructional book or manual (for example, for new software or a new automobile), or go to a Web site that features lengthy instructions for consumer goods, and create a set of 3-×-5–inch laminated cards or a four- to eight-page booklet that will be easy to follow and thus encourage consumers to follow instructions.

5. Locate two sets of assembly, how-to-use, or cleaning instructions from products that you have recently purchased. Key the instructions on your word processor (or scan them with OCR software). Using the insert-comment technique explained in Chapter 5 (Digital Tips: Using Word Processing to Review Collaborative Documents, page 136), critique the instructions you have copied, then, using the Writing Instructions in Plain Language checklist on page 433, compare their use of plain language. Discuss ways that the instructions could have been improved and comment on what is well written.

6. Write two sets of instructions on how to get from the closest airport to your school's student center. Assume your audience is made up of two groups of potential students: native speakers of English and nonnative speakers of English. (See

Chapter 8, Understanding the Principles of Business Communication, for helpful information on international communication strategies.)

7. Imagine that you are the Web master for a large online chat group that is visited by thousands of people each day. You have been concerned about visitors conducting themselves unprofessionally by doing things like attacking others, linking your site with other sites, and trying to sell products and services to other visitors. Define your site's topic and purpose, then create a list of at least ten instructions regarding conduct for your site and explain the penalties for ignoring the instructions.

8. Collect examples of instructions that are written using ambiguous words like "might" or "may" and revise them using explicit words.

9. Many supermarkets and other large retailers now offer self-checkout systems that encourage customers to scan, pay for, and bag their merchandise themselves. These systems allow the store to place employees in other areas where one-on-one attention is needed, and they reduce the need to hire more cashiers. Imagine that you work for a company that manufactures these checkout systems. Write a set of instructions for store managers that will help them prevent the following problems that could discourage customers from using the equipment (*Hint*: Many of these problems could be prevented before the customer has to face them):

- The customer is unfamiliar or uncomfortable with the self-checkout system.
- The customer scans the bar code, but the product does not appear in the register's inventory database.
- The customer has difficulty following the steps needed to work the self-checkout system (for example, he or she can't figure out how to use the scales to weigh produce).

▓ Collaborative Classroom Projects

ON THE WEB

For more collaborative classroom projects, go to Chapter 12, bedfordstmartins.com/ writingthatworks

1. In groups of four to six, write assembly instructions for a product in the classroom. For example, assume that the instructor's desk needs to be assembled. Write an introduction, a required equipment and materials section, a procedure section, and a conclusion. Share your instructions with the class.

2. For any of the exercises or projects in this chapter that ask you to create instructions, conduct a usability test with protocols as a means of checking the usability of those instructions. Sit next to your usability test participants as they comment aloud while they follow the instructions and perform the tasks. This should reveal their thought processes, attitudes, and reasons for decision-making, which should help you determine areas of helpfulness or confusion in your instructions. Form groups of three or four, as directed by your instructor.

▓ Research Projects

ON THE WEB

For extra research projects, go to Chapter 12, bedfordstmartins.com/ writingthatworks

1. Numerous chemicals are used in the cleaning of educational institutions' bathrooms, offices' carpeting, and so on. For this assignment, research and write a formal report on the cleaning products used by your institution's cleaning or

maintenance crews. Include formal-report elements based on your instructor's specific directions.

a. Begin by interviewing the director of maintenance (or someone in a similar position) at your institution about the kinds of cleansers and chemicals used for specific types of cleaning. Ask about the precautions needed and specific instructions given to those who work with these chemicals. Ask about the amount and cost of these products on a monthly or yearly basis.

b. Next, inquire about training given to employees in the use of these chemicals (your Human Resources Department may conduct this training). Ask how much training and instruction is offered and what subjects are covered. Ask if any special sessions are offered to nonnative speakers or readers of English.

c. Research "green," or environmentally friendly, products that can be used in place of more toxic cleansers. Be sure to address the ability of such cleansers to clean heavily populated environments, the potential cost of such products, and the training or instruction needed for their use.

Write a formal report to the head of maintenance that summarizes your findings, makes recommendations on product safety and worker training and instruction, and recommends a course of action regarding the use of traditional cleansers, environmentally friendly cleansers, or a combination of both. Include a graph or chart with your report.

2. As explained in this chapter, warning words, symbols, icons, and labels are increasingly standardized, although industry practices do vary. Certain signal words in boldface and their corresponding colors are becoming standards in North America, like **DANGER** in red, **WARNING** in orange, and **CAUTION** in yellow. And certain icons, like the no-smoking symbol depicted in Figure 12–7, are universally understood. Research appropriate icons that you could place in the formal report described in Research Project 1. For example, what icons and signal words with corresponding colors would you use, or would you create, that might represent a dangerous bathroom-cleaning product used by your university? How would you differentiate it for a product that might be less toxic but is still dangerous if ingested? Report your findings to your instructor in a memo.

3. Explore the following two Web sites to discover how they use illustrations to help convey their messages to the consumer: SafetyStore at <www.safetystore.com/>, an online catalog of safety and preparedness products, and the U.S. Coast Guard, Office of Boating Safety at <www.uscg.mil/USCG.shtm>. Make a list of the variety of illustrations used and their individual purposes. Analyze the style of text that accompanies the illustrations. Determine the goals of these sites and whether these sites accomplish their goals. Support your conclusions with examples, as directed by your instructor.

4. Imagine that you give how-to-travel seminars for people in different occupational fields who will be flying on airlines throughout the United States. In your earlier seminars, some people were confused about what is allowed in carry-on luggage and what has to be checked into the cargo bay. You decide to create lists for your seminar attendees that break down acceptable and prohibited items by the following categories: male and female models traveling to fashion shoots, semiprofessional athletes traveling to their sporting events, construction vendors heading for conventions, and martial artists heading to competitions. Using the list of per-

mitted and prohibited carry-on items from the Transportation Security Adminis-tration at <www.tsa.gov/public/display?theme=177>, create two handouts for one or two of the groups above, complete with the appropriate symbols or icons, to ac-commodate members of these groups that include the following:

a. English-speaking American travelers
b. American immigrants and international travelers who are not familiar with symbols and icons used in this country and for whom English is a second language

13 | Writing Proposals

AT A GLANCE: Proposals

This chapter discusses the audience for, the management and organization of, and the writing strategies used to develop the following kinds of proposals:

- Internal proposals / 454
  - Routine / 454
  - Formal / 454
- External proposals / 463
  - Solicited / 463
  - Unsolicited / 463
  - Grant and research / 468
  - Sales / 475
- Time-sensitive proposals / 488
- Requests for proposals / 490

A proposal is a document written to persuade members of an organization that what is proposed will benefit them by solving a problem or fulfilling a need. When you write a proposal, therefore, you must convince your audience that they need what you are proposing, that it is practical and appropriate, and that you are the right person or organization to provide the proposed product or service. To persuade your organization's management to make a change or an improvement or perhaps to fund a project you would like to launch, you would write an *internal proposal*. To persuade someone outside your company to agree to a plan or take a course of action, you would write an *external proposal*, such as a sales proposal. A *sales proposal* seeks to convince a potential customer to purchase your products or services. A *grant proposal* requests funding for projects solicited by government agencies, research foundations, educational institutions, and other nonprofit organizations.

VOICES IN THE WORKPLACE

Ensuring Proposals Are Clear and Well Supported

Licensed mental health counselor Sarah Schwerdel emphasizes the importance of grant proposals to her agency's counseling services: "When writing a proposal . . . have a very clear idea of key concepts, as well as strategies and goals you are hoping to achieve. The proposal needs to be thorough and supported by relevant research."

Planning and Writing Proposals

Regardless of the type of proposal you write—internal, external, sales, or grant—begin by considering whether your company or organization can complete the project being proposed. Do you have the right staff expertise and facilities to address questions about your competence to complete the project effectively, on time, and within the agreed-on budget? If not, can you get the necessary help elsewhere? If you can perform the task required, you are ready to plan and draft the proposal.

Audience and Purpose

Writing a persuasive and even complex proposal can be simplified by composing a concise statement of exactly the problem or opportunity that your proposal is designed to address. Stating the problem or opportunity concisely helps you and your readers understand the value, scope, and limitations of your proposed solution.

Put yourself in your readers' position—ask what their needs and goals are and how your proposal can benefit them or their institution. Consider what information would convince you to make the decision you are asking them to make. Then, being as specific as possible, identify the following:

1. Sufficient background information to describe the extent of the problem (if the information is based on research, cite your sources)
2. The methods or optional approaches to be used in achieving the proposed solution
3. Information about equipment, materials, and staff requirements
4. An itemized list of costs
5. A schedule for completing the project broken down into separate tasks

Each of these items is central for a persuasive and complete proposal; you can see detailed examples of each in the figures later in this chapter. As you consider what your readers will want to know, also assess their positions in the organization reviewing your proposal. You will have more than one reader because proposals usually require more than one level of review and approval. Each will assess the proposal from the perspective of his or her responsibilities in the organization.

- *Executives* and other high-level decision makers, for example, will want to know the long-term benefits of what you propose, as well as the amount of money, the number of personnel, and the timetable that your plan requires.

- *Managers* will need to evaluate your credibility and consider how your plan addresses their problem. They will also need to know how they would put your plan into action. They would be responsible for site preparation, staff training and motivation, and the schedule.

- *Technical staff* will need even more information on how to put your plan to work and will focus on the sections in your proposal that cover your previous experience and the proposed detailed solution, including the work plan, schedule, blueprints, and diagrams.

ON THE WEB

For more help with writing proposals, go to Chapter 13, bedfordstmartins.com/ writingthatworks

---

▶ CONSIDERING AUDIENCE AND PURPOSE

Writing Proposals

- ▪ Is your audience a manager within your organization (for an internal proposal) or a potential customer outside your organization (for an external proposal)?

- ▪ Does your proposal answer clearly the following questions?
    - What problem does your proposal address?
    - What do you propose to do?
    - What benefits does your proposed plan offer?
    - How will you implement your plan?
    - When do you plan to undertake and complete it?
    - How much do you estimate it will cost?
    - How long will it take?

- ▪ Does your proposal address the functional needs of those who must evaluate it by including
    - A summary in nontechnical language for decision makers?
    - A description of the proposed solution, budget, schedule, and training requirements for managers?
    - Technical details and visuals of the proposed solution for the specialists who must assess your degree of expertise to perform the work?

- ▪ Is the language professional and respectful?

- ▪ Is the proposal written, organized, and submitted exactly as specified in the request for proposals?

- ▪ Have you carefully revised material used from your workplace to fit seamlessly into the proposal?

Project Management

Companies that depend on the work generated by proposals are frequently faced with the need to prepare high-quality, persuasive proposals under tight deadlines. To meet these aims, companies assemble proposal-writing teams. Collaborative teams like these are usually headed by a project leader to guide the process, organize the content, and ensure that the deadline is met.

The team begins by creating a broad outline of the proposal, dividing it into sections, and ensuring that each section is assigned to a team member on the basis of subject-area expertise. The team also searches the company's files for existing content—such as standard language for a product description or a company profile—that can be adapted for the proposal underway. The project manager then establishes a schedule that includes due dates for drafts of each section, reviews of the drafts, a revision cycle, management review, and preparation of the final proposal.

Repurposing Content (Boilerplate)

Repurposing is the copying or converting of existing content, such as written text and visuals, from one document into another for a different purpose. In the workplace, this process saves time because content that often requires substantial effort to develop need not be recreated for each new use.

The process of repurposing may be as simple as copying and pasting content from one document to another. Note, however, that content can be repurposed exactly as it is written only if it fits the scope, audience, and purpose of the new document. If not, adapt the content to fit its new context. If you are writing a sales proposal, for example, and you need to describe the specifications of a product, you may be able to use the same specifications posted at your company's Web site. For narrative content, however, you may need to adapt the verb tense, voice, tone, and point of view to fit the context of a proposal aimed to persuade a potential customer.

Discuss sources of existing material useful to your proposal in team planning meetings and store them in electronic folders, on network drives, or on internal Web sites for sharing with other team members.

ETHICS NOTE

In the workplace, repurposing content within an organization does not violate copyright because the organization owns the information it creates and can share it freely across the company. Likewise, a writer in an organization may use and repurpose material in the public domain and, with some limitations, content that is licensed under Creative Commons, as described at <http://creativecommons.org/about/>.

In the classroom, of course, the use of content or someone else's unique ideas without acknowledgment or the use of someone else's exact words without quotation marks and appropriate credit is plagiarism.

◆ *See pages 180–181 in Chapter 6, Researching Your Subject.*

Each member of the team is responsible for researching and drafting his or her assigned segment of the document. Keeping the client's needs and the proposal's purpose in mind, each member should review the other team members' work and offer advice to help improve it.

Individual writers then evaluate their colleagues' reviews and accept, reject, or build on their suggestions. When each segment is finalized, the project manager consolidates all of the completed drafts into a final master copy.

◆ *For a detailed overview of the collaborative writing process, see Chapter 5, Collaborative Writing.*

For additional guidance on preparing a proposal on a tight schedule, see Meeting the Deadline: The Time-Sensitive Proposal on pages 488–490.

WRITER'S CHECKLIST
Writing Proposals with a Team

✔ Hold a planning meeting with the proposal team to assign work and establish due dates for all tasks.

✔ Assign a team member to each section to ensure that it is complete, consistent, and complies with the requirements of the request for proposals.

✔ Set priorities so that the most important sections of the proposal receive adequate attention and are on schedule.

✔ Delegate work to ensure that subject-area experts are available within the schedule established.

✔ Schedule the project so that work begins on the sections that will take the longest, doing as many sections as possible simultaneously.

✔ Repurpose existing content as extensively as possible, *being careful to adapt it to the prospective customer.*

✔ Select the best medium to communicate among proposal team members.

✔ Track the status of each part of the proposal carefully, sending periodic reminders about upcoming deadlines.

Organization

Any proposal—whether it is internal or external or whether it is short and uncomplicated or long and complex—should be planned and organized carefully. The organization of internal proposals varies according to topic and scope of coverage. Figures 13–1 through 13–5 illustrate two typical examples. For external or grant proposals, follow guidance in the request for proposals exactly when organizing the proposal. (See Requests for Proposals on pages 490–492.) The samples throughout this chapter are representative of proposals used in a variety of workplace settings.

Persuasive Writing

A proposal, by definition, is persuasive writing because you are attempting either to convince your readers to do something or to believe that you are the right person or firm to provide a product or service. Your goal is to prove to your readers that they need what you are proposing to do and that it is practical and appropriate. For an unsolicited proposal, you may even need to convince your readers that they have a problem serious enough to require a solution. You would then offer your solution by first building a convincing case, demonstrating the validity of your approach.

In persuasive writing, how you present your ideas is as important as the ideas themselves. Avoid ambiguity, do not wander from your main point, and, above all, never make false claims. Support your appeal with relevant facts, statistics, and examples. Your supporting evidence must lead logically, even inevitably, to your conclusions and your proposed solution—that is, begin with the most important evidence and end with valid but secondary evidence. Finally, cite the relevant sources of information used to support your position. Doing so gives your arguments strong credibility.

◆ *For a detailed overview of researching and citing evidence and supporting information, see Chapter 6, Researching Your Subject.*

ETHICS NOTE

As you develop the points in your proposal, be careful to acknowledge any contradictory evidence or potentially conflicting opinions; doing so allows you to anticipate and overcome objections to your proposal and even helps you to support your argument. By acknowledging negative details or opposing views, you not only gain credibility but also demonstrate good ethics.

The tone of your proposal should be positive, confident, and tactful. The following example, addressed to the Qualtron Corporation, is inappropriate because of its condescending tone:

▶   The Qualtron Corporation needs to consider the potential problem of not having backup equipment available when a commercial power failure occurs. The corporation would also be wise indeed to give a great deal more consideration to the volume of output expected per machine.

The following version of the same passage is positive, confident, and tactful:

▶   To prevent damage to essential Qualtron equipment in the event of a commercial power failure, we recommend a system redesign to upgrade Qualtron's existing backup power supply. The backup configuration proposed is based on a technical analysis of the output of each machine and takes into account future system growth. For example, . . .

WRITER'S CHECKLIST
Writing Persuasive Proposals

✔   Analyze your audience carefully to determine how to best meet your readers' needs or requirements.

✔   Write a concise purpose statement to clarify your proposal's goals.

✔   Emphasize the proposal's benefits to readers and anticipate their questions or objections.

✔   Incorporate evidence to support the claims of your proposal, being careful to cite your sources.

✔   Divide the writing task into manageable segments and develop a work schedule.

✔   Review the descriptions of proposal sections and their uses in this chapter.

✔   Select an appropriate, visually appealing format (see Chapter 7, Designing Effective Documents and Visuals).

✔   Use a confident, positive tone throughout the proposal.

▧ Internal Proposals

The purpose of an internal proposal is to suggest a change or an improvement within an organization. An internal proposal, often in memo format, is sent to a superior within the organization who has the authority to accept or reject the proposal. Internal proposals are typically reviewed by one or more departments for cost, practicality, and potential benefits. Two common types of internal proposals—routine and formal—are often distinguished from each other by the frequency with which they are written and by the degree of change proposed.

◆ *The telecommuting proposal by Christine Thomas (see Figure 1–6) is an example of an internal proposal.*

Routine Internal Proposals

Routine internal proposals are the most frequent type of proposal and typically include small spending requests, requests for permission to hire new employees or increase salaries, and requests to attend conferences or purchase new equipment. In writing routine proposals, highlight any key benefits to be realized.

Figure 13–1 shows a typical internal proposal. It was written as a memo by a plant safety officer to the plant superintendent and recommends changes in specific safety practices at the company.

Formal Internal Proposals

Formal internal proposals usually involve requests to commit relatively large sums of money. They are usually organized into sections that describe a problem, propose a solution and recommendation, and offer to implement the recommendation. The body, in turn, is further divided into sections to reflect the subject matter. The proposal may begin with a section describing the background or history of an issue and go on to discuss options for addressing the issue in separate sections.

The introduction of your internal proposal should establish that a problem exists and needs a solution. This section is sometimes called a "problem statement." (Internal proposals are sometimes referred to as *problem-solution memos*.) If the audience is not convinced that there is a problem, your proposal will not succeed. After you identify the problem, summarize your proposed

Memo

To: Harold Clurman, Plant Superintendent
CC: Carla Hernandez, Supervisor, Group 333
From: Fred Nelson, Safety Officer   *Fn*
Date: August 4, 2010
Subject: Safety Practices for Group 333

Many accidents and near-accidents have occurred in Group 333 because of the haz-   *Introduction that*
ardous working conditions in this area. This memo identifies those hazardous   *states a problem*
conditions and makes recommendations for their elimination.

Hazardous Conditions

Employees inside the factory must operate the walk-along crane through aisles that
are frequently congested with scrap metal, discarded lumber, and other refuse from
the shearing area. Many surfaces in the area are coated in oil.

The containers for holding raw stock and scrap metal are also unsafe. On many of the   *Detailed explanation*
racks, the hooks are bent inward so far that the crane cannot fit into them properly   *of the problem*
unless it is banged and jiggled in a dangerous manner. To add to the hazard, employees in the press group do not always balance the load in the racks. As a result, the
danger of falling metal is great as the unbalanced racks swing practically out of control overhead. These hazards endanger employees in Group 333 and also employees
in the raw-stock and shearing areas because the crane passes over these areas.

Hazards also exist in the yard and in the chemical building. Dumping strip metal
into the scrap bins is the most dangerous practice of all. To dump this metal, the
tow-motor operator raises the rack over the edge of the scrap-metal bin and rotates
the forks to permit the scrap metal to fall from one end of the rack. As the weight
shifts, the rack slams into one of the tow-motor forks (raised 12 feet above the
ground). This method has resulted in two tow-motor tip-overs in the past month.   *Additional details*
In neither incident was the driver injured, but injuries are very likely. Group 333
employees must also dump tubs full of scrap metal from the tow motor into the
10-foot-high scrap bins. Because of the unpredictable way the metal falls from
the tubs, employees have received many facial cuts and body bruises. In winter
weather, all employees have been cut and bruised in falls that occurred as they were
climbing up on scrap bins covered with snow and ice to dump scrap from pallets
that had not been banded.

Finally, nearly all Group 333 employees who handle the caustic chemicals report
damaged clothing and ruined shoes. Poor lighting in the chemical building (lights
20 feet above the floor), storage racks positioned less than two feet apart, and container caps incorrectly fastened have made these accidents impossible to prevent.

1

Figure 13–1   Routine Internal Proposal (continued)

Recommendations

Recommended solution

To eliminate these hazards as quickly as possible, I recommend that the following actions be taken:

1. Group 333 supervisors must rigorously initiate and enforce a policy to free aisles of obstructions.
2. All dangerous racks must be repaired and replaced.
3. The Engineering Group must develop a safe rack dumper.
4. Heavy wire-mesh screens must be mounted on the front of all tow motors.
5. Group 333 employees must not accept scrap in containers that have not been properly banded.
6. Illumination must be increased in the chemical building, and a compulsory training program for the safe handling of caustic chemicals must be scheduled.

Conclusion

I would like to meet with you and the supervisor of Group 333 before the end of the month, as your schedule permits. You will have my complete cooperation in working out all of the details of the proposed recommendations.

2

Figure 13–1 **Routine Internal Proposal** (continued)

solution and indicate its benefits and estimated total cost. Notice how the introduction in Figure 13–2 states the problem directly and then summarizes the writer's proposed solution.

The body of your internal proposal should offer a practical solution to the problem and provide the details necessary to inform and to persuade your readers. In the body, you will itemize the problem you are addressing; the methodology of your proposed solution; information about equipment, materials, and staff; cost breakdowns; and a detailed schedule. Figure 13–3 on pages 458–460 shows the body of the internal proposal introduced in Figure 13–2.

The conclusion of your internal proposal should tie everything together, restate your recommendation, and close with a spirit of cooperation (offering to set up a meeting, supply additional information, or provide any other assistance that might be needed). Keep your conclusion brief, as in Figure 13–4 on page 461.

If your proposal cites information that you obtained through research, such as published reports, government statistics, or interviews, follow the conclusion with a works-cited list that provides complete publication information for each source, as in Figure 13–5 on page 462.

◆ *For guidance on researching and citing background information, see Chapter 6, Researching Your Subject.*

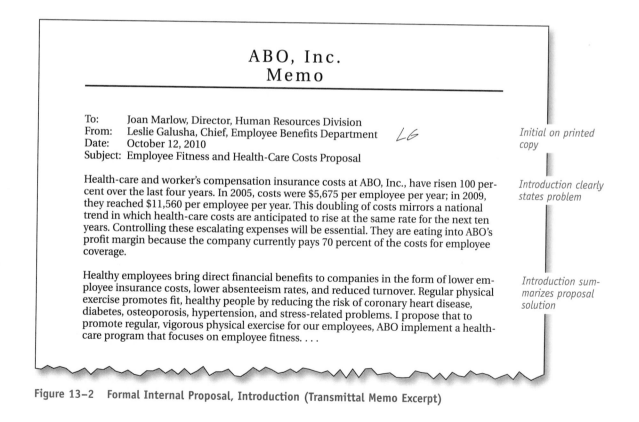

ABO, Inc.
Memo

To: Joan Marlow, Director, Human Resources Division
From: Leslie Galusha, Chief, Employee Benefits Department *LG*
Date: October 12, 2010
Subject: Employee Fitness and Health-Care Costs Proposal

Initial on printed copy

Health-care and worker's compensation insurance costs at ABO, Inc., have risen 100 percent over the last four years. In 2005, costs were $5,675 per employee per year; in 2009, they reached $11,560 per employee per year. This doubling of costs mirrors a national trend in which health-care costs are anticipated to rise at the same rate for the next ten years. Controlling these escalating expenses will be essential. They are eating into ABO's profit margin because the company currently pays 70 percent of the costs for employee coverage.

Introduction clearly states problem

Healthy employees bring direct financial benefits to companies in the form of lower employee insurance costs, lower absenteeism rates, and reduced turnover. Regular physical exercise promotes fit, healthy people by reducing the risk of coronary heart disease, diabetes, osteoporosis, hypertension, and stress-related problems. I propose that to promote regular, vigorous physical exercise for our employees, ABO implement a health-care program that focuses on employee fitness. . . .

Introduction summarizes proposal solution

Figure 13–2 **Formal Internal Proposal, Introduction (Transmittal Memo Excerpt)**

Joan Marlow   2   Employee Fitness Proposal

Problem of Health-Care Costs

Information explaining extent of problem

The U.S. Department of Health and Human Services recently estimated that health-care costs in the United States will triple by the year 2017. Corporate expenses for health care are rising at such a fast rate that, if unchecked, in eight years they will significantly erode corporate profits.

According to Health and Human Services, people who do not participate in a regular and vigorous exercise program incur double the health-care costs and are hospitalized 30 percent more days than people who exercise regularly. Nonexercisers are also 41 percent more likely to submit medical claims over $10,000 at some point during their careers than are those who exercise regularly.

Information explaining extent of problem

Citations identify sources of information in MLA style

These figures are further supported by data from independent studies. A model created by the National Institutes of Health (NIH) estimates that the average white-collar company could save $596,000 annually in medical costs (per 1,000 employees) just by promoting wellness. NIH researchers estimated that for every $1 a firm invests in a health-care program, it saves up to $3.75 in health-care costs (Goetzel 342). In an overview of studies that evaluated the benefits of company wellness programs, the Public Health & Health Policy Institute of Wisconsin reported that "an unhealthy lifestyle or modifiable risk factors . . . account for at least 25 percent of employee health-care expenditures" (Zank and Friedsam 1).

Proposed Solutions for ABO

The benefits of regular, vigorous physical activity for employees and companies are compelling. To achieve these benefits at ABO, I propose that we choose from one of two possible options: build in-house fitness centers at our warehouse facilities or offer employees several options for membership at a national fitness club.

In-House Fitness Center

Explanation of proposed solution

Building in-house fitness centers would require that ABO modify existing space in its five warehouses and designate an area outside for walking and running. To accommodate the weight-lifting and cardiovascular equipment and an aerobics area would require a minimum of 4,000 square feet. Lockers and shower stalls would also have to be built adjacent to the men's and women's bathrooms.

Figure 13–3   Formal Internal Proposal, Body (continued)

The costs to equip each facility are as follows:

1	Challenger 3.0 Treadmill	$4,395	*Required*
3	Ross Futura exercise bicycles @ $750 each	$2,250	*equipment*
1	CalGym S-370 inner thigh machine	$2,250	*and materials*
1	CalGym S-325 outer thigh machine	$2,250	
1	CalGym S-260 lat pull-down machine	$2,290	
1	CalGym S-360 leg-extension, combo-curl	$1,900	
1	CalGym S-390 arm-curl machine	$2,235	
1	CalGym S-410 side-lat machine	$1,950	
1	CalGym S-430 pullover machine	$2,110	
1	CalGym S-440 abdominal machine	$2,250	*Breakdown of costs*
1	CalGym S-460 back machine	$2,250	
1	CalGym S-290 chest press	$2,000	
1	CalGym S-310 pectoral developer	$1,950	
10	5710321 3-wide lockers @ $81 each	$810	
4	5713000 benches and pedestals @ $81 each	$324	
	Carpeting for workout area	$3,000	
3	showers each, men's/women's locker room	$15,000	
	Men's and women's locker-room expansion	$15,000	
	Remodeling expenses	$450,000	
	Total per ABO site	$514,214	
	Grand Total	**$2,571,070**	

At headquarters and at the regional offices, our current Employee Assistance Program staff would need to be available several hours each workday to provide instructions for the use of exercise equipment. Aerobics instructors can be hired locally on a monthly basis for classes. The Buildings and Maintenance Department staff would clean and maintain the facilities.

Required staff

Fitness-Club Membership

Offering a complimentary membership to a national fitness club for all employees can also help reduce company health-care costs. AeroFitness Clubs, Inc., offers the best option for ABO's needs. They operate in over 45 major markets, with over 300 clubs nationwide. Most important, AeroFitness Clubs are located here in Bartlesville and in all four cities where our regional warehouses are located.

Explanation of proposed solution

AeroFitness staff are trained and certified in exercise physiology and will design individualized fitness programs for our employees. They offer aerobics classes for all levels, taught by certified instructors. Each club also features the latest in resistance exercise equipment from Nautilus, Universal, Paramount, and Life Fitness. Most AeroFitness facilities provide competition-size swimming pools, cushioned indoor running tracks, saunas, whirlpools, steam rooms, and racquetball courts.

Figure 13–3   Formal Internal Proposal, Body (continued)

AeroFitness offers a full range of membership programs that include corporate discounts. The basic membership of $600 per year includes the following:

- Unlimited use of exercise equipment
- Unlimited aerobics classes
- Unlimited use of racquetball, sauna, and whirlpool facilities
- Free initial consultation with an exercise physiologist for exercise and nutrition programs
- Free child care during daytime working hours

The club offers a full range of membership programs for companies. ABO may choose to pay all or part of employee membership costs. Three membership program options are available with AeroFitness:

- *Corporate purchase.* ABO buys and owns the memberships. With 10 or more memberships, ABO receives a 35-percent discount.

     ABO costs: $600 per employee × 1,200 employees – 35% discount = $468,000 per year.*

Breakdown of costs

- *Corporate subsidy.* Employees purchase memberships at a discount and own them. With 10 or more memberships, employees and the company each pay one-half of annual membership dues and receive a 30-percent discount off annual dues. The corporation also pays a one-time $50 enrollment fee per employee.

     ABO costs: $300 per employee × 1,200 employees – 30% discount = $252,000 per year. The one-time enrollment fee of $50 per employee adds $60,000 to first-year costs.*

- *Employee purchase.* Employees purchase memberships on their own. With five or more memberships, employees receive 25 percent off regular rates. Club sales representatives conduct an on-site open-enrollment meeting. Employees own memberships.

     ABO costs: None.

*Assumes that all employees will enroll.

Figure 13–3   Formal Internal Proposal, Body (continued)

Joan Marlow   5   Employee Fitness Proposal

Conclusion and Recommendation

I recommend that ABO, Inc., participate in the corporate membership program at AeroFitness Clubs, Inc., by subsidizing employee memberships. By subsidizing memberships, ABO shows its commitment to the importance of a fit workforce. Club membership allows employees at all five ABO warehouses to participate in the program. The more employees who participate, the greater the long-term savings in ABO's health-care costs. Building and equipping fitness centers at all five warehouse sites would require an initial investment of over $2.5 million. These facilities would also occupy valuable floor space—on average, 4,000 square feet at each warehouse. Therefore, this option would be very costly.

Enrolling employees in the corporate program at AeroFitness would allow them to attend on a trial basis. Those interested in continuing could then join the club and pay half of the membership cost, less a 30-percent discount on the $600 yearly fee. The other half of the membership fee ($300) would be paid for by ABO. If an employee leaves the company, he or she would have the option of purchasing ABO's share of the membership to continue at AeroFitness or selling their half of the membership to another ABO employee wishing to join AeroFitness.

Implementing this program will help ABO, Inc., reduce its health-care costs while building stronger employee relations by offering employees a desirable benefit. If this proposal is adopted, I have some additional thoughts about publicizing the program to encourage employee participation. I look forward to discussing the details of this proposal (including the implementation schedule for each option) with you and answering any questions you may have.

Conclusion restates recommendation

Conclusion closes with spirit of cooperation

Figure 13–4   Formal Internal Proposal, Conclusion

Joan Marlow   6   Employee Fitness Proposal

Works Cited

Works-cited section lists research sources in MLA style

Centers for Medicare & Medicaid Services. "Projected." *National Health Expenditure Data.* CMS, 2006. Web. 20 Sept. 2010.

Goetzel, R. Z., et al. "Health Care Costs of Worksite Health Promotion Participants and Nonparticipants." *Journal of Occupational and Environmental Medicine* 40.4 (1998): 341–46. *PubMed.* Web. 18 Sept. 2010.

Kozar, Marcie. "Re: Company Costs for Nonexercisers." Message to the author. 15 May 2010. E-mail.

United States. Dept. of Health and Human Services. "Physical Activity Fundamental to Preventing Disease." *Office of the Assistant Secretary for Planning and Evaluation.* Dept. of Health and Human Services, 20 June 2002. Web. 12 Sept. 2010.

Zank, Daniel, and Donna Friedsam. "Employee Health Promotion Programs: What Is the Return on Investment?" *Issue Brief.* Wisconsin Public Health & Health Policy Institute. Sept. 2005. Web. 12 Sept. 2010.

Figure 13–5   Works-Cited Page of a Formal Internal Proposal

WRITER'S CHECKLIST
Creating Internal Proposals

✔ Prepare your proposal for someone in your organization with the power to act on it.

✔ Describe the problem clearly, providing any essential technical or historical background to clarify why the problem exists.

✔ Offer your solution in sufficient detail so that a decision maker can evaluate your approach.

✔ Note any resource requirements necessary for a solution (personnel, equipment, materials).

✔ Provide a schedule for implementing the solution.

✔ Specify the benefits expected to result from your solution.

▨ External Proposals

External proposals are prepared for clients and customers outside your company. They are either submitted in response to a request for goods and services from another organization (a solicited proposal) or sent to them without a prior request (an unsolicited proposal). Research and grant proposals, a type of external proposal, are usually submitted to nonprofit organizations, which include medical and research institutions, as well as to local, state, and federal government agencies, to request funding to support research that could benefit the funding organization.

Solicited Proposals

To find the best method of doing a job and the most qualified company to do it, procuring organizations commonly issue a request for proposal (RFP) or an invitation for bids (IFB) that asks competing companies such as yours to bid for a job. An RFP may be rigid in specifying how the proposal should be organized and what it should contain, but it is normally quite flexible about the approaches that bidding firms may propose. Ordinarily, the RFP simply defines the basic work that the procuring organization needs and leaves it up to the proposers to put forth their method of performing the work economically and within their stated schedule. An IFB, however, is restrictive, binding the bidder to produce an item or a service that meets the exact requirements of the agency or company. (For guidance in preparing RPFs, see Requests for Proposals on pages 490–492.)

When you respond to an RFP or IFB, pay close attention to any specifications in the request governing the preparation of the proposal and follow them carefully. Such specifications usually state how the proposal should be organized, the kind of technical expertise required, the basis for calculating cost estimates, the location of the work site, and the like. Figure 13–6 shows a short solicited sales proposal that responds to a property-management company's IFB on a landscaping project.

Unsolicited Proposals

Unsolicited proposals are those submitted to a company without a prior request and are not as unusual as they may sound: Companies often operate for years with a problem they have never recognized (unnecessarily high maintenance costs, for example, or poor inventory-control methods). You might prepare an unsolicited proposal for such a company if you were convinced that the potential customer could realize substantial benefits by adopting your solution to a problem. You could also propose that a company purchase your services if the company does not provide them (Figure 13–7 on pages 465–467). Of course, you would need to convince the customer of the need for what you are proposing and that your solution would be the best one. Many unsolicited proposals are preceded by a letter

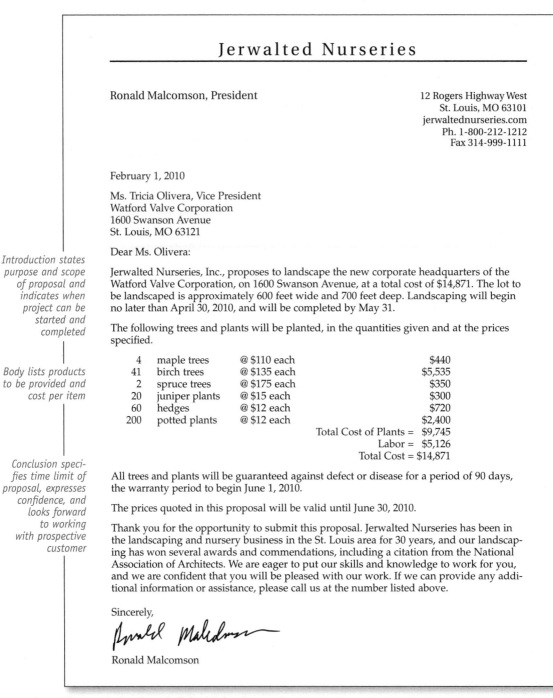

Jerwalted Nurseries

Ronald Malcomson, President

12 Rogers Highway West
St. Louis, MO 63101
jerwaltednurseries.com
Ph. 1-800-212-1212
Fax 314-999-1111

February 1, 2010

Ms. Tricia Olivera, Vice President
Watford Valve Corporation
1600 Swanson Avenue
St. Louis, MO 63121

Dear Ms. Olivera:

Introduction states purpose and scope of proposal and indicates when project can be started and completed

Jerwalted Nurseries, Inc., proposes to landscape the new corporate headquarters of the Watford Valve Corporation, on 1600 Swanson Avenue, at a total cost of $14,871. The lot to be landscaped is approximately 600 feet wide and 700 feet deep. Landscaping will begin no later than April 30, 2010, and will be completed by May 31.

The following trees and plants will be planted, in the quantities given and at the prices specified.

Body lists products to be provided and cost per item

4	maple trees	@ $110 each	$440
41	birch trees	@ $135 each	$5,535
2	spruce trees	@ $175 each	$350
20	juniper plants	@ $15 each	$300
60	hedges	@ $12 each	$720
200	potted plants	@ $12 each	$2,400
		Total Cost of Plants =	$9,745
		Labor =	$5,126
		Total Cost =	$14,871

Conclusion specifies time limit of proposal, expresses confidence, and looks forward to working with prospective customer

All trees and plants will be guaranteed against defect or disease for a period of 90 days, the warranty period to begin June 1, 2010.

The prices quoted in this proposal will be valid until June 30, 2010.

Thank you for the opportunity to submit this proposal. Jerwalted Nurseries has been in the landscaping and nursery business in the St. Louis area for 30 years, and our landscaping has won several awards and commendations, including a citation from the National Association of Architects. We are eager to put our skills and knowledge to work for you, and we are confident that you will be pleased with our work. If we can provide any additional information or assistance, please call us at the number listed above.

Sincerely,

Ronald Malcomson

Ronald Malcomson

Figure 13–6   Short Solicited Sales Proposal

Longo's Shoe Repair

1211 Erie Street
Hobard, OH 44425

longoshooz.com
Phone: 331-467-0333

March 15, 2010

Mr. Harry Rice
General Manager
JK Sports, Inc.
12100 Hickory Pike
Willington, OH 44428

Dear Mr. Rice:

Longo's Shoe Repair Shop congratulates you on the grand opening of JK Sports!
We would like to offer you our services as the area's leading repair shop for baseball and softball gloves. We currently hold five-year contracts with the Locker
Room and the S & S Baseball Express store. We also value your time and offer
the convenience of pickup and delivery on all orders.

Introduction states purpose of the proposal and establishes the company's reputation

Repair Procedures

We evaluate each glove and estimate the cost of repair based on the degree of
damage and the estimated time of repair. If the actual cost exceeds the estimated
cost by more than $5, we will call you to discuss the reason for the additional
cost and will proceed only upon your approval. Most repairs will be confined to
the section damaged, but if the glove is old and the strings appear weak, we will
re-string the glove to ensure its fitness for continued use.

The type of glove will also affect price. Catchers' mitts are typically the most expensive to repair because of their heavy use and the additional string they require.
Likewise, first basemen's gloves and softball gloves are larger than hardball field-
ers' gloves and require more lace to repair, even for minor damage.

Special Repair and Care

Our shop is unique in the area because of the range of repairs we can make as
well as the extra care we give each glove before it is returned to the customer.
We are a shoe shop, so we have the necessary sewing machines and workmanship

Figure 13–7   **Short Unsolicited Sales Proposal** (continued)

Mr. Harry Rice   2   March 15, 2010

capabilities to fix any torn or worn-away leather that may need to be stitched together or patched with matching leather.

Once a glove has been repaired, we fully condition it. The inside of the glove will be treated with Dr. Glove's Foam System, which helps protect against the sweat and dirt that crack leather and cause increased wear. The outside of the glove is then treated with Easton Oil, which keeps the glove soft, pliant, and resistant to dirt. We also provide instructions to the glove owner to keep the glove oiled throughout the playing season and to oil it again for off-season storage.

New Gloves

New gloves need to be broken in quickly. To assist owners, we recently expanded our services to include two new glove preparation methods. The first method involves a chemical-dip process over a two-day period to mold the glove into shape. The procedure is 100 percent safe for the leather and enhances the leather's softness. The cost is $55 for catchers' mitts and $48 for all other gloves.

The second system is a foam-and-oven treatment. The glove is coated with a specialty foam and baked for a specified time. The process takes one day and costs $50 for all types of gloves. Both of these systems are proven effective and time-saving compared to the break-in time normally required.

Cost Guidelines and Equipment

Body details the product line, prices, and specific features

We charge an initial $21 for each repair job and $12 per hour after the initial hour. We also include the cost of supplies in the total bill. Supplies are priced as follows:

- 2-foot 10-gauge string $2.50
- 3½-foot 10-gauge string $3.75
- 2-foot 12-gauge string $3.25
- 3½-foot 12-gauge string $4.10
- 2 x 4 leather patch $3.00
- 3 x 5 leather patch $3.75
- Waxed thread $0.16 per inch

The string gauge used depends on the glove manufacturer and location of the repair. Repairs to the web area always require 12-gauge string.

Figure 13–7   Short Unsolicited Sales Proposal (continued)

Mr. Harry Rice 3 March 15, 2010

We also feature special rates for bulk orders—for repair orders of 10 or more gloves, we fix the tenth glove free! And remember, we value your time, so we offer free pickup and delivery on all orders.

Recommendation and Qualifications

We hope that our reputation for top-quality services encourages you to consider our company as your first choice for glove repairs. Our 40 years of experience and our equipment, tools, and staff expertise account for our reputation as the premier shop for the fine-detailed work that goes into every glove we repair. The added glove conditioning and break-in services we believe enhance this reputation.

Persuasive conclusion showcases company's skill and experience and extends an offer to follow up with more information

We welcome your review of this offer and look forward to establishing good working relations with you, your staff, and your customers. I would be pleased to meet with you or send any additional information you request. Please contact me at the shop during business hours, Monday through Friday, 8 a.m. until 5 p.m., or by e-mail at vlongo@longoshooz.com.

Sincerely,

Vincent Longo

Vincent Longo,
Proprietor

Figure 13–7   **Short Unsolicited Sales Proposal** (continued)

ON THE WEB

For a description of
the purpose and or-
ganization of typical
requests for proposals,
as well as a sample
RFP, go to Chapter 13,
bedfordstmartins.com/
writingthatworks

of inquiry that specifies the problem or unmet need to determine whether there
is any potential interest. If you receive a positive response, you would conduct a
detailed study of the prospective client's needs to determine whether you can be
of help and, if so, exactly how. You would then prepare a formal proposal on the
basis of your study.

ETHICS NOTE

Keep in mind that, once submitted, a sales proposal is a legally binding document
that promises to offer goods or services within a specified time and for a specified
price. Many sales proposals also note that the offer is valid for a limited period (usually 90 days).

Grant and Research Proposals

Grant and research proposals are written to nonprofit organizations to request the
approval of and funding for projects that solve a problem or fulfill a need. For example, a professor of education might submit a research proposal to the state or
federal Department of Education to request funding for research on the relationship of class size to educational performance; similarly, a community center
might submit a grant proposal to obtain funding from a local government agency
for an after-school job-training program.

Many government agencies, private foundations, and other nonprofit groups
solicit research and grant proposals. Granting organizations typically post opportunities, along with detailed application guidelines, on their Web sites, and they
usually specify their own requirements for the format and content of proposals, as
shown in Figure 13–8. Always research the grant-making organization first to familiarize yourself with its areas of interest and its purpose in granting the funding.
Because organizations looking for funding often pursue multiple grants, tailor
your grant or research proposal to each specific audience by carefully following
the guidelines provided by the granting agency. In addition, remember that proposals must always be persuasive: Explain your project's goals, your plan for
achieving those goals, and your qualifications to perform the project.

Although application guidelines may differ from one organization to another,
grant proposals generally require the following sections at a minimum:

ON THE WEB

For samples of
research and grant
proposals, as well as
the full text of this
grant proposal,
go to Model
Documents Gallery,
bedfordstmartins.com/
writingthatworks

- Cover letter
- Title page
- Introduction/summary
- Literature review
- Project narrative
- Statement of need

- Project description
- Project outcomes
- Budget
- Schedule
- Conclusion

Request for Seed Grant Proposals

Discovery Park
Purdue University
West Lafayette, IN 47907
2008

Purpose

Discovery Park requests seed grant proposals from Purdue faculty and staff. A total of $300,000 has been allocated to fund seed grants for proposals that catalyze new high impact activities at Purdue. This program is not meant to fund complete projects, but rather to provide the necessary support to start new efforts that will be supported longer term by other funding sources. All funded project teams are expected to submit a proposal to an external funding agency through Discovery Park, or to receive support from an outside organization (e.g., company) for continuation of the project effort.

Eligibility

Anyone certified by the Office of the Vice President for Research to serve as a Principal Investigator to an outside agency may submit a proposal. The proposed team may include personnel from outside of Purdue.

Proposals: The deadline for receipt of proposals is _5:00 p.m., Tuesday, January 15, 2008._ Proposals should be submitted as a single pdf file attachment to an e-mail message addressed to Marty R. at *****@purdue.edu. Projects should have a start date no earlier than March 1, 2008, and include expenditure of all funds by May 1, 2009.

Proposals are to be attached to a completed University Proposal Submission Form, and should follow this sequence:

Page 1. Face page, including:
- Proposal title
- Principal investigator, with signature
- Partnering Discovery Park Centers
- Total budget
- Project period

Pages 2-6. Research plan, limited to 5 pages, single-spaced, one inch margins, and no smaller than 11 point font. Proposals must address:
- The review criteria listed below.
- What extramural funding will be pursued on the basis of the proposed activity.
- A plan for routinely meeting with the identified Discovery Park partners to monitor and direct project activity, further develop synergy, maximize impact, and discuss toward project goals.

Page 7. References.

Page 8. Support letter from a Discovery Park Center Director or Managing Director specifying the nature of the partnership. For example, Discovery Park Centers can provide project management support, business office support, assistance in preparing

Figure 13–8 Request for a Grant Proposal (General and Specific Requirements).
Source: Purdue University, Office of the Vice President for Research <www.purdue.edu/Research/vpr/funding/docs/dp_seed_grant_RFP-HCK.pdf>.

Cover Letter

Usually a page long, the cover letter should identify who you are and your affiliation. It should specify the grant for which you are applying, summarize the proposed project, and include the amount of funding you are requesting. End the letter by expressing your appreciation for the opportunity to submit the proposal and include information about how you can be reached. The letter should include a subject line with the grant title in addition to the address of the recipient, date of submission, salutation (Dear . . .), and complimentary close (Sincerely), as in Figure 13–9.

Title Page

The title page is the grant-proposal cover. On a single page, show the title of the project, names of team members and their affiliations, date submitted, and name of the recipient's organization, as shown in Figure 13–10 on page 472.

Introduction/Summary/Abstract

The introduction, also called the Summary or Abstract, is your proposal at a glance. It briefly describes in a page the problem to be solved in the language used in the request for proposals, as in Figure 13–11 on page 472. Most important, your introduction should sketch the expected outcomes of your grant proposal, answering the question, What will you achieve? For a research proposal, you may also describe your proposed research methods in a separate paragraph: interviews, questionnaires, videotapes, observations, and so on.

Literature Review

◆ *For additional information about creating literature reviews or for a sample literature review, see pages 174–204 in Chapter 6, Researching Your Subject.*

The literature review allows reviewers of your proposal to assess your familiarity with current research in the field, as shown in Figure 13–12 on page 472. Is your research up to date? thorough? pertinent? Be selective in listing sources, which may include journal articles and books as well as interviews, broadcasts, blogs, and other sources. A literature review will also reveal whether conclusive research has already been done in an area or whether competing programs have successfully addressed the same problem. Some or all of the sources may be annotated to establish their scope and pertinence.

Project Narrative

The project narrative is the heart of the proposal. It's where you describe in detail the scope of the work, expected outcomes, list of tasks, schedule from start to finish, and proposed cost. The detailed problem statement must be specific and thorough. The excerpt shown in Figure 13–13 on page 473 from a grant proposal states the problem and includes pertinent data.

Project Description

The project-narrative section usually includes details of how the research will be conducted (the methodology), as in the excerpt shown in Figure 13–14 on page 473 from the reading-performance proposal.

October 6, 2010

Ms. Joan Atwater
Executive Director
ABC Foundation
13 Hill Street
Boston, MA 02116

Subject: Read to Succeed! Program

Dear Ms. Atwater:

Orchard Middle School is pleased to present this proposal for your review. We look forward to partnering with you to provide a reading intervention program for our students with poor reading skills called Read to Succeed! Orchard Middle School has over 50 at-risk students with a reading performance of at least two years behind their current grade level. The objective of the Read to Succeed! program is to help all students with poor reading skills learn to read at grade level and increase their reading speed, comprehension, and reading attention span.

Summary of program and objective

Last year, we ran a pilot Read to Succeed! program with a small group of students with poor reading skills and have seen dramatic improvements, with most of the students increasing their reading ability by one or two grade levels. . . .

We have seen measurable success, and we are now seeking to expand our Read to Succeed! program to address the needs of all at-risk students in the Orchard Middle School. Our proposal requests $16,504 in funding to obtain the software, hardware, and training necessary to equip the Orchard Middle School resource room with five assistive reading systems, each including a computer, a scanner, and assistive reading software.

Funding request

We appreciate ABC Foundation taking an interest in helping our students develop their reading skills through our new reading program! Please call me at 888-555-1212, ext. 342, or e-mail me at jhazelton@oms.edu if you require any further information or have any questions concerning this proposal.

Contact information

Thank you.

Jennifer Hazelton

Jennifer Hazelton

Special Education Coordinator
Orchard Middle School
387 Pine Hill Road
Orchard, VT 02331

Figure 13–9   Grant-Proposal Cover Letter. *Source:*

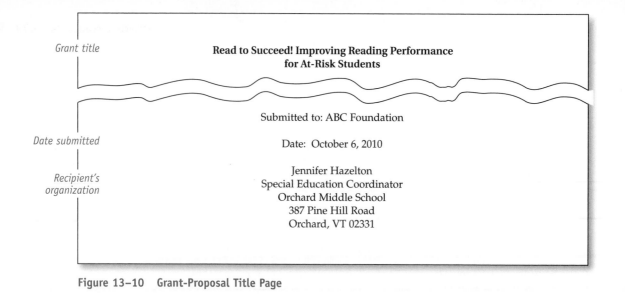

Grant title **Read to Succeed! Improving Reading Performance for At-Risk Students**

Submitted to: ABC Foundation

Date submitted Date: October 6, 2010

Recipient's
organization

Jennifer Hazelton
Special Education Coordinator
Orchard Middle School
387 Pine Hill Road
Orchard, VT 02331

Figure 13–10   Grant-Proposal Title Page

Project Abstract

Purpose and expected
outcomes

The Orchard Middle School, in Orchard, Vermont, is seeking a grant to expand our Read to Succeed! program with the objective of helping all our at-risk students increase their reading skills and be able to read at grade level using the same classroom textbooks and materials as their peers. The objective is that by the end of the year the students will have at least doubled their reading speed and will have improved their reading skills by one to two grade levels. The Read to Succeed! program features computers equipped with assistive reading software and text scanners for reading instruction. Funding in the amount of

Funding request $16,504 is requested for staff training and to purchase the required software and hardware for the school's resource room.

Figure 13–11   Grant-Proposal Introduction

References

Selective program
research source in
APA format

Elkind, J. (1998). *A study of the efficacy of the Kurzweil 3000 reading machine in enhancing poor reading performance*. Portola Valley, CA: Lexia Institute.

Heckler, L., Burns, L., Katz, L., & Elkind, J. (2002). Benefits of assistive reading software for students with attention disorders. *Annals of Dyslexia*, 52, 223–335.

Wise, B., Olson, R., & Murray, C. (1993). Using computer-based phonological awareness and reading instruction. *Annals of Dyslexia*, 45, 99–122.

Figure 13–12   Grant-Proposal References Section (Excerpt)

Statement of Need

Orchard Middle School has 276 students, 59 of whom have been determined to be at risk in their reading performance for a variety of reasons, including learning disabilities, such as attention deficit disorder (ADD) and dyslexia, or other language difficulties based on economic status. Orchard Middle School is eligible for Title 1 funds, and if these students are not given an opportunity to improve their reading skills, they are, as studies show, more likely to be truant and drop out of school.

Scope of proposal

Figure 13–13   Grant-Proposal Statement of Need

Project Outcomes

Having discussed the preparation for the program and how the participants will be evaluated, the grant must describe the outcomes, or deliverables, of the proposal. It must describe what results the organization can expect based on the time, labor, and funding it has invested in the program. In this case, the outcomes are stated as quantifiable objectives, as in Figure 13–15 on page 474. This section is also called "objectives."

Budget

Include a budget narrative section that provides a detailed listing of costs for personnel, equipment, building renovations, and other grant-related expenses. This information must be clear and accurate. List costs in a format easily grasped by those evaluating the data, as shown in Figure 13–16 on page 474. If your proposal is approved, you are being entrusted with funds belonging to someone else, and you are accountable for them. Your cost estimates may also be subject to changes

Program Description

The Orchard Read to Succeed! program will enable at-risk students to improve their reading skills through the use of five computers equipped with scanners and assistive reading software. Students using this innovative reading system will be able to use all their classroom materials, including textbooks, providing them access to the general curriculum. The students will increase their reading speed and comprehension, which will help them obtain classroom subject proficiency. Included in the Read to Succeed! program will be a day of training for the reading specialist and classroom teachers on the features and use of the Kurzweil 3000 software.

Specific program details

Figure 13–14   Grant-Proposal Program Description

Goals and Objectives

General program objectives

The goal of the Read to Succeed! program is to enable at-risk students and students with learning and reading disabilities to improve their reading skills to the point where they can succeed in school and develop the reading skills that will prepare them for high school and postsecondary education. Studies have shown that poor readers, those reading at a grade level or more behind, are more likely to be disruptive in the classroom, truant from school, and at risk of dropping out of high school.

The main objectives of the Read to Succeed! program include the following:

Quantifiable program objectives

1. Providing a measurable increase in reading speed, comprehension, and attention span. The objective is for the students to double their reading speed and increase their reading skills by one to two grade levels by the end of the school year.
2. Enabling poor readers to access the general curriculum through the use of assistive reading technology that will scan and read their textbooks and other classroom materials.
3. Providing learning-disabled students with a multisensory reading alternative that will help them increase their reading speed to the point where they can read on their own.
4. Helping learning- and reading-disabled students stay in their regular classroom with their peers so that they can continue learning in a least-restrictive environment.

Figure 13–15   Grant-Proposal Goals and Objectives Statement

Budget

The budget includes funds for a Lab Pack containing five copies of Kurzweil Educational System's Scan/Read Color software, along with five computers and scanners. They will provide five independent assistive reading workstations. This combination will give students the greatest flexibility in using their textbooks and other classroom materials.

Detailed list of program requirements

	Price	Quantity	Total
Kurzweil Scan/Read Lab Pack (Color) 5-Pack	$7,095	1 (5-Pack)	$7,095
Software Maintenance Agreement (SMA)	$709	1 (5-Pack)	$709
Epson 300 Scanner	$300	5	$1,500
Dell PC with Monitor	$1,200	5	$6,000
Training	$1,200	1 day	$1,200
Total			**$16,504**

Figure 13–16   Grant-Proposal Budget Narrative

over which you have no control, such as price increases for equipment, software, or consulting assistance. The project may also require ongoing funding following completion of the grant's tasks. Either estimate such costs or note that they will appear in a Future Funding section.

Schedule

Prepare a schedule of tasks that need to be performed to complete the project. Arrange them as bulleted points in sequence from first to last with due dates for each. Schedules can also be presented in table format, as shown in Figure 13–17.

Conclusion

The conclusion is a brief wrap-up section that emphasizes the benefits or advantages of your project. This section gives you one more opportunity to give the funding organization a reason why your proposal merits its approval. This is also the place to express your appreciation for the opportunity to submit the proposal.

Finally, note the time frame during which the proposal is valid and close with a statement of your willingness to provide further information.

ON THE WEB

For useful Web sources for grant-proposal preparation, go to Chapter 13, bedfordstmartins.com/ writingthatworks

Activity	Date	
Submit grant proposal	October 2010	*Program timeline and dates*
Expected grant notification	December 2010	
Obtain hardware and software	January 2011	
Set up Kurzweil 3000 program	January 2011	
Training session for teachers	February 2011	
Student introduction	February 2011	
Test initial reading speed	February 2011	
Begin first 12-week phase	March–May 2011	
Test reading improvement	June 2011	
Prepare project results report	July 2011	

Figure 13–17   Grant-Proposal Time Line

Sales Proposals

The sales proposal, a major marketing tool for business and industry, is a company's offer to provide specific goods or services to a potential buyer within a specified period of time and for a specified price. The primary purpose of a sales proposal is to demonstrate that the prospective customer's purchase of the seller's products or services will solve a problem, improve operations, or offer other benefits.

Sales proposals vary greatly in length and sophistication. Some are a page or two written by one person, others are many pages written collaboratively by several people, and still others are hundreds of pages written by a proposal-writing team. A short sales proposal might bid for painting the outside of a single-family home, a sales proposal of moderate length might bid for the installation of a network operating system for a small company, and a very long sales proposal might bid for the construction of a multimillion-dollar shopping center or sports complex. Short sales proposals are often written on standardized forms that are available from office-supply and stationery stores.

Your first task in writing a sales proposal is to find out exactly what your prospective customer needs. Then determine whether your organization can satisfy that customer's needs. If appropriate, compare your company's strengths with those of competing firms, determine your advantages over them, and emphasize those advantages in your proposal. For example, say a small biotechnology company is bidding for the contract to supply several types of medical test kits to a hospital. The proposal writer who believes that the company has a better-qualified staff than its competitors might include the résumés of the key people who would be involved in the project as a way of emphasizing that advantage.

Although the simple sales proposal typically follows the introduction-body-conclusion pattern, the long sales proposal contains more parts to accommodate the increased variety of information that it must present. The long sales proposal may include some or all of the following sections:

- Cover, or transmittal, letter (Figure 13–18)
- Title page
- Executive or project summary (Figure 13–19)
- General description of products (Figure 13–20)
- Detailed solution or rationale (Figure 13–21)
- Cost analysis (Figure 13–22 on page 482)
- Delivery schedule or work plan (Figure 13–22 on page 483)
- Site-preparation description (Figure 13–23)
- Training requirements (Figure 13–24)
- Statement of responsibilities (Figure 13–25)
- Description of vendor (Figure 13–26 on page 486)
- Organizational sales pitch (optional) (Figure 13–26 on page 487)
- Conclusion (optional) (Figure 13–27)
- Appendixes (optional)

Optional sections may be included at the discretion of the proposal-writing team. A conclusion, for example, may be added to a very long proposal as a convenience to the reader, but it is not mandatory. A site-preparation section, how-ever, is essential if the work proposed requires construction, remodeling, or such preparatory work as facility rewiring before equipment can be installed.

A long sales proposal begins with a cover letter—sometimes called a *trans-mittal letter*—that expresses your appreciation for the opportunity to submit your proposal and for any assistance you may have received in studying the customer's requirements. The letter should acknowledge any previous positive association with the customer. Then it should summarize the recommendations offered in the proposal and express your confidence that they will satisfy the customer's needs. Figure 13–18 shows the cover letter for the proposal illustrated in Figures 13–19 through 13–27—a proposal that the Waters Corporation of Tampa provide a com-puter system for the Cookson's chain of retail stores.

A title page and an executive summary—sometimes called a *project sum-mary*—follow the cover letter. The title page contains the title of the proposal, the date of submission, the company to which it is being submitted, your company's name, and any symbol or logo that identifies your company. The executive sum-mary is addressed to the executive who will ultimately accept or reject the pro-posal and should summarize in nontechnical language how you plan to approach the work. Figure 13–19 shows the executive summary of the Waters Corporation proposal.

If your proposal offers products as well as services, it should include a general description of the products, as shown in Figure 13–20. In many cases, product de-scriptions will already exist in other company publications; be sure to check your company's files or server before drafting a description from scratch.

Following the executive summary and the general description, explain exactly how you plan to do what you are proposing. This section, called the *detailed solu-tion*, or *rationale*, will be read by specialists who can understand and evaluate your plan, so you can feel free to use technical language and discuss complicated concepts. Figure 13–21 on page 481 shows one part of the detailed solution ap-pearing in the Waters Corporation proposal, which included several other appli-cations in addition to the payroll application. Notice that the detailed solution, like the discussion in an unsolicited sales proposal, begins with a statement of the customer's problem, follows with a statement of the solution, and concludes with a statement of the benefits to the customer. In some proposals, the headings "Problem" and "Solution" are used for this section.

A cost analysis and delivery schedule are essential to any sales proposal. The cost analysis, or budget, itemizes the estimated cost of all the products and ser-vices that you are offering; the delivery schedule—also called a *work plan*—com-mits you to a specific timetable for providing those products and services. Figure 13–22 on page 482 shows the cost analysis and delivery schedule of the Waters Corporation proposal.

If your recommendations include modifying your customer's physical facili-ties, you would include a site-preparation description that details the modifica-tions required. In some proposals, the headings "Facilities" and "Equipment" are used for this section. Figure 13–23 on page 484 shows the site-preparation section.

◆ For additional guid-ance on writing cover letters and transmittals, see page 321 in Chapter 9, Writing Business Correspon-dence, and page 388 in Chapter 11, Writing Formal Reports.

◆ For more advice on preparing a title page, see pages 389–390 in Chapter 11, Writing Formal Reports.

◆ For a discussion of executive summaries, see pages 398–400 in Chapter 11, Writing Formal Reports.

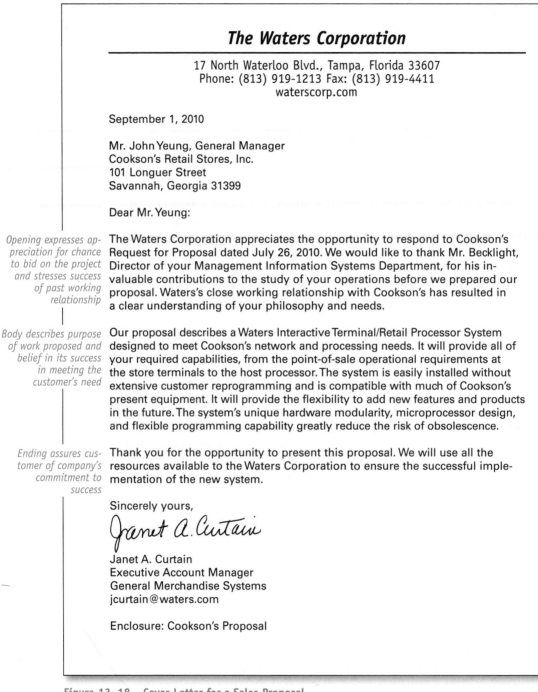

The Waters Corporation

17 North Waterloo Blvd., Tampa, Florida 33607
Phone: (813) 919-1213 Fax: (813) 919-4411
waterscorp.com

September 1, 2010

Mr. John Yeung, General Manager
Cookson's Retail Stores, Inc.
101 Longuer Street
Savannah, Georgia 31399

Dear Mr. Yeung:

Opening expresses appreciation for chance to bid on the project and stresses success of past working relationship

The Waters Corporation appreciates the opportunity to respond to Cookson's Request for Proposal dated July 26, 2010. We would like to thank Mr. Becklight, Director of your Management Information Systems Department, for his invaluable contributions to the study of your operations before we prepared our proposal. Waters's close working relationship with Cookson's has resulted in a clear understanding of your philosophy and needs.

Body describes purpose of work proposed and belief in its success in meeting the customer's need

Our proposal describes a Waters Interactive Terminal/Retail Processor System designed to meet Cookson's network and processing needs. It will provide all of your required capabilities, from the point-of-sale operational requirements at the store terminals to the host processor. The system is easily installed without extensive customer reprogramming and is compatible with much of Cookson's present equipment. It will provide the flexibility to add new features and products in the future. The system's unique hardware modularity, microprocessor design, and flexible programming capability greatly reduce the risk of obsolescence.

Ending assures customer of company's commitment to success

Thank you for the opportunity to present this proposal. We will use all the resources available to the Waters Corporation to ensure the successful implementation of the new system.

Sincerely yours,

Janet A. Curtain
Executive Account Manager
General Merchandise Systems
jcurtain@waters.com

Enclosure: Cookson's Proposal

Figure 13–18 **Cover Letter for a Sales Proposal**

The Waters Proposal   September 1, 2010

EXECUTIVE SUMMARY

The Waters 319 Interactive Terminal/615 Retail Processor System will provide your management with the tools necessary to manage people and equipment more profitably with procedures that will yield more cost-effective business controls for Cookson's.

Opens with overview of the proposed system

The equipment and applications proposed for Cookson's were selected through the combined effort of Waters and Cookson's Management Information Systems Director, Mr. Becklight. The architecture of the system will respond to your current requirements and allow for future expansion.

The features and hardware in the system were determined from data acquired through the comprehensive survey we conducted at your stores in February of this year. The total of 71 Interactive Terminals proposed to service your four store locations is based on the number of terminals currently in use and on the average number of transactions processed during normal and peak periods. The planned remodeling of all four stores was also considered, and the suggested terminal placement has been incorporated into the working floor plan. The proposed equipment configuration and software applications have been simulated to determine system performance based on the volumes and anticipated growth rates of the Cookson's stores.

Summarizes scope of system proposed

The information from the survey was also used in the cost justification, which was checked and verified by your controller, Mr. Deitering. The cost effectiveness of the Waters 319 Interactive Terminal/615 Retail Processor System is apparent. Expected savings, such as the projected 46 percent reduction in sales audit expenses, are realistic projections based on Waters's experience with other installations of this type.

Ends with projected cost savings of interest to the executive reader

Figure 13–19   Executive Summary of a Sales Proposal

The Waters Proposal   September 1, 2010

GENERAL SYSTEM DESCRIPTION

The point-of-sale system that Waters is proposing for Cookson's includes two primary Waters products. These are the 319 Interactive Terminal and the 615 Retail Processor.

Waters 319 Interactive Terminal

Detailed breakdown of system components and functions essential for technical readers

The primary component in the proposed retail system is the 319 Interactive Terminal. It contains a full microprocessor, which gives it the flexibility that Cookson's has been looking for.

The 319 Interactive Terminal provides you with freedom in sequencing a transaction to suit your needs rather than limiting you to a preset list of available steps or transactions. The terminal program can be adapted to provide unique transaction sets, each designed with a logical sequence of entry and processing to accomplish required tasks. The 319 Interactive Terminal also functions as a credit-authorization device, either by using its own floor limits or by transmitting a credit inquiry to the 615 Retail Processor for authorization.

Data-collection formats have been simplified so that transaction editing and formatting are much more easily accomplished. The information systems manager has already been provided with documentation on these formats and has outlined all data-processing efforts that will be necessary to transmit the data to your current systems. These projections have been considered in the cost justification.

Waters 615 Retail Processor

The Waters 615 Retail Processor is a server-based system designed to support the Waters family of retail terminals. The processor will reside in your data center in Buffalo. Operators already on your staff will be trained to initiate and monitor its activities.

Software

Additional system details for technical specialists

The Retail III software used with the system has been thoroughly tested and is operational in many Waters customer installations. The software provides the complete processing of the transaction, from the interaction with the operator on the sales floor through the data capture on disk in stores and in your data center.

Retail III provides a menu of modular applications for your selection. Parameters condition each of them to your hardware environment and operating requirements. The selection of hardware will be closely related to the selection of the software applications.

-2-

Figure 13–20   General-Description-of-Products Section of a Sales Proposal

The Waters Proposal   September 1, 2010

PAYROLL APPLICATION

Current Procedure

Your current system of reporting time requires each hourly employee to sign a time
sheet; the time sheet is reviewed by the department manager and sent to the Payroll
Department on Friday evening. Because the week ends on Saturday, the employee must
show the scheduled hours for Saturday and not the actual hours; therefore, the department manager must adjust the reported hours on the time sheet for employees who
do not report on the scheduled Saturday or who do not work the number of hours
scheduled.

A primary system feature described in problem-solution form

The Payroll Department employs a supervisor and three full-time clerks. To meet
deadlines caused by an unbalanced work flow, an additional part-time clerk is used
for 20 to 30 hours per week. The average wage for this clerk is $10.31 per hour.

Advantage of the Waters System

The 319 Interactive Terminal can be programmed for entry of payroll data for each
employee on Monday mornings by department managers, with the data reflecting actual
hours worked. This system would eliminate the need for manual batching, controlling,
and data input. The Payroll Department estimates conservatively that this work
consumes 30 hours per week.

Hours per week	30
Average wage (part-time clerk)	×10.31
Weekly payroll cost	$309.30
Annual Savings	$16,083.60

*Supporting cost analy-
sis illustrates company
savings*

Elimination of the manual tasks of tabulating, batching, and controlling can save 0.25
hourly units. Improved work flow resulting from timely data in the system without data-
input processing will allow more efficient use of clerical hours. This would reduce payroll
by the 0.50 hourly units currently required to meet weekly check disbursement.

Eliminate manual tasks	0.25
Improve work flow	0.50
40-hour unit reduction	1.00
Hours per week	40
Average wage (full-time clerk)	12.62
Savings per week	$509.80
Annual Savings	$26,509.60
TOTAL ANNUAL SAVINGS:	**$42,593.20**

Figure 13–21   Detailed Solution of a Sales Proposal

The Waters Proposal   September 1, 2010

COST ANALYSIS

This section of our proposal provides detailed cost information for the Waters 319 Interactive Terminal and the Waters 615 Retail Processor. It then multiplies these major elements by the quantities required at each of your four locations.

<u>319 Interactive Terminal</u>

	Price	Maintenance (1 year)
Terminal	$2,895	$167
Journal Printer	425	38
Receipt Printer	425	38
Forms Printer	525	38
Software	220	—
Totals	**$4,490**	**$281**

The following breakdown itemizes the cost per store:

<u>Store No. 1</u>

Breakdown of hardware, software, and maintenance costs

Description	Quantity	Price	Maintenance (1 year)
Terminals	16	$68,400	$4,496
Backup Memory Pack	1	350	147
Laser Printer	1	2,490	332
Software	16	3,520	—
Totals		**$74,760**	**$4,975**

-4-

Figure 13–22 Cost Analysis and Delivery Schedule of a Sales Proposal (continued)

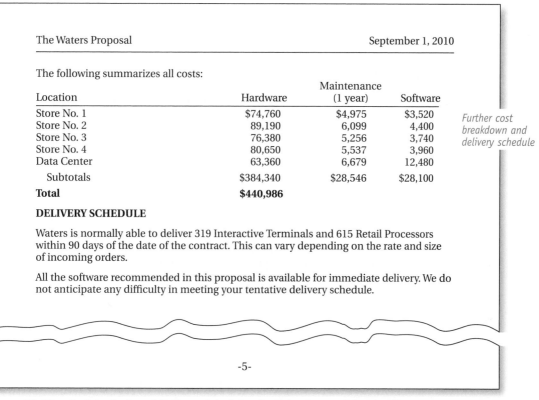

The Waters Proposal   September 1, 2010

The following summarizes all costs:

Location	Hardware	Maintenance (1 year)	Software
Store No. 1	$74,760	$4,975	$3,520
Store No. 2	89,190	6,099	4,400
Store No. 3	76,380	5,256	3,740
Store No. 4	80,650	5,537	3,960
Data Center	63,360	6,679	12,480
Subtotals	$384,340	$28,546	$28,100
Total	**$440,986**		

Further cost breakdown and delivery schedule

DELIVERY SCHEDULE

Waters is normally able to deliver 319 Interactive Terminals and 615 Retail Processors within 90 days of the date of the contract. This can vary depending on the rate and size of incoming orders.

All the software recommended in this proposal is available for immediate delivery. We do not anticipate any difficulty in meeting your tentative delivery schedule.

-5-

Figure 13–22   Cost Analysis and Delivery Schedule of a Sales Proposal (continued)

If the products and services you are proposing require training the customer's employees, your proposal should specify the required training and its cost. Figure 13–24 on page 485 shows the training requirements section of the Waters proposal.

To prevent misunderstandings about what you and your customer's responsibilities will be, you should draw up a statement of responsibilities (Figure 13–25 on page 486), which usually appears toward the end of the proposal. Also toward the end of the proposal is a description of the vendor, which gives a profile of your company, its history, and its present position in the industry. The description-of-the-vendor section typically includes a list of people or subcontractors and the duties they will perform. The résumés of key personnel may also be placed here or in an appendix. Following this description, many proposals add what is known as an organizational sales pitch. To this point, the proposal has attempted to sell specific goods and services. The sales pitch, striking a somewhat different chord, is designed to sell the company and its general capability in the field. The sales pitch promotes the company and concludes the proposal on an upbeat note. Figure 13–26 on page 487 shows the vendor-description and sales-pitch sections of the Waters proposal.

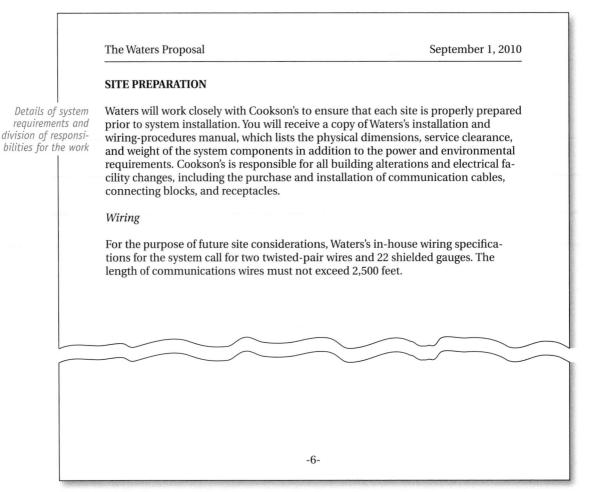

The Waters Proposal   September 1, 2010

SITE PREPARATION

Details of system requirements and division of responsibilities for the work

Waters will work closely with Cookson's to ensure that each site is properly prepared prior to system installation. You will receive a copy of Waters's installation and wiring-procedures manual, which lists the physical dimensions, service clearance, and weight of the system components in addition to the power and environmental requirements. Cookson's is responsible for all building alterations and electrical facility changes, including the purchase and installation of communication cables, connecting blocks, and receptacles.

Wiring

For the purpose of future site considerations, Waters's in-house wiring specifications for the system call for two twisted-pair wires and 22 shielded gauges. The length of communications wires must not exceed 2,500 feet.

-6-

Figure 13–23   Site-Preparation Section of a Sales Proposal

ON THE WEB

For a complete, annotated version of the proposal shown in Figures 13–18 through 13–27, as well as the RFP to which the proposal responded, go to Model Documents Gallery, bedfordstmartins.com/writingthatworks

Some long sales proposals include a conclusion section that summarizes the proposal's salient points, stresses your company's strengths, and includes information about whom the potential client can contact for further information. It may also end with a request for the date the work will begin should the proposal be accepted. Figure 13–27 on page 488 shows the conclusion of the Waters proposal.

Depending on length and technical complexity, some proposals include appendixes made up of statistical analyses, maps, charts, tables, and résumés of the principal staff assigned to the project. Appendixes to proposals should contain only supplemental information; the primary information should appear in the body of the proposal.

The Waters Proposal   September 1, 2010

TRAINING

To ensure a successful installation, Waters offers the following training course for
your operators.

Interactive Terminal/Retail Processor Operations

Course number: 8256
Length: three days
Tuition: $500.00

*Employee training
costs and length*

This course provides the student with the skills, knowledge, and practice required
to operate an Interactive Terminal/Retail Processor System. Online, clustered, and
stand-alone environments are covered.

We recommend that students have a department-store background and that they
have some knowledge of the system configuration with which they will be working.

-7-

Figure 13–24   Training-Requirements Section of a Sales Proposal

RESPONSIBILITIES

Based on its years of experience in installing information-processing systems, Waters believes that a successful installation requires a clear understanding of certain responsibilities.

Waters's Responsibilities

Generally, it is Waters's responsibility to provide its users with needed assistance during the installation so that live processing can begin as soon thereafter as is practical.

- Provide operations documentation for each application that you acquire from Waters.
- Provide forms and other supplies as ordered.
- Provide specifications and technical guidance for proper site planning and installation.
- Provide adviser assistance in the conversion from your present system to the new system.

Division of tasks between customer and vendor

Customer's Responsibilities

Cookson's will be responsible for the suggested improvements described earlier, as well as the following:

- Identify an installation coordinator and system operator.
- Provide supervisors and clerical personnel to perform conversion to the system.
- Establish reasonable time schedules for implementation.
- Ensure that the physical site requirements are met.
- Provide personnel to be trained as operators and ensure that other employees are trained as necessary.
- Assume the responsibility for implementing and operating the system.

-8-

Figure 13–25   Statement-of-Responsibilities Section of a Sales Proposal

The Waters Proposal   September 1, 2010

DESCRIPTION OF VENDOR

The Waters Corporation develops, manufactures, markets, installs, and services total business information-processing systems for selected markets. These markets are primarily in the retail, financial, commercial, industrial, health-care, education, and government sectors.

Statements of the vendor's history and commitment to its core business to highlight its experience and reputation

The Waters total-system concept encompasses one of the broadest hardware and software product lines in the industry. Waters computers range from small business systems to powerful general-purpose processors. Waters computers are supported by a complete spectrum of terminals, peripherals, and data-communication networks, as well as an extensive library of software products. Supplemental services and products include data centers, field service, systems engineering, and educational centers.

The Waters Corporation was founded in 1934 and presently has approximately 26,500 employees. The Waters headquarters is located at 17 North Waterloo Boulevard, Tampa, Florida, with district offices throughout the United States and Canada. For a comprehensive listing of Waters products and services, visit our Web site at waterscorp.com.

WHY WATERS?

Corporate Commitment to the Retail Industry

Waters's commitment to the retail industry is stronger than ever. We are continually striving to provide leadership in the design and implementation of new retail systems and applications that will ensure our users of a logical growth pattern.

Research and Development

Over the years, Waters has spent increasingly large sums on research-and-development efforts to ensure the availability of products and systems for the future. In 2009, our research-and-development expenditures for advanced-systems design and technological innovations reached the $70 million level.

Leading Point-of-Sale Vendor

Waters is a leading point-of-sale vendor, having installed over 150,000 units. The knowledge and experience that Waters has gained over the years from these installations ensure well-coordinated and effective systems implementations.

-9-

Figure 13–26   Description-of-Vendor and Sales-Pitch Sections of a Sales Proposal

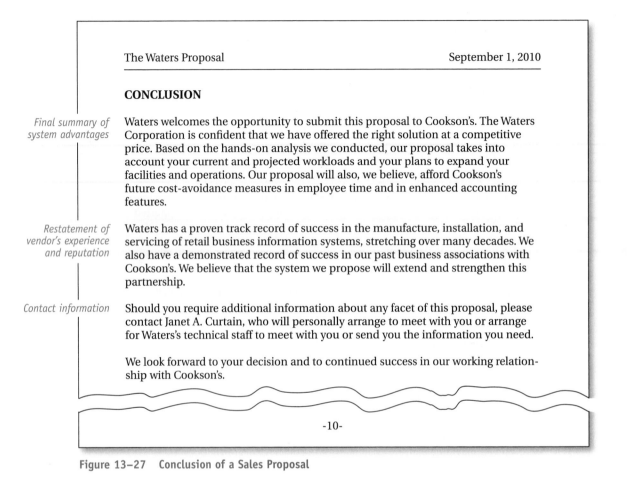

Figure 13–27   Conclusion of a Sales Proposal

The following text appears within the figure:

The Waters Proposal   September 1, 2010

CONCLUSION

Final summary of system advantages — Waters welcomes the opportunity to submit this proposal to Cookson's. The Waters Corporation is confident that we have offered the right solution at a competitive price. Based on the hands-on analysis we conducted, our proposal takes into account your current and projected workloads and your plans to expand your facilities and operations. Our proposal will also, we believe, afford Cookson's future cost-avoidance measures in employee time and in enhanced accounting features.

Restatement of vendor's experience and reputation — Waters has a proven track record of success in the manufacture, installation, and servicing of retail business information systems, stretching over many decades. We also have a demonstrated record of success in our past business associations with Cookson's. We believe that the system we propose will extend and strengthen this partnership.

Contact information — Should you require additional information about any facet of this proposal, please contact Janet A. Curtain, who will personally arrange to meet with you or arrange for Waters's technical staff to meet with you or send you the information you need.

We look forward to your decision and to continued success in our working relationship with Cookson's.

-10-

■ MEETING THE DEADLINE: The Time-Sensitive Proposal

Proposal writers must give top priority to meeting the procuring organization's deadline, while also producing a high-quality, persuasive proposal likely to receive favorable evaluations. The following time-management strategies can help toward meeting these goals.

1. *Hold an initial planning session.* The project manager should hold a planning meeting with the project coordinator, the compiler, the budget specialist, and the key subject-matter specialists to introduce the project team members, set priorities, determine and delegate tasks, set milestone deadlines for each task, and decide the most effective way to create and exchange drafts: e-mail, wikis (collaborative project Web sites), faxing, and the like.

2. *Assign coordinators.* During the planning meeting, the project manager should choose a writing coordinator to organize the creation and production of text and graphics, and a compiler (often an administrative assistant) to integrate all sections and elements of the final proposal and to make sure that those sections and elements adhere to the potential customer's requirements in the request for proposal.

3. *Set priorities.* The sections or features likely to weigh most heavily during the prospective customer's evaluation of the proposal should receive the most attention from the writers and the most space in the final product. Make this determination at the beginning of the project. These sections tend to be longer than sections of lesser importance. For example, for a ten-page proposal that includes four sections, the two most important sections might be four pages each, while the two least important sections might be one page each.

4. *Delegate tasks.* To expedite research and writing, assign more than one person to work on each section, and allow them to work out a way to collaborate efficiently to meet the deadline for submitting their section. This strategy works best when the contributors have diverse schedules and areas of specialization. Often, two or three subject experts coauthor parts of a single section, and the writing coordinator edits the resulting draft for clarity and coherence.

5. *Work out a schedule.* During the initial planning session, determine how much time each task is likely to require. Start work immediately on tasks likely to take longer to complete, but also begin to collect other important pieces, such as résumés, biographies, and project descriptions. Decide which tasks can be done simultaneously and which tasks must precede others. When establishing a schedule, work backward from the proposal deadline, leaving at least a day for the proposal to reach its destination by express delivery, half a day before that for collecting company signatures and making multiple copies of the proposal, and half a day before that for last-minute edits and proofreading.

6. *Use repurposed material.* When possible, import into the proposal standard pieces of information from previous proposals, such as résumés, descriptions of past projects, and company goals and accomplishments. This is known as boilerplate material. For additional information about the use of boilerplate, see page 181 in Chapter 6.

7. *Track progress and deadlines.* Use e-mail or phone messages periodically to send out reminders about deadlines or prompt someone to deliver material that you need right away. Hold interim meetings if doing so will speed up your work. If interim task deadlines are missed and you need information, materials, or finished products immediately, ask everyone on the project team to abandon other projects to devote full-time and extra hours to the proposal effort so that you can meet the final deadline.

8. *Hold a lessons-learned meeting, if necessary.* Even when these strategies are used, problems can arise that jeopardize the quality of your proposal or your ability to meet the final deadline. After sending the proposal, hold a debriefing session in which you identify those problems and plan strategies for avoiding them when planning and writing future proposals.

▥ Requests for Proposals

When a company or another organization needs a task performed or a service provided outside its staff expertise or capabilities, it seeks help from vendors that can provide the expertise or capabilities needed. The company seeking help usually makes its requirements known to potential vendors by issuing a request for proposals. The RFP details the company's requirements so that vendors can evaluate whether to bid on the project.

The details provided in an RFP permit vendors to understand your needs and enable you to determine from their responses which vendor to select to meet your requirements. Although RFPs lay out your requirements, they usually do not specify how these requirements are to be met.[1] Potential vendors prepare proposals to describe their solutions for meeting your requirements; you then choose from among them the one that best suits your needs, budget, and schedule.

RFP Structure

Like proposals, RFPs vary in length, formality, and structure. Some are a page or two, and others run to hundreds of pages. The scope of information included and even the terminology used to describe specific sections vary with the type of task or service being solicited. For example, RFPs involving computer systems usually include a "Technical Requirements" section, specifying site-preparation requirements and describing the current technical infrastructure at the company issuing the RFP. The purpose and context of RFPs also vary. Each RFP involves unique legal, budgetary, confidentiality, and administrative considerations. The following sections describe typical components for RFPs.

Information About Your Company

One section of an RFP should describe your company's mission, goals, size, facility locations, position in the marketplace, and possibly a brief company history. It should also provide your company contact information. This section parallels the "Description of Vendor" section in proposals (see Figure 13–26).

---

[1]A related document is an invitation for bids. An IFB strictly defines the quantity, type, and specifications for an item that an organization, such as a government agency, intends to purchase.

Project Description

Another section, sometimes called "Scope of Work" or "Workscope Description," describes the deliverable (the project or service) you need, with a detailed list of requirements. For example, an RFP prepared by a pharmaceutical company soliciting training for its sales representatives about a new drug divided the project description into three sections:

- Target audience (members of sales staff and their technical background and computer experience)
- Content (specific curriculum and length of training)
- Deliverable (in-person training, CD-ROM, or Web page, using video, audio, and animation)

Vendors responding to this RFP would organize their proposals in line with these requirements. For some projects, requirements can be described in a summary statement, as shown in the following examples.

▶ The project deliverable will be a questionnaire to be mailed to approximately 400 adults regarding their consumer experiences with various health-care providers.

▶ The deliverable will be a networked online forms package for approximately 1,200 employees, permitting information to be completed online, stored in a database, routed via e-mail, and printed on paper. The package shall be integrated into the company's current network environment at its headquarters facility.

The project description may also indicate whether the deliverable must be created new or can be obtained commercially and adapted to the project's needs. For example, if the project involves software development, the description may state whether the requesting company prefers commercially available software or expects the vendor to develop unique software for the project. The project-description section can also specify other details such as a project-management plan and any warranty or liability requirements.

Delivery Schedule

For complex projects lasting a month or longer, specify the time allotted for the project and a proposed schedule of tasks.

Proposal Description

Many RFPs provide format requirements for proposals, such as how the proposal should be organized; the number of copies expected; whether an electronic file is required; where, the date by which, and to whom the proposal should be sent; and how it should be sent (registered mail, courier service, etc.). Some companies even provide an electronic proposal template for vendors to follow.

Vendor Qualifications

Most RFPs request information about the vendor as well — a summary of the vendor's experience, professional certifications, number of employees, years in business, quality-control procedures, awards and honors, and the like. An RFP may require references of recent customers as well as financial references. The RFPs usually require that vendors submit the résumés of the principal employees assigned to the project.

Proposal-Evaluation Criteria

The proposal-evaluation section informs vendors of the criteria you will use to select the company to work for you. Will you decide solely on cost? a combination of cost and vendor past performance? technical expertise? Many companies organize the criteria by importance or weight while others grade proposals with a point system and include a table of criteria, each of which is given a point value on a scale of either 100 or 1,000 total points, as in the following sample:

▷   Proposal-Evaluation Criteria

CRITERIA	POINTS
Administrative	50
Technical	700
Management	100
Price	100
Presentation and demonstration	50
Total	**1,000**

ON THE WEB

To view the RFP that accompanies the sample Waters proposal, see Model Documents Gallery, bedfordstmartins.com/ writingthatworks

Appendixes

Some RFPs include one or more appendixes or "Attachments." These may include sample forms and questionnaires, a sample contract, technical information about a company's server and workstation configurations, workflow-analysis diagrams, dates and times when vendors can visit the work site before finalizing their proposals, and other essentials too detailed for the body of the RFP.

ETHICS NOTE

If your RFP contains any company-confidential information, you could include a legally binding nondisclosure statement for vendors to sign before you send the full RFP. Many companies also include a guarantee not to open proposals before the due date and never to disclose information in one vendor's proposal to a competing vendor.

CHAPTER 13 SUMMARY: WRITING PROPOSALS

A proposal

- Is written to persuade a reader to follow a plan or course of action.
- Is written from the perspective and needs of the audience.
- Is produced by a collaborative team of specialists when the proposal is complex.
- Consists of the following parts (and may include additional parts, based on the needs of your topic and specifications of the request for proposals):
  - The problem you propose to solve and your solution to it
  - The dates on which you propose to begin and complete work
  - Any special benefits of your proposed approach
  - The total cost of the project
  - Any previous positive association between your company and the potential customer (if a sales proposal)
  - What products and services you are offering (if a sales proposal)
  - How the job will be done
  - The procedures you propose to use to perform the work
  - The materials you will use (if applicable)
  - The schedule for each stage of the project
  - Detailed costs
  - The benefits of your solution, products, or services that persuade the reader to take action
  - Your confidence in your ability — or, if a sales proposal, of your company's ability — to carry out the project
  - Your willingness to provide further information
  - The advantages of your company over its competitors
  - Your appreciation for the opportunity to submit the proposal
  - The time period during which the proposal is valid
  - A list or description of any supplemental materials

An internal proposal

- Is written to a manager within your organization.
- Is usually written to persuade management to make a change or an improvement or to fund a project that you would like to launch.

An external proposal

- Is written to a potential client outside your organization.
- May be solicited or unsolicited.
- Might be written to persuade a potential customer to purchase your company's products or services.
- May be short or long, depending on the complexity of the topic.
- Is often time sensitive and must be produced by a collaborative writing team under the pressure of a tight deadline.

A grant proposal

- ▨ Is written to a nonprofit organization — government agency, educational or research institution, or private foundation.
- ▨ Is solicited in a grant request for proposals that specifies exactly how the grant proposal should be organized and what it should contain.
- ▨ May offer assistance with a project that requires an investigation or research into an issue.
- ▨ May be required to explain the expected outcomes of the project — "What will you achieve?"
- ▨ Is always required to be submitted by a specified date.

A request for proposals

- ▨ Is written by an organization to solicit proposals from outside vendors for a service or product.
- ▨ Describes its requirements and expected deliverable in sufficient detail for vendors to respond with realistic solutions.
- ▨ Provides format requirements on what the proposal should include and how it should be organized.
- ▨ Includes evaluation criteria to inform vendors of the organization's selection criteria for their proposals.

ON THE WEB

For an online quiz on proposals, go to Chapter 13, bedfordstmartins.com/ writingthatworks

▨ Exercises

1. Address an internal proposal to your supervisor, recommending that your company begin a tuition-refund plan or specific technology-training program. Propose at least three major advantages to having either of these educational programs, and present them in decreasing order of importance.

2. You are a landscaping contractor and would like to respond to the following RFP, which appears in your local newspaper:

   ▸ Lawn-mowing agreement for the Town of Augusta, Oregon. Weekly mowing of 5 miles of Route 24 median and sidings, 10 acres in Willoughby Park, and 23 acres at Augusta Memorial Golf Course, May 30 through September 30. Proposals are due April 30.

   Write a proposal in which you estimate the number of labor-hours the contract would require, what you would charge, the ability of your staff and equipment to do the job, your firm's experience and qualifications, and the weekly schedule that you propose to follow.

3. Write a proposal letter to change a specific rule or regulation of an organization to which you belong, such as your school, religious organization, professional association, or fitness club. List the current rule or regulation, then present your proposed changes and explain the advantages of your new rule. Address your short proposal to the president or head of the organization.

4. Imagine that you work as a proposal writer for an electronics company that makes specialized equipment for the U.S. Navy. You have been informed that should your

company win a contract next year, a record will be kept of your performance assessments and evaluations. Both positive and negative information will be recorded, such as quality reviews, over-budget cost reports, user comments, and technical successes and failures (see <www.cpars.navy.mil> for detailed information on the Navy's Contractor Performance Assessment Reporting System). Draft an internal proposal to your boss detailing this new information and suggesting procedures and processes that could be put into place so that your company's performance assessments and evaluations will be positive.

5. As a human resources coordinator of a large company, you've noticed an increase in the number of employee medical emergencies, some serious, over the past two years. Write an internal proposal memo to your supervisor, offering plans that would (1) contribute to employees' good health and (2) help employees respond to medical emergencies. Plans for improving employees' health could include a more comprehensive medical-benefits package, on-site health screening, stress-management and nutrition counseling, and corporate memberships to fitness centers. Plans for helping employees handle medical emergencies could include on-site CPR and first-aid training. Explain the benefits of each solution you propose.

6. Imagine that you run your own business and want to expand your client base. First, choose a small business concept that interests you and identify a service or product that such a business might provide. Prepare a one-page cost analysis for a sales proposal that you would submit to a prospective client. Your cost analysis should be clearly written and well formatted, and it should include the following breakdown for the project:

- Cost of personnel or labor
- Cost of overhead
- Cost of new equipment
- Total cost of project

Submit any amounts you wish in these categories and change the category titles as needed. Each category except total cost must contain at least four different line items. For example, cost of personnel or labor might include the hourly rate for the time the company president will spend on this project and the cost of other staff specialists required on the project. Overhead might include the cost of support staff, supplies, company vehicles, and so forth. The cost of new equipment would include the cost of items purchased solely for the client. Although you may use any numbers you wish in the line items, all subtotals should equal the total cost when added together.

7. In Exercise 7 in Chapter 10, you were asked to imagine that you were a consultant hired by a company that creates security systems for the average homeowner. Although its new wireless surveillance camera was supposed to work in low light and transmit pictures up to 100 meters, your tests revealed that the camera's picture and sound quality were negatively impacted by the interference of other electrical equipment in the house, such as baby monitors, microwave ovens, and cordless phones. Static noises and jumping lines made it nearly impossible to understand the sound and picture.

Now, imagine that you are the head of the security systems company's development team. Based on the test report you wrote for Exercise 7 in Chapter 10, write an internal proposal to the head of the company detailing the test results and requesting funds to hire an electronics consultant who specializes in solving such problems.

8. Identify a problem that you feel needs to be solved either at work or at school. For example, the increasing number of students and limited number of parking spaces are causing a major parking problem. Or sealed windows in your office building are creating sick-building syndrome, and many employees are getting ill more frequently and for longer periods of time. Your assignment is to write a proposal offering a solution to the problem. (Your instructor may want to approve your topic selection.) Assume that your proposal is internal, and include the following in your proposal:

   a. Transmittal letter
   b. Executive summary
   c. Introduction, body, and conclusion
   d. Cost analysis (you may invent the numbers)
   e. Time line or schedule of delivery
   f. Description of vendor

   Your completed proposal will be seven to ten pages long, with the executive summary less than one page, single-spaced. Your introduction, body, and conclusion will be approximately three pages of text, 1½-spaced. Insert at least two visuals within the text.

ON THE WEB

For more collaborative classroom projects, go to Chapter 13, bedfordstmartins.com/ writingthatworks

■ Collaborative Classroom Projects

1. In teams of three to five members, review the description of the vendor included in Figure 13–26, and develop and design an organizational sales pitch. Referring back to this chapter, develop a rough draft, including an original layout and design created by your team. Set priorities for the information to be included and be creative in the manner you choose to present the information. Take 45 minutes to one hour to complete this assignment.

2. In teams of five to seven members, develop an internal proposal asking the dean's office to upgrade or expand a facility, technology, or course offering (or another topic approved by your instructor). Your proposal is due in three weeks. Spend 45 minutes developing a plan for completing your group's proposal. Refer to Meeting the Deadline: The Time-Sensitive Proposal on pages 488–490.

   a. Your team will need to assign a project manager, a writing coordinator, a compiler, and a budget specialist.
   b. Once chosen, the project manager will begin the session by introducing team members, setting priorities, and determining and delegating tasks.
   c. In a collective effort, make a list of the tasks that will need to be completed.
   d. Decide what sections will be included in the proposal.
   e. Develop a time line, including scheduling and sequencing of the tasks. Include any other details you feel are relevant as you develop your plan.

   As directed by your instructor, present your plan for how your team will meet the deadline orally to the class or submit the plan in writing to your instructor. Submit the finished proposal to your instructor.

Research Projects

ON THE WEB

For extra research projects, go to Chapter 13, bedfordstmartins.com/ writingthatworks

1. Many government and research proposals have very specific instructions on the format and content of each proposal. For example, a proposal's instructions may specify the number of characters per inch allowed in the text, and the size of the margins and number of lines allowed per page. Assume that you and three other classmates are interested in pursuing a career as professional grant writers for medical and educational institutions. Research at least six specific grants dealing with medical or educational products or research. Create a report of your findings (review Chapter 10, Writing Informal Reports) that gives many examples of the instructions you found and also explains why agencies that fund research projects would be so specific about such seemingly inconsequential details.

2. For Exercise 2 in Chapter 10, you wrote an investigative report detailing back injuries and worker's compensation claims at a large online retailer. Research warehouse equipment companies and manufacturers of safety equipment and use your findings to create an internal proposal that comments on such issues as the design of warehouse equipment, especially the kind that transports heavy boxes, and makes suggestions for the purchase of new equipment that would help the warehouse workers prevent injuries.

3. Your high-tech company is interested in changing its security procedures to include biometric verification technology. Employees' fingerprints or retina patterns (or both) would now be scanned before they could enter top-secret areas. You have been asked to investigate at least three Web sites of companies that provide this kind of technology. Write a proposal letter to your boss that details how the technology works, the cost, and the advantages over traditional security methods.

4. Assume that you run the Adult Basic Education (ABE) program at your local county jail. Your job is to offer instructional and support services that will help incarcerated adult students improve their literacy and English-speaking skills through the high school level, to the point that they are ready, upon their release, to continue and succeed in postsecondary education. Search the Web for educational grants that might help you meet your goals. You may apply for funds to address potential courses in ABE, literacy, pre-adult secondary education, English for speakers of other languages (ESOL), preliteracy ESOL, and adult diploma classes, among others.

   a. Begin by searching the Web site of your state's Department of Education, then move to the federal agencies. Create a report of at least three sources of funding available, what they give money for, and the requirements for applying for the funding. (These may include required forms, like letters of intent and budget details.) Also note all of the deadlines.

   b. Draft a proposal to your state's Department of Education that answers the questions in Considering Audience and Purpose: Writing Proposals on page 450.

   c. Now rework your proposal draft according to the Writing Persuasive Proposals checklist on page 453–454. Remember that you are arguing that your program has the greatest need and offers the most for its students, so persuasive writing is essential. (You won't be rewriting the proposal in a specific format for a specific funding source unless you wish to, but rather reworking the existing draft.)

Giving Presentations and Conducting Meetings

AT A GLANCE: Presentations and Meetings

Although most of this book covers the principles of writing that work in business and industry, much workplace information is communicated orally as well, and the components of such communications—listening and responding effectively—are both critically important. This chapter offers practical guidelines for the following:

- Preparing and delivering presentations / 499
  - Determining your purpose / 499
  - Analyzing your audience / 500
  - Gathering information / 500
  - Structuring your presentation / 500
  - Using visual aids / 504
  - Delivering your presentation / 511
  - Reaching global audiences / 515
- Listening / 516
- Conducting productive meetings / 523
  - Planning a meeting / 523
  - Running a meeting / 527
  - Taking minutes / 530

Writing and presentations have much in common. Both must be logically organized and are most effective when clear and succinct. However, much is different between writing and presentations, and this chapter explores those elements unique to oral communication. Oral communication is most widely used in the workplace for giving presentations and in conducting meetings. Central to the success of both is effective listening.

VOICES IN THE WORKPLACE

Engaging Your Audience

Paul B. Greenspan spends much of his time doing presentations for prospective and established clients of EMC Corporation: "A good presenter uses techniques to minimize the amount of work the audience has to do. Use arresting visuals and avoid long, bulleted lists that basically duplicate [your] notes. Body language is also important—how you use your arms, how you gesture. The 'big' gesture that may seem exaggerated to the presenter looks natural to the audience. . . . The day of the 'droning, talking head' with an inch-thick stack of transparencies is gone forever."

■ Preparing and Delivering Presentations

The steps required to prepare an effective presentation parallel the steps you follow to write a document: (1) Determine your purpose and analyze your audience, (2) find and gather the facts to support your point of view and proposal, and (3) logically organize your information. However, because presentations are intended for listeners, not readers, your manner of delivery, the way you organize the material, and your supporting visual aids require as much attention as your content.

ON THE WEB

For more help with giving presentations and conducting meetings, go to Chapter 14, bedfordstmartins.com/ writingthatworks

Determining Your Purpose

Every presentation is given for a purpose—to share information, to urge an audience to take action, to analyze data, to present solutions to a problem. To determine the purpose of your presentation, use these questions as a guide: What do I want my audience to know? What do I want my audience to believe? What do I want my audience to do when I have finished the presentation? Based on the answers to these questions, write a purpose statement that answers the questions *what* and *why*.

▶ The purpose of my presentation is to explain to my classmates the various tasks I performed last semester as a part-time volunteer at the Maplewood Adult Day Care Center [*what*] so that other members of the class will consider becoming volunteers at Maplewood [*why*].

▶ The purpose of my presentation is to convince my company's chief information officer of the need to improve the appearance, content, and customer use of our company's Web site [*what*] so that she will include additional funds in the budget for site-development work next fiscal year [*why*].

Keep in mind that the context of the presentation will affect your purpose and your audience's reaction to it. Will your audience be expecting you to address an existing company or industrywide issue important to the members of your audience? Will your organization's goals, expectations, even jargon be appropriate

◆ *For a fuller discussion of determining purpose, analyzing an audience, considering your context, and gathering information, see pages 5–11 in Chapter 1, Assessing Audience and Purpose.*

when you address outside groups? Will your gestures and use of eye contact be appropriate for your audience's background or cultural frame of reference? These and other matters make up the context affecting the success of your presentations.

Analyzing Your Audience

Once you determine the desired end result of the presentation, analyze your audience so that you can tailor your presentation to their needs. Answer the following five questions about your audience:

1. What is their level of experience or knowledge about your topic?
2. What is their general educational level and age?
3. What is their attitude toward the topic you are speaking about, and—based on that attitude—what interests, concerns, fears, or objections might they have?
4. Are there subgroups among them that might have different concerns or needs?
5. What questions might they ask about this topic?

Sales representatives in a briefing on a new product line will likely be positive and enthusiastic. But townspeople being briefed at a public meeting about cleanup options for a toxic waste site near their town will be wary or even frightened. Tailor your presentation accordingly.

Gathering Information

Once you have focused the presentation, find the information that will support your point of view or the action you propose. Give the audience only the information necessary to accomplish your goals; too much information will overwhelm them and too little information will leave them either with a sketchy understanding of your topic or with the feeling that they need more information to support the course of action you wish them to take. And what kind of information will be most persuasive? Will the audience expect data-centered information, like specific facts, figures, and statistics? Or will quotations from subject experts or even anecdotes be more convincing? Your topic will affect the information you present, but so will the makeup of your audience.

Structuring Your Presentation

Structure your presentation for listeners. Listeners remember openings and closings best because listeners are freshest at the outset and refocus their attention as you wrap up your remarks. Take advantage of this pattern. Give your audience a brief overview of your presentation at the beginning, use the body to develop your ideas, and end with a summary of what you covered and, if appropriate, a call to action.

Introduction

The introduction to your presentation may include an opening—something designed to catch and focus the audience's attention. The following opening *defines a problem*:

▷ You have to write an important report, but you'd like to repurpose the bulk of an old report into your new one. The problem is that you don't have an electronic version of the old report. You'll have to re-key many pages. You groan because that seems an incredible waste of time. Have I got a solution for you!

Notice how this opening appeals to the audience member, addressing him or her directly, and describes a common work-related problem. Once it captures the audience's attention, it leads into the body of the presentation (the "solution").

You could also use any of the following types of openings:

- *An attention-getting statement*: As many as 50 million Americans have high blood pressure.
- *A rhetorical question*: Would you be interested in a full-sized computer keyboard that is waterproof, is noiseless, and can be rolled up like a rubber mat?
- *A personal experience*: As I sat at my computer deleting my eighth junk e-mail of the day, I decided to find a way to eliminate this time-waster.
- *An appropriate quotation*: According to researchers at the Massachusetts Institute of Technology, "Garlic and its cousin the onion confer major health benefits—including fighting cancer, infections, and heart disease."

Following your opening, set the stage for your audience by giving an overview of the presentation. The overview may include general or background information that your audience will need in order to understand the more detailed information in the body of your presentation. It may also be an overview of how you've organized the material.

▷ This presentation explains the options available to you, the employees of Acme Corporation, for making payroll contributions to a long-term retirement plan that will enhance the income you will receive from Social Security and pension benefits.

▷ This presentation will answer your questions about the following:
- How much can I save?
- How much does Acme contribute to the plan?
- What are my investment options?

◆ *For additional examples of openings, see pages 84–86 in Chapter 3, Writing the Draft.*

Body

In the body of your presentation, persuade your audience of the validity of your conclusion. If you are addressing a problem, demonstrate that the problem exists and offer a solution or range of possible solutions. If your introduction stated that the problem was low profits, high costs, outdated technology, or high employee absenteeism, for example, you might use the following approach:

- Offer a solution.
    - Increase profits by lowering production costs.
    - Cut overhead to reduce costs.
    - Upgrade existing technology to improve productivity.
    - Offer employees more flexibility in their work schedules or other incentives.
- Prove your point.
    - Gather the facts and data you need.
    - Present the facts and data using easy-to-understand visual aids. (The next section, Using Visual Aids, discusses this topic in more detail.)
- Call for action.
    - Convince your audience to agree, to change their minds, or to do something.
- Anticipate questions ("How much will it cost?") and objections ("We're too busy now. When will we have time to learn the new software?") and be ready for them.

Closing

Your closing should achieve the goals of your presentation. If your purpose is to motivate the members of your audience to take action, ask them to do what you want them to do; if your purpose is to get your audience to think about something, summarize what you want them to think about. Many presenters make the mistake of not actually closing—they simply quit talking, shuffle papers around, and then walk away.

Because your closing is what your audience is most likely to remember, it is the time to be strong and persuasive. Returning to the retirement savings plan example on page 501, consider the following possible closing:

▷   This is the first step toward your future security.
- Decide how much you can save each month.
- Remember Acme's contribution.
- Choose the investment options that best fit your needs.
- ENROLL NEXT WEEK!

This closing brings the presentation full circle and asks the audience to act on the information provided in the presentation—exactly what a closing should do. And it is courteous to end by thanking the members of the audience for their time and attention.

Transitions

Transitions, which may be no longer than a sentence or two, let the audience know that you're moving from one topic to the next. They also prevent a choppy, disjointed presentation and provide you, the speaker, with assurance that you know where you are going and how to get there. They should appear between the introduction and the body, between the points in the body, and between the body and the closing.

▶ Before getting into the specifics of the fund families available to you, I'd like to describe the investment goals and strategies of each. That information will provide you with the background you'll need to compare the differences among them to make an informed decision about what works best for you.

It is also a good idea to pause for a moment after you've delivered a transitional line between topics to let the audience members shift gears with you. Remember, they don't know where you're headed and—unlike in a written report—they cannot flip ahead to see what's coming next.

Figure 14–1 illustrates the typical pattern of a workplace presentation, although the number of slides and their content will vary, depending on the speaker's

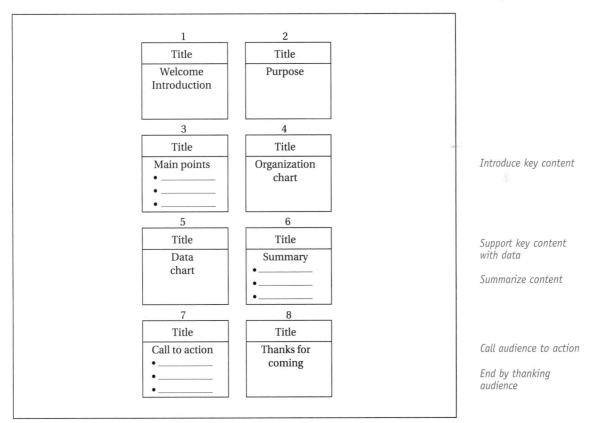

Figure 14–1   Pattern for a Typical Presentation

topic. The complete presentation for the savings and investment program is shown in Figure 14–2. Note the conciseness and layout of the language and visuals.

WRITER'S CHECKLIST
Organizing a Presentation

✔ When preparing a presentation, follow the same guidelines that you follow for writing.

✔ Use a logical structure that includes an introduction, a body, and a conclusion.

✔ Be clear, direct, and precise.

✔ Support your presentation with specific examples.

✔ Use transitions between subtopics to help your listeners understand how the parts are related.

Using Visual Aids

Well-planned visual aids can clarify and simplify your message because they communicate clearly, quickly, and vividly. They are also attention-getting devices that help retain audience interest. Charts, graphs, and illustrations greatly increase audience understanding and retention of the information, especially for complex issues and technical information that could otherwise be misunderstood or glossed over by your audience. A bar graph, pie chart, diagram, or concise summary of key points can eliminate misunderstanding and save many words.

Keep visuals as simple as possible for presentations by including only essential information. Bear in mind that presentation audiences have less time to absorb complex visuals than readers do. Tables, for example, are ideal for showing detailed data (budget expenditures, production output, staff hours worked) but are poor at showing trends and overviews of these data. Instead, use a chart or graph to show the data and discuss important details orally.

Use text sparingly on slides. Instead of blocks of text, use bulleted or numbered lists, keeping them parallel in meaning and grammatical form. Use numbered lists if sequence matters or bulleted lists if it does not. And limit bulleted or numbered lists to five or six items per slide.

The slide should contain no more than 40 to 45 words. Any more will clutter the slide and force you to use a smaller type size, which could impair the audience's ability to read the information. The slide should list only the key points you wish to cover. You can provide additional background and context out loud for what's on the slide—it is an oral presentation, after all.

◆ *Use the guidelines for preparing visuals discussed in Chapter 7, Designing Effective Documents and Visuals.*

You can create and present your visual aids in a variety of media, including computer presentation software; flip charts, whiteboards, and chalkboards; overhead transparencies; 35mm slides; and handouts. Note that visuals in presentations require titles; however, they generally do not need figure numbers because you will refer to them in the proper sequence during the presentation.

EMPLOYEE BENEFITS

Acme Corporation

Presented by Laura Phelps

Office of Human Resources

June 2010

Cover slide for presentation information — who, what, when

Savings and Investment Program

Are You Saving Enough for Your Future?

This presentation will explain our options for contributing to the employee savings plan through payroll deductions.

Acme Corporation considers this program a long-term retirement-oriented plan to enhance your retirement security above the level of your pension and Social Security benefits.

-1-

Introductory slide with overview of topic and attention-getting statement

Acme Corporation
Savings and Investment Program

Questions to Ask Yourself

- How much can I save?
- How much does Acme Corporation contribute?
- What are my investment options?

-2-

Rhetorical questions to pique audience interest and announce organization of information

Figure 14–2   Sample Presentation (continued)

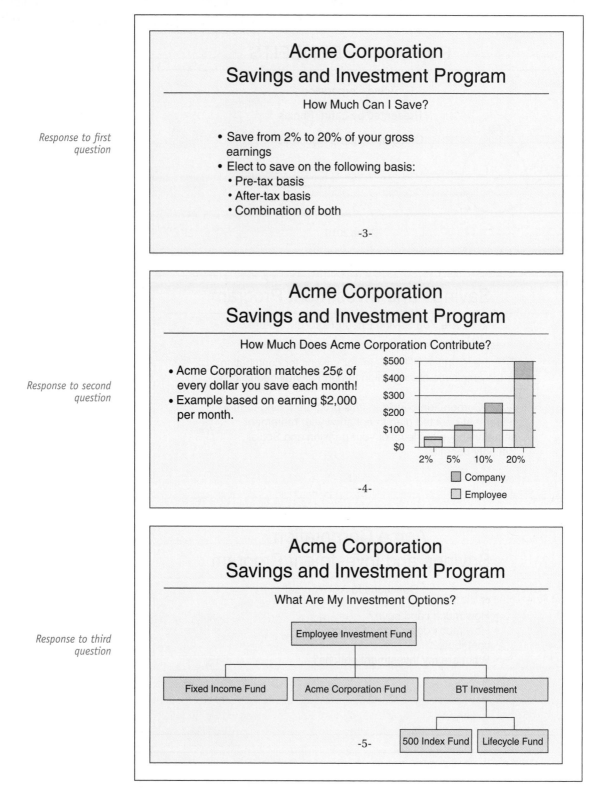

Response to first question

Response to second question

Response to third question

Figure 14–2 Sample Presentation (continued)

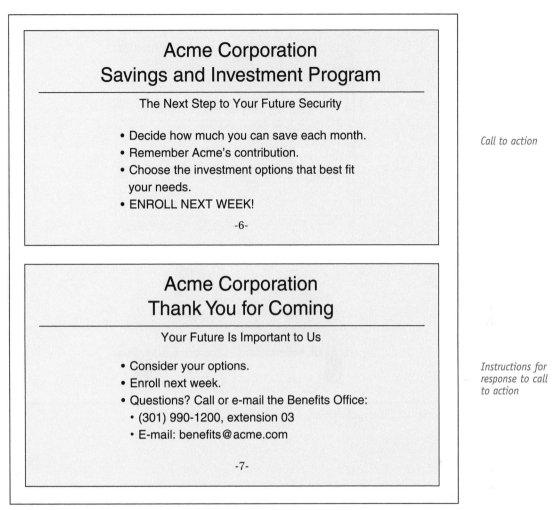

Call to action

Instructions for
response to call
to action

Figure 14–2   Sample Presentation (continued)

Using Presentation Software

Visual information in workplace presentations is frequently displayed on computer monitors, for a small audience, or by projectors connected to a laptop computer, for larger audiences (Figure 14–3).

Presentation software, such as PowerPoint, Corel Presentations, Freelance Graphics, and other packages, permits you simultaneously to create your slides as you write your presentation. You can import content, charts, and graphs from other files, and you can use standard templates and other aids that help you design effective visuals. Possible enhancements include a selection of layouts, typefaces, background textures and colors, as well as clip-art images, sound (including music), and video (such as animation) from outside sources, such as the Internet. Avoid using too many enhancements, however, because they could distract viewers from your message. (Figure 14–4 shows a slide that uses a bulleted list and clip art.)

Laptop computer, projector, and pull-down screen

Figure 14–3   Computer-Presentation Setup

Figure 14–4   Presentation Slide with Bulleted List and Clip Art

Presentation software also makes it possible to convert a presentation to Web format and post it to your company's intranet site, a feature that makes your slides accessible to your colleagues during or after your presentation.

Be sure to integrate your visuals with your presentation when you rehearse. Practice loading the presentation and anticipate any technical difficulties that might arise. Should you encounter a technical snag during the presentation, stay calm and give yourself time to solve the problem. If you can't, say so and move on. As a backup, carry a copy of your electronic presentation printed onto transparencies in case there's a problem with the computer projection system. Also carry an extra copy of your presentation on a disk for backup.

Using Flip Charts, Whiteboards, and Chalkboards

Flip charts are large sheets of white paper bound like a tablet and fastened to the top of an easel (Figure 14–5). The charts are ideal for smaller groups in a conference room or a classroom. The presenter writes on the sheets with colored felt-tip pens, often during the presentation. To avoid distracting your audience by writing as you speak, prepare text and sketches ahead of time on a series of sheets and flip through them during your presentation. Flip charts are also an ideal medium for brainstorming with your audience. You can fill sheet after sheet with ideas, tape them on the walls for everyone to see, and use a clean sheet or sheets to organize the ideas into an outline for follow-up work.

ON THE WEB

For a helpful tutorial on creating effective slides, see bedfordstmartins.com/ writingthatworks and select *Tutorials*, Preparing Presentation Slides. For links to additional information and tutorials for using presentation software, select *Web Links*.

ON THE WEB

For another example of presentation slides, go to Model Documents Gallery, bedfordstmartins.com/ writingthatworks

Figure 14–5 Flip Chart

Whiteboards and chalkboards, common to classrooms, are convenient for creating impromptu sketches and for jotting notes during your presentation. If your presentation requires extensive notes or complex drawings, create them before the presentation to minimize audience impatience. Ensure before the presentation that you have ample chalk or marking pens and an eraser. If you need to keep ideas that will be erased because you're running out of space, assign someone in the audience to record them for future reference.

Using Overhead Transparencies and Slides

Transparencies are page-sized sheets of clear plastic on which the text and graphics for your presentation are copied, using a computer printer or copy machine. During the presentation, you place the transparencies on an overhead projector (Figure 14–6), and the images are projected onto a screen or blank wall. The images can range from black text on clear film to multicolored computer images.

Figure 14–6   Overhead Projector and Transparency Sheet

You could, depending on the complexity of the topic, create a series of overlays to cover selected areas and then remove them to reveal the next key point or illustration in the presentation. You can also lay a sheet of paper over a list of bulleted items on a transparency, uncovering them one at a time as you discuss each point, to focus audience attention on each one in the sequence.

Slides are 2-by-2–inch 35mm film color transparencies inserted into a carousel and projected onto a screen or a blank wall. Color transparencies are especially useful if you need to include photographs in your presentation. (The individual screens produced using presentation software are also called slides.)

Overhead transparencies and slides are best seen in a darkened room, unlike flip charts and chalkboards or whiteboards, which are best seen in a fully lighted room.

> **DESIGNING YOUR DOCUMENT**
> ## Creating Slides for Presentations
>
> - Use bulleted or numbered lists instead of blocks of text. Use numbers if sequence is important and bullets if it is not. And keep lists to no more than five or six items per slide.
> - Limit text to no more than 40 to 45 words. (See Figure 14–4.)
> - Make your slides consistent in type style, type size, and spacing.
> - Use a type size readable by members of the audience in the back of the room. Type should be no smaller than 30 point bold. For headings, 45 or 50 point is better.
> - Use graphs and charts rather than tables to show data trends. Use only one or two graphs or charts per slide; otherwise, the data will look cluttered and may be hard to see.
> - Ensure that the contrast between your text and background is sharp. (See Figure 14–3.) Use light backgrounds with dark lettering and avoid textured or fancy "wallpaper" backgrounds.
> - Aim for 12 or fewer slides per presentation. More than that will tax any audience's concentration.
> - Don't read the text on your slides word for word. Instead, summarize the content of the slide and cover salient points in detail.

Using Handouts

Handouts typically are paper copies of your presentation slides, although they may be a summary of key points; supporting data in tables, charts, and graphs; or other supplementary information. They benefit you and your audience by reinforcing what is said and by permitting your listeners to take notes and retain the material for future reference. They are usually distributed before the presentation for your audience to review.

Delivering Your Presentation

Once you have outlined and drafted your presentation and prepared your visuals, you are ready to practice your delivery.

Practicing Your Presentation

Familiarize yourself with the sequence of the material—major topics, notes, and visuals—in your outline. Once you feel comfortable with the content, you're ready to practice the presentation itself.

Practice on your feet and out loud.   Try to practice in the room where you'll give the presentation to learn the idiosyncrasies of the room: acoustics, lighting, how the chairs will most likely be arranged, where the electrical outlets and switches are located, and so forth. Practicing out loud is more effective than just rehearsing mentally because you process the information in your mind many times faster than you can possibly speak it. Rehearsing out loud will make clear exactly how long your presentation will take and will highlight any problems, such as awkward transitions. Rehearsing also helps you to eliminate or reduce verbal tics, such as "um," "you know," and "like," as well as helping you determine how loudly you need to speak based on the size of the room.

Practice with your visuals.   Be sure to integrate your slides, transparencies, or other visuals into your practice sessions. This will help your presentation go more smoothly. Operate the equipment (computer, slide projector, or overhead projector) until you're comfortable with it. Even if things go wrong, being prepared and having practiced will give you the confidence and poise to go on. You can also use your visuals as cues to the next point you wish to make.

Videotape your practice session.   Videotape is a very effective and sometimes embarrassing way to catch what you are doing wrong. The tape will reveal how you present your material from the audience's perspective. If you do not have access to a video recorder, at the very least use an audio recorder to evaluate your vocal presentation. Another effective technique is to ask a friend or colleague to watch you rehearse and comment on your delivery.

WRITER'S CHECKLIST
Practicing Your Presentation

✔ Practice out loud and, if possible, in the room where you'll deliver the presentation.

✔ Incorporate your visuals as you practice, using the computer, slide projector, or overhead transparencies.

✔ Videotape or audiotape your practice session and evaluate it critically, or have a colleague or classmate observe and comment.

✔ Because the meaning of gestures differs greatly from culture to culture, carefully choose and rehearse those that you will use during your presentation.

✔ Practice your presentation in front of colleagues or friends and have them watch for any gestures that could be misinterpreted by your audience.

Using Delivery Techniques That Work

In addition to your words and message, nonverbal communication can engage and motivate your audience. If you want your audience to share your point of view, show them your enthusiasm for your topic. Your words will have more staying power when you deliver them with physical and vocal animation. Be sure to make eye contact; use movement and gestures; and vary your vocal inflection, pace, and projection.

Make eye contact.   The best way to establish rapport with your audience is with eye contact. For smaller audiences, make eye contact with as many people as possible. In a large audience, directly address those people who seem most responsive to you in different parts of the audience. Address each person separately, and focus your attention on him or her for several seconds before moving on. Doing so helps you establish rapport with your audience by holding their attention. It also gives you important visual cues as to how you're doing. Are people engaged and actively listening? Do they look puzzled, or are they staring at the floor? These cues may tell you that you need to speed up or slow down the pace of your presentation.

Use movement and gestures.   Animate your presentation with physical movement. The easiest way to integrate movement into your presentation is to step to the screen and point to a visual as you discuss it. Touch the screen with the pointer and turn back to the audience before beginning to speak (touch, turn, and talk). If you are using an overhead projector, you can place the pointer directly on the overhead so that it casts a shadow that points to the appropriate item on the screen. Otherwise, simply take a step or two to one side or to the other after you have been talking for a minute or so. This type of movement is most effective at transitional points between major topics or after pauses for emphasis. Too much movement, however, can be distracting—so try not to pace or wave your arms. Hand gestures will come more naturally during your presentation if you include them in your practice sessions.

Adjust your vocal inflection, pace, and volume.   Your voice can be an effective tool in communicating your sincerity, enthusiasm, and command of your topic. Use it to your advantage to project your credibility. *Vocal inflection* is the rise and fall of your voice at different times, such as the way your voice naturally rises at the end of a question ("You want it *when*?"). Keep your audience's attention by using this pattern as you would in a conversation. Do not fall into a monotone speech pattern that can hypnotize your audience and make them drowsy. Vocal variety also allows you to highlight differences between key and subordinate points in your presentation.

Pace is the speed at which you deliver your presentation. If you speak too fast, your words will run together, making it difficult for your audience to follow you. If you speak too slowly, the audience will get impatient and their minds may wander.

Speak up to be heard. If anyone in the audience cannot hear you, your presentation has been ineffective for that person. If the members of your audience have to strain to hear you, they may give up trying to listen. You can correct for these problems by practicing out loud, with or without a microphone, with someone listening from the back of the room.

CONSIDERING AUDIENCE AND PURPOSE

Engaging Your Audience When Speaking

- Establish rapport and trust by looking into the eyes of as many audience members as possible.

- Use your voice to communicate sincerity and enthusiasm, and, above all, do not speak in a monotone. Project your voice so that you're heard by everyone, and pace your delivery so that your words don't run together.

- Be animated, moving to the screen to emphasize points and gesturing naturally.

- Hold the interest of your audience by looking at your notes as little as possible. (Never read directly from your notes.)

- Deliver your talk from a prepared outline on slides rather than memorizing it word for word. This way, your delivery

  - sounds more natural and less monotonous.

  - helps audience attention and comprehension.

  - enables more eye contact with your audience, which helps convey your interest in and enthusiasm for the topic.

Dealing with Presentation Anxiety

Everyone experiences nervousness before a presentation. Survey after survey reveals that dread of speaking in front of others ranks among the top five fears for most people. Typical reactions to this stress include shortness of breath, a racing heartbeat, trembling, perspiration, and even nausea. Some people react by clearing their throats repeatedly, tugging at their clothing or earlobes, or moving continuously during the presentation. Instead of letting this stress inhibit you, focus on channeling your nervous energy into a helpful stimulant. That is, if you can't eliminate your stress entirely, manage it. The best way to master this feeling is to know your topic thoroughly. If you know what you are going to say and how you are going to say it, you will gain confidence and reduce anxiety as you become immersed in your subject.

Rehearsing your presentation will help. Do so alone or, if possible, in front of one or more listeners. If you're anxious because you may forget something or get lost during your delivery, you may find it helpful to write out the presentation in full, put it aside, and rehearse using only brief notes. If you falter, refer to your written version. After a practice session, imagine yourself in front of your audience delivering your material point by point. Begin by saying to yourself, "My subject is important. I am ready. My listeners are here to listen to what I have to say." If you cannot remember every point you wish to make during the practice presentation, review your notes or visuals. These will trigger your memory both as you imagine the presentation and when you're actually giving it.

You can use several techniques to quell the butterflies immediately before a presentation. Fill your lungs with a deep breath and hold it for a count of ten. Then exhale and repeat, doing so several times or until you feel your body begin to relax.

Tensing and relaxing muscles is another effective stress reducer. Clench both fists tightly and count to ten while inhaling and then exhale. Repeat several times until your stress begins to diminish.

During the presentation, do not be upset if you say the wrong word, refer to the wrong visual, or otherwise do something unplanned. Simply take a deep breath, correct your mistake, and move forward. Do not refer to your mistake unless you must—chances are that the audience will think you are moving according to plan.

Reaching Global Audiences

The prevalence of multinational corporations and multinational trade agreements, the increasing diversity of the U.S. workforce, and even increases in immigration have made the ability to reach audiences with varied cultural backgrounds an essential skill. The multicultural audiences for your presentations may include clients, business partners, colleagues, and current and potential employees and customers of varied backgrounds.

Presentations to global audiences involve special challenges. As with all materials intended for global readers and listeners, keep your language simple and consistent. Don't call something a "ratio" in one place and a "rate" in another. Puns and wordplay may entertain a U.S. audience but will likely confuse foreign listeners. State the main points of your presentation often and in the identical language each time. Follow these guidelines whether you are addressing an audience for whom English is a second language or speaking through an interpreter. As you deliver your presentation, speak slowly and deliberately, enunciating clearly and pausing often. Keep in mind the following additional points about delivering presentations:

- Bland is better than colorful. Avoid idioms ("dog and pony show," "barking up the wrong tree"), jargon ("emoticons," "debugging"), and acronyms. They will put an unnecessary impediment between you and your audience. Avoid U.S.-centered examples of business, political, or sports figures unless they are essential to your discussion. They will not be understood and, worse, they will suggest to your audience that your perspective about the world is narrowly focused on the United States.

- Do not use the trite sports metaphors that are all too common in American speech ("slam dunk," "touchdown," "home run"). They will puzzle the members of your international audience and suggest to them that you are insensitive about their culture and customs.

- Jokes can backfire even with U.S. audiences, so they are especially tricky with international listeners. If you think that humor is important to your message, try it out on someone familiar with the languages and cultures of your audience beforehand and revise accordingly.

◆ *For additional information and tips on communicating with multicultural audiences, see page 70 in Chapter 3, Writing the Draft; and pages 250–256 in Chapter 7, Designing Effective Documents and Visuals; and pages 343–351 in Chapter 9, Writing Business Correspondence.*

- With U.S. audiences, maintaining eye contact enhances the speaker's credibility and connectedness with the audience. In some Asian cultures, however, making direct eye contact is seen as an invasion of privacy. For these listeners, try instead to sweep your gaze across them rather than looking at anyone too long.

> ### CONSIDERING AUDIENCE AND PURPOSE
>
> ### Evaluating Your Presentation
>
> ■ Have you analyzed the purpose of your presentation so that it focuses on what you want your audience to know, to believe, or to do when they leave?
>
> ■ Do you know the makeup of your audience so that your presentation accommodates their level of knowledge of, experience with, and attitude toward your topic?
>
> ■ Is your presentation structured in the best sequence for an audience of listeners?
>
> ■ Are your presentation's visual aids concise, informative, and visible to everyone in the room?
>
> ■ Have you practiced your presentation so that your delivery is animated, shows mastery of the topic, can be heard by everyone, and is not rushed?
>
> ■ For international audiences, is your presentation free of U.S.-centered idioms, references, and jargon?

▦ Listening

An equally important counterpart to a good presentation is active listening. Active listening enables you to understand an instructor's directions, a speaker's presentation, a manager's goals, and a customer's needs and wants. Above all, it lays the foundation for cooperation. Productive communication occurs when both the speaker and the listener focus clearly on the content of the message and attempt to eliminate as much interference as possible.

Fallacies About Listening

Most people assume that because they can hear, they know how to listen. In fact, *hearing* is passive and *listening* is active. Hearing voices in a crowd or a ringing telephone requires no analysis and no active involvement. We hear such sounds without choosing to listen to them—we have no choice but to hear them. Listening, however, requires taking action, interpreting the message, and assessing its worth. Listening also requires that you consider the context of messages and the differences in meaning that may be the result of differences in the speaker's and the listener's occupation, education, culture, language, sex, ethnicity, or other factors. The more carefully you listen, the better you will communicate with managers, colleagues, and clients in all settings, whether in a phone conversation, face-to-face, in a meeting, or during a presentation.

Steps to More Effective Listening

To listen more effectively (1) make a conscious decision to listen actively, (2) think about your purpose for listening, (3) take specific actions to listen more efficiently, and (4) adapt to the situation.

Make a Conscious Decision

The first step to effective listening is simply making up your mind to do so. Effective listening requires conscious effort, something that does not come naturally. To listen actively, the well-known precept is true: "Seek first to understand and then to be understood."[1] If you follow this rule, you may find it easier to take the steps or the time required to ensure that you are indeed exerting a conscious effort to listen effectively.

Define Your Purpose

To listen effectively, you must know *why* you're listening. Focusing on your purpose will help manage the most common problems people have with listening: drifting attention, formulating a response while the speaker is still talking, and interrupting the speaker. When you know a situation will require active listening, take the time to focus on the following questions:

- What kind of information do I hope to get from this conversation or meeting?
- How will this information benefit me?
- Do I need to act on this information in some way?
- What kind of message do I want to send while I'm listening? Is it understanding? determination? flexibility? competence? patience?
- Do I foresee any problems, such as boredom, wandering attention, anger, or impatience?
- How can I keep these problems from preventing me from listening effectively?

Take Specific Actions

Become a responder rather than a reactor. A *responder* is a listener who slows down the communication to be certain that he or she is accurately interpreting the speaker. A *reactor* simply says the first thing that comes to mind, without

---

[1]Steven R. Covey, *The 7 Habits of Highly Effective People: Powerful Lessons in Personal Change*, 15th ed. (New York: Free Press, 2004).

checking to make sure that he or she accurately understands the message. Take the following actions to help you become a responder and not a reactor.

- Aim to be impartial when evaluating a message. For example, do not dismiss a message because you dislike the speaker or are distracted by the speaker's appearance, mannerisms, or accent.
- Slow down the communication by asking for more information or by paraphrasing the message before you offer your thoughts. Paraphrasing lets the speaker know that you are listening, gives the speaker an opportunity to clear up any misunderstanding, keeps you focused, and helps you remember the discussion.
- Listen with empathy by putting yourself in the speaker's position or looking at things from the speaker's perspective. Try to understand the speaker's feelings, wants, and needs—appreciate his or her point of view. When people feel they are being listened to, they tend to respond with appreciation and cooperation.
- Take notes while you are listening. Note-taking provides several benefits. It helps you stay focused on what the speaker is saying, especially during a presentation or lecture. It helps you remember what you've heard because you reinforce the message by writing it. (You can also check the notes at a later date, when you need to recall what was said.) Finally, it communicates to the speaker that you are listening and that you are interested in what he or she is saying.

> ▶ **CONSIDERING AUDIENCE AND PURPOSE**
>
> ### Listening Effectively
>
> - Make a conscious decision to become a better listener.
> - Define your purpose for listening in a given situation:
>   - What kind of information do you want from this exchange?
>   - How can you use this information?
> - Block out background distractions to focus on the message.
> - Screen out personal biases or preconceptions that may hinder an impartial evaluation of the message.
> - Slow down the speaker by asking for more information or by paraphrasing the message before responding to the speaker.
> - Take notes to help stay focused on what the speaker is saying.
> - Adapt to the situation.

Adapt to the Situation

Listening at peak efficiency at all times is not necessary. When someone stops you in the hall for an idle conversation, you may legitimately listen without giving the conversation your full attention. Even during a lecture, you may be listening for specific information only. However, if you are on a team project where the success of the project depends on everyone's contribution, pay close attention. Doing so enables you to gather information important to the project as well as other nuances, such as the ongoing relationships among team members.

◼ MEETING THE DEADLINE: The Time-Sensitive Presentation

When you need to prepare a presentation under a tight deadline, it helps to follow a structured approach—one that will enable you to work efficiently, reduce anxiety, and feel confident in what you have to say. As you begin this process, remember that your goal is to create and deliver a logically organized and visually appealing presentation that is appropriate for your audience, fulfills your purpose, and is appropriate in scope.

Use the following guidelines to help you plan, create, practice, and deliver a presentation that will satisfy you and your audience while meeting your deadline.

Part I: Planning Your Presentation (45 Minutes)

Focus on each of the following points as you prepare your presentation:

1. *Know the purpose of your presentation.* Think of what you want your audience to know, to believe, or to do as a result of your presentation. Write a purpose statement that defines the scope of your presentation and indicates what you plan to cover. After writing your purpose statement, think about how to introduce your topic, decide what key points will explain your topic, and choose a closing point that will make a clear statement to your audience.

2. *Analyze your audience.* While considering the needs of all your listeners, concentrate on the key decision makers in your audience and gear your presentation toward them. Based on your audience, decide how technical your presentation will be, use language suitable to your listeners' level of expertise, and avoid jargon.

3. *Gather your information.* Your presentation probably covers a topic you have already written about in a proposal or report. Organize all relevant information on your topic into one electronic file. If this is not possible, collect hard copies of the materials into a folder.

4. *Plan your delivery time frame.* As you plan and develop your presentation, remember that you will need to get your points across within a set time period. Whether your presentation is scheduled for five minutes or an hour, think of your main points in relation to your time frame.

5. *Structure the content of your presentation.* Outline what you want to say in a logical manner that will achieve your goals and meet the needs of your listeners. Plan how many slides or transparencies you will need to convey your message. For a five-minute presentation, you will need no more than five to ten slides. If you decide to work with five slides, plan to discuss these for about a minute each. For ten slides, plan to discuss each for about 30 seconds. Some slides—those covering key points and benefits—will require more time than, say, an introductory slide. Consider the following structure:

Slide 1	Introduce yourself.
Slide 2	Introduce your topic.
Slide 3	State your purpose.
Slides 4–6	State and explain your key points—points that will inform or persuade your audience.
Slides 7 and 8	Explain how what you propose will benefit your listeners.
Slide 9	Close by reviewing the most important parts of your presentation. Choose carefully what you want your listeners to remember most.
Slide 10	Thank your listeners for their attention. Credit outside sources, if necessary, and include your contact information.

Part II: Creating Your Presentation (90 Minutes)

Given your time frame, use your energy wisely when preparing your slides or visuals.

- Use simple transparencies or work within one of PowerPoint's basic templates to create your slides.

- To write your notes simultaneously, work in the Notes Page option, available under View in the menu.

- For each slide, cover no more than five to seven ideas or "bullet points."

- Keep your slides uncluttered and easy to read, even from the back of the room.

- Import existing charts and graphs to your presentation, but don't spend time creating and designing new ones. If time permits, add inoffensive clip art where appropriate or a tasteful color background (use light background colors to ensure a contrast between the type and the background). If not, focus on the clear presentation of your content. (*Note*: For visuals you are unable to import but that are important, bring printouts to hand out to your audience.) See Figure 14–7.

What Are the Benefits to Employees?

- Access The Sports Center for $20/month— includes all athletic facilities, whirlpool, and sauna.

- Support of personal trainers or massage therapists, for an additional $15/month.

- Free cholesterol and blood-pressure screening.

- Free nutrition and weight-management counseling.

- Employee incentive "wellness points" that earn discounts on fitness gear and clothing at The Sports Center Shop.

-2-

This slide appears on-screen for the audience

The Healthy Life Program offers your employees one of the best and most affordable wellness packages available nationwide. For modest monthly fees, your employees can become members of The Sports Center and Day Spa, a facility that won the "Best of Chicago" award in 2009, and that was recently rated #1 by *In-Shape Magazine.* Here they can enjoy numerous benefits that include not only a generous offering of classes such as aerobics, spinning, kickboxing, Pilates, and yoga, all taught by top-notch instructors—but they will also enjoy the support of the highly qualified personal trainers, nutrition counselors, and health-care professionals on staff. We do all we can to make sure our members approach exercise, diet, and lifestyle change safely and sensibly.

The Notes pages give you a space in which to expand the ideas of your slide with concrete details; they do not appear on-screen

Figure 14–7   Notes Page of a PowerPoint Presentation

- Once your slides are complete, work within the Notes Page to write the text of your presentation. You can later print out your notes for practice or for reference if you need them when delivering your presentation.

- Preview and evaluate your slides by selecting Slide Sorter (under View in your menu bar). Edit, rearrange, delete, or add to slides and visuals as needed. See Figure 14–8.

Part III: Practicing Your Presentation (45 Minutes)

Focus on the following points as you rehearse your presentation:

- Practice your delivery at least three times.
- Time yourself and make any necessary adjustments. If you edit your presentation at this point, practice it again at least twice.

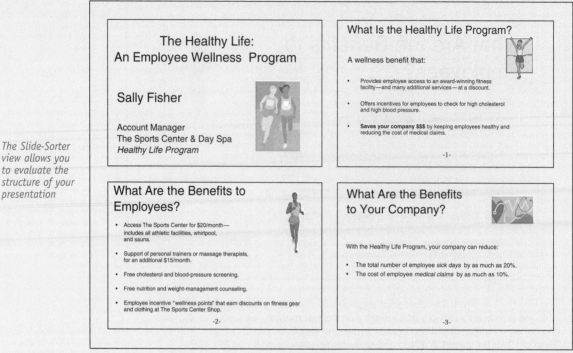

The Slide-Sorter view allows you to evaluate the structure of your presentation

Figure 14–8   Slide-Sorter View of a PowerPoint Presentation

- Use your time constructively. If you find yourself worrying, practice again or mentally run through your slides and key points.

- Avoid memorizing your presentation. A spontaneous delivery will be more credible and engaging to your audience.

- The night before your presentation, choose and prepare attire that is appropriate and professional.

- Try to visit the room where you will be presenting beforehand, preferably a day ahead of time. If this is not possible, arrive at least 45 minutes before your presentation. Check out the presentation equipment—making sure it is in good working order and that you know how to operate it. Evaluate the setup of the room, the lighting, and the temperature, and make any necessary adjustments.

Part IV: Delivering Your Presentation (allotted time)

Keep the following points in mind while delivering your presentation.

- Speak energetically. Your enthusiasm will energize your listeners and help persuade them to consider what you propose.

- Refer to your slides during your presentation, but don't read them word for word—what you say should provide detail and depth to what appears on the screen.
- Know what you want to say about each slide. If necessary, refer to the notes you created when you developed your slides. Tape notes for each slide onto index cards for a less-intrusive way to check them during the presentation.
- Use vocal inflection to emphasize key points; a monotone voice will put your audience to sleep.
- Breathe deeply. Bringing oxygen to the brain keeps you composed and mentally sharp and helps you to speak slowly and more clearly.

Conducting Productive Meetings

Meetings are a fact of workplace life. Though essential, they are seldom looked forward to. They can be time-consuming and even stressful if the topic is contentious or if there are personality conflicts among participants. None of these potential concerns is avoidable entirely, but the suggestions in this section will help you minimize or avoid them.

In basic terms, a meeting is a face-to-face exchange among a group of people who have come together for a common purpose—to make a contribution to a collective effort. A meeting requires planning and preparation, just as writing and oral presentations do.

Planning a Meeting

For a meeting to be successful, determine the focus of the meeting, decide who should attend, and choose the best time and place to hold it. Prepare an agenda for the meeting and determine who should take the minutes.

What Is the Purpose of the Meeting?

The first step in planning a meeting is to focus on your desired outcome. Ask yourself what those attending want to know, to believe, or to do as a result of attending the meeting.

Suppose you called a meeting of your sales staff to design a sales campaign to launch a new scanner model successfully. In response to the questions in the previous paragraph, you could jot down the following answers:

▶ As a result of this meeting:
  - I want the salespeople *to know* that this scanner can increase their sales considerably.

- I want the salespeople *to believe* that this is the best scanner on the market and that their customers want it.
- I want the salespeople *to offer* their ideas for the sales campaign.

Once you focus on your desired outcome, use the information to write a purpose statement for the meeting that answers the questions *what* and *why*.

▶ The purpose of this meeting is to gather ideas from the sales force [*what*] that will create an effective sales campaign for our new scanner model [*why*].

Who Should Attend?

Invite to the meeting only those who can contribute to fulfilling your planned outcome. If a meeting must be held without some key participants, send or e-mail the agenda to them prior to the meeting and ask for any contributions they would like to make. If employees from regional offices or other geographic locations need to participate, they can do so by speakerphone or a video link. Circulate the meeting minutes to everyone, including those who could not attend, following the meeting.

When Should the Meeting Be Held?

Schedule a meeting when all or most of the key people can be present. The time of day and the length of the meeting can affect its outcome. Consider the following when planning your meeting:

- Be mindful that people need Monday morning to focus on the upcoming week.
- Note that people need Friday afternoon to focus on completing the current week's tasks.
- Avoid the hour following lunch because most people feel sleepy then.
- Avoid early morning meetings because attendees may be delayed by traffic and everyone likes a few minutes in the morning to check messages, get a cup of coffee, and so on.
- Include adequate breaks in meetings scheduled to last longer than two hours so that attendees can check their messages, make important phone calls, or use the restroom.
- Avoid meetings during the last 15 minutes of the day. You can be assured of a quick meeting, but it is likely that no one will remember what went on.
- Schedule meetings at a time convenient to those participating remotely by speakerphone in different time zones.

Where Should the Meeting Be Held?

If the meeting involves in-house personnel only, hold the meeting in the office of the most senior member, or in a conference room, if you need more space. For meetings with clients, vendors, or other outside personnel, having a meeting in your office or conference room can give you an advantage. You feel more comfortable, and your guests' newness to the surroundings may give you an edge. Agreeing to hold the meeting at their location, however, signals your cooperation. For balance, especially for first-time gatherings, meet at a neutral site, such as at an off-site conference center. That way, no one has a distinct advantage and attendees often feel freer to participate.

What's on the Agenda?

A tool for focusing participant attention, the agenda is an outline of the issues the meeting will address. Never begin a meeting without an agenda, even if that agenda is only a handwritten list of topics you want to cover. Distribute the agenda a day or two before the meeting so that those attending have time to prepare or gather the necessary materials. For a longer meeting in which participants will make a presentation or need to be prepared to discuss an issue in detail, try to distribute the agenda a week or more in advance. If you have no time to distribute the agenda early, however, be sure to distribute it at the beginning of the meeting.

The agenda should cover only a few major items: the names of attendees, the time and place of the meeting, and the topics to be discussed. If people are presenting material, the agenda should indicate the amount of time allotted for each speaker. Finally, the agenda should give the start and stop times for the meeting so that participants can plan the rest of their day. Figure 14–9 shows a sample agenda.

Sales-Meeting Agenda

Purpose: To Get Input for a Sales Campaign for the New Scanner

Date: May 10, 2010

Place: Conference Room 14-C

Time: 9:30 a.m.–11 a.m.

Attendees: Advertising Manager, Sales Manager and Reps, Customer Service Manager

Topic	Presenter	Time
The Scanner	Bob Arbuckle	9:30–9:45
The Sales Strategy	Mary Winifred	9:45–10:00
The Campaign	Maria Lopez	10:00–10:15
Discussion	Led by Dave Grimes	10:15–11:00

What, where, when, who details

Topics of meeting, presenters, and periods scheduled

Figure 14–9   Meeting Agenda

If distributed in advance of the meeting, the agenda should be accompanied by a memo or an e-mail message that invites people to the meeting. The message should include the following:

- The purpose of the meeting. Everyone should know not only exactly why this meeting is being held but also what you hope to accomplish.
- The meeting start and stop times. People need this information so that they will know how to budget their time. A word of warning: When you advertise an ending time for the meeting, be sure to end it on time unless everyone agrees to extend the meeting beyond the promised stop time.
- The date and place.
- The names of the people invited. Knowing the names of everyone who will be attending often affects how people prepare for the meeting.
- Instructions on how to prepare for the meeting. Participants may need to prepare differently, so tell them collectively and individually how to get ready for the meeting.

Figure 14–10 shows an e-mail message transmitting a meeting agenda.

ON THE WEB

For links to Web sites with information on groupware and whiteboard software, go to Chapter 14, bedfordstmartins.com/ writingthatworks

---

@ **DIGITAL TIPS:** **Conducting Meetings from Remote Locations**

When participants cannot meet face to face, consider holding a videoconference or Web conference using groupware or whiteboard software. Groupware allows meeting participants having the proper equipment at remote locations to perform collaborative activities, such as sharing documents, participating in real-time discussions, or commenting on documents. Whiteboard software allows participants to write on an interactive LCD panel as though they were in a room with a whiteboard. Writings are then displayed on each participant's screen and can be saved or printed.

▶ **CONSIDERING AUDIENCE AND PURPOSE**

Attending Meetings

- Be punctual. When attending a meeting, always arrive several minutes early. Being aware of time shows that you acknowledge the value of another person's time.
- Be attentive. If you are new to the organization, spend time listening and observing, but do speak.
- Share your ideas even if they differ from those expressed by other attendees; meetings are considered an opportunity for everyone to share ideas.
- Feel comfortable responding as your ideas come to you. Also, because meetings are considered a place for brainstorming, don't be too concerned about expressing your thoughts in complete sentences or in perfect grammatical form.

Subject:	Planning Meeting
Date:	Mon, 03 May 2010 13:30:12 EST
From:	Susan Chaney <schaney@millenniumscanners.com>
To:	Advertising Manager, Sales Manager, Sales Representatives, Customer Service Manager
Attachments:	⫻ Sales Meeting Agenda.doc (29 KB)

Announces what, when, who, where

Purpose of the Meeting

The purpose of this meeting is to get your ideas for the upcoming introduction and sales campaign for our new scanner.

Date, Time, and Location

Date: May 10, 2010
Time: 9:30 a.m.–11:00 a.m.
Place: Conference Room E (go to the ground floor, take a right off the elevator, third door on the left)

Attendees

The groups addressed above.

Meeting Preparation

Everyone should be prepared to offer suggestions on the following items:

- Sales features of the new scanner
- Techniques for selling the scanner
- Customer profile of potential buyers
- FAQs — questions customers may ask
- Anticipated support services (maintenance, supplies)

Transmits agenda (attached) and preparation instructions

Agenda

Please see the attached document.

Figure 14–10   E-mail Message Transmitting an Agenda

Running a Meeting

To lead a successful meeting, follow your agenda—the topics that must be covered and the outcomes that you wish—and ensure that you have invited the right people with the necessary information. Equally important, keep in mind how the personalities of those attending a meeting may affect its success. Members of any group are likely to vary greatly in their personalities and attitudes. Most of the time you need only be tactful and diplomatic in your dealings with everyone in attendance, and the meeting will go well. Begin by setting an example for the group by listening carefully and by encouraging participants to listen to each other. (Review the section about listening earlier in this chapter.) To create an environment in which people listen to each other, adopt a "you" attitude by being considerate of other people's points of view.

1. Consider the feelings, thoughts, ideas, and needs of others; don't ignore other points of view.
2. Make others feel valued and respected by listening and responding to them.
3. Respond positively to the comments of others whenever possible.
4. Consider communication styles and approaches different from your own, particularly those of people from other cultures.

Despite your best efforts, you will encounter people whose personalities hinder effective communication during the meeting. The following guidelines should help you to deal with these potential impediments and keep the group's focus on successfully working through the agenda.

- *The interruptive person.* An interruptive person rarely lets anyone finish a sentence and can intimidate the group's quieter members. Tell that person in a firm but nonhostile tone to let the others finish what they are saying in the interest of getting everyone's best thinking. By addressing the issue directly, you signal to the group the importance of putting its common goals first.

- *The negative person.* A negative person generally has difficulty accepting change and will often oppose a new idea or project. If left unchecked, this attitude can demoralize the group as a whole. Of course, not all negative views are invalid. As long as the negative person is making valid points, ask the group for its suggestions as to how to remedy the issues being raised. When these issues are outside the agenda of the meeting in progress, let everyone know that you will schedule a separate meeting to discuss these issues. Then move to the next item on the agenda. If the person's points are not valid, you may need to schedule a separate meeting with this person to sort out any misunderstandings.

- *The rambling person.* The rambling person cannot collect his or her thoughts quickly enough to state them succinctly. Although such participants can cause impatience, their thoughts may be of value. You can help by restating or clarifying their ideas. Quite often, the person will nod in agreement, and you can move on. Try to strike a balance between providing your own interpretation and drawing out the person's intended meaning.

- *The quiet or nonparticipating person.* This person may be reluctant to speak in a group setting or may be simply deep in thought. At an appropriate moment, ask for this person's thoughts on the topic at hand, being tactful so as not to cause embarrassment. You could also go around the table asking everyone by name if he or she has any thoughts on an issue instead of beginning with the quiet person. This gives such a person time to collect his or her thoughts. Another approach is to ask such a person *before the meeting* to jot down his or her thoughts on the meeting agenda for use during the meeting.

- *The territorial person.* The territorial person fiercely defends his or her group against all threats—real and perceived—and may fail to cooperate with members of other departments or companies. To deal with this situation, point out that although the individual's territorial concerns may be valid, everyone is working for the same organization and its overall goals take precedence.

Dealing with Conflict

Despite your best efforts, conflict is inevitable. Keep in mind, however, that conflict is also potentially valuable; when managed positively, it can stimulate creative thinking by challenging complacency and showing ways to achieve goals more efficiently or economically.

Try to deal with conflict so that its benefits are retained and its negative effects are minimized. First, be sure that those involved in the conflict are aware of any areas of agreement, and emphasize these areas to establish common ground. Then identify any differences and ask why they exist. If facts seem to be at issue, determine which are correct. If goals differ, encourage each party to try to look at the problem from the other person's point of view. You can take any of a number of approaches to resolve a conflict, including the following:

- *Noncombative tactics.* Avoid accusations, threats, or disparaging comments, and emphasize common interests and mutual goals. Praise conciliatory acts and express a desire for harmonious relations. This can have a very disarming effect on an aggressive person.

- *Persuasion.* Try to convince the other party to accept your point of view. How successful this is likely to be will depend on your credibility and on the other person's willingness to consider your views. Provide facts or previous practices to support your position. Point out how your position benefits the other person (if true). Show how your position is consistent with precedent, prevailing norms, or accepted standards. Tactfully point out any overlooked costs, any disadvantages, or any errors in logic in the other party's point of view.

- *Bargaining.* Exchange concessions until a compromise is reached. Compromising means settling for half a victory rather than risking an all-out win-or-lose struggle. A compromise must provide each side with enough benefits to satisfy minimal needs.

- *Collaborating.* Each side accepts the other's goal as well as its own, and works to achieve the best outcome for both. For such a win-win approach to succeed, each side must understand the other's point of view and discover the needs that must be satisfied. A flexible, exploratory attitude is a prerequisite for collaboration. Trust must be high, but collaborating to resolve conflict often leads to creative results. Define the problem, then define alternative solutions, and then select the one that provides both sides with the most benefits.

Making a Record of Decisions and Assignments

Many organizations and committees keep official records of their meetings; such records are known as *minutes*. If you are running the meeting, delegate the minute-taking to someone else in advance, who will take careful notes during the meeting. The minute taker then writes and distributes the minutes before the next meeting. At the beginning of each meeting, attendees vote to accept the minutes from the previous meeting as prepared or to revise or clarify specific items.

Not all meetings require formal notes, but it can be helpful to record major decisions made, tasks assigned, or information needed to complete a discussion at a later date. For a standing committee, either rotate responsibility for taking minutes or assign someone permanently to the task.

If you are assigned to write minutes, keep them brief and to the point. Give complete information on each topic concisely and go on to the next one. Keep abstractions and generalities to a minimum and, most important, be specific. If you are referring to a nursing station on the second floor of a hospital, say "the second floor nursing station," not simply "the second floor." Following a set format, such as that shown in Figure 14–11, will help you to keep the minutes concise. To avoid future misunderstandings, the minute taker should write down each assignment, the person responsible for it, and the due date.

In addition to the minute taker, meeting participants must also record decisions and assignments in the course of the meeting. Someone may be assigned to record decisions on flip charts for this purpose (see Figure 14–5). Information on the charts can be revised for clarity later and distributed to those who attended. Another option is to use a laptop computer to record decisions and assignments

> ### ▶ CONSIDERING AUDIENCE AND PURPOSE
>
> ## Planning and Conducting Meetings
>
> - Develop a purpose statement to focus your thoughts.
> - Invite only those essential to fulfilling the purpose of the meeting.
> - Select a meeting time and place convenient to all attendees.
> - Create an agenda and distribute it a day or two before the meeting.
> - Assign someone to take notes and make clear what the notes should include.
> - Follow the agenda to keep everyone focused on the purpose of the meeting and the time available.
> - Be respectful of the views of others and their ways of expressing those views.
> - Review the strategies in this chapter for dealing with attendees whose style of expression in some way prevents your getting everyone's best thinking.
> - Deal with conflict positively to maximize its benefits.
> - Ensure that meeting minutes record major decisions; assignments; other due dates; and, if necessary, the date, time, and location of a follow-up meeting.
> - Close the meeting by reviewing all decisions and assignments.

WARETON MEDICAL CENTER
DEPARTMENT OF MEDICINE

Minutes of the Monthly Meeting of the Credentials Committee

DATE: April 20, 2010

PRESENT: M. Valden (Chairperson), R. Baron, M. Frank, J. Guern, L. Kingston,
          L. Kinslow (Secretary), S. Perry, B. Roman, J. Sorder, F. Sugihana

Meeting attendees

Dr. Mary Valden called the meeting to order at 8:40 p.m. The minutes of the previous meeting were unanimously approved, with the following correction: the secretary of the Department of Medicine is to be changed from Dr. Juanita Alvarez to Dr. Barbara Golden.

Meeting opening time, a correction, and acceptance of previous minutes

Old Business

None.

New Business

The request by Dr. Henry Russell for staff privileges in the Department of Medicine was discussed. Dr. James Guern made a motion that Dr. Russell be granted staff privileges. Dr. Martin Frank seconded the motion, which passed unanimously.

Terse coverage of topics and decisions

Similar requests by Dr. Ernest Hiram and Dr. Helen Redlands were discussed. Dr. Fred Sugihana made a motion that both physicians be granted all staff privileges except respiratory-care privileges because the two physicians had not had a sufficient number of respiratory cases. Dr. Steven Perry seconded the motion, which passed unanimously.

Dr. John Sorder and Dr. Barry Roman asked for a clarification of general duties for active staff members with respiratory-care privileges. Dr. Richard Baron stated that he would present a clarification at the next scheduled staff meeting, on May 17.

Dr. Baron asked for a volunteer to fill the existing vacancy for Emergency Room duty. Dr. Guern volunteered. He and Dr. Baron will arrange a duty schedule.

There being no further business, the meeting was adjourned at 9:15 p.m. The next regular meeting is scheduled for May 17, at 8:40 p.m.

Meeting adjournment time

Respectfully submitted,

Leslie Kinslow   MARY VALDEN

Leslie Kinslow   Mary Valden, M.D.
Medical Staff Secretary   Chairperson

Signatures of minute taker and committee chairperson

Figure 14–11   Minutes of a Monthly Meeting

and to have these notes projected on a screen so that participants can see what is being recorded. The electronic document can be revised for clarity and distributed to all attendees by e-mail or on paper. It can also serve as the basis for official meeting minutes.

ETHICS NOTE

Because minutes can be used to settle disputes, they must be accurate, complete, and clear. When approved, minutes become the official record of decisions made at the meeting and can be used as evidence in legal proceedings.

Remember that meeting minutes may be used in the future by a lawyer, judge, or jury who probably won't be familiar with the situation you are describing—and that you may not be available to explain what you wrote or you may not remember any of the details of the situation. After all, the reason for taking minutes is to create a permanent record that will be available should it be needed.

The minutes must list all meeting attendees, so, unless you know everyone there, circulate a lined sheet of paper at the beginning of the meeting so that people can write their names and titles or organizations for you to incorporate into the minutes. Request e-mail addresses, too, for distribution of the minutes. Be specific when you refer to people. Instead of using titles ("the chief of the Marketing Division"), use names and titles ("Florence Johnson, chief of the Marketing Division"). If a member of the committee is to report to the committee at its next meeting, state the member's name and the topic so that there is no uncertainty about the assignment and who is responsible for it. Be consistent in the way you refer to people. Do not use a title when referring to one person (Mr. Jarrell) and first and last name when referring to another (Janet Wilson). It may be unintentional, but a lack of consistency in titles or names may imply a deference to one person at the expense of another. Minutes should always be objective and impartial.

When you have been assigned to take the minutes at a meeting, go adequately prepared. A laptop computer is an ideal tool for this task. If you handwrite the minutes, bring more than one pen and plenty of paper. If it is convenient, you may bring a tape recorder as backup to your notes. Bring the minutes of the previous meeting and any other necessary material. Take memory-jogging notes during the meeting and then expand them with the appropriate details immediately after the meeting. Remember that minutes are primarily a record of specific actions taken, although you may sometimes need to summarize what was said or state the essential ideas in your own words.

Closing the Meeting

Set aside five or ten minutes before closing the meeting to review all decisions and assignments by having the minute taker read them aloud. Doing so helps the group focus on what they have collectively agreed to do. This period also allows for any questions to be raised or misunderstandings to be clarified and promotes everyone's agreement about the group's decisions. Set a date by which everyone at the meeting can expect to receive the minutes. Finally, thank everyone for their participation and close the meeting on a positive note.

WRITER'S CHECKLIST
Writing Minutes of Meetings

Include the following information in meeting minutes:

✔ The name of the group or committee holding the meeting

✔ The topic of the meeting

✔ The kind of meeting (a regular meeting or a special meeting called to discuss a specific subject or problem)

✔ Names of attendees and their titles or organizations

✔ The place, time, and date of the meeting

✔ A statement that the chair and the secretary were present or the names of any substitutes

✔ A statement that the minutes of the previous meeting were approved or revised

✔ A list of any reports that were read and approved

✔ All the main motions that were made, with statements as to whether they were carried, defeated, or tabled (vote postponed), and the names of those who made and seconded the motions (motions that were withdrawn are not mentioned)

✔ A full description of resolutions that were adopted and a simple statement of any that were rejected

✔ A record of all ballots with the number of votes cast for and against resolutions

✔ The time the meeting was adjourned (officially ended) and the place, time, and date of the next meeting, if any

✔ The recording secretary's signature and typed name, and, if desired, the signature of the chairperson

CHAPTER 14 SUMMARY: GIVING PRESENTATIONS AND CONDUCTING MEETINGS

In planning a presentation, ask the following questions:

▪ What is my purpose?

▪ Who is my audience?

▪ What amount of information should I prepare to adequately cover the topic for my audience in the time available?

In preparing the presentation:

▪ Gather the needed information.

▪ Decide how to organize the information.

▪ Structure the presentation around this organization.

▪ Decide on the types of visuals you will need.

In rehearsing your presentation:

▪ Become familiar with your presentation.

▪ Practice on your feet, out loud, and with your visuals.

▪ Videotape your practice sessions, if possible, and review the video for posture, gestures, and voice, as well as for content.

▪ Try to rehearse in the room where the presentation will take place to familiarize yourself with its layout.

When delivering the presentation:

▪ Remember that nervousness before a presentation is normal.

▪ Show enthusiasm for your topic through the effective use of movement, eye contact, gestures, and your voice.

To maximize your effectiveness as a listener:

▪ Adapt your level of concentration to the situation.

▪ Take the time to understand what the speaker is saying before speaking yourself.

▪ Acknowledge the speaker through questions and gestures.

▪ Define what you need or hope to take away from listening to someone else.

▪ Consciously work to control yourself from letting boredom, distractions, anger, or other impediments affect you.

In conducting effective meetings:

▪ Determine the purpose of the meeting.

▪ Decide who should be invited.

▪ Determine the best time and place for the meeting.

▪ Create and distribute an agenda before the meeting.

▪ Select someone to take minutes.

▪ Manage different types of people effectively to achieve the best outcome for the group.

▪ Deal with conflict positively by adopting noncombative tactics, persuasion, bargaining, or collaborating.

▪ Review all decisions made and assignments to participants at the close of the meeting.

To record the minutes of a meeting:

▪ Be prepared to record the proceedings—a laptop computer is ideal. Also bring minutes from the previous meeting and any other necessary materials, like handouts.

▪ Be accurate, complete, and clear because minutes of a meeting may be used to settle disputes or as evidence in legal proceedings. Follow a set format for taking notes.

▪ Be concise and avoid generalities.

▪ Be specific and consistent when referring to people, places, and events.

▪ Be objective and impartial, avoiding adjectives and adverbs that suggest either good or bad qualities.

▪ Record tasks and the names of attendees who will perform these tasks.

▪ Expand your notes immediately after the meeting, adding appropriate details, if necessary.

ON THE WEB

For an online quiz on presentations and meetings, go to Chapter 14, bedfordstmartins.com/ writingthatworks

▨ Exercises

ON THE WEB

For additional exercises, go to Chapter 14, bedfordstmartins.com/ writingthatworks

1. Select a topic for a presentation and write a purpose statement that is based on your answers to the three questions discussed on page 499: (1) What do I want my audience to know? (2) What do I want my audience to believe? and (3) What do I want my audience to do? Possible topics include the following:

   • Should Congress censor the Internet?
   • Describe a policy you would like to see changed or an initiative you would like to see implemented on your campus. (Examples could include (1) more parking spaces; (2) additional campus safety measures—e.g., more emergency call boxes; (3) more focus on hands-on health care for introductory nursing classes; (4) on-campus voting polls for local and national elections; (5) ecologically friendly laundry facilities in dormitories.)
   • Are printed books a thing of the past?
   • What responsibility do businesses have toward the public?
   • Should local, state, and federal governments tax Internet purchases?
   • Should school cafeterias ban hamburgers, hot dogs, pizza, and soft drinks?
   • Would you and one or more partners stand a better chance of business success if you opened a coffee kiosk (in a hospital lobby, in a shopping mall, or on a busy street corner, for example) or if you invested in and ran a coffee shop for a coffee-chain franchise (Seattle's Best, Starbucks, Cosi, and so on)?

2. Complete the following statements about the audience for the presentation topic you selected for Exercise 1:

   a. The experience or level of knowledge that my audience currently has about my subject is _____. Based on their existing knowledge, I should _____.
   b. The general educational level of my audience is _____. Based on their general educational level, I'll need to _____.
   c. The type of information I should provide this audience to achieve my objective is _____.
   d. Some of the questions that the audience may have throughout the presentation include the following:
      • _____
      • _____
      • _____

3. Continuing with the presentation topic you used in Exercises 1 and 2, prepare an introduction for your presentation that includes the following:

   • An interesting opening
   • A statement of purpose
   • An explanation of how you are going to present the topic (method of development)

4. Using the same presentation topic and materials from Exercises 1, 2, and 3, create a closing for your presentation that asks your audience to take a specific action or that summarizes the main points and restates the purpose of your presentation.

5. Prepare an outline for the presentation you've been working on in the previous four exercises. Use at least four headings and three subheadings under each

heading. Include an opening, an introduction, a body, and a closing. Next, prepare at least six transparencies using bullet statements and keywords that will help keep the audience focused during your presentation. For this assignment, concentrate on using effective text and clip art, if desired, when preparing each transparency. You will discover that your finished product serves not only as an aid to your presentation but as an outline for you to follow during the presentation, possibly eliminating the need for notes.

6. Add two of the following to the set of visuals you prepared for Exercise 5: table, chart, graph, map, or pictorial other than clip art.

7. Write a brief explanation of the impact that the audience has on any presentation you might prepare. Consider the following:

   • How does the education or reading level of the audience guide your choices in what information to include and how you will convey it?
   • If the audience shares your field or major, how will that affect your choices in what information to include and how you will convey it?
   • How might your understanding of your audience affect the purpose of your presentation? How do your purpose and understanding of your audience affect the way that you organize your presentation? (It may be helpful to review pages 31–33 in Chapter 2, Organizing Your Information.)

8. A popular expression used to describe ineffective presentations is "death by PowerPoint." Whether the problem lies with the presentation or the presenter, examples include pointlessly long presentations, presenters who read each slide word for word, cluttered slides in a tiny font, or presentations that are either too plain and boring or too filled with distracting text animations. Using at least three of the presentation exercises or projects that are offered in this chapter, write a memo to the class cautioning your classmates against "death by PowerPoint" and suggesting how to avoid it. Give specific examples of where the PowerPoint creator could go wrong in each instance.

9. Attend a lecture on campus given by a speaker with whom you are likely to disagree (you may also choose to attend a lecture on a topic about which you have a strong opinion). Take to the presentation the list of the points about listening on page 518. As you listen to the presentation, make brief notes of your reactions; for example, note when you are tempted to be distracted by the speaker's appearance, mannerisms, or accent. Immediately after the presentation, expand your notes and review this chapter for advice on listening. Turn your observations of your own use of listening techniques into a report on how using them can help others listen better.

ON THE WEB

For more collaborative classroom projects, go to Chapter 14, bedfordstmartins.com/ writingthatworks

▣ Collaborative Classroom Projects

1. During a presentation, verbal, visual, and nonverbal communications affect your audience. To make a positive impression on your audience and to keep their attention, you must convey your genuine enthusiasm for your topic. With this principle in mind, take turns in front of the class introducing yourselves and explaining what you plan to accomplish in your career. Speak for no more than three minutes, and pay attention to the nonverbal communication signals that you and

your classmates use. Do some students seem more excited about their future careers than others? Do some seem bored? Think about which gestures and expressions work well and which should be avoided while speaking.

2. Plan a meeting, to take place outside class, to organize a particular class activity or trip; to decide on a specific policy; or to vote on a specific campus, national, or international issue. The meeting will require the participation of everyone in your class. As a group, determine what you expect to achieve at the meeting and prepare a short agenda. Appoint a meeting facilitator to keep the meeting focused and a meeting secretary to record the minutes. At the meeting, maintain an atmosphere in which students listen to each other and practice adopting the "you" attitude, as discussed on pages 527–529. When the meeting is concluded and decisions have been made or actions decided, write a brief analysis of the interaction that occurred during the session. What, if anything, could have been improved? Did the environment encourage participation?

Research Projects

ON THE WEB

For extra research projects, go to Chapter 14, bedfordstmartins.com/writingthatworks

1. PowerPoint has been heralded and criticized by many scholars and experts. Prepare a five-minute presentation in which you give the history of PowerPoint and describe the reasons people support and denigrate the tool. Be sure to both paraphrase and directly cite each of the experts you use as a source. Structure your presentation so that the introduction has an attention-getting opening, a body that presents your research, and a closing that summarizes major points and asks your audience to ponder some of the major issues with PowerPoint.

2. Research cataracts, the most popular surgeries used to correct them, and the costs and benefits associated with each surgery. Create a visual presentation that could be used by an ophthalmologist to inform new cataract patients about their surgical options. Assume these patients have vision problems already and adjust the slides accordingly.

3. Imagine that you are the chief executive officer for a national property group interested in building a shopping mall in your state. You have several national and international chain stores interested in establishing stores in your mall, so you want to establish your mall in a county where customers of various economic and racial demographics reside. Begin by going to the U.S. Census Bureau Web site at <www.census.gov>, selecting the regional office closest to you, and clicking the "Regional Fun Facts" link for your state. Look at the demographics for your state and explore the data from several local counties. Narrow your choice to two counties that offer the best customer base for the type of mall you are considering. Prepare a table, graph, or chart on a transparency or in PowerPoint, comparing relevant information regarding the two counties and listing the U.S. Census Bureau as your source. The transparency should be simple, with a font large enough for an audience to read it from a distance. Be ready to share the visuals and your recommendation with the class.

4. Imagine that you work with several other college students at a carpet cleaning company that puts coupons in local flyers and newspapers to solicit business. Potential customers often call to discuss their carpets and schedule a free

consultation. Employees take turns answering the phones when the receptionist is on break, but Lee and Janice let the phone ring four or five times before picking it up because they like to finish what they're doing before beginning what could be a long discussion. If another employee accidentally transfers a call to Lee, he bounces it back to the front desk or transfers it to Janice so that he can focus on something else. Because Janice is on the phone all day, she often has to eat at her desk, and occasionally answers the phone mid-chew. Sometimes Janice stops by Lee's desk to ask him about orders; Lee usually puts his hand over the receiver before answering her. Because Lee, Janice, and others like them will soon be fired unless they improve their telephone skills, you have decided to hold a meeting to address the problem.

a. Determine what the purpose of your meeting is and who should attend it.
b. Search the Web for at least three sites that describe proper phone etiquette, then create a list of what employees should be doing to create a good impression to potential customers.
c. Use your list to prepare an agenda for the meeting.
d. Keeping in mind that employees are sensitive to criticism and that you want to maintain a positive attitude among the staff—but that you also want to solve the phone etiquette problem—write a transmittal memo that will be distributed with the meeting agenda.

15 | Writing for the Web: Rhetorical Principles

AT A GLANCE: Web Content

This chapter offers guidance in the following areas to help you write and organize Web content, and it emphasizes the importance of collaborating closely with a site's Web master to optimize content for speed and accessibility:[1]

- ▪ Writing for rapid consumption / 540
- ▪ Crafting content for the Web / 540
- ▪ Highlighting information / 549
- ▪ Enhancing access to content / 552
- ▪ Repurposing existing content / 554
- ▪ Protecting the privacy of your users / 555
- ▪ Documenting sources of information / 557
- ▪ Contributing to collaborative and multimedia content / 558

Given the pervasiveness of Web technology in the workplace for news, marketing, research, and shopping, you will likely contribute content to your company or organization Web site. You may be asked to create a blog for customer relations, develop answers for an FAQ page, write a product description, and more. Writing for the Web is very much like writing for print: You need to understand your purpose and your audience, carefully research your subject, organize your thoughts, use plain language, and make your text free of typographical or grammatical errors. Familiarize yourself with the site's existing overall design and content areas. Before submitting your content, review recently published material at the site to get a sense of the site's purpose and audience and how your content works in relationship to both.

However, writing for the Web is different from writing for other media—and more challenging—because your audience is scanning a computer screen and expects to get information quickly and efficiently. Moreover, you may have a global audience, and competing sources of information are only a click or two away. For these reasons, ease of access to your content will

---

[1]In the workplace, the Web master or site designer maintains site-wide technical and design standards. On campus, your instructor or the campus computer support staff can guide you on standards for posting content.

VOICES IN THE WORKPLACE

Respect How Your Users Read Online

Annika Tamura, Design Director at Boston.com, a regional Web site that provides content for the online *Boston Globe*, observes after site usability tests, that "people read differently online. They jump around and read short amounts. . . . We needed to label and organize information [for the *Boston Globe*] into logical groupings that made it clear if a section was about news or travel. . . . Respect that information is what people come to your site for."

be affected by how it's written and organized, the speed at which it loads to your readers' screens, and even the language translation options available at your site.

Writing for Rapid Consumption

ON THE WEB

For Web-design resources, go to Chapter 15, bedfordstmartins.com/ writingthatworks

People read text on Web sites differently than they read text on paper. Reading rates on the Web slow by 25 percent and more compared with rates for reading paper text, in part because of eyestrain caused by the flickering monitor. Few people read Web content word for word. Most—up to 80 percent—scan the screen for what interests them or for what they need. Depending on interest and number of words per page, Web readers spend between 25 and 80 seconds per page.[2] And although motivated readers slow down to read medical, financial, or how-to information, for example, most people scan and read rapidly. Given the reader's brief attention span and other features unique to Web sites, you must plan and organize your information to promote ease of use and comprehension.

Crafting Content for the Web

Whether you plan to write original content for a Web site or repurpose content from an existing document, use the following guidelines to plan and organize your text and graphics.

Using the Inverted Pyramid

Begin with the bottom line—your conclusions—by using the inverted-pyramid method traditionally used by journalists to organize your writing. State your conclusions or most important points before providing the detailed background

---

[2]Jakob Nielsen's Alertbox, "How Little Do Users Read?" May 6, 2008, <http://useit.com/alertbox/ percent-text-read.html>.

information—facts, data, and logic—to support them. Most Web readers skim content and may not scroll to the bottom of a page, so the inverted-pyramid presentation of information promotes speed of access to your content. Placing the most important information at the beginning allows readers to grasp what is significant without having to read to the end. Of course, you still need to provide the background details, explanations, documentation, and other information essential to your content for readers wishing for the additional level of detail. You can also reduce the amount of background information on a page by linking to second- or third-level content elsewhere. (This technique is described in detail on pages 545–548.) Placing your most important ideas first also optimizes your content for Web searches because search engines scan the first several paragraphs of a Web page, in addition to other relevant site information, like paragraph headings. Figure 15–1 depicts this method in principle and Figure 15–2 shows how it works in practice.

◆ *The inverted-pyramid method is also described on pages 44–45 in Chapter 2, Organizing Your Information.*

Using a Simple Style and an Appropriate Tone

If you want your ideas to make an impact on the Web, your writing style must be plain, honest, and to the point. Web users are looking for information, not unsupported claims—whether you are describing a product (such as a digital camera) or a public policy idea (such as charter schools). To this end, avoid promotional language that inflates the claims of the product or idea but provides no corroborating information to support those claims.

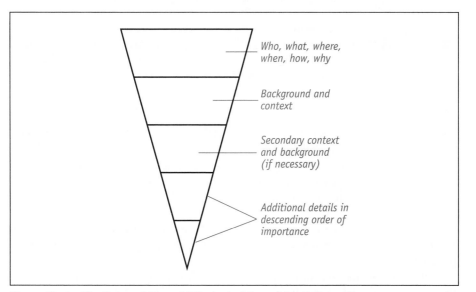

Figure 15–1 The Inverted-Pyramid Method of Organizing Information

Answers what, when, where, why

Answers why and describes scope of activity

Expands context by describing additional scope of activity

Concludes with secondary (background) details

Figure 15–2 Press Release at a Web Site, Using the Inverted-Pyramid Presentation of Information. *Source:* Department of Energy, <www.doe.gov>.

UNSUPPORTED CLAIM	Amco's All-in-One Mini Sound System is the best product in its class on the Internet! Buy one today!
SUPPORTED CLAIM	Amco's All-in-One Mini Sound System is a proven leader in compact systems based on <u>industry tests</u> and was voted the #1 mini sound system for 2009 by *Audio Magazine*.

Note that the improved version links directly to the source of the evidence (*industry tests* and *Audio Magazine*) that supports the company's claims about the product.

Like e-mail, the Web often invites informality. Remember that regardless of the technology used to reach your reader, your words and tone represent your company or project. Eliminate any biased or sexist language and resist the temptation to insert unnecessary and inappropriate humor in any writing—Web or otherwise—intended for the public. Also avoid puns, which suggest too much informality and can confuse your international readers. This guidance applies equally to the language of the captions and callouts for graphics.

◆ *For comprehensive guidance on style, tone, and the avoidance of biased language, see Chapter 4, Revising the Draft.*

Writing Concisely

Revise your text for conciseness. Your readers will appreciate your effort because they are looking for useful content in a hurry. Concise content also reduces reader eyestrain caused by prolonged reading on a computer screen. Use the following guidelines to achieve conciseness:

- Cover one idea in each paragraph.
- Begin each paragraph with a topic sentence.
- Try to limit each paragraph to three or four sentences.
- Aim for short sentences with simple sentence structure; use concrete nouns and active verbs.
- Use plain language.

Figure 15–3 provides depicts a page on the Web site of the Mayo Clinic, a world-renowned medical facility, which explains the importance of exercising the body's core muscles. Because it provides how-to information, the language must be detailed and accurate. Even so, it can be made concise and organized for ease of reading. The page is effective because each paragraph is introduced by a pertinent heading, opens with a topic sentence, and covers one facet of the subject in plain language. The page integrates an informative visual as well.

◆ *For additional guidelines on using topic sentences, achieving conciseness, and using plain language, see Chapter 4, Revising the Draft.*

Chunking Content

Another way to focus reader attention is to break up dense blocks of text by dividing them into short paragraphs so that they stand out and can be quickly scanned and absorbed. Each chunked passage should coherently focus on one facet of your topic. Identify such passages with captions or headings that announce the topic and help the reader decide at a glance whether to read the material. Include links for more detailed secondary or background information to avoid slowing readers not interested in that level of information. Use the inverted-pyramid principle to organize these passages.

The pages shown in Figures 15–2 and 15–3 both effectively divide their content into short paragraphs and include links to additional material. Each paragraph in Figure 15–2 focuses on one point and, for ease of access, is set off from the others by white space. The use of headings for the short paragraphs in Figure 15–3 makes the information even easier to scan. Note the link to a visual (core

Heading signals topic coverage

Concise definition of the concept with illustration

Short bulleted paragraphs "chunk" content

Each paragraph describes one facet of the routine

Thumbnail of illustration

Figure 15–3   Web Page Featuring Chunked Content.   *Source:* Mayo Clinic, <www.mayoclinic.com>.

muscle group) to clarify the concept being described. The passages in both figures are grouped in a logical sequence for the information covered.

Linking to Internal Content

Use *hyperlinks*—words or images that act as gateways to other content areas—to expand access to your information. These links work best to provide facts, data, charts, glossaries, or documentation to support or expand coverage of information on the screen, such as a link to the research article or an illustration. They give readers quick access to material and save them the trouble of having to scroll through screen after screen to locate content.

If your coverage on a single page stretches beyond two or three screens, as for a short report, booklet, or pamphlet, create a table of contents for it at the top of the Web page. Hyperlink each heading in the table of contents to the same heading further down the page. Make sure these links are visible on the first screen so that readers need not scroll down to see them. Use hyperlinks to connect the headings in the table of contents to their locations in the document so that the reader can access a specific section quickly and easily, as shown in Figure 15–4. The reader can either scroll down to read the whole document or use the hyperlinks in the table of contents to access a piece of the information quickly and easily. Depending on the overall site design, the complete document may even be located at a different part of the site, such as in a collection of similar documents, thus eliminating the need for the reader to scroll down a single screen to review it.

In addition to informational links, Web pages also include navigational links that move visitors through a document and site. For lengthy content on a single page, for example, include directional cues, such as links at convenient breaks so that users can get to the top of the page without having to scroll.

▲
Back to Top

These links are placed between text passages where they do not interrupt readers. Most sites use standardized navigational links whose meanings are usually described at the site's Help page. Consult with the Web master for site standards on their use.

Use links to focus user attention, not distract it. Keep to a minimum hyperlinks *within* text paragraphs. Otherwise, they are visually distracting (underlined or colored) and make scanning the text difficult. Embedded links also tempt readers to leave the page before reaching the end of your content. Figure 15–5 on page 547 shows a page from a site that contains too many distracting links embedded in the text. Rather than embedding hyperlinks throughout the body of your text, combine them into short, well-organized lists that are introduced with explanatory text. Be sure to inform readers where the link will take them. In some cases, the title of the link is self-explanatory: <u>Glossary</u> or <u>For Additional Information</u>. At other times, you need to add a brief explanatory passage:

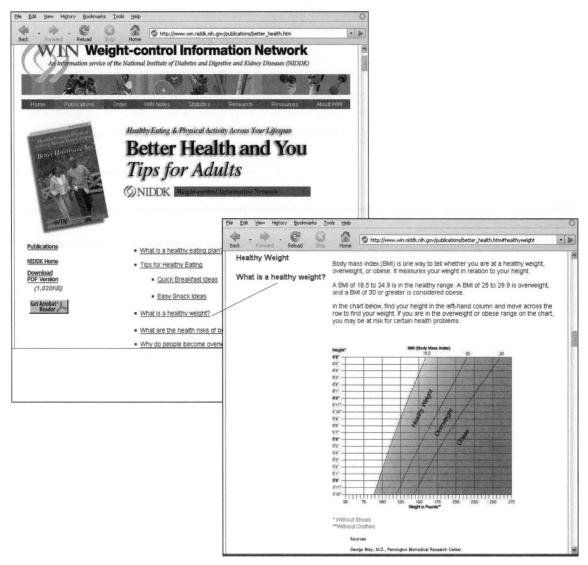

Figure 15–4   Table of Contents Linking to Content on the Same Web Page.
Source: National Institutes of Health, <www.nih.gov>.

▷   Refer to the section on <u>Plug-ins, Viewers, and Other Tools</u> for information on icons associated with document formats, such as PDFs, used at this site.

You can place lists of hyperlinks periodically throughout your document to break up large blocks of text or you can place a list of links at the end of your document, as you would with footnotes. Finally, avoid cuing readers with the phrase "Click Here." The phrase offers no useful information and is considered a Web cliché.

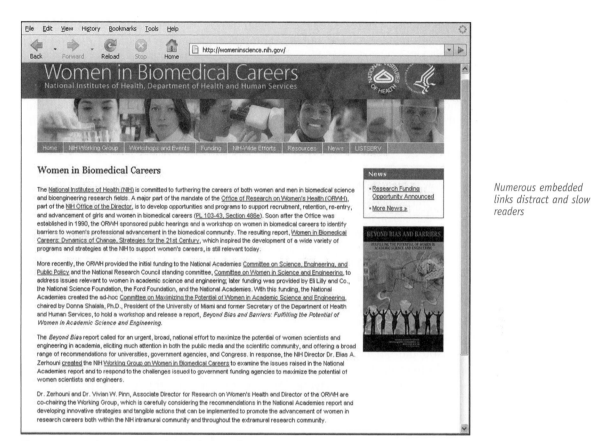

Figure 15–5   Overuse of Embedded Links (Links Underlined for Emphasis).
Source: National Institutes of Health, <http://nih.gov>.

Numerous embedded links distract and slow readers

AVOID   To learn more about our company, <u>Click Here</u>.

BETTER   Learn more about the <u>XYZ Corporation</u>.

Linking to External Content

Links to external (or outside) sites can be an invaluable way of expanding your content. However, be sure to review such sites and their content carefully before linking to them. Is the site's author or sponsoring organization reputable? Is the content accurate and current? Does the site date-stamp its content (such as "This page was last updated on January 12, 2010")? Is the information unbiased?

Some Web sites request that you ask their permission before linking to them. To determine a site's policy in this regard, review its <u>About Us</u> page, usually accessible from the homepage. Although linking to another site can be done electronically without the other site being aware of the link, your organization may have a policy of asking permission of outside sites before linking to them. In either case, e-mail a request to the site's Web master asking for permission. Check with your site's Web master to find out if standardized language exists for making such requests.

Link directly to the page or specific area of an external site that is relevant to your users and be sure that your writing provides a clear context for why you're sending your readers there and what they will find. The following passage appears at the Web site for the Nuclear Regulatory Commission (NRC). It directs users to a non-NRC site to obtain automatic updates about business opportunities with the agency.

▶   **How to Identify Potential Contract Opportunities**

NRC publicizes and posts proposed business opportunities valued at greater than $25,000 on the <u>FedBizOpps</u> [EXIT] Web site. Once at this site, select "Vendors," select "NRC" from the pull-down menu, and select "Posted Dates," which takes you into NRC business opportunities. From here, select the posted opportunity you are interested in. You may also register at <u>FedBizOpps</u> [EXIT] to receive any further notifications about address, Solicitation Number, and select the "Subscribe to Mailing List" button at the bottom of the page. By registering with FedBizOpps, your company can be notified via e-mail of procurement opportunities the day they are posted.

Note the [EXIT] label in this passage. Many sites place an icon or a text label next to links to external sites to inform users that they are leaving the host site. Other sites show pop-up text, saying, "You are now leaving the XYZ Corporation site. <u>Continue</u> or <u>stay</u>?" A site's Help page may explain the purpose of the practice, such as the following passage:

▶   **Exit [EXIT]**

The Exit icon is placed directly after an external link to let you know that the link is going to take you away from the NRC site. These links are provided as a service and do not imply any official endorsement of or responsibility for the opinions, ideas, data, or products presented at these locations or guarantee the validity of the information provided. (For more information, refer to the <u>Site Disclaimer</u>.)

Check with your Web master or site administrator about site policy for these notices if your content includes links to external sites.

Once you link to another site, you are responsible for checking frequently to ensure that the content remains accurate and current—or that it hasn't disappeared. It may be corporate or organizational legal policy at your site to post a disclaimer, such as the following, to inform users that information at external sites is not under your control and may at times be erroneous.

◆ *For detailed guidance on reviewing outside sites and other Internet sources of information, see the Evaluating Online Resources checklist on page 174.*

▶   *Disclaimer*: The XYZ Corporation cannot guarantee the accuracy, completeness, or reliability of all information on non-XYZ servers and Web sites to which the XYZ site links.

WRITER'S CHECKLIST
Crafting Content for the Web

✔ Organize content from the top down—begin with your most important point, adding supporting details and background information in descending order of importance.

✔ Present ideas as concisely as possible and express them in plain language.

✔ Support all claims with facts.

✔ Chunk dense blocks of text into shorter passages that stand out for ease of reading and introduce them with informative headings.

✔ Create hyperlinks to additional information to reduce content on your page and to enrich coverage of your topic.

✔ Review hyperlinks periodically to ensure that their content continues to be relevant to your purposes.

Highlighting Information

Writing and organizing text for rapid consumption are essential first steps to promoting ease of access to your content. You can further augment access through a variety of highlighting techniques, some common to printed text and some unique to Web content.

Using Headings and Subheadings

Headings reduce the complexity of text by highlighting structure and showing organization. They also signal breaks in coverage from one topic to the next. Readers use them to scan rapidly for meaningful information on-screen as well as in printed documents. Set off headings in boldface or another text attribute, such as color, on a separate line either directly above or in the left margin directly across from the text they describe. Figure 15–3 on page 544 uses headings effectively to introduce and divide content.

◆ For additional guidance about the use of headings to highlight content, see pages 213–215 in Chapter 7, Designing Effective Documents and Visuals, and pages 403–408 in Chapter 11, Writing Formal Reports.

Using Bulleted and Numbered Lists

Like headings, bulleted and numbered lists break up dense paragraphs. They also reduce text length and highlight relevant content instead of embedding it within paragraphs. Bulleted lists show readers that the items displayed are parallel in importance. Numbered lists inform readers immediately that the sequence of your information is crucial. Regardless of the form the list takes, make all items in it grammatically parallel.

Note that not all text passages should be broken into bulleted lists. Doing so would make your pages look like a PowerPoint presentation but without a speaker to fill in the context for the bulleted points. Lists without supporting explanatory text lack coherence. The bulleted items in Figure 15–3 are effective because they

◆ *For more informa-tion about creating numbered and bulleted lists, see page 105 in Chapter 4, Revising the Draft.*

focus reader attention on specific core exercise techniques following a general in-troduction to the topic.

Giving Directional Cues

Avoid navigational cues that make sense on the printed page but not on a Web screen, such as "as shown in the example below" or "in the graph at the top of this page." Phrases like these can be confusing when there is no real reference for "above" and "below," and no "top" or "bottom" of the document. Instead, position links so that they are tied directly to the content to which they pertain. For ex-ample, insert links that take readers directly to the content you want them to see. (See the sample <u>Back to Top</u> link on page 545.)

The terms *next* and *previous* can also cause confusion. Use these terms only when you know users accessed your page from an immediately preceding page. These terms are, however, used appropriately to navigate through PDF files.

Providing Keywords for Content Retrieval

One challenge of writing for the Web is making sure that your desired audience can find your page. To increase the odds that Web search engines will locate your site, be specific in describing your important points. Using keywords throughout your text will help the search engine find your page.

NO KEYWORDS	**Remembering Our Founder** We are proud to introduce a new commemorative coin honoring our company's founder and president. The item will be available on this Web site after December 1, 2010, which is the 100th anniversary of our first sale.
WITH KEYWORDS	**Reynolds Commemorative Coin on Sale** The new *Reynolds* commemorative coin features a portrait of *George G. Reynolds*, the founder and president of *Reynolds Corporation*. The *coin* can be purchased on our Web site (<<u>www.reynoldswidgetcorp.com/coin.htm</u>>) after December 1, 2010, in honor of the 100th anniversary of the sale of the first *Reynolds widget*.

By using words in the text and heading such as "Reynolds," "George G. Reynolds," and the "coin" instead of "our company's," "our founder," and "the item," you will give the search engines specific information that they, in turn, can give to users. The revised paragraph also includes a link to the company's Web site for ease of access to those wishing to purchase the coin.

Using Graphics and Typography

The way your content looks on the screen when published will be affected by the site's existing design. The page will likely display a banner at the top, featuring the organization or company name; navigational toolbars at the top, bottom, or left side of the screen; links to other content areas; and other elements. The site's de-sign standards may affect the line length of your text (such as single or double columns); the default type sizes and styles in use at the site; and the preferred for-mat for graphics files, color, and a variety of other features. Meet with the site's Web master to ensure that your content fits smoothly into the existing design and that it is consistent with site technical and design standards.

Graphics

As with print publications, your audience and purpose should determine *why* graphics are important to your content. At times, graphic elements—photo-graphs, line drawings, animations, or videos—provide visual relief from dense text and are appealing and motivational, as in the introduction to Figure 15–4 on page 546. For the most part, however, use only images that illustrate essential in-formation, as in Figure 15–3 on page 544. Because users depend on the site for ac-cessible and visually clear information, use graphics that load as quickly as pos-sible and be mindful that for some users with modem-only access, large or high-resolution graphics, like color photographs or animated images, can cause long delays as they download to the user's system. For high-resolution graphics that are essential, consider using thumbnails—images reduced to 10 to 15 per-cent of the original file size for quick access. Note the effective use of a thumbnail image of core muscles in Figure 15–3. Work with the site Web master to optimize all graphics for speed of access. Ask about the preferred file-compression for-mat—JPEG, GIF, or other—for visuals you submit. Also consider giving visitors a graphics-free option for quicker access to your content.

Font Size and Style

Font sizes and styles affect screen legibility. Computer screens display fonts at lower resolutions than in most printed text. Thus, sans serif fonts work better for text passages on-screen because serifs "fuzz out" on low-resolution monitors, adversely affecting legibility and causing eyestrain. Consult with your Web mas-ter about the site's font preferences and review the text of your content on an in-ternal browser for legibility before posting it for public access. Be aware, how-ever, that even with your best efforts to ensure legibility, the user's browser, operating system, and font preferences can affect how your text looks on the user's screen.

Line Length

Line length also affects legibility. Short line lengths reduce the amount of eye move-ment and eyestrain necessary to scan text. The optimal line length is approximately half the width of the screen.[3] To achieve this length, draft text that's between 50 and

---

[3]Patrick L. Lynch and Sara Horton, *Web Style Guide: Basic Design Principles for Creating Web Sites*, 3rd ed. (New Haven, CT: Yale University Press, 2008), 192, 215. See also <www.webstyleguide.com/type/lines.html>.

◆ *For more information about type sizes and styles, see pages 212–213 in Chapter 7, Designing Effective Documents and Visuals.*

70 characters, or 10 to 12 words to a line. Longer lines make it difficult for readers to locate the next line of text at the left margin, particularly for single-spaced paragraphs. Finally, as with printed material, do not use all-capital letters or boldface type for blocks of text. They slow reader speed and comprehension.

Special Font Characters

For content that contains special or international characters, consult with the Web master about the best way to submit the files for HTML coding. These characters include, among others, bullets, dashes, and asterisks; symbols for chemical and mathematical equations; or fonts and accent marks for non-English languages. In general, aim for consistency to establish a visual sense of unity and to provide visual cues that help visitors find information.

DESIGNING YOUR DOCUMENT
Highlighting Information

- Use headings and subheadings to introduce text passages, to signal changes in topics, and to provide visual breaks on the page.
- Use bulleted lists to display text in an easy-to-scan format when the ideas are parallel in meaning.
- Use numbered lists to display content when the sequence of the information matters.
- Make all bulleted and numbered lists grammatically parallel.
- Provide hyperlinks to additional content rather than written directions for finding it elsewhere on the site.
- Use keywords to describe important content so that Web search engines will find your page.
- Select graphics that are essential to your audience and purpose.
- Optimize graphics files so that they download quickly.
- If you cannot avoid large file sizes, use thumbnails of your graphics on your page that link to the original-size image.
- Use appropriate font styles, sizes, and line lengths to enhance the legibility of your content.

▦ Enhancing Access to Content

The techniques discussed in the previous sections will help you organize and present text and graphics for the Web that are easy for your audience to understand. This section describes your responsibility as a content provider to ensure that your information is accessible to people with disabilities and that it meets the needs of international users.

Ensuring Access for People with Disabilities

Many of the advantages of Web sites include colorful graphics, animation, and streaming video and audio. However, these design elements can be barriers to people with impaired vision or hearing or those who are color blind. To overcome these barriers to your content, discuss the following strategies with the site Web master or site-accessibility specialist.

- Avoid frames, complex tables, animation, JavaScript, and other design elements that are incompatible with text-only browsers and adaptive technologies, such as voice or large-print software.[4]
- Provide HTML versions of pages and documents whenever possible because this format is most compatible with the current generation of screen readers.
- Include closed captions for audiovisual files or text-equivalent captions that describe the graphic elements of your content (for example, "Photograph of Harriet V. Sullivan, President, HVS Accounting Services").
- Design for the reader who is color blind using captions and other text to make meaning independent of color (Green, labeled *G*, means *All Safe*).

Implementing these measures requires the expertise of a Web-technology specialist. However, as the content provider, you will be expected to write text captions for all graphics and sound features—as described in the third item of the preceding list. You may also want to offer different options for site visitors, such as full-graphics, light-graphics, and text-only versions of your content. Discuss these options with the Web master.

Finally, arrange with the site Web master to have your content tested for accessibility. A complete list of Web-accessibility evaluation tools is located at <www.w3.org/WAI/ER/tools/complete>.

ON THE WEB

For guidelines for improving Web-site accessibility, go to Chapter 15 at bedfordstmartins.com/ writingthatworks

Considering International Users

Consider the needs of international readers if they are part of your target audience. You need not write simplistic prose to do so, nor do you need to write separate versions of your content for domestic and international readers. As with other writing aimed at readers of English as a second language, you would, review your text to eliminate expressions and references that make sense only to someone very familiar with American English. Avoid expressions such as "throw in the towel" and "a no-brainer." Likewise, when appropriate, express dates, clock times, and measurements consistent with international practices.

◆ *For more information about international usage of dates, times, and measurements, see Chapter 9, page 347.*

---

[4]Adaptive technologies, such as screen readers, use software to activate a voice synthesizer that reads aloud the text and captions for nontext elements (e.g., graphics) on a computer screen.

◆ *For more on interna-*
tional audiences, see the
following:
- *Writing for an Inter-*
  national Audience,
  page 70
- *Using Visuals to*
  Communicate
  Internationally,
  pages 250–256
- *Writing International*
  Correspondence, pages
  343–351
- *Reaching Global*
  Audiences, pages
  515–516

Choose visual content carefully, too. Opt for symbols and icons, colors, representations of human beings, and captions that can be easily understood. And use graphics, including video files, that load quickly. Some international users have modem-only access, and for them large, high-resolution, and video files can cause long delays as they download to the user's system. (See "Using Graphics and Typography," pages 550–552, for additional information.)

Finally, consider providing links to online translation sites for your international users. Your site Web master will likely provide information about online translation tools. If not, a selective listing of free translation sites is available at <http://websearch.about.com/od/internetresearch/a/translate.htm >.

CONSIDERING AUDIENCE AND PURPOSE

Enhancing Access to Content

- Work with your site's Web master or accessibility specialist to provide content—text, graphics, audio—that is compatible with adaptive technologies used by people with disabilities.

- Create captions that accurately describe the graphics and audio features of your content.

- Describe color-coded content so that its meaning can be understood independent of color.

- Test your content for accessibility using an appropriate site listed at <www.w3.org/WAI/ER/tools/complete>.

- Create text, graphics, and units of measurement to accommodate international readers.

■ Repurposing Existing Content

You may be asked to submit existing content to a Web site. It may be a report, user manual, or parts of a policy-and-procedure handbook. In its original form, the content will be organized to be read in the sequence written for paper publication. If the document is lengthy, it makes sense to retain the document's original sequence and page layout. If you shorten or revise your original document for posting on the Web, footnote or otherwise mark the Web content accordingly, as in the following example, so that readers will know that it differs from the original.

▷ *The data in Appendix A of this report are updated monthly and vary from the data in the printed report, which is published each February.

Documents posted on the Web are frequently converted to PDF files to display the pages on-screen exactly as they appear on paper. Readers can read the PDF version online, download it to a hard drive, or print it in whole or in part.

Regardless of format or version used, do the following before you prepare existing paper documents for public availability on a Web site:

- Review the document for compliance with your organization's publishing policies:
  - Is it appropriate for public access?
  - Is it consistent with current policies and practices for the organization's products and services?
  - Does it contain proprietary and privacy information that must be protected or deleted?
- Obtain permission for Web publication if the document contains copyrighted text, tables, or images. (Some copyright holders require separate permissions for paper and Web publication of their content.)
- Contact the site Web master about the preferred electronic file format in which to submit the document for coding and posting: Microsoft Word, PageMaker, PDF, FrameMaker, or other format.
- Ask the Web master to optimize any slow-loading graphics files for quicker access.
- Review the coded document on an internal Web site *before* it is posted to the public site to ensure that it is the correct version, that no information is missing, and that all links work and go to the right places.

If your document is long, assume that users will print it to read offline. Consult your site's Web master about creating a single-file version of the document to optimize printing.

@

DIGITAL TIPS: Using PDF Files

Converting documents such as reports, articles, and brochures to PDF files allows you to retain the identical look of the printed documents. The PDF pages will display on-screen exactly as they appear on the printed page. Readers can read the document online, download and save it, or print it in whole or in part. For more on this topic, see <bedfordstmartins.com/writingthatworks> and select *Digital Tips*, "Using PDF Files."

Protecting the Privacy of Your Users

You may find it necessary to collect user information at your site. You may ask users, for example, to respond to a questionnaire that you've posted, to subscribe to a service, to sign up for a newsletter or special offer, to comment on a document, or to give you general feedback about your page. Many users also submit unsolicited e-mail questions to Web sites about some aspect of the site. Be aware that most Internet users wish to have information about themselves—name, residential and e-mail addresses, phone number, credit-card number, personal opinions, and the like—kept confidential. In response to this concern, all reputable Web sites post a privacy notice—usually on the homepage—informing users about how it intends to handle the solicited and unsolicited information from individuals received at the site.

If you plan to collect such information on your page or if your page has a <u>Contact Us</u> link, ask the site Web master to put a link on your page to the site-wide privacy statement. As an example, the privacy policy in Figure 15–6, excerpted from the NRC's Web site, appears on its homepage (<www.nrc.gov>) and other locations throughout the site where the public can contact or submit information to the agency.

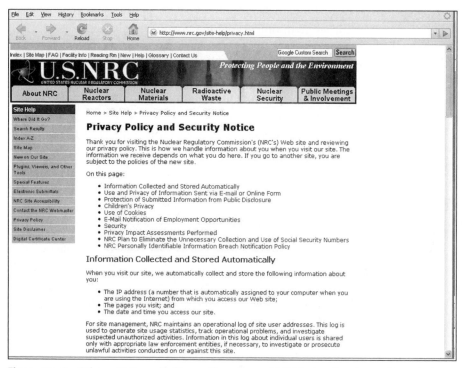

Figure 15–6   Privacy Statement (Excerpt).   *Source:* U.S. Nuclear Regulatory Commission, <www.nrc.gov>.

Some corporate privacy statements describe their policy for sharing user information, such as subscriber lists, with third parties for marketing purposes. Informing users of this practice is both candid and ethical. These sites often give users the opportunity to refuse permission to use their addresses for marketing, as in the following example:

▶ **Opt Out Choice**
Our users are given the opportunity to "opt out" of having their information used for purposes not directly related to our site at the point where we ask for the information. For example, our order form has an "opt out" mechanism so that users who buy a product from us but don't want any marketing material can keep their e-mail address off our lists.

Although important to keep confidential, user information (search patterns, content feedback, questions about goods and services) is a valuable source of information about the public's use of a site. The Web server, for example, can log data on site usage (number of users accessing a page, duration of their stay, etc.). This and other kinds of feedback are collected and compiled anonymously and can be used to make helpful revisions to your content.

CONSIDERING AUDIENCE AND PURPOSE

Protecting the Privacy of Your Users

- Provide users with a link to the site's privacy statement, particularly if you solicit comments or provide an e-mail link for unsolicited comments.
- Inform users if you intend to use their information for marketing or if you intend to share their information with third parties.
- Give visitors the option of refusing permission to have their information used for marketing.

Documenting Sources of Information

As with print publications, you must document and acknowledge outside sources of information or of help received—text, images, streaming video, and other multimedia material. If any of this source material is copyrighted, you must seek prior approval before using it. Likewise, you may use material in the public domain and, with some limitations, content that is licensed under Creative Commons, as described at <http://creativecommons.org/about/>. Documenting sources at your site has at least two major advantages: (1) It discloses where you obtained your information, thereby bolstering the site's credibility, and (2) it allows users to locate that source, if necessary. The site should also document information in the public domain, such as publications and Web sites of the federal government.

Site credibility is further enhanced by acknowledging help received in the creation or review of content at the site. Note the passage in the third paragraph of the Weight-Control Information Network of NIH's Web site, shown in Figure 15–7.

◆ *For guidance on the use and documentation of source material, including electronic information, see Chapter 6, Researching Your Subject.*

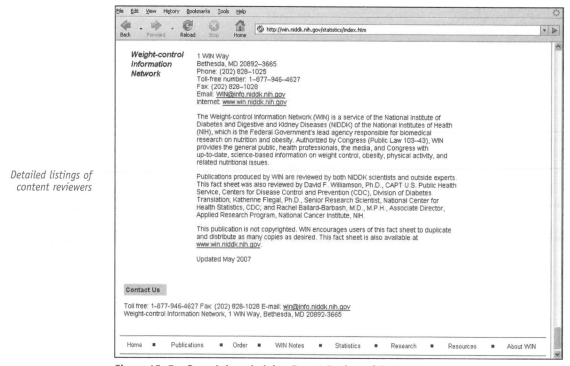

Detailed listings of content reviewers

Figure 15–7   Page Acknowledging Expert Review of Content.   *Source:* National Institutes of Health, <www.nih.gov>.

These acknowledgments attest to the accuracy, quality, and objectivity of the information provided.

■ Contributing to Collaborative and Multimedia Content

A growing number of Web genres have become the focus of social and workplace interaction for the public and special-interest users. They include distinct Web genres, like blogs, that encourage the exchange of ideas and opinions among users interested in consumer goods, politics, technology, job opportunities, sports, and much more. They also include Web-based platforms, like wikis, that enable writers to collaborate on a writing project. The best-known example of a wiki is the online encyclopedia Wikipedia. FAQs (frequently asked questions), although not unique to Web writing, have become a popular feature of corporate and organizational Web sites. By highlighting the information most commonly sought by users of an organization's products and services, FAQs save time and frustration for site users. Podcasting, a Web-based multimedia genre, is another important means of distributing a variety of workplace, educational, medical, and leisure-pursuit information to interested audiences.

Blogs

A blog (short for "Web log") is a Web-based journal for posting opinions, information, and responses to other bloggers on subjects of mutual interest to them. Blog sites may also include links to relevant Web sites or post documents and audiovisual files. Blog entries are displayed in reverse chronological order with the most recent post first. The usefulness of a blog stems in large part from the immediate interactivity it offers target audiences. That is, anyone can submit a comment or question to a blog and have the organizational sponsor or other interested bloggers respond to it. All these postings are displayed and become part of on ongoing "conversation" about a topic. And because it is an ongoing activity, readers who follow blogs expect the postings to be useful and to appear routinely. So posting blog entries and keeping them current requires a substantial commitment of time and effort. Sporadic postings and dated information will hurt you and your organization's credibility.

Organizational Blogs

Companies, local governments, and nonprofit organizations create blogs to help meet such goals as attracting and retaining clients or customers: promoting and obtaining feedback on their products and services; and even developing a sense of community among their customers, employees, citizens, and others. Unlike Web sites, which usually present a formal perspective on an organization, blogs provide an informal and interactive forum for organizations to communicate directly with a target audience. Organizations can create both external and internal blogs.

External blogs are publicly available on the Internet both for an organization's customers or clients and for executives, spokespeople, or employees to share their views. Blogs help build credibility for an organization because customers know they can "chat" with an organization's representative and exchange current information instead of relying on information in published documents and on Web sites. Tesla Motors, for example, has an external blog where company marketing and engineering officials present information about their electric car as well as read and respond to the opinions from bloggers about the car. Figure 15–8 shows a Tesla Motors blog by its chief technical officer.

Internal blogs are usually created for employees and can be accessed only through the organization's intranet site. Such internal blogs may serve as newsletters and help achieve the following organizational goals:

- Provide opportunities for employees to discuss issues or concerns
- Encourage employee participation in upcoming events or initiatives
- Share employee and community news, such as promotions, wedding and birth announcements, community outreach activities, and more

Figure 15–8   Corporate Blog

Writing for Organizational Blogs

Write blog entries in an informal, conversational style—use contractions, the second person (you), and the active voice.

▷   Check out the latest concept for our new dashboards—we've added more space. Is the console large enough to hold your Starbucks and iPod? Let us know what you think.

Keep your sentences and paragraphs short, as with other Web writing. Your readers will appreciate short entries that help them find relevant information quickly. Use bulleted lists, italics, and other layout-and-design elements, such as boldface and white space, to organize contents. Keep headlines short and direct to catch attention and increase the blog's visual appeal and readability. Before publishing, proofread your entry carefully for grammar, spelling and typos, and formatting errors.

Enhance the value of the site by linking to other sites that post related information, documents, and audiovisual and other interactive files. And establish your credibility by identifying the sources of your ideas and quotations.

The Wall Street Journal

▶   A ~~major newspaper~~ reported today that our company is in merger talks with Acme
       ^

Infrastructure, Inc.

ETHICS NOTE

Because organizations expect employees to assume full responsibility for the content they post on a company blog, you must maintain high ethical standards.

- Do not post information that is confidential, proprietary, or sensitive to your employer.
- Do not attack competitors or other individuals (such as employees, other bloggers, or shareholders).
- Do not post content that is profane, libelous, or harassing, or that violates the privacy of others.
- Do not plagiarize. Obtain permission, as needed, for any material that is protected by copyright, and cite your sources.
- Obtain your supervisor's permission before publishing to ensure that the content, tone, and Web links are compatible with organizational policy.

Tagging Blog Postings

Consider using "tags" at your site. Tags are keywords that identify the subject of each blog post. They are usually listed following the blog post and link to all other posts on that topic. The tags listed in Figure 15–9 on page 562 indicate popular topics for postings at a blog site discussing solar-powered wireless Internet access in San Francisco.

Tags are important for two reasons. (1) Tags permit users to retrieve by topic the postings not visible on the homepage. Older blog postings are usually filed so that only recent posts appear on the homepage. (2) Tags can be picked up by search engines and social-networking bookmarking sites such as <del.icio.us>. Tagging allows your site to become "visible" to external users seeking information discussed at your site's blog.

Many blogs allow users to add tags. Called a "folksonomy," user-generated tags can broaden the site's keywords and benefit both routine visitors and search-engine effectiveness. The disadvantages of user-generated tags, however, include misspelled words and arbitrary terms that can reduce the site's "visibility" to search engines.

First entry by blog sponsor on that date

Tags link to other blog posts on that topic for future searches

Figure 15-9   Blog Post Showing Keyword Tags

Wikis

Wikis are Web sites that host collaborative writing projects. They allow users to edit or comment on the content and organization of a document. Wikis may be used for public-access collaborative reference works (like Wikipedia) or for Internet-only sites maintained by a company. Users become Web authors by using the system's writing and editing software to post comments or questions to drafts of existing documents. These features are especially useful for a group of collaborators developing a report or paper. Wiki sites also track all edits so that users can see who revised what. Wikis differ from blogs in that they permit all users to both change and comment on content (like Wikipedia), whereas blogs permit users only to comment on the content posted by the site's author.

In the workplace, wikis can be used for a variety of purposes, including coauthoring and co-editing documents, sharing and distributing information, managing projects, and providing communication spaces for clients and customers. They are especially helpful when collaborators are geographically separated, and they simplify the process of tracking multiple versions of a draft because the system displays all changes to it by author and date.

ON THE WEB

For more detailed advice on creating and editing documents in a wiki, go to bedfordstmartins.com/writingthatworks and select *Digital Tips*, "Using Wikis for Collaborative Work."

◆ *For additional information about using wikis for collaborative writing, see pages 132–133 in Chapter 5, Collaborative Writing.*

Podcasts

Podcasts are audio files about a specific topic that are created in .mp3 format for distribution over the Internet. They can be downloaded for listening onto a computer, an MP3 player, or an iPod. One main advantage of podcasts is that the audience can play them when and where they wish—their home or office computer or on an MP3 player anywhere else. Video podcasts, possible with some MP3 players, are also becoming an ideal means of distributing how-to information.

Podcasts support many valuable functions in educational and workplace settings. Educators use them to distribute lectures, class assignments, foreign-language lessons, and demonstrations. Students in turn can podcast presentations, class diaries, and interviews, to cite a few examples of their use. Audio podcasts can be augmented with such visual elements as presentation slides and videos.

With their flexible audiovisual capability and their portability, podcasts are an increasingly popular workplace medium to distribute product information to customers and clients as well as technical how-to information to employees at remote work sites.

When creating a podcast, use some of the same techniques important to a successful presentation. Begin by preparing the script: Analyze the audience; gather and organize the information; and note where to integrate visuals, including videos. Rehearse your delivery, recording it for playback and analysis. Is your voice clear? Is your tone enthusiastic? sincere? credible? Then record the audio for posting.

ON THE WEB

For a sampling of podcast tutorials on the Internet, go to Chapter 15, bedfordstmartins.com/writingthatworks

◆ *For detailed guidance in preparing and delivering a presentation, see pages 499–516 in Chapter 14, Giving Presentations and Conducting Meetings.*

FAQs (Frequently Asked Questions)

A list of frequently asked questions and their answers provides information that readers would likely ask about products, services, or other information presented on a Web site or in customer-oriented brochures or instructions. Presenting commonly sought information in one place, FAQs save readers from searching through an entire Web site or document to find what they need.

A good FAQ list helps a company or an organization spend less time answering phone calls and e-mail questions. It can also help create a positive impression with customers because it acknowledges that their time is valuable. Note, however, that an FAQ list is no substitute for solving problems with a product or service.

ETHICS NOTE

If customers are experiencing numerous problems because of a faulty product design or programming flaw, you need to work with the company's product developers to correct the problem rather than try to skirt it with an FAQ list.

Questions to Include

Develop the list of questions and their answers by brainstorming with colleagues who regularly are in contact with customers. They are in the best position to know what customers ask. Study other FAQ lists your customers might review for products or services. Can you find the answers quickly, or must you scroll through many pages to find them? Consider how the questions are organized: Are they separated into logical categories or listed in random order? Is it easy to differentiate the question from the answer? Do the answers provide too much or too little information?[5] For Web FAQ lists, do the answers link to useful content at other sites?

List your questions in decreasing order of importance so that readers can obtain the most important information first. If you have a number of questions that are related to a specific topic, group them into categories and identify each category with a heading. You could also create a table of contents for the FAQ to help readers locate topics relevant to their interests.

Placement

Locate your FAQ list for ease of reader access. For Web sites, the FAQ page is usually linked from the homepage either in a directory or with a text link for easy access. The site Web master will provide guidance for site placement. In printed documents, such as brochures, FAQs are often highlighted and placed on a separate page following the main body.

---

[5]For examples of FAQs, search with QueryCat at <querycat.com>, which offers the "largest database of frequently asked questions."

WRITER'S CHECKLIST
Developing FAQs

✔ *Focus on your reader.* Write your questions and answers from a "you" point of view and use a positive, conversational tone.

✔ *Divide long FAQ lists.* Group related questions under topic headings. For long on-line FAQ lists, consider including only questions with links to separate pages, each containing an individual question and answer.

✔ *Distinguish questions from answers.* Use boldface for questions and use white space to separate questions from answers. Minimize use of multiple colors, italics, or other formatting styles that can make the list difficult to read at a glance.

✔ *Keep questions and answers concise.* If a question has a long answer, add a link to a separate Web page or refer to an appropriate page number in a printed document.

✔ *Keep the list updated.* Review and update FAQ lists at least monthly—or more frequently if your content changes often. Make it possible for your customers to submit questions they would like to see added to the FAQ list.

CHAPTER 15 SUMMARY: WRITING FOR THE WEB

Use the following revision checklist to make sure that content you develop or adapt for the Web is crafted for ease of reading by site visitors and is accessible to people with disabilities as well as to international users.

▪ Plan, organize, and write Web content that can be grasped quickly, using the following techniques:

- Use the inverted-pyramid method to organize content top down so that key points and conclusions appear first.

- Develop content that is accurate, backed by supporting evidence, and expressed in a tone appropriate for your audience.

- Write concisely and use plain-language principles consistent with your content.

- Break up dense blocks of text into smaller paragraph-length passages that are sequenced by the inverted-pyramid method.

- Expand access to your information by hyperlinking it to content at your or other Web sites.

▪ Augment access to your content using the following highlighting techniques:

- Introduce topics with headings and subheadings to signal the shift from one topic to another.

- Use bulleted and numbered lists to further break up dense blocks of text and focus reader attention on relevant points.

- Use directional cues appropriate to a Web page and avoid those that make sense only in printed material.

- Highlight introductory passages with key terms and concepts that allow search engines to locate your content.

- Select graphics pertinent to your audience and purpose, and optimize them for quick access.
- Choose type sizes and fonts to enhance legibility.
- Limit line length to promote ease of scanning.

■ Provide for the special needs of people with disabilities and international site visitors by adhering to the following guidelines:

- Create content compatible with adaptive technologies.
- Use language, units of measurement, and graphics that are consistent with the practices of international and U.S. site visitors.
- Be mindful of modem-only access in many parts of the world and work with the site Web master to tailor graphic and audiovisual content accordingly.

■ Submit a previously published document to a Web site according to the following guidelines:

- Submit the document in the most suitable file format for the site.
- Inform site users if the Web version is abridged or otherwise differs from the printed version.
- Obtain prior permission to publish works that contain copyrighted text or graphics.
- Examine the document on an internal Web server for accuracy and effectiveness before it is posted for public access.
- For a long document, post a single file version for users wishing to print the document.

■ Inform site users of how or whether their privacy is protected if they submit solicited or unsolicited information to you.

■ Give credit to outside sources of content at your site, including approval to use copyrighted material.

When creating a blog, adhere to the following guidelines:

■ Write in a conversational tone.

■ Keep entries short and focused on the topic.

■ Link to important topic-related information.

■ Identify information sources to enhance site credibility.

■ Tag blog postings to ease user and search-engine access to topical content.

■ Ensure that organizational postings are in line with organizational norms, values, and policies.

Consider using a wiki for a collaborative project in the following situations:

■ There are several content providers or reviewers.

■ Some or all collaborators are geographically separated.

■ Tracking multiple versions of a document draft is important.

Consider creating a podcast in the following situations:

■ The information is suitable to audio or audiovisual treatment.

■ The information is intended for an audience in need of a how-to presentation in a portable format.

Use the following guidelines when creating and posting an FAQ list:

■ Develop questions based on customer and client concerns.

ON THE WEB

For an online quiz on writing for the Web, go to Chapter 15, bedfordstmartins.com/ writingthatworks

■ Organize questions in a pattern logical to the topic, putting the most important concerns before secondary concerns.

■ Use plain language—answers are of no value if they cannot be understood.

■ Exercises

1. Bring in a report, a research paper, or an essay written for another course and rework it so that it is appropriately chunked for online reading. Use appropriate captions and headings.

2. Review the reworked research paper or essay that you prepared for Exercise 1 and note places where you could link elements in your text to existing Web sites. Find Web sites to link to and list them on a separate page.

3. As your instructor directs, post a report, a research paper, an essay, or another text you have already written to your personal or class Web site. (Review Repurposing Existing Content on pages 554–555 before you begin.) You can also use your text from Exercise 1.

4. Using this textbook (or a textbook from another class that you are taking) as a model, analyze the use of headings, subheadings, white space, models and examples, visuals, and so on. Note the consistency in the use of these and other textual elements. Do they invite the reader to continue to read from section to section and chapter to chapter? Present your findings to the class.

5. Imagine that you are a writer who wants to publish an online book because it is much less expensive to present your book in a PDF file and let readers print the pages than it is to print a hard-copy book yourself. Create an idea for your book, then create the specifications for the design of the pages, including font sizes, heading styles, line width, and so on. Use your findings from Exercise 4 to help in your design choices.

6. For Collaborative Classroom Project 2 in Chapter 8, you created an information sheet that explains to donors how to deduct a car donation to a local nonprofit organization on their taxes. Revise this information sheet into content to be posted on the nonprofit organization's Web site. Remember that tax information is often very wordy and difficult to follow, so you will need to be strategic about presenting it online. Review the Highlighting Information checklist on page 552 before you begin.

7. Many companies have intranets that they use to share information with employees as well as selected vendors and clients. For Exercise 9 in Chapter 12, you were asked to write a set of instructions to help supermarket managers assist customers who use self-checkout systems. Rework those instructions for uploading to the system manufacturer's intranet site. Consider adding links as well as highlighting techniques, like directional cues.

8. For Research Project 4 in Chapter 13, you were asked to research and apply for a grant to fund an Adult Basic Education program at your local county jail. Assume

that your organization received the grant. Using the example of the press release in this chapter as a model (Figure 15–2), write a press release that announces your organization's success in obtaining the grant and telling readers how the funds will be used to further the organization's mission. Use the inverted-pyramid structure explained on pages 540–541.

ON THE WEB

For more collaborative classroom projects, go to Chapter 15, bedfordstmartins.com/ writingthatworks

■ Collaborative Classroom Projects

1. In groups of three or four students who share your major, bring to class information from three Web sites that you might use to research a career of your choice. Print out relevant pages from each site and together review the guidelines in this chapter for documenting sources of information. Draft a list of questions to consider when evaluating online text as a research resource specific to your field. Evaluate and compare each of the sites that your group members have found and decide which sites would be the most reliable for career research. Write a brief group summary of your findings to share with the class.

2. Assume that you and two other students are consultants who work with various groups who represent disabled people. One of your tasks is to write letters to companies whose Web sites do not adhere to Web-accessibility standards, explaining that because disabled customers cannot use their sites, the companies are losing potential business.

   Before the next class, decide on a type of company to investigate (for example, insurance companies, movie theaters, grocery stores, and so on), then run several of the companies' Web sites through a Web-accessibility tool at <www.w3 .org/WAI/ER/tools/complete> (you will need to know their URLs). Print the results and bring them to class. As a group, analyze your findings, looking closely at quality and accessibility. Which of these companies would you write to in order to explain Web-site accessibility? What changes would you suggest be made to the site and why?

ON THE WEB

For extra research projects, go to Chapter 15, bedfordstmartins .com/writingthatworks

■ Research Projects

1. For your major department's Web site, write an online article that describes five databases to which your college library has access that are pertinent to your field of study.

2. For Exercise 2 in Chapter 10 and Research Project 2 in Chapter 13, you prepared reports about back injuries and worker's compensation at the warehouse of a large online retailer and proposed ways to improve employee safety. Now assume that you work for the Human Resources Department of this company and you want to create a page for the company intranet to explain safe lifting procedures.

   a. Begin by researching ways to safely lift heavy objects. Remember that you will need to cite your sources. (You may use any research you've already completed as a starting point.) You also want to consider what sources (if any) you might link to from your page.

b. Consider your audience for this page: You may have workers who speak English as a second language or who have low literacy skills, for example. It may be prudent to use more graphics than text. (Review Chapter 7, Designing Effective Documents and Visuals.) Remember that many graphics on the Web are copyrighted: Be sure to determine if you need permission before cutting and pasting any images into your document.

c. Draft your page either in hard copy (through thumbnail sketches) or in a Web-site design program if you have access to one. Then, with a classmate, conduct a usability test (see Chapter 12, Writing Instructions) of your instructions. Take any comments regarding the page layout into consideration as well.

d. Finish your page.

3. On the Web, you can find several sites that explain how things work. (One excellent resource is <www.howstuffworks.com>.) Review the guidelines in this chapter for creating documents and integrating visuals, then

a. Choose an electronic object, such as a cell phone or digital camera, and explore how it works. Print the explanation of how the object works and evaluate both the explanation and the Web page, according to the criteria described in this chapter.

b. Mark up the Web-page layout and the explanation, indicating any changes you would make to improve its design. You may focus on one aspect of the explanation, such as its use of chunking, or many aspects. Feel free to sketch out your ideas.

c. Write a memo to your instructor in which you explain what does and does not work for the original design of the Web page and the explanation, supporting your ideas with information in this chapter. Specify how your changes would improve the document's design. Attach to your memo the marked-up printout of the explanation and any sketches you've created.

4. Many local convention and visitors-bureau sites describe local attractions, provide listings of educational institutions in the area, recommend shopping and art areas, and so on. Go to such a Web site and analyze the material already on the site. Then get the name and e-mail address of the site's Web master and write a letter to that person with ideas for stories on colorful characters or events or places in the city that would be relevant for that site.

16 Finding the Right Job

AT A GLANCE: The Job Hunt

The search for a job can be logically divided into five steps, each of which is covered in this chapter:

- Determining the best job for you / 571
- Preparing an effective résumé / 578
- Writing an effective letter of application / 602
- Doing well in the interview / 609
- Sending follow-up correspondence / 613
- Sending a resignation letter or memo / 615

You have enviable advantages as you look for a job. You've prepared for the world of work with an education, training, and experience. You have desirable skills to offer—some directly applicable to a specific job, others more general that are applicable regardless of the job. (The writing skills acquired in this and other classes are also applicable across a broad range of occupations. The Writing @ Work portfolio on pages 261–272 illustrates how writing plays an important role in a wide variety of professions.) Your awards, honors, extracurricular activities, and life experiences all demonstrate these broadly applicable abilities and your willingness to take on challenging work—in an office, a laboratory, a hospital, a community clinic, an industrial site, or a wilderness area.

Whether you are applying for your first professional job, changing jobs, or returning to the job market after an absence, you'll need to be systematic and persistent in your job search. Occasionally a desirable job comes your way without much effort, but the odds are against that happening. As well prepared as you may be, you need to plan your job search carefully. The detailed guidance in this chapter will increase your chances of translating your skills into a successful job search.

Before you begin your search for a job, do some serious thinking about your future. Decide first what you would most like to be doing now. Then think about the kind of work you'd like to be doing two years from now and five years from now. Once you have established your goals, you can begin your job hunt with greater confidence because you'll have a better idea of what kind of position you are looking for and in what companies or other organizations you are most likely to find that position.

VOICES IN THE WORKPLACE

Knowing Your Audience and Purpose

Sherri Pfenning, senior career counselor at the University of Wisconsin–Milwaukee Career Development Center, stresses the importance of honing your résumé for the right audience and purpose: "Your résumé is a commercial, just like the commercials you see on TV or anywhere else. For a commercial to be successful, the creator has to know both the product and the audience inside out. Advertisers adapt product language and packaging to successfully attract the interest of different audiences. Likewise, you need to know what you are trying to sell with your résumé, what your audience is buying, and how to adapt the language of your résumé regarding your skills and qualities to attract the interest of different employer groups you approach."

Determining the Best Job for You

Begin by assessing your skills, interests, and abilities. Next, consider your career goals and values. Ask yourself questions like the following: What courses have I most enjoyed? Does helping others interest me? How important are career stability and a certain standard of living? Where do I want to live? Do I prefer working independently or collaboratively?[1]

Once you've reflected on and brainstormed about the type of work that's right for you, a number of sources can help you locate the job you want:

- Networking
- Campus career services
- Web resources
- Advertisements
- Trade and professional journal listings
- Private and temporary employment agencies
- Internships
- Government employment agencies
- Letters of inquiry and informational interviews

Finding the job that's right for you may take many months. If you face unemployment during this period, consider working for a temporary employment agency, as described on page 575.

ON THE WEB

For more advice on finding the right job, go to Chapter 16, bedfordstmartins.com/writingthatworks

◆ Brainstorming is discussed on pages 9–10 in Chapter 1, Assessing Audience and Purpose.

---

[1]A good source for stimulating your thinking is the most recent edition of *What Color Is Your Parachute? A Practical Manual for Job-Hunters & Career Changers* by Richard Nelson Bolles, published by Ten Speed Press and updated annually.

Networking

Networking is communicating with people who might provide useful advice about your intended career or connect you with potential employers. They may be people already working in your chosen field, contacts in professional organizations and volunteer groups, professors and former employers, family members, friends, or neighbors; any of them might direct you to exactly the job lead you need. Use your contacts to expand your network of contacts. Consider that of all open positions, an estimated 80 percent are filled through networking.[2] Networking frequently takes place online too, via e-mail, discussion groups, and social-networking Web sites; see "Web Resources" below for more information.

Campus Career Services

Visiting your school's career center—and working with a counselor who understands your strengths and interests—is a great way to begin your job search. Career centers often hold job fairs and workshops on such topics as preparing your résumé for your particular field and doing well in an interview; they also offer other job-finding resources on their Web sites. In addition, recruiters from business, industry, and government often visit college job-placement offices to interview prospective employees. Recruiters will also keep your school's career counselors aware of current employment needs and current job openings. Career counselors can not only help you in the brainstorming phase of your career selection but also put you in touch with the best, most current resources—identifying where to begin your search and saving you time.

Web Resources

Using the Internet can enhance your job search in a number of ways. In addition to providing access to job listings in newspapers and professional journals, the Web provides a wealth of sites that give advice about careers, job seeking, and résumé preparation; several sites make it possible to search job listings, post your résumé, and apply for positions confidentially. Social networking sites are also growing in importance for job-search and career-networking opportunities; although many students regularly use social-networking sites for friendships and casual communication, don't overlook their value during the job search. The following sites include job-search and career-networking guidance as well as job listings.

- America's Job Bank at <www.ajb.dni.us>
  Sponsored by the U.S. Department of Labor, America's Job Bank is a comprehensive listing of job postings categorized by state. It also contains

---

[2]From JobStar Central, an online job-search guide hosted by the *Wall Street Journal* at <http://jobstar.org>.

such information as salary and demographic employment profiles for job seekers interested in relocating to another region.

- Monster at <www.monster.com>
  One of the best-known sites, Monster.com contains such information as career advice and job postings (including international listings). Specialized pages cater to the interests of occupational groups.

- CollegeGrad.com at <www.collegegrad.com>
  CollegeGrad.com is a site for the entry-level job seeker. It has user-friendly design links to sections on résumés, cover letters, interviews, and negotiations; explains what to do when you get an offer; and posts an E-Zine for job hunters.

- Riley Guide: Employment Opportunities and Job Resources on the Internet at <www.rileyguide.com>
  The Riley Guide contains introductions and annotated links to resources by career field, employer type, and location. It also has sections on résumé preparation and online recruiting.

- What Color Is Your Parachute? JobHuntersBible.com at <www.jobhuntersbible.com>
  What Color Is Your Parachute? is a site for job seekers and career changers based on the best-selling book of the same name by Richard N. Bolles. It provides such resources as an interactive test for career counseling, tips for using the Internet, tips for preparing an effective résumé, and links to job postings and other useful sites.

- LinkedIn at <www.linkedin.com>
  This site combines job-search and business networking opportunities for professionals. Site users can post a professional profile of accomplishments that can be accessed by potential employers, clients, and service providers. The profile forms the hub of a network of trusted contacts who, in turn, bring their own trusted connections so that profiles may be linked to hundreds of contacts with shared career interests and needs. Such social-networking sites allow users to expand their contact base considerably, perhaps connecting with colleagues or friends of friends in a chosen field of interest. The site also posts job listings.

In addition to these resources, always visit the Web sites of companies you are interested in. Not only do they help you learn about the company's background and current activities, but most corporate Web sites also list job openings, provide instructions for applicants, and offer other information, such as descriptions of employee benefits. Many Web sites include an option that allows you to e-mail your cover letter and résumé directly to the appropriate department or person.

Also consider exploring Internet discussion groups and blogs that relate to your career interests. These sites can provide a useful way to keep up with the trends in your profession and with general employment conditions over time—

ON THE WEB

For job-hunting tips, sample documents, and links to these and several other job-search sites, go to **bedfordstmartins.com/ writingthatworks** and select *Finding an Internship or Job* and *Web Links.*

◆ *See also pages 166–171 in Chapter 6, Researching Your Subject.*

◆ *Before you create your own Web site, see the introductory material on pages 540–557 in Chapter 15, Writing for the Web.*

and some also post job openings that may be appropriate for you. One resource for finding professional discussion groups is Google Groups, organized by subject and available at <http://groups.google.com>. A topical listing of blogs can be found at <http://technorati.com>.

Finally, consider posting your résumé on your personal Web site. Although posting your résumé on an employment database will undoubtedly attract more potential employers, and often be targeted for a specific job, including your résumé on your own site has benefits. For example, you might provide a link to your site in e-mail correspondence or provide your Web site's URL in an inquiry letter to a prospective employer. If you use a personal Web site, however, it should contain only material that would be of interest to prospective employers, such as examples of your work, awards, and other professional items. If you decide to post your résumé on the Web, keep in mind the advice regarding electronic résumés on pages 587–592.

Employment specialists suggest that you spend time on the Web later in the evening or very early in the morning so that you can focus on in-person contacts during working hours.

ETHICS NOTE

Many employers now routinely check the Web (including personal sites, blogs, and social-networking sites such as Facebook and Friendster) for materials posted by and about job candidates and current employees. Remember that your Web presence is available for anybody to see and that you must maintain a professional demeanor when searching for a job. Be very careful that you do not post any comments, photographs, videos, or links that a potential employer may find objectionable or inappropriate. Even seemingly harmless materials, such as pictures from a party or expressions of support for a particular sports team, could compromise your chances of being considered for employment.

Advertisements

In addition to posting job openings at their Web sites, many employers advertise in the classified sections of print and online newspapers as well as on general-purpose classified-ad sites such as Craigslist at <http://craigslist.org>. Occasionally, newspapers print special supplements that provide valuable information on résumé preparation, job fairs, and other facets of the job market. Check the Sunday editions or help-wanted Web pages of major newspapers for the widest selection of employment listings. Keep in mind that a position may be listed under various classifications. A clinical medical technologist seeking a job, for example, might find the specialty listed under "Medical Technologist," "Clinical Medical Technologist," or "Laboratory Technologist." Depending on a hospital's or a pathologist's needs, the listing could be even more specific, such as "Blood Bank Technologist" or "Hematology Technologist." So try to read or search all areas that may be pertinent to your interests.

As you read the ads, take notes on such things as salary ranges, job locations, job duties and responsibilities, and even the terminology used in the ads to describe the work. A knowledge of the words and expressions that are generally used to describe a particular type of work can be helpful when you prepare your résumé and letters of application. Using the appropriate terminology is especially important for résumés that you submit electronically. (See "Electronic Résumés" on pages 587–592.)

Trade and Professional Journal Listings

In many industries, trade and professional associations publish periodicals of interest to people working in specific occupations. Such periodicals (print and online) often contain job listings. If you were seeking a job in forestry, for example, you could check the job listings in the *Journal of Forestry*, published by the Society of American Foresters. To learn about the trade or professional associations for your occupation, consult resources on the Web, such as Google's *Directory of Professional Organizations*, or online resources offered by your library or campus career office. You may also consult the following references at a library: *Encyclopedia of Associations*, *Encyclopedia of Business Information Sources*, and *National Directory of Employment Services*.

◆ *See also pages 158–166 in Chapter 6, Researching Your Subject.*

ON THE WEB

For access to professional organizations and publications, go to Chapter 16, bedfordstmartins.com/ writingthatworks

Private and Temporary Employment Agencies

Private employment agencies are organizations in business to help people find jobs—for a fee. Reputable agencies provide you with job leads, help you organize your job search, and supply information on companies doing the hiring.

Choose a private employment agency carefully, preferably through a personal recommendation. Some are very well established and reputable; others are not. Check with your local Better Business Bureau and with friends, acquaintances, or your school's career office before you sign an agreement with a private employment agency. Before signing a contract, be sure you understand who is paying the agency's fee. Often the employer pays the agency's fee; however, if you have to pay, make sure you know exactly how much. As with any written agreement, read the fine print carefully.

If you are interested in—but not certain about—a professional area, consider working in that area as a temporary or part-time employee. A temporary placement agency could match you with a temporary job in your field, lasting anywhere from a few days to six months or longer. Even as a short-term member of a support staff, you can gain valuable experience that can help you decide whether a particular profession is right for you. Temporary work in a professional area will also build your network of contacts while you continue your job search. Finally, temporary work may lead to a permanent position; if you prove to your manager and colleagues that you are serious about the industry and an asset to their department, you may be in a good position if a permanent job opens up.

ON THE WEB

For access to employment agencies approved by the Better Business Bureau, go to Chapter 16, bedfordstmartins.com/ writingthatworks

Internships

As you evaluate job options, consider taking an internship. An entry-level position lasting anywhere from six weeks to an entire semester, an internship provides you with the opportunity to gain experience in a field of your choice. These positions offer you a variety of career benefits by allowing you to do the following:

- Try a position without making a permanent commitment.
- Explore a field to clarify your career goals while getting on-the-job experience.
- Develop skills and gain experience in a new field or industry.
- Evaluate a prospective employer or firm.
- Acquire a mentor in the workplace.
- Benefit from networking contacts for future job opportunities.
- Gain access to professional references.
- Be eligible for a job offer based on the employer's satisfaction with your work.

Almost all types of workplace organizations have internship programs: companies; law firms; nonprofit organizations (such as educational institutions, public interest groups, museums, foundations, political parties, think tanks, and research facilities); local, state, and federal government agencies; and more. The experience you gain will depend on the type of organization you join. Small organizations may expose you to a great variety of tasks; larger organizations may rotate participants through several departments or positions. Although many firms offer salaries or stipends, some, like nonprofit organizations, may not.

During your internship, keep a journal of tasks performed and job responsibilities that you can include in your résumé or portfolio. You may have created a brochure, designed or posted content to a Web site, created a poster, input data to a spreadsheet or database, used your computer skills to troubleshoot problems for the office, tracked and reported on industry trends, or organized a conference. Whatever the task, be sure to make note of it. These accomplishments are of interest to prospective employers.

To locate internship opportunities, begin with your Career Office on campus. That office posts such opportunities on its Web site. If location is important, the listings will yield the most positions in the vicinity of your campus. Otherwise, simply typing "internship opportunities" into an Internet search engine will yield hundreds of internship opportunities for all types of organizations in the United States and abroad.

Government Employment Services

Local, state, and federal government agencies offer many employment services. Local government agencies are listed in telephone and Web directories under the name of your city, county, or state. For detailed information on the trends of over 250 occupations, see the most recent edition of the *Occupational Outlook Handbook*, published by the U.S. Department of Labor at <http://bls.gov/OCO>. For information about jobs with the federal government, contact the U.S. Office of Personnel Management at <http://usajobs.opm.gov/>.

ON THE WEB

For access to government employment resources, go to Chapter 16, bedfordstmartins .com/writingthatworks

Letters of Inquiry and Informational Interviews

If you would like to work for a particular firm, write and ask whether it has any openings for people with your qualifications. Normally, you should send the letter either to the director of human resources or to the department head; for a small firm, however, you may write to the head of the firm. Your letter should present a general summary of your employment background or training. (See Writing an Effective Letter of Application on pages 602–608.)

In your letter of inquiry, ask if you can meet with someone for an informational interview and whether you may bring your résumé with you. Some organizations welcome the opportunity to talk with prospective employees, even when they have no immediate job openings. It's a way for them to assess fresh talent, promote their firm, and expand their file of eligible prospects. You could also request an informational interview from one of your networking contacts. Although the interview is informal, dress appropriately and do some homework beforehand: What's the firm's core business or mission and its size? Does the firm plan to expand? (Review the list of topics discussed in Doing Well in the Interview on pages 609–612.) Use the interview as an opportunity to practice your interview skills, to learn about accepted workplace standards, and to gain insight into the organization's expectations for prospective employees.

Job-Search Record Keeping

As you pursue a job, keep a paper or an electronic record of your search to track your progress. Include copies of job ads, the dates they were published, the period during which applications will be accepted, copies of application letters, versions of your résumé (if you revised it for specific jobs), notes requesting interviews, and the names of important contacts. Keep the contact information for interviews and the dates they were held: who, what, when, and where. Also note salient facts about interviews, such as type of work, salary offers, promotion potential, benefits, and assistance with student loans. Use these records to compare job options and as a reminder for any follow-up questions.

■ Preparing an Effective Résumé

A résumé is a summary of your qualifications and your main tool for finding a job.[3] Generally limited to one page (or two if you have a great deal of experience), your résumé itemizes the qualifications that you can mention only briefly in your application letter. The information in your résumé is key to helping employers decide whether to contact you for a personal interview. It can also serve as the source for specific questions asked during an interview.

Because résumés form the basis for a potential employer's first impression, make sure that yours is well organized, carefully designed, consistently formatted, easy to read, and free of errors. Keep the following guidelines in mind.

- Consider first an organization that highlights your strengths and fits your goals, as suggested by the examples shown in this chapter.
- Experiment to determine a layout and design that is attractive and uncluttered.
- Be consistent. Be sure to use, for example, the same date formats (5/2010 or May 2010), punctuation, and spacing throughout.
- Proofread carefully, verify the accuracy of the information, and have at least one other person — preferably your instructor or someone in your professional field — review it.
- Use a high-quality printer and high-grade paper.
- For electronic résumés, use an accessible file format.

◆ See also pages 210–219 in Chapter 7, Designing Effective Documents and Visuals, and pages 115–116 in Chapter 4, Revising the Draft.

Analyzing Your Background

In preparing to write your résumé, determine what kind of job you are seeking. Then ask yourself what information about you and your background would be most important to a prospective employer in the field you have chosen. On the basis of your answers, decide what details to include in your résumé and how you can most effectively present your qualifications. Brainstorm about yourself and your background, answering the following questions:

- What college or colleges did you attend? What degree(s) do you hold? What was your major field of study? What was your grade point average? What academic honors have you been awarded? What particular academic projects reflect your best work?

---

[3]A detailed résumé for someone in academic and scientific areas is often called a *curriculum vitae* (also *vita* or *c.v.*). It may include education, publications, projects, grants, and awards as well as a full work history. Outside the United States, the term *curriculum vitae* is often used as a synonym for the word *résumé*.

- What internships or jobs have you held? What were your principal and secondary duties in each of them? When and for how long did you hold each job? Have you been promoted? Be sure to list any work-study, summer, or volunteer jobs as well.

- What skills have you developed that potential employers value and seek in ideal job candidates? What projects or accomplishments reflect your important contributions? What language and computer skills do you have?

- What other experiences and activities would be of value in the kind of job you are seeking? Consider extracurricular activities that have contributed to your learning experience; leadership, interpersonal, and communication skills you have developed; or any collaborative work you have performed.

Use your answers as a starting point and let one question lead to another. Because you are brainstorming, don't censor your answers; record all of your experiences and accomplishments. As you organize your résumé, you can winnow items that are less relevant or outdated. Moreover, try to be specific, including quantifiable answers. *How many* projects did you handle per year? *How much* money did you raise? *What percentage* of new business did you bring in?

If you are returning to the workplace after an absence, most career experts say that it is important to acknowledge the gap in your career rather than try to hide it. That is particularly true if, for example, you are reentering the workforce because you have devoted a full-time period to care for children or dependent adults. Do not undervalue such work. Although unpaid, it often provides experience that develops important time-management, problem-solving, organizational, and interpersonal skills. Figure 16–1 illustrates how you might reflect such experiences in a résumé.

Primary Child-Care Provider, 2007 to 2010
  Furnished full-time care to three preschool children at home. Instructed in beginning scholastic skills, time management, basics of nutrition, arts, and swimming. Organized activities, managed household, and served as neighborhood-watch captain.

Home Caregiver, 2008 to 2009
  Provided 60 hours per week in-home care to Alzheimer's patient. Coordinated medical care, developed exercise programs, completed and processed complex medical forms, administered medications, organized budget, and managed home environment.

Highlights the organizational and time-management responsibilities of unpaid home care

Figure 16–1   Unpaid Experience Included in a Résumé

If you have done volunteer work during such a period, list that experience. Volunteer work often results in the same experience as full-time, paid work, a fact that your résumé should reflect, as in Figure 16–2. As with a paid job, be specific about what you accomplished in the position.

Emphasizes the coordination, organizational, and funds-management skills of volunteer tasks

School Association Coordinator, 2009 to 2010
Managed special activities of the Briarwood Elementary School Parent-Teacher Association. Planned and coordinated meetings, scheduled events, and supervised fund-drive operations. Raised $70,000 toward refurbishing the school auditorium.

Figure 16–2   Volunteer Experience Included in a Résumé

Organizing Your Résumé

A number of different organizational patterns can be used effectively. The following categories are typical—which you choose should depend on your experience and goals, the employer's needs, and any standard practices in your profession.

Heading (name and contact information)

Job objective (also called Profile) (optional)

Qualifications summary

Education

Employment experience

Related skills and abilities

Honors and activities

References

Portfolios (optional)

Whether you place education or employment experience first depends on the job you are seeking and which credentials would strengthen your résumé more. If you are a recent graduate without much work experience, you would list education first. If you have years of job experience, including jobs directly related to the kind of position you are seeking, you would list employment experience first. In your education and employment sections, list the most recent experience first, the next most recent experience second, and so on. This is known as reverse chronological order.

The Heading

At the top of your résumé, include your name, address, telephone number (home or cell), and e-mail address. Make sure that your name stands out on the page. A centered heading usually works best (Figure 16–3). If you have both a school address and a permanent home address, place your school address on the left side of the page and your permanent home address on the right side of the page. Place both underneath your name, as shown in Figure 16–4.

CONSUELA B. SANDOVAL
6819 Elm Street
Somerville, Massachusetts 02144
(617) 635-1552
cbsand@cpu.fairview.edu

Figure 16–3   Centered Résumé Heading

VIKRAM L. MATHUR

SCHOOL
148 University Drive
Bloomington, Indiana 47405
(812) 652-4781
mathur2@iu.edu

HOME (AFTER JUNE 2010)
1482 Marengo Lane
Nashville, Tennessee 37204
(615) 343-0406
vlmathur@yahoo.com

Figure 16–4   Résumé Heading for a Student with Two Addresses

Job Objective

The job objective frames the material in a résumé and helps the reader quickly understand your goal. If you decide to include an objective, use a heading such as "Objective," "Employment Objective," "Career Profile," or "Job Profile." State your immediate goal and, if you know it, the direction that you hope your career will take. Try to write this section in no more than three lines, and tailor it to the specific job for which you are applying, as illustrated in the following examples:

- A full-time computer-science position aimed at solving engineering problems and contributing to a management team.

- A position addressing the physical and mental health concerns of women, such as family planning, career counseling, or crisis management.
- Full-time management of a high-quality local restaurant.
- A summer medical research position providing opportunities to assess clinical trial protocols and findings.

Keep in mind that the objective section is optional. Although some potential employers prefer to see a clear employment objective in résumés, many employment specialists counsel against them because they can have the unintended consequence of limiting your options. If you are responding to a specific advertisement or job posting, stating the objective can be useful in showing employers that your skills and experiences can meet their needs; however, if you are sending out a résumé blindly, consider leaving off the objective.

Qualifications Summary

Sometimes called a *summary statement* or *career summary*, a qualifications summary can include skills, achievements, experience, or personal qualities that make you especially well suited to a position. You can simply call this section "Qualifications." To capture a prospective employer's attention, you may use a headline, such as "Award-Winning Senior Financial Analyst," as shown in Figure 16–14 on page 597.

Education

List the college(s) you have attended, the degrees you received and the dates you received them, your major field(s) of study, and any academic honors you have earned (Figure 16–5). Include your grade point average only if it is 3.0 or higher — or include your average in your major if that is more impressive. List courses or independent work only if they are relevant to the job you seek. Mention your high school only if you want to call attention to special high school achievements, awards, projects, programs, internships, or study abroad.

Employment Experience

The two most common ways to organize employment experience are in reverse chronological order and by category of professional experience, although both approaches may be combined if the job history warrants it. Using reverse chronological order, begin with your most-recent job and work backward under a single major heading called "Experience," "Employment," "Professional Experience," or the like (Figure 16–6). You could, alternatively, organize your experience functionally by clustering similar types of jobs or experience into one or several sections with specific headings such as "Management Experience," "Major Accomplishments," or "Summary of Qualifications" (Figure 16–7 on page 584).

One type of arrangement might be more persuasive than the other, depending on the situation. For example, if you are applying for an accounting job but have no specific background in accounting, you would probably do best to list past and present jobs in chronological order, from most to least recent. If you are

EDUCATION

Georgia Institute of Technology, Atlanta, GA
Bachelor of Science in Engineering (expected June 2010)
Cumulative Grade Point Average: 3.46 out of possible 4.0

*College, degree, and
field of study*

> *Related Courses*
> Methods of Digital Computations
> Differential Equations
> Graphic Display
> Software Design

*Related courses
pertinent to job*

> *Activities and Honors*
> Phi Chi Epsilon—Honor Society for Women in Business and Engineering
> Society of Women Engineers—Secretary-Treasurer (2008–2009)
> American Institute of Industrial Engineers—Secretary (2008–2009)
> Engineering Science Club
> Doris Harlow Scholarship recipient (2007, 2008)
> Dean's List six of eight semesters

*Activities and honors
to highlight
accomplishments*

Figure 16–5   Education Section of a Résumé

EMPLOYMENT EXPERIENCE

Computer Systems International, Atlanta, Georgia
ASSISTANT TRAINING DIRECTOR
September 2008 to Present
> Prepared professional training program for the Design, Data Entry, and
> Engineering departments.

*Reverse chronological
listing of job experience*

Vacationland Amusement Park, Toccoa, Georgia
CHIEF LIFEGUARD
April 2006 to August 2008
> Supervised three other lifeguards and trained them in emergency first-aid
> techniques.

Figure 16–6   Employment Experience Organized in Reverse Chronological Order

Opens with qualifica-tions and career accomplishments

Uses active verbs to describe experiences

Lists job history and volunteer work follow-ing qualifications and accomplishments

SUMMARY OF QUALIFICATIONS

SPANISH-LANGUAGE SKILLS
- Fluent speaking, reading, and writing in Spanish (native language is English)
- Judged highly proficient in medical vocabulary and interpreting by Harvard Pilgrim Health Care
- Write and report in Spanish for *Siglo 21*, a newspaper based in Lawrence, Massachusetts
- Translate newspaper articles from English to Spanish

INTERPERSONAL SKILLS
- Conduct culturally appropriate bilingual interviews under stressful conditions
- Trained to remain calm and focused when talking to people at the scene of fires, crimes, and in the wake of family tragedies
- Bicultural as well as bilingual

COMMUNICATION SKILLS
- Relay speakers' words and ideas to others with accuracy and speed
- Write press releases for the largest immigrant advocacy group in Massachusetts

EMPLOYMENT HISTORY

Freelance reporter and copy editor, Boston, Massachusetts	2007–present
Reporter, *News & Record*, Greensboro, North Carolina	2005–2007
Reporter, *Gaston Gazette*, Gastonia, North Carolina	2003–2005
Reporter, *Press & Standard*, Walterboro, South Carolina	2001–2003

VOLUNTEER WORK

Writer, Mass. Immigrant and Refugee Advocacy Coalition, Boston, Massachusetts	2007–present
Interpreter, blood drives and United Way campaigns, Greensboro, North Carolina	2005–2007
Intake worker, El Vínculo Hispano, Siler City, North Carolina	2003–2005
English as a Second Language teacher, Walterboro, South Carolina	2001–2003

Figure 16–7 **Employment Experience Organized Functionally**

applying for a supervisory position and have had three supervisory jobs in addi-tion to two nonsupervisory positions, you might choose to create a single section called "Supervisory Experience" and list only your three supervisory jobs. Or, you could create two sections—"Supervisory Experience" and "Other Experience"—and include the three supervisory jobs in the first section and your nonsupervi-sory jobs in the second section.

The functional résumé groups work experience by types of workplace activities or skills rather than by jobs in chronological order. Organization by function is useful for applicants who want to stress certain skills important to the prospective employer or industry or who have been employed at only one job and want to demonstrate the diversity of their experience in that position. Functional arrangement is also useful if you are changing careers and want to highlight transferable skills. However, many employers are suspicious of functional résumés because they can be used to hide a poor work history, such as excessive job hopping or extended unemployment gaps. Functional elements can be combined with a chronological arrangement by using a qualifications summary or skills category, as shown in Figure 16–7.

ETHICS NOTE

Be truthful. The consequences of giving false information in your résumé could be serious. The truthfulness of your résumé reflects not only your personal ethics but also the integrity with which you would represent an employer.

In general, follow these conventions when working on the "Experience" section of your résumé. Use the brainstorming list you created earlier, deciding which work experiences and skills are relevant for the specific job or organization to which you are applying.

- Include jobs or internships when they relate directly to the position you are seeking. Although some applicants choose to omit internships and temporary or part-time jobs, including such experiences can make a résumé more persuasive if they have helped you develop specific, relevant skills.

- Include volunteer experiences, such as taking on a leadership position in a college organization or directing a community-service project, if they demonstrate that you have developed skills valued by potential employers. Such skills might include supervisory roles, entrepreneurial positions, or fund-raising experience.

- List military service as a job; give the dates served, the duty specialty, and the rank at discharge. Discuss military duties if they relate to the job you are seeking.

- For each job or experience, list both the job title and company name. Throughout each section, consistently begin with either the job or the company, depending on which will likely be more impressive to potential employers.

- Under each job or experience, provide a concise description of your primary and secondary duties. If a job is not directly relevant, provide only a job title and a brief description of duties that helped you develop skills valued in the position you are seeking. For example, if you were a lifeguard and now seek a management position, focus on supervisory experience or even experience in averting disaster to highlight your man-agement, decision-making, and crisis-control skills.

- Use action verbs (for example, "managed" rather than "as the manager") and state ideas succinctly, as shown in Figure 16–7 on page 584. Even though the résumé is about you, do not use "I" (for example, instead of "I was promoted to Section Leader," use "Promoted to Section Leader").

- Focus as much as possible on your achievements in your work history ("Increased employee retention rate by 16 percent by developing a train-ing program"). See also Figure 16–8. Employers want to hire doers and achievers.

Announces student's official job title

Identifies supervisory roles

Uses active verbs

Emphasizes student's achievements and quantifies her con-tributions to the organization

Vague, Lackluster Résumé
Student Volunteer Council
   I helped sign up new members for community volunteer projects.
Baker Library
   I worked in the archives.

Concise, Active Résumé
Vice president, Student Volunteer Council
   Organized recruitment drive for over 30 different community-service proj-ects; raised campuswide participation by 25%.
Research fellow, Baker Library
   Catalogued and photographed new collection of historical documents for university archives.

Figure 16–8   Vague Job Description Revised for Clarity

Related Skills and Abilities

Employers are interested in hiring applicants with a variety of skills or the ability to learn new ones fairly quickly. Depending on the position, you might list in a skills section items such as fluency in a foreign language; writing and editing abil-ities; specialized technical knowledge; equipment or mechanical training; or computer skills, including knowledge of specific languages, software, and hard-ware, as well as Web sites created. Also include relevant social-networking activi-ties (hobby, school club, volunteer work), such as blogs, podcasts, and profiles; these activities can highlight your technical and writing skills, but be sure they will portray you in a professional light.

Honors and Activities

List honors and unique activities near the end of your résumé. Include student or community activities, professional or club memberships, awards received, or works published. Be selective; do not duplicate information given in other cate-gories, and include only information that supports your employment objective. Depending on which skills or activities you want to emphasize, use a heading such as "Activities," "Honors," "Professional Affiliations," or "Publications and Memberships."

References

Avoid listing references unless that is standard practice in your profession or your résumé is sparse. Instead, use the phrase "References available upon request" to signal the end of a long résumé, or write "Available upon request" after the heading "References" as a design element to balance a page. In any case, you should have a separate list of references to give to prospective employers after interviews; your list should include the main heading "References for [your name]" and the names, affiliations, titles, and contact information for each of your references. Do not give anyone as a reference without first obtaining his or her permission.

Portfolios

The résumé may also state that a "Portfolio is available upon request." Portfolios have traditionally been used by artists and writers to illustrate their work. However, a portfolio also may provide samples of your most impressive written work (reports, proposals, presentations), copies of letters of praise, certificates that attest to special abilities, newspaper clippings, a CD of a Web site you created, and other items that visually display your accomplishments and potential contributions to a prospective employer. Present your portfolio professionally and attractively in a folder or binder; if you create a Web résumé, you can post your portfolio with it (see "Electronic Résumés" on pages 587–592). For an interview, it is best to bring a portfolio containing ten items or fewer.

Salary

Avoid listing the salary you desire in your résumé. On the one hand, you may price yourself out of a job you want if the salary you list is higher than a potential employer is willing to pay. On the other hand, if you list a low salary, you may not get the best possible offer. (See "Salary Negotiations" on page 612.)

Electronic Résumés

In addition to the traditional paper résumé, you can post a Web-based résumé. You may also need to submit a résumé through e-mail to a potential employer to be included in an organization's database. As Internet and database technologies converge, remain current with the forms and protocols that employers prefer by reviewing popular job-search sites, such as HotJobs at <http://hotjobs.yahoo.com> and Monster.com at <www.monster.com>.

Scannable and Plain-Text Résumés

Large companies often electronically scan résumés into a database, which allows them a time-saving way to screen a large pool of applicants for job openings. With this practice in mind, be prepared to submit your résumé in more than one format. In addition to the traditional paper résumé, prepare and submit a no-frills, or plain-text, version for ease of scanning.

ON THE WEB

For further advice on portfolios, go to Chapter 16, bedfordstmartins.com/ writingthatworks and select *Web Links,* "Kimeldorf Library."

◆ *For additional information about fonts and page design, see pages 212–213; 216 and Digital Tips: Designing Documents with a Word Processor on page 214.*

DESIGNING YOUR DOCUMENT

Formatting the Résumé

Make your first impression count. To do so, use the following guidelines for designing an easy-to-read résumé that will highlight your qualifications and get you noticed.

Paper and Printing

- Use 8½-by-11-inch high-quality bond paper in white, ivory, or light gray.
- Use 1-inch margins all around.
- Print in black ink on one side only.
- Use a good-quality printer so that text is crisp and clear.

At-a-Glance Look

- Ensure that each section is balanced proportionally on the page with the other sections.
- In addition to 1-inch margins, use ample white space consistently to prevent a cluttered look:
  - Separate each section with sufficient white space so that it stands out from the elements above and below it.
  - Single space within sections.
  - Double space or, if space permits, triple space between sections.
  - Indent the second line within a section when it continues the previous line.

Font Size and Design

- Use no more than two font styles.
- Select fonts to identify different levels of information.
- Use sans serif fonts for headings and serif fonts for text.
- Use **bold face**, *italics*, <u>underlining</u>, and ALL CAPITALS sparingly for emphasis; do not overdesign.
- Use font sizes to differentiate headings from text: 10 to 13 points for text and 14 to 20 points for headings.
- Use bullets to signal a new topic within each section and to emphasize individual items, such as each job responsibility, accomplishment, college course, or internship position.
- Be consistent and uniform throughout:
  - Use the same fonts and design features—bullets, indentions, text boxes, capital and lowercase letters, and other elements.
  - Show headings, date formats, punctuation, and spacing consistently, as well.
- Consider alternative methods of creating the résumé:
  - Use a résumé template in your word-processing package.
  - Have a professional graphic designer create your résumé.

@

DIGITAL TIPS: Creating a Résumé Using a Template

Microsoft Word and Corel WordPerfect offer templates for a variety of résumé styles.

- Click on File/New/Templates in your toolbar and follow the guidance provided. Note that the templates may be stored on your computer or accessed through a Web site.
- Select from a variety of ways to organize and present the content:
  - Entry level—Elegant
  - Chronological—Contemporary
  - Functional—Professional
- Adapt the template to your needs or preferences by applying an array of design features:
  - Add lines across the page.
  - Change fonts.
  - Standardize headings.
- Spell-check before printing. Proofread carefully.

A plain-text version is easier to scan than the traditional résumé because OCR (optical character recognition) scanning software does poorly in recognizing unusual typefaces, graphics, boxes, and other typographic and design features common in traditional paper résumés. The easiest way around these limitations is to format a version of your résumé as a plain-text file (.txt) or to use ASCII-compatible[4] characters so that it can be read accurately across most applications and systems.

A scannable résumé is normally mailed to an employer in paper form, scanned, and downloaded into a company's searchable database. Avoid decorative, uncommon, or otherwise fancy typefaces; use simple font styles (a sans serif font such as Arial) and sizes for text and headings between 10 and 14 points. Use white space generously because scanners use it to recognize where one topic has ended and another has begun. Although a paper résumé is best kept to one page, you need not limit an electronic résumé to a single page. However, keep the résumé as simple, clear, and concise as possible. Use white or off-white paper and do not fold it for mailing because a scanner can misread a folded line. Scan such a résumé yourself in OCR to make sure there are no problems.

Some employers request ASCII or plain-text résumés via e-mail, which they can add directly to their résumé database without scanning. ASCII résumés also allow employers to read the file regardless of the type of software they are using. You can copy and paste such a résumé directly into the body of the e-mail message. You may also include a section in such a résumé titled "Keywords" (or perhaps

---

[4]ASCII (pronounced ăs´-kēy) is an acronym for American Standard Code for Information Interchange and is the most basic format for transferring files between different programs. In word-processing terms, it can be thought of as unformatted text.

@

DIGITAL TIPS: Preparing an ASCII Résumé

When preparing an ASCII document, proper formatting is critical. Keep the following points in mind:

- Do not use word-processing elements, such as graphic lines or boxes, bullets, underlining, italics, or boldface.
- Avoid uncommon typefaces; use simple font styles and sizes between 10 and 14 points.
- Create horizontal lines by using a series of hyphens or asterisks (up to 60 characters).
- Replace bullets with hyphens or asterisks, and use white space between sections rather than indenting.
- Set the margins so that you do not exceed 65 characters per line, including spaces.
  - Use the space bar instead of tabs and column formats.
  - Align everything to the left margin.
  - Use hard returns, not the word-wrap feature, to insert line breaks.
- Save your document as an ASCII or MS-DOS text using the .txt extension (for example, "resume.txt").

For more on preparing an ASCII résumé, go to bedfordstmartins.com/writingthatworks and select *Digital Tips*, "Preparing an ASCII Résumé."

give a descriptive name, such as "Areas of Expertise"). Keywords, also called *descriptors*, allow potential employers to search the database for such terms to screen for qualified candidates. So be sure to use keywords that are the same as those used in the employer's descriptions of the jobs that best match your interests and qualifications. This section can follow the main heading or appear near the end of your résumé. Figure 16–9 is an example of a plain-text résumé that demonstrates the use of keywords for electronic searches.

E-mail–Attached Résumés

An employer may request or you may prefer to submit a résumé as an e-mail attachment to be printed out by the employer. If so, consider using a relatively plain design and sending the résumé as a rich text format (.rtf) document. Or, if precise design is important, send the résumé as a PDF file that will preserve the fonts, images, graphics, and layout. You can attach this file to an e-mail message that will then serve as your application letter.

◆ *See also Digital Tips: Using PDF Files on page 555.*

Web Résumés

Another option is to post your résumé on your own Web site. Doing so makes it available to potential employers at their convenience—you need only send them

DAVID B. GROENING
6819 Locustview Drive
Topeka, Kansas 66614
(913) 233-1552
dbgroening@cpu.fairview.edu

JOB OBJECTIVE
Work as a programmer with writing, editing, and training responsibilities,
leading to a career in information design management.

KEYWORDS
Programmer, Operating Systems, Unipro, Newsletter, Graphics,
Cybernetics, Listserv, Professional Writer, Editor, Trainer, Instructor,
Technical Writer, Tutor, Designer, Manager, Information Design.

Keywords listed in a separate section

EDUCATION
** Fairview Community College, Topeka, Kansas
** Associate's Degree, Computer Science, June 2006
** Dean's Honor List Award (six quarters)

Asterisks replace bullets

RELEVANT COURSE WORK
** Operating Systems Design
** Database Management
** Introduction to Cybernetics
** Technical Writing

EMPLOYMENT EXPERIENCE
** Computer Consultant: September 2005 to Present
Fairview Community College Computer Center: Advised and trained
novice users; wrote and maintained Unipro operating system
documentation.
** Tutor: January 2004 to June 2005
Fairview Community College: Assisted students in mathematics and
computer programming.

Line width limited to 65 characters

SKILLS AND ACTIVITIES
** Unipro Operating System: Thorough knowledge of word-processing,
text-editing, and file-formatting programs.
** Writing and Editing Skills: Experience in documenting computer
programs for beginning programmers and users.
** Fairview Community Microcomputer Users Group: Cofounder and
editor of monthly newsletter ("Compuclub"); Listserv manager.

All lines begin at left margin

FURTHER INFORMATION
** References, college transcripts, a portfolio of computer programs,
and writing samples available upon request.

Figure 16–9   Résumé in ASCII Format

your Web address. A Web résumé can also be updated as often as necessary without the need to mail updates to everyone. Perhaps the chief advantage of a Web résumé is that it allows you to create an electronic portfolio linked to samples of your work—reports, articles, graphics projects, presentations, and the like. An interactive résumé with links to the portfolio will work only if you create an HTML (hypertext markup language) version of your work. If you wish to post a résumé and portfolio without hyperlinks, you could use a plain-text version or PDF image file instead. If you plan to post your résumé on your own Web site, keep the following points in mind:

- Follow the general advice for writing for the Web, outlined in Chapter 15, Writing for the Web.
- View your résumé on several browsers to see how it looks.
- Just below your name, you may wish to provide a series of internal links to such important categories as "Experience" and "Education."
- Consider building a multipage site for displaying a work portfolio, publications, reference letters, and the like.
- If privacy is an issue, include an e-mail link ("mailto") at the top of the résumé rather than your home address and phone number.

Make the most of posting your résumé on your own Web site by e-mailing links to potential employers. Keep in mind that personal Web sites are by their nature less effective than commercial services that attract recruiters with their large databases of candidates.

Sample Résumés

The sample résumés in this section are provided to stimulate your thinking about how to tailor your résumé to your own job search. Before you design and write your résumé, look at as many samples as possible, and then organize and format your own to best suit your previous experience and your professional goals and to make the most persuasive case to your target employers.

- Figure 16–10 presents a conventional résumé in which a recent college graduate is seeking an entry-level position.
- Figure 16–11 on page 594 shows a résumé with a variation of the conventional headings to highlight professional credentials.
- Figure 16–12 on page 595 shows a résumé that focuses on the applicant's management experience.
- Figure 16–13 on page 596 focuses on how the applicant advanced and was promoted within a single company.
- Figure 16–14 on page 597 illustrates how an applicant can organize a résumé by combining functional and chronological elements.

PEGGY EDWARDS
144 Elm Street, Apt. 4
West Orange, New Jersey 07052
(973) 741-0134
peggy-edwards@hotmail.com

Heading with name and contact information

OBJECTIVE   To work at a local health department as a Registered Environmental Health Specialist.

EDUCATION   Montclair State University, Upper Montclair, New Jersey
B.S., Health Education (concentration in Community Health), 2010
Magna Cum Laude (GPA: 3.75/4.0)

Essex County Community College, West Caldwell, New Jersey
A.S., Social Sciences, 2007

Education and listing of course work appropriate for a recent graduate

RELATED COURSES:
- Public Health
- Health Promotion
- Environmental Health
- The Teaching of Health
- School Health and Community Service
- Environment and Public Health

HONORS:
Dean's List, Phi Theta Kappa, Golden Key National Honor Society

RELATED EXPERIENCE   *Intern, Bergen County Health Department, 1/2009–4/2009*
(North Bergen, New Jersey)
Conducted Chapter 12 food inspections, reviewed septic plans, and responded to community complaints under the supervision of trained health inspectors.

Internship and part-time job experience relevant to a recent graduate

Substitute Health Teacher, West Orange High School, 9/2006–1/2007
(West Orange, New Jersey)

Dental Assistant, Daniel R. Korb, D.D.S., P.A., 8/2005–3/2006
(Cedar Grove, New Jersey)
Took dental radiographs of all patients, sterilized instruments, and sanitized rooms.

LICENSES   New Jersey Registered Environmental Health Specialist
New Jersey Dental Radiologist
New Jersey Commercial Driver's license with air-brake endorsement

Licenses related to job objective

REFERENCES   Furnished upon request

Figure 16–10   Résumé for an Entry-Level Position

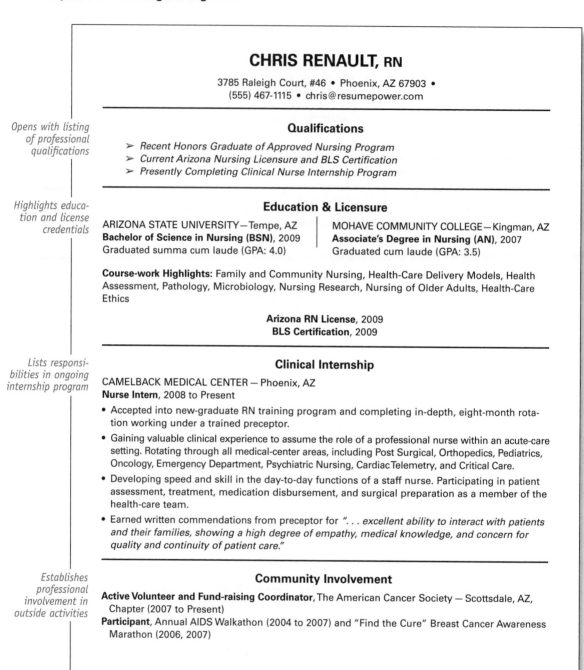

Opens with listing of professional qualifications

Highlights education and license credentials

Lists responsibilities in ongoing internship program

Establishes professional involvement in outside activities

CHRIS RENAULT, RN

3785 Raleigh Court, #46 • Phoenix, AZ 67903 •
(555) 467-1115 • chris@resumepower.com

Qualifications

➢ *Recent Honors Graduate of Approved Nursing Program*
➢ *Current Arizona Nursing Licensure and BLS Certification*
➢ *Presently Completing Clinical Nurse Internship Program*

Education & Licensure

ARIZONA STATE UNIVERSITY—Tempe, AZ
Bachelor of Science in Nursing (BSN), 2009
Graduated summa cum laude (GPA: 4.0)

MOHAVE COMMUNITY COLLEGE—Kingman, AZ
Associate's Degree in Nursing (AN), 2007
Graduated cum laude (GPA: 3.5)

Course-work Highlights: Family and Community Nursing, Health-Care Delivery Models, Health Assessment, Pathology, Microbiology, Nursing Research, Nursing of Older Adults, Health-Care Ethics

Arizona RN License, 2009
BLS Certification, 2009

Clinical Internship

CAMELBACK MEDICAL CENTER — Phoenix, AZ
Nurse Intern, 2008 to Present

• Accepted into new-graduate RN training program and completing in-depth, eight-month rotation working under a trained preceptor.

• Gaining valuable clinical experience to assume the role of a professional nurse within an acute-care setting. Rotating through all medical-center areas, including Post Surgical, Orthopedics, Pediatrics, Oncology, Emergency Department, Psychiatric Nursing, Cardiac Telemetry, and Critical Care.

• Developing speed and skill in the day-to-day functions of a staff nurse. Participating in patient assessment, treatment, medication disbursement, and surgical preparation as a member of the health-care team.

• Earned written commendations from preceptor for *". . . excellent ability to interact with patients and their families, showing a high degree of empathy, medical knowledge, and concern for quality and continuity of patient care."*

Community Involvement

Active Volunteer and Fund-raising Coordinator, The American Cancer Society — Scottsdale, AZ, Chapter (2007 to Present)
Participant, Annual AIDS Walkathon (2004 to 2007) and "Find the Cure" Breast Cancer Awareness Marathon (2006, 2007)

Figure 16–11 Résumé, Highlighting Professional Credentials. Prepared by Kim Isaacs, Advanced Career Systems, Inc.

ROBERT MANDILLO
7761 Shalamar Drive
Dayton, Ohio 45424
(513) 255-4137
mand@juno.com

OBJECTIVE

A management position in the aerospace industry with responsibility for developing new designs and products.

MANAGEMENT EXPERIENCE

MANAGER, ENGINEERING DRAFTING DEPARTMENT — May 2004–Present
Wright-Patterson Air Force Base, Dayton, Ohio

Supervise 17 drafting mechanics in support of the engineering design staff. Develop, evaluate, and improve materials and equipment for the design and construction of exhibits. Write specifications, negotiate with vendors, and initiate procurement activities for exhibit design support.

SUPERVISOR, GRAPHICS ILLUSTRATORS — June 1991–April 2004
Henderson Advertising Agency, Cincinnati, Ohio

Supervised five illustrators and four drafting mechanics after promotion from Graphics Technician. Analyzed and approved work-order requirements. Selected appropriate media and techniques for orders. Rendered illustrations in pencil and ink. Converted department to CAD system.

EDUCATION

BACHELOR OF SCIENCE IN MECHANICAL ENGINEERING TECHNOLOGY, 1991
Edison State College, Wooster, Ohio

ASSOCIATE'S DEGREE IN MECHANICAL DRAFTING, 1989
Wooster Community College, Wooster, Ohio

PROFESSIONAL AFFILIATION

National Association of Mechanical Engineers and Drafting Mechanics

REFERENCES

References, letters of recommendation, and a portfolio of original designs and drawings available online at <www.juno.com/mand>.

Begins with job experience relevant to prospective employers

Education and affiliations emphasize rigorous preparation in field and continuing professional interests

Figure 16–12   Résumé for an Applicant with Management Experience

CAROL ANN WALKER
1436 West Schantz Avenue
Laurel, Pennsylvania 17322
(717) 399-2712
caw@yahoo.com

FINANCIAL EXPERIENCE

KERFHEIMER CORPORATION, Philadelphia, Pennsylvania

Job-experience opening highlights promotion

Senior Financial Analyst, June 2005–Present
Report to Senior Vice President for Corporate Financial Planning. Develop manufacturing cost estimates totaling $30 million annually for mining and construction equipment with Department of Defense.

Financial Analyst, November 2002–June 2005
Developed $50-million funding estimates for major Department of Defense contracts for troop carriers and digging and earth-moving machines. Researched funding options, resulting in savings of $1.2 million.

FIRST BANK, INC., Bloomington, Indiana

Planning Analyst, September 1997–November 2002
Developed successful computer models for short- and long-range planning.

EDUCATION

Ph.D. in Finance: expected, June 2010
The Wharton School of the University of Pennsylvania

M.S. in Business Administration, 2001
University of Wisconsin–Milwaukee
"Executive Curriculum" for employees identified as promising by their employers.

B.S. in Business Administration (*magna cum laude*), 1997
Indiana University
Emphasis: Finance   Minor: Professional Writing

PUBLISHING AND MEMBERSHIP

Published "Developing Computer Models for Financial Planning," *Midwest Finance Journal* 34.2 (2007): 126–36.

Association for Corporate Financial Planning, Senior Member.

REFERENCES

References and a portfolio of financial plans are available upon request.

Figure 16–13   Advanced Résumé, Showing Promotion within a Single Company

―――― CAROL ANN WALKER ――――

1436 West Schantz Avenue • Laurel, PA 17322
(717) 399-2712 • caw@yahoo.com

Award-Winning Senior Financial Analyst

Astute senior analyst and corporate financial planner with 11 years of experience and proven success enhancing P&L scenarios by millions of dollars. Demonstrated ability to apply critical thinking and sound strategic/economic analysis to multi-dimensional business issues. Advanced computer skills include Hyperion, SQL, MS Office, and Crystal Reports.

Opens by highlighting career accomplishments and functional areas of expertise

---

Financial Analyst of the Year, 2008

Recipient of prestigious national award from the Association for Investment Management and Research (AIMR)

Areas of Expertise

- Financial Analysis & Planning
- Forecasting & Trend Projection
- Trend/Variance Analysis
- Comparative Analysis

- Expense Analysis
- Strategic Planning
- SEC & Financial Reporting
- Risk Assessment

Career Progression

KERFHEIMER CORPORATION–Philadelphia, PA   2002 to Present

Senior Financial Analyst, June 2005 to Present
Financial Analyst, November 2002 to June 2005

Rapidly promoted to lead team of 15 analysts in the management of financial/SEC reporting and analysis for publicly traded, $2.3-billion company. Develop financial/statistical models used to project and maximize corporate financial performance. Support nationwide sales team by providing financial metrics, trends, and forecasts.

Continues with chronological history that features accomplishments

Key Accomplishments:

- **Developed long-range funding requirements crucial to firm's subsequent capture of $1 billion** in government and military contracts.
- **Facilitated a 45% decrease in company's long-term debt** during several major building expansions through personally developed computer models for capital acquisition.
- **Jointly led large-scale systems conversion to Hyperion**, including personal upload of database in Essbase. Completed conversion without interrupting business operations.

Figure 16–14   Advanced Résumé, Combining Functional and Chronological Elements. (continued)
Prepared by Kim Isaacs, Advanced Career Systems, Inc.

———————————— CAROL ANN WALKER ————————————

Résumé • Page Two

Career Progression (*continued*)

FIRST BANK, INC.–Bloomington, IN   1997 to 2002

Planning Analyst, September 1997 to November 2002
Compiled and distributed weekly, monthly, quarterly, and annual closings/financial reports, analyzing information for presentation to senior management. Prepared depreciation forecasts, actual-vs.-projected financial statements, key-matrix reports, tax-reporting packages, auditor packages, and balance-sheet reviews.

Key Accomplishments:

• **Devised strategies to acquire over $1 billion at 3% below market rate.**
• **Analyzed financial performance for consistency to plans and forecasts**, investigated trends and variances, and alerted senior management to areas requiring action.
• **Achieved an average 23% return on all personally recommended investments.** Applied critical thinking and sound financial and strategic analysis in all funding options research.

Education

THE WHARTON SCHOOL OF THE UNIVERSITY OF PENNSYLVANIA (Philadelphia)

Ph.D. in Finance Candidate, Expected June 2010

UNIVERSITY OF WISCONSIN (Milwaukee)

M.S. in Business Administration, May 2001

INDIANA UNIVERSITY (Bloomington)

B.S. in Business Administration, Emphasis in Finance
(*magna cum laude*), May 1997

Affiliations

• Association for Investment Management and Research (AIMR), Member, 2004 to Present
• Association for Corporate Financial Planning (ACFP), Senior Member, 2002 to Present

Portfolio of Financial Plans Available on Request
(717) 399-2712 • caw@yahoo.com

Figure 16–14   Advanced Résumé, Combining Functional and Chronological Elements. (continued)
Prepared by Kim Isaacs, Advanced Career Systems, Inc.

During your job search, apply for as many positions as possible that are acceptable to you and for which you qualify. However, be careful to adapt your core résumé to the specific requirements of each job listing before you submit it. Note how the applicant, Joshua Goodman, tailors the two résumés in Figures 16–15 and 16–16 on pages 600–601 in response to two different job listings for a graphic designer. Both résumés are formatted in an unconventional style to highlight his graphic-design skills. The ABC Services listing (Figure 16–17 on page 602) describes a candidate who can use graphics and desktop-publishing software to produce printed products ("ads, brochures, signs, flyers, etc."). Joshua's résumé (Figure 16–16) focuses on his experience with this work under Graphic-Design Experience. Note that this focus for the listing in Figure 16–18 on page 602 gives equal coverage to his graphic- and Web-design capabilities in response to the XYZ Group's listing for someone with both skills. He specifically inserts a new section (Web-Design Experience) for this purpose. And to highlight the Web-design experience, he changes the reverse chronological order of the résumé in Figure 16–15. If he's interviewed by ABC Services and asked about Web design, he can discuss his background then.

ON THE WEB

For more examples of résumés with helpful annotations, go to Model Documents Gallery, bedfordstmartins.com/ writingthatworks

Layout and design of résumé reflect candidate's graphic-design skills

Joshua S. Goodman
222 Morewood Avenue
Pittsburgh, PA 15212
(878) 111-1234
jgoodman@aol.com

OBJECTIVE

A position as a graphic designer with responsibilities in information design, packaging, and media presentations.

EDUCATION

Carnegie Mellon University, Pittsburgh, Pennsylvania
BFA in Graphic Design — May 2007.

Graphic Design
Corporate Identity
Industrial Design
Graphic Imaging Processes
Color Theory
Computer Graphics
Typography
Serigraphy
Photography
Video Production

Relevant course work

EMPLOYMENT EXPERIENCE

Job experience highlights qualifications for position described in Figure 16–17

Assistant Designer • Dyer/Khan
Los Angeles, California
Summer 2008, Summer 2009
Assistant Designer in a versatile design studio. Responsible for design, layout, comps, mechanicals, pre-press production for four-color posters, booklets, brochures, etc.
Clients: Paramount Pictures, Mattel Electronics, and Motown Records.

Highlights publications experience from design through the print-production cycle

Graphic Designer • Barton & Barton
Los Angeles, California
Summer 2007
Graphic Designer for advertising firm. Designed Web sites and created templates for two corporate clients. Created interactive banners and screen interfaces to facilitate online advertising for three corporate clients.

Features graphic design background

COMPUTER SKILLS

XML, HTML, JavaScript, Forms, Macromedia Dreamweaver 8, Macromedia Flash 4, Photoshop CS4, Image Ready (Animated GIFs), CorelDRAW, DeepPaint, iGrafx Designer, MapEdit (Image Mapping), Scanning, Microsoft Access/Excel, QuarkXPress.

Production Assistant • Grafis
Los Angeles, California
Summer 2006
Production assistant at fast-paced design firm. Assisted with comps, mechanicals, and miscellaneous studio work.
Clients: ABC Television, A&M Records, and Ortho Products Division.

ACTIVITIES

Member, Pittsburgh Graphic Design Society; Member, The Design Group

Figure 16–15   Résumé Tailored to a Job Listing for a Traditional Graphic Designer (for ABC Services, see Figure 16–17 on page 602)

Joshua S. Goodman
222 Morewood Avenue
Pittsburgh, PA 15212
(878) 111-1234
jgoodman@aol.com

OBJECTIVE

A position as a graphic designer with responsibilities in Web and document design, packaging, and media presentations.

EDUCATION

Carnegie Mellon University, Pittsburgh, Pennsylvania
BFA in Graphic Design — May 2007.

Web Design
Computer Graphics
Graphic Design   *Relevant*
Corporate Identity   *course work*
Industrial Design   *as recent*
Graphic Imaging Processes *graduate*
Color Theory
Typography
Serigraphy
Photography
Video Production

WEB-DESIGN EXPERIENCE

Revised version of résumé targets job listing requiring Web-design skills and experience

Graphic Designer • Barton & Barton
Los Angeles, California
Summer 2007
Planned major revision of advertising firm's corporate Web site. Designed Web sites and created templates for two corporate clients. Created interactive banners and screen interfaces to facilitate online advertising.

Separate Web section calls attention to key experience, even though not most recent chronologically

GRAPHIC-DESIGN EXPERIENCE

Assistant Designer • Dyer/Khan
Los Angeles, California
Summer 2008, Summer 2009
Assistant designer in a versatile design studio. Responsible for design, layout, comps, mechanicals, and project management.
Clients: Paramount Pictures, Mattel Electronics, and Motown Records.

Production Assistant • Grafis
Los Angeles, California
Summer 2006
Production assistant at fast-paced design firm. Assisted with comps, mechanicals, and miscellaneous studio work.
Clients: ABC Television, A&M Records, and Ortho Products Division.

COMPUTER SKILLS

CorelDRAW, DeepPaint,   *Highlights*
Dreamweaver, iGrafx   *Web-software*
Designer, MapEdit (Image   *capabilities*
Mapping), Scanning, Microsoft
Access/Excel, QuarkXPress,
PageMaker, Illustrator, Adobe
Acrobat Writer, MS Word.

ACTIVITIES

Member, Pittsburgh Graphic Design Society; Member, The Design Group.

Figure 16–16   Résumé Tailored to a Job Listing for a Graphic Designer with Web-Development Experience (for XYZ Group, see Figure 16–18)

GRAPHIC DESIGNER

ABC Services, Inc., a hospitality management company located in Anywhere, USA, is in search of a full-time graphic designer able to multitask and proficient in Adobe PageMaker, Illustrator, Photoshop, Acrobat, and Word to create ads, brochures, signs, flyers, etc. Must be familiar with print process and IBM platforms. ABC offers great benefits, competitive salary, and flexible work environment. Please send résumé and salary requirements to ABC Group, etc.

Figure 16–17   Job Listing for a Traditional Graphic Designer (ABC Services)

GRAPHIC DESIGNER

The XYZ Group, a prestigious scientific organization located in Anyplace, USA, seeks a graphic designer. Position requires an experienced and creative graphic designer with strong concept and design skills to work on a wide range of projects, including logos, brochures, posters, annual reports, and Web-site design. Candidate must be able to manage many projects simultaneously and work with minimal supervision on all aspects of projects from start to finish. Must have good interpersonal skills for interaction with a wide variety of staff and volunteers to ensure timely production of all projects.

Candidates must have expert-level knowledge of PageMaker, Photoshop, and Illustrator/FreeHand in the Windows environment and Adobe Dreamweaver (current release). Must have previous print-buying experience. Web-page development experience, good proofreading skills, and scanner experience are essential. Bachelor's degree in graphic design, fine arts, communications, or related field with a minimum 3–5 years' recent experience using all required skills. Send cover letter and résumé, including salary history, to XYZ Group, etc.

Figure 16–18   Job Listing for a Graphic Designer with Web-Development Experience (XYZ Group)

■ Writing an Effective Letter of Application

When applying for a job, you almost always need to submit an application or a cover letter with your résumé. The letter of application is essentially a sales letter in which you market your skills, abilities, and knowledge. Therefore, your application letter must be persuasive. The successful application letter accomplishes four tasks: (1) it catches the reader's attention favorably by describing how your skills will contribute to the organization, (2) it explains which particular job interests you and why, (3) it convinces the reader that you are qualified for the job by drawing your reader's attention to particular elements in your résumé or portfolio, and (4) it requests an interview.

◆ *For a discussion of sales letters, see pages 325–330 in Chapter 9, Writing Business Correspondence.*

Opening Paragraph

In the opening paragraph, provide context and show your enthusiasm.

1. Indicate how you heard about the opening. If you have been referred to a company by an employee, a career counselor, a professor, or someone else, be sure to mention this even before you state your job objective ("I recently learned from Ms. Jodi Hammel of an opening in your firm").

2. State your job objective and mention the specific job title ("I am writing to apply for the position of district manager"). Those who make hiring decisions review many application letters. To save them time while also calling attention to your strengths as a candidate, state your job objective directly in your first paragraph.

3. Explain why you are interested in the job and demonstrate your initiative as well as knowledge of the organization by relating your interest to some facet of the organization. ("This position interests me greatly not only because your firm is number one in the region but also because I am impressed with Advertising Media's Employee Development Program.")

Note how the following opening paragraph cites where the position was advertised, states the position title, and expresses interest in line with a career objective.

▶ Dear Mr. Lupert:

In the February 24, 2010, issue of the *Butler Gazette*, I learned that you have summer technical training internships available. This opportunity interests me because I have the professional and educational background necessary to make positive contributions to your firm.

Body Paragraphs

In the second paragraph (and third, if necessary), show through examples that you are highly qualified for the job. Limit each of these paragraphs to just one basic point that is clearly stated in the topic sentence. For example, your second paragraph might focus on work experience and your third paragraph on educational achievements. Don't just *tell* readers that you're qualified—*show* them by including examples and details. Come across as proud of your achievements and refer to your enclosed résumé, but do not simply summarize your résumé. Indicate how (with your talents) you can make valuable contributions to the company you are interested in, such as "I was the national winner of TI's 'Outstanding Customer Service Award' for 2005, 2006, and 2007. I have strong contacts with key buyers at all the major firms in our industry."

Note how the following two paragraphs from the application letter for an internship position give specific examples of project experience, provide information on course work and degree goals, reference the enclosed résumé, and emphasize how these experiences can contribute to the company.

▶ My professional experiences are representative of my abilities. My current project, a computer tutoring system that teaches LISP (an artificial intelligence programming language), is the first of its kind and is now being sold across the country to corporations and universities. I work with a team to test and revise our work until we have solved each problem. I have also developed leadership and collaborative skills that I could contribute to a summer position at Applied Sciences. As a cofounder of a project to target and tutor high school students with learning disabilities, I organized and implemented many of the training and tutoring sessions. My ability to take the initiative on challenging projects would be a valuable asset to your company.

Pursuing degrees in industrial management and computer science has prepared me well to make valuable contributions to your goal of successfully implementing new software. Through varied courses, described in my résumé, I have the ability to learn new skills and to interact effectively in a technical environment. I would look forward to applying all these abilities at Applied Sciences, Inc.

Closing Paragraph

In the final paragraph, request an interview. Let the reader know how to reach you by including your phone number or e-mail address. End with a statement of goodwill, even if it is only "thank you."

▶ I would appreciate the chance to interview with you at your earliest convenience. If you have questions or would like additional information, contact me at (435) 228-3490 any Tuesday or Thursday after 10 a.m. or e-mail me at <sennett@excepr.com>. Thank you for your time.

Sincerely,

Molly Sennett

Molly Sennett

Enclosure: Résumé

See also pages 115–116 in Chapter 4, Revising the Draft.

Proofread your letter carefully. Research indicates that if employers notice even one spelling, grammatical, or mechanical error, they often eliminate the candidate from consideration immediately. Such errors give employers the impression that you lack writing skills or that you are generally sloppy and careless in the way you present yourself professionally.

WRITER'S CHECKLIST
Writing a Letter of Application

✔ In the opening paragraph:

– Indicate how you heard about the opening.

– State your job objective and interest in the job.

– Mention the job title.

✔ In the body of the letter:

– Cite project and previous employment experiences that demonstrate your qualifications for the job.

– Indicate how college course work, your degree, and pertinent training add to your qualifications for the job.

– Refer to your enclosed résumé.

– Explain how your qualifications and achievements can contribute to the prospective employer.

✔ In the closing paragraph:

– Request an interview.

– Provide your phone number and e-mail address so that you can be contacted.

– End with a goodwill statement.

Sample Letters

The three sample application letters shown in Figures 16–19 through 16–21 follow the application-letter structure described in this section. Each is adapted according to emphasis, tone, and style to fit its particular audience.

- In Figure 16–19 on page 606, a college student seeks an internship in a retail business.

- In Figure 16–20 on page 607, a recent college graduate applies for a job in graphic design.

- In Figure 16–21 on page 608, a person with many years of work experience applies for a job as a district manager.

ON THE WEB

For more sample cover letters, go to Model Documents Gallery, bedfordstmartins.com/ writingthatworks

From: Marsha S. Parker <msparker@ubi.edu>
To: Patrice C. Crandall <pcrandall@abels.com>
Sent: Monday, February 22, 2010 10:47AM
Subject: Application for Summer Internship
Attachment: 📄 Parker_Resume.doc

Dear Ms. Crandall:

I have learned from your Web site that you are hiring undergraduates for summer internships. Such an internship appeals to me because Abel's buyer-training program impressed me as I researched the industry.

The professional and analytical qualities that my attached résumé describe match the job description on your Web site. My experiences with the Alumni Relations Program and the University Center Committee have enhanced my communication and persuasive abilities and my understanding of compromise and negotiation. For example, in the alumni program, I persuaded both uninvolved and active alumni to become more engaged with the direction of the university. On the University Center Committee, I balanced the students' demands with the financial and structural constraints of the administration. With these skills, I can ably assist the members of your department with their summer projects and successfully juggle multiple responsibilities.

I would appreciate the opportunity to meet with you to discuss your summer internship further. If you have questions or would like to speak with me, please contact me at (412) 863-2289 any weekday after 3 p.m or you can e-mail me at <msparker@ubi .edu>. Thank you for your consideration.

Sincerely,

Marsha S. Parker

Opens by demonstrating initiative in researching the company, locating the program, and noting its value to the applicant's career

Continues by linking the applicant's personal characteristics to tangible accomplishments

Figure 16–19   Application Letter Sent as an E-mail Message from a College Student Applying for an Internship

222 Morewood Ave.
Pittsburgh, PA 15212
April 16, 2010

Ms. Judith Castro
Director, Human Resources
Natural History Museum
1201 S. Figueroa Street
Los Angeles, CA 90015

Dear Ms. Castro:

I have recently learned from Jodi Hammel, a graphic designer at Dyer/Khan, that you are recruiting for a graphic designer in your Marketing Department. Your position interests me greatly because it offers me an opportunity both to fulfill my career goals and to promote the work of an internationally respected institution. Having participated in substantial volunteer activities at a local public museum, I am aware of the importance of your work.

Opens by referencing a personal contact at the firm

I bring strong up-to-date academic and practical skills in multimedia tools and graphic arts production, as indicated in my enclosed résumé. Further, I have recent project management experience at Dyer/Khan, where I was responsible for the development of client brochures, newsletters, and posters. As project manager, I coordinated the project time lines, budgets, and production with clients, staff, and vendors.

Continues with a strong emphasis on recent experience and accomplishments

My experience and contacts in the Los Angeles area media and entertainment community should help me make use of state-of-the-art design expertise. As you will see on my résumé, I have worked with the leading motion picture, television, and music companies—that experience should help me develop exciting marketing tools Museum visitors and patrons will find attractive. For example, I helped design an upgrade of the CGI logo for Paramount Pictures and was formally commended by the Director of Marketing.

Refers to enclosed résumé

Could we schedule a meeting at your convenience to discuss this position further? Call me any weekday morning at 412-555-1212 (cell) or e-mail me at <jgoodman@aol.com> if you have questions or need additional information. Thank you for your consideration.

Sincerely,

Joshua S. Goodman

Joshua S. Goodman

Enclosure: Résumé

Figure 16–20   Application Letter from a Recent Graduate Applying for a Graphic-Design Job

522 Beethoven Drive
Roanoke, VA 24016
November 15, 2010

Ms. Cecilia Smathers
Vice President, Dealer Sales
Hamilton Office Machines, Inc.
6194 Main Street
Hampton, VA 23661

Dear Ms. Smathers:

Opens by referencing a personal contact at the firm

During the recent NOMAD convention in Washington, one of your sales representatives, Karen Jarrett, informed me of a possible opening for a district manager in your Dealer Sales Division. My extensive background in the office-systems industry makes me an ideal candidate for the position.

Continues with a concise career summary

I was with Technology, Inc., Dealer Division from its formation in 1998 until TI's merger and reorganization last year. During that period, I was involved in all areas of dealer sales, both within Technology, Inc., and through personal contact with a number of independent dealers. From 2003–2008, I served as Dealer Sales Manager and Special Representative. As described in the enclosed résumé, I was the national winner of TI's "Outstanding Customer Service Award" for 2006, 2007, and 2008. I have strong contacts with key buyers at all the major firms in our industry.

Closes with contact information

I would be happy to discuss my qualifications in an interview at your convenience. Please telephone me at (804) 449-6743 or e-mail me at <gm302.476@sys.com>.

Sincerely,

Gregory Mindukakis

Gregory Mindukakis

Encloses a résumé

Enclosure: Résumé

Figure 16–21 Application Letter from an Applicant with Many Years of Experience

Doing Well in the Interview

Preparing a professional résumé and writing an effective letter of application are essential to obtaining a job interview; that preparation helps you understand your strengths as a potential employee and articulate your career objectives. Nevertheless, the interview is often the most difficult part of the job search because it is so pivotal in the hiring process. A job interview may last for 30 minutes, or it may take several hours; it may be conducted by one person or by several, either at one time or in a series of interviews, in person, by phone, or by teleconference. Because it is impossible to know exactly what to expect, be as prepared as possible. If you are interviewed by phone, set aside a time and place where you won't be interrupted, and have your résumé and note-taking tools (notepad, computer) available.

Before the Interview

The interview is not a one-way communication. It presents you with an opportunity to ask questions of your potential employer and to demonstrate your knowledge of the position and the organization itself. In preparation, learn everything you can about the company before the interview by answering the questions listed in the Learning About Employers checklist on page 611. You can obtain information from the company's Web site, current employees, company literature, and the business section of local and national newspapers, such as the *New York Times*, the *Los Angeles Times*, the *Wall Street Journal*, and the *Washington Post* (available online and in the library). You may be able to learn about the company's size, sales volume, product line, credit rating, branch locations, subsidiary companies, new products and services, building programs, and other such information from its annual reports; publications such as *Moody's Industrials* at <www.moodys.com>, *Dun and Bradstreet* at <www.dnb.com>, *Standard & Poor's* at <www.standardandpoors.com>, and *Thomas' Register* at <www.thomasnet.com>; and other business reference sources a librarian might suggest. What you cannot find through your own research, ask your interviewer. Now is your chance to make certain that you are considering a healthy and growing company. It is also your chance to show your interest in the company and find out as much as possible about company-employee relations, including opportunities for career growth. To that end, you may want to ask your interviewer some or all of the following questions:

- Is there a probationary period for new employees?
- How often are employees formally evaluated on their performance?
- Does the company require training or certification?
- Does the company fund career-related training and outside education?
- Does the position I'm applying for have promotion potential?

Finally, as a way of gaining insight into how the company operates, you could ask your interviewer how he or she started at the company—if time permits.

Try to anticipate the questions your interviewer might ask, and prepare your answers in advance. Be sure you understand a question before answering it, and avoid responding too quickly with a rehearsed answer—try to answer in a natural and relaxed manner. Interviewers typically ask the following questions:

- What are your short-term and long-term occupational goals?
- Where do you see yourself five years from now?
- What are your major strengths and weaknesses?
- Do you work better with others or alone?
- How do you spend your free time?
- What accomplishments are you particularly proud of and why?
- Why are you leaving your current job?
- Why do you want to work for this company?
- Why should I hire you?
- What salary and benefits do you expect?

Some of these questions are difficult. Give them careful thought, try to be as concrete as possible by offering examples when appropriate, and remember that there is no one correct answer.

Many employers use behavioral interviews. Rather than traditional, straight-forward questions, the behavioral interview focuses on asking the candidate to provide examples or respond to hypothetical situations. Interviewers who use behavior-based questions are looking for specific examples from your experience. Prepare for the behavioral interview by recollecting challenging situations or problems that were successfully resolved. Examples of behavior-based questions include the following:

- Can you tell me about a time when you experienced conflict on a team?
- If I were your boss and you disagreed with a decision I made, what would you do?
- How have you used your leadership skills to bring about change?
- Can you tell me about a time when you failed and what you have learned from the experience?

Be sure that you arrive for your interview at the appointed time. In fact, it is usually a good idea to arrive early because you may be asked to fill out an application before you meet your interviewer. Read the application form before filling it out, and proofread it when you are finished. Not only does the application form provide the company with a record for its files, but it also gives the company an opportunity to see how closely you follow directions, how thoroughly you complete a task, and how well you express your ideas in writing. Always bring extra copies of your résumé and samples of your work (if applicable). Some of the people you meet may not have a copy of your résumé, and it contains much of the same information the application asks for: personal data, work experience, and education.

Finally, bring a tablet and pen or PDA to record pertinent information. Do not, however, bring a laptop computer—doing so creates a distraction and a barrier between you and your interviewer.

ON THE WEB

For online access to major national newspapers and other business references, go to Chapter 16, bedfordstmartins.com/writingthatworks, and select *Web Links*.

WRITER'S CHECKLIST
Learning About Employers

As you search for information about potential employers, use these questions as a guide.

✔ What kind of organization is it? Is it for profit? nonprofit? governmental? educational?

✔ Does it provide a service or product? If so, what kind?

✔ How diversified are its products, services, or goals?

✔ How large is the business? How large are its assets?

✔ Is it locally owned? Is it a subsidiary of a larger organization? Is it expanding?

✔ How long has it been in business?

✔ Where will you fit in?

During the Interview

The interview actually begins before you are seated: What you wear and how you act make a first impression. In general, dress simply and conservatively, avoid extremes in fragrance and cosmetics, be well groomed, and never chew gum.

Behavior

First, thank the interviewer for his or her time, express your pleasure at meeting him or her, and remain standing until you are offered a seat. Then sit up straight (good posture suggests self-assurance), look directly at the interviewer, and try to appear relaxed and confident. If you feel nervous during the interview, use that nervous energy to your advantage by channeling it into alertness. Listen carefully and record important information in your memory. Jot down a few facts and figures as needed, but do not attempt to take extensive notes.

◆ *See also the discussion on listening on pages 516–519 in Chapter 14, Giving Presentations and Conducting Meetings.*

Responses

When answering questions, don't ramble or stray from the subject. Say only what you must to answer each question properly and then stop, but avoid giving just yes or no answers—they usually don't permit the interviewer to learn enough about you. Some interviewers allow a silence to fall just to see how you will react. The burden of conducting the interview is the interviewer's, not yours—and he or she may interpret your rush to fill a void in the conversation as a sign of insecurity. If such a silence makes you uncomfortable, be ready to ask pertinent questions about the company from your prepared list. If the interviewer overlooks important points, such as the probationary period or promotion potential, bring them up.

Interviewers look for a degree of self-confidence and understanding of the field in which the applicant is applying for a job, as well as genuine interest in the field, the company, and the job. Less is expected of a beginner, but even a newcomer must show some self-confidence and command of the subject. One way to communicate your interest in the job and company is to ask questions. Interviewers respond favorably to applicants who can communicate and present themselves well.

Salary Negotiations

Although it is better to negotiate salary after you have a job offer or certainly late in the interview, you may be asked, "What are your salary requirements?" You cannot answer such a question without solid preparation. Make sure that you are aware of prevailing salaries in your field so that you will be better prepared to discuss salary. If you are a recent graduate, it is usually unwise to attempt to bargain. Many companies have inflexible starting salaries for beginners.

First, your goal should be to work toward a win-win situation for you and your prospective employer. Avoid overemphasizing money because it tends to make your potential loyalty to an organization suspect. The issue is not simply one of dollar amounts but of your own job satisfaction and what value you can bring to your employer. Consider the following guidelines:

- Seek advice ahead of time from a professional with relevant experience about the typical salary ranges for similar positions.

- Determine the lowest salary you would accept, perhaps based on your most recent employment.

- Consider possible fringe benefits that would be valuable to you (health care, paid education and training) and the firm's opportunities for promotion.

ON THE WEB

For links to Web sites offering useful resources for salary negotiations, see Chapter 16, bedfordstmartins.com/ writingthatworks, and select *Web Links*.

If questioned directly about salary, you can give an answer such as, "I was considering a range of $____ to $____, but that would also depend on the benefits available and the potential or timetable for promotions or salary increases." Remember, it's always acceptable to say to a prospective employer that you would like to think about an offer.

Conclusion

At the conclusion of the interview, thank your interviewer for his or her time. Indicate that you are interested in the job (if true), and try to get an idea of when you can expect to hear from the company (do not press too hard). Reaffirm friendly contact with a firm handshake.

■ Sending Follow-up Correspondence

After you leave the interview, review your notes for accuracy and fill in any gaps while the information is fresh—it may be helpful in comparing job offers. As soon as possible after the interview (no later than two days), send the interviewer a note of thanks in a brief letter or e-mail message. Such notes often include the following:

- Your thanks for the interview and to individuals or groups that gave you special help or attention during the interview
- The name of the specific job for which you interviewed
- Your impression that the job is attractive, if true
- Your confidence that you can perform the job well
- An offer to provide further information or answer further questions

Figure 16–22 shows a typical example of follow-up correspondence. If you have not heard back from the company about the status of your application in two

---

From: pming@juno.com (Philip Ming)
To: vallone@infosystems.com
Subject: Re: Employment Interview
Sent: 14 May 2010 3:59:56 PM Eastern Daylight Time

Dear Mr. Vallone:

Thank you for the informative and pleasant interview we had yesterday. Please extend my thanks to Mr. Wilson of the Media Group as well.

Opens with an expression of appreciation

I came away from our meeting most favorably impressed with Information Systems. I find the position of ACR Designer in the Medical Division to be an attractive one and feel confident that my qualifications would enable me to perform the duties to everyone's advantage.

Continues with a strong statement of interest in the job

If I can answer any further questions, please let me know.

Sincerely yours,

Philip Ming

```
====================
```
Philip Ming
9672 Patton Drive
Kearney, NE 68849
(308) 841-9782
```
====================
```

Ends with relevant contact information

Figure 16–22   Follow-up E-mail Thanking the Interviewer

weeks, send another brief and courteous letter or e-mail message. Beyond that period, it is the responsibility of the company to contact you.

If you are offered a job you want, accept the offer verbally and write a brief letter of acceptance as soon as possible—certainly within a week. The organization of such a message is simple. Begin by accepting the job you have been offered. Identify the job by title and state the exact salary so that there will be no confusion on these two important points. The second paragraph might go into detail about moving dates and the time for reporting to work. The details will vary, depending on the nature of the job offer. Conclude with a statement that you are looking for-

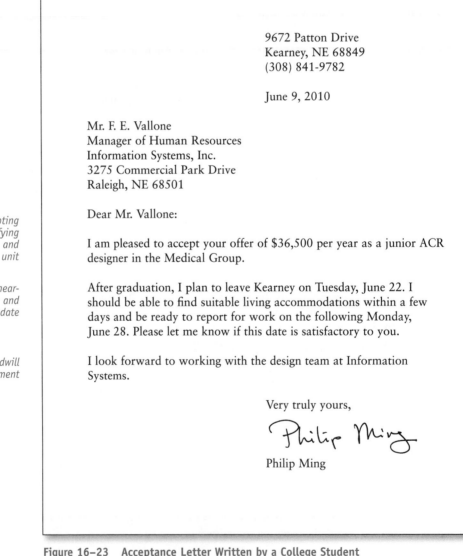

Opens by accepting job and verifying the salary, title, and organizational unit

Continues with near-term schedule and start date

Ends with goodwill statement

9672 Patton Drive
Kearney, NE 68849
(308) 841-9782

June 9, 2010

Mr. F. E. Vallone
Manager of Human Resources
Information Systems, Inc.
3275 Commercial Park Drive
Raleigh, NE 68501

Dear Mr. Vallone:

I am pleased to accept your offer of $36,500 per year as a junior ACR designer in the Medical Group.

After graduation, I plan to leave Kearney on Tuesday, June 22. I should be able to find suitable living accommodations within a few days and be ready to report for work on the following Monday, June 28. Please let me know if this date is satisfactory to you.

I look forward to working with the design team at Information Systems.

Very truly yours,

Philip Ming

Philip Ming

Figure 16–23   **Acceptance Letter Written by a College Student**

ward to working for your new employer, as in the acceptance letter written by a college student in Figure 16–23.

Because you will probably have applied to more than one company or organization, you will need to write a letter of refusal if you receive more than one job offer. Be especially tactful and courteous because the employer you are refusing has spent time and effort interviewing you and may have counted on your accepting the job. It is also possible that you may apply for another job at this company in the future. Figure 16–24 is an example of a job-refusal letter. It acknowledges the consideration given the applicant, offers a logical reason for refusal of the offer, and then concludes on a pleasant note.

◆ *For additional advice on writing refusal letters, see pages 283–289 in Chapter 8, Understanding the Principles of Business Communication, and pages 330–331 in Chapter 9, Writing Business Correspondence.*

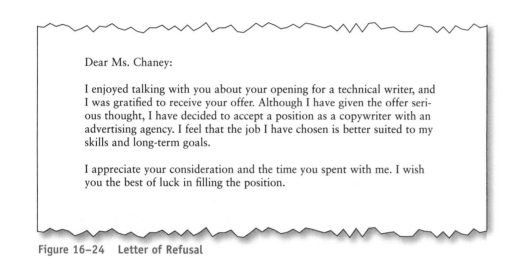

Dear Ms. Chaney:

I enjoyed talking with you about your opening for a technical writer, and I was gratified to receive your offer. Although I have given the offer serious thought, I have decided to accept a position as a copywriter with an advertising agency. I feel that the job I have chosen is better suited to my skills and long-term goals.

I appreciate your consideration and the time you spent with me. I wish you the best of luck in filling the position.

Opens with a tactful reason for refusing the job offer

Closes by acknowledging the effort of the prospective employer

Figure 16–24   Letter of Refusal

Sending a Resignation Letter or Memo

When you are planning to leave a job, for any reason, you usually write a resignation letter or memo to your supervisor or to an appropriate person in the Human Resources Department.

- Start on a positive note, regardless of the circumstances under which you are leaving.
- Consider pointing out how you have benefited from working for the company or say something complimentary about the company.
- Comment on something positive about the people with whom you have been associated.
- Explain why you are leaving in an objective, factual tone.
- Avoid angry recriminations because your resignation will remain on file with the company and could haunt you in the future when you need references.

◆ *For strategies concerning negative messages, see pages 283–289 in Chapter 8, Understanding the Principles of Business Communication.*

ON THE WEB

For another sample resignation letter, go to Model Documents Gallery, bedfordstmartins.com/ writingthatworks

Your memo should give enough notice to allow your employer time to find a replacement. It might be no more than two weeks, or it might be enough time to put your files in order and train your replacement. Some organizations may ask for a notice equivalent to the number of weeks of vacation you receive. Check the policy of your employer before you begin your letter.

The sample resignation letter in Figure 16–25 is from an employee who is leaving to take a job offering greater opportunities. The resignation memo in

227 Kenwood Drive
Austin, TX 78719
January 6, 2010

R.W. Johnson
Director of Metallurgy
Hannibal Laboratories
1914 East 6th Street
Austin, TX 78702

Dear Mr. Johnson:

Positive opening

My three years at Hannibal Laboratories have been an invaluable period of learning and professional development. I arrived as a novice, and I believe that today I am a professional—primarily as a result of the personal attention and tutoring I have received from my superiors and the fine example set by both my superiors and my peers.

Reason for leaving

I believe, however, that the time has come for me to move on to a larger company that can give me an opportunity to continue my professional development. Therefore, I have accepted a position with Procter & Gamble, where I am scheduled to begin on January 25. Thus, my last day at Hannibal will be January 22. I will be happy to train my replacement during the next two weeks.

Positive closing

Many thanks for the experience I have gained and best wishes for the future.

Sincerely,

J. L. Washburne

J. L. Washburne

Figure 16–25   Resignation Letter to Accept a Better Position

MEMO

To: T. W. Haney, Vice President, Administration
From: L. R. Rupp, Executive Assistant   *LR*
Date: February 9, 2010
Subject: Resignation from Winterhaven, effective March 2, 2010

My five-year stay with the Winterhaven Company has been a very
pleasant experience, and I believe that it has been mutually beneficial.

Positive opening

Because the recent restructuring of my job leaves no career path open
to me, I have accepted a position with another company that I feel will
offer me greater advancement opportunities. I am, therefore, submitting my resignation, to be effective on March 2, 2010.

Reason for leaving

I have enjoyed working with my coworkers at Winterhaven and wish
the company success in the future.

Positive closing

Figure 16–26   Resignation Memo under Negative Conditions

Figure 16–26 is written by an employee who is leaving under unhappy circumstances; notice that it opens and closes positively and that the reason for the resignation is stated without apparent anger or bitterness.

CHAPTER 16 SUMMARY: FINDING THE RIGHT JOB

Follow these five steps for finding a job:

- Determine the best job for you.
- Prepare an effective résumé.
- Write an effective letter of application.
- Conduct yourself professionally during the interview.
- Send a follow-up message after the interview.

Research the following sources of information and options for locating jobs:

- Campus career center
- Web resources
- Tips from family, friends, and acquaintances
- Letters of inquiry
- Informational interviews
- Advertisements in newspapers
- Advertisements in trade and professional journals
- Private and temporary employment agencies

■ Internships

■ Local, state, and federal agencies

Plan your résumé carefully.

■ Determine the type of job you seek and compile a list of prospective employers.

■ Consider the type of information about you and your background of most importance to potential employers.

■ Determine, based on this information, the details that should be included and the most effective way to present them.

Write an effective letter of application.

■ Catch the reader's attention.

■ Create the desire for your services.

■ Include a brief summary of your qualifications for the specific job for which you are applying.

■ State when and where you can be reached.

Follow these steps to prepare for a job interview:

■ Learn everything you can about your prospective employer.

■ Arrive on time.

■ Highlight those strengths most useful to the job for which you are applying.

■ Demonstrate your knowledge of your field.

■ Send the interviewer a brief note of thanks after the interview.

When you receive a job offer, write one of the following letters:

■ If you plan to accept the offer, send a letter of acceptance as soon as possible after you receive the offer.

■ If you plan to refuse, send a letter as soon as possible refusing the offer but expressing your appreciation for the organization's time and effort in considering you.

Follow these guidelines in preparing a letter or memo of resignation:

■ Begin and end the message on a positive note.

■ Explain the reason for your departure factually and objectively.

■ Give at least two weeks' notice (and preferably longer) to allow your employer to prepare for your departure.

ON THE WEB

For an online quiz on finding the right job, go to Chapter 16, bedfordstmartins.com/ writingthatworks

ON THE WEB

For additional exercises go to Chapter 16, bedfordstmartins.com/ writingthatworks

■ Exercises

1. Write a letter or an e-mail message to a past or present teacher, employer, or other appropriate person, asking permission to use him or her as a job reference. Be prepared to explain in class why you think this person is especially well qualified to comment on your job qualifications.

2. Obtain a sample résumé at your school's career-development center or local copy center. Annotate and write a brief critical analysis of the résumé for your instructor, pointing out its strong points and how it might be improved in content, organization, or design.

3. List five specific features a company or other employer would need to have to make you interested in working for it. Next, list what you would want to gain from your work experience, such as learning more about a specific technology that interests you.

4. Following the guidelines on pages 587–592, create a résumé to send in response to an electronic posting advertising a summer position in your field of study. Submit your résumé either on a disk or as an e-mail attachment, or both, as required by your instructor.

5. Using the guidelines in this chapter, write a letter of application and a résumé in response to an advertisement for a job you will be qualified for when you graduate. Use high-quality white bond paper and make sure the letter and résumé are error- and blemish-free.

6. Assume that you have been interviewed for the job in Exercise 5. Write a follow-up letter expressing thanks for the interview.

7. If your current résumé is prepared by job chronology, prepare a second résumé — a functional résumé — that not only organizes work experience by type but also helps you identify important skills, abilities, or experiences. Follow the guidelines on pages 580–587. Your instructor may ask you to submit your chronological résumé with your functional résumé.

8. Review your existing résumé to make sure that the verbs and nouns in your job descriptions are consistent and parallel in structure. (See page 104 in Chapter 4, Revising the Draft.)

9. Create an ASCII, or a plain-text, résumé that you could send via e-mail or upload to your Web site. (Use the guidelines provided in Digital Tips: Preparing an ASCII Résumé on page 590.)

Collaborative Classroom Projects

ON THE WEB

For more collaborative classroom projects, go to Chapter 16, bedfordstmartins.com/ writingthatworks

1. Divide into groups of four to six classmates who share your major area (or a similar area) of study. Appoint a group leader and a recorder. For the first 30 minutes, brainstorm a list of action words that could be used to describe your collective skills, abilities, and experiences, and which could work well in a résumé to be used to apply for a job in your field. During the next 15 minutes, brainstorm a list of positions that you could apply for when you graduate. Be ready to share your information with your classmates.

2. Working in pairs, spend 20 minutes during which you play the role of the job interviewer, while your partner plays the role of the interviewee. Then switch roles for the next 20 minutes. Begin by referring to the interview section of this chapter, and decide the name and type of company where you are interviewing, the position, and other details about the job. Include the following questions in the interview:

   - What are your short-term and long-term professional goals?
   - What are your major strengths and weaknesses?
   - Why do you want to work for our company?
   - What are your personal career goals?

- What accomplishment are you particularly proud of? Describe it.
- Why should I hire you?

In conclusion, consider what answers you would change in preparation for your next interview.

ON THE WEB

For extra research projects, go to Chapter 16, bedfordstmartins.com/ writingthatworks

■ Research Projects

1. Research three major employers in your field and, in an outline format, answer the following questions about each:

   a. What kind of an organization is it?
   b. Is it a for-profit or nonprofit organization?
   c. Does it provide a service or services? If so, what kind(s)?
   d. What does its mission statement reveal?
   e. How large is the business? How large are its assets?
   f. Is it locally owned? Is it a subsidiary of a larger operation? Is it expanding?
   g. How long has it been in business?
   h. If it is government employment, at what level or in what sector is it?
   i. Where would you fit in?

   You can obtain information from the Internet, current employees, company literature such as employee publications, and the business section of back issues of local and national newspapers (available in the library and on the Web).

2. Imagine that you work for a large consulting company that has been hired to give a presentation in several European countries on how to seek employment in the United States. You've received several samples of would-be applicants' résumés and have noticed many differences between the structure of their résumés and what is expected in the United States. Research job hunting and résumé writing strategies used in two other countries of your choice, then create a presentation on American-style résumé writing for job seekers from those countries (review Chapter 14, Giving Presentations and Conducting Meetings). Be sure to address the following issues:

   - The use of the title "motivation letter" instead of "cover letter"
   - The inclusion of an applicant's date of birth, marital status, and children on résumés
   - Personal photographs
   - Chronological order versus reverse chronological order
   - Spelling
   - College-level education described as "tertiary" education
   - Paper size

3. Review the Web sites of at least three online college or university placement centers, including the one hosted by your school. These centers offer links and general job-search information and can be helpful as you plan your own specific job search. Begin with the Center for Career Opportunities at Purdue University at <www.purdue.edu>. Write a brief analysis of at least three career-planning sites you reviewed (including the URLs). Be ready to share your results with the class.

4. Find information about the future employment potential of graduates in your major field of study by using at least five Web sources. In a brief memo to your instructor, answer the following questions about your major field:

    a. Based on current indicators, what are the job projections in your field in this country?
    b. Is there a worldwide demand for people in your field?
    c. Do employees in your field have an opportunity to advance?
    d. In your field, is there a wide range in salary expectations based on geographic location?
    e. What other relevant information can you provide?

PART 4

Revision Guide: Sentences, Punctuation, and Mechanics

Sentences   625

Sentence Faults   625
Pronouns   627
Adjectives and Adverbs   632
Verbs   635

Punctuation   643

Commas   643
Semicolons   648
Colons   649
Apostrophes   650
Quotation Marks   653
Periods   654
Question Marks   655
Exclamation Marks   656
Parentheses and Brackets   656
Hyphens   657
Dashes   659
Ellipses   660
Slashes   661

Mechanics   662

Capitalization   662
Numbers   664
Abbreviations   667
Italics   668

English as a Second Language (ESL)   670

Count and Mass Nouns   670
Articles   671
Prepositions   672
Gerunds and Infinitives   673
Adjective Clauses   673
Verb Tenses   673
Helping Verbs   674
Conditional Sentences   675

MARK/SYMBOL	MEANING	EXAMPLE	CORRECTED TYPE
↶	Delete	the ~~manager's~~ report	the report
∧	Insert	the report (manager's)	the manager's report
dots (let)	Let stand	the manager's report	the manager's report
≡ (cap)	Capitalize	the monday meeting	the Monday meeting
/ (lc)	Lowercase	the Monday Meeting	the Monday meeting
∼ (tr)	Transpose	the cover lettre	the cover letter
⊂	Close space	a loud speaker	a loudspeaker
#	Insert space	a loudspeaker	a loud speaker
¶	Paragraph	...report. The meeting...	...report. The meeting...
⌒	Run in with previous line or paragraph	...report. The meeting...	...report. The meeting...
— (ital)	Italicize	the New York Times	the *New York Times*
∼∼ (bf)	Boldface	Use boldface sparingly.	Use **boldface** sparingly.
⊙	Insert period	I wrote the e-mail	I wrote the e-mail.
⌃	Insert comma	However we cannot...	However, we cannot...
=	Insert hyphen	clear cut decision	clear-cut decision
—/M	Insert em dash	Our goal productivity	Our goal—productivity
⌃ or :|	Insert colon	We need the following	We need the following:
⌃ or ;|	Insert semicolon	we finished we achieved	we finished; we achieved
⌄ ⌄	Insert quotation marks	He said, I agree.	He said, "I agree."
⌄	Insert apostrophe	the managers report	the manager's report

Proofreaders' Marks

Sentences

A sentence is the most fundamental and versatile tool available to writers, but sentence faults and issues with pronouns, adjectives, adverbs, and verbs can cause difficulties for your readers. To help you avoid these problems, this section describes common sentence errors and how to correct them.

■ Sentence Faults

Sentence-level errors, like inaccurate facts or incomplete information, can confuse, irritate, or even mislead your readers. These errors can make your meaning hard to determine or, even worse, alter the meaning entirely. Grammatically, the most serious sentence problems are run-on sentences, comma splices, sentence fragments, and dangling and misplaced modifiers.

Run-on Sentences and Comma Splices

An independent clause expresses a complete thought by itself. Although it might be part of a larger sentence, it can stand alone as a separate sentence:

▷   The training division will offer three new courses.

▷   Interested employees should sign up by Wednesday.

When two independent clauses are joined without any punctuation, the result is a *run-on*, or *fused, sentence*. When two independent clauses are joined with only a comma, the result is called a *comma splice* or *comma fault*. Either problem can be corrected by (1) making two sentences, (2) joining the two clauses with a semicolon (if they are closely related and balanced in meaning), (3) joining the two clauses with a comma and a coordinating conjunction, or (4) subordinating one clause to the other.

◆ *For tips on subordinating clauses effectively, see pages 103–104 in Chapter 4, Revising the Draft.*

RUN-ON	The training division will offer three new courses interested employees should sign up by Wednesday.
COMMA SPLICE	The training division will offer three new courses, interested employees should sign up by Wednesday.
CORRECT	The training division will offer three new courses. Interested employees should sign up by Wednesday. [two sentences]
CORRECT	The training division will offer three new courses; interested employees should sign up by Wednesday. [semicolon]
CORRECT	The training division will offer three new courses, *so* interested employees should sign up by Wednesday. [comma plus coordinating conjunction]
CORRECT	*When* the training division offers the new courses, interested employees should sign up for them. [one clause subordinated to the other]

Sentence Fragments

A sentence fragment is an incomplete grammatical unit that is punctuated as a sentence.

FRAGMENT	And quit his job.
SENTENCE	He quit his job.

A sentence fragment lacks either a subject or a verb or is a subordinate clause or phrase. Sentence fragments are often introduced by relative pronouns (*who, whom, whose, which, that*) or subordinating conjunctions (such as *although, because, if,* and *while*). When you use these introductory words, you must combine the dependent clause that follows with a main clause to form a complete sentence.

▶ The new manager instituted several new procedures. ~~Although~~ she didn't obtain approval for them with Human Resources.

, although

A sentence must contain a main, or finite, verb; verbals (gerunds, participles, and infinitives) cannot function as verbs. The following examples are sentence fragments because they lack main verbs.

FRAGMENT	*Providing* all employees with disability insurance.
SENTENCE	The company *provides* all employees with disability insurance.
FRAGMENT	*To work* a 40-hour week.
SENTENCE	Most of our employees *work* a 40-hour week.

Explanatory phrases beginning with *such as, for example, because,* and similar terms may lead to sentence fragments.

▶   The staff wants additional benefits. ~~For example,~~ the use of company cars.
         , such as

Dangling and Misplaced Modifiers

Phrases that do not clearly and logically refer to the correct noun or pronoun are called *dangling modifiers*. Correct this problem by adding the appropriate noun or pronoun for the phrase to modify or by rewriting the phrase as a clause.

▶   While eating lunch, the generator malfunctioned.
       I was

▶   After finishing the negotiations, ~~dinner was relaxing.~~
                                      we relaxed at dinner.

A *misplaced modifier* refers, or appears to refer, to the wrong word or phrase. Avoid this problem by placing modifiers as close as possible to the words they modify. Position each modifier carefully so that it says what you mean.

▶   We ~~just~~ bought the property for expansion.
                            just

▶   Our copier was used to duplicate materials ~~for other departments~~ that needed to be reduced.
       for other departments

A *squinting modifier* is located between two sentence elements and might refer to either one. To eliminate the ambiguity, move the modifier or revise the sentence.

▶   ~~The~~ union agreed ~~during the next week~~ to return to work.
    During the next week, the

▶   The union agreed during the next week ~~to return to work.~~
                                          to return to work

▪ Pronouns

A *pronoun* is used as a substitute for a noun (the noun for which a pronoun substitutes is called the *antecedent*). An unclear link between a pronoun and its antecedent can sometimes cause confusion.

Pronoun Case

Grammatical case indicates the functional relationship of a noun or a pronoun to the other words in a sentence. The case of a pronoun is always determined by its function in a phrase, clause, or sentence. If it functions as the subject, it is in the subjective case; if it functions as an object, it is in the objective case; if it reflects possession or ownership and modifies a noun, it is in the possessive case. The subjective case can indicate the person or thing acting (*He* sued the vendor), the person or thing acted on (*He* was sued by the vendor), or the topic of description (*He* is the vendor). The objective case can indicate the thing acted on (The vendor sued *him*) or the person or thing acting but in the objective position (The vendor was sued by *him*). The possessive case indicates the person or thing owning or possessing something (It was *his* company).

Singular	*Subjective*	*Objective*	*Possessive*
First person	I	me	my, mine
Second person	you	you	your, yours
Third person	he, she, it	him, her, it	his, her, hers, its

Plural	*Subjective*	*Objective*	*Possessive*
First person	we	us	our, ours
Second person	you	you	your, yours
Third person	they	them	their, theirs

Determining Case

One test to determine the proper case of a pronoun is to try using it with a transitive verb that requires a direct object—a person or thing to receive the action expressed by the verb. *Hit* is a useful verb for this test. If the pronoun would logically precede the verb, use the subjective case; if it would logically follow the verb, use the objective case.

▹ *She* hit the volleyball. [subjective case]
▹ The volleyball hit *her*. [objective case]

An *appositive* is a noun or noun phrase that follows and amplifies another noun or noun phrase. A pronoun appositive takes the case of its antecedent.

▹ Two systems analysts, *Joe and I*, were selected to represent the company.

[*Joe and I* is in apposition to the subject, *systems analysts*, and therefore must be in the subjective case.]

▹ The systems analysts selected two members of our department—*Joe and me*.

[*Joe and me* is in apposition to *two members*, the object of the verb *selected*, and therefore must be in the objective case.]

The reverse situation can also present problems. To test for the proper case when the pronouns *we* and *us* are followed by an appositive noun that defines them, try the sentence without the noun.

SENTENCE	(*We/us*) pilots fly our own airplanes.
INCORRECT	*Us* fly our own airplanes.
	[The incorrect usage sounds wrong.]
CORRECT	*We* fly our own airplanes.
	[The correct usage sounds right.]

To determine the case of a pronoun that follows *as* or *than*, mentally add the words that are omitted but understood.

▶ The other sales representative is not paid as well as *she* [is paid].
  [You would not write, "*her* is paid."]

▶ His partner was better informed than *he* [was informed].
  [You would not write, "*him* was informed."]

If pronouns in compound constructions cause problems, try using them singly to determine the proper case.

▶ In his report, Jamel thanked Sam and (*me/I*).
▶ In his report, Jamel thanked *Sam*.
▶ In his report, Jamel thanked *me*.

Using *Who* or *Whom*

Writers are often unsure whether to use *who* or *whom*. *Who* is the subjective case form, whereas *whom* is the objective case form. When in doubt about which form to use, substitute a personal pronoun to see which one fits. If *he, she,* or *they* fits, use *who*.

▶ *Who* is the training coordinator?
  [You would say, "*She* is the training coordinator."]

If *him, her,* or *them* fits, use *whom*.

▶ It depends on *whom*?
  [You would say, "It depends on *them*."]

Pronoun Reference

A pronoun should refer clearly to a specific antecedent. Avoid vague and uncertain references.

▷   *, which was a big one,*
   We got the account after we wrote the proposal. ~~It was a big one.~~

For coherence, place pronouns as close as possible to their antecedents.

▷   *, praised for its design, is   .*
   The office building next to City Hall ~~was praised for its design.~~

A general (or broad) reference or one that has no real antecedent is a problem that often occurs when the word *this* is used by itself.

▷   *experience*
   He deals with personnel problems in his work. This helps him in his personal life.

Another problem is a hidden reference, which has only an implied antecedent.

▷   *the   of ketone bodies*
   A high-lipid, low-carbohydrate diet is "ketogenic" because it favors ~~their~~ formation.

Do not repeat an antecedent in parentheses following the pronoun. If you feel you must identify the pronoun's antecedent in this way, rewrite the sentence.

AWKWARD   The senior partner first met Bob Evans when he (Evans) was a trainee.

IMPROVED   Bob Evans was a trainee when the senior partner first met him.

Pronoun-Antecedent Agreement

A pronoun must agree, or correspond in form, with its antecedent in person, gender, and number.

Person

A pronoun must agree with its antecedent in person. For example, use either the third person or the second person. Don't mix them.

INCORRECT   *Employees* must sign the logbook when *you* enter a restricted area.

CORRECT   *Employees* must sign the logbook when *they* enter a restricted area.

CORRECT   *You* must sign the logbook when *you* enter a restricted area.

Gender

A pronoun must agree with its antecedent in gender.

▷   *Isabel* was wearing *her* identification badge, but *Tom* had to clip *his* on before they could pass the security guard.

Traditionally, a masculine pronoun was used to agree with antecedents that include both sexes, such as *everybody, nobody, one, person, someone,* or *student.*

However, to avoid the implied sexual bias in such usage, use the following alternatives:

GENDER BIAS   *Everybody* completed *his* report on time.

FREE OF BIAS   *Everybody* completed *his or her* report on time.

FREE OF BIAS   *Everybody* completed a report on time.

Often, the best solution is to rewrite the sentence in the plural; but be sure to make all related objects plural too. Do not, however, resort to a plural pronoun when the antecedent is singular.

INCORRECT   *Everybody* completed *their* reports on time.

                       [The antecedent, *Everybody*, is singular, but the pronoun, *their*, is plural.]

CORRECT   The *employees* completed *their* reports on time.

                       [The antecedent, *employees*, is plural; the pronoun, *their*, is also plural.]

◆ *See also page 111 in Chapter 4, Revising the Draft.*

ESL Tips

Using Possessive Pronouns

In many languages, possessive pronouns agree in number and gender with the nouns they modify. In English, however, possessive pronouns agree in number and gender with their antecedents. Check your writing carefully for agreement between a possessive pronoun and the word, phrase, or clause to which it refers.

▶ The *woman* bought *her* brother lunch.
▶ *Robert* sent *his* mother flowers on Mother's Day.

Number

A pronoun must agree with its antecedent in number.

▶ Although the typical *engine* runs well in moderate temperatures, ~~they~~ *it* often stall *s* in extreme cold.

In formal English, indefinite pronouns (*anybody, anyone, anything, each, either, everybody, everyone, everything, neither, nobody, none, no one, somebody, someone,* and *something*) are considered singular and must be referred to by singular pronouns.

INCORRECT   When *someone* has conducted research, *they* are likely to write an effective report.

You can use the following options for revision: (1) replace the plural pronoun with *he or she* or *his or her*; (2) make the antecedent plural; or (3) rewrite the sentence so that no problem of agreement exists.

CORRECT	When *someone* has conducted research, *he or she* is likely to write an effective report.
CORRECT	When *writers* have conducted research, *they* are likely to write an effective report.
CORRECT	A writer who has conducted research is likely to write an effective report.

Collective nouns may be singular or plural, depending on meaning.

CORRECT	The *staff* prepared *its* annual report.
	[*Staff* refers to the group as a single unit.]
CORRECT	The *staff* returned to *their* offices after the meeting.
	[*Staff* refers to members of the group as individuals.]

A compound antecedent joined by *or* or *nor* is singular when both elements are singular and plural when both are plural. If one of the antecedents is singular and the other plural, the pronoun agrees with the nearer antecedent.

CORRECT	Either the *receptionist* or the *secretaries* should go on *their* lunch breaks.
CORRECT	Either the *secretaries* or the *receptionist* should go on *his or her* lunch break.

A compound antecedent with its elements joined by *and* requires a plural pronoun.

CORRECT	The *architect* and the *designer* prepared *their* plans.

▒ Adjectives and Adverbs

An adjective modifies or describes a noun or pronoun. An adverb modifies the action or condition expressed by a verb. An adverb may also modify an adjective, another adverb, or a clause.

Comparatives and Superlatives

The three degrees of comparison are called the *positive* (the basic form of the adjective or adverb), the *comparative* (showing comparison with one other item), and the *superlative* (showing comparison with two or more other items).

Most adjectives and adverbs show the comparative form with the suffix *-er* for two items and the superlative form with the suffix *-est* for three or more items.

▶ The first report is *long*. [adjective in positive form]

▶ The second report is *longer*. [adjective in comparative form]

▶ The third report is *longest*. [adjective in superlative form]

▶ This copier prints *fast*. [adverb in positive form]

▶ This copier prints *faster* than the old one. [adverb in comparative form]

▶ This copier prints the *fastest* of the three tested. [adverb in superlative form]

Many two-syllable adjectives and most three-syllable adjectives are preceded by the word *more* or *most* to form the comparative or the superlative.

▶ The new Media Center is *more* impressive than the old one. It is the *most* impressive in the country.

Most adverbs with two or more syllables end in *-ly*, and most adverbs ending in *-ly* are compared by inserting the comparative *more* or *less* or the superlative *most* or *least* in front of them.

▶ Her sales rose *more quickly* last quarter than those of any other company's sales representative.

▶ *Most surprisingly*, the engine failed during the final test phase.

A few adjectives have irregular forms of comparison (*much, more, most; little, less, least*). A few irregular adverbs require a change in form to indicate comparison (*well, better, best; worse, worst; far, farther, farthest*).

Absolute words (such as *unique, perfect, exact,* and *infinite*) are not logically subject to comparison, especially in workplace writing, where accuracy and precision are often crucial.

▶ We modified our mission statement to more ~~exactly~~ _{closely} reflect our long-term goals.

Placement

Within a sentence, adjectives may appear before the nouns they modify (the attributive position) or after the nouns they modify (the predicative position).

▶ We negotiated a *bigger* contract than our competitor did.
  [attributive position]

▶ We negotiated a contract *bigger* than our competitor's.
  [predicative position]

Using Adjectives

In English, unlike many other languages, adjectives have only one form. Do not add -s or -es to an adjective to make it plural.

▶ the *long* letter
▶ the *long* letters

Likewise, adjectives in English do not change to show gender.

▶ The *tall* man (masculine noun)
▶ The *tall* woman (feminine noun)
▶ The *tall* building (neuter noun)

Capitalize adjectives of origin (city, state, nation, continent).

▶ the *Venetian* canals
▶ the *Texas* legislature
▶ the *French* government
▶ the *African* continent

In English, verbs of feeling (for example, *bore, interest, surprise*) have two adjectival forms: the present participle (*-ing*) and the past participle (*-ed*). Use the present participle to describe what causes the feeling. Use the past participle to describe the person who experiences the feeling.

▶ We heard the *surprising* election results.

[The *election results* cause the feeling of surprise.]

▶ The *surprised* candidate found out she had lost the election.

[The *candidate* experienced the feeling of surprise.]

Adjectives follow nouns in English in only two cases: when the adjective functions as a subjective complement, as in:

▶ That project is not *finished*.

and when an adjective phrase or clause modifies the noun, as in:

▶ The project *that was suspended temporarily* has a new deadline.

In all other cases, adjectives are placed before the noun.

When there are multiple adjectives, the order illustrated in the following example would apply in most circumstances, with some exceptions. (Normally, do not use a phrase with so many stacked modifiers.)

The six extra-large rectangular brown cardboard takeout containers...

determiner | number | comment | size | shape | color | material | qualifier | noun

An adjective is called a predicate adjective when it follows a linking verb, such as a form of the verb *to be.* By completing the meaning of a linking verb, a predicate adjective describes, or limits, the subject of the verb.

▶ The job is *easy.*

▶ The manager was very *demanding.*

An adjective also can follow a transitive verb and modify its direct object (the person or thing that receives the action of the verb).

▶ They painted the office *white.*

An adverb may appear almost anywhere in a sentence, but its position can affect meaning. Avoid placing an adverb between two verb forms where it will be ambiguous because it can be read as modifying either.

AMBIGUOUS	The man who was making calculations *hastily* rose from his desk and left the room.
	[Did the man calculate hastily or did he rise hastily?]
IMPROVED	The man who was making calculations rose *hastily* from his desk and left the room.
IMPROVED	The man who was *hastily* making calculations rose from his desk and left the room.

▨ Verbs

A verb is a word or group of words that describes an action (The copier *jammed* at the beginning of the job), states the way in which something or someone is affected by an action (He *was disappointed* that the proposal was rejected), or affirms a state of existence (She *is* a district manager now). This section focuses on those areas of verb usage that can cause inexperienced writers problems.

Subject-Verb Agreement

Agreement, grammatically, means the correspondence in form between different elements of a sentence. A verb must agree with its subject in person and number.

▶ *I am* going to approve his promotion.

[The first-person singular subject, *I*, requires the first-person singular form of the verb, *am*.]

▶ His *colleagues are* envious.

[The third-person plural subject, *colleagues*, requires the third-person plural form of the verb, *are*.]

Intervening Words

Subject-verb agreement is not affected by intervening phrases and clauses.

▷ *One* in twenty hard drives we receive from our suppliers *is* faulty.
[The verb, *is*, must agree in number with the subject, *one*, not *hard drives* or *suppliers*.]

The same is true when nouns fall between a subject and its verb.

▷ Only *one* of the emergency lights *was* functioning.
[The subject of the verb is *one*, not *lights*.]

▷ *Each* of the managers *supervises* a statewide region.
[The subject of the verb is *each*, not *managers*.]

Note that *one* and *each* are normally singular.
Modifying phrases can obscure a single subject.

▷ The *advice* of two engineers, one lawyer, and three executives *was* obtained prior to our making a commitment.
[The subject of the sentence, *advice*, requires the single verb, *was*.]

Inverted Word Order

Inverted word order can confuse agreement between subject and verb.

▷ From this work *have come* several important *improvements*.
[The subject of the verb is *improvements*, not *work*.]

Collective Subjects

Subjects expressing measurement, weight, mass, or total often take singular verbs even though the subject word is plural. Such subjects are treated as a unit.

▷ *Four years is* the normal duration of the apprenticeship program.

However, when such subjects refer to the individual items that make up the unit, a plural verb is required.

▷ If you're looking for oil, *three quarts are* on the shelf in the garage.

Similarly, collective subjects take singular verbs when the group is thought of as a unit. They take plural verbs when the individuals are thought of separately.

▷ The *committee is* holding its meeting on Thursday.

▷ The *majority are* opposed to delivering their reports at the meeting.

Compound Subjects

A compound subject is composed of two or more elements joined by a conjunction such as *and, or, nor, either . . . or,* or *neither . . . nor.* Usually, when the elements are connected by *and,* the subject is plural and requires a plural verb.

▷   *Chemistry and finance are* prerequisites for this course.

If the elements connected by *and* form a unit or refer to the same person, however, the subject is regarded as singular and takes a singular verb.

▷   Peaches and cream *is* his favorite dessert.
▷   His accountant and business partner *prepares* the tax forms.
     [His accountant is also his business partner.]

A compound subject joined by *or* or *nor* requires a singular verb with two singular elements and a plural verb with two plural elements.

▷   Neither the doctor nor the nurse *is* on duty.
▷   Neither the doctors nor the nurses *are* on duty.

A compound subject with a singular and a plural element joined by *or* or *nor* requires that the verb agree with the element closer to it.

▷   Neither the office manager nor the *accountants were* there.
▷   Neither the accountants nor the *office manager was* there.

Indefinite Pronouns

Indefinite pronouns such as *some, none, all, more,* and *most* may be singular or plural, depending on whether they are used with a mass noun (*Most* of the oil *has* been used) or with a count noun (*Most* of the drivers *know* why they are here). Mass nouns are singular, and count nouns are plural. Other words, such as *type, part, series,* and *portion,* take singular verbs even when they precede a phrase containing a plural noun.

◆ *See also pages 670–671.*

▷   A *series* of meetings *was* held about the best way to market the new product.
▷   A large *portion* of most annual reports *is* devoted to promoting the corporate image.

Relative Pronouns

A relative pronoun (*who, which, that*) may take either a singular or a plural verb, depending on whether its antecedent is singular or plural.

▷   He is an *auditor* who *takes* work home at night.
▷   He is one of those *auditors* who *take* work home at night.

Singular Nouns Ending in -s

Some abstract nouns are singular in meaning though plural in form; examples include *mathematics*, *news*, *physics*, and *economics*.

▷ Textiles *is* an industry in need of import quotas.

▷ Statistics *is* a branch of mathematics that analyzes and interprets data based on samples and populations.

Some words, such as the plural *jeans* and *scissors*, cause special problems.

▷ The *scissors were* ordered last week.
   [The subject is the plural *scissors*.]

▷ A *pair* of scissors *is* on order.
   [The subject is the singular *pair*.]

Book Titles

A book with a plural title requires a singular verb.

▷ *Monetary Theories is* a useful source.

Subject Complements

A *subject complement* is a noun or an adjective in the predicate of a sentence following a linking verb. The number of a subject complement does not affect the number of the verb—the verb must always agree with the subject.

▷ The topic of his report *was* rivers.
   [The subject of the sentence is *topic*, not *rivers*.]

Voice

In grammar, *voice* indicates the relation of the subject to the action of the verb. When the verb is in the *active voice*, the subject acts; when it is in the *passive voice*, the subject is acted on. Because the active voice is generally more direct, more concise, and easier for readers to understand, use the active voice in most cases.

▷ *The agency*
   It was reported ~~by the agency~~ that the new model is defective.

◆ For additional guidance on choosing between active and passive voice, see pages 101–102 in Chapter 4, Revising the Draft.

Whether you use the active or the passive voice, be careful not to shift voices in a sentence.

▷ David Cohen corrected the inaccuracy as soon as ~~it was identified by~~ the editor.
   identified it

he does not permit them
▶ The captain permits his crew to go ashore, but ~~they are not permitted~~ to go downtown.
^

Mood

Mood in grammar indicates whether a verb is intended to make a statement or ask a question, give a command, or express a hypothetical possibility.

The *indicative mood* states a fact, gives an opinion, or asks a question.

▶ The setting *is* correct.
▶ *Is* the setting correct?

The *imperative mood* expresses a command, suggestion, request, or plea. In the imperative mood, the implied subject *you* is not expressed.

▶ *Install* the wiring today.
▶ Please *let* me know if I can help.

The *subjunctive mood* expresses something that is contrary to fact, conditional, hypothetical, or purely imaginative; it can also express a wish, a doubt, or a possibility. In the subjunctive mood, *were* is used instead of *was* in clauses that speculate about the present or future, and the base form (*be*) is used following certain verbs, such as *propose*, *request*, or *insist*.

▶ If we *were* to close the sale today, we would meet our monthly quota.
▶ The senior partner insisted that she *be* in charge of the project.

The most common use of the subjunctive mood is to express clearly that the writer considers a condition to be contrary to fact. If the condition is factual, use the indicative mood.

SUBJUNCTIVE	If I *were* president of the firm, I would change several hiring policies.
INDICATIVE	Although I *am* president of the firm, I don't control every aspect of its policies.

Do not shift haphazardly from one mood to another within a sentence; to do so makes the sentence unbalanced as well as ungrammatical.

INCORRECT	*Reboot* the computer first [imperative]; then you *should empty* the cache [indicative].
CORRECT	*Reboot* the computer first [imperative]; then *empty* the cache [imperative].
CORRECT	You *should reboot* the computer first [indicative]; then you *should empty* the cache [indicative].

Determining Mood

In written and especially in spoken English, there is an increasing tendency to use the indicative mood where the subjunctive traditionally has been used. Note the differences between traditional and contemporary usage in these examples:

Traditional (Formal) Use of the Subjunctive Mood

▶ I wish he *were* here now.
▶ If I *were* going to the conference, I would room with him.
▶ I requested that she *show* up on time.

Contemporary (Informal) Use of the Indicative Mood

▶ I wish he *was* here now.
▶ If I *was* going to the conference, I would room with him.
▶ I requested that she *shows* up on time.

As a speaker of English, you are faced with a choice: Do you use the subjunctive and, with some groups of people, sound sophisticated or intellectual? Or, do you use the indicative and, with other groups, sound uneducated? The answer might be to master both uses and be able to move freely between the different groups. In business and technical writing, however, it is best to use the more traditional expressions.

Tense

Tense is the grammatical term for verb forms that indicate time distinctions. English has six simple tenses: present, present perfect, past, past perfect, future, and future perfect. Each tense also has a corresponding progressive form.

Tense	Basic Form	Progressive Form
Present	I start	I am starting
Present perfect	I have started	I have been starting
Past	I started	I was starting
Past perfect	I had started	I had been starting
Future	I will start	I will be starting
Future perfect	I will have started	I will have been starting

Use the *simple present tense* to represent action occurring in the present, without any indication of time duration (I *use* the calculator); to present actions or conditions that have no time restrictions (Water *boils* at 212°F); or to indicate habitual action (I *pass* the coffee shop every day). A general truth is always expressed in the present tense (Time *heals* all wounds). In addition, the present tense can be used as a "historical present" to make things that occurred in the past more vivid (Dow Jones *Reaches* a Record High).

Use the *present perfect tense* to describe something from the recent past that has a bearing on the present—a period of time before the present but after the simple past. The present perfect tense is formed by combining the present tense of the helping verb *have* with the past participle of the main verb (We *have finished* the draft and can now revise it).

To indicate an action that took place entirely in the past, use the *simple past tense*. The past tense is usually formed by adding *-d* or *-ed* to the root form of the verb (We *closed* the office early yesterday).

To indicate that one past event preceded another, use the *past perfect tense*, which is formed by combining the helping verb *had* with the past participle of the main verb (He *had finished* by the time I arrived).

Use the *simple future tense* to indicate a time that will occur after the present. The helping verb *will* (or *shall*) is used along with the main verb. (I *will finish* the

---

ESL Tips

Using the Progressive Form

English uses the progressive form, particularly the present progressive, more frequently than other languages do. The progressive form of the verb is composed of two features: a form of the helping verb *be* and the *-ing* form of the base verb.

PRESENT PROGRESSIVE	I *am updating* the Web site.
PAST PROGRESSIVE	I *was updating* the Web site last week.
FUTURE PROGRESSIVE	I *will be updating* the Web site regularly.

The present progressive is used in three ways:

1. To refer to an action that is in progress at the moment of speaking or writing

    ▶ My assistant *is taking* the meeting minutes.

2. To highlight that a state or an action is not permanent

    ▶ The office temp *is helping* us for a few weeks.

3. To express future plans

    ▶ The summer intern *is leaving* to return to school this Friday.

The past progressive is used to refer to a continuing action or condition in the past, usually with specified limits.

▶ I *was failing* calculus until I got a tutor.

The future progressive is used to refer to a continuous action or condition in the future.

▶ We *will be monitoring* his condition all night.

Verbs that express mental activity or the senses of sight, smell, touch, sound, and taste are generally not used in the progressive.

▶ I *believe* the defendant's testimony.

job tomorrow.) Do not, however, use the future tense needlessly; doing so merely adds complexity.

▶   This system ~~will be~~ *is* explained on page 3.

▶   When you press this button, the feeder ~~will move~~ *moves* the paper into position.

Use the *future perfect tense* to indicate an action that will be completed at the time of or before another future action. It is formed by linking the helping verbs *will have* to the past participle of the main verb. (He *will have driven* 400 miles by the time he returns.)

Be consistent in your use of tense. The only legitimate shift in tense records a real change in time. Illogical shifts in tense will only confuse your readers.

▶   Before he visited the branch office, the manager ~~meets~~ *met* with the staff.

Punctuation

Punctuation is a system of symbols that helps the reader to understand the intention of a sentence and the structural relationships within it. Misuse of punctuation can cause your reader to misunderstand your meaning. Marks of punctuation may link, separate, enclose, terminate, classify, and indicate omissions from sentences. Most of the 13 punctuation marks can perform more than one function. Their use is determined by grammatical conventions and by the writer's intention.

■ Commas

The *comma* (,) appears more frequently than any other mark of punctuation because it has such a wide variety of uses: it can link, enclose, and separate sentence elements. Used with care, the comma can clarify and emphasize how ideas fit together; used carelessly, it can cause confusion.

Linking Independent Clauses

Use a comma before a coordinating conjunction (*and, but, or, nor*, and sometimes *so, yet*, and *for*) that links independent clauses.

◆ *See also semicolons, pages 648–649.*

▶ The new microwave disinfection system was delivered, *but* the installation will require an additional week.

However, if two independent clauses are short and closely related—and there is no danger of confusing the reader—the comma may be omitted. Both of the following examples are correct.

▶ The cable snapped and the power failed.
▶ The cable snapped, and the power failed.

Introducing Elements

Clauses and Phrases

Generally, place a comma after an introductory clause or phrase, especially if it is long, to identify where the introductory element ends and where the main part of the sentence begins.

▶ *Because of limited vaccine production capacity for this year's strain of influenza,* we are urging that high-risk patients be given priority for available vaccine supplies.

A long modifying phrase that precedes the main clause should always be followed by a comma.

▶ *During the first series of field-performance tests at our Colorado proving ground,* the new engine failed to meet our expectations.

When an introductory phrase is short and closely related to the main clause, the comma may be omitted.

▶ *In two seconds* a 5°C temperature rise occurs in the test tube.

A comma should always follow an absolute phrase, which modifies the whole sentence.

▶ *The tests completed,* we organized the data for the final report.

Words

Certain types of introductory words are followed by a comma. One example is a transitional word or phrase (*however, in addition*) that connects the preceding clause or sentence with the thought that follows.

▶ *Furthermore,* steel can withstand a humidity of 99 percent, provided there is no chloride or sulfur dioxide in the atmosphere.

▶ *For example,* this change will make us more competitive in the marketplace.

When adverbs closely modify the verb or entire sentence, they should not be followed by a comma.

▶ *Perhaps* we can still solve the turnover problem. *Certainly* we should try.

A proper noun used in an introductory direct address is followed by a comma, as is an interjection (such as *oh, well, why, indeed, yes,* and *no*).

▶ *Nancy,* enclosed is the article you asked me to review. [direct address]

▶ *Yes,* I will ensure that your request is forwarded. [interjection]

Quotations

Use a comma to separate a direct quotation from its introduction.

▶ Morton and Lucia White said, "People live in cities but dream of the countryside."

Do not use a comma when giving an indirect quotation.

▶ Morton and Lucia White said that people dream about country life, even though they live in cities.

◆ *See also Quotation Marks, pages 653–654, and Quoting from Your Sources, pages 176–177.*

Enclosing Elements

Use commas to enclose nonrestrictive and parenthetical sentence elements. Nonrestrictive elements add subordinate information about the things they modify; parenthetical elements also insert extra information into the sentence. Each is set off by commas to show its loose relationship with the rest of the sentence.

▶ Our new Detroit factory, *which began operations last month*, should add 25 percent to total output. [nonrestrictive clause]
▶ We can, *of course*, expect their lawyer to call us. [parenthetical element]

Similarly, enclose a nonrestrictive participial phrase (any form of a verb used as an adjective) within commas.

▶ The lathe operator, *working quickly and efficiently*, finished early.

In contrast, restrictive elements—as their name implies—restrict the meaning of the words to which they apply and cannot be set off with commas.

▶ The boy *in the front row* is six years old. [restrictive]
▶ The boy, *who is sitting in the front row*, is six years old. [nonrestrictive]

In the first sentence, *in the front row* is essential to the sentence: The phrase identifies the boy by his location. In the second sentence, the relative clause *who is sitting in the front row* is incidental: The main idea can be communicated without it.

An appositive phrase (which reidentifies another expression in the sentence) is enclosed in commas.

▶ Our company, *the Blaylok Precision Tool Company*, is doing well this year.

Separating Elements

Items in a Series

Although the comma before the last item in a series is sometimes omitted, it is generally clearer to include it.

▶ Random House, Bantam, Doubleday, and Dell were individual publishing companies before the industry's restructuring.

[Without the final comma, *Doubleday and Dell* might refer to one company or two.]

Phrases and clauses in coordinate series are also punctuated with commas.

▶ Plants absorb noxious gases, act as receptors of dirt particles, and cleanse the air of other impurities.

When phrases or clauses in a series contain commas, separate them with semi-colons.

▶ Our new products include amitriptyline, which has sold very well; dipyridamole, which has not sold well; and cholestyramine, which was just introduced.

Adjectives

When adjectives modifying the same noun can be reversed and make sense, or when they can be separated by *and* or *or*, they should be separated by commas.

▶ The drawing was of a *modern, sleek, swept-wing* airplane.

When an adjective modifies a phrase, no comma is required.

▶ She was investigating the *damaged inventory-control system.*

[The adjective *damaged* modifies the phrase *inventory-control system.*]

Never separate a final adjective from its noun.

▶ He is a conscientious, honest, reliable/worker. [omit comma]

Dates

A full date that is written in the month-day-year format uses a comma preceding and following the year.

▶ Note that November 30, 2020, is the payoff date for the bond.

◆ *See also page 347 in Chapter 9, Writing Business Correspondence.*

Do not use commas for dates in the day-month-year format, which is used in many parts of the world and by the U.S. military.

▶ Note that 30 November 2020 is the payoff date for the bond.

Do not use commas if only the day or the year is included.

▶ The target date of May 2011 is optimistic, so I would like to meet on March 4 to discuss our options.

Numbers

Use commas to separate the elements of Arabic numbers.

▶   1,528,200 feet

However, because many countries use the comma as the decimal marker, use periods or spaces rather than commas in international documents.

▶   1.528.200 feet *or* 1 528 200 feet

Addresses

Commas are conventionally used to separate the elements of an address written on the same line (but they are not inserted between the state and the zip code).

▶   Kristen James, 4119 Mill Road, Dayton, Ohio 45401

Use commas to separate elements of geographic names.

▶   Toronto, Ontario, Canada

Names

Use a comma to separate names that are reversed or that are followed by an abbreviation of an earned title, such as Ph.D., M.D., and C.P.A.

▶   Smith, Alvin
▶   Jane Rogers, Ph.D.

In current usage, however, no comma is necessary before abbreviations of personal and corporate names (such as Jr., Sr., and Inc.).

▶   Ray Aragon Jr.
▶   Grace Inc.

Using Commas with Other Punctuation

When a comma should follow a phrase or clause that ends with words in parentheses, the comma always appears outside the closing parenthesis.

▶   Although we left late (at 7:30 p.m.), we arrived in time for the keynote address.

Commas always go inside quotation marks.

▶   The operator placed the discharge bypass switch at "normal," which triggered a second discharge.

A comma should not be used with a dash, an exclamation mark, a period, or a question mark.

▷   "Have you finished the project?/" I asked. [omit comma]

Avoiding Unnecessary Commas

Writers often add commas where they do not belong because they assume that a pause should be indicated by a comma. It is true that commas usually signal pauses, but it is not true that pauses *necessarily* call for commas.

Be careful not to place a comma between a subject and its verb or between a verb and its object.

▷   The wet weather across the region/makes spring planting difficult. [omit comma]

▷   The firm employs/four writers, two artists, and one photographer. [omit comma]

Do not use a comma between the elements of a compound subject or a compound predicate consisting of only two elements.

▷   The chairman of the board/and the president prepared the press release. [omit comma]

▷   The manager revised the schedules/and improved morale. [omit comma]

Placing a comma after a coordinating conjunction (*and, but, for, nor, or, so, yet*) is an especially common error.

▷   We doubled our sales, but/we still did not dominate the market. [omit comma]

Do not place a comma before the first item or after the last item of a series.

▷   We purchased new office furniture, including/desks, chairs, and tables. [omit comma]

▨ Semicolons

The *semicolon* (;) links independent clauses or other sentence elements that are of equal weight and grammatical rank. The semicolon indicates a longer pause than a comma would, but not so long a pause as a period would.

Two closely related independent clauses can be linked by a semicolon.

▷   No one applied for the position; the job was too difficult.

The relationship between the two statements should be so clear that a reader will understand why they are linked without further explanation. Often, such clauses balance or contrast with each other.

▷   Our last supervisor allowed only one long break; our new supervisor allows two short ones.

Use a semicolon between two main clauses connected by a coordinating conjunction (*and, but, for, or, nor, yet, so*) if the clauses are long and contain other punctuation.

▶ In most cases these individuals are corporate executives, bankers, or Wall Street lawyers; but they do not, as the economic determinists seem to believe, simply push the button of their economic power to affect fields remote from economics.

A semicolon should be used before conjunctive adverbs (such as *therefore, moreover, furthermore, indeed, in fact, however*) that connect independent clauses.

▶ I won't finish today; moreover, I doubt that I will finish this week.

Do not use a semicolon between a dependent clause and its main clause. Elements joined by semicolons must be of equal grammatical rank or weight.

▶ No one applied for the position, even though it was heavily advertised.

Colons

The *colon* (:) is a mark of anticipation and introduction that alerts the reader to the close connection between the first statement and the one following.

▶ We carry three brands of watches: Timex, Swiss Army, and Omega.

Do not, however, place a colon between a verb and its objects.

▶ The three fluids for cleaning pipettes are, water, alcohol, and acetone. [omit colon]

Do not use a colon between a preposition and its object.

▶ I would like to be transferred to, Tucson, Boston, or Miami. [omit colon]

A colon can link one statement to another that develops, explains, amplifies, or illustrates the first, including two independent clauses.

▶ Any large organization must confront two separate, though related, information problems: It must maintain an effective internal communication system, and it must maintain an effective external communication system.

Occasionally, a colon may be used to link an appositive phrase to its related statement if special emphasis is needed.

▶ Only one thing will satisfy Mr. Sturgess: our finished report.

Colons separate citation elements and time designations.

▷ 3:144 [refers to page 144 of volume 3]

▷ *Microsoft MapPoint 2009.* Redmond, WA: Microsoft, 2008. CD-ROM. [separates location and name of publisher]

▷ *The Black Swan: The Impact of the Highly Improbable* [separates a book's title and subtitle]

▷ 9:30 a.m.

In a ratio, the colon indicates the proportion of one amount to another and replaces *to*.

▷ The cement is mixed with the water and sand at a ratio of 7:5:14.

A colon follows the salutation in business correspondence, even when the salutation refers to a person by first name.

▷ Dear Ms. Jeffers:

▷ Dear Frank:

The first word after a colon may be capitalized if it begins a complete sentence, a formal resolution or question, or a direct quotation.

▷ The conference attendance was low: We did not advertise widely enough.

Begin a subordinate element following a colon with a lowercase letter.

▷ We have only one way to stay within our present budget: to reduce expenditures for research and development.

▪ Apostrophes

An *apostrophe* (') is used to show possession; to mark the omission of letters; and sometimes to indicate the plural of numbers, letters, and acronyms.

Showing Possession

A noun or pronoun is in the possessive case when it represents a person, place, or thing that possesses something. Possession is generally expressed with *'s* (the *report's* title), with a prepositional phrase using *of* (the title *of the report*), or with the possessive form of a pronoun (*our* report). Practices vary for some possessive forms, but the following guidelines are widely used in business writing. Above all, be consistent.

◆ *See also Pronoun Case, pages 627–629.*

Singular Nouns

Most singular nouns indicate possession with *'s*.

▶ a *manager's* office
▶ the *company's* stock value
▶ the *witness's* testimony
▶ the *bus's* schedule

When pronunciation is difficult or when a multisyllable noun ends in a *z* sound, you may use only an apostrophe.

▶ *New Orleans'* levee reconstruction plans

Plural Nouns

Plural nouns that end in *-s* or *-es* show the possessive case with only an apostrophe.

▶ the *managers'* reports
▶ the *companies'* joint project
▶ the *witnesses'* reports
▶ the *buses'* schedules

Plural nouns that do not end in *-s* or *-es* show the possession with *'s*.

▶ *children's* clothing
▶ *women's* resources
▶ *men's* lockeroom

Compound Nouns

Compound nouns form the possessive with *'s* following the final letter.

▶ the *vice president's* proposal
▶ the *editor-in-chief's* desk

Plurals of some compound expressions are often best expressed with a prepositional phrase (presentations of the *editors-in-chief*).

Coordinate Nouns

Coordinate nouns show joint possession with *'s* following the last noun.

▶ *Fischer and Goulet's* partnership was the foundation of their business.

Coordinate nouns show individual possession with *'s* following each noun.

▶ The difference between *Barker's* and *Washburne's* test results was statistically insignificant.

Possessive Pronouns

The possessive pronouns (*yours, its, his, her, ours, whose, theirs*) do not require apostrophes. (Even good systems have *their* flaws.) *Its* is a possessive pronoun and does not use an apostrophe; *it's* is a contraction of *it is* and does not show possession.

▶ *It's* important that the sales department meet *its* quota.

Indicating Possession

English expresses possession in two ways: *'s* and *of.*

Use *'s* with personal names, personal nouns, collective nouns, and animals. (Use just an apostrophe for plural nouns that end with *s.*)

▶ *Joan's* class
▶ the *receptionist's* lunch hour
▶ the *government's* pension plan
▶ the *employees'* stock portfolios

You can also use *'s* (or just an apostrophe) with some inanimate nouns: geographical and institutional names, nouns that refer to time, and nouns of special interest to human activity.

▶ the *company's* investors
▶ *today's* agenda
▶ a *week's* rest
▶ *business'* influence on politics

Use *of* with inanimate objects and measurements.

▶ the title *of* the monthly report
▶ a cup *of* coffee
▶ the length *of* the memo

Indicating Omission

An apostrophe is used to mark the omission of letters or numbers in a contraction or a date (*can't, I'm, I'll;* the class of *'10,* the crash of *'29*). Although this usage is in no sense wrong, it is less formal than the longer forms and should be applied sparingly in business and professional writing.

Forming Plurals

An apostrophe can be used in forming the plurals of letters, words, or lowercase abbreviations if confusion might result from using *s* alone.

▶ The search program does not find *a*'s and *i*'s.
▶ *I*'s need to be distinguished from the number 1.
▶ Check for any *c.o.d.*'s.

Generally, however, add only *s* (in Roman type) when referring to words as words or capital letters (which should be set in italics).

▶ Five *and*s appear in the first sentence.
▶ The applicants received *A*s and *B*s in their courses.

Do not use an apostrophe for plurals of abbreviations with all capital letters (DVDs) or a final capital letter (ten Ph.D.s) or for plurals of numbers (7s, the late 1990s).

▧ Quotation Marks

Quotation marks (" ") are used to enclose direct repetition of spoken or written words. Quotation marks have other special uses, but they should not be used for emphasis.

Identifying Quotations

Enclose in quotation marks anything that is quoted word for word (a direct quotation) from speech or written material.

▷   She said at this morning's staff meeting, "I want the progress report before three o'clock."

◆ *For tips on achieving emphasis, see pages 101–106 in Chapter 4, Revising the Draft.*

Do not enclose indirect quotations—usually introduced by the word *that*—in quotation marks. Indirect quotations paraphrase a speaker's words or ideas.

▷   She said that she wanted a copy of the progress report by three.

◆ *See also Paraphrasing, pages 178–179.*

Material quoted directly and enclosed in quotation marks cannot be changed from the original unless you show the change in brackets.

Use single quotation marks (' ') to enclose a quotation that appears within another quotation.

▷   John said, "Jane told me that she was going to 'stay with the project if it takes all year.'"

◆ *For further information on incorporating quoted material and inserting comments, see Avoiding Plagiarism and Copyright Violations, pages 180–181; Quoting from Your Sources, pages 176–178; Brackets, pages 656–657; and Ellipses, page 660.*

Setting Off Words, Phrases, and Titles

Words and Phrases

Use quotation marks to set off special words or terms only to point out that the term is used in context for a unique or special purpose (that is, in the sense of the term *so-called*).

▷   A remarkable chain of events caused the sinking of the "unsinkable" *Titanic* on its maiden voyage.

Slang, colloquial expressions, and attempts at humor, although infrequent in workplace writing, should not be set off by quotation marks unless they indicate a direct quote.

▷   Our first six months in the new office amounted to little more than a ⌃shakedown cruise⌃ for what lay ahead. [omit quotation marks]

Titles of Works

◆ *See also Italics, pages 668–669.*

Use quotation marks to enclose titles of short stories, articles, essays, chapters of books, radio and television programs, and songs. However, do not use quotation marks for titles of books and periodicals, which should appear in italics.

> Did you see the article "No-Fault Insurance and Your Motorcycle" in last Friday's *Wall Street Journal*?

Using Quotation Marks with Other Punctuation

Commas and periods always go inside closing quotation marks.

> "We hope," said Ms. Abrams, "that the merger will be announced this week."

Semicolons and colons always go outside closing quotation marks.

> He said, "I will pay the asking price"; this was a real surprise to us.

◆ *See also use of quotation marks with question marks, page 656.*

All other punctuation follows the logic of the context: If the punctuation is part of the material quoted, it goes inside the quotation marks; if the punctuation is not part of the material quoted, it goes outside the quotation marks.

ESL Tips

Using Quotation Marks with Other Punctuation

The use of quotation marks and other punctuation in U.S. and Canadian English differs from usage in some languages.

Style of quotation marks
▶ "exceptional" *not* „exceptional" *or* «exceptional»

Comma inside closing quotation mark
▶ "as a last resort," *not* "as a last resort",

Period inside closing quotation mark
▶ "to the bitter end." *not* "to the bitter end".

Semicolon or colon outside closing quotation mark
▶ "there is no doubt"; *not* "there is no doubt;"

■ Periods

A *period* (.) usually indicates the end of a declarative or an imperative sentence. Periods may also end questions that are actually polite requests and questions to which an affirmative response is assumed. (Will you please send me the financial statement.)

Use a comma, not a period, after a declarative sentence that is quoted in the context of another sentence.

▶ "The project has every chance of success," she stated.

A period is, by convention, placed inside quotation marks.

◆ *See also Quotation Marks, pages 653–654, and Quoting from Your Sources, pages 176–178.*

▶ He stated clearly, "My vote is yes."

If a sentence ends with an item in parentheses, the period should follow the end parenthesis.

▶ The institute was founded by Harry Denman (1931–1992).

When a complete sentence within parentheses stands independently, however, the end punctuation goes inside the final parenthesis.

▶ The project director listed the problems her staff faced. (This was the third time she had complained to the board.)

When a sentence ends with an abbreviation that ends with a period, do not add another period.

▶ Please meet me at 3:30 p.m.

■ Question Marks

The *question mark* (?) has several uses, but most often ends a sentence that is a direct question or request.

▶ Where did you put the tax report?
▶ Will you e-mail me if your shipment does not arrive by June 10?

Use a question mark to end a statement that has an interrogative meaning—a statement that is declarative in form but asks a question. (The tax report is finished?)

Question marks may follow a series of separate items within an interrogative sentence.

▶ Do you remember the date of the contract? its terms? whether you signed it?

Use a question mark to end an interrogative clause within a declarative sentence.

▶ It was not until July (or was it August?) that we submitted the report.

Retain the question mark in a title that is being cited, even if the sentence in which it appears has not ended.

▶ *Can Investments Be Protected?* is the title of her book.

◆ *See also Periods, pages 654–655.*

Never use a question mark to end a sentence that is an indirect question.

▷ He asked me where I put the tax report?

When used with quotations, the placement of the question mark is important. If the writer is asking a question, the question mark belongs outside the quotation marks.

▷ Did she say, "I don't think the project should continue"?

◆ *See also Quoting from Your Sources, pages 176–178 in Chapter 6, Researching Your Subject.*

If the quotation itself is a question, the question mark goes inside the quotation marks.

▷ She asked, "Do we have enough funding?"

If both cases apply—the writer is asking a question and the quotation itself is a question—use a single question mark inside the quotation marks.

▷ Did she ask, "Do we have enough funding?"

▦ Exclamation Marks

The *exclamation mark* (!) indicates strong feeling, urgency, elation, or surprise (*Hurry! Great! Wow!*). However, it cannot make an argument more convincing, lend force to a weak statement, or call attention to an intended irony.

An exclamation mark can be used after a whole sentence or an element of a sentence.

▷ This meeting—please note it well!—concerns our budget deficit.

When used with quotation marks, the exclamation mark goes outside, unless what is quoted is an exclamation.

▷ The paramedics shouted, "Don't touch the victim!" The bystander, according to a witness, "jumped like a kangaroo"!

In instructional writing, the exclamation mark is often used in cautions and warnings (*Danger! Stop!*).

▦ Parentheses and Brackets

Parentheses (( )) and *brackets* ([ ]) are used to enclose explanatory or digressive words, phrases, or sentences.

Material in parentheses often clarifies or defines the preceding text without altering its meaning.

▷ She severely bruised her shin (or *tibia*) in the accident.

Parentheses are also used to enclose numerals or letters that indicate sequence.

▶ The following sections deal with (1) preparation, (2) research, (3) organization, (4) writing, and (5) revision.

The primary use of brackets is to enclose a word or words inserted by the writer or an editor into a quotation.

▶ The text stated, "Hypertext systems can be categorized as either modest [not modifiable] or robust [modifiable]."

Use brackets to set off a parenthetical item that is already within parentheses.

▶ We should be sure to give Randolph Chaney (and his brother Scott [1912–1982]) credit for his part in founding the institute.

Parenthetical material does not affect the punctuation of a sentence. If a parenthesis or bracket appears at the end of a sentence, the ending punctuation should appear after the parenthesis or bracket. Likewise, a comma following a parenthetical word, phrase, or clause appears outside the closing parenthesis or bracket.

▶ She severely bruised her shin (or *tibia*), and he tore the cartilage (or *meniscus*) in his knee.

When a complete sentence within parentheses stands independently, however, the ending punctuation goes inside the final parenthesis.

▶ The project director listed the problems her staff faced. (This was the third time she had complained to the board.)

■ Hyphens

The *hyphen* (-) serves both to link and to separate words. The hyphen joins compound words (able-bodied, self-contained, self-esteem), forms compound numbers from twenty-one through ninety-nine, and divides fractions when they are written out (three-quarters).

Linking Modifiers

Two- and three-word modifiers that express a single thought are hyphenated when they precede a noun.

▶ It was a *well-written* report.

However, a modifying phrase is not hyphenated when it follows the noun it modifies.

▶ The report was *well written.*

If each of the words can modify the noun without the aid of the other modifying word or words, do not use a hyphen.

▶ a *new digital* printer

If the first word is an adverb ending in *-ly*, do not use a hyphen.

▶ a *privately* held company

A hyphen is always used as part of a letter or number modifier.

▶ 9-inch, A-frame

In a series of unit modifiers that all have the same term following the hyphen, the term following the hyphen need not be repeated throughout the series; for greater smoothness and brevity, use the term only at the end of the series.

▶ The third-, fourth-, and fifth-floor rooms were recently re-carpeted.

Separating Prefixes and Suffixes

When a prefix precedes a proper noun, use a hyphen to connect the two.

▶ pre-Internet
▶ anti-Americanism
▶ post-Newtonian

A hyphen may (but does not have to) be used when the prefix ends and the root word begins with the same vowel. When the repeated vowel is *i*, a hyphen is almost always used.

▶ re-elect
▶ re-enter
▶ anti-inflationary

A hyphen is used when *ex-* means "former."

▶ ex-partners
▶ ex-wife

The suffix *-elect* is connected to the word it follows with a hyphen.

▶ president-elect

Hyphens identify prefixes, suffixes, or syllables written as such.

▶ *Re-*, *-ism*, and *ex-* are word parts that cause spelling problems.

Other Uses

Hyphens separate letters showing spelling (or misspelling).

▶ In his letter, he spelled "believed" b-e-l-e-i-v-e-d.

To avoid confusion, some words and modifiers should always be hyphenated. *Re-cover* does not mean the same thing as *recover*, for example; the same is true of *re-sent* and *resent*, *re-form* and *reform*, *re-sign* and *resign*.

Hyphens are also used to divide words at the end of a line. Avoid dividing words if possible; however, if you must divide them, consult a dictionary.

Dashes

The *dash* (—) is a versatile, yet limited, mark of punctuation. It is versatile because it can perform all the functions of punctuation (to link, to separate, to enclose, and to show omission). It is limited because it is especially emphatic and easily overused. Use the dash cautiously, therefore, to indicate more informality, emphasis, or abruptness than the conventional marks would show.

A dash can indicate a sharp turn in thought.

▶ The project will end October 30—unless we receive additional funds.

A dash can indicate an emphatic pause.

▶ The project will begin—after we are under contract.

Sometimes, to emphasize contrast, a dash is also used with *but*.

▶ We completed the survey quickly—but the results were not accurate.

A dash can be used before a final summarizing statement or before repetition that has the effect of an afterthought.

▶ It was hot near the annealing ovens—unbearably hot.

A dash can be used to set off an explanatory or appositive series.

▶ Three of the applicants—John Evans, Rosalita Fontiana, and Kyong-Shik Choi—seem well qualified for the job.

Dashes set off parenthetical elements more sharply and emphatically than commas or parentheses.

▶ Only one person—the president—can authorize such activity.
▶ Only one person, the president, can authorize such activity.
▶ Only one person (the president) can authorize such activity.

Use dashes for clarity when commas appear within a parenthetical element.

▶ Retinal images are patterns in the eye—made up of light and dark shapes, in addition to areas of color—but we do not see patterns; we see objects.

A hyphen can stand for *to* or *through* between letters, numbers, and locations.

▶ pp. 44–46

▶ The Detroit–Toledo Expressway

▶ A–L and M–Z

The first word after a dash is never capitalized unless it is a proper noun. When keying in the dash, use two consecutive hyphens (--), with no spaces before or after the hyphens.

Ellipses

An *ellipsis* indicates the omission of words from quoted material; it is indicated by three spaced periods called *ellipsis points* (. . .). When you use ellipsis points, omit marks of internal punctuation at the point of omission, unless they are necessary for clarity or the omitted material comes at the end of a quoted sentence.

ORIGINAL TEXT	Promotional material is sometimes charged for, particularly in high volume distribution to schools, although prices for these publications are much lower than the development costs when all factors are considered.
WITH OMISSION AND ELLIPSIS POINTS	Promotional material is sometimes charged for . . . although prices for these publications are much lower than the development costs. . . .

Notice that the final period is retained and what remains of the quotation is grammatically complete.

When the omitted part of the quotation is preceded by a period, retain the period and add the three ellipsis points after it.

ORIGINAL TEXT	Of the 172 major ethics cases reported, 57 percent were found to involve unsubstantiated concerns. Misinformation was the cause of unfounded concerns of misconduct in 72 cases.
WITH OMISSION AND ELLIPSIS POINTS	Of the 172 major ethics cases reported, 57 percent were found to involve unsubstantiated concerns. . . .

◆ *See also Quoting from Your Sources, pages 176–178 in Chapter 6, Researching Your Subject.*

Do not use ellipsis points when the beginning of a quoted sentence is omitted.

▶ The ethics report states that "26 percent of the total cases reported involved incidents partly substantiated by ethics officers as serious misconduct."

Slashes

The *slash* (/)—called a variety of names, including *slant line, diagonal, virgule, bar,* and *solidus*—both separates and shows omission.

The slash can indicate alternatives or combinations.

▷ David's telephone numbers are (333) 549-2278/2235.

▷ Check the on/off switch before you leave.

The slash often indicates omitted words and letters.

▷ miles/hour (miles per hour)

▷ w/o (without)

In fractions and mathematical expressions, the slash separates the numerator from the denominator ($3/4$ for three-fourths; x/y for x over y).

Although the slash is used informally with dates (5/11/10), do not use this form in international communications because many countries in Europe reverse the day-month order using this system. Thus, 5/11/10 would mean November 5, 2010, rather than May 11, 2010.

The forward slash (/) is often used to separate items in the URL (uniform resource locator) addresses for sites on the Internet (<bedfordstmartins.com/writingthatworks>). The backward slash (\) is used to separate parts of computer file names (<c:\myfiles\reports\annual10.doc>).

Mechanics

Certain mechanical questions tend to confound the writer on the job. Should a number be written as a word or figure? How are acronyms used? Should a date be stated day-month-year or month-day-year? These and other questions frequently arise when you are writing a letter or report. This section will help you answer such perplexing questions.

■ Capitalization

The use of capital, or uppercase, letters is determined by custom. They are used to call attention to certain words, such as proper nouns and the first word of a sentence. Use them carefully, especially when they affect a word's meaning (march/March, china/China, turkey/Turkey).

Proper Nouns

Proper nouns name specific persons, places, things, concepts, or qualities and are capitalized (Business Writing 205, Microsoft, Pat Wilde, Peru).

Common Nouns

Common nouns name general classes or categories of people, places, things, concepts, or qualities rather than specific ones and are not capitalized (business writing, company, person, country).

First Words

The first letter of the first word in a sentence is always capitalized. (Of the plans submitted, ours is best.) The first word after a colon is capitalized when the colon introduces an independent clause or a complete sentence.

▶ The meeting will address only one issue: What is the firm's role in environmental protection?

If a subordinate element follows the colon or if the thought is closely related, use a lowercase letter following the colon.

▶   We kept working for one reason: the approaching deadline.

The first word of a complete sentence in quotation marks is capitalized.

▶   Peter Drucker said, "The most important thing in communication is to hear what isn't being said."

The first word of a complete sentence enclosed in dashes, brackets, or parentheses is not capitalized when it appears as part of another sentence.

▶   We must make an extra effort in safety this year (accidents last year were up 10 percent).

In correspondence, the first word in the salutation (Dear Mrs. Markels) and complimentary close (Sincerely yours,) are capitalized, as are the names of recipients.

Specific Groups

Capitalize the names of ethnic groups, religions, and nationalities (Native American, Christianity, Mongolian). Do not capitalize the names of social and economic groups (middle class, working class, unemployed).

Specific Places

Capitalize the names of all political divisions (Ward Six, Chicago, Cook County, Illinois). Capitalize the names of geographic divisions (Europe, Asia, North America, the Middle East). Do not capitalize geographic features unless they are part of a proper name.

▶   The mountains in some areas, such as the *Great Smoky Mountains*, make cell-phone reception difficult.

The words *north*, *south*, *east*, and *west* are capitalized when they refer to sections of the United States. They are not capitalized when they refer to directions.

▶   I may travel *north* when I relocate, but my family will remain in the *South*.

Specific Institutions, Events, Concepts

Capitalize the names of institutions, organizations, and associations (U.S. Department of Health and Human Services). An organization usually capitalizes the names of its internal divisions and departments (Aeronautics Division, Human Resources Department). Types of organizations are not capitalized unless they are part of an official name (a business communication association; Association for Business Communication). Capitalize historic events (the Great Depression of the 1930s). Capitalize words that designate holidays, specific eras, months, or days of the week (Labor Day, the Renaissance, January, Monday). Do not capitalize seasons of the year (spring, autumn, winter, summer).

Titles of Works

Capitalize the initial letters of the first and last words of the title of a book, an article, a play, or a film, as well as all major words in the title. Do not capitalize articles (*a, an, the*) or coordinating conjunctions (*and, but, for, or, nor, yet, so*), unless they begin or end the title (*The Lives of a Cell*). Capitalize prepositions within titles only when they contain more than four letters (*Between, Within, Until, After*), unless you are following a style that recommends otherwise. The same rules apply to the subject line of an e-mail message or a memo.

Professional and Personal Titles

Titles preceding proper names are capitalized (Ms. Berger, Senator McCain). Appositives following proper names normally are not capitalized (John McCain, *senator* from Arizona). However, the word *President* is capitalized when it refers to the chief executive of a national government.

Job titles used with personal names are capitalized (Ho-shik Kim, *Division Manager*). Job titles used without personal names are not capitalized (The *division manager* will meet us tomorrow).

Use capital letters to designate family relationships only when they occur before a name (my *uncle*; *Uncle* Fred).

Abbreviations, Letters, and Units

Capitalize abbreviations if the words they stand for would be capitalized, such as M.B.A. (Master of Business Administration). Also capitalize the following:

- Letters that serve as names or indicate shapes (vitamin B, T-square, U-turn, I-beam)
- Certain units, such as parts and chapters of books and rooms in buildings, when specifically identified by number (Chapter 5, Ch. 5; Room 72, Rm. 72)

Minor divisions within such units are not capitalized unless they begin a sentence (page 11, verse 14, seat 12).

■ Numbers

The standards for how to express numbers in workplace writing vary; however, unless you are following an organizational or a professional style manual, observe the following guidelines.

Words or Numerals

Write numbers from zero through ten as words, and write numbers above ten as numerals.

▶ I rehearsed my presentation *three* times.

▶ The meeting was attended by *150* people.

Do not follow a word representing a number with a numeral in parentheses that represents the same number. Doing so is redundant.

▶ Send five ~~(5)~~ copies of the report.

Spell out numbers that begin a sentence, even if they would otherwise be written as numerals. If spelling out such a number seems awkward, rewrite the sentence so that the number does not appear at the beginning.

　　　　Last month, 273
▶ ~~Two hundred seventy-three~~ defective products were returned ~~last month.~~

Spell out approximate and round numbers.

▶ We've had *over a thousand* requests this month.

　　In most writing, spell out ordinal numbers, which express degree or sequence (first, second; but 27th, 42nd), when they are single words (our *third* draft) or when they modify a century (the *twenty-first* century). However, avoid ordinal numbers in dates on correspondence (use March 30 or 30 March, not March 30th).

　　When several numbers appear in the same sentence or paragraph, write them the same way, regardless of other rules and guidelines.

▶ The company employs *271* people, leases *7* warehouses, and owns *150* trucks.

Money

In general, use numerals to express exact amounts of money. (We charge $28.95 per unit.) Use words to express indefinite amounts of money. (The printing system may cost several thousand dollars.) Use numerals and words for rounded amounts of money over one million dollars; use numerals alone for more complex or exact amounts.

▶ The contract is worth $6.8 million.

▶ The corporation paid $2,452,500 in taxes last year.

Plurals

Indicate the plurals of numerals by adding *-s* (7s, the late 1990s). Form the plural of a written number (like any noun) by adding *-s* or *-es* or by dropping *-y* and adding *-ies* (elevens, sixes, twenties).

Measurements

Express units of measurement as numerals (3 miles, 45 cubic feet, 9 meters). When numbers run together in the same phrase, write one as a numeral and the other as a word.

    ▶   The order was for ~~12~~ *twelve* 6-inch pipes.

Generally give percentages as numerals and write out the word *percent*. (Approximately *85 percent* of the land has been sold.) However, in a visual, like a figure or table, use a numeral followed by a percent symbol (*85%*).

Express fractions as numerals when they are combined with whole numbers (27 1/2 inches, 4 1/4 miles). Spell out fractions when they are expressed without a whole number (one-fourth, seven-eighths). Always write decimal numbers as numerals (5.21 meters).

Time and Dates

Express hours and minutes as numerals when a.m. or p.m. follows (11:30 a.m., 7:30 p.m.). Spell out time that is not followed by a.m. or p.m. (four o'clock, eleven o'clock).

In the United States, dates are usually written in a month-day-year sequence (August 11, 2010). Never use the strictly numerical form for dates (8/11/10) in business writing because the date is not always immediately clear, especially in international correspondence.

ESL Tips

Punctuating Numbers

Some rules for punctuating numbers in American English are summarized as follows.

Use a comma to separate numbers with four or more digits into groups of three, starting from the right.

▶ 2,500
▶ 57,890 cubic feet
▶ $187,291

Do not use a comma in years, house numbers, zip codes, and page numbers.

▶ June *2010*
▶ *92401* East Alameda Drive
▶ The zip code is *91601*
▶ Page *1204*

Use a period to represent the decimal point (*4.2* percent; *$3,742,097.43*).

Addresses

Spell out numbered streets from one to ten unless space is at a premium (East Tenth Street). Write building numbers as numerals. The only exception is the building number *one* (4862 East Monument Street; One East Monument Street). Write highway numbers as numerals (U.S. 40, Ohio 271, I-94).

Documents

In manuscripts, page numbers are written as numerals, but chapter and volume numbers may appear as numerals or as words (page 37, Chapter 2 or Chapter Two, Volume 1 or Volume One). Express figure and table numbers as numerals (Figure 4 and Table 3).

■ Abbreviations

Abbreviations are shortened versions of words or combinations of the first letters of words (Corp./Corporation, URL/*uniform resource locator*). Abbreviations that combine the first letter or letters of several words—and can be pronounced as words—are called *acronyms* (PIN/*personal identification number*, laser/*light amplification by stimulated emission of radiation*). Abbreviations and acronyms, if used appropriately, can be convenient for both the writer and the reader. Like symbols, they can be important space savers in workplace writing.

Abbreviations and acronyms are useful only when your readers understand them. Some abbreviations, for example, can have several different meanings (NEA stands for both the National Education Association and the National Endowment for the Arts in the United States; British readers would associate it with the Nuclear Energy Association). When in doubt, spell it out.

Names of Organizations

A company may include in its name a term such as *Brothers, Incorporated, Corporation,* or *Company.* If the term is abbreviated in the official company name that appears on letterhead stationery or on its Web site, use the abbreviated form: *Bros., Inc., Corp.,* or *Co.* If the term is not abbreviated in the official name, spell it out in writing, except with addresses, footnotes, bibliographies, and lists where abbreviations may be used. Likewise, use an ampersand (&) only if it appears in the official company name. For names of divisions within organizations, terms such as *Department* and *Division* should be abbreviated (*Dept., Div.*) only when space is limited.

Measurements

Except for abbreviations that may be confused with words (*in.* for *inch* and *gal.* for *gallon*), abbreviations of measurement do not require periods (*yd* for *yard* and *qt* for *quart*). Abbreviations of units of measure are identical in the singular and plural: 1 *cm* and 15 *cm* (*not* 15 *cms*). Some abbreviations can be used in combination with other symbols (°*F* for *degrees Fahrenheit* and *ft*² for *square feet*).

The following list includes abbreviations for the basic units of the International System of Units (SI), the metric system. This system not only is standard in science but also is used in international commerce and trade.

Measurement	Unit	Abbreviation
length	meter	m
mass	kilogram	kg
time	second	s
electric current	ampere	A
thermodynamic temperature	kelvin	K
amount of substance	mole	mol
luminous intensity	candela	cd

ON THE WEB

For additional definitions and background, see the National Institute of Standards and Technology Web site at <http://physics.nist.gov/cuu/Units/units.html>.

Personal Names and Titles

Personal names generally should not be abbreviated: Thomas (*not* Thos.) and William (*not* Wm.). An academic, civil, religious, or military title should be spelled out and in lowercase when it does not precede a name. (The *captain* wanted to check the orders.) When they precede names, some titles are customarily abbreviated (*Dr.* Smith, *Mr.* Mills, *Mrs.* Katz).

An abbreviation of a title may follow the name; however, be certain that it does not duplicate a title before the name (Angeline Martinez, Ph.D. *or* Dr. Angeline Martinez, *not* Dr. Angeline Martinez, Ph.D.). When addressing correspondence and including names in other documents, spell out titles (The Honorable Mary J. Holt; Professor Charles Martin). Traditionally, periods are used with academic degrees, although they are sometimes omitted (M.A./MA, M.B.A./MBA, Ph.D./PhD).

ON THE WEB

For links to Web sites specifying standard abbreviations and acronyms, including U.S. Postal Service abbreviations, see bedfordstmartins.com/writingthatworks and select *Web Links*.

■ Italics

Italics is a style of type used to denote emphasis and to distinguish foreign expressions, book titles, and certain other elements. *This sentence is printed in italics.* Italic type is signaled by underlining in a manuscript submitted for publication or where italic font may not be available, such as in e-mail messages. Italicize words that require special emphasis in a sentence. (Contrary to projections, sales have *not* improved.) Do not overuse italics for emphasis, however. (*This* will hurt *you* more than *me*.)

◆ *For more effective ways to achieve emphasis, see pages 101–106 in Chapter 4, Revising the Draft.*

Foreign Words and Phrases

Foreign words and phrases that have not been assimilated into the English language are italicized (*sine qua non, coup de grâce, in re, in camera*). Foreign words that have been fully assimilated into the language need not be italicized. A word may be considered assimilated if it appears in most standard dictionaries and is familiar to most readers (cliché, etiquette, vis-à-vis, de facto, siesta).

Titles

Italicize the titles of separately published documents, such as books, periodicals, newspapers, pamphlets, brochures, legal cases, and movies.

▷ *Turning Workplace Conflict into Collaboration* by Joyce Richards was reviewed in the *New York Times*.

Italicize the titles of compact disks, DVDs, plays, long poems, paintings, sculptures, and musical works.

CD-ROM	*Computer Security Tutorial on CD-ROM*
PLAY	Arthur Miller's *Death of a Salesman*
LONG POEM	T. S. Eliot's *The Waste Land*
MUSICAL WORK	Gershwin's *Porgy and Bess*

Do not italicize the titles of holy books and legislative documents (Old Testament, Magna Carta).

◆ *See also Quotation Marks, pages 653–654.*

Proper Names

The names of ships, trains, and aircraft (but not the companies or governments that own them) are italicized (U.S. Aircraft Carrier *Independence*; U.S. Space Shuttle *Endeavor*). Craft that are known by model or serial designations are not italicized (DC-7; Boeing 747).

Words, Letters, and Numerals

Words, letters, and numerals discussed as such are italicized.

▷ The word *inflammable* is often misinterpreted.

▷ The *S* and *6* keys on my keyboard do not work.

Subheads

Subheads in a report are sometimes italicized.

▷ *Training managers.* We are leading the way in developing first-line managers who not only are professionally competent but . . .

◆ *For guidance on using italics as a design element, see page 213 in Chapter 7, Designing Effective Documents and Visuals.*

English as a Second Language (ESL)

ON THE WEB

For Web sites and electronic grammar exercises intended for speakers of English as a second language, see bedfordstmartins.com/ writingthatworks and select *Web Links* and *Exercise Central.*

Learning to write well in a second language takes a great deal of effort and practice. The most effective way to improve your command of written English is to read widely beyond the reports and professional articles your job requires, such as magazines, newspapers, essays, novels, biographies, short stories, or any other writing that interests you. In addition, listen carefully to native speakers on television, on the radio, and in person. Do not hesitate to consult a native speaker of English, especially for important writing tasks, such as e-mail messages, memos, and reports. Focus on those particular areas of English that give you trouble.

This section is a guide to some of the common problems nonnative speakers experience when writing English. For additional help, ask a native speaker or refer to the earlier sections of this guide.

> **ESL Tips**
>
> **Finding Additional ESL Guidance in *Writing That Works***
>
> Most of the information in this revision guide will be helpful to writers of English as a second language; however, the entries listed in the index under "ESL Tips" address specific issues that often cause problems.

■ Count and Mass Nouns

Count nouns refer to things that can be counted (tables, pencils, projects, reports). *Mass nouns* (also called *noncount nouns*) identify things that cannot be counted (electricity, water, air, loyalty, information). This distinction can be confusing with words like *electricity* and *water*. Although we can count kilowatt-hours of electricity and bottles of water, counting becomes inappropriate when we use the words in a general sense, as in "*Water* is an essential resource." Count nouns have plural forms; mass nouns do not. Following is a list of common mass nouns.

acid	coffee	information	precision
advice	education	knowledge	research
air	electricity	loyalty	technology
anger	equipment	machinery	transportation
biology	furniture	money	water
business	health	news	weather
clothing	honesty	oil	work

This distinction between whether something can or cannot be counted determines the form of the noun to use (singular or plural), the kind of article that precedes it (*a, an, the,* or no article), and the kind of comparative adjective it requires (*fewer* or *less, many* or *much,* and so on).

■ Articles

This discussion of articles applies only to common nouns (not to proper nouns, such as the names of people) because count and mass nouns are always common nouns.

The general rule is that every count noun must be preceded by an article (*a, an, the*), a demonstrative adjective (*this, that, these, those*), a possessive adjective (*my, your, her, his, its, their*), or some expression of quantity (such as *one, two, several, many, a few, a lot of, some, no*). The article, adjective, or expression of quantity appears either directly in front of the noun or in front of the whole noun phrase.

▶ Beth read *a* report last week. [article]

▶ *Those* reports Beth read were long. [demonstrative adjective]

▶ *Their* report was long. [possessive adjective]

▶ *Some* reports Beth read were long. [indefinite adjective]

The articles *a* and *an* are used with count nouns that refer to one item of the whole class of like items.

▶ Matthew has *a* pen. [Matthew could have *any* pen.]

The article *the* is used with nouns that refer to a specific item that both the reader and the writer can identify.

▶ Matthew has *the* pen. [Matthew has a *specific* pen that is known to both the reader and the writer.]

The article *the* is used with the superlative form of adjectives and adverbs.

▶ His report was *the* best the board had ever read.

Do not use *the* with the comparative form.

▶ Which of these two restaurants is ~~the~~ better?

When making generalizations with count nouns, writers can either use *a* or *an* with a singular count noun or use no article with a plural count noun. Consider the following generalization using an article.

▶ *An* egg is a good source of protein. [any egg, all eggs, eggs in general]

However, the following generalization uses a plural count noun with no article.

▶ Eggs are good sources of protein. [any egg, all eggs, eggs in general]

When you are making a generalization with a mass noun, do not use an article in front of the noun.

▶ Sugar is bad for your teeth.

■ Prepositions

Prepositions are words that help connect nouns or pronouns to other parts of a sentence. They help to specify a relationship between items.
The word *on* is used with days of the week.

▶ We have staff meetings *on* Mondays.

At is used with hours of the day and with noon, night, and dawn.

▶ We leave work *at* 5:00.
▶ Lunch will be served *at* noon.

In is used with other parts of the day and with months, years, and seasons.

▶ I check my e-mail *in* the morning.
▶ I started to work for the firm *in* May.

The word *on* indicates a surface on which something rests.

▶ The files are *on* the desk.

At refers to an area or to a place.

▶ My assistant is *at* her desk.

In indicates a place that is inside an enclosure.

▶ The documents are *in* the file folder.

Gerunds and Infinitives

Nonnative writers are often puzzled by which form of a verbal (a verb used as another part of speech) to use when it functions as the direct object of a verb—or a complement. No structural rule exists for distinguishing between the use of an infinitive or a gerund as an object of a verb. Any specific verb may take an infinitive as its object, others may take a gerund, and yet others take either an infinitive or a gerund. At times, even the base form of the verb is used.

▶ He enjoys *working.* [gerund as a complement]

▶ She promised *to fulfill* her part of the contract. [infinitive as a complement]

▶ The president had the manager *assign* her staff to another project. [basic verb form as a complement]

To make such distinctions accurately, rely on what you hear native speakers use or what you read. Many ESL texts contain chapters on infinitive and gerund usage that list verbs with their appropriate complements.

Adjective Clauses

Because of the variety of ways adjective clauses are constructed in different languages, they can be particularly troublesome for nonnative writers of English. The following guidelines will help you form adjective clauses correctly.

Place an adjective clause directly after the noun it modifies.

who is standing across the room
▶ The tall woman is a vice president of the company ~~who is standing across the room.~~
    ^   ^

The adjective clause *who is standing across the room* modifies *woman,* not *company,* and thus comes directly after *woman.*

Avoid using a relative pronoun with another pronoun in an adjective clause.

▶ The man who ~~he~~ sits at that desk is my boss.

Verb Tenses

To determine which verb tense to use, consider the time in which the action you are describing occurs in relation to other actions.

◆ For an overview of how to choose the appropriate tense, see pages 640–642.

Present Perfect

Because it is so closely related to the past tense, the present perfect tense remains one of the most problematic of all tenses. In general, use the present perfect tense to refer to events completed in the past that have some implication for the present.

PRESENT PERFECT   She *has revised* that report three times.

                            [She might revise it again.]

When a specific time is mentioned, however, use the simple past.

SIMPLE PAST   I *wrote* the letter yesterday morning.

                            [The action, *wrote*, does not affect the present.]

Use the present perfect with a *since* or *for* phrase to describe actions that began in the past and will continue in the present.

▶   This company *has been* in business *for* seventeen years.

▶   This company *has been* in business *since* I was a child.

Present Progressive

◆ *See ESL Tips: Using the Progressive Form on page 641.*

The present progressive tense is especially difficult for those whose native language does not use this tense. The present progressive tense is used to describe some action or condition that is ongoing (or in progress) in the present and may continue into the future.

PRESENT PROGRESSIVE   I *am searching* for an error in the document.

                            [The search is occurring now and may continue.]

In contrast, the simple present tense more often relates to habitual actions.

SIMPLE PRESENT   I *search* for errors in my documents.

                            [I regularly search for errors, but I am not necessarily searching at this moment.]

■ Helping Verbs

In English, 23 helping verbs (forms of *have*, *be*, and *do*) may also function as main verbs. In addition, nine modal verbs (*can, could, may, might, must, shall, should, will, would*) function only as helping verbs. *Have*, *be*, and *do* change form to indicate tense; the nine modals do not.

   The following guidelines will help you determine the proper use of modals. One-word modals do not change form to show a change in subject.

▶   I *could* quit. She *could* quit.

Most two- and three-word modals do change form, like other helping verbs.

▶   I *have to* finish the project. She *has to* finish the project.

Never use *to* between a one-word modal and the main verb.

▶   I can ~~to~~ type.

    [Most of the two- and three-word modals include *to*, as in *ought to drive*.]

Never use two one-word modals together.

▶   I might ~~could~~ work tomorrow.

■ Conditional Sentences

In *conditional sentences*, clauses that follow the words *if, when,* and *unless* show whether the result is possible or real, depending on other circumstances. Conditional sentences have two parts: a subordinate clause that begins with *if, when,* and *unless,* and a main clause that expresses a result.

A *prediction* foretells something based on conditional circumstances. Use a present-tense verb within the *if* clause. The clause that expresses the result is formed with a modal helping verb (usually *will*) and the base form of the verb.

▶   *If* you treat employees fairly, they *will be* more productive.

A *fact* explains a factual relationship between two or more occurrences. Use the same verb tense in both the conditional clause and the result clause.

▶   When it *snows,* I *leave* for work an hour earlier.

▶   When the chairperson *started* the meeting, he *welcomed* all new employees.

A *hypothetical sentence* explains that a result is impossible, did not happen, or is unlikely to happen. Use a past-tense verb within the *if* clause, and *would, could,* or *might* in the result clause.

▶   *If* I were CEO, I *would take* three months' vacation every year.

Acknowledgments *(continued from the copyright page)*

Figure 3–8: Steve Coffel and Karyn Feiden. Illustration for Explanation of a Process. From *Indoor Pollution* by Steve Coffel and Karyn Feiden. Copyright © 1990 by Steve Coffel and Karyn Feiden. Used by permission of Ballantine Books, a division of Random House, Inc., and Barbara Lowenstein Associates.

Figure 3–13: "Definition by Analogy" excerpt from Gerald J. Alred, Charles T. Brusaw, and Walter E. Oliu, *The Business Writer's Handbook*, Eighth Edition. Copyright © 2005 by Bedford/St. Martin's. Reprinted by permission of Bedford/St. Martin's.

Figure 4–1: "Abstract-to-Concrete Words" from Gerald J. Alred, Charles T. Brusaw, and Walter E. Oliu, excerpts from *The Business Writer's Handbook*, Eighth Edition (p. 7). Copyright © 2005 by Bedford/St. Martin's. Reprinted by permission of Bedford/St. Martin's. Ron S. Blicq. "An Integrated Collaborative Writing Project" from *Collaborative Technical Writing: Theory and Practice*, edited by Richard Louth and Martin Scott (Association of Teachers of Technical Writing, 1989). Adapted with permission of Ron S. Blicq.

Figures 7–1 and 7–2: "Page Illustrating Design" and "Layout Choices." From Gerald J. Alred et al., *The Professional Writer*, figure L–4. Copyright © 1991 by Bedford/St. Martin's. Reprinted with the permission of Bedford/St. Martin's.

Figure 7–12: "Distorted and Distortion-Free Expressions of Data" from Gerald J. Alred, Charles T. Brusaw, and Walter E. Oliu, *The Business Writer's Handbook*, Eighth Edition (p. 254). Copyright © 2005 by Bedford/St. Martin's. Reprinted by permission of Bedford/St. Martin's.

Figure 7–25: "Exploded-View Drawing." From Xerox Corporation, *WorkCentre XD Series User Guide*, page 6. Copyright © Xerox Corporation. Used with permission.

Figure 7–37: Two ISO symbols from John Perry, "Graphical symbols to address consumer needs," *ISO Bulletin* (March 2003): 10–11. © International Organization for Standardization (ISO). This material is reproduced from ISO/IEC Guide 74 with permission of the American National Standards Institute (ANSI) on behalf of ISO. No part of this material may be copied or reproduced in any form, electronic retrieval system or otherwise or made available on the Internet, a public network, by satellite or otherwise without the prior written consent of the ANSI. Copies of this standard may be purchased from the ANSI, 25 West 43rd Street, New York, NY 10036, (212) 642-4900, <http://webstore.ansi.org>. Standards Institute.

Figure 8–3: Figure C–13 on page 118 of Gerald J. Alred, Charles T. Brusaw, and Walter E. Oliu, *The Business Writer's Handbook*, Ninth Edition. Copyright © 2009 by Bedford/St. Martin's. Reprinted by permission of Bedford/St. Martin's.

Page 297: Scott Adams, *Dilbert* cartoon, "My derogatory and condescending e-mail will set things right." Copyright © 1999 by United Features Syndicate. Reprinted with the permission of United Media.

Figure 8–7: Figure I–4 on page 266 of Gerald J. Alred, Charles T. Brusaw, and Walter E. Oliu, *The Business Writer's Handbook*, Ninth Edition. Copyright © 2009 by Bedford/St. Martin's. Reprinted by permission of Bedford/St. Martin's.

Figure 8–8: Figure M–4 on p. 326 of Gerald J. Alred, Charles T. Brusaw, and Walter E. Oliu, *The Business Writer's Handbook*, Ninth Edition. Copyright © 2009 by Bedford/St. Martin's. Reprinted by permission of Bedford/St. Martin's.

Figure 8–9: Figure M–5 on p. 327 of Gerald J. Alred, Charles T. Brusaw, and Walter E. Oliu, *The Business Writer's Handbook*, Ninth Edition. Copyright © 2009 by Bedford/St. Martin's. Reprinted by permission of Bedford/St. Martin's.

Figure 9–8: "A Gift for Registering" e-mail. Copyright © 2003 by cartoonbank.com. All rights reserved. Reprinted with permission.

Figure 10–5: Trip Report Memo, "Trouble-Shooting Trip to Garcia Tractor Co., Caracas, Venezuela, June 8–11, 2006," adapted from a Visit Report prepared by Johan De Beer, Mitsubishi Engines, N.A.

Figures 11–1, 11–2, 11–3, 11–4, 11–5, 11–6, 11–8, 11–9, 11–10, 11–13, and 11–14: "Formal Report." Reprinted with the permission of Susan Litzinger, a student at Pennsylvania State University, Altoona.

Figure 11–10: Five Graphs: "Reported Ethics Cases," "Major Ethics Cases in 2004," "Disposition of Substantiated Major Ethics Cases in 2005," "Minor Ethics Cases," and "Mode of Contact in Reported Ethics Cases in 2005." From Gerald J. Alred, Charles T. Brusaw, and Walter E. Oliu, *The Business Writer's Handbook*, Eighth Edition (pp. 226–229). Copyright © 2005 by Bedford/St. Martin's. Reprinted by permission of Bedford/St. Martin's.

Figure 12–4: "Visual Instructions Created for International Customers" from Rubbermaid Home Products, Rubbermaid Frame Shelf Kit (Product Number 4B03). Copyright © 2004 by Rubbermaid Home Products. Reprinted by permission.

Figure 12–5: "Introduction for Instructions" from Sony Corporation, "About This Manual" from *Home Theater System Manual* (2003). Copyright © 2003 by Sony Corporation. Reprinted with the permission of Sony Corporation. Used by permission of Sony Electronics, Inc.

Page 435: "Mr. Yuk" Logo, <www.mryuk1.com>, is the copyrighted symbol of the Pittsburgh Poison Center at the University of Pittsburgh Medical Center. Reprinted with permission from the Pittsburgh Poison Center, University of Pittsburgh Medical Center.

Figure 12–9: "Installation of Kenmore Waste Disposers." Copyright © 1997 by Sears, Roebuck and Company, Hoffman Estates, Illinois. Reprinted with permission.

Figure 12–11: "Quick Set Up Poster." Copyright © 2009 Hewlett Packard Development Company Ltd. Reproduction rights granted by Hewlett Packard Company. Reprinted with permission. All rights reserved.

Figures 13–9, 13–10, 13–11, 13–12, 13–13, 13–14, 13–15, 13–16, and 13–17: Kurzweiledu.com. "Sample Grant Proposal Cover Letter, Cover Page, Introduction, References Section (excerpt), Statement of Need, Program Description, Goals and Objectives Statement, Budget Narrative, Timeline." From <http://www.kurzweiledu.com/files/proof_resources _grant1.pdf> (pp. 2–8). Used with the Permission of Cambium Learning, Inc., Kurzweil.

Figure 15–3: Two Screenshots: "Mayoclinic.com: Tools for Healthier Lives. Core Exercises" and "Enter Core Exercises." Used with permission from mayoclinic.com. All rights reserved.

Figure 15–8: Two Screenshots: Corporate blog, Teslamotors.com. Reprinted by permission of Tesla Motors.

Figure 15–9: Three Screenshots from <www.cleantechnica.com>. Including the article "Free Solar-Powered Wi-Fi Coming to a Town Near You." Written by Jerry James Stone. Reprinted by permission of Green Options Media.

Figure 16–7: "Employment Experience Organized Functionally." Reprinted with the permission of Chris Helms.

Figure 16–10: "Résumé for an Entry-Level Position." Reprinted with the permission of Peggy Edwards.

Figures 16–11 and 16–14: "Résumé (Highlighting Professional Credentials)," and "Advanced Résumé (Combining Functional and Chronological Elements)." Prepared by Kim Isaacs, Advanced Career Systems, Inc. Reprinted by permission.

Figure 16–20: Fig. A–9 on p. 41 of Gerald J. Alred, Charles T. Brusaw, and Walter E. Oliu, *The Business Writer's Handbook*, Ninth Edition. Copyright © 2009 by Bedford/St. Martin's. Reprinted by permission of Bedford/St. Martin's.

Figure 16–25: Fig. R–3 on p. 468 of Gerald J. Alred, Charles T. Brusaw, and Walter E. Oliu, *Handbook of Technical Writing*, Ninth Edition. Copyright © 2009 by Bedford/St. Martin's. Reprinted by permission of Bedford/St. Martin's.

Index

abbreviations
  capitalization of, 664
  in e-mail messages, 296
  guidelines for using, 667–68
  in inside addresses, 309
  in instant messages, 301, 302
  list of, 389, 396
  for measurements, 667–68
  for names and titles, 668
  for names of organizations, 667
  plural form of, 652
  spelling out, in abstracts, 393
  in titles of works, 389
absolute words and phrases, 633, 644
abstracts, 165
  descriptive, 390, 392
  in formal reports, 386, 390–94
  for grant proposals, 470
  guidelines for, 394
  informative, 390–92, 393
Academic Search Premier, 157, 161
acceptance letters, 614–15
accessibility, of Web pages, 551, 552–54, 565–66
accident reports, 36, 76, 370–73
accuracy
  of content, 96
  of graphic elements, 223
  in informal reports, 361
  of research sources, 173
  in revision process, 115–16
  in test reports, 374
acknowledgment letters, 321, 324
acknowledgments, in preface, 396
acronyms
  guidelines for using, 667
  spelling out, in abstracts, 393
action, calling for in presentations, 502
active listening, 516–18
active voice, 638–39
  for emphatic writing, 101
  ESL tips for, 102
  first-person point of view and, 106–7
  for instructions, 432, 433
  in résumés, 586

addresses
  inside business letters, 306–9, 313
  commas in, 647
  numbers in, 667
  on résumés, 581
adjective clauses, 673
adjectives, 632–35
  articles with, 671–72
  commas with, 646
  comparative forms of, 632–33, 671–72
  with count nouns, 671
  ESL tips for, 634, 673
  placement of, 633–35
  predicate, 635
  using multiple, 634
  See also modifiers
adjustment letters, 336–39, 340–41
Adobe Acrobat, 136
Adobe portable document format. *See* PDF files
adverbs, 632–35
  comparative forms of, 632–33, 671–72
  conjunctive, 649
  ending in -*ly*, 633
  introductory, 644
  placement of, 635
  See also modifiers
affectation, avoiding, 112–13, 281, 346
age bias, 111–12
agenda, meeting, 525–26, 527, 530
agreement
  pronoun-antecedent, 630–32
  subject-verb, 635–38
  See also subject-verb agreement
American Psychological Association style. *See* APA style
America's Job Bank, 572–73
ampersands, 667
Amura, Annika, 540
analogy, in definitions, 80, 82
analytical reports, 386
annual reports, 386
antecedents
  agreement with pronoun, 630–32
  defined, 627
  references to, 629–30

anxiety, presentation, 514–15
APA style, 182–92
  documentation models for, 186–90
  example of, 191–92
  in-text citations, 182–84
  for quoted material, 178
  references list, 184–86, 411
APA Style Guide to Electronic References, 182
apostrophes, 650–53
  for forming plurals, 652–53
  indicating omissions, 652
  possessive case and, 650–52
appendixes
  in formal reports, 415
  in RFPs, 492
  in sales proposals, 483, 484
  in technical reports, 69
appositives, 628, 645, 649
argument. *See* persuasion
articles (*a, an, the*)
  ESL tips for, 671–72
  in titles of works, 664
articles (periodicals)
  currency of, 158
  documenting, 175, 187, 188, 197–98
  evaluating, 171–74
  in library databases, 159, 161–63, 164
ASCII résumés, 589–90, 591
assignments
  after meetings, 530
  understanding time-sensitive, 293
asterisks, 297
attention-getting statement, opening with, 501
audience
  analyzing, in draft writing, 67–75
  assessing needs of, 4–5, 6–7, 14
  for business communication, 275, 276, 280
  catching interest of, 84
  choosing visuals for, 220–23
  considering point of view of, 68
  for formal reports, 386
  global audiences, 70, 250–56, 343–51
  goodwill tone for, 282, 283
  for informal reports, 359
  for inquiry letters, 322, 325
  for instructions, 422, 423–28, 431, 436
  as listeners, 500–501, 513, 514, 518
  organizing information for, 31–33, 35, 57–58
  for presentations, 499–500, 516, 519
  for proposals, 449–50
  questions to ask about, 7, 67, 72, 500
  for résumés, 571
  revision process and, 96
  for sales letters, 325–26
  word choice and, 108–9
  writing for multiple, 68–70, 386, 387, 449–50
  writing style and, 281
  writing to persuade, 70–71, 72–74
  "you" viewpoint and, 282
  See also global audiences
author/date method of documentation, 182

authors
  authority of, 172–73
  corporate, documenting, 184, 187, 188, 194, 197, 198
  multiple, documenting, 183, 186, 193–94, 197
  multiple works, documenting, 183, 193
  online sources, documenting, 188, 198
  in references list, 185
  unknown, documenting, 184, 187, 188, 194, 198
  in Works Cited list, 195

background information
  in cover letters, 323
  in openings, 288, 360
  in presentations, 501
  in process explanations, 76
  in proposals, 449
  for research topics, 157
  for time-sensitive messages, 293
  on Web sites, 541
back matter, for formal reports, 414–17
bad-news correspondence. *See* negative messages
banners, 550
bargaining, in conflict management, 529
bar graphs, 233–35
  common uses for, 221, 233
  for schedules, 139, 140, 235
bias, in research sources, 173
biased language, 110–12, 543. *See also* sexist language
bibliographies, 165
  in formal reports, 414–15
  See also documentation of sources
biology style manuals, 203
bitmapped (raster) programs, 251
Blazon, Beth, 422
blind courtesy copy (*bcc:*), 292, 296, 312
Bloglines, 170
blogs, 559–62
  defined, 559
  documenting, 189, 199
  ethical considerations, 561
  evaluating sources from, 172
  guidelines for, 566
  internal and external, 559
  for job resources, 573–74
  organizational, 559–61
  RSS feeds, 169–70
  tagging posts, 561–62
  writing style for, 560–61
body
  of business letters, 310, 313
  of formal reports, 396–414
  of informal reports, 360, 373, 379
  of job application letters, 603–4
  of presentations, 502
  of proposals, 457, 458–60
  of tables, 225

body movement, in presentations, 513
body parts, depicting for international
        audiences, 252–54
boilerplate material, 451, 489
        See also repurposed content
boldface type
    for emphasis, 106, 213, 435
    for headings, 215
books
    documenting, 175, 186–87, 188, 197, 198
    evaluating, 171–74
    in references list, 186
    searching library catalogs for, 159–61
    in Works Cited list, 195
Boolean operators, 170
boxes, for highlighting, 105, 213, 215
boxheads, 225
brackets, 653, 656–57
brainstorming
    in business research, 149
    for formal reports, 386
    in presentations, 509
    in résumé writing, 578–79
    using live chat, 133
    in writing process, 9–10, 294
Bramlage, Steve, 26
brochures/pamphlets, documenting, 190, 200
buffers, in negative messages, 284, 330
bulleted lists, 504, 508, 510, 511, 549–50, 588
business communication
    business letters, 278
    e-mail messages, 277
    faxes, 278
    guidelines for, 276–77, 313–15
    importance of, 275
    instant messaging, 277–78
    meetings, 279
    memos, 278
    selecting appropriate medium, 71, 277–80,
        313–14
    style and tone for, 280–83
    telephone and conference calls, 278–79
    videoconferences, 279
    voice-mail messages, 279
    Web communications, 280
business correspondence, 320–52
    acceptance letters, 614–15
    acknowledgment letters, 321, 324
    adjustment letters, 336–39, 340–41
    clarity and emphasis in, 290–91
    collection letters, 339–43, 344–45
    complaint letters, 331–36, 337
    cover letters, 321, 322, 323, 388
    direct patterns for, 283–84
    effective structure for, 283–93, 314
    e-mail messages, 295–301
    good news messages, 284, 286, 314
    goodwill tone for, 282, 283
    guidelines for, 313–15, 352
    headings in, 290–91
    indirect patterns for, 284–88

inquiry and response letters, 321–25
instant messaging, 301–3
international, 250–56, 343–51, 352
job application letters, 602–8
lists in, 290
negative messages, 284–88, 330–43, 352
observing protocol, 291–92, 296
openings and closings, 288–89
reader-focused letters, 284, 285
refusal letters, 330–31, 332–35, 615
resignation letters, 615–17
routine and positive letters, 321–30, 352
sales letters, 325–30
style and tone for, 280–83, 314
subject lines, 84, 291
time-sensitive letters, 293–95, 314
types of, 320
writing style for, 281
"you" viewpoint in, 282
        See also business communication; business
            letters; e-mail messages; memos
business letters
    body of, 310
    complimentary closes, 311, 313, 663
    continuing pages, 311, 313
    end notations, 312
    format guidelines for, 306–13
    full-block style, 306, 307
    guidelines for writing, 315
    headings, 306–9
    informal reports as, 358
    inside addresses, 306–9
    investigative reports as, 365
    letterhead stationery for, 278, 280, 306, 307,
        311
    modified-block style, 306, 308
    openings and closings, 84, 85, 288–89
    organizing information for, 26
    salutations, 309–10, 663
    signature blocks, 311
    uses for, 277, 278, 280, 313
        See also business correspondence
business resources, online, 170–71

campus career services, 572
Canale, Debra, 65
capitalization, 662–64
    of abbreviations, 664
    of adjectives, 634
    all, for emphasis, 106, 213
    with colons, 650, 662–63
    common nouns and, 662
    in e-mail messages, 296, 297
    of first words, 662–63
    for headings, 409
    of institutions, events, concepts, 663–64
    of letters and units, 664
    of name titles, 664
    of proper nouns, 662
    of specific groups, 663
    of specific places, 663

capitalization (*cont.*)
  style guidelines for, 132
  in subject lines, 291
  of titles of works, 664
captions
  for graphic elements, 224, 230
  for highlighting, 215, 220
  for Web design, 543, 553
career services, campus, 572. *See also* job
    search
case, pronoun, 627–29
cause and effect analysis, 76, 82–84, 90
cautions. *See* warnings
CD-ROM publications, documenting, 189, 199
cell phones, 278–79
chalkboards, 510
charts
  documenting, 189, 199
  flip charts, 509
  flowcharts, 244–47
  organizational, 247
  for presentations, 504, 507, 509, 511, 520
  See also graphs; visuals
chemistry style manuals, 203
Chicago Manual of Style, 131
chronological organization, 13, 35, 36, 38,
    39, 57
  for résumés, 582–83
  for trip reports, 34
chunking content, in Web writing, 543–45
citation-management software, 163
citations. *See* in-text citations
claim letters. *See* complaint letters
clarity
  in business writing, 290–91
  in document design, 209
  illustrating for, 436–38
  in revision process, 114
classification
  in formal definitions, 79
  as organizational method, 35, 40–44, 45,
    46, 57
clauses
  adjective, 673
  introductory, 644
clip-art images, 243, 507, 508, 520
closings
  building goodwill with, 283, 284, 286, 287, 331
  in business writing, 289
  complimentary, in letters, 311, 313, 663
  in draft writing, 86–87
  in e-mail messages, 298
  in job application letters, 604
  for meetings, 532–33
  for presentations, 502
  See also conclusions
coherence, 97–101
  paragraph unity, 97–98
  use of transitions, 98–100
collaborating, in conflict management, 529

collaborative writing projects, 129–42
  advantages and disadvantages of, 130–31
  computer technology for, 132, 133, 136, 137,
    563
  conflict in, 137–38
  defined, 129–30
  formal reports, 387
  for global audiences, 134, 136
  guidelines for, 132, 134, 138, 142, 452
  leadership in, 139–41, 387, 451
  with other departments, 141–42
  planning stage, 131–32, 134
  proposals, 451–52
  reasons for doing, 129
  research and writing stages, 133
  review and revision in, 134–36
  review transmittal sheets for, 139, 141
  scheduling, 131, 139–41, 451
  style and format guides for, 131–32, 139
  team functions in, 131–37
  using e-mail in, 137, 295
  writing process for, 129–30
collection letters, 339–43, 344–45
collective nouns
  agreement with pronoun, 632
  agreement with verb, 636
CollegeGrad.com, 573
colons
  capital letter following, 650, 662–63
  common usage for, 649–50
  with quotation marks, 654
  in salutations, 309, 650
color
  cultural differences in use of, 252, 256, 436
  designing for color-blind, 553
  for highlighting, 215–16, 436
  in photographs, 249–50
  in presentation visuals, 520
  for warning signal words, 435
columns
  in document design, 214, 216, 218, 219
  graphs using, 221, 238–41
command sentences, for instructions, 432
commas, 643–48
  in addresses, 647
  with adjectives, 646
  avoiding unnecessary, 648
  with coordinating conjunctions, 625, 626,
    643, 648
  for dates, 646
  for direct address, 644
  for enclosing elements, 645
  for introductory elements, 644–45
  for linking clauses, 625, 626, 643
  in names and titles, 647
  with numbers, 647, 666
  with other punctuation, 647–48, 654
  for quoted material, 645
  for separating elements, 645–47
  for series of items, 645–46, 648

comma splices, 625–26
common knowledge, 180
common nouns, 662, 671
company description, in RFPs, 490
comparative modifiers, 632–33, 671–72
comparison
    as organizational method, 13, 32, 33, 35,
        51–57, 58
    as transitional device, 99
complaint letters, 331–36, 337
    organization for, 333
    resources for sending, 336
    responding to, 336–39, 340–41
completeness, revising for, 96
complimentary closes, in business letters,
        311, 313, 663
compound constructions
    agreement with pronoun, 632
    agreement with verb, 637
    commas with, 648
    possessive form of, 651
    pronouns in, 629
compound words, hyphens for, 657
comprehension tests, for instructions, 443
computer technology
    checking format consistency, 116
    clip-art images, 243, 507, 508, 520
    for collaborative writing, 132, 133, 136, 137,
        563
    electronic résumés, 587–92
    Find-and-Replace command, 14, 120
    grammar and spell checkers, 14, 115, 120,
        295
    graphics software, 251, 252
    for layout and format, 132
    for meeting minutes, 530–32
    presentation software, 507–9, 520–21
    print preview feature, 306
    for remote meetings, 526
    revision process and, 14, 115, 120
    RSS (really simple syndication), 169–70
    saving and tracking versions, 66, 133
    word processors, 14
    See also digital tips; word-processing
        programs
conciseness
    in abstracts, 392–93
    active voice for, 101
    in closings, 86
    in instructions, 432
    in revision process, 109–10
    in Web writing, 543
conclusions
    in executive summaries, 398
    false, 83
    in formal reports, 386, 410, 412–13
    in grant proposals, 475
    in informal reports, 360, 362, 373, 379
    in instructions, 431
    in proposals, 457, 461

    in sales proposals, 476–77, 484, 488
    as transitional device, 99
    See also closings
conditional sentences, 675
conference calls, 279. See also meetings
confidence, developing, 65, 131
confidentiality
    e-mail messages and, 296
    questionnaires and, 154
    Web page users and, 555–57
conflict
    in collaborative writing projects, 137–38
    in meetings, 529
conjunctions
    for compound subjects, 637
    as transitional devices, 99
    See also coordinating conjunctions
conjunctive adverbs, for linking clauses, 649
Connery, Brian, 130
consistency
    in collaborative writing, 132
    in document design, 209, 213
    for graphic elements, 223
    with numbers, 665
    in résumé writing, 578, 588
    for verb mood, 639
consumer instructions, 425–27
content
    accuracy of, 96
    revising for, 96–97
context
    assessing, in writing process, 5, 8
    guidelines for, 8
    for lists, 290
    in opening statement, 84
    of presentations, 499–500
    in refusal letters, 330
    selecting medium and, 277
    word choice and, 108–9
contractions, 347, 349, 652
contrast, as transitional device, 99
conversational voice, 74, 281. See also
        informal style
cooling period, in writing process, 95, 276
coordinate nouns, 651
coordinating conjunctions
    commas with, 643, 648
    for linking clauses, 625, 626, 643, 649
    in titles of works, 664
copy notations (cc:). See courtesy copy
copyright permissions, 175, 180–81, 225, 451,
        555, 557
Corel Presentations, 507
costs
    in grant proposals, 473–75
    in proposals, 449, 457
    in sales letters, 326–27
    in sales proposals, 477, 482–83
count nouns, 670–72
courtesy copy (cc:), 292–93, 296, 301, 312

cover letters
  background information in, 323
  in business writing, 321
  for e-mail attachments, 296, 321
  for faxes, 278
  for formal reports, 322, 388
  for grant proposals, 470, 471
  for questionnaires, 154, 157
  for sales proposals, 477, 478
coworkers, instructions for, 424, 425, 426
Craigslist, 574
Creative Commons, 451, 557
cultural differences
  learning about, 70
  symbols and, 254–55
  writing style and, 343–46
  See also global audiences; international
      communication
currency, of research sources, 158, 173
curriculum vitae, 578*n*
cutaway drawings, 242

dangling modifiers, 627
dashes, 648
  common usage for, 659–60
  for emphasis, 106, 659
databases
  documenting sources from, 188, 196, 198
  library, 157, 159, 161–63, 164, 165
  résumé, 574, 587–90
  search strategies for, 161–63, 164
  storing search results, 163
dates
  apostrophes with, 652
  in business letters, 309, 313
  commas with, 646
  in international correspondence, 347,
      666
  numbers in, 666
  slashes in, 661
  on title page, 389, 390
deadlines
  in collaborative writing, 131
  time-sensitive messages, 293–95
  time-sensitive presentations, 519–23
  time-sensitive proposals, 451, 488–90
  in writing process, 65–66
decimal numbering system outline, 28–30,
      408
decreasing order of importance organization,
      13, 34, 35, 44–45, 47, 48, 57
definitions
  for elements in visuals, 223
  extended, 79–80, 81, 82
  formal, 79
  glossaries, 415
  informal, 79
  for technical terminology, 114
  what-it-is-not, 80–82
  as writing strategy, 76, 79–82, 90

delivery schedule
  in RFPs, 491
  in sales proposals, 477, 482–83
Demers, Robert, 281
demonstrative adjectives, 671
dependent clauses, for subordination, 102,
      675
description
  organizing patterns for, 38–40
  using illustrations for, 79, 80, 81
  whole-to-parts method of, 79
  as writing strategy, 75, 77–79, 89
descriptive abstracts, 390, 392
descriptors, in electronic résumés, 590
design. *See* document layout and design;
      format guidelines; Web writing and
      design
details
  in description, 77–79
  inappropriate level of, 108, 109
development methods. *See* organizational
      methods; writing strategies
dictionaries
  documenting, 187, 197
  for research, 165
digital tips
  ASCII résumés, 590
  away-from-desk e-mail messages, 300
  checking format consistency, 116
  collaborative writing software, 133
  creating indexes, 416
  creating simple tables, 228
  creating styles and templates, 364
  for document design, 14, 214
  for draft writing, 66
  e-mailing research questions, 150
  formatting outlines, 34
  grammar and spell checkers, 115
  graphics software, 251, 252
  instant messaging, 303
  managing e-mail messages, 301
  organizing and highlighting instructions,
      424
  report formatting, 387
  résumé templates, 589
  reviewing collaborative documents, 136
  for revision process, 14, 115, 120
  sending e-mail attachments, 297
  software for remote meetings, 526
  storing search results, 163
  using e-mail for collaborative projects, 137
  using PDF files, 555
  using search engines, 170
  word processors, 14
  See also computer technology; Internet
      research; Web writing and design;
      word-processing programs
dimensional-column graphs, 238–41
direct address, commas for, 644
directional cues, on Web pages, 545, 550

directional signs, cultural differences in, 255–56
direct observation. *See* observation, in research
direct quotations, 176, 645, 653. *See also* quoted material
direct statements, 105
direct style
  for business writing, 283–84, 285, 314
  global audiences and, 70, 343
  for instructions, 432–33
  See also style, writing
disabilities, people with
  bias against, 111–12
  designing Web pages for, 553, 566
discussion groups, electronic
  documenting sources from, 189, 199
  evaluating sources from, 172
  for job resources, 573–74
diversity, acknowledging, 256. *See also* global audiences; international communication
division and classification organization, 32, 33, 35, 40–44, 45, 46, 57
documentation of sources, 181–204
  APA style, 182–92
  citation-management software, 163
  in collaborative writing, 132
  copyright violations and, 180–81
  ethical considerations, 181, 225, 414
  examples of, 191–92, 201–2
  in formal reports, 411, 414
  in-text citations, 178, 182–84, 193–94
  MLA style, 193–202
  multimedia sources, 189–90, 199–200
  online sources, 175, 184, 188–89, 194, 196, 198–99
  other style manuals for, 203–4
  for paraphrases, 178
  personal communications, 184, 190, 199, 200
  in persuasive writing, 453
  plagiarism and, 180, 294, 414
  printed sources, 175, 186–87, 197
  public domain materials, 181, 451, 557
  purpose of, 181–82
  references list (APA), 184–86, 192
  for summaries, 179
  taking notes for, 175
  for visuals, 225, 230
  for Web writing, 557–58
  Works Cited list (MLA), 194–96, 202, 457, 462
document layout and design, 210–20
  for business letters, 306–13
  checking format consistency, 116
  columns, 216, 218
  creating thumbnail sketches, 216, 217
  digital tips for, 14, 214
  for e-mail messages, 297–98

for formal reports, 387
guidelines for, 209–12, 220, 256–57
headings, 213–15, 403–8, 409
highlighting devices, 213–16, 220
illustrations, 219
importance of, 116
for instructions, 436–42
integrating visuals with text, 219, 220–24, 256–57
lists, 219
margins, 116, 214, 218, 219
for memos, 303–5
page design, 216–20
for presentation slides, 507, 511
for résumés, 578, 588
templates for, 214, 364, 387
typography, 212–13, 214, 220
visuals, 220–56. *See also* visuals
white space, 116, 216–19
  See also format guidelines; Web writing and design
Dogpile, 169, 170
draft writing, 64–90
  analyzing audience during, 67–75
  for business writing, 276
  closings, 86–87
  in collaborative writing, 132, 133
  developing confidence, 65
  development strategies for, 75–84
  digital tips for, 66
  establishing role and voice in, 71–74
  example of, 87–89
  for formal reports, 386
  guidelines for, 67, 75, 89–90
  guidelines for evaluating, 96–97
  for international audiences, 70
  introduction to, 64–65
  for memos, 15–16
  for multiple audiences, 68–70
  opening statements, 84–86
  persuasive communication, 70–71, 72–74
  saving and tracking versions, 66, 133
  time-management tactics for, 65–67
  for time-sensitive messages, 294–95
  See also writing process
drawings, 241–44
  close-ups with enlarged details, 437, 439
  cutaway, 242
  in description, 79, 80, 81
  exploded-view, 242, 243
  guidelines for, 242
  in process explanation, 76–77, 78
  sources for, 243
  uses for, 221
  See also illustrations; visuals
dummy, 216

EBSCOhost, 161
education, on résumés, 580, 582, 583
electronic résumés, 587–92

electronic sources. *See* Internet research; online sources
ellipses, 177, 660
Ellis, Howard, 223
e-mail messages, 295–301
   attaching résumés, 589, 590
   attachments in, 296, 297, 298
   away-from-desk messages, 300
   for collaborative writing projects, 137, 295
   confidentiality and, 296
   courtesy copies, 292–93, 296, 301
   design considerations, 297–98
   documenting, 184, 189, 199
   guidelines for, 314–15
   ineffective use of, 14, 71
   informal reports as, 358
   managing, 301
   memos as, 303
   multisubject, avoiding, 291
   negative messages, 286–88
   observing netiquette rules, 296–97
   observing protocol, 291–92
   organizing information for, 26
   for research questions, 150
   responding to, 296, 298, 301
   reviewing, 295–96, 301
   sales letters as, 328, 329, 330
   salutations and closings in, 298
   signatures for, 297, 299, 300
   style and tone for, 295
   subject lines in, 291, 296
   trip reports as, 374
   uses for, 277, 280, 295, 298, 313
   See also business correspondence
embedded links, 545, 547
emoticons, 297
empathy, in listening process, 518
emphasis, 101–6
   active and passive voice for, 101–2
   in business writing, 290–91
   direct statements for, 105
   guidelines for, 106
   highlighting devices for, 213–16
   lists for, 104–5
   order of importance organization for, 105
   parallel structure, 104
   sentence subordination for, 102–3
   typographical devices for, 52, 105–6, 668
   varied sentence length for, 105
employment. *See* job search
employment agencies, 575
employment experience, 580, 582–86
employment interviews. *See* job interviews
enclosure notations, 312
Encyclopaedia Britannica, 163
Encyclopedia of Careers and Vocational Guidance, The, 163–65
encyclopedias, 163–65, 187, 197
end notations, in letters, 312

English as a Second Language (ESL), 670–75
   active and passive voice, 102
   adjective clauses, 673
   adjectives, 634
   articles (*a, an, the*), 671–72
   conditional sentences, 675
   count and mass nouns, 670–71
   determining mood, 640
   gerunds and infinitives, 673
   helping verbs, 674–75
   indicating possession, 652
   possessive pronouns, 631
   prepositions, 672
   punctuating numbers, 666
   quotation marks, 654
   stating an opinion, 107
   supporting an argument, 96
   verb tense, 641, 673–74
equipment and materials
   in instructions, 430–31
   in proposals, 449, 457
ERIC (Educational Resources Information Center), 163
ethics notes
   acknowledging opposing opinions, 9, 71, 453
   avoiding bias, 110
   confidentiality issues, 154, 296
   documenting sources, 181, 225, 414
   FAQs, 564
   highlighting advantages, 103
   I and *we* usage, 107
   instant messaging, 303
   job-related writing, 21
   minute-taking, 532
   organizational blogs, 561
   persuasive strategies, 31, 71
   plain-language laws, 112
   primary research, 149, 151, 154
   quoted material, 177
   repurposing content, 451
   résumé writing, 585
   RFPs, 492
   sales writing, 327, 468
   sending blind copies, 292
   taking responsibility, 102
   trouble reports, 370
   warnings and cautions, 434
   Web presence, 574
   Web versions of formal reports, 411
   word choice, 109
   writer's voice, 75
ethnic bias, 111–12
evidence
   in cause and effect analysis, 83, 90
   linking to, on Web sites, 542
   in persuasive writing, 453
   in presentations, 502
   in sales letters, 330

examples
    in definitions, 79, 81
    in opinions, 107
    as transitional device, 99
exclamation marks, 648, 656
executives, writing for, 450
executive summaries
    for formal reports, 386, 398–400
    for sales proposals, 477, 479
    for technical reports, 69
Expanded Academic ASAP, 163
experience. *See* personal experience
explanatory notes, in formal reports, 408–9
explanatory phrases, as fragments, 626–27
exploded-view drawings, 242, 243
extended definitions, 79–80, 81, 82
external proposals, 463–88
    defined, 448
    grant and research proposals, 468–75
    guidelines for, 493–94
    sales proposals, 475–88
    solicited proposals, 463, 464
    unsolicited proposals, 463–68
    See also grant proposals; sales proposals
eye contact
    global audiences and, 516
    in presentations, 513

face-to-face meetings, 277, 279, 280, 314. *See also* meetings
fact, conditional sentence as, 675
FAQs (frequently asked questions), 558, 564–65, 566–67
faxes, 278, 280, 313
feasibility studies, 386
feedback, in collaborative writing, 130, 136
figures
    in formal reports, 394, 410
    list of, 224, 386, 394
    numbered, 224, 410, 667
    See also visuals
film/video, documenting, 189, 199
first draft. *See* draft writing
first-person point of view, 106, 113
flexibility
    in collaborative writing, 133
    in draft writing, 66–67
flip charts, 509, 530
flowcharts, 222, 244–47
"folksonomy," 561
follow-up correspondence, in job search, 613–15
fonts, 211, 212, 551. *See also* typography
footers, 213, 214, 215
footnotes
    explanatory, 408–9
    in tables, 225
    type size for, 213
foreign words, italics for, 668–69

foreword, in formal reports, 395
formal definitions, 79
formal internal proposals, 454–62
formal reports, 385–417
    abstracts, 390–94
    appendix, 415
    back matter, 414–17
    bibliography, 414–15
    body, 396–414
    collaborative writing of, 129
    conclusions, 386, 410, 412–13
    cover letters, 321, 322, 388
    defined, 358, 386–87
    executive summary, 398–400
    explanatory notes, 408–9
    foreword, 395
    format guidelines for, 385, 387
    front matter, 389–96
    glossary, 415
    guidelines for, 417
    headings in, 403–8, 409
    index, 415–17
    introductions, 400–403
    investigative reports, 365
    list of abbreviations and symbols, 396, 398
    list of figures and tables, 394
    multiple audiences for, 68–70, 386, 387
    numbering visuals, 410
    outlines for, 26
    posted on Web sites, 411
    preface, 396, 397
    recommendations, 386, 410–11, 412–13
    references list, 411, 414
    table of contents, 394, 395
    text section of, 403–10
    title page, 389–90, 391
formal style, 74, 281
    as affectation, 112
    business letters and, 278, 306
    See also style, writing
format guidelines
    for business letters, 306–13
    for business writing, 277
    for collaborative writing, 131–32
    customizing templates, 214, 364, 387
    for drawings, 242
    for e-mail messages, 297–98
    for formal reports, 385, 387
    for informal reports, 360, 362, 364, 365, 373
    for meeting minutes, 530, 531
    for memos, 303–5
    for outlines, 34
    for résumés, 588
    See also document layout and design
fractions, 666
fragments, sentence, 626–27
Freelance Graphics, 507
freewriting, 66
frequently asked questions. *See* FAQs

front matter, for formal reports, 389–96
full-block style, for letters, 306, 307, 313
functional résumés, 582–85
future perfect tense, 640, 642
future progressive tense, 641
future tense, 640, 641–42

gender
  pronoun-antecedent agreement in, 630–31
  sexist language and, 111, 630–31
general-to-specific organization, 32, 35, 47, 50, 58
geographical names
  capitalization of, 663
  commas with, 647
gerunds, 626, 673
gestures
  cultural connotations of, 252–54, 256
  in presentations, 499, 512, 513
Gilpin, Deborah, 6
GIS (geographic information systems) software, 165
global audiences
  graphics for, 250–56
  instructions for, 427–28, 429, 436
  language for, 346–47, 427, 428
  presentations for, 515–16
  translation sites for, 554
  use of color and, 252, 256, 436
  Web design for, 543, 553–54, 566
  writing for, 68, 70, 343–51
  See also international communication
GlobalEDGE, 169
glossaries, 386, 415
good news messages, 284, 286, 314
goodwill
  in acknowledgment letters, 321
  in adjustment letters, 336, 339
  in business writing, 282, 283
  in closings, 283, 284, 286, 287, 331
  instructions and, 422
  in negative messages, 330
Google, 166, 167
Google Groups, 574
Google Maps, 169
Google Reader, 170
government employment services, 577
government resources
  documenting, 190, 200
  documents and reports, 171
  online, 171
  opinion polls, 171
  as public domain, 181
  statistical sources, 171
  style standards for, 203
grammar checkers, 14, 115, 120
grant proposals, 468–75
  application guidelines, 468–69
  defined, 448, 468
  guidelines for, 494

structure for, 468, 470–75
graphic elements
  in formal reports, 410
  for international communication, 250–56
  typefaces for, 212
  in Web design, 551, 554
  See also drawings; illustrations; visuals
graphics software, 251, 252
graphs, 228–41
  bar, 233–35
  dimensional-column, 238–41
  line, 228–32, 241
  picture, 238
  pie, 235–37
  for presentations, 504, 507, 511, 520
  versus tables, 228, 229
  uses for, 220, 221–22
  See also visuals
Greenspan, Paul B., 499
group names, capitalization of, 663
groupware, 526

handbooks, 165
hand gestures, cultural connotations of, 254
handouts, in presentations, 511, 520
headers, 213, 214, 215
  for second pages, 305, 311
headings
  for business letters, 290–91, 306–9
  decimal numbering system for, 408
  defining styles for, 14, 132
  in formal reports, 403–8, 409
  guidelines for, 403
  for highlighting, 213–15, 220
  for instructions, 428–30
  levels of, 403, 408, 409
  in memos, 303
  placement of, 215
  in résumés, 581
  typeface and size for, 212, 213, 215, 669
  in Web writing, 543, 549
helping verbs, 674–75
highlighting devices
  in document design, 211, 213–16, 220
  for e-mail messages, 297–98
  for emphasis, 52, 105–6, 290–91
  for warnings and cautions, 434–35, 436
  for Web writing, 549–52
  word-processing features for, 424
historical present verb tense, 640
HotJobs, 587
HTML (hypertext markup language) format, 592
humor, 653
  global audiences and, 515
  Web writing and, 543
Hurd, Steven, 95
hyperlinks
  on blog sites, 561
  embedded, 545, 547

hyperlinks (*cont.*)
  to external content, 547–48
  to internal content, 545–47
  listing, 546
hyphens, 657–59
  for modifiers, 657–58
  other uses for, 659
  with prefixes and suffixes, 658
hypothetical sentence, 675

I (pronoun)
  in job-related writing, 106–7, 113
  in résumés, 586
icons
  for global audiences, 215, 255, 256
  for highlighting, 215
  uses for, 222
  in warnings, 435, 436
idioms, 346, 347, 515, 553
illustrations
  callouts in, 79, 81
  in description, 79, 80, 81
  in document design, 219
  in process explanation, 76–77, 78
  See also drawings; visuals
image, organizational, 210, 211–12, 275, 280
imitation, affectation and, 113
imperative mood, 74, 639
  for instructions, 432, 433
importance. *See* decreasing order of
        importance organization; increasing
        order of importance organization;
        inverted-pyramid method, for Web
        writing
imprecision, affectation and, 113
impression, affectation and, 112–13
incident reports, 370–73
increasing order of importance organization,
        13, 35, 45–47, 49, 57, 105
indefinite pronouns, 631–32, 637
independent clauses
  joining, 625–26, 643
  in run-on sentences, 625–26
indexes
  creating with word processor, 416
  for formal reports, 415–17
  library, 161–63
indicative mood, 639–40
indirect quotations, 176, 645, 653. *See also*
        quoted material
indirect style
  in international communication, 346
  for negative messages, 284–88, 314, 346
  See also style, writing
infinitives, 626, 673
Infomine, 169
informal definitions, 79
informal reports, 358–79
  accuracy in, 361
  audience for, 359

body, 360, 379
collecting information for, 359
conclusions, 360, 362, 379
defined, 358
format guidelines for, 360, 362, 364, 365,
        373
guidelines for, 379
introductions, 360, 379
investigative reports, 365–69
note taking for, 359
periodic reports, 361–62, 364–65, 366–67
planning and writing, 358–60
progress reports, 361–64
recommendations, 360, 362, 365, 373, 379
test reports, 374–78
trip reports, 373–74, 375–76
trouble reports, 370–73
types of, 361
informal style
  for blogs, 560
  in business writing, 74, 281
  for e-mail messages, 295
  for sales letters, 328
  for Web writing, 542–43
  See also style, writing
information
  collecting, for reports, 359
  establishing scope of, 4, 11–12
  gathering, for presentations, 500, 519
  gathering, for time-sensitive memo, 293–94
  generating and gathering, 4, 8–11
  organization of, 12–13, 25–58. *See also*
        organization
  sources for, 11
  See also research
*Information Processing: Documentation
        Symbols and Conventions for Data,
        Program, and System Flowcharts,
        Program Network Charts, and System
        Resources Charts* (ISO publication),
        246
information-processing flowcharts, 246
information surveys, 392
informative abstracts, 390–92, 393
in-house materials, 181
initiation, affectation and, 113
inquiry letters, 321–25
  audience and purpose for, 322, 325
  forwarding, 325, 326
  for job opportunities, 577
  responding to, 325, 327
  for unsolicited proposals, 468
insecurity, affectation and, 113
instant messaging (IM)
  confidentiality and, 296
  ethical considerations, 303
  guidelines for, 315
  privacy and security issues, 303
  uses for, 277–78, 280, 295, 313
  writing and managing, 301–3

Institutional Review Board (IRB), 149
instructions, 422–44
    audience and purpose for, 31–32, 68, 422,
        423–28, 431, 436
    for consumers, 425–27
    for coworkers, 424, 425, 426
    design principles for, 210–11, 436–42
    direct and concise language for, 432–33
    guidelines for, 443–44
    for international audiences, 427–28, 429
    organization of, 31–33, 34–36, 424, 428–31
    planning, 423–31
    two-tier approach to, 438–42
    usability tests for, 442–43
    visuals in, 428, 429, 436–42
    warnings and cautions in, 106, 432, 433–36
    writer's accurate understanding of, 423
    writing process for, 432–36
intercultural communication, 346. *See also*
        global audiences; international
        communication
interjections, 644
internal proposals, 454–62
    body, 457, 458–60
    conclusions, 87, 457, 461
    defined, 448, 454
    formal, 454–62
    guidelines for, 462, 493
    introductions, 454–57
    problem statements, 454–57
    routine, 455–56
    See also proposals
international audiences. *See* global audiences
international communication, 343–51
    appropriate and inappropriate examples of,
        347–51
    collaborative writing and, 134, 136
    color usage in, 252, 256, 436
    considering audience for, 68, 70, 134
    cultural differences in connotation and,
        252–56
    cultural symbols and, 254–55
    dates, time, and measurement in, 347, 666
    graphics in, 250–56
    guidelines for, 352
    icons for, 215, 255, 256
    indirectness in, 346
    instructions, 427–28, 429
    international standards for, 246, 252, 255,
        347, 428, 435
    language and usage in, 346–47
    salutations for, 298, 346, 347
    translations for, 343, 427, 428, 554
    Web design for, 543, 553–54, 566
    writing style differences, 343–46
International Organization for
        Standardization (ISO), 246, 255, 428
International System of Units (SI), 668
Internet. *See* Internet research; Web sites; Web
        writing and design

Internet Public Library, 169
Internet research, 11, 166–71
    business and government resources, 170–71
    documenting, 175, 184, 188–89, 196, 198–99
    evaluating sources, 171–74
    job resources, 572–74
    for legal research, 149
    metasearch engines, 169, 170
    search engines, 166, 167, 170
    subject directories, 157, 158, 166, 168, 169
    web-based tools, 169–70
    See also library research; research; search
        strategies
Internet Scout Project, 169
internships, 576, 585
interruptive person, in meetings, 528
interviews
    conducting, 151–52
    determining sources for, 150
    documenting, 184, 190, 200
    ethical considerations, 151
    guidelines for, 151–52
    note taking for, 151, 152
    preparing for, 151
    for research, 11, 149, 150–52
    for usability testing, 443
    using e-mail for, 150
    See also job interviews
in-text citations
    APA style, 182–84
    MLA style, 193–94
intimidation, affectation and, 113
introductions
    in business writing, 288–89
    for formal reports, 400–403
    for grant proposals, 470, 472
    for informal reports, 360, 373, 379
    for instructions, 430
    for presentations, 501
    for proposals, 454–57
    for technical reports, 69
    See also openings
introductory elements
    commas with, 644–45
    as fragments, 626
inverted-pyramid method, for Web writing,
        540–41
inverted word order, subject-verb agreement
        with, 636
investigative reports, 76, 365–69, 379, 386
invitation for bids (IFBs), 463
italics
    in e-mail messages, 298
    for emphasis, 106, 213, 668
    for foreign words, 668–69
    guidelines for using, 668–69
    for proper names, 669
    for subheads, 669
    for titles of works, 669
    for words, letters, numerals, 669

jargon
  correct use of, 114, 433
  global audiences and, 346, 347, 515
job application letters, 602–8
  guidelines for, 605
  objectives of, 602–3
  organization of, 603–4
  samples of, 605–8
job interviews, 609–12
  asking questions in, 609–10
  behavioral interviews, 610
  behavior during, 611–12
  concluding, 612
  follow-up correspondence for, 613–15
  informational, 577
  learning about employers, 609, 611
  preparing for, 609–11
  requesting, 604
  responding to questions in, 610, 611–12
  salary negotiations, 612
job objectives, 581–82, 603
job resignation letters, 615–17
job search, 570–618
  acceptance and refusal letters, 614–15
  application letters, 602–8
  establishing goals, 570, 571
  guidelines for, 617–18
  internships, 576, 585
  interviewing, 609–12
  professional Web presence and, 574
  record keeping for, 577
  rejection letters, 331, 334
  resources for, 571–77
  résumés for, 578–602. See also résumés
job titles, capitalization of, 664
journalism, style standards for, 203
journals
  documenting articles in, 187, 196, 197
  for job search, 575
  for library research, 166
  See also articles (periodicals)
JSTOR, 163

key words and phrases
  blog post tags, 561–62
  for electronic résumés, 589–90
  for online searches, 162, 163, 164, 166, 170
  repetition of, for transitions, 99–100
  in Web writing, 550

laboratory reports, 36, 374–78
Ladwig, Susan U., 149
language, 107–14
  avoiding affectation, 112–13, 346
  avoiding wordiness, 109–10
  biased, 110–12
  context and word choice, 108–9
  for global audiences, 346–47, 427, 428
  jargon, 114
  plain, 112–14, 433, 541

  sexist, avoiding, 110–11, 543, 630–31
  technical terminology, 113–14
  for warnings and cautions, 434
law style manuals, 203
layout. See document layout and design; Web
    writing and design
leadership, in collaborative writing projects,
    139–41, 387, 451
lecture/speech, documenting, 200
letterhead stationery, 278, 280, 306, 307, 311,
    313
letters. See business letters
letters (alphabet)
  capitalization of, 664
  hyphens with, 658, 659
  italics for, 669
  plural form of, 652
Lexis/Nexis Academic, 163
Librarians' Internet Index, 169
library research, 11, 158–66
  catalogs for locating books, 159–61
  common library terms, 165–66
  evaluating sources, 171–74
  for job resources, 575
  periodical databases, 157, 159, 161–63,
    164
  reference works, 160, 163–65
  storing search results, 163
  subject directories, 166, 168
  types of resources, 158–59
  using library homepage, 159, 160, 166
  See also Internet research; research
line graphs, 228–32, 241
  avoiding visual distortion in, 230, 232
  guidelines for, 230
  single and double, 231
  uses for, 221–22
line length, in Web writing, 551–52
line spacing, in business letters, 310, 313
LinkedIn, 573
links. See hyperlinks
listening, 516–19
  active, 516–17
  defining purpose of, 517
  fallacies about, 516–17
  guidelines for, 518
  in meetings, 527–28
  to presentations, 500–501, 513, 514
  steps to effective, 517–19, 534
lists
  of abbreviations and symbols, 389, 396, 398
  brainstorming, 9–10
  bulleted and numbered, 504, 510, 511,
    549–50
  in business writing, 290, 295, 303
  in document design, 219
  for emphasis, 104–5
  of figures and tables, 224, 386, 394
  guidelines for using, 105
  of hyperlinks, 546

lists (*cont.*)
  for organizing ideas, 5, 12–13
  overuse of, 104–5, 290
  in presentation visuals, 504, 510, 511
literature reviews, in grant proposals, 470, 472

magazines
  documenting articles in, 187, 196, 197, 198
  for library research, 166
  page layout for, 219
managers, writing for, 450
manuals, 165. *See also* instructions
maps, 247–48, 249
  documenting, 189, 199
  guidelines for creating, 248
  online sources, 169
  uses for, 221
margins, in document design, 116, 132, 214,
    218, 219, 306, 313, 588
mass nouns, 670–71, 672
McGraw-Hill Encyclopedia of Science and
    Technology, 165
measurements
  abbreviations for, 667–68
  agreement with verb, 636
  in international correspondence, 347
  specifying, in visuals, 224
  words versus numerals, 666
mechanics
  abbreviations, 667–68
  capitalization, 662–64
  defined, 662
  italics, 668–69
  numbers, 664–67
medical style manuals, 203
medium
  listing in documentation, 196
  selecting appropriate, 8, 71, 277–80, 313–14
meetings, 523–33
  agenda for, 525–26, 527, 530
  closing, 532–33
  conducting, 527–33, 534
  conference calls, 279
  conflict in, 529
  determining attendees, 524
  guidelines for attending, 526
  lessons-learned, 490
  minute-taking for, 530–32
  planning for, 523–27, 530
  problem personalities in, 528–29
  purpose of, 523–24, 530
  site for, 524–25
  software for remote meetings, 526
  time and duration of, 524
  uses for, 277, 279, 280, 314
memos
  additional pages, 305
  courtesy copies, 292–93
  format guidelines for, 303–5
  guidelines for, 315

informal reports as, 358
internal proposals as, 455–56
investigative reports as, 365, 368–69
multisubject, avoiding, 291
negative messages, 286–88
observing protocol, 291–92, 305
openings, 84–85
organizing information for, 26
systematic writing of, 14–20
transmittal, 388
trip reports as, 374, 375–76
trouble reports as, 370, 371–72
uses for, 278, 280, 303, 313
See also business correspondence
Metacrawler, 169, 170
metasearch engines, 169, 170
microform, 166
mind mapping software, 170
Mindomo, 170
minutes of meetings, 139
  delegating, 530
  ethical considerations, 532
  guidelines for taking, 530–32
  organizing patterns for, 36
misplaced modifiers, 627
MLA Handbook for Writers of Research Papers,
    182
MLA style, 182, 193–202
  documentation models for, 197–200
  example of, 201–2
  guidelines for online sources, 196
  in-text citations, 193–94
  medium consulted, 196
  for quoted material, 178
  Works Cited list, 178, 194–96, 411, 414
modal verbs, 674–75
Modern Language Association style. *See* MLA
    style
modest tone, 283
modified-block style, for letters, 306, 308, 313
modifiers, 632–35
  avoiding redundancy with, 109
  dangling, 627
  hyphenated, 657–58
  as introductory elements, 644
  misplaced, 627
  squinting, 627
  subject-verb agreement and, 636
  for subordination, 102
  See also adjectives; adverbs
money, words versus numerals for, 665
Monster.com, 573, 587
mood, verb
  consistency of, 639
  ESL tips for, 640
  types of, 639
Mueller, Ulrike, 136
multimedia content
  documenting sources, 189–90, 199–200
  in Web design, 558–59

multivolume works, documenting, 186, 187, 193, 195, 197

names and titles
    abbreviations for, 668
    in business letters, 309–10
    capitalization of, 664
    commas in, 647
    first names, 298, 309, 346, 347, 668
    job titles, 664
    in meeting minutes, 532
    on title page, 389, 390
National Atlas, 169
navigational tool bars, 550–51
negative messages
    indirect style for, 284–88, 314, 346
    organization for, 330–31
    reader's point of view in, 331
    types of, 330–43
    See also specific types
negative person, in meetings, 528
netiquette rules, for e-mail, 296–97
networking, for job search, 572
newsletter, thumbnail sketches for, 216
newspaper advertisements, for job search, 574–75
newspaper articles
    currency of, 158
    databases for, 157
    documenting, 187, 196, 198
New York Times Index, 163
noncombative tactics, for conflict management, 529
noncount nouns, 670–71
nonrestrictive elements, enclosing, 645
note taking
    for informal reports, 359
    for interviews, 151, 152
    while listening, 518
    for meeting minutes, 532
    for organizing ideas, 12–13
    for organizing short documents, 26
    for research, 174–76
nouns
    collective, 632
    common, 662, 671
    compound, 632, 651
    coordinate, 651
    count and mass, 670–72
    possessive, 650–51
    proper, 662, 669
    singular, ending in -s, 638
Noyes, David, 361
number agreement
    pronoun-antecedent, 631–32
    subject-verb, 635–38
numbered lists, 504, 511, 549–50
numbers
    in addresses, 667
    ESL tips for, 666

for figures and tables, 224, 410, 667
guidelines for using, 664–67
hyphens with, 657, 658, 659
italics for, 669
measurements, 666
ordinal, 665
page numbers, 389, 390, 392, 396, 415, 667
plural form of, 653, 665
punctuation with, 647, 650, 666
slashes in, 661
times and dates, 666
words versus numerals, 665
See also measurements

objective case, of pronouns, 627–28
observation, in research, 149, 152
Occupational Outlook Handbook, 577
omissions
    apostrophes for, 652
    ellipses for, 177, 660
    in quoted material, 177
    slashes for, 661
online sources
    documenting, 175, 184, 188–89, 190, 194, 196, 198–99
    evaluating, 171–74
    library catalogs, 159–61
    periodical databases, 161–63, 164
    search engines and subject directories, 166–70
    See also Internet research; library research
openings
    buffers, 284, 330
    in business writing, 288–89
    in draft writing, 84–86
    for international communication, 346, 347, 349
    for job application letters, 603
    for presentations, 501
    for process explanations, 76
    tone for, 289
    See also introductions
opinions
    acknowledging opposing, 9, 71, 453
    stating, 107
oral communication, 498
    listening process, 516–19
    managing conflict and, 529
    problem personalities and, 528–29
    See also meetings; presentations
order of importance organization, 13
    decreasing, 44–45
    increasing, 45–47, 105
organization, 25–58
    considering audience and purpose, 31–33, 57–58
    digital tips for, 424
    for formal reports, 403–10
    for grant proposals, 470–75
    guidelines for, 58

organization (*cont.*)
  importance of, 25–26
  for negative messages, 330–31
  outlining, 26–34
  of presentations, 500–504, 520
  for proposals, 452
  of résumés, 580–87
  revising, 96–97
  for sales proposals, 476–88
  in systematic writing, 12–13
  for time-sensitive messages, 294
  for Web writing, 540–41
organizational charts, 222, 247
organizational methods, 32, 34–57
  cause and effect analysis, 82–84
  chronological, 36, 38, 39
  common approaches, 35, 57–58
  comparison, 51–57
  decreasing order of importance, 44–45, 47, 48
  definitions, 79–82
  description, 77–79, 80, 81
  division and classification, 40–44, 45, 46
  general-to-specific, 47, 50
  increasing order of importance, 45–47, 49, 105
  for instructions, 32, 34–36, 428–31
  inverted-pyramid method, 540–41
  for persuasion, 32, 45
  process explanation, 76–77, 78
  sequential, 34–36, 37
  spatial, 36–40, 41–42
  specific-to-general, 50, 51
organizational names
  abbreviations for, 667
  capitalization of, 663
  on title page, 389, 390
organizational rank, business communication and, 291–92
outlining, 26–34
  advantages of, 26
  for business writing, 276
  for classification, 45
  in collaborative writing, 131, 133, 451
  for comparison, 53, 56
  decimal numbering system, 28–30
  digital tips for, 14, 34
  in formal reports, 386
  guidelines for, 30–31
  impact of purpose and audience on, 31–33
  including graphic elements in, 223
  organizational patterns for, 32–33, 34–57
  peer review of, 26
  for reports, 359
  in revision process, 96
  Roman numeral outline, 26–28, 29–30
  for spatial description, 41
  for specific-to-general organization, 51
  using for draft writing, 64
overhead transparencies, 510–11, 520

pace, in presentations, 513
padded phrases, avoiding, 109–10
page design, 216–20. *See also* document layout and design; format guidelines; Web writing and design
page numbers
  for appendixes, 415
  for body of report, 396
  for front matter, 389, 390, 392, 396
  general guidelines for, 667
paint graphics programs, 251
paragraphs
  length of, 98
  transitions between, 100
  transitions within, 99–100
  unity in, 97–98
  in Web writing, 543
  writing effective, 97–101
parallel structure, 104, 295, 393
paraphrasing
  in listening process, 518
  in research, 176, 178–79, 183
parentheses, 647, 655, 656–57
parenthetical citations. *See* in-text citations
parenthetical elements
  capitalization for, 663
  enclosing, 645, 656–57, 659–60
part-by-part pattern, of comparison, 52, 56–57
participial phrases, 645
participles, 626, 634
passive voice, 638–39
  emphasis and, 101–2
  ESL tips for, 102
  pronouns and, 106–7
  responsibility and, 102, 286–87
  in test reports, 374
  uses for, 101–2
past perfect tense, 640, 641
past progressive tense, 641
past tense, 640, 641, 674
pauses
  commas for, 648
  dashes for indicating, 659
  in presentations, 503
PDF files, 550, 554, 555, 590
peer reviewing. *See* reviewing, peer
peer writing team. *See* collaborative writing projects
people, depicting for international audiences, 252–54
Pepetto, Robert, 331
percentages, 666
periodicals
  for library research, 166
  in references list, 186
  in Works Cited list, 196
  See also articles (periodicals)
periodic reports, 361–62, 364–65, 366–67, 379
periods, 648, 654–55, 666

person
  pronoun-antecedent agreement in, 630
  subject-verb agreement in, 635
  See also point of view
personal communication, documenting, 184,
      190, 199, 200
personal experience
  opening with, 501
  as primary research, 150
  on résumés, 579
personal names. *See* names and titles
persuasion
  acknowledging opposing opinions, 71, 453
  of audience, 68, 70–71, 72–74, 89
  in conflict management, 529
  ethical considerations, 31, 71
  organizing patterns for, 32, 45
  in presentation closings, 502
  in proposals, 448, 452–54
  respectful tone for, 289
  in sales proposals, 87
  supporting arguments, 96
Pfenning, Sherri, 571
photographs, 248–50
  digital, 249
  highlighting objects in, 249
  uses for, 221, 242
  using color, 249–50
  in Web design, 551
  See also visuals
phrases
  absolute, 644
  for clarifying meaning, 110
  introductory, 644
  padded, 109–10
  for subordination, 102
physical appearance, of document, 116. *See
      also* document layout and design
pictograms, 238
pictorial flowcharts, 244, 245
picture graphs, 222, 238
pie graphs, 222, 235–37
places, capitalization of, 663
plagiarism, 175, 180–81, 294, 414, 451
plain language guidelines, 112–14, 427, 433,
      541
plain-text résumés, 587–90
planning
  in collaborative writing, 131–32, 134
  guidelines for, 5
  for informal reports, 358–60
  instructions, 423–31
  meetings, 523–27, 530
  proposals, 449–54
  for time-sensitive messages, 293–94
  for time-sensitive presentations, 519–20
  for time-sensitive proposals, 488–90
  See also organization; schedules
plurals
  apostrophes for forming, 652–53

of numbers, 653, 665
  possessive case of, 651
  pronoun, 628
podcasts
  documenting, 190, 200
  in Web design, 558–59, 563, 566
point of view
  acknowledging opposing, 9, 71, 453
  considering audience's, 68
  in job-related writing, 106–7, 113
  personal versus impersonal, 106–7
  "you" viewpoint, 282
  See also person
politeness, in business communication, 283,
      347
political divisions, capitalization of, 663
political science style manuals, 203
portfolios, for job search, 587, 592
positive tone, 283
possessive adjectives, 671
possessive case
  apostrophes for, 650–52
  ESL tips for, 652
  nouns, 650–51
  pronouns, 628, 631, 650, 651
PowerPoint, 507, 520–21
prediction, conditional sentence as, 675
preface, in formal reports, 396, 397
prefixes
  affectation and, 112
  hyphenated, 658
prepositional phrases, for showing
      possession, 650, 651
prepositions
  ESL tips for, 672
  in titles of works, 664
presentations, 499–516
  body of, 502
  closings, 502
  considering audience and purpose,
      499–500, 514, 516, 519
  delivery techniques, 511–15, 522–23, 534
  delivery time frame for, 520
  engaging audience, 499, 514
  evaluating, 516
  gathering information for, 500, 519
  giving brief overview, 500, 501
  for global audiences, 515–16
  guidelines for, 504, 512, 533–34
  introductions, 501
  organization of, 500–504, 520
  organizing patterns for, 47
  practice techniques, 511–12, 521–22, 534
  presentation anxiety, 514–15
  presentation software, 507–9, 520–21
  sample of, 505–7
  time-sensitive, 519–23
  transitions in, 503
  typical pattern for, 503–4
  See also presentation visual aids

presentation visual aids, 504–11
  flip charts, 509
  handouts, 511, 520
  overhead transparencies and slides, 510–11, 520
  practicing with, 512
  presentation software, 507–9, 520–21
  whiteboards and chalkboards, 510
present perfect tense, 641, 673–74
present progressive tense, 641, 674
present tense, 640, 674
pretentious language, 112–13, 346
primary research, 149–57
  interviewing, 150–52
  observation, 152
  personal experience, 150
  questionnaires, 152–57
print sources
  documenting, 186–87, 197
  evaluating, 171–74
  using library, 158–66
prioritizing, for time-sensitive proposals, 489
privacy issues
  for e-mail messages, 296
  for instant messaging, 303
  on Web pages, 555–57
problem statements
  in presentation openings, 501
  in proposals, 449, 454–57, 470, 473, 477
process explanation
  flowcharts for, 244–47
  illustrations for, 76–77, 78
  organization of, 34–36, 76–77
  as writing strategy, 75, 76–77, 89
  See also instructions
product/service descriptions
  in proposals, 451
  in sales letters, 326
  in sales proposals, 477, 480
professional journals, for job search, 575
professional names. *See* names and titles
progressive tenses, 640, 641, 674
progress reports, 361–64, 379
  information surveys, 392
  openings and closings for, 86
  series of, 362
project descriptions, in RFPs, 491
project narrative, in grant proposals, 470, 473
project outcomes, in grant proposals, 473, 474
project reports. *See* periodic reports; progress reports
promotional correspondence, 325–30. *See also* sales letters
Prono, Judy, 387
pronouns
  antecedents, agreement with, 630–32
  antecedents, references to, 629–30
  case of, 627–29
  in compound constructions, 629

  defined, 627
  for direct writing, 433
  ESL tips for, 631
  following *as* or *than*, 629
  indefinite, 631–32, 637
  in job-related writing, 106–7, 113
  possessive case, 628, 631, 650, 651
  relative, 637
  sexist language and, 111, 630–31
  singular and plural, 628
  as transitional device, 99–100
  we/us usage, 628–29
  who/whom usage, 629
proofreading, 115–16
  for format consistency, 116
  for global audiences, 346–47
  of job application letters, 604
  proofreaders' marks, 116, 136, 624
  in stages, 115–16
proper nouns, 662, 669
proposals, 448–94
  audience and purpose for, 449–50
  collaborative writing of, 451–52
  correspondence rejecting, 331, 332, 335
  cover letter for, 321
  defined, 448
  documenting sources in, 453, 457, 462
  external, 463–88
  grant and research, 468–75
  guidelines for, 453–54, 462, 493–94
  internal, 454–62
  organization of, 452
  outlines for, 26
  persuasive writing in, 452–54
  planning and writing, 449–54
  purpose statement for, 449
  repurposed content for, 451
  requests for (RFPs), 463, 490–92
  time-sensitive, 488–90
  See also external proposals; internal proposals; sales proposals
protocols
  in business communication, 291–92, 296
  for usability testing, 443
publication information
  in references list, 185, 186
  in Works Cited list, 195
Publication Manual of the American Psychological Association, 131, 182
public domain materials, 181, 451, 557
punctuation, 643–61
  apostrophes, 650–53
  brackets, 656–57
  colons, 649–50
  commas, 643–48
  cultural connotation of, 255
  dashes, 659–60
  ellipses, 660
  exclamation marks, 656

punctuation (*cont.*)
  hyphens, 657–59
  parentheses, 656–57
  periods, 654–55
  question marks, 655–56
  quotation marks, 653–54
  semicolons, 648–49
  slashes, 661
purpose
  in business writing, 276
  determining, 4–6
  in draft writing, 75
  in effective listening, 517, 518
  of informal report, 359, 360
  of inquiry letters, 325
  for instructions, 423–28, 431
  of meetings, 523–24, 526, 530
  method for closing and, 87
  in opening statement, 84
  organizing information for, 31–33, 57–58
  of presentations, 499–500, 516, 519
  for proposals, 449–50
  for research, 157
  for résumé, 571
  in revision process, 96
  statement of, 5–6, 14, 31–32, 66, 449, 499,
    524
  stating, in formal reports, 400
  of visuals, 220–23
  voice and, 74

qualifications summary, in résumés, 582
question marks, 648
  common usage for, 655–56
  cultural connotation and, 255
questionnaires, 11, 149, 152–57
  advantages and disadvantages of, 152–53
  ethical considerations, 154
  guidelines for, 157
  preparing and designing, 153–57
  sample of, 154–56
  selecting recipients for, 153
  on Web pages, 555
questions
  FAQs, 564–65
  for interviews, 151, 610, 611–12
  opening with, 501
  for paragraph transitions, 100
  in presentations, 502
  for research, 157, 158
quiet person, in meetings, 528
quotation marks, 653–54
  capitalization and, 663
  for direct quotations, 176, 653
  ESL tips for, 654
  with other punctuation, 647, 654, 655, 656
  for search engines, 170
  for setting off words and phrases, 653–54
  single, 653

  for titles of works, 654
quoted material
  block indent for, 178
  deletions and omissions in, 177, 660
  direct quotations, 176
  documenting, 182–84, 193–94
  ethical considerations, 177
  incorporating into text, 177–78
  indirect quotations, 176
  inserting clarifying comments, 177, 657
  opening with, 501
  punctuation for, 645, 653–54

racial bias, 111–12
radio programs, documenting, 189–90, 199
rambling person, in meetings, 528
readers. *See* audience
Readers' Guide to Periodical Literature, 163
reading practices, cultural differences in, 255
recommendations
  in closings, 86, 87
  in executive summaries, 398
  in formal reports, 386, 410–11, 412–13
  in informal reports, 360, 362, 373, 379
  in proposals, 457
redundancy, avoiding, 109
references, in résumés, 587
references list (APA), 184–86, 192, 411. *See also*
    documentation of sources
reference works, library, 160, 163–65
refusal messages, 330–31, 332–35, 615
relative pronouns
  in adjective clauses, 673
  agreement with verb, 637
  in sentence fragments, 626
religious bias, 111–12
religious symbols, cultural connotations and,
    255, 256
remote meetings, 526
repetition, of key words and phrases, 99–100
reports
  defined, 358
  documenting, 190
  See also formal reports; informal reports
repurposed content
  for proposals, 451, 489
  on Web sites, 554–55
  See also boilerplate material
requests for proposals (RFPs), 463, 490–92
  appendixes, 492
  company description, 490
  ethical considerations, 492
  grant proposals, 469
  guidelines for, 494
  project descriptions, 491
  proposal descriptions, 491
  proposal-evaluation criteria, 492
  structure for, 490
  vendor qualifications, 492

research, 148–205
 avoiding plagiarism and copyright
  violations, 180–81
 for collaborative writing, 133
 developing search strategy, 157–58
 documentation of sources, 132, 181–204
 ethical considerations, 149, 151, 154
 evaluating sources, 158, 171–74
 for formal reports, 386
 guidelines for, 204–5
 Institutional Review Board and, 149
 Internet research, 166–71
 interviewing, 150–52
 library research, 158–66
 literature reviews, 470
 note taking in, 174–76
 observation, 152
 paraphrasing, 178–79
 primary, 149–57
 questionnaires, 152–57
 quoting sources, 176–78
 secondary, 157–71
 summarizing, 179–80
 types of, 11
 using personal experience, 150
 See also documentation of sources; Internet
  research; library research
research proposals, 468–75
research reports, 386
resignation letters, 615–17
respectful tone, 283, 289
responder, listener as, 517–18
responses
 to e-mail, 296, 298
 to inquiry letters, 325, 327
 to job interview questions, 610, 611–12
responsibility
 avoiding, with passive voice, 102, 287
 for business writing, 277
 statement of, in sales proposals, 483, 486
restrictive elements, 645
résumés, 578–602
 adapting to specific job listings, 599–602
 analyzing background for, 578–80
 audience for, 571
 databases for, 574, 587–90
 design guidelines for, 588
 education, 580, 582, 583
 electronic résumés, 587–92
 e-mail-attached, 589, 590
 employment experience in, 580, 582–86
 ethical considerations, 585
 guidelines for writing, 578
 headings in, 581
 honors and activities section, 586–87
 job objectives in, 581–82
 organizing, 580–87
 personal experience in, 579
 portfolios with, 587, 592
 posting on Web site, 574, 590–92

qualifications summary, 582
 references in, 587
 samples of, 592–602
 scannable and plain-text, 587–90, 591
 skills and abilities section, 586
 templates for, 589
 volunteer experience in, 580, 585
 See also job search
reviewing, peer
 in collaborative writing, 130, 134–36
 of formal reports, 387
 for memos, 15
 of outlines, 26
 in professional journals, 166
 for revision process, 95
review transmittal sheets, 139, 141
revision process, 94–121
 accuracy in, 115–16
 active and passive voice, 101–2
 avoiding affectation, 112–13
 biased language, 110–12
 for business writing, 276
 checking format consistency, 116
 clarity in, 114
 coherence, 97–101
 in collaborative writing projects, 134–36
 conciseness in, 109–10
 content and organization, 96–97
 digital tips for, 14, 115, 116, 120
 emphasis in, 101–6
 essential elements of, 94–95
 evaluating draft, 96–97
 example of, 116–19
 for formal reports, 386–87
 guidelines for, 95, 96–97, 100–101, 114,
  120
 for memos, 15–17
 paragraph unity, 97–98
 parallel structure, 104
 physical appearance, 116
 plain language guidelines, 112–14
 point of view, 106–7
 proofreading, 115–16
 subordination of sentences, 102–3
 for time-sensitive messages, 294–95
 use of transitions, 98–100
 using jargon, 114
 using lists, 104–5
 using technical terminology, 113–14
 word choice, 108–9
 writing effective paragraphs, 97–101
 versus writing process, 64, 89
RFPs. *See* requests for proposals
rhetorical question, opening with, 501
*Riley Guide: Employment Opportunities and
 Job Resources on the Internet*, 573
Roman numeral outline, 26–28, 29–30
rough draft. *See* draft writing
routine internal proposals, 454, 455–56
RSS (really simple syndication), 169–70

rules (lines)
    for highlighting, 213, 215
    in tables, 225
run-on sentences, 625–26

salary
    information on résumés, 587
    negotiations, 612
sales brochures
    audience and purpose for, 31–32
    example of draft for, 87–89
    organizing material for, 31–33
    persuasion in, 32
    revision process for, 116–19
sales letters, 325–30
    ethical considerations, 327
    guidelines for, 330
    identifying audience for, 325–26
    mentioning costs in, 326–27
    product/service descriptions, 326
sales pitch, in sales proposals, 483, 487
sales proposals, 475–88
    collaborative writing of, 129
    conclusions, 87
    defined, 448, 475–76
    ethical considerations, 468
    long, 476–88
    short, 464–67, 476
    structure for, 476–88
    unsolicited, 465–67
    See also proposals
salutations
    in business letters, 309–10, 313
    capitalization in, 663
    in e-mail messages, 298
    in international correspondence, 298, 346,
        347
    to multiple recipients, 310
    punctuation for, 309, 650
sans serif typeface, 212, 215, 551, 588
scannable résumés, 587–90
schedules
    bar graphs for, 139, 140, 235
    in collaborative writing, 131, 139–41, 451
    for draft writing, 65–66
    in grant proposals, 475
    for meetings, 524
    organizing patterns for, 36
    in proposals, 449, 457
    in RFPs, 491
    in sales proposals, 477, 482–83
    for time-sensitive messages, 293–95
    for time-sensitive presentations, 519–23
    for time-sensitive proposals, 488–90
schematic diagrams, 222
Schwerdel, Sarah, 449
Scirus, 169
scope
    describing in opening, 360
    establishing, 4, 11–12

in outlines, 26
of research topic, 158
stating, in formal reports, 400
screening (shading), for highlighting, 215–16
search engines, 166, 167, 170
    optimizing content for, 541, 550
    See also Internet research
search strategies
    advanced searches, 166, 167
    developing effective, 157–58
    keyword searches, 162, 163, 164, 166
    for library catalogs, 159–61
    for library databases, 161–63, 164
    multiple search terms, 159
    for search engines, 166, 170
    setting search limits, 161
    storing database search results, 163
secondary research, 157–71. See also Internet
        research; library research
second-person point of view, 106
semicolons
    common usage for, 648–49
    for linking clauses, 625, 626, 648–49
    with quotation marks, 654
    for series of items, 646
sentence faults, 625–27
sentences, 625–42
    in abstracts, 392–93
    comma splices in, 625–26
    conditional, 675
    dangling and misplaced modifiers in, 627
    fragments, 626–27
    in international correspondence, 346
    length of, 105, 294, 433
    modifier usage, 632–35
    parallel structure, 104, 295
    pronoun problems in, 627–32
    revising and polishing, 294–95
    run-on, 625–26
    subordination in, 102–3, 625, 626
    transitions between, 99–100
    verb usage, 635–42
    in Web writing, 543
sequential organization, 34–36, 37, 57
    illustration of, 436–38
    for instructions, 32, 33, 428, 431
    transitional words for, 99
series of items, punctuating, 645–46, 648,
        655
serif typeface, 212
sexist language, 110–11, 543
    avoiding in occupational descriptions, 110
    avoiding in salutations, 310
    pronoun usage and, 111, 630–31
"shop talk," 114
signal words, for warnings, 434–35
signatures
    for business letters, 311
    for e-mail messages, 297, 299, 300
    for internal communications, 292

signatures (*cont.*)
   for printed memos, 305
   in sales letters, 328
simple tenses, 640–42
site-preparation section, in sales proposals, 477, 484
slang, 653
slashes, 661
slides, presentation, 510–11, 520–21
social networking sites
   for job resources, 572
   professional Web presence and, 574
social work style manuals, 204
solicited proposals, 463, 464
solutions
   detailed, in sales proposals, 477, 481
   in presentations, 502
sources
   acknowledging, 180
   currency of, 158
   evaluating, 158, 171–74
   for research interviews, 150
   for time-sensitive messages, 293–94
   See also documentation of sources; online sources; print sources; research
spatial organization, 34, 35, 36–40, 41–42, 57
specific-to-general organization, 35, 50, 51, 58
spell checkers, 14, 115, 120, 295
sports metaphors, avoiding, 515
SPSS (statistical package for the social sciences), 165
squinting modifiers, 627
staff requirements, in proposals, 449, 457, 485
statement of need, in grant proposals, 473
statistical sources, 165, 171
status reports. *See* periodic reports
step-by-step sequence. *See* sequential organization
stub column, 225
style, writing, 280–83
   audience and, 281
   cultural differences in, 343–46
   direct and indirect patterns, 283–88
   informal versus formal, 281
   for instructions, 432–33
   for Web writing, 541–43
   See also direct style; formal style; indirect style; informal style
style standards
   APA style, 182–92
   for collaborative writing, 131–32, 139
   list of, 203–4
   MLA style, 193–202
subheads
   italics for, 669
   style guidelines for, 403, 408, 409
   in Web writing, 549
subject
   identifying, in opening, 84, 288
   introducing, in reports, 400, 403

subject complements, 634, 638
subject directories, 157, 158, 166, 168, 169. *See also* Internet research
subjective case, of pronouns, 627–28
subject lines
   capitalization in, 291, 664
   catching audience interest with, 84
   in e-mail messages, 291, 296
   guidelines for, 291
   for trouble reports, 373
subject-verb agreement, 635–38
   with collective subjects, 636
   with compound subjects, 637
   with indefinite pronouns, 637
   intervening words and, 636
   inverted word order and, 636
   for plural book titles, 638
   with relative pronouns, 637
   singular nouns ending in -*s*, 638
   for subject complements, 638
subjunctive mood, 639–40
subordinating conjunctions, in sentence fragments, 626
subordination
   in abstracts, 393
   avoiding excessive, 103
   in conditional sentences, 675
   for emphasis, 102–3
   ethical considerations, 103
   for run-on sentences, 625, 626
suffixes
   affectation and, 112
   hyphenated, 658
summaries
   abstracts, 390–94
   in closings, 86, 87
   for grant proposals, 470, 472
   for paragraph transitions, 100
   in research, 176, 179–80
   See also executive summaries
superlative modifiers, 632–33, 671–72
surveys, 443
symbols
   cultural differences in, 254–55, 256, 347
   defining, 223
   depicting warnings and cautions, 434–35
   flowchart, 244–47
   international standards for, 246, 255, 347, 428, 435
   list of, 389, 396, 398
   proofreaders' marks, 624
   uses for, 222
synonyms, in informal definitions, 79

table of contents
   in formal reports, 386, 389, 394, 395
   for Web writing, 545, 546
tables, 224–28
   for comparison, 51, 52
   continued, 225, 227, 228

tables (*cont.*)
   design guidelines for, 228
   digital tips for, 228
   elements of typical, 224–26
   in formal reports, 394, 410
   versus graphs, 228, 229
   informal, 226, 228
   list of, 224, 394
   numbered, 224, 410, 667
   for presentations, 504
   screening (shading) in, 216
   uses for, 220, 221
   See also visuals
tags, for blog posts, 561–62
team projects. *See* collaborative writing
      projects
technical staff, writing for, 450
technical terminology
   as affectation, 112
   appropriate use of, 68, 113–14
   graphics for, 251
   in international correspondence, 346
technical writing
   in collaborative projects, 129
   in formal reports, 386, 389
   list of abbreviations and symbols for, 396, 398
   for nonspecialists, 32
   outline for, 28–30, 408
   in proposals, 450
   report subsections for, 68–70
   SI unit abbreviations, 668
technology symbols, cultural differences in,
      255
telephone and conference calls, 277, 278–79,
      280, 313
television programs, documenting, 189–90,
      199–200
templates
   for collaborative writing, 132
   for correspondence, 306
   for document design, 214, 387
   for informal reports, 364, 365
   for presentation slides, 507
   for résumés, 589
tense. *See* verb tense
terminology
   in graphic elements, 223
   for job search, 575
   library terms, 165–66
   See also glossaries; jargon; technical
      terminology
territorial person, in meetings, 529
test reports, 374–78, 379
text
   of formal reports, 403–10
   integrating visuals with, 219, 220–24, 256–57
   in presentation visuals, 504, 511
third-person point of view, 106
thumbnail images, on Web sites, 551
thumbnail sketches, for page design, 216, 217

time
   colons in, 650
   in international correspondence, 347
   numbers in, 666
   as transitional device, 99
time-line graphs, 140, 235. *See also* bar
      graphs
time-management tactics
   for draft writing, 65–67
   for time-sensitive messages, 293–95, 314
   for time-sensitive presentations, 519–23
   for time-sensitive proposals, 488–90
time order. *See* chronological organization
title page
   for formal reports, 389–90, 391
   for grant proposals, 470, 472
   for sales proposals, 477
titles
   catching audience interest with, 84
   for visuals, 225, 504
   See also job titles, capitalization of;
      names and titles; title page; titles
      of works
titles of works
   capitalization of, 664
   italics for, 669
   plural, agreement with verb, 638
   question marks in, 655
   quotation marks for, 654
   in references list, 185
   type size for, 213
   in Works Cited list, 195
tone, 280–83
   in adjustment letters, 336, 338
   building goodwill, 282, 283
   in collection letters, 342–43
   direct versus indirect, 283–88
   for openings, 289
   in proposals, 453
   in sales letters, 328
   for Web writing, 542–43
   "you" viewpoint, 282
topic sentences
   in abstracts, 392
   paragraph unity and, 97–98
   placement of, 98
trade journals
   for gathering information, 11
   for job search, 575
training requirements, in sales proposals, 483,
      485
transitional devices, 98–100
   list of common, 99
   between paragraphs, 100
   for presentations, 503
   punctuating, 644
   between sentences, 99–100
transitive verbs, 628, 635
transmittal review sheets, 139, 141. *See also*
      cover letters

trip reports, 373–74, 375–76, 379
openings for, 360
organizing patterns for, 34, 36
trouble reports, 370–73, 379
ethical considerations, 370
guidelines for, 373
revision process for, 373
typography
for e-mail, 297–98
for emphasis, 52, 105–6
for headings, 403, 408, 409
for highlighting, 213
for presentation slides, 511
in print document design, 211, 212–13, 214, 220
for résumés, 588, 589, 590
special and international characters, 552
typeface and size, 212–13
for Web design, 551–52

units of measurement
abbreviations for, 667–68
capitalization of, 664
unpublished data, documenting, 190
unsolicited proposals, 453, 463–68
usability testing, for instructions, 149, 442–43

vague messages, 290
vector graphics programs, 251
vendor description, in sales proposals, 483, 487, 490
vendor qualifications, in RFPs, 492
verbals, 626, 673
verbs, 635–42
action, in résumés, 586
active and passive voice of, 101–2, 638–39
defined, 635
ESL tips for, 640, 641, 673–75
helping, 674–75
linking, 635, 638
modal, 674–75
mood of, 639–40
objects of, 673
in sentence construction, 626
transitive, 628, 635
See also subject-verb agreement
verb tense
ESL tips for, 641, 673–74
progressive, 640, 641
simple, 640–42
videoconferences, 279, 280, 314
viruses, computer, 297
visually impaired readers, typefaces for, 212
visuals, 209, 220–56
bar graphs, 233–35
captions for, 215, 220, 224, 230, 232
chart for choosing appropriate, 221–22
clip art, 243, 507, 508, 520

close-ups with enlarged details, 437, 439
color and screening for, 215–16
computer graphics, 251, 252
designing and integrating with text, 219, 220–24, 256–57
dimensional-column graphs, 238–41
documenting sources of, 225, 230
drawings, 241–44
ethical considerations, 230
flowcharts, 244–47
in formal reports, 386–87, 410
graphs, 228–41
guidelines for using, 223–24, 257
in instructions, 76–77, 78, 428, 429, 436–42
for international communication, 250–56
international graphic standards, 246, 252, 255, 428, 435
line graphs, 228–32
maps, 247–48
numbered, 224, 410, 667
organizational charts, 247
photographs, 248–50
pictograms, 238
pie graphs, 235–37
for presentations, 504–11, 520–21
tables, 224–28
in test reports, 374
for warnings and cautions, 434–35
in Web design, 543–45, 551, 554
See also icons
Vohs, John, 130
voice
active and passive, 101–2, 638–39
ESL tips for, 102
establishing writer's, 71–74
in presentations, 513, 522, 523
See also active voice; passive voice
voice-mail messages, 279, 280, 314

warnings
emphasizing, 106, 656
ethical considerations, 434
for global audiences, 250
in instructions, 432, 433–36
language for, 434
symbols and signal words for, 434–35
we (pronoun), in job-related writing, 107
web-based tools, 169–70
Web sites
accessibility of, 551, 552–54, 565–66
for business communication, 280, 314
for collaborative writing, 133
copyright permissions from, 181
documenting sources from, 184, 188, 196, 198
domain names, 170
formal reports posted on, 411
for job resources, 572–74, 575

Web sites (*cont.*)
   posting résumés on, 574, 590–92
   for research, 158
   See also Internet research; online sources;
      Web writing and design
Web-technology specialist, 553
Web writing and design, 539–67
   blogs, 559–62, 566
   bulleted and numbered lists in, 549–50
   chunking content in, 543–45
   collaborative and multimedia content,
      558–65
   conciseness in, 543
   directional cues, 545, 550
   documenting sources of information,
      557–58
   enhancing access to content, 552–54,
      565–66
   enhancing site credibility, 557–58
   FAQs, 564–65, 566–67
   graphic elements, 543–45, 551, 554
   guidelines for, 549, 552, 554, 565–67
   headings and subheadings in, 543, 549
   highlighting information in, 549–52
   for international users, 543, 553–54, 566
   inverted pyramid method for, 540–41
   line length for, 551–52
   linking to external content, 547–48
   linking to internal content, 545–47
   listing hyperlinks, 546
   optimizing for content retrieval, 541, 550
   optimizing printing, 555
   for people with disabilities, 553, 566
   plain language for, 541
   planning and organizing content, 540–49,
      565
   podcasts, 563, 566
   posting an existing document, 554–55, 566
   posting presentation slides, 509
   posting résumés, 574, 590–92
   protecting user privacy, 555–57
   providing keywords for search engines,
      550
   reader attention span and, 540
   style and tone for, 541–43
   typography for, 551–52
   using color images, 249, 551
   wikis, 563, 566
What Color Is Your Parachute? (Web site),
   573
whiteboards, 510
whiteboard software, 526
white space
   in document design, 14, 116, 132, 216–19
   surrounding visuals, 224, 247
who, whom, 629
whole-by-whole pattern, of comparison, 52–55
whole-to-parts method, of description, 79

Wikipedia, 165, 558
wikis
   for collaborative writing, 133, 563
   documenting, 189, 199
   evaluating sources from, 172
   in Web design, 558, 563, 566
word choice
   context and, 108–9
   ethical considerations, 109
   general versus specific terms, 108–9
   See also language
wordiness, avoiding, 109–10
word order, for emphasis, 52
word placement, for instructions, 433
word-processing programs
   for collaborative writing projects, 132, 136
   for creating tables, 228
   designing documents with, 214, 424
   digital tips for, 14
   draft writing with, 66
   index feature of, 416
   for layout and format, 132
   outline feature of, 14, 34
   templates, 364, 387, 589
   using ASCII format, 590
   See also computer technology; digital tips
words
   absolute, 633
   foreign, 668–69
   introductory, 644
words used as words
   italics for, 669
   plural form of, 652
work environment, preparing, 66
workplace writing. *See* writing at work
Works Cited list (MLA), 178, 194–96, 202, 411,
   414, 457, 462. *See also* documentation
   of sources
"writing appointments," 65–66
writing at work, 261–72
   casting agencies, 269
   elementary education, 266
   ethical considerations, 21
   microbiology, 268
   nursing, 262–64
   public relations, 267
   radio disc jockey, 265
   research consulting, 271–72
   structural engineering, 270
writing process
   assessing audiences' needs, 4–5, 6–7
   for business communication, 276–77
   for collaborative writing, 129–30, 133
   considering context of, 8
   determining purpose, 4–6
   establishing role and voice in, 71–74, 75
   establishing scope, 11–12
   example of, 14–20

writing process (*cont.*)
    generating and gathering information, 8–11
    guidelines for, 21
    for international audiences, 68, 70, 343–51
    for multiple audiences, 68–70, 386, 387,
        449–50
    planning, 5
    versus revision process, 64, 89
    systematic approach to, 4–13
    See also draft writing; writing at work
writing strategies
    cause and effect analysis, 82–84
    defined, 75–76, 89–90

definitions, 79–82
description, 77–79, 80, 81
process explanation, 76–77, 78
See also organizational methods
writing style. *See* style, writing
WWW Virtual Library, 169

Yahoo! 167
"you" viewpoint
    in business writing, 282
    in meetings, 527–28